LOOKING
FOR GOD

PALMETTO
PUBLISHING
Charleston, SC
www.PalmettoPublishing.com

LOOKING FOR GOD
Copyright © 2024 by George H. Elder, PhD

Hardcover ISBN: 979-8-82292-237-2
Paperback ISBN: 979-8-82292-238-9
eBook ISBN: 979-8-8229-4099-4

GEORGE H. ELDER, PhD

LOOKING FOR GOD

*Dreams and
Contemplations On Being*

To the University of New Hampshire,

a place where possibilities become realities.

FOREWORD

Searching for the source of our existence has been a driving force since humanity first became aware, and few are the exceptions from the quest. The paths followed vary, but the goal of existential enlightenment is often the same. For example, the Shakers had a vibrant colony along the shores of New Hampshire's Mascoma Lake in Enfield, just a few miles from my home in West Lebanon. Their pursuit of exuberant, expressive dance instead of conjugal intimacy ensured the faith would eventually wither, but other searches for religious insight have been more popular and enduring. For better or worse, New Hampshire's John Smith (Latter-day Saints) of Derryfield and Mary Baker Eddy (Church of Christ, Scientist) of Tilton helped spawn major religious movements that persist. In addition, Vermont's Brigham Young (Latter-day Saints) of Whitingham, along with many others from New Hampshire and Vermont, helped shape Mormonism.

Yet why should these spiritual quests be the case? I believe the majesty and splendor of New Hampshire and Vermont's physical settings cause many to ponder the roots of our being. Fall colors inspire us, for here we can find a multi-hued mountainous terrain that stretches as far as the eyes can see. The region is also crisscrossed with small and large rivers and dotted with countless lakes and ponds. The visage can serve as a portal to some sublime speculations, which was the context in which I was raised. One can easily glimpse the Divine here, wherever she or he looks.

Like many, I have surveyed innumerable sources for inspiration and insights into what many call God and some dub existence. This quest has led me to examine mythopoetic accounts, pantheism, monotheism, Hinduism, Buddhism, Christianity, Islam, empiricism, science, rationalism, and other philosophies. Of course, these notions are all seen through the lens of my personal experiences, with the general focus being an attempt better to understand the universe and our roles within it.

At the very least, searching for and seeking to understand existence's sources and machinations provides them with an ideational presence of sorts. Indeed, thinking about thinking allows ideas like the ones you are pondering while reading this line to exist. The processes involved in such contemplations form links between the material, energetic, and metaphysical. In fact, seeking to understand the nature of being could be life's essential purpose, our *raison d'être*. We are stardust, coalesced, and reformed in fashions that allow us to reflect on the source of our existence.

To accomplish this end, we must fully use our various perceptual abilities. This takes us to one of the ways insights are gleaned. Clearly, we learn much from books, education, and life experiences, but we also have other tools at our disposal. All people dream, and some of us vividly recall these experiences. A few claim to travel through time and space during astral dreams and visions, carried far by imagination's impetus. I am such a dreamer, although some maintain I'm just a bit daft. However, the dreams I will relate within the following text actually happened. I recorded them long ago when my faculties were much more capable. Age has weathered my mind and body, making a once stout fortress into something akin to a bucket of sand.

Although a debatable choice, I will present these dreams within the context of a fictionalized dialogue, which shows how much I have slipped over the years. A straightforward narrative would have been more conventional and easier to write, but rapidly switching perspectives via multiple characters with disparate viewpoints and backgrounds is enlightening and enjoyable. "Alex," my avatar, reveals things about himself and human nature that can be uncomfortable, savage, and disconcerting. He was certainly not a happy-happy-joy-joy kind of fellow. Indeed, it is hard to describe me/Alex as sane, and I led a wayward and wanton life until I became a coach at the University of New Hampshire (UNH). Before that, I was "disturbed." Anyone could be who sought to find the nature of existence within dreams. I even dared look for what many call God, and you will join me on this trek. It is one of many spiritual adventures, some of which have proven prophetic.

I was systematic as my lucid dream capacities developed, constantly pushing to see more and to go further. Yet we must be careful of what we seek, for the visions that are found can be more than haunting. Some were utterly terrifying and violent, occasionally leaving me more mystified than edified. I became reclusive and temperamental, ever prone to conflict and despair.

In my madness, however, I found numerous insights into our roles within an ever-changing universe that may aid your personal quest.

I felt compelled to record the more spectacular dream events several years ago. They began in early childhood and persisted for nearly 40 years. I cannot say why or how they happened with any certainty, but the dreams may have resulted from cortical anomalies. Indeed, I was plagued by "complicated migraines" throughout my life, and these grew to include neurological symptoms by my thirties and forties. There were seizure-like events, long periods of dysarthria, and much worse. My balance began deteriorating by age forty, and some memory functions gradually declined. The doctors say my brain is now markedly atrophic in various areas, and by sixty-five, my memories started fading. If one were to speak to me today, it is very doubtful I'd recall the conversation, let alone who I spoke with. Yet my work was rescued, such as it is.

In that I am somewhat defective, why should my ramblings be of interest? Well, I'm not pretty, but I have a slight sense of humor, fair intellect, and am honest by most measures. I'm also a good storyteller and have written numerous published articles and books. In addition, I was highly educated by academic standards, all the way to PhD level. As for work experiences, I was a bouncer, custodian, window washer, college teacher, drug addict, collegiate coach, writer, weightlifter, and upper-level scholar. I was, and am, deeply religious, yet I do not subscribe to any major religion.

My main lesson about formal education was that many folks within the academy tend to believe that they're pretty damn bright. In fact, the silly sots are sure of it. Yes, I've met many Mensa-level folks and was once considered of that ilk. Ah, but thinking we're bright is an illusion, an act of banal egotism. Hey, there is much more that we do not know than we will or can ever learn. So, like Socrates, I am forever ignorant but eager to seek knowledge.

Happily, Chucky W. taught me humility at a young age, and the lesson sunk in. Now, Chucky had some developmental problems, and several of us would-be wiz kids considered him a "retard." Like many, we were sometimes a cruel and bigoted bunch of children, insensitive to the extreme. However, our fifth-grade homeroom teacher sought to put us in our place regularly. In fact, she would often stump us on an almost daily basis by asking the class odd questions. For example, she once asked, "When the milkman puts milk on the porch steps on a cold winter morning, why does the glass sometimes break?"

Oh, we bright kids came up with answers about cold making glass brittle, and some offered that tire vibrations from passing cars may cause the fragile glass to crack. Meanwhile, Chucky was waving his hand to beat the band and making excited "Oh, ooh, ohhh," sounds. This went on for about five or ten minutes, with all our answers being shot down in flames. Finally, the teacher called on Chucky. He exclaimed, "Milk is like water! And the water gets bigger when it freezes." The classroom roared with laughter, at least until our teacher said, "That is correct, Charles.

The water in the milk freezes and expands. This causes the jar to break because it cannot expand to contain its contents. Excellent job, Charles!"

I was stunned but never has a question been so enlightening in so many ways. And though I was to eventually get a BS in pre-Physical Therapy (UNH), Master's in Writing (UNH), and PhD in Speech Communication (Penn State), the lesson has remained. Sadly, I saw the same story played out *ad nauseam*, bight people thinking they know more than they do. Once, my Penn State peers discussed who was or wasn't "a player" in our PhD program . . . as if any of us were fit to make such judgments. I shook my head and left the room, having been considered a marginal student at best. However, I knew enough to understand that I was not fit to judge, a lesson many of my kith had yet to grasp.

As fate would have it, my dissertation was the first thesis published as a hard-cover book in over 30 years in my department, and I graduated with high honors. However, I knew there was no future for me in the academy. I was too moody and impolitic, being very much my father's son and a free-spirited child of New Hampshire's Upper Valley. If I thought an idea was bunk, I would say so; often quite crudely. Thus, I became a writer who successfully avoided making much money from the habitude.

See how easily I get distracted? My train of thought often runs off the tracks, but that's a good thing, given the subject matter of this book. Following the dreams, we will examine a series of essays and short works designed to entertain, inform, and get a rise out of readers. Some of these ramblings may not be your cup of tea. For example, the philosophy chapter entitled *Plato on Number and Word Salads* (57) can be tedious, while a few of Part IV's Chapters on Time and Space are barely intelligible. My bad. Indeed, I considered putting the Philosophy and Time and Space chapters at the very end of the book, hoping they would not drive readers away. Well, skip over those bits if you want because there is much to choose from.

We will examine philosophy, nature, nurture, love, interesting characters, politics, and questions about time and space. We will explore the human condition and zoom through the cosmos on the wings of imagination. Many of the essays have a rustic perspective for reasons already explained. However, the writing style shifts. It runs from tedious academic to down-home Upper Valley, my natural voice.

Oh, I will rankle some of you about various subjects and stylistic choices, as is my typical wont. Others may find my views objectionable, flawed, or annoying, but I hope one doesn't read books merely to find consensus with the writer. We read to become engrossed in thought, periods when time disappears, and we are wrapped tightly within a type of communion that transcends time and space. We become bound to the now, a rapture we can share via Aristotle, Dante, and numerous others. After all, I may be dead and gone by the time these lifeless symbols are processed by you and given meaning. And here these words are, opening conceptual gates via the agency of your thoughts while you ponder and opine.

Moreover, you will extend whatever humble insights I can offer based on your past, current situation, and ongoing moods. And that advancement of wisdom, when all is said and done, is the purpose of this text. It is a primer that you will take to much more elevated heights than I could ever achieve. In fact, I believe those reading these words can prevent the utterly catastrophic future revealed in some of the dreams. That is because the person reading this text has the power of creation coursing throughout his or her being. So, let us now go to a mountainside in rural New Hampshire and begin our journey of discovery.

TABLE OF CONTENTS

PART I

DREAMS

1

The Past Is Prologue

Mirai (mr-ai) appreciated being invited to the hike, although it was proving much more arduous than anticipated. Nonetheless, rewards for the effort dazzled her senses. Fall's vibrant graces spread far and wide with a wealth of splendid hues pleasing her eyes and crisp cool air filling her lungs. The climb had become surreal, something beyond the physical. As the muscles in her legs throbbed, Mirai relished the moment, finding the journey up and down the slopes of New Hampshire's Mount Major far more spiritual than physical. She gazed in awe at the rippling surface of nearby Lake Winnipesaukee, reflecting the sun in a spectacular array of shimmering light. It was a sublime vista.

As Mirai and her two companions headed up the trail, she wanted to tell them how enthralled she was by the experience.

1.1 View of Lake Winnipesaukee from the top of a Mount Major trail in New Hampshire

Alas, she could not speak, although Mirai's hearing was very acute. Sign language allowed her some expressive communion, assuming others could grasp her meaning. Yet she was bringing up the rear of the tiny convoy, and her hands were well out of sight. It seemed rude to capture her companions' attention via whistling. That was her usual means of saying, "Pay attention," but nature's chorus need not be so harshly disturbed. A dreary happenstance of genetics deprived Mirai of any semblance of speech at inception. Medical experts said the disorder was due to a FOX B1C2 genetically induced deviation in her expressive phonetic articulatory loop . . . whatever that means. She found the explanations tedious and unnecessary because various toxins had long made chromosomal anomalies commonplace in her community. To be different was not different.

There were no regrets. Mirai trooped through childhood, adolescence, and adulthood, eventually becoming a gifted scholar at Oxford's Institute of Temporal Dynamics. She became the quintessential historian and a widely published author. She basked in praise of those in the know. She was fulfilled and happy. However, her vocal incapacity had one vexing drawback: some people ignored her. Her present companions, Verity and Alex, were tolerably attentive. They had even learned sign language to discern what Mirai was communicating. Mirai found it endearing, happy evidence that true friends would do what they must to commune.

Still, it was a lonely existence. Furthermore, Mirai was far from her native soil, albeit within an increasingly desolate and searing environment. No hikes along bucolic trails had been possible for hundreds of years in the dead lands surrounding British Columbia's Prince George. However, its 1,890-foot elevation made it immune from the rising seas' relentless incursions into coastal regions. Safe havens were at a premium for Mirai and her kindred, and most opted for cooled air, shaded abodes, and artificial settings. To hazard a casual walk through nature was to risk health and life.

Nevertheless, home is where the heart is. She especially missed her mother. When Mirai was a child, her mother would brush Mirai's hair one hundred times each night while singing beautiful songs from her native Japan. The melodies became locked in Mirai's mind, their echoes comforting her on lonely days. She sometimes felt so alone and irretrievably distant from anyone who cared that she wept.

The tiny caravan soon stopped in an opening adjacent to a small, fast-running brook. The pleasant refrain of rushing water provided a welcome accompaniment to the songbirds' chorus. Mirai marveled at a swift dragonfly's intricate wings and iridescent metallic sheen as it gently lit upon a rock that broke the stream's surface. The scene was a visual ode to joy, a singular moment of delight. She smiled, thankful for the sight. There was no such life where she lived.

Mirai sat on a lichen-covered boulder to rest and bathe in the warm sunlight. Yes, the climb was a test, but the surrounding scenery was worth the journey. Her light blue athletic pants and matching fleece pullover had resisted the increasing chill. Still,

1.2 Mirai marveled at a swift dragonfly's intricate wings and iridescent metallic sheen.

the sun's rays were a welcome supplement. She closed her eyes to focus on the sounds, marveling at nature's chorus. Was there a pattern in the disparate sounds? She wondered if the babbling water and chirping birds were in harmony. Her musings were quickly distracted.

"Are you sure this is the right place?" Alex whined, trying to catch his breath. His face was red, and perspiration penetrated his coal-black sweat suit, dripping off his shaggy head and face. He was a stout 37-year-old who was far more comfortable hefting large objects in a gym than trekking up and down mountain slopes. Yet he was not a nonathletic roly-poly. Hidden beneath Alex's massive portage was a powerful body forged by years of heavy weightlifting and exercise. Dieting, on the other hand, was not his forte.

Mirai found Alex petty and crude at times. He could also become overly emotional, which made a poor bedfellow to an essentially confrontational nature. However, it was clear that he appreciated and deeply valued her friendship, as he made countless efforts to curry Mirai's favor. She recalled her thirty-second birthday party, a time of too much wine and celebration. When his eyes and hers became locked, as with lovers, she felt her heart race. He was also intuitive and intelligent, which drew Mirai to him. Alex could read her work with understanding. Indeed, he was one of the few who could accept her contention that the arrow of time did not always fly in one direction.

"Yes, *mon ami*, Verity is positive this place it is," Verity said while carefully surveying the area. "Madame Leonedria has to be close by. She could not have moved the cave, not the one she lives in. Verity is certain her home is near this tree beside the petite brook. Yet she cannot find it. *C'est un impossible!* Perhaps we should climb over the ridge."

Alex shook his head while wiping away sweat from his brow with a small towel. "No eff'n way!" he grumbled. "No more climbing. I swear we've been over every damn inch of this mountain!"

"You cannot find anything good if you give up so easily," Verity replied. She turned to Mirai and signed, "Mirai, are you so tired as this fat one?"

Mirai chuckled and shook her head. It was evident that Alex wanted Verity passionately, yet Verity was elusive. She was a diminutive beauty, graced by curly raven hair, a deep tan, and classical Mediterranean facial features. She wore a red spandex jumpsuit and a tight beige jacket emphasizing a curvaceous figure. It was an attribute Verity flaunted with enthusiasm, a flame to all moths.

Alex glanced at Mirai and smiled. He understood that she possessed a depth of thought that few could imagine. Alex found that beautiful mind more than ample compensation for her verbal deficit. Nonetheless, he often pondered about the compensatory neural substrates that sustained Mirai's insights. Such intellectual tedium was his usual way. To Alex, the biomechanical underpinning of thought was just as essential as thought itself. He believed that all things have a rationalistic basis, and he was setting out to prove that point in his dissertation project. Alex would demonstrate how communication changed people's minds in the neuroanatomical sense. He thus studied the neurosciences in a depth that few could manage, including many medical doctors. There were discernable reasons for all things if one looked.

Alex turned to Verity and sighed. "How did I ever let you talk me into this? The whole idea is ridiculous when I think about it."

"Why is it ridiculous to seek good counsel?" Verity shot back. "Mirai, she feels and loves nature, does she not? You ask for the direction and purpose in life, and Verity needs advice from the wisest person she has ever known."

"But from an old gypsy lady who sells trinkets and fortunes on a mountainside?" Alex gasped while sucking in some deep breaths. "Good Lord, I can hardly breathe."

"Look at you! You sweat like a pig," Verity sneered.

"Pigs don't sweat," Alex scoffed. "Horses sweat."

"Yes, but you are much fatter than the horse," Verity said. "Mount Major, she is not so tall! She is just 545 meters. Yet you cannot manage even this! *C'est un shameful*, Alex. Verity says this because your friend she is, but you must lose the weight."

Mirai laughed, ever amused by her friends' nearly constant bickering. They loved each other despite their many differences, but Mirai knew Alex and Verity would never become lovers. Alex was staid, focused, and contentious. Verity was effervescent and capricious. They shared passion and fiery dispositions, which worked against bridging their profound differences.

As for herself, Mirai welcomed Alex's affections, as evidenced by his letters and the occasional flowers he brought her. Despite his coarseness and occasional flashes of anger, Alex was a kind soul. Yet Mirai wasn't sure she liked Alex enough to break her usual reticence concerning intimacy, nor did her mission protocols include that possibility. To Mirai, there was an ideal. Sex and love were two different things. She believed that one of the objects of life was to discover where they merged, where the plural becomes singular. She sensed Alex held the same view. However, Verity was attracted to any bright light that caught her eye. Ah, but Mirai was happy with their friendship and greatly valued it.

Alex flashed a wry grin and continued his squabbling. "No friend would ask a fat man to clamber all over a damn mountainside," he exclaimed. "This pack I'm carrying sure as hell doesn't help! The thing must weigh over 50 pounds. I'm ditching it for a while."

Verity chuckled. "Ah, but Verity also has the pack back! And Mirai, she, too, has the pack. The weight is no problem because we are in fine condition."

"You call those wimpy things backpacks?" Alex asked. "They're less than half the size of mine."

"And you are over twice the size of Verity and Mirai together. Now stop the whining and let Verity think. Why cannot the cave we find?"

Alex heaved the bulky pack off his shoulder and set it on the ground. With a heavy sigh, he shrugged his well-muscled shoulders and rolled them backward and forward, relieved of an irritating burden. Curious, he bent over and opened the backpack to examine its contents.

"I should have eff'n watched you fill this miserable thing," he growled, shaking his head. "Food! I'm carting cans, bottles, and fruit up a goddamn mountain. And I'm bringing them to someone who doesn't seem to exist!"

"Oh, Madame Leonedria most certainly exists," Verity insisted. "We talked for hours on a day like this. When we find her, you will cherish the journey. Of this, Verity is sure. Plus, it is simply *savoir-faire* to bring her the supplies. After all, she is too old to carry heavy bags up the slopes."

Alex rolled his eyes before sealing the heavy backpack. He knew it was pointless to argue with Verity. He looked at Mirai and asked, "Are you doing OK?"

Mirai nodded, pleased that Alex was always attentive to her needs. She could read lips, mouth words, and hear, but signing was far more precise. Indeed, she always signed when expressing herself, especially in the present company. To be sure, Alex and Verity could quickly discern her intended meaning, albeit they made some mistakes.

"I am tired," Mirai deftly signed. "This hike is much harder than anticipated. But I am glad we're here. What a beautiful place! It is like a cathedral of life."

"Agreed," Alex replied. "If one has to be lost, this is the place to be. Of course, if we knew what we were looking for, it would help."

Most people allowed Mirai to disappear into the background due to her affliction. They only paid lip service to her welfare, and she had few true friends. Life was much different where she was born and raised. There, friends and family surrounded her with love and attention. They easily communed with Mirai while she grew strong in mind and body. It was also a safe home, albeit far more cloistered and restrictive than she liked. Curiosity and education soon lured her from the nest and into Oxford's prestigious halls. Yet she was to go further afield, for Mirai had sailed onto the dangerous seas of time and space.

Her family had begged her to stay home because there could be no return from the primitive past. But she was on a special mission, albeit a one-way venture. Hers was a flight into history's making, requiring years of careful planning, training, and special permits. Mirai would examine how relatively minor past actions could shape massive changes in the future. Such intrusions inevitably produce ripples, which is why they were prohibited. However, rare cases were deemed existential necessities. To be sure, the book you are reading would only exist if the mission succeeded. Yes, Verity came to find you.

The technical and monetary cost of manipulating the time-space continuum was horrendous, and the bickering between the Temporal Governors and academics left all involved at odds. However, several historical records indicated a temporal intrusion had definitely taken place involving Mirai, and thus causality became the essential issue. The mission was reluctantly approved, with a temporal transition of 1,052 years taking mere seconds. Yet events immediately went differently than planned after Mirai materialized. It was one thing to examine the past from a distant perspective but quite another to immerse yourself in it.

Relevant records and a manufactured biography had been meticulously prepared and planted, and Mirai's abilities swiftly earned the praise of employers and her fellow academics. Sadly, Mirai soon found herself within lonely scholarly contexts that were difficult at best. However, she needed to establish credentials, and this took time. She was alone and isolated from any support, doing her best to fit into the existential milieu of a distant past. The mission planners had anticipated the problems involved but not the mind-numbingly tedious and petty barriers between Mirai and her assignment.

Mirai's life became consigned to an unending series of research fellowships instead of a proper job, with her mission eventually taking her to the University of New Hampshire. After all, this was where the incursion took place, at least according to the available records. Oh, the powers at UNH knew she was top of the class. She dazzled them with papers, insights, and theories. But how could she teach? Two attempts to do so via PowerPoint presentations and handouts earned very poor student evaluations. The students sought to hear her words rather than read them. Alas, youth is often more intolerant than many surmise. Hence, Mirai's peers and superiors paid her little mind. She couldn't truly become one of the anointed with bad student reviews. Yet her name was prominent when department heads boasted to deans about how many papers their staff produced. To be sure, her publishing record alone led Mirai to precisely where she wanted to be, the intended focus of her historical assignment. Everything was going as planned for her to be with Alex, Verity, and you, the reader. Now and here was the optimal time and place.

Mirai glanced over at Alex, having to squint due to the blinding sun. Alex cared deeply about her, an unanticipated and unfortunate happenstance concerning her undertaking. They met during a tempestuous interdepartmental conference. The subject was mass lectures versus small class settings. Mirai noted Alex was strident in defending small classes, even to the point of rudeness; he found her attractive and brilliant. Thus began a friendship bordering on unexpressed passion. Alex visited Mirai's tiny cubicle for long communions, patiently striving to learn and understand sign language. Yes, he loved her after a fashion. She mused about the future should Alex forsake his futile quest for Verity. Perhaps he is the one, she thought, although she knew the Temporal Governors would disapprove.

Alex's huffing and puffing pulled Mirai from her thoughts. "Look, I asked for your help in finding answers to questions about God, existence, and all of that," he conceded to a barely interested Verity. "I took your word that this person we're looking for is wise beyond all others. But we've spent hours searching, and I can barely move. Please, let's call it a day."

"To find anything worth having, one must spend time and effort, *mon ami*," Verity chided while waving a dismissive gesture toward Alex. She pointed to herself. "Verity, she comes to this mountain many times. Only once has she come upon Madame Leonedria. But this one occasion was enough to change Verity's entire life! It allowed her to see the new perspectives."

Alex raised his arms in frustration. "Sometimes, I barely understand your perspectives because they shift with the wind. What's true today may be false tomorrow. It all depends on how you feel or whom you're talking with. Verity, this Leonedria woman is an itinerant, a gypsy! For all we know, she's gone or dead."

"She cannot die," Verity insisted.

"Anything that lives can die!" Alex scoffed. "Now, let's go back to the car! The sun is getting low, and mid-September isn't a good time to spend a night on the slopes. We don't have a tent, and descending in the dark can be dangerous. Look, we have to head back."

Mirai knew Alex was correct, at least about the current situation. He grew up in rural New Hampshire and was familiar with nature's vagaries. Conversely, Mirai grew up in a protected subterranean environment, albeit highly artificial. There were no trees, bugs, or animals. Nor was there a threat of her freezing to death or falling off a slope. She stood and stared at Verity. She hoped Verity would see sense in what Alex was saying. Instead, she detected complete desperation in Verity's countenance. Fear and uncertainty were traits she had seldom seen in Verity. It wasn't reassuring.

"We cannot leave!" Verity cried. "We will not leave! Verity must find Madame Leonedria for her reasons *particulière*. But what is wrong? This place is most definitely the right one. Verity knows this is the place! Madame Leonedria, where are you?" she shouted. "Please! We must see you! *Respondez, s'il vous plait.*" Tears rapidly filled her eyes.

Mirai walked to Verity and held her hand. Alex hovered over them and placed a hand on Verity's shoulder.

"There's no need to get upset," he softly intoned. "We'll try again in a couple—"

Verity angrily shoved Alex's hand away.

"No, no, no! We must find her now!" Her eyes were wild and frantic. "MADAME, PLEASE! WE HAVE THE FOOD AND THE—"

"Don't be yelling like that," Alex said. "Someone will think we're—"

"What does Verity care about what people think?" Verity angrily interjected. She fought back tears, but they flowed nonetheless. "If we do not find her, then Verity is . . . she is . . ."

Mirai looked into Verity's frantic face and softly massaged her shoulders, offering what comfort she could. She knew Verity was fundamentally unstable, but she was essential in what the historical records indicated would transpire.

Alex was perplexed. He was clumsy, not knowing what to do or say. "Oh, damn, please don't cry!" he implored. "We're all tired and overwrought. But it'll be all right." He gently grasped Verity's hand. "We'll go back home and try again in—"

"Do not p-p-patronize Verity!" Verity yelled. "And let go of her hand! Oh, Verity has s-s-searched and searched for Madame so many times. For seven years, she carried the food and money up this mountain. And for seven years, she has only the tears to show. Yet let me tell you, Madame Leonedria is here! We talked! We talked for much time in her cave. Verity knows Madame is here."

"Of course she is," Alex said, knowing how volatile Verity could become. "Maybe we just picked the wrong time of year to find her."

"Or perhaps 'we' didn't," someone interjected, causing the trio to turn around. A matronly older woman was hobbling toward the small group, assisted by a tall, richly carved walking stick. Her voice was strong and clear, far more so than her 70-year-old apparent age indicated.

1.3 Madame Leonedria suddenly appeared dressed in ornate Gypsy attire.

2

She Who Knows

Mirai was shocked. She pondered how this elderly woman could so abruptly enter the clearing without having been noticed. It seemed she had just appeared. But how? That issue aside, Mirai knew that Madame Leonedria was supposed to become involved in the events unfolding. That is what the records recovered from the Mount Lebanon Cemetery indicated would happen. She studied the dainty old lady, with some of her former peers at Oxford contending that Madame Leonedria was a transtemporal being. A few scholars even believed her to have been involved in events stretching back for several millennia. It was all a great mystery.

The woman carried a sizeable ornate handbag and wore a long, colorful dress. Mirai thought the gaudily-hued panels and trim were as Mexican in style as those of a gypsy. Her delicately embroidered floral-pattern blouse was covered with a tightly crocheted blue shawl that came down to the waist. A blue scarf tied tightly over her white hair completed the attire. She wore a wealth of jewelry that caught the declining sunlight—dangling earrings, necklaces, and bracelets.

She may indeed be a gypsy, Mirai thought, at least in this rendition of reality. Then Mirai suddenly sensed something very odd. She discerned the old woman could comprehend her thoughts. This was anticipated by the mission planners, but Mirai still found the intrusion disturbing. The old woman smiled at her, a warm and knowing grin that seemed to melt the years from her face.

"Very pleased to meet you, Mirai," she said while hobbling up and briefly taking her hand. "Yes, you are the future's folly looking back. Thus, the silence you're blessed with. The writer thought he was clever to include you and your undertaking. It was an ideal means of exposition that could change a dialogue into—"

"Madame? Madame Leonedria?" Verity interjected, her words more hopeful than sure.

"You scared the hell out of me," Alex exclaimed to Madame. "Where did you come from?"

"Don't we all come from the same place?" Madame Leonedria replied. "Oh, but I've been here for some time. Please forgive me for startling you, sir. I thought it most unlikely I could surprise people calling my name."

She reached into her oversized purse and rummaged around before finally pulling out a simple clay pipe. It was of evident antiquity and humble design.

"Could I interest you in this fine clay pipe?" she asked. "It was made by an Onagunga shaman over 600 years ago. He was a progenitor of the wise and noble sachem Passaconaway. Like you, he enjoyed vision quests. This pipe gave him some limited service in achieving that end. Please feel its fine texture. Perhaps you can imagine some of the thoughts of its former user."

Alex took the pipe and examined it closely, swearing he could feel its heat and detect the faint smell of marijuana in the bowl. He thought this will make a fine keepsake and pondered how much it would cost.

"No, this is not right," Verity said while shaking her head. "No, no, no, no! You cannot be Madame Leonedria!"

"Yet you can be Verity," the woman replied.

"But you are too young," Verity insisted. "The white hair, bright dress, bags, and voice are almost identical. Yet the face, she is much younger. C'est un impossible!"

"Such linear thinking, my dear," Madame Leonedria said with a smile. "You should have changed enough since our last meeting to avoid that pitfall. Our perspectives, not our appearances, define what was, is, and will be. Perhaps you've not been communing with Mirai enough. But still, it's nice seeing you, as it will be when I'm older and you're younger." Madame

Leonedria turned to Alex. "Now you, sir, I sense you're a highly educated man, or at least that's what you would have me say."

"I would?" Alex replied, taking his attention from the pipe.

"But of course," Madame Leonedria said. "After all, you're writing these lines. Well, you think you are. For some reason, you want the reader to know that you've studied many ancient philosophers. You've also read several modern theorists, although you do not find the moderns illuminating. Please don't have me list them. That tedium comes from your ego and not my thought. And yes, you studied the Bible and many other religious texts. Alas, you've yet to find much solace in these efforts. Then came a turn toward science and a long search into the physical processes sustaining thought. You garnered advanced degrees along the way and have written much.

"Despite all you've learned, you realize how little you know. Some may find this the first tiny step toward wisdom. Yet you still need to figure out who you are and why you're here! Yes, you're as bewildered as my dear Verity. Furthermore, you're as lost as some of those who are reading these lines. You search for life's purpose and meaning and how best to spend your remaining time and energy. Sadly, we're only granted a precious few moments to discover life's great mysteries, and your moments are running out."

"There's no doubt about that," Alex sadly said. "I've squandered decades. Now the corporeal 'me' is slip-sliding away."

"Though you are young and powerful in this fantasy," Madame Leonedria said. She gently touched Alex's face. "I know how tired you truly are, dear child. I understand how difficult it is for you to craft these lines. All things follow a path, be the course direct or not. You began this trek as so much stellar debris that had found a sentient form. Yes, coalesced dust gave rise to the thoughts from which it came. For many years the insights garnered along your path have eluded description. Yes, you tried, but there was a litany of failures. Now this sublime task calls to you one last time."

Alex furrowed his brow in confusion. "Look, we just came up Mount Major to—"

"Oh, that's just a petty plot device," Madame Leonedria interrupted with a dismissive wave. "We're going beyond that. In fact, you had forsaken this trek. You were unsure how to tell a story beyond your capacity to express, yet you've always had enough arrogance to commit these words to paper." She gently chuckled. "It's as if they could perpetuate some grand insight you've stumbled upon. How typically male, my son. Child, to have ever been is to always be from one perspective or another, written words or not. However, you're plagued by doubts and are forever unsure. Let's hope those with us can discern what is meaningful from what is shallow conjecture. Now, let us get back to the business at hand. If you don't like the pipe, perhaps this crystal is of more interest. Just a moment now."

Madame Leonedria busily searched through her bag, and Mirai pondered why Verity looked so confused and desperate. From Mirai's perspective, everything was history. Only time, space, and location dictate the past, present, and future. Everything Madame Leonedria said made perfect sense. This was especially so from the context of a being who had already experienced the story, be it the past informing the future or the future reflecting on the past. It was fundamental Temporal Dynamics 101. Her thoughts were distracted by Madame Leonedria's ongoing efforts.

"Give me some time to find it in my bag," Madame Leonedria intoned while groping deep within the oversized purse. "Yes, I know it's in here, somewhere. Ah, here it is!"

She carefully pulled out a crystal sphere about the size of a baseball. It glistened in the sunlight, reflecting the rays in a scintillating assortment of colors.

"Isn't it lovely?" the Madame said while holding up the glittering globe. "Look at the sphere from this angle. Note that it appears almost without substance. Ah, but if one rotates the globe ever so slightly, there is a great vision to behold! Yes, see how a hoard of tiny, sparkling lights emanates from within when one gazes into the crystal. They begin in the center and spread outwards in all directions! They flourish and dim. They dance around one another in elegant patterns. Then we rotate the globe again! And now there is nothing except a void that grows as dark as the looming night."

"I-I-I," Alex stuttered, his eyes wide.

"Verity's ring!" Verity interrupted. "Do you still have the ring?"

"One transaction at a time, dear Verity," Madame Leonedria sternly intoned. She turned to Alex. "Now, sir, I believe you've seen this item before."

"In a dream! I saw it during a dream as a child," he said.

"Yes, you did," Madame Leonedria replied. "The globe fascinated you then, but you were far too young to understand its deeper meanings. Ah, but now you know what this gem represents, this universe from within and where it resides from without. That became clear eons ago. Yes, that was after you began studying the nature of being. Well, at least in as much as your kind currently understands being. This is much the same path Mirai has walked. However, she has more profound perspectives than you, my son.

"Yet how can one have experienced a conceptual metaphor during youth that only acquired meaning decades later? Where did the insight come from? Or was it always within, born in the flesh? Ah, I see the question still plagues you. How little you understand the nature of what we are. Be that as it may, perhaps flashes from your youth, such as this globe, don't mean much to you, Alex. So, let us reconsider the pipe. That may be more to your liking and needs. It is certainly consistent with your nature."

Alex shook his head and glanced at Verity. "This is very disconcerting, Verity," he said. "The normal barriers that define an episode's plot and context are breaking down."

"No, this is her way, *mon ami*!" Verity said. "She is the ultimate sage. Yes, you are most certainly Madame Leonedria."

"Of course I am," Madame Leonedria noted, gently dipping her head. She turned to Alex while returning the globe to her pouch. "If the globe and pipe are not compelling, kind sir, perhaps some jewelry is in order. It hasn't been an outstanding season for jewelry. I have a few bracelets, pendants—"

"The ring!" Verity interjected. "Verity must back buy the ring! Verity brought you all this food!" She excitedly rummaged through her backpack, pulling out various items. "Here! See the fine loaves of bread and fruits? The oranges were picked just one day ago in Florida. Verity had them flown to New Hampshire just for Madame."

"They're fine oranges, indeed," Madame Leonedria said while accepting one of the fruits. She smelled the orange and smiled broadly before stowing it in her bag. "I've always enjoyed fresh citrus fruit, my dear."

Verity quickly turned to Alex. "Alex, open the pack back. Hurry, hurry!" Alex dutifully obeyed and pulled items from the backpack while Verity described them. "Yes, Madame, we have so much for you. See, look at all we have brought! We have the fine Chablis, port, sauce, and some chocolate. A-a-and Verity, she also brought money!" Verity unzipped the right pocket of her pants and pulled out a thick wad of rolled bills. "Look, look, here are a hundred thousand-dollar bills. And Verity also has the check for . . ."

Mirai was intrigued by Verity's desperation. She pondered how precious this mysterious ring must be. It was the first she'd heard of any unique ring, but it was apparent that it meant a lot to Verity. However, Alex was not amused.

"Put those bills away!" he insisted, glancing around for possible interlopers. "What the hell are you thinking? It's foolish to carry that much—"

"Useless paper," Madame Leonedria interjected. She shook her head and stared deeply into Verity's eyes. "I've no need for such excessive trivia, child. You should know that! And what good are checks up here, my dear? Should I have a friendly black bear cash them?"

"Please, Madame Leonedria! Please, please, please!" Verity implored while tears trickled down her cheeks. "Verity will give you anything for the ring. Anything! She has borrowed against her inheritance. She has walked up this mountain and searched for you endlessly."

"But you traded the jewel for so little," Madame Leonedria observed. "I believe you wanted a sandwich at the time. Yes, I had a small booth just outside my abode. It was a fine baloney-and-cheese sandwich, though hardly worth what you offered."

"No, no, no! You gave Verity much more when we talked," Verity cried. "You gave her a chance to see and live in the moment, the perspective present. But, but s-s-she forgot—"

Verity broke down, weeping inconsolably. Mirai rushed over to offer comfort, but Madame Leonedria interposed herself. She spoke gently while holding the crying Verity close.

"Oh, come here, my dear," she intoned. "Let me hold you. Let those tears flow. Don't censor your soul. Never do that."

"It was Mama's wedding ring," Verity sobbed. "A-and Verity—"

"Found the trinket a mere encumbrance, an unwanted responsibility," Madame Leonedria said while rubbing Verity's back. She pulled away slightly and added, "Perhaps you shouldn't have disregarded the ring's symbolism. I well recall our talk, my child. You were lost and desperate, Verity, like your friend Alex. You didn't like being bound by the past. Furthermore, you were uncertain about the future. You thought a stronger sense of subjectivity would provide comfort in a universe of constant change. Such a perspective would give you a means of living in the moment. Ah, but I warned you about where rejecting the symbols of the past would lead."

Then Madame Leonedria reached into her pocket and pulled out a tiny gold ring graced by a humble diamond. She studied the small jewel for a moment. "This little ring is a symbol of love. Love is an idea that can give life profound meaning. Granted, the meanings symbols access can bind our ways of perceiving, thinking, and acting. They can even drive us toward believing the eternal exists." She looked into Verity's moist eyes and added, "Yet look at what happens when we give up our links to the past. Now you feel empty. One moment becomes the next, and there is nothing to connect them. There is no continuity, no context, nothing to hold onto. You have become a child of the now, a slave of the present. I told you this would happen, did I not?"

"You did, but the memory, she always fades," Verity explained.

"Without memories, we are truly adrift," Madame Leonedria said. "We become trapped in the present, separated from the past, and orphaned in the future. Now you wish to be whole."

"Y-y-yes! Please!" Verity begged. "Please, help make Verity whole. She has brought you—"

"Nothing of value except her insights," Madame Leonedria added. "Here, let me dry your tears." She dabbed away the wetness on Verity's face with a brightly patterned handkerchief.

"Verity now sees that being is as related to thought as thought is to being," Verity observed. "They are one and the same."

"Yes, and parts of being are the aspects of time—past, present, and future," Madame Leonedria explained. "That is the true value of this little ring." She held out the ring to Verity. "For these many years, I have kept this tiny gem, for I knew its call would bring you this way. Please, take back what you should never have given up so easily. Be whole again."

Verity joyously accepted the diminutive ring and placed it on her little finger. "Oh! Ah, it is, it is a—"

"Substance that can act as a symbol," Madame Leonedria said. "The symbol can unlock a meaning. And, meaning can—"

"Help shape being and thought!" Verity gleefully observed. While studying the small ring, her eyes widened, and long dormant memories sparked anew. "Ah, I can see! I can see the past again! Verity sees Mama's eyes light up when she talks about the night Papa gave her this *petite* ring! She can smell the Christmas meal cooking in the oven! Oh, and we laugh and smile during the *fêtes d'anniversaire*. Mama, she dances with Papa. They float across the floor! *C'est magnifique!* It all comes back—sights, sounds, conversations, feelings, joy, and sadness! Oh, thank you, Madame Leonedria. Thank you so very much. I have been so—"

"So reckless with what you were and will become," Madame Leonedria observed. "Had you lost those memories, the symbol would also mean nothing. That's a lesson the Egyptians taught us." She turned to Mirai and seemed to peer deep into her soul.

Mirai was momentarily stunned, suddenly distracted from watching her friend Verity cry joyfully. She wished she had an item to channel such vivid and strong emotions.

"Yes, Mirai, these thoughts could have been more efficiently expressed," Madam Leonedria said. "Alas, the writer is limited in talent and only slightly insightful. Yet you understand that our dear Alex is passionate, despite his tedious quest for technical knowledge. You know that because you understand time far better than he does. Whether Alex is worthy or not of your affection and kind attention remains an open question."

Mirai nodded, happy to finally commune with an understanding soul sans sign language. She watched Madame pull her shawl tighter.

"It's getting chilly out here, children," the Madame observed. "My joints can't tolerate the cold as well as they do when I'm younger. Let us retire to my abode, but please return the pipe, Alex."

"Here you go," Alex said while returning the object to Madame. "I will definitely be buying that."

"We shall discuss that later," Madame Leonedria said before returning the pipe to her bag. She surveyed the darkening sky and said, "We must make haste. Get your packs ready, and we shall proceed. Oh, and don't look so perplexed, sir. You know exactly what's going on. After all, you're writing these lines."

"Yeah, I'm the writer and not a particularly good one," Alex said.

"That much is clear," Madame Leonedria said. "The urge to get thoughts on the page exceeds your capacity to record them properly. Furthermore, your memory is now such that grammar and punctuation are spotty. Nonetheless, perhaps you are adequate for the task at hand. We shall see."

"This piece is taking on a life of its own," Alex said. "But I'm tired of being called 'sir.' I prefer 'Alex.'"

"If you insist on a *nom de plume*," Madame Leonedria said. "And the author's name you were pondering for this book is ridiculous. Dear me . . . Justan Mann? Ludicrous. Some doubt the word of a person who uses false names instead of his or her given one, my dear 'earth-worker.'"

"I always liked the name, Alex," he said. "Have since I was a kid." He dutifully loaded foodstuffs into his pack, adding, "Plus, I don't care about having my actual name used or remembered. That's not why we're here. Moreover, I don't owe you any justifications for my choices."

"How testy!" Madame Leonedria replied. "Ah, your true nature comes shining through. Yet we have to get going. Now gather these supplies, children, and let us seek shelter. We'll have to hurry because the walk is quite a distance."

Mirai cinched her pack and watched Alex load items into his bag, noting it was heavy. But he hefted the load onto his back and shoulders effortlessly. She mused at how powerful Alex was. He could be a nearly perfect combination of thought and body if not for his appetites. He could quickly devour an entire large pizza and keep going. Mirai saw firsthand what the excesses were doing to him, a far starker lesson than any historical record could offer. She knew his coming years of misery, a painful life bound to a walker and mobility devices. Ultimately, Mirai knew Alex would reach out to her, not Verity. Verity was an ephemeral creature of the self. She was someone many could find, but none could own. Her musings were cut short.

"There is not so much more to hike," Verity said while tightening the straps on her backpack. "The cave, I know it was right here."

"'Was' and 'is' are two different things, Verity, though they are cousins," Madame Leonedria said. "Being linear in time and space is restraining. Much of our identity is bound to the memories symbols can unlock, constraining and ambiguous though they are. But at least you've found your 'I' voice again, not that you needed more ego, my dear. Come, we can't dally. I sense a cold front, and tonight the snow may fly."

Mirai was ready to go.

3

Into the Gloom

Twilight was giving way to darkness while the small group proceeded. Madame Leonedria took the lead, followed by Verity and Mirai. Alex brought up the rear, glancing incessantly at the surroundings lest some danger should appear. Mirai fretted about stumbling through the wooded and rock-strewn landscape under such conditions. One could easily break an ankle or leg. However, the stars were coming out with a rising full moon that slowly provided some feeble light. Still, the forest's canopy was like an umbrella in places, casting pitch-black shadows that hid the surroundings. Mirai nervously glanced back at Alex, who understood her growing concerns.

"Keep your arms out to the side and front," he warned. "And put your feet down gently! A hole or rock can ruin our

3.1 Preparing for a dangerous night hike

fun. The trees and bushes will help keep us on the path, but at least the cold will keep the ticks away. Hate those things. Damn, this was supposed to be a day trip, yet here we are. Lead on, Madame."

"But of course," Madame Leonedria said, taking slow, shuffling strides into the woods. "Follow closely, children. Don't you wish you had written a light source into the script, Alex?"

"No doubt about that," Alex replied. "Hell, I can barely see the way ahead. God help us if we run into a bear."

Mirai froze, terrified by the sudden prospect of slashing claws and gnashing teeth. The occasional briars were proving vexing enough, but a bear? While preparing for the mission, she had read about the powerful apex predator, but encountering such a beast was deemed improbable. Or was it?

Alex nearly bumped into her. "Don't stop like that!" he exclaimed. "I almost ran you over."

"Stop talking about bears!" Madame Leonedria said. "You're scaring the poor child. The only bears around here are my friends, Mirai. I assure you that they'll let us be. Now, no more delays! Pay attention to the path."

"If the bear comes, she will definitely eat the fattest first. That is most certainly you, *mon ami*," Verity said with a chuckle.

The group moved slowly ahead, eventually coming to a less wooded section. This improved their ability to see, although it was still a hazardous hike. Alex sighed. He fretted more about his friends than bears or other threats.

"I've been through surrealistic adventures before," he said to relieve the fear he had aroused. "But nothing like a nighttime walk along a rocky mountain trail."

"Yes, you had many adventures, *surréaliste*," Verity said with a smile. "You were the heavy drug user."

"Drugs alone don't make for surrealism," Alex said. "There are also religions, astrophysics, conversations—"

"And dreams," Madame Leonedria interjected. She leaned heavily on her stick, and Verity moved close in case the elderly woman needed help. Madame poked her stick ahead into the encompassing gloom and said in a sing-song tone, "The adventures in your mind confused you far more than those experienced when awake. That's why we're walking this path. You've been seeking answers for decades, and they have led to this rather precarious trek." The Madame paused momentarily, then carefully navigated the path step by step. "Please watch your step going over these rocks, children. And stay close! This section is very dark, with some dangerous drop-offs to our left. One could easily fall 20 meters or more."

"Oh, crap!" Alex nervously said. "You mean cliffs?"

"As a young man, you once ran up these slopes," Madame Leonedria observed. "I believe you had taken some hallucinogens, perhaps LSD."

"It was a stupid thing to do," Alex confessed. "I climbed hand over hand up a rock face, oblivious to the danger."

"You, *mon ami*?" Verity asked. "This, I do not believe."

"I wasn't always a porker," Alex said. "I would gain and lose 100 pounds regularly. I was lusting after some young lady, like a dog in heat. I think her name was Ginger or something similar. That was many years ago. Things change, Verity. They change all the time."

"They certainly do," Madame Leonedria said. "When you were a child, your imagination could soar high, Alex. Now you're grounded by illness and lassitude. We'll have to work on that."

Mirai enjoyed the shared information, especially Madame Leonedria's insights into Alex's past. It was unclear how she knew these details, but Mirai surmised telepathy was involved. She recalled looking through one of Alex's photo files while visiting his apartment one day. He had indeed changed radically in size and form over the years. There were pictures of him as a lithe and athletic man, and then others documented him being much beefier, his shoulders and chest filled with muscle from lifting heavy weights. In one photo, he hoisted 420 pounds overhead, yet obesity had long assumed ascendance.

Mirai thought it a shame, though admonitions were useless.

The light continued dimming, and Mirai struggled to adjust her vision, with waves of fear periodically washing through her body. Mirai shivered slightly, noting the growing cold and fearing the increasing darkness. Yes, it would be terrible to tumble down the jagged rock-laced slopes. A fall in this situation would have dire consequences. However, the prospect of a sudden animal attack was utterly terrifying. Yes, the records she studied indicated that this would not happen, but history often had a way of being poorly recorded. This was a frightening adventure that would long be remembered.

"Madame, I am very . . . *très fatigué, très, très,*" Verity said, her voice strained by exhaustion.

"I know, my dear," Madame Leonedria said while slowly proceeding. "You're exhausted and need to rest. Verity, you've reestablished connections with the past and are thus much more than you recently were. This can be a considerable burden for anyone. Such is memory's weight. Such is the price of continuity. But be of cheer. We've only a short way to go."

"Shoot, I thought you said this was a long journey," Alex said.

Madame Leonedria stopped abruptly and turned to face Alex's shadowy form. She angrily pointed her walking stick toward him. "I don't suffer fools lightly, Alex!" she sternly said. "You know that traveling even 10 feet can be an odyssey, especially for one who cannot walk! Yes, you've seen that before."

"Don't yell at me!" Alex shot back. "I know all too well how painful a single step can be. I've been injured many times tossing around weights and—"

"Now you're writing these lines as an enfeebled old cripple," Madame Leonedria scolded. "You couldn't manage even a few feet of this path as you truly are. Yes, you should better understand the effects of time and distance!" She turned to Mirai. "One day, you'll have to educate this shallow man. It will not be easy."

Mirai nodded, knowing that reaching into Alex's past had already produced a technical and ethical cost. Changing the past always did. Furthermore, she pondered whether reordering him in form and thought was more prudent. The mission was to ensure this adventure was recorded and shared with those who could help forge a better legacy for their progeny. That prospect would be improved if Alex's many faults could be corrected. It would be a matter of preserving what was worthy within the context of a new present. Indeed, Alex's foibles could be eliminated. Genetic and experiential manipulations would do the trick. Then again, what would the resultant product be? It would certainly not be Alex. The current journey should dictate the best path to pursue. If more temporal manipulations were made, this moment—four people and a host of readers on top of a mountain in New Hampshire—might not exist. It was a conundrum, one that her presence had created.

"He would rather be reordered in your present," Madame Leonedria said, once again peering into Mirai's mind. "He detests this timeline. Come, children," she demanded while gesturing ahead. The group plodded along while Madame Leonedria provided occasional tips regarding the trail. The encompassing gloom was now darkness, and sounds of shuffling footsteps and snapping twigs filled the night air. Briars occasionally grabbed at the party's legs, with each step presenting new challenges.

"My abode is just beyond that tree up ahead," Madame said after some time. "It's the large spruce on our left. Careful of the loose rocks! One can easily break a leg here."

Madame Leonedria finally stopped in a small clearing and sighed. She leaned heavily on her stick and stared at a patch of barely discernable lilac bushes. Verity, Mirai, and Alex soon joined her, out of breath and somewhat dizzy from the journey.

"Goodness, that lilac bush in the middle has overgrown the entrance to my abode," the Madame observed. "Oh, these are the changes that nature brings."

"The pack back; she is so heavy," Verity whined.

"Are you all right?" Alex asked.

"She'll be fine, as will we all," Madame Leonedria said. "I left a small lamp hanging from this large maple tree. It may have fallen, so help me find it."

The group fumbled around the great tree like blind monks seeking to understand an elephant by feeling its surfaces and appendages. Mirai stumbled over an object and grabbed onto the tree's trunk to save herself from a nasty spill. She reached down and felt a round metallic form. It had a handle on the top, although Mirai could not discern what it was. She whistled loudly.

"Mirai?" Verity said. "The lamp you did find?"

Mirai felt Madame Leonedria's hand touch her arm. Then the old woman quickly reached down, and the object disappeared from Mirai's hand.

"Excellent, Mirai," she said. "Now, let me find a lighter in this pack. I always carry one."

"I definitely should have written in a flashlight," Alex quipped as Madame Leonedria rummaged through her bag.

"Nonsense," she said. "Groping in the darkness is an appropriate metaphor. Those with us can easily deduce its meaning. Ah, here we go!"

Madame Leonedria pulled out a barbecue lighter and clicked it alight. The tiny flame drove away the darkness, illuminating her craggy face and casting shadows this way and that. She handed the small lantern to Verity and opened the faceplate.

"Hold this lamp still while I try to light it, dear," she said. "That's right. Now Alex, see if you can push that bush out of our way. The night's chill is upon us, but my abode is very comfortable."

"No problem," Alex said. He walked up to the large bush and took a few deep breaths. Then Alex pushed mightily against its tangled upper trunk, snapping branches and rustling leaves heralding his efforts. "Wow, this thing's really rooted," he grunted. Alex placed a foot against the cave's opening for leverage and pushed harder against the bush. The stubborn shrub finally gave way with a sharp cracking sound.

"There it goes," he said. "Come on. We should be able to squeeze through this space. You first, Madame. Then Verity and Mirai. I'll bring up the rear."

"Let me help you, Verity," Madame Leonedria said. While entering the cave, she lent her a hand, saying, "You'll soon have a place to rest those burdens."

4

Definitely not Plato's Cave

Mirai was surprised by what she saw upon entering the cave. There was order in this place, more of a large, comfortable room than a hermit's stark grotto. The abode's surfaces were strikingly smooth. They seemed seared out of the living rock by an instrument employing tremendous heat. Suitable devices were available in Mirai's era to craft such a dwelling, but this was another time and place. Indeed, most habitats were subterranean in Mirai's epoch, safe from heat and solar radiation. Yet the current period was in the distant past when Earth was far more welcoming. Perhaps Madame Leonedria was more than a gypsy, much like Mirai's peers had surmised.

Mirai surveyed the room's details while Madame Leonedria lighted more lamps. Various nooks and crannies of different sizes were neatly laid into a roughly 30-foot-diameter circular chamber. Two entry doors served small adjacent rooms, albeit too dark to see their contents. Mirai presumed one of the spaces was a bathroom. Books, cases, bedding, boxes, and numerous keepsakes were stored within the open orifices with ample lamps and candles, giving evidence of a scholar's chambers. In the middle was a large open hearth with a sooty hood reaching down from the ceiling. Neatly cut and stacked firewood and dusty ashes proved that the heating and cooking facilities were well used. A few plush chairs and a humble humpback couch surrounded the hearth. Small tables stood between the chairs, providing ample surfaces for food, libations, and books. Dressers, dining tables, and chairs abutted some of the walls by the internal portals.

Mirai's attention was quickly drawn to numerous glistening objects and artifacts. Some were formed of brass, bronze, silver, and colored glass. Many were of apparently great antiquity and would be rare in any collection. Exquisitely made Persian rugs and ornate wall hangings completed the setting.

Alex quickly entered and took stock of the surroundings, although the exhausted Verity had seen it all before.

"*Mon Dieu*, look at *ma mère's* ring!" she exclaimed with a broad smile as her half-closed eyes fixated on the long-sought jewel. Her joy was palpable.

Madame Leonedria lit a few of the larger lamps, their flickering light reflecting off the small diamond.

"Yes, it is the tiny diamond," Verity said. "But she glows in the lamplight, *n'est pas?* It was Mama's smallest ring. My papa,

41

he gave it to her when they first got married. He was not a rich man then. Ah, but this simple, minuscule ring meant more to Mama than all the great jewels Papa ever gave her. How she loved this little one! And how I miss her."

"She is wherever you look, Verity, and especially within your heart," Madame Leonedria advised. "Let us start a fire to drive away the cold, children. Come, place some wood in the hearth." She picked up kindling and placed it in the hearth's center. "See, we start with small branches. We'll add larger pieces of wood as the fire takes hold."

Mirai, Verity, and Alex joined Madame Leonedria in the task. She used the lighter to begin a small fire in the assembled mass's center, with the hearth's hood capturing the rising smoke. The growing flames snapped and popped while the firewood's moisture surrendered to the growing heat. Mirai and Alex added a few larger pieces of wood, with all enjoying the radiant heat. Verity stretched and yawned, taking a seat and still studying her ring. She smiled while musing, enthralled by rekindled memories sparking to life.

"That's all right, but please be judicious," Madame advised. "This firewood will have to last us an eon or two. Oh, and please forgive the Spartan surroundings. As you can see, I've little need for luxury," the Madame said.

"Wow, this place is a rush!" Alex said while examining the room's details. The walls were as smooth as glass, and he admired the excellent handiwork in the recessed alcoves and furniture.

"There's everything a person would need for a comfortable life in here—inlaid beds, dining tables, counters . . ."

"The cave is exactly as Verity remembers," Verity said. "Oh, there are a few things changed. Still, the boxes, furniture, and items scattered around are the same. Madame, *excusez-moi*, but I must take the nap. Just a little one."

"I know, dear," Madame Leonedria said. "Here, let me help you with that pack. All of you, please put your packs on the table beside the sink. We can sort out their contents later."

Alex and Mirai did as ordered and placed their bags on the table. When Alex glanced at Verity, he recognized that look on her face—droopy eyes and cheeks. He was somewhat concerned about her, as was his wont. She was obviously exhausted. Indeed, they were all tired after a nine-hour hike, but Verity also had emotional stress weighing her down.

Mirai, too, was feeling fatigued. She had not experienced such an arduous trek since her ill-fated tenure as a Nature Scout when she was 10. Her team's task was to locate and preserve plant and animal life in the arid wilderness surrounding their families' subterranean shelters, a sometimes-dangerous job. Alas, Mirai's affliction proved insurmountable, her peers finding sign language too much of a task to learn. As usual, Mirai slowly vanished into the background. She eventually fled into the world of books and computer screens. Now, she simply listened to Madame Leonedria and Verity talking while soaking up the fire's growing warmth. Alex added a few larger pieces of wood as the flames took hold.

"Look at you!" Madame Leonedria said while taking Verity's hand. "You're tired but finally at rest."

"*C'est vrai*," Verity agreed. "I am the complete woman!"

"You are, dear child!" Madame Leonedria agreed. She gestured toward an ample alcove adjacent to one of the internal doors. "There's a very comfortable sleeping chamber by that water bowl, and you surely need a respite. Curl up on the blankets and rest your burden. The hearth will warm your bones while sweet sleep calls."

Mirai watched Verity drag herself to the chamber and dutifully settle in. She noted that the couch and a large adjacent nook would be just as comfortable. They were undoubtedly inviting. However, she was also keen on communing with this wise old woman. Mirai was bound up in a narrative that offered the promise of learning, a nearly constant quest for her. She also intended to be in this place at this particular time. All was going as planned. Madame Leonedria spread a comforter over Verity, who was rapidly falling asleep.

The old woman walked over to Alex and Mirai, her eyes gleaming in the burgeoning firelight. "The cost of this exposition is pages and pages, Alex," she warned. "Only a few of them have any higher meaning, as in our groping through the darkness to find a safe haven. Now, pour us all some drinks from the Chablis that Verity brought. You'll find glasses in that wooden box beside the table. They're from Florence. Please don't drop them!"

"Where do you want these supplies?" Alex said while searching through Verity's packs and placing their contents on the table and nearby counters.

"It doesn't matter," Madame Leonedria said. "Mirai, please give me that loaf of rye bread Alex pulled out. My goodness, I can smell it from here! It will make a fine accompaniment to the wine."

Mirai dutifully obeyed. She found a cutting board, knife, and reusable paper plates while Alex pulled a large bottle of Chablis from the bag. It was a nightmare for him to open the bottle. His bumbling efforts greatly amused Mirai, and she finally helped him manage the task. Alex then took three glasses from their elegant wood box and carefully set them on the table. He marveled at their engraved scenes and intricate gilding, each glass displaying a different classical theme.

"Wine and bread are an excellent repast, and Verity has an excellent taste in bread," Madame said. She sat close to the hearth and continued speaking while Alex and Mirai completed their duties. "When Verity and I met, the sandwich I offered had superb-tasting rye bread. It was very similar to that loaf she brought. At the time, Verity had no money to pay for my services. Oh, I warned her not to part with the ring. The conversation was payment enough. After all, we are nothing without someone to commune with."

"These glasses are exquisite. I'd hate to break one," Alex nervously said while filling each two-thirds with wine. The elegant glasses were gilded at the top and bottom with an ornate grape-vine design that only a master craftsman could have created.

"They were a gift from a Florentine prince who had lost his wife to the plague," Madame Leonedria said while rearranging the hearth's firewood with an iron poker. "He found consolation in being inconsolable. I helped him discover a different path, and he was very grateful. Yes, finding suitable paths is my purpose. I suspect Mirai already knows that from her historical studies. Come, children, let us sit at the hearth and talk. Ah, and add that other bottle of Chablis to our repast, the one beside the sink. I have a feeling we may be here for a while."

"We'll use that fancy tray you found above the sink to bring over the wine and bread," Alex advised Mirai. He cautiously placed the glasses, bread, and bottles on the tray. "It's hefty, so I'll carry it. We'll set up on that small table beside the chair Madame is sitting on. I know you prefer comfy chairs like the red one, so I'll take the couch."

"Logistics, logistics," Madame Leonedria said. "The ancients did away with much of that via using dialogue alone, Alex. Yet you took this dreary turn toward exposition instead of that approach. So, here we are, over 45 pages in, although we've hardly moved any great distance."

Mirai smiled while following Alex to the hearth. She knew he had failed countless times to tell this particular story. Indeed, the current effort could well go the way of all the others, although part of Mirai's mission was to ensure the text was completed. Yet this was also his last attempt. Time and increasingly ill health had exacted their cost on Alex's embodiment. Worse, his mind was slipping. He had trouble finding names and was increasingly clumsy. Parts of his brain had become atrophic, though the cause was unknown to him. Alex's essence was "slip-sliding away," as he liked to say, but Mirai knew Alex was dedicating the story to her and her kind. She would thus do everything possible to help him tell it, temporal regulations be damned.

Alex put the tray on the table. He briefly paused and watched Madame Leonedria cut thick slices of bread, one of his favorite foods. She laid them out on the paper plates, ready to serve. Mirai sat to the left of Madame Leonedria on a plush, comfortable chair. She enjoyed its soft felt surfaces and snuggled into its warm embrace. Now, this was comfort incarnate. Alex sprawled out on the couch to her right, his mass sinking into the soft cushions.

"Expository writing generally sucks," Alex said. "Yet I thought the subplots and contextual shifts could tell stories in their own right. Still, this approach is tedious."

"We can't have that in a tale about purpose and being," Madame Leonedria said. "Debate stimulates insights. Ah, but those silent souls with us will take what we say much further than we can imagine."

"I hope so," Alex said. "You know, Mirai is what this story is actually about. She's the readers' progeny many times removed. I begged her to come with us."

"It was my choice," Mirai signed. She took a sip of wine and added, "However, having the decision foisted upon me caused terrible discord. Your time capsule caused no end to consternation, but here I am."

"I apologize," Alex said. "Verity and I thought your presence here was necessary. It makes the narrative harder to write since you can't speak. That's because you're deeper than these words can ever relate. Yeah, you think way beyond the text."

"Grasping the future is never easy," Madame Leonedria said. "Mirai and her kind found this work, much like you planned, Alex." She handed out the wine and bread. "She'll obviously answer your call. Nevertheless, we have to pay attention to the people reading these lines. They're the ones who have to act. Hmmm, and there is one in particular. I can sense her . . . and another. These people are in our presence, yet distinct from it physically. Yes, I can almost see those with us. Granted, most readers are far less removed in terms of perspective than Mirai."

"Well, we're all linked now," Alex said. He glanced at Mirai and asked, "Do you think this can work?"

She shrugged and took another sip of wine.

"Faint heart wins naught," Alex said. He turned to Madame and said, "You're right about me being lost, Madame. I'm not even sure how to proceed with our discussion."

"Why the cave setting, Alex?" Madame Leonedria asked. "Are these shadows dancing on my walls supposed to remind us of Plato's grand allegory?"

"As in worldly things being mere shadowy renditions of the perfect ideas underlying them?" Alex said.

"Examining that idea will distract us from this book's purpose," Mirai signed. "All this to explore a twenty-four-hundred-year-old allegory?"

"Well, we have to examine where the thoughts reside that are part and parcel of the reader, me, you, and all else," Alex explained. "But that is not what this cave setting is about. This is a point of departure."

"Dear me, this isn't going to be a treatise on metaphysics!" Madame Leonedria said. "Most readers don't want that, and neither do I!"

"Besides, our shared reality is far more complex than you know," Mirai signed. "Even during your day, the standard model of particle physics contained 61 fundamental constituents. People from my era know our existence is much more elaborate than this."

"Oh, I agree we can't go there, Mirai," Alex said. "That takes us into complexities that have nothing to do with this book's purpose. But sharing the basic ideas we're expressing can be challenging. Symbols like these words cannot cast metaphorical shadows without the impetus of learning, memory . . ."

Mirai whistled loudly, shook her head, and raised an open hand. It was her insistent cue that the conversation was off track. She knew Alex's mind tended to race and then abruptly jump topics.

"Quite right," Madame Leonedria said as she nodded toward Mirai. "Alex just deleted 452 words about the ancients that served no purpose. It is appropriate that you're with us, Mirai. You'll keep the conversation on track, so to speak. Let our context act as a point of departure from the conventional. Allow the narrative to unfold as it will, Alex. You're a writer guiding us on a vision quest. The readers have been led to my humble home. They sit with us at this hearth, feel the fire's warmth, and share our repast and conversation. Rest assured, most care little about Plato and the ancients. Even fewer want to delve into advanced physics.

"Many of them are seeking to learn and find purpose. In fact, that's why they've chosen to be with us. Isn't that what was promised on the book cover? They read these words and become one with our thoughts. You're unsure how to proceed, Alex, but I find that promising. Many of those with us are also confused about the nature of existence and our roles within it."

"That's exactly why we're here," Alex said.

"Oh, we're here for much more than that!" Madame Leonedria said. "We're here to share what you've seen about the readers' future. Fears and doubts about their prospects nag you." She sipped the wine and paused for a moment before continuing. "You've witnessed what the readers will face. Yet you question the dreams and visions that bring us together. Perhaps they were just fantasies. Maybe they were the products of delusion and not truth. If so, why have so many of them come to be? You wonder whether they are warnings or premonitions, the possible versus the fated."

"Those goddamn dreams give me no rest!" Alex exclaimed. He shook his head in frustration. "I have flashbacks of them all the damn time. For over 30 years, I've struggled to tell this story! I write and rewrite it, but the text is never good enough! Draft after draft with nothing ever being finished. Mirai knows it!"

Mirai nodded and signed, "It's a work in progress, though it never seems completed."

"Do you think a project like this can ever be truly finished?" Madame Leonedria asked.

"No," Alex sadly said. "Oh, I've already published the dreams in a semi-scientific treatise. But that was not the intended audience! I wanted us to commune with the person who is reading this sentence right now. Besides, that book costs way too much at $135 per copy! It was a wasted effort."

Mirai whistled and quickly signed a terse reply. "You learned from brain imaging studies that dreams and imagination share many functional roots. Ergo, the dreams were derived from some of the same processes used to craft this book."

"That's true, Mirai," Alex said. "However, there is a more pressing impetus now. By all rights, I shouldn't even be here. The physical me should have died about 10 years ago. Or was it twelve? But as promised, I'll finish this project."

"Perhaps," Madame Leonedria said. "We all hang by threads and most assuredly do not hang forever."

Mirai nodded, still miffed about Alex's carelessness. If he genuinely cared about their friendship or the future, why didn't he care about himself? After all, how could anyone claim to love another if that person couldn't love him or herself? She glared at Alex, and he looked down.

"You can be pissed off to the max, but the book is underway," Alex said. "I'm keeping my word." He paused and looked into Mirai's angry face, his eyes growing moist. "In reality land, every day is constant eff'n pain! Yet here I am, thinking of you and what we must accomplish. Now, let's focus on our task."

"What a contradiction you are," Mirai signed. "It seems to me a book about dreams shouldn't be much of a challenge for a writer. Dreams are narratives. They're stories or much like them."

"Those dreams are not simple stories!" Alex exclaimed. "You know that! And there is much about them that I'm not sure of. Granted, dreams and imagination are cohorts, but was I being guided by mere illusions, or was it some higher truth that moved me? Were the dreams just passing fantasies, or was there something far more profound involved?"

"Questioning your own insights and motives is promising, especially on a quest such as this," Madame Leonedria observed. "You sought to see the nature of what is and will be. The visions were disturbing. Where do they come from? Why you?"

"Exactly!" Alex said. "Why such a fallible and angry fuck-up? I've seen mysteries and paradoxes that defy interpretation, like the globe you showed me. I've even spoken with God or something very close to it. But who would believe such a thing? And who the heck am I to relate the story? I have—"

"The same strengths and weaknesses as those listening to our conversation," Madame Leonedria interrupted. "Stop this dithering, Alex! The readers can discern the truth. I know you intend to tell it; that's not the issue. I believe you question your abilities to tell the story."

"He always does," Mirai signed.

Alex sighed. "It's more than doubt! I don't want to mislead the person reading these words. That would be the worst possible outcome. Look, I've spent years studying the sciences and humanities. However, the events in my dreams go way beyond anything I've studied or experienced in the material world. How does one write about experiences that defy description?"

"Enough self-doubts!" Madame Leonedria said. "Your concerns mix with the angst over so many failed efforts. Moreover, you hate wine and wonder why you wrote it into the script. Fine. Enjoy the bread, my diabetic friend. But please leave your tedious doubts behind! The reader yearns to be informed, not distracted. Start by letting us know how your journey to this place began. Tell us about the earliest dreams you can recall."

5

The Evolution of a Dreamer

The fire crackled and popped, casting dancing shadows throughout the room. Alex sank deeper into the cushions while pondering his earliest dreams. His eyes lit up as recollections came to light, and he leaned forward.

"Well, I often dreamt of flying when I was a kid. Most people have similar dreams. They're cross-cultural and ubiquitous. Some Freudian researchers once believed they're caused by emerging sexual urges. That idea was mere supposition, the stuff of early humanistic psychology."

5.1 The author experienced both lucid and astral dream states

"It's all about telling the story, Alex, and not explaining every detail," Madame Leonedria said. "Get to the dreams, child. Did you like them?"

"You bet!" Alex said with a smile. "How I looked forward to them!"

"Do me a favor, Alex," Madame Leonedria said. "Put yourself into a present-tense voice while explaining a past-tense experience. Relive the events."

"I'll try," Alex said. He closed his eyes and peered deep within, his tale slowly unfolding . . .

"Wow, I'm soaring way above my house. But where should I go? Oh, what about crossing the Connecticut River! Yeah! I can fly above the forests and the fields of Vermont. Nana lives out there. All the roofs and streets can be seen from way up here. But which way should I go? There's Main Street! And the road to the right leads to the river, so we should head that way. But I'm too high, so I will go down a little.

"There is the steel trestle bridge between West Lebanon, New Hampshire, and White River Junction, Vermont. Yep, we're going the right way. As we descend, the flaking green paint and rivets on the bridge come into view. Wow, there must be a gazillion rivets on the bridge! They're very rusty. I can also see swirling eddies and whirlpools in the river. Oh, don't get stuck in them! No way. There are big trees up ahead I could crash into.

"I better go higher real fast! Whew, that was close! We barely cleared those elm trees. The treetops, the roofs, the roads below . . . everything is so clear. I can even see boulders, road lines, and chimneys on the roofs. The wind blows on my face, and I feel motion when I turn or change height. This is wicked neat! I wonder where these dreams will lead."

"You knew you were dreaming," Mirai signed. "An early sign of metacognition?"

"Perhaps," Madame Leonedria said. "I'm more concerned with Alex's storytelling at this stage. I believe reliving the dreams is the best way to proceed."

"They will still be reconstructions," Mirai signed. "All memories are reconstructions and often deviate slightly with every recall."

"Memories can be imperfect, yet here you are, my dear," the Madame stated. "You must have felt the trek was worth the cost." She turned to Alex and smiled. "I noticed the occasional fear, Alex. Tell me about that."

"I've always feared heights," Alex observed. "It runs in my family. Nonetheless, I kept trying to fly higher, faster, and farther. Then one night when I was about seven or so . . . well, I got lost. It was terrifying."

"Active voice, child," Madame Leonedria said.

Alex looked down, speaking with increasing emotion while he continued his story.

"W-w-what am I going to do? The moon is out. But it's way too dark up here to see where we are. Gosh, why did I have to go so far and so high? And which way leads back home? I could crash into a plane or something. There's a clearing over there just below the slope of that big hill! Yeah! Let's land there and figure out how to get home. Oh, be careful going down! No, don't land on the road! Go for that clearing to the left of it. Slow down more and go around those bushes! Slower! Slow, slow, slow! There we go. Now land easy! There! I can feel the ground.

"It's cold here. I bet some big animals are in those woods. And don't go near that dirty water! This place must be on the far side of White River Junction, just beyond the Veterans' Hospital. That's where we probably are. I don't know. But it's dark, and I'm too tired to fly anymore. How am I going to get home? We'll have to walk, but which way do we go? And what if a bear or wild dog gets me? It's best to hide in that thicket over there. Yeah, we'll wait here until dawn. Then, I can find some help.

"Yuck! This place is all muddy! We're in a swamp, and my feet are getting wet. Some of the reeds and cattails are taller than me. I could get caught in quicksand or drown. I want to wake up! I want to . . . no! Don't cry! Something could hear us! Shhh, just stay really still.

"Gee, I'm thinking about things while in a dream. But is this a dream? Maybe we're really here, lost in this dirty place! Yeah, this may be real. Stars are twinkling up above. I feel the night's chill and hear crickets chirping. And those are peepers in the water, lots and lots of them. The long grass and bushes feel prickly, and my feet are soaked. I want to wake up! This is scary!"

Alex looked up at Mirai and the Madame, his chest heaving. "Eventually, I did awaken."

"Did you notice the shifts from the 'I' to the 'we' voice?" Mirai signed. "When we examined earlier versions of this text, the 'we' voice was exclusive."

"The 'we' perspective drove my editors crazy," Alex laughed. "It's a passive-expressive mode. Dale also claimed the 'we' voice can indicate deception during interviews. That put me right off my feed. But 'we' is how I've usually perceived things. It's how I speak to myself while thinking. The use of the 'I' voice was her idea. You can see I resisted it and still do. Besides, the perspective shifts add variety, albeit at the cost of consistency."

"We're the sum of many parts," Madame Leonedria observed. "I, Mirai, Verity, and the readers are also in your mind, so perhaps the 'we' voice is appropriate. You certainly memorized that event in great detail."

"I was terrified!" Alex said. "I can still recall it as an actual event, even after 60-odd years. At this stage, I began to blur the distinctions between reality and thought. The experience was powerful enough to become trapped in memory's net. The processes that cause emotional dreams to be so vividly memorized are known, but you two will get angry if I discuss science."

"Stop acting like a child!" Mirai angrily signed. "However, don't drone on to the detriment of the story you're trying to tell."

"Sound advice," Alex said. "When we experience strong emotions, our bodies release stress hormones. These can aid memory formation. However, excessive amounts of the hormones often impair memory. This is probably an innate defense response. After all, the complete recall of very traumatic memories can have negative consequences. That's the essence of post-traumatic stress disorder. Of course, I had no such insights at the time. As for the source of flying dreams, there are numerous theories, but damn few facts."

"Perhaps flying dreams reflect what our youthful thoughts can do, although the 'how' and 'why' questions beg for explanations," Madame Leonedria said.

"I studied the literature and came up with a few ideas," Alex replied.

"Don't get us sidetracked!" Mirai signed.

"I'll be brief," Alex replied. "I look at early flying dreams in terms of cortical development. For example, children have a superabundance of neurons and synaptic connections, far more than adults. These are slowly winnowed as we mature. In effect, the brain modifies itself while we grow. These changes continue until 21 or so. However, the early abundance of synaptic connections may have some advantages. It could allow our young minds to process information in more synesthetic fashions than are possible after we mature."

"Synesthetic?" Madame Leonedria scoffed.

"Most of our listeners and readers aren't familiar with this term, nor should you be burdening them," Mirai signed. "Here is where you always go wrong! You get lost in irrelevant details, and the story suffers. This isn't a science treatise!" she added, her agile fingers almost dripping with disdain for Alex's approach.

"I'm sure the readers don't want to wade through layers of jargon, but this is important," Alex noted. "Synesthesia happens when a particular sensory or upper-level cortical pathway automatically activates another path. It's like a cross-wiring event. For instance, some folks process specific numbers similarly to how most analyze unique colors. Others perceive certain sounds as evoking distinct emotional feelings or sensations. The phenomenon has been amply demonstrated and has a very high incidence among poets and people of that ilk.

"Simply put, when young, we may recall event sensations in fashions that far exceed what can be managed in later life. For example, during youth, we remember a car ride. While doing so, the recall of seeing objects flying by may become enmeshed with a simultaneous memory of feeling movement. To be sure, these are memories wrapped in sensations! All the more so in dream states. In fact, there's a tremendous capacity for imaginative information processing when we're young. Sadly, only some can enlist that ability when they're older. Maturity makes our minds more compartmentalized and efficient, but we lose something precious during the transition."

"Indeed, we do," Madame Leonedria said. "And it can take eons to reacquire the capacity."

"I had no such insights at the time," Alex said. "My dreams also became more elaborate over time. Of course, that's perfectly normal. As the flying dreams proliferated, I also experienced many instances of *déjà vu*. I suppose that's only natural. As our brains mature, we garner more memories. These can be activated by sights, sounds, and other sensory cues we may not consciously perceive. It's hard to say whether my dreams or life experiences were the sources of these *déjà vu* effects. There was also something more unusual that occurred." Alex paused for a moment. "Damn, I'm not comfortable talking about it."

"Then I'm positive we should discuss it," Madame Leonedria said. "Was it related to *déjà vu* events?"

"Not exactly," Alex said. "How should I put this? Well, my life has been riddled with what can best be called 'perspective shifts.' I don't know how else to describe them, although this will sound crazy as hell. These stretch back to my earliest memories."

"They occurred during waking hours?" Madame Leonedria asked.

"Always," Alex replied. "Their development probably overlapped with changes in my dream states. After all, when our imagination expands enough to construct flying perspectives, other perceptual abilities could also become manifest."

"It would help if you could provide a few examples," Madame Leonedria said.

"The perspective shifts were sudden and unexpected," Alex said. "They also came with an overpowering sensation of detachment. I could be on the slopes of Mount Lebanon, in my yard, or playing on a neighbor's lawn. Suddenly, I would feel a kind of linkage with another point of view or time. The events are hard to explain. It seemed like I was outside myself."

"As in, removed from your own mind?" Mirai signed.

"It was more like looking at a reflection of what I was doing from a distant viewpoint," Alex explained. "I could actually see myself pondering the odd connections while they occurred. I could watch my expressions and body position shift while the event unfolded."

"Many of us sense having been somewhere before," Madame Leonedria observed.

"Oh, the occurrences were much different than that," Alex said. "The earliest recallable event happened when I was about three or four. I was playing on our front porch with my two sisters. Light snow covered the landscape, and I was bundled up, safe from winter's chill. I saw myself holding onto the porch's railing and peering through the spindles. I marveled at the effect. It was like witnessing a prisoner in an old-fashioned jail. There was no understanding of why or how it happened, but the event became locked in my memory.

"Similar perspective shifts happened that involved a nap with my grandmother, watching myself stare at Christmas lights, being terrified during a fierce thunderstorm, and making drawings for a grade school project on the Civil War. In all cases, I was watching myself. The events weirded me out at first. I pondered while I was pondering, unsure of how I could possibly be seeing myself while the episodes unfolded. However, I grew accustomed to the detached feeling."

"Didn't your young mind find this odd?" Mirai signed.

"For years, I found the experiences disturbing," Alex said. "I wasn't sure what was happening, although I didn't regard these perspective shifts as mystical or magical. Imagining ourselves from an external point of view is now an area of much research. Psychologists call it 'allocentric perception.' Yet these were spontaneous experiences. They were not dedicated tasks in a lab setting. Hell, I have no idea what stimulated them."

"One such as you will always seek rational explanations," Madame Leonedria said.

"I have for years," Alex said. "The only possible answer is ongoing cognitive and sensory-processing activity. But what sparked it? The triggers for internal memory activation are many. They could even include abnormal cortical electrical activity, as in epilepsy or altered neurotransmitter concentrations. Activity can also be triggered via external energy sources. For example, focused electromagnetic impulses can trigger memory-processing resources."

"It seems they were daydreams, Alex," Mirai observed.

"I'm not so sure," Alex said. "I've long wondered if your lot had anything to do with them. After all, you being here demonstrates the future can inform the past."

"Why would you think my peers or I would be involved in those events?" Mirai signed.

"Oh, we'll get to that," Alex promised. "Many other things were going on during that time that impacted my dreams and thoughts. For example, my family life dictated that I become withdrawn and fearful."

"Explain why," Mirai signed. "Those with us need to know, but be brief!"

"It will piss off my family if I do that," Alex advised.

"Honesty risks discord," Madame Leonedria observed. "And I know you once abandoned this project because of that risk. But don't we owe the reader the truth as we perceive it?"

"We do," Alex confessed, briefly shaking his head. "You see, my father, Henry, drank a lot. Yeah, he was frequently loud and abusive when I was a child. The man was tormented. He would scream, swear, and smash furniture during drunken escapades. It was awful. While his hurricane raged, my mother tried being its serene eye. She was a place of comfort during the storms.

"I recall Dad breaking a rocking chair my mother comforted me in. I then found solace hiding under a dining room pedestal table . . . until he destroyed it. I grew to dread his presence, his ceaseless tirades. There was nowhere left to go but inside. Fear plagued my thoughts and daily life. In time, the fear turned to anger. Then the anger morphed into hatred. Sickness overtook my heart, and the seeds of a sociopath were being sown.

"I drew pictures of people being tortured. I was so cruel to animals that it shamed me. I set fires. I tried to burn down our house . . . twice. My mother held my hand to a fire on the stove at a young age. She wanted me to fully understand the damage my growing sickness could cause others. I was terrified. The event was so traumatic that I cannot recall the pain. Ma claimed the deed served the purpose, although it was an extreme measure."

"All of that truly happened?" Mirai signed.

"Of course it did!" Alex tersely replied. "And I know some readers get turned off by such admissions. A few are thinking, 'Wow, this guy is a psychopath!' Well, life ain't all lollipops and roses for some folks! The past is what it is. We do the best we can to live with it and soldier on. Besides, I owe those with us the complete truth."

"You were angry when you related your father's behavior, Alex," Madame Leonedria observed. "After all these years, you still hold on to the rage."

"I know," Alex sadly said. "That's why I'm alone. My history and thoughts are jumbled and twisted. I can be a moody and nasty son-of-a-bitch at times, that's for sure. I'm hardly the person who should be telling a story that leads to God's door."

"We'll see where it leads," Madame Leonedria said. "We're all children of our circumstances, Alex. They made you different from the norm. I suspect you know that. Perhaps you've always felt this way."

"We're all unique in one way or another," Alex admitted. "I felt more trapped than anything else. It was like I was living out a script that had been written for me."

"You didn't feel there were any choices?" Mirai signed.

"Not for me," Alex said. "I begged my mom to get a divorce in middle school, but she wouldn't do it. She loved Dad, no matter what. So, yeah, I was trapped."

"There must have been some happy moments," Madame Leonedria observed. "Weren't there birthday parties? Wasn't Christmas a time of joy and wonder? Surely, your mother read stories to you?"

"Yes, Ma did read many stories," Alex said. "And as I learned the narrative form, my dreams changed too. They took on narrative patterns. In fact, by the age of seven or eight, a huge shift occurred in my dreams. I discovered an escape from sadness and despair! I crafted a wonderful fantasy realm within my dreams. These events were as vivid and realistic as daily experiences. They soon assumed a serial structure."

"Interesting," Mirai signed. "Please elaborate."

Alex sat up and took a sip of wine. "The earliest I can recall involved a recurring series of dreams about children who played by a riverbank. I must have been seven or so at the time. The events were like a weekly TV serial; only the episodes played out in my head. But they were very realistic. In fact, these dreams became integral parts of my reality. There were plot twists, but the setting and characters became very familiar. They were my friends, and I looked forward to visiting them.

"I can still see their faces. Each had a distinct and lively personality. There was a worrier, a questioner, a comedian, and many others. Their names elude me now. We met in a small, unpainted barn with spider webs in its doorway. We'd play hide-and-seek in the straw piles or race through the nearby fields and forest. Sometimes, we strolled down trails that led to the river. The water there was dark, deep, and turbulent. I was afraid to go near it. There was a tire affixed to a branch that hung over the river. But only the big kids used that.

"My mother grew up adjacent to the Connecticut and White River confluence. When I was a child, we often visited her old homestead. I probably picked up on those memories and used them to create my dream world of escape."

Alex wrung his hands together and glanced down at the floor. "The most unusual aspect of those dreams is that the children aged over time, much like I did. Then I became arrogant about my abilities to withdraw into this conscious dream world." He paused and shook his head. "Unfortunately, my haughtiness had unexpected repercussions. Man, did I mess up."

"Please go on," Mirai signed, "though you seem uncomfortable."

"I am," Alex confessed. "Anyway, during one of these dreams, we were gathered together in the barn when some older children drifted in. I usually regarded them as a vague threat. However, they never hurt me or others during these wonderful fantasies. They were just bigger. In any event, I decided to impress the older kids with my knowledge."

"First person active voice, Alex," Madame Leonedria said. "Put us into the dream as it happened. What did you say to the older children?"

"I was so damn prideful," Alex said. "Give me a moment to recall the essentials."

Alex ran his hands through his hair and furrowed his brow. He bit his lower lip in concentration. "I remember telling the older kids, 'You know, we're all in a dream. I'm the dreamer! Yep, this is my dream, but I'm unsure how it works.'

"Oh, oh! My friends seem surprised. They're upset by my revelation. The little girl over in the corner is crying.

'It's no big deal. Please don't worry,' I say.

"It's not working. And those big kids look angry. This could get bad. That big kid in the light brown shirt is furious! He has freckles and dirty blond hair. Gosh, he must be 12 or 13. Man, he's got his fists clenched!

'Why did you have to tell her that?' he growls.

'I didn't mean anything bad!'

"I don't know what to say or do. All the kids have downcast expressions. Oh, what have I done? I feel terrible. It's like I blabbed a big secret.

'I am so sorry! I didn't mean anything bad!' I shout.

"They won't even look at me. Why? Why did I have to show off?

"Sadly, that was the end of my adventures with the river kids," Alex sighed. He looked at Mirai and saw a sense of uneasiness in her eyes. "I never dreamt of them again, though I searched for the group in many dreams. I greatly regretted the incident and still do."

"As well you should," Mirai signed. "Arrogance has a price."

"Why do you think the series ended?" Madame Leonedria asked.

"I was in the initial stages of learning how to master and manipulate dream narratives," Alex replied. "The experts call it 'lucid dreaming.' One becomes aware of objects and events while in a dream state. There's also a capacity to consciously discern thoughts and thought processes. Lastly, the dreamer develops self-awareness. That's the capacity to act deliberately and exert influences within the dream. The narrative form has great power, but it can be fragile. It's one thing to be content while playing a part in an unfolding story. It's another to bring an outside perspective into the account that violates the plotline."

"It is much like the person who screams, 'God is dead!' during a High Mass," Madame Leonedria noted. "The intrusion can violate a story's form and expectations. It can even shatter an entire pattern of thought."

"This is a common effect of pushing the knowing-you're-in-a-dream technique too far," Mirai signed. "Did you think you were special because of these serial dreams?"

"Not at all," Alex said. "I presumed everyone had dreams like mine. Anyone reading these sentences can use the dream-consciousness approaches discussed here. The key element is the conscious realization that one is within a dream, which is a big step for some. Still, many readers will have experienced these kinds of events. However, individual predispositions and experiences are critical factors in their evolution."

"I wonder whether the perspective shifts were also evolving as you aged," Madame Leonedria remarked. "They seem to mirror some of your dream developments."

"They did," Alex said. "A very memorable experience happened when I was eight or nine. I was standing by a trellis on a neighboring apartment's back lawn. Quite suddenly, I saw myself. I knew at once that the image was from an outside perspective. It made me wonder if my ongoing thoughts emanated from within my body or were being manipulated from the outside. I tried to discern how this distant point of view operated. The odd state accorded a marvelous linkage, although with whom or what was unclear.

"There was something profound to be learned from the experience. So, I strived to determine what it was. It was clear that the occurrence could instill ideas. But from where? I sensed the event was bound by rules and regulations, although these still needed to be gleaned. Indeed, I failed to grasp any deeper meaning. It all ended in a muddle."

"Did these experiences follow any kind of order?" Madame Leonedria asked. "Did they build on one another?"

"Yeah, to an extent," Alex explained. He fidgeted and added, "A powerful event occurred while I was in the house's yard directly adjacent to my family's home. I saw myself stop and look up, pondering where the influence was coming from. A familiar presence was communing with me via thought.

"This had happened in past instances, but that time was different. My personal sense of self moved into the mind of the watcher. We melded, or so it seemed, and I wondered whether the experience came from within or outside my body. Yet the event threw in a new twist. I glimpsed, or more likely imagined, what the other entity was doing. It was like I was in an outside viewer's mind."

"As in an actually seeing from another person's point of view?" Madame Leonedria asked.

"Exactly!" Alex explained. "My thoughts were one with the observer's, a shared consciousness. I knew the outside observer was distinct from me, but our thoughts had become enmeshed. I sensed he understood our shared consciousness situation and desperately wanted to correct it. I saw the man's hands busily adjusting complex equipment bedecked with displays. There was a problem with the machine. It had something to do with energy fluctuations or oscillations. That's what I gleaned from the discussion that was going on.

"A plotline began unfolding. Of course, this was not unlike my serial dreams. I heard disjointed bits of a panicked discussion between the observer I was one with and another fellow. He seemed to be a perplexed coworker. A dial came into sharp focus; it had three calibrated sections served by a single measuring needle. The goal was for the indicator to be in the central red section of each dial. However, something was wrong and needed to be fixed.

"Then, the linkage was abruptly broken. I suddenly zoomed back to seeing myself again, standing on the lawn. I felt like a lab animal. So now I'm putting you on the spot, Mirai. Was that your kin? Has the future been tweaking me?"

"Tweaking?" Mirai signed. "These thoughts we're sharing with the reader are changing perceptions. Is that what you mean by 'tweaking'? Is tweaking a deliberate manipulation or an aspect of happenstance?"

"Ha, you're so damn political," Alex said, shaking his head. "Does your kin have the capacity to shift thoughts?"

"Anyone has that capacity!" Mirai angrily signed. "It's called communication! That is what we're doing right now! Did the future directly intervene? Is that what you want to know?" She grew angry and glared at Alex with fiery eyes. "You tried to manipulate us!" she signed, fingers gesturing fast and furious. "This text, your diaries . . . they all included several acts of blatant manipulation. You wanted a power that you already had! You begged us for what has been destroying your mind! Yet you wanted even more. You wanted to join us!"

"To escape my time!" Alex said. "Yes, that's true enough. Nevertheless, the event with the machines gave me a reason to believe there was external causation! Mirai, you know that event wasn't based on imagination alone."

"You've done your best to make it that way," Mirai signed.

"It's hard not to love you," Alex said. "I do so with every fiber of my being. Be that as it may, I regarded the machine perspective shift as a net plus. I gleaned a few more insights into the odd experiences. However, I was no closer to understanding whether these perspective shifts were artifacts of imagination or external causation."

"Perhaps there was a relationship between the serial nature of your perspective shifts and those found in your dreams," Madame Leonedria said. "There was a general tendency to unfold ongoing and increasingly elaborate plotlines."

"That's a distinct possibility," Alex said.

"It's much more likely than the future interfering with the past," Mirai noted. "There are also ample life experiences and even genetics to consider. These played into the dreams you relate."

"I'm sure you're right," Alex replied. "However, there seems to be something beyond all that. My father didn't know about some of these dreams, although we had discussed several. He appeared to discern that they would one day be put into this text. Oddly, he even seemed to grasp his role in shaping my thoughts, dreary and traumatic though the experiences were. He spoke with me when he was close to death. He lay there, lamenting his drinking and raging. His voice was raspy and weak.

"He grabbed my hand and said, 'I had to do those things. I had to. And someday, you'll understand why.' Flashes of some of the dreams came to mind even while he spoke. Yeah, I knew exactly what he was talking about. It was like I could see inside his mind. His torment taught me lessons I would one day share with others. He knew that relating his and my shared misery could help some people find salvation from the storm, or so it seemed. Yet there had been too much anguish and turmoil! God, how I hated him."

"That hate has left you a bitter old man, the very thing your father wished to avoid," Madame Leonedria said. She shook her head and looked down. "I find that surprising. Your mother was a loving woman. You've even assigned me her baptismal name."

"She was kind," Alex said. "My mother tried to free my burden, even to the end. She was dying of pancreatic cancer, and I had just finished recording these dreams. They were unpolished, and it was clear that she would never have a chance to read the work. At one point, I gazed down on her failing, cancer-ravaged body. I told her how angry I was with God for her pain.

"In a weary and strained voice, she said, 'No, you must never do that, my son. You must learn how to love.'

"Love was her way, and that impetus had long held the family together. I read her some of these very words, including this sentence. After all, her influence helped stimulate this manuscript's creation. She faded quickly over the next few days, but at least her insights will touch other minds and hearts."

"It's a pity you didn't take your mother's advice about learning to forgive and forget," Madame Leonedria said. "Trauma can blind us, Alex. Flashes of furniture being smashed, slurred insults, and angry screams still echo through your mind."

"Like when my father said, 'Fuck you and fuck your birthday'!" Alex growled. "Dad was too damn drunk to make it up the stairs. He repeatedly drilled those words into my soul while I helped him to his bed." Alex's eyes narrowed, and teeth clenched. "Could a fucking apology erase all that? *Could it?*"

"You always say there are reasons for everything," Mirai signed.

"Yeah, there were reasons!" Alex said angrily, his voice growing loud and strident. "Henry was the victim of his own father's brutality. Hell, he was beaten for poor grades or spelling mistakes! I mean, he was whipped! His father was an intolerant intellectual, a beast of the self. He was also a man of utterly savage disposition. Dad was ridiculed and abused for even minor offenses. All this was the handiwork of a prideful bigot from the Old South. He wouldn't even attend my dad's wedding. No son of his would marry a temperamental Latin!

"I also understood how the father's sins are borne by the son. Still, this knowledge didn't quell the hatred and anger growing within. Understanding cannot stop trauma's fires. They still rage to this very day! In the end, the cycle of hatred is forged by torment and fed by its memories. Believe me, I learned how to hate."

"That's the basis for your sociopathic tendencies," Mirai signed. "We found it odd that you confessed this early in the text. This is especially so in a book that seeks to appeal to our readers' higher natures. This was a risky tactic."

"Alex regards himself as a reflection of his kind," Madame Leonedria said. "He is someone with humanity's strengths and flaws." She leaned forward and added, "As your mother often said, 'Hatred is binding and blinding.' However, your father's behavior was one of the keys to this domain of thought we're now sharing with others. The turmoil he caused helped spark your visions."

"The cost was terrible!" Alex replied, a tear rolling down his cheek. "His actions made me withdraw from life, to flee deep inside."

"Said the author who often fails to understand what he is writing and why he is writing it," Madame Leonedria said. She took a deep sip of wine. "Listen, my child, you're not alone in bearing life's wounds. Several of those reading these lines have also felt the same stings. Some have been shot, stabbed, raped, and far worse. They've known abuse that you cannot even imagine! They've become one with us and seek to understand what you clearly do not.

"Your wounds have driven you into this refuge wherein we strive to find and share meaning with others. This includes those who can still escape the trap that has ensnared you. They need to seek help, much like you've refused to. Advising others to learn how to forgive is the first step in coming to terms with much of life's suffering," Madame Leonedria said.

Mirai nodded, signing, "We have had to forgive those who did nothing to save the world we must inhabit! That includes some of those who are reading this book."

"How can one learn to forgive when traumatic memories haunt us?" Alex roared. "They constantly tear at us, reminding us of misery and pain at every turn. Forgive and forget is a stu-pid-ass bromide! Should a woman forgive a rapist? Should a young man forgive a sexual predator? That torment does not melt away!" he fumed.

"How the hatred has poisoned you!" Madame Leonedria said. "That same hatred infests humanity, and this is an unde-niable truth. Wars rage and people starve because of hate! Try to learn from your father and begin by forgiving him." She loudly slammed an open hand on the table and pointed at Alex. "Yet your eyes grow wide even now, and a snarl mars your face. How can the readers rise above hate when you cannot? Yes, memory is one with reality for many trauma victims. Misery becomes as fresh and present as remembering. You've become trapped with-in a cycle that keeps turning on itself! It can grow into a whirl-wind that sweeps away everything good. Tell me, where is your wife? Do you have a child to bear your name? There is nothing but these words! That is what your hatred and anger have done! That is what they can do to entire worlds! A sad past can destroy both the present and future."

"Enough!" Alex bellowed. "Yeah, I'm tormented, and per-haps I'll always be. This is a brutally painful part of the text for me. But if these words help others, they are worth the mis-ery. They sure as hell burn me to the core. I'll get this fucking project done if it kills me! I've transformed some of my hate into dedication. That's why we're here! Is that what you want me to say? Is that what you want me to tell the readers? Is this enough anguish?"

"You tell me," Madame Leonedria said, gritting her teeth. "You're writing the lines. As I've explained, you're not alone in harboring the anger and resentment wrought by festering memories. Perhaps one day, you will see deeply enough to glimpse the beauty within. Perhaps those who are sharing our conversation will too. You and they could then perceive that new experiences can provide happy memories that counteract the bad. That is a choice that everyone has. It will be so while the spark of life remains."

There was silence for a moment except for the crackling fire.

"Here, let me refresh your drink," Madame Leonedria said, breaking the silence.

"No thanks; I hate wine," Alex said.

"Perhaps that's the subconscious reason you wrote it into the script," Madame Leonedria said. "Given your experiences with alcohol, it's no wonder you've chosen to avoid drink. In any case, we've just started on our journey. I'm particularly interested in the dream where you saw this."

She reached into her bag and pulled out the crystal globe.

6

The Dreamer Learns

The globe glittered and was warm to the touch. Various hues occasionally sparked to life from discrete and tiny points of light within the orb while they swirled around one another in circles. There was an underlying order here, though it was difficult to grasp or describe.

"May I hold it?" Alex asked.

"Of course," Madame Leonedria said, handing him the glittering object. "Be aware that the knowledge it contains can have a terrible price. Yes, it has great attraction, as does a female black widow for its mate."

"I saw a larger and more sophisticated version of this globe in a dream," Alex explained. "It was from a long dream series, which began soon after the river kids disappeared from the scene. The series must have started when I was about 10 and lasted into my late twenties.

"The dream site was midway up the west slope of Mount Lebanon, well behind our house. In those days, the area was sprawling with thick woods and a few rocky fields, although it is developed today. In my dreams, I walked through the forest and marveled at the ladyfingers and other wildflowers. Crickets chirped, and the soft carpet of leaves squished underfoot. It was a pleasant refuge from the storm of my everyday family life.

"In one dream, I found a simple white ranch house partially surrounded by a post-and-rail fence. A dark-haired boy about my age was playing in the front yard. His name was Roger, and I sensed we shared similar misery. Lord knows how I knew this, but I did. Whereas my pain involved my father, his appeared to be derived from his white-haired mother. Oh, she was in no way mean to me, and Roger never said she hurt him. I also recall her feeding us tasty little treats like cookies and brownies. Perhaps I only imagined she harmed Roger to strengthen my identification with him. Then again, her maternal instincts might have been so powerful that they stifled him. To be sure, she was constantly in the background, or so it seemed.

"In any event, dreams about Roger were a huge step up in reality and clarity. I could feel, touch, and manipulate objects. I could talk with Roger about our shared dream state, and he would respond with questions."

"Please give us an example," Mirai signed.

Alex nodded. "In one dream, Roger asked, 'How do you know this is a dream? And maybe it's me and not you who is having it.'

"I answered, 'Well, I'm going to wake up soon, and you'll be gone. That's how it always goes.'

'How do you know your waking up isn't my going to sleep?'

'Because I can go into the woods where you live when I'm awake, and your house isn't there!'

'Perhaps we live in different times or places but share the same dreams.'

'That would be neat! Do you think that's what happens?' I asked. I had never thought of my dreams occurring within the concurrent context of another person's thoughts and ideas. Plus, the notion Roger and I could commune with each other despite being in far different times and locations was intriguing. He was a rush."

"He sounds like the kind of friend every curious child would want to have," Mirai noted.

"That he was," Alex said. "Roger was far smarter than I. He discussed being in two places at once and other mysterious things. He tried to explain these concepts by way of complex mathematical terms. They made absolutely no sense to my young mind. Nonetheless, he patiently wrote formulas on a notepad. Unfortunately, I couldn't grasp what they meant. They're only vague memories now. I should have recorded them then but didn't see the point. It wasn't like they made any sense to me. Perhaps the memories could be retrieved by hypnosis. Yet I've little faith in recovered memories."

"Those formulas could have been illuminating," Mirai signed.

"How could a character in your dream possibly know more than you did?" Madame Leonedria asked.

"We discussed how Roger came to know so much," Alex said. "He told me a wise, old uncle had taught him many things. I never met the man. He was apparently a professor of some sort who was on perpetual sabbatical. His uncle had stored several fascinating teaching machines in Roger's home, secured in an off-limits room. Clearly, we weren't to disturb his possessions while he was away. Moreover, we would be punished by Roger's mother for doing so. Still, kids will be kids! In one dream, Roger and I snuck into the room. Shelves lined the walls and went up to the ceiling. They were loaded with books, papers, and various black boxes."

"Relive the experience," Madame Leonedria advised. "Look back into the dream."

"Give me a moment," Alex said. He closed his eyes and tried to visualize when he came across the globe. In a soft voice, he said. "Yeah, we're in the room. It's a bit dark. Shhh, we must make fewer sounds, or we'll be discovered. Roger unclips the latches of a big box on one of the lower shelves and carefully removes the cover. The container houses a large crystal globe mounted atop a short pedestal. The assembly is affixed to a sturdy metal base and is quite heavy. The base plate has a complicated control device built into it. Numerous dials and buttons can modulate the sphere's inner display, and Roger explains what they do. There are also engraved charts on the base, though I need help to understand what they say.

'Wait till you see this!' Roger softly says.

"Roger manipulates the controls, and the results are marvelous! From a point within the display's center suddenly arises a rapidly multiplying host of tiny glittering lights. They spread outward, quickly filling most of the sphere. The lights coalesce and separate. They're bound in a waltz of sorts that forms delicate weblike patterns. The lights grow bright and then dim while spreading outward. Then the entire cycle repeats itself, going back to a single point. Therein, it begins anew.

'Wow! That's really cool, Roger! What does it mean?' I whisper.

'Everything!'

'Everything?'

"Help is needed to understand what the teaching tool is designed to demonstrate, but I am more interested in the device's beauty. Roger is patiently trying to explain what the globe's operations represent. He's talking about energy, mass, gravity, and time. Finally, Roger gives up. He advises, 'Why don't you try looking at one particular point in the globe? Something amazing will happen!'

"I do as asked, and I'm awestruck by the results. The deeper I peer into the display, the more detailed the view becomes. It's like a telescope is zooming into an ever-smaller bit of the universe. Galaxies appear before long. Within the galaxies, wink star clusters. Within these clusters, I see solar systems. Planets circle around stars and moons around planets. Roger tells me that on some of these planets are those who can see our world. We're separated by time and space but united by shared thoughts.

'The deeper one looks, the more one sees. The more one sees, the greater the passage of time,' Roger says. He tries to explain the details involved, and I pretend to understand. Yet to me, the device is only a plaything!"

Alex continued to gaze into Madame Leonedria's small sphere, seemingly lost in its magic.

"It was a wondrous apparatus," he observes. "Several years later, I grasped some connections while studying special relativity theory, albeit superficially. There was no higher understanding of the dream's implications while experiencing it. Yet Roger put up with my ignorance. He showed me several other machines. I sure wasn't up to the task of understanding the principles they were designed to demonstrate. The details of the devices escape me now. Oh, there was a neat apparatus that could cause sound and light to emanate from distant locations. It was a directed-energy-transference mechanism, an utterly fascinating tool. Once again, I viewed the machine as a very cool toy."

"Interesting," Mirai noted. "Were these prescient dreams?"

"Good question," Alex said. "I don't have a great answer for where the insights came from. I suspect that knowledge is inherent in being. Perhaps knowledge exists as unrealized potentials that imagination can occasionally grasp and bring to light."

"Part of your tripartite scheme of mass, energy, and thought," Madame Leonedria said. "Tell us more about Roger."

"Dreams involving Roger occurred for many years," Alex said. "Much as with the river kids, we both aged simultaneously. I instantly recognized the dream settings when they occurred. However, the usual narrative sporadically tossed in a few wrinkles that kept my interest. For example, Roger was not always home. Well, that's what his mother would claim. In fact, I once snuck into the house when no one was inside so I could peruse the black boxes."

"Such was your quest for hidden knowledge," Madame Leonedria said with a smile.

"True enough," Alex said. "Anyway, Roger's mom returned, and she must have seen me running out the back door. It was a close call. I still ponder what would have happened if she'd caught me."

"An extended developmental narrative," Mirai deftly signed. "It seems to have dynamic elements."

"Yes, the plots were constantly evolving," Alex said. "Roger also changed a lot over time, as do we all. He became more engrossed in various interests and was at home far less often. Unlike the river kids, his departure was not abrupt. My last visit with him was in the late 80s, perhaps a bit later. Let's try to go back to that dream. Give me a minute."

"Take your time, Alex," Madame Leonedria said.

"I'm walking the familiar path to Roger's house," Alex said while reliving the event. "Ah, he is in the front yard. He's reclining on a comfortable lawn couch beneath a big sun umbrella.

A clunky cellular phone is lying atop a table by his side. A few other lawn chairs are close by. Ha, he's grown a mustache! Oh, it looks like Roger is glad to see me.

'It's been a long time,' he says with a smile.

'How's your mother doing?' I ask.

'I'm fine,' she says while exiting the house. She's carrying a tray with two glasses of ice-cold lemonade. She is wrinkled and hobbled by age but still attentive.

'Please sit and have a glass of lemonade,' she says. 'I'm sure you and Roger have a lot to discuss.'

"I sit in one of the lawn chairs and take a sip from the sweet nectar. It is cold and tart. Roger and I exchange pleasantries and engage in some philosophical banter. Roger's mother retreats into the house, leaving us to talk.

'I've been reading a lot of Plato lately,' I advise.

'Oh, Platonic metaphysics. I prefer Aristotle myself,' Roger says nonchalantly.

'I figured you would. Aristotle didn't accept the need to postulate a transcendental noumenal realm for perfect and timeless ideas. You know, as in his concept of the Forms.'

'It was a terrible idea!' Roger laughs. 'Can you tell me why?'

'Well, it separates aspects of thought from those who think. It makes ideas distinct from our universe, although they somehow participate in our shared reality. Exactly how this happens is never spelled out.'

'It's where the concept leads that's a more serious concern.'

"The phone rings, and Roger picks it up.

'If it's at 35.6, it's time to sell. Dump the funds into IBM,' Roger says into the receiver. Then he puts the phone down and smiles. 'Now, where were we?'

"I can hold my own a lot better than during our childhood. In fact, I can do better than hold my own. Roger actually seems impressed. However, telephone calls continue to interrupt our conversation. The messages are about various stock prices and rates. Roger has gone the way of the dollar. He has such an incredible intellect. Yet there he is, though, spending all his time making money. It's sad. I'm tired of waiting for him to finish the incessant calls.

'It seems like you're too busy to talk right now. Maybe I'll see you later,' I say.

"He waves goodbye while talking on the phone. The stroll back onto the tree-lined path is full of sadness and regret and thus ends the dream." Alex searches the Madame's eyes for a reaction. "Perhaps I'll see Roger again one day," he said, "though we seem to be headed in different directions."

"I presume your perspective shifts were also becoming more elaborate," Mirai signed.

"They had been for a long time," Alex grumbled. "I recall a Fourth of July event when I was about 11 or 12. I attended a movie where small gifts were handed out. Mine was a plastic powder horn, a singularly useless and unwanted present. Afterward, I stood facing our home in the yard outside 9 Highland Avenue. I had disassembled the toy to find something useful. My perspective suddenly shifted, and I saw myself holding the toy's pieces. Similar experiences had happened many times before, but few with such clarity.

"Anyway, I watched myself standing on the lawn and looking toward my now-external perception. It was roughly 20 feet off to my physical body's right and elevated by about 15 to 20 feet. I sensed a familiar presence. It was like a conduit that linked me with a very distant perspective. As usual, it seemed as if I were within the mind of someone who was communing with me from afar.

"I could discern bits of information filtering through. In fact, some intriguing thoughts were gleaned while the event unfolded. The critical perceptions were that time and space are not rigidly interrelated. Some gaps or holes allow them to leak into one another. I suspect that's one reason Mirai is here. I sought more information while striving to comprehend the source of the odd event.

"At the time, I didn't fully understand the content of the perspective shift. The universe seems abuzz with knowledge and insights, although accessing this information requires directed thought. I regret not having the foresight to write down the details of the experience. It drifted away but left a distinct memory. The perspective shifts experienced between the ages of 10 and 25 parallel the developments in my dreams. However, I could only glean vague generalities from the shifts. That wasn't the case in the dreams. For example, Roger shared specific and detailed insights, although they were well beyond my understanding then."

"As some still are," Mirai signed. "Isn't that the nature of imagination?"

"I tend to avoid mystification and the like," Alex said. "No, I'm unsure about the source of these perspective shifts. Nor do I know how or whether they shaped my evolving dreaming states. However, once the capacity was instilled, it persisted. There are several dozen frozen moments like those I described earlier."

"So, we have a dreamer who maintains a running narrative," Madame Leonedria says. "Complex technical and philosophical material is involved, only a scattering of which is committed to memory."

"Well, I got the gist of many things right away," Alex said. "Yet a peculiarity of some dreams is that their subject matter was only understood years later. Lord knows where the ideas actually came from, as was the case with the crystal globe. The concepts presented in that dream were many years beyond my comprehension at the time. And it isn't like I could control or understand some of the material within the dreams. The underpinnings of this phenomenon are unclear, but I theorize that most dreams are related to the narrative forms we learn through stories and experience."

"You studied this area in depth, Alex," Madame Leonedria said.

"I believe all things have a rational basis," Alex replied. He returned the globe to Madame Leonedria, adding, "I do not fear searching for it."

"Perhaps you should elaborate, Alex," Madame Leonedria said. "Yet be cautious, or you'll drive the reader away."

"Yeah, my usual boring self," Alex chuckled. "Our abilities to form abstract connections while dreaming may be related to what I call 'narrative templates.' They're like construction forms that one pours concrete into; only the concrete here consists of memories. The fundamental forms involved help maintain memory-processing tendencies. You know, if X occurs, it is linked to Y, and so on. These templates are created when our brains are exposed to regularly experienced tales, stories, and experiences. They are collapsed into neuronal assemblies that support prototypical event, time, and spatial schemas."

"Few readers like wading through passages like that!" Mirai signed. "Give us some practical examples, but be brief!"

"OK, OK," Alex huffed. "We have all heard several 'once-upon-a-time' quest stories. Eventually, we create a narrative template that guides our associations and expectations during a dream. Thus, story event X happens during time Y and at location Z. In an archetypal story, the hero fights a dragon that guards a castle before rescuing a captive from one of its towers. The dragon, castle, and captive theme can be fleshed out from existing memories during a dream. Subsequently, Uncle Ralph may be perceived as the dragon. This is especially true if he is seen as aggressive and assertive. A familiar school could be the castle, and a sibling may be the captive. Thus unfolds a unique combination that fills in the various blanks of a staid storyline.

"We can form narrative templates to deal with everyday episodes and events. These include attending church, eating at restaurants, celebrating holidays, and other recurring experiences. These templates are given physical presence within distinct but interconnected memory-processing assemblies. Some of these assemblies contain links to sensory memories and the like. Others are related to time, place, actions, and even cognitive-processing resources. Theoretically, if one or more elements within a given template are activated during a dream, it can activate an entire storyline. The template's connections with various collateral memory resources can be readily recruited to organize and fill in elements as a dream unfolds."

"Does the reader need to know this?" Madame Leonedria asked.

"It beats the hell out of believing in mysticism!" Alex said with a sneer. "When I was young, dreams were the stuff of mystery and wonder. However, most are not. The majority are the byproducts of recently activated memories. These are related to occurrences that happen during our daily lives. The activated memories tie into a narrative form during a dream, and away we go. Moreover, the forms we develop are capable of integrating some abstract concepts. In essence, the activated forms plug in associated memories to help a dream make sense, fantastic though the story be. As the narrative proceeds, its trajectory is modified via each activated memory element. A new memory can be fashioned if the dream is recalled, as in a painting created with existing colors. This new memory can then form the subsequent basis for additional dream events. Each modifies the next as various new and existing elements are added."

"Yes, a plausible mechanism to explain your serial dreams," Mirai signed. "Each is built upon its predecessor."

"That's high praise coming from you," Alex said. "I imagine this is also where some kinds of clairvoyance come from. The basic structure of most narrative forms is probability-based. After all, the structure is initially created from regularly occurring experiences. However, there is an ongoing process of associational activations as a dream unfolds. Missing elements within the form can be supplied by activating any number of causally or temporally related memories. The narrative forms thus allow formerly disparate memory elements to become linked during dreams. Something new arises. Nonetheless, it's an offspring of a probability-based mechanism."

"Perhaps, but dreams can contain unique connections," Mirai signed. "They can even include things that could not exist, such as flying lions."

"Very true," Alex admitted. "Ultimately, all memories are based on associations. Some unique dream occurrences may be part of a capacity to recognize things within a dreamscape that are not typically accessible to consciousness. After all, our brains usually process hordes of inputs that accompany normal sensory environments and events when we're awake. Sleep quells the storm and allows the imagination to dominate."

"Ah, ever the scientist!" Madame Leonedria said. "There's no doubt that nurture can derive the story and the event templates you describe. Perhaps these templates and prior experiences can sustain some kinds of dream formation. However, doesn't nature also play a role? Indeed, cannot the universe itself inform us during dreams? Your mother had the power to see, as do many others. Some are with us right now. Could there be a genetic linkage?"

"It's possible," Alex conceded. "My mother didn't like talking about it, but she had many prescient dreams. Ma's father warned her that she would be badly hurt in one of them. Nonetheless, he insisted that everything would be all right. The next day or so, our old coal furnace had a flashback that scorched my mother's eyes, face, and hands, covering them in second-degree burns. Oh, those burns were terrible. I recall the daily application of vile-looking ointments. Nonetheless, Ma's eyes and skin healed without a scar.

"In another dream, Ma's father told her that she would have a daughter and that the daughter was to be named Mary Louise. Sure enough, my mother gave birth to a daughter several months later. Of course, she was superstitious enough to name her Mary Louise. She had countless dreams like that. Ma never saw them as anything other than normal, although her Catholic religiosity usually stifled her desire to discuss them. She even dreamed about the Virgin Mary and was foretold about her death."

"Those dreams don't fit your narrative schema ideas," Madame Leonedria said. "They deal with the unknowable, things outside our normal experiences. Could there be more to dreams, fancy, and imagination than your understanding of science can grasp?"

"They're definitely predictive, but I detest mysticism," Alex said. "I truly do."

"Yet you love fantasy, my ersatz scientist." Madame Leonedria smiled. "Isn't that what has drawn us together? Some could find that a contradiction. This is especially so since you made me your mother's alter ego, albeit a being beyond time as humans experience it. Please tell me, where do premonitions come from?"

"I think they're a child of imagination," Alex said. "But like you have observed, some break the narrative form. This is especially true concerning time."

"As in the future informing the past," Mirai signed. "Isn't that why I'm here?"

"That was the plan," Alex replied. "Ah, but you're not cooperating."

"Would you expect the future to behave as a well-trained pet?" Mirai signed.

"I suppose not," Alex said with a smile. "I've sought the underpinnings of premonitions and prophecy for years, but science doesn't deal well with the subjects. Hell, if it's not testable, it doesn't exist. That's the scientific method, and that's why some despise it. The methodology is an intellectual straightjacket, although it has some graces. But it just can't deal with ESP, premonitions, and the like—too many uncontrollable variables. Lengthy books are written on foresight, but precious few offer profound accounts of how it occurs."

"Then speculate," Mirai signed.

"Speculation feels like penance," Alex replied. "The only mechanism I can deduce is based on memory activations and probability. This can lead us to the door of prophecy. Yet there is more to it."

"Many of us have had dreams that came true," Madame Leonedria observed. "Indeed, most of our readers are directly or indirectly familiar with them. They can be very disconcerting, and I'm positive you've experienced them. Why not give us some examples?"

"That's easy enough," Alex said. "One night, I dreamt of an open grave that had a headstone with the name 'Mary' imprinted on it. The grave had a door serving it. I knew the decision to open that door was being made—that was clear to me. The next day, I learned Uncle Pat had passed. At the time, I didn't know he was close to death. As it turned out, Uncle Pat had asked his kids to let him slip away instead of calling the doctors. He opened death's door to return to the woman he loved. That woman's name was Mary."

"If you didn't know he was close to death, why was his presence in your mind?" Mirai signed.

"I have no idea," Alex said. "On another occasion, I dreamt my father and another man were in a large, muddy depression made by a heavy earth-moving machine. They wore purple hospital garb, so I knew the dream was about Dad being sick. At the time, he suffered from a massive staph infection following a hip replacement and was clearly dying. The condition had gone too far. In the dream, my father was lying in the depression, with his bad hip and leg mired in the muddy water. Dad wasn't concerned about the situation and seemed happy to see me. The other man was wheelchair-bound and stuck in the messiest part of the hole.

"The Veterans' hospital was nearby, so I went into the hollow and lifted my old man up. His weak arm wrapped feebly around my shoulders, and his weight was easy to bear. I carried him up the muddy grade and to the hospital's door. Upon proceeding through the entrance, *bang* . . . I abruptly woke.

"Later that day, my brother, Peter, called to tell me Dad had just died. But that wasn't a surprise. I knew he was gravely ill. So, it stood to reason that the dream was nothing out of the norm. The real surprise came during the funeral.

"The priest was crowing about bringing my father back into the Christian fold. Then he mentioned another person who'd passed away on the same day as Dad. It sounded as though this man knew my father. I asked my sister, Nancy, who the man was. She told me he was a wheelchair-bound man, and his image blazed into my mind. I can still picture him hunched over and looking into his lap. His hands are folded together as if in prayer. Perhaps he's holding a rosary, but I can't make the object out. Though I never saw him during my worldly life, I knew his face."

"This certainly doesn't fit the narrative form idea," Mirai signed. "It contains elements that were not derived from actual memories. How could your mind have constructed that old man? The dream also predates the actual occurrences. When reading your diary, we noted several such dreams."

"Yeah, prophetic dreams bother me," Alex said. "Some are inexplicable. For example, another prescient dream came before visiting the Hershey Medical Center. The doctors were going to repair some herniated cervical discs. Man, I was in constant pain. Anyway, the dream's setting was in the attic of our home. I was struggling to carry my old Sears mattress down the narrow stairway. The bed was bulky and unusually heavy, although the load was manageable. I glanced up the attic stairs as I neared the bottom. There was Dad, bending down and looking at me. He was dressed in white clothing that seemed almost aglow.

"He smiled and said, 'You must be strong to carry your own bed.'

"Then came the flash of a dream years earlier when I found myself an enfeebled cripple who couldn't speak clearly. I thought the operation could have complications, but I was wrong. I was told that day my neck could be repaired, but a more serious problem was afoot. The magnetic-resonance imaging (MRI) scan showed cortical atrophy in some regions. The doctor said the pattern indicated the early stages of a neurological disease called multiple system atrophy. It slowly turns people into cripples, though doctors now think another degenerative process is in play. It's all the same. My neurons are wasting. Perhaps part of my subconscious discerned there was something beyond the disc problems in play. After all, there was ongoing fatigue, clumsiness, and dizziness too. However, the dream coinciding with the diagnosis was disconcerting."

"I would think so," Mirai signed. "Furthermore, you only have suppositions for what caused the forewarning."

"Yeah, that's the way it is," Alex confessed. "It's unclear what spawned the premonition. Moreover, they recently discovered those crushed cervical disks set up a degenerative process in my spinal cord that's progressing. Go figure!"

"The ride is difficult," Madame Leonedria said. "Yet we would not be here if you could not manage it."

"Being confined to a bed is slowly becoming a reality, but I'll get my work done," Alex insisted. "Even as these words are typed, my fingers fumble about for the keys, and a wheelchair sits beside me. Yet this book will be completed, come what may. Past sins devour my future, but so be it! Ultimately, most of us are reduced to lying in bed. And yeah, we must be strong enough to bear it."

"So, here we are," Madame Leonedria observed. "However, you've still not explained how such dreams happen."

"I don't understand how or why these dreams about the future happen," Alex said. "I saw images of my cat, Fred, right before he died. In one dream, I saw several red-lettered examination grades with the exact scores received on my college midterms. I even envisioned reading these words to my mother while she was dying, not that they could ease her pain. There have been dozens of these portents. They leave me more confused than enlightened.

"I've learned enough to invent rationalistic explanations. They correlate with what we know from neuropsychological and mnemonic standpoints. Those with us can judge whether anything beyond that is worth considering. I suspect there is. I believe that future events can be known through probability analysis or metaphysical resources. They are in the realm of future fact, and all knowledge is accessible through ideas, insights, imagination, and dreams. The 'how' questions remain enigmatic. However, some readers have either experienced foreknowledge or know someone who has. I was hoping Mirai could provide some illumination."

"How could a linear thinker possibly understand temporal dynamics, Alex?" Mirai signed. "You're trapped in the present-tense perspective. It separates the future from the past, but that need not be. Tell me, Alex, how much does a thought weigh?"

"Oh, no, you don't!" Alex said with a dismissive hand wave. "One can easily contend massless patterns sustained by processes X, Y, and/or Z can inculcate knowledge. The next step is to claim such patterns are not bound by niceties such as the speed of light and time. This will take us to how thoughts can transcend the boundaries that normally apply to corporeal existence. Nah, it's pure speculation."

"So close-minded," Mirai signed. She smiled and added, "Yet you see no inconsistency in having trans-temporal characters in this text."

"I'm consistently inconsistent," Alex said with a smile. "However, prophecy has a knowable basis, and time will reveal what it is. If knowledge is transtemporal and accessible, then finding a functional basis is possible. Some processes may involve how time and thought interact during dream states. That's how you may work, Mirai, but I suspect there is something more to you than imagination alone. It's not like I can fully understand the principles involved. Well, not yet!"

"Can we ever distill prophecy into any single essence?" Madame Leonedria asked. "Are prophets merely good storytellers, or have they been touched by what some call God? Whatever the answer, we have to move on, child. Suffice it to say that one of the reasons this text dissatisfies you is because it seeks unknowable truths. Still, pushing the boundaries is your way. Given this inclination, one surmises you strived to find answers within dreams."

"I did indeed," Alex said. Before he continued, he took a moment to relish in the warmth of the fire, the sound of wood crackling, and to appreciate the wonderment of it all.

7

Metaphysical Experiments

"Between the ages of 17 and 23, I conducted a long series of dream experiments," Alex said. "As you'll see, they eventually led to uniquely lucid states. The experiences were more the stuff of reality than fantasy. I felt the breeze and the sun's warmth. I witnessed nature's splendid hues and textures. Of course, the thoughts emanated from within, yet often touched upon what was unknown. I could probe moral, ethical, and spiritual issues. However, I often found no answers. All the while, there was a constant desire to expand this capacity. I wanted to test and expand its limits. Moreover, the experiences were often terrifying."

"The unknown can be frightening," Madame Leonedria said. "Nonetheless, that's what most of us are compelled to explore. After all, the mundane offers us few prospects of discovering anything new and meaningful."

"There is no better word than 'experimentation' to describe this period," Alex said. "However, the trials could only be conducted when I was in a particular state. Dreams are especially vivid and well-remembered during that cusp between sleep and wakefulness, at least for me. This started happening a lot during my college years. One event stands out from the others. Unlike many previous experiences, there was no precursor or building sense that my consciousness dwelled in a dream. Instead, I unexpectedly found myself in the back seat of a powerful red convertible. The sleek car raced up a winding road that hugged a steep mountainside. The details remain fresh."

"Put us in the event, Alex," Madame Leonedria said.

"It's late, perhaps one in the morning or so," Alex said. He gently rocked while speaking. "The car's motion and speed are palpable. Yeah, this is one of those unique dreams. The night air is warm, almost uncomfortably so. These turns make me somewhat dizzy, but it's an invigorating ride. I don't much like this slope we're driving on, though. It's a long way down to the canyon floor. Yeah, we're in a desert, or so the terrain appears.

"Wow, the woman beside me is drop-dead gorgeous! Elegant, stunning beauty, with earrings that glisten in the moonlight. It's dark, but she's a brunette, wearing her hair up in a nice 'do. A white gown accentuates her fine figure. Oh, she's perfection incarnate. How sweet is this?

"But I'm not appropriately dressed to be with her! Good Lord! I'm wearing sweats and training shoes, typical coaching attire. It's like being a barbarian among the cultured elite. Of course, that's what I am. How the hell did I end up in this situation?

"Hey, I can hear chatter and laughter from the couple in the front seat. They're talking about having had a great time. These people must have come from a formal dinner party or some similar soiree. Fine evening apparel garbs the woman in front. Oh, and the driver is in a nice tuxedo. Yeah, I'm definitely out of place here.

"I know we're all within a dream, even though it's very realistic. I love this, and my awareness is becoming more acute by the second. Hmmm, let's take advantage of this state while it lasts.

'This is quite a dream,' I say, but no one replies.

"This event is different from previous dreams. It's not so much a fantasy as an actual experience. Perhaps I'm free of all constraints. There's also this odd sense of power. It's a kind of energy that feeds into conscious thought, like the power of this car zipping along the road. It's very alluring. This dream is unique, but the state may not last long. This could be the ideal time to ask for some answers.

'I know we're in a dream. I don't know where you come from or why I'm here. But there's a question that's been haunting me. I want to know if God exists.'

"They look surprised, but no one answers. The evening's gaiety is evaporating. *How do I go about this?*

'Look, I'm not trying to wreck anyone's good time. All I'm looking for is an answer. It doesn't have to be right.'

'I'm not sure,' replies the woman in the front seat.

'Who is?' the driver adds with a shrug.

'Perhaps he knows,' she replies.

'No way, we're not going there!' the driver insists. 'It's a long way from where we are.'

"I lean forward and ask, 'Who is this person you speak of?'

'He knows everything,' the lady notes.

'But his place is out of our way,' the driver adds.

'Please take me! My time here may not last,' I beg.

'We may as well.'

'If we must,' the driver reluctantly says. 'But it's a long drive.'

'Thanks for helping me.'

"The girl beside me looks angry. She won't even glance my way. Man, I've wrecked the festive mood. But what choice is there? It's an important question. It's *the* question! Yet this trip is taking a while. The drive goes on and on, although this landscape is beautiful! I should say something. Nah, these people seem upset enough. The woman beside me is still ticked off, wearing a silent frown. I hate imposing on folks, but what else can we do?

"Ah, we're taking a side road and ascending a steep grade. This reminds me of the road up Mount Washington, minus the trees. Lots of twists and turns and some very precarious slopes. I do not like this too much. Oh, an elegant house up ahead is built into the side of this mountain we're ascending. Yikes, this is a treacherous landscape! It isn't the best place to put a home, although this is more of an estate than a house. The driver parks on an oversized lot in front of the home.

"Hmmm, real nice place. It's a low-set, rambling, single-floor structure with many windows and dark-stained woodwork. Part of it overhangs the slope, rather perilously so. The lights are on, so perhaps someone is home.

'There you go,' the driver says.

'You guys want me to go in there?'

'We don't have the answers,' the woman in the front seat explains.

'What if you guys take off and I get stranded?'

'You wanted to come here,' she replies.

"The woman beside me says with a pout, 'Just go in.'

More effort should have been made to communicate with her. No time to fret about that now. I could get stranded, that's for sure. Well, I should find this fellow they spoke of and get some answers.

"Damn, this car isn't easy to exit. It's built very low to the ground. It's great for navigating turns but lousy for much else. *Clunk.* There we go. Now stretch the legs a bit.

'Don't be shy,' the driver says.

'I won't be.'

"Nice stonework on the walkway, but I'd better check out the car. Yeah, it's still there. The woman who was beside me is sitting on the fender. She still looks sad. I feel guilty as hell. What the heck? Why is she putting on sunglasses at night? They're milling around the vehicle and chattering; they'll be here for a while.

"The door is wide open. I'd like to know what to do.

'Is anyone here?' I ask meekly.

"No answer. What to do? What do my friends think? I turn toward them, and the driver gestures for me to enter.

"Faint heart wins naught, but let's look before we leap. The scene is so real, so tangible. There's track lighting built into the ceiling, modern-looking stainless-steel chairs with leather-covered seats, and a big glass-surfaced coffee table.

'Is anyone here?' I whisper.

"No answer, but what a place! Wow! Look at the landscapes outside those huge windows! The moonlight bounces off desert slopes and massive towering buttes. Oh, and we are up there! Goodness, I was right about part of this place overhanging a mountainside. Holy bejesus! It's a long way down to the valley's floor. What a perch we're atop. This place is unbelievable!

"Maybe someone is inside one of the rooms. Let's check it out. Whew, there're lots of rooms here and a few long hallways. The kitchen sprawls on the left, and this must be the living room. These enormous windows are a rush! If I can find the guy who lives here, there'll be much to discuss. The living room's carpet feels soft under my feet. Wow, I hear my footsteps on this hallway's wooden floor. My sneakers squeak when I turn, though they aren't marking the floor. This dream is a blast, but finding this dude is a problem.

'Please, is anyone here?'

"There are still no replies, but this place is palatial! Here I am, checking out all these rooms in a stranger's home. What happens if I walk into someone's bedroom and they're sleeping? And what if the owner returns? It wouldn't be good if he found me rummaging through his home uninvited. Well, there's no other reason the door would have been left open. So, here I am, full of power and ability. In addition, everything in this state is precise and detailed. Yet there are no answers!

"What to do? Returning to the living room and waiting for this guy is best. Huge place, but we're headed in the right direction. Here we are. Let's sit on that leather chair and think about all this. Ah, there we go. Oh, yeah, nice and comfy.

"It isn't easy to fathom what this experience means. Well, finding out whether God exists is difficult. This mystery guy was supposed to know the answer, but he's not even here! Hmmm, that could mean something in itself. Perhaps it's futile to depend on supposedly wise or famous people for insights. This is probably a path we have to walk on our own. Hmmm, maybe my companions will know where the owner is. Yeah, asking them is a good idea. This is a great place to hang out, but let's return to the car.

"Damn it! They've taken off, just as I feared. Son of a bitch! I've been abandoned, lost in a desert at night. Well, that's OK. Let's just keep walking until I awake. Yeah, we're treading down a dark, deserted road. It's a bit scary, but there's nothing to be upset about . . . unless some demonic coyote attacks me. It's only a partial loss, though. A conceptual bridge has been crossed. I can now bring full consciousness into a dream. I'm no longer bound to one reality, one sense of perspective. Lord knows where this will lead. I hear my feet striking the pavement and keep going.

"This feels like a long walk, and I can barely see. Hot as hell out here, too. Do these experiences come from outside or from within? I'm always wondering about that, although the answer doesn't matter. These kinds of dreams will eventually provide insights. This one has failed so far, but the act of looking allows one to see. If so, I'm on the right track to finding our Maker. It's just a matter of time.

"When this notion comes to mind, I'm flung back into consciousness. I was tossed from one reality to another without any transition whatsoever. It was a strange, detached sensation. I awoke as though I'd never been asleep."

"You were at UNH when this dream happened?" Mirai signed.

"I was," Alex said. "I was a drug-addled undergrad and a pitiful student."

"You've always been immature, Alex," Madame Leonedria observed. She raised an eyebrow at him. "I sense there was more to this dream than you gleaned while in it."

"You bet," Alex replied. "What's particularly odd about the experience was that I saw the hilly nocturnal landscape we passed about 10 years later. It was while I was living in southern California. I traveled from Camarillo to Fresno to see a friend's weightlifting meet. The desert flora and terrain are unlike anything in New Hampshire, which added to the sense of *déjà vu*."

"Once again, how could the future possibly inform the past?" Mirai signed, a smile crossing her lips.

"You know more about that than I," Alex said. "So, stop teasing. But thus began a period in which I made several attempts to push these dream states to their limits. I even conducted metaphysical experiments within the dreams while they occurred."

"You were determined to understand thoughts about thought," Madame Leonedria observed.

"I was," Alex said. "One dream, in particular, stands out from the others. At the time, I was a resident of UNH's Congreve Hall. Oh, I loved that place. Great party dorm. Anyway, I was fast asleep in my ground-floor room. Like others in the series, this dream didn't have precursors indicating a lucid state was unfolding. Instead, I abruptly realized that I was having a conscious dream."

"Then relive it," Madame Leonedria said. "Take us through the experience."

Alex nodded and closed his eyes briefly.

"Gosh, I'm holding a beer and listening to tunes. This is my dorm room. But who are these guys I'm partying with? One has an unkempt beard and wears a red flannel shirt and blue jeans. He's tall and has broad facial features. He's got a large belly but is a big guy overall. He looks Greek, kind of like my friend Jim. The other dude has fine, dark hair, a preppy white sweater, and is a slight fellow. They're sitting on chairs, sucking down brews, and smoking weed. I've no idea who these guys are, but they seem pleasant enough. Ah, I can taste the tang of this beer. The sweet smell of marijuana permeates the air. I feel the vibrations from the speakers as they pound out 'Lucy in the Sky with Diamonds.' Wow, this is an excellent experience.

'Hey, this is great! I'm getting buzzed in a dream!' I say.

'Yeah, it's a good time,' the bearded guy replies.

"He takes a long drag from the joint and then passes it to his friend. He reaches for his pack of cigarettes and taps them on the desk. The preppy takes a hit and then sips his drink. 'And we're just getting started,' he says.

'Shouldn't I know your names?' I ask while taking the joint.

'You'd just forget them,' one replies.

'You're probably right, especially if I keep puffing on this.'

'It's kick-ass stuff.'

'That's for sure. Hey, I would like to know if you are characters I created for this dream. Or are you external souls who found their way into my imagination?'

'I was wondering the same thing about you,' the short guy replies.

'But this is a dream,' I observe.

'Hey, it's all a big dream, man,' the bearded fellow rumbles. He yanks out a cigarette and lights it. 'It doesn't begin or end or come from the outside or inside. It simply is.'

'Ah, this is great. I don't know how long we've got together. But I will remember you two, even if I don't know your names.'

'What's in a name? I read that somewhere,' the preppy dude says.

Through puffs of smoke, our furry friend laughs a deep guffaw. He says, 'You couldn't have read it for one of our classes!' Both the willowy guy and I crack grins. We talk for a long time. However, the dream is a transient experience, which we all realize. I lament that our time together is short.

'I'm going to wake up in a bit, and you guys will be gone, maybe for good.'

My pal waves a broad hand through the smoke filtering from his mouth. He squints at me, his eyes reduced to slits and his cheeks red as cherries.

'But it's been a good time,' he says, 'and time is all we got!'

'Usually, I ask about God in these kinds of things. But let's try something different.'

'Why?' the small man asks.

'Well, I've been doing dream experiments. I'd like to borrow a pack of your cigarettes if you don't mind. I'll put them under my pillow and see if they're still there after this dream ends.'

'Hey, this is my last pack! But here you go.'

'That's kind of you. I'll just tuck the pack right in here.'

'It isn't going to work.' He scratches his dark, curly beard. 'It's the wrong time and the wrong place.'

'Well, this is my room, so we're all set spatially.'

'But since this is a dream, those cigarettes are thoughts,' the skinny guy says. 'A thought probably has a pattern, but it's not tangible.'

7.1 Making a thought real must take a shitload of energy, and thus the expeiment failed

'It must take a shit-load of energy to make a thought tangible,' our shaggy friend comments. 'And you're only going to remember about half of what we've discussed.' He stubs out his last cigarette.

'You guys are probably right, but it's worth a shot.'

'Yeah, but they're my last cigarettes. And now I'm buttless!'

"We laugh and go on to discuss things that elude my memory. I awoke a short while later, and the experiment failed—no cigarettes under my pillow. Still, most of those semi-philosophical dreams were enjoyable experiences."

"Concepts regarding temporal dynamics, as they relate to metaphysics, were in play during this dream," Mirai signed. "The pattern-of-thought concept one of your friends mentioned was fascinating. A better question might have been related to what sustains the pattern. You claim thought is one with matter and energy; that begs a detailed explanation of which aspects of being a thought partakes in. What material elements or energies create and sustain our thought patterns? Are they biological alone? But once generated, can our thoughts travel beyond their source? I also found other aspects of the dream intriguing. For example, why would it require more energy for a thought to become a reality than during the normal dynamics between matter and energy?"

"I don't think most of those with us care much about these details," Madame Leonedria observed.

"Patterns of thought can be found by tracing bioelectrical energy signatures in neurons," Alex said, paying no heed to Madame Leonedria's advice. "Yet there is more to it than just that. I wanted to transform that metaphysical pack of cigarettes into a corporeal reality. Ultimately, this is about how the constituents of atoms and various forms of energy eventually give rise to sentient life forms that can manipulate being by applying ideas. The process begins with particle physics and what sustains and guides the interactions between its various elements. Are they purely random or directed processes? If directed, what sustains the impetus? Then we move on to molecular genetics, and—"

"Enough of this twaddle!" Madame Leonedria loudly insisted. "Think about the needs of the readers! You and Mirai can discuss these issues among yourselves. Let us get back to the subject at hand! What Alex described is a lucid dream. As we've discussed, they typically involve the capacity to experience dreams as conscious events. Ah, but these are mere precursors to what can follow. Once consciousness is grasped during dreams, it can soar to all places on imagination's wings."

"There's no better way of putting it," Alex said. "The literature calls them 'astral events,' not that they're well understood. Indeed, some dismiss their existence."

"You know better, child," Madame Leonedria said.

"I know that dreams can open doors," Alex said. "During my experimental phase, a series of powerful and often frightening dream states occurred. They involved a palpable sense of energy and movement. The dreams usually included a unique type of consciousness and being that existed without any discernable form or boundaries. It was similar to the mountain-car-ride dream without the vehicle metaphor. The dreams are like traveling through the universe at incredible speeds."

"The quintessential essence of the astral state," Mirai signed.

"There's no doubt about that," Alex said. "Some of those events were absolutely terrifying." Alex took a sip of wine, pursing his lips due to its unpleasant taste. He leaned forward, using numerous hand gestures while his narrative continued.

8

Astral States

"The dreams often open with my being within a state of crystal-clear consciousness. My mind is awake and active, although my body feels adrift. There is usually darkness around me. It's like I've been removed from our shared reality, albeit that one is not without abilities. For example, I can move my being in any direction. After moving for any significant distance, a sense of acceleration occurs. This is accompanied by a feeling of energy that flows into one's being, as odd as that sounds. The events typically include a humming noise that slowly increases in pitch and intensity if the movement is maintained. It's like a high-powered engine revving up. The sense of motion and energy flow cannot be fully described. The faster I go, the more power streams in. The more power I have, the greater my velocity becomes. It's an

8.1 Astral states took the author through time and space

utterly intoxicating feedback loop. On the downside, the state can easily become painful and exhausting."

"What causes the pain and fatigue?" Mirai signed.

"I really don't know," Alex replied. "During the acceleration phase, there's a vexing sensation of pressure. I'm not sure what it is."

"Acceleration increases mass and thus resistance," Mirai noted.

"That would imply I'm accelerating a mass," Alex said. "But these are thoughts, Mirai. Thoughts don't have mass."

"That which generates thoughts often does," Mirai noted. "Moreover, neuronal impulses themselves are—"

"Enough speculation, children!" Madame Leonedria interrupted with a dismissive wave. "Continue describing the state, Alex."

"The resistance is a bear to overcome," Alex said. "It's a penetrating counterforce that rips at one's being. There's a battle between speed and friction. Or perhaps inertia and force are involved. In any case, it hurts like hell. At times, the clarity of consciousness and control is striking. However, when the acceleration/power loop becomes too great, the sense of pressure and disorientation become unbearable. Sometimes, my head ached so much during the experiences that I would awake. That was no fun at all. It was like having a migraine on steroids. There would be dizziness and nausea, altogether unpleasant. These were vastly different and far more powerful states than the flying dreams from my childhood."

"Perhaps we should examine the history of these events," Madame Leonedria said. "After all, they've led us to this cave, along with those reading these lines."

"They have indeed," Alex said. "The first dream of this kind occurred just before I began conducting my consciousness experiments in college. One night, the nebulous state I described came upon me. It was like floating in deep space, divorced from earthly sensations. Yet, I could move at will. And when I did so, there came the alluring energy feedback. I was both scared and attracted by the sensations. It's impossible to describe the sense of acceleration or the exhilaration caused by the power coursing through my being. It's intoxicating, like being part of an infinitely powerful machine. These feelings are so far beyond everyday experiences that there is no equivalent. I think astronauts and fighter pilots probably feel something similar, but it is unique.

Regarding cognition and capabilities, it's as if I could do everything and go all places.

"I swiftly pressed the acceleration phase and then abruptly penetrated a barrier. I do not know what the obstacle was, but a setting instantly formed. My senses rapidly became attuned, and I found myself adrift. I was thousands of feet above my West Lebanon, New Hampshire, home, surrounded by the gloom of night. Not a fan of heights, I was both enthralled and frightened. Yet, it was evident I could go anywhere. With this knowledge came a perceptual clarity that allowed me to discern the location of those like me. They appeared as brilliant points of light dotting the landscape below. These beacons were few, but they shone far brighter than the city and residential illumination.

"I was drawn to New York City because I sensed the powerful presence of another dream flyer, a woman. Her thoughts attracted me like a lure, and I soon raced toward her presence through the encompassing darkness. Nocturnal landscapes, lighted cities, and car-speckled streets zipped by beneath me. In a few moments, New York came into view, a 250-mile metaphysical foray taking mere seconds. It seemed wise to descend and slow down while approaching her towering apartment building. Upon entering the building's parking garage, I continued decelerating while zooming through walls, hallways, and a door. Solid objects posed no resistance. They were penetrated without impact, if one can envision such a thing. As soon as her immediate presence was sensed, *bang* . . . I awoke."

"I believe a few of those with us have had similar astral experiences," Madame Leonedria said. "Others are contemplating how to induce the states. Be careful where you tread, dear hearts. There are texts about achieving such states, but some have dangerous advice. Knowing your inclinations, Alex, I wager the experiences eventually drove you to research their foundations."

"I'm still working on it," Alex said. "My research indicates that these events are uncommon, and I could not fully instill or control the states for some time. A few claim they can do as they wish in astral states, but that differs from my experience. However, they're recorded in almost every culture, so the capacity may be inherent. The states are characterized by the sense of leaving one's body. Many claim our physical and astral forms are two distinct but related entities. Yeah, some even contend our astral form is actually our soul. The 'soul' can roam the ethereal astral plane in that theory. This is akin to a metaphysical realm. It's supposedly an intermediary place between Earth and heaven that is the purview of souls and angels."

"Do you subscribe to that view?" Mirai signed.

"Of course not!" Alex indignantly replied. "Unfortunately, there's very little scientific literature addressing the idea. Instead, astral events are lumped together with lucid dreams. Their rarity also ensures there won't be much future research. Moreover, there is a problem differentiating them from lucid flying dreams. Some associate the events with narcolepsy, epilepsy, and the like. In my case, they could even be caused by migraines or degenerative processes. For the most part, astral dreams are re-garded as bunk within and outside the scientific community. To be sure, many folks mock the whole idea. Of course, scientists often scorn things they don't fully understand or cannot test. Some are little more than willful bigots."

"So, says a man who worships at the altar of science," Madame Leonedria observed. "Then how do you explain them?"

"I wouldn't believe they existed had I not experienced them," Alex said. "I know they're imagination-based. The cog-nitive processes that sustain our imagination's forays into day-dreams, dreams, and astral states may open cognitive gateways. These may allow perceptions that go beyond those mediated by the senses. This is where memory and cognition interact sans sensory input. So, we're talking about thoughts about thoughts about thoughts."

Mirai signed, "We call that collateral—"

"No!" Madame Leonedria sternly intoned. "Foreknowledge is a dangerous thing. You should know better!"

Mirai looked down, duly chastened.

"You had better be good, Mirai," Alex said with a smile. "We can't have you corrupting the timeline too much! Be that as it may, I don't regard astral dreams as mystical or bunk. They're born of the processes that create thought. How much they ex-tend beyond those processes is the question. Perhaps the ability can be fostered if people experience dreams similar to what I did. I've also pondered whether my experiences with peyote, LSD, and mushrooms could have stimulated these events."

"That is a possibility we considered when examining these dreams," Mirai signed.

"I tend to doubt the events were drug-related," Alex said. "Drugs hindered my progress. In fact, I seldom dreamt at all when intoxicated. Moreover, my conscious contemplations were disjointed and trivial when stoned or tripping. Granted, some current shamans use drugs to stimulate visions. The ancients sure did, and some of the methods were detailed . . . such as fasting. All that is under the rubric of dream induction. My experience indicates that hallucinogens and other drugs aren't a good way to increase cognitive capacities or perceptions, let alone stimulate dreams. Oh, one thinks great and wondrous insights are happening when intoxicated. That's for sure. But try reading a text that was written while tripping when you're sober. It will lack continuity, depth, and any meaningful insights. It's word-hash, for the most part, a bloody waste of time."

"These are interesting views for a self-confessed drug addict," Madame Leonedria said. "Are they honest?"

"Everything I'm writing is honest!" Alex indignantly replied. "Drugs ended up being a dead end for me. Some have other views, but I had several painful experiences. I saw deaths and violence, no end to the misery. I wasted years getting high, and the habit offered no higher insights. For me, it was just gratuitous self-indulgence. Yeah, I liked getting buzzed for its own sake, but there was no higher purpose other than that."

"Yet you still take drugs," Madame Leonedria noted. "As do many of those with us."

"To each his or her own," Alex said. "Look, I'm no reformed zealot! My corporeal self takes sixteen pills and six or seven injections daily to stay alive. It's no fun at all. A few puffs of pot help me sleep when the pain is too great. Regardless of that, I began my vision quests before I started using hallucinogens and their cousins. Moreover, I continued it well after I stopped using them."

"Still, we should not dismiss their possible effects, Alex," Madame Leonedria observed.

"Agreed," Alex said. "We're the sum of all our experiences. That doesn't mean I want those with us to drop a few hits of acid to stimulate dream formation."

"We should return to examining the actual astral states," Mirai signed. "We're getting off point."

"Astral states were rare and random," Alex said, "and I couldn't control them for some time. I could manipulate the acceleration and direction to a degree, but there was little consistency. Nor could I induce the states by any means, though I easily recognized when they were happening. Once in a while, the acceleration phase failed, and I became disoriented. The pain was also a nuisance. Nonetheless, this didn't stop me from seeking kindred spirits when the events happened, including the woman in New York. I was drawn to the other dream flyers as an insect is to light. Perhaps I merely imagined similar dreamers were at hand. In any event, there is a barrier I could never quite cross. Well, at least concerning finding my way into another person's presence."

"Ah, Venus is disharmonious with you, Alex," Madame Leonedria said.

"It sure seems to be," Alex said. "Despite this, I continued experimenting with thought travel. When I penetrated the counterforce barrier, the dreams occasionally led to visions and insights. Some were profound. One of my attempts ended in a bizarre dream about probability, although the details weren't clear or coherent. The general theme was that whatever can be will be, given enough time and the right conditions. Ergo, a possibility, however remote, needs only time and the correct context to become a reality. I saw eggs turning into chickens and then chickens back into eggs. Another time, I went so fast that I tasted blood, although the barrier remained intact. It was a harrowing and exhausting experience. I had a headache for days.

"Perhaps these dreams led to the cortical degeneration they say I'm experiencing. Hell, I can't even walk a straight line anymore. In fact, I'm typing this text with two fingers, and one of them keeps missing the damn keys! The right hand also spazzes at times, and that is pissing me off. It's frustrating as hell. They tell me dementia has set in, but every coin has two sides. In fact, my cortical anomalies and genetics probably helped foster the dream states. For example, my dad had migraines, and Ma was a seer. That combination might have made these lucid states possible. Who the hell knows?

"Another causal agent could be the dream experiments I conducted. In effect, my almost systematic attempts to accelerate consciousness while dreaming could have achieved some success.

The neurophysiological processes involved need to be clarified. The massive recruitment of neuronal resources is involved, along with employing synesthesia. There was also cerebellar involvement during these dreams, as in sensing movement. The sensation of speed and motion is incredible. How brain chemistry and vascular anomalies feed into all this is unclear. Once again, cause and effect are unknown."

"Nature and nurture are difficult to tease apart, and perhaps it's folly to do so," Madame Leonedria said. "Even so, one such as you will always test limits."

"I definitely did that," Alex said, "despite the pain associated with the experiences."

"What about your perceptual shifts? Did these continue?" Mirai signed.

"They still do!" Alex said. "I'm unsure about the cause of these perspective shifts. Nor do I know how or whether they impacted my dream states. But once the capacity was instilled, it persisted. There are several dozen frozen moments like those described earlier. These include one shared with a dear friend. Oh, she was a woman I could have loved. Hell, I should have! She reminds me of you, Mirai."

"Please explain," Mirai signed.

"Stacey was brilliant!" Alex's eyes lit up. "She was a mathematician and every bit as crazy as I am. Oh, and she was hot! I mean, nice figure and beautiful face. Ah, but I was too immature to see what could have been. So, it all melted away into dim memories and regrets. Well, we seldom get do-overs.

"Anyway, Stacey and I were on a bus going to a local mall. I must have been in my late 20s at the time. There was frost on the window that formed a fascinating crystalline landscape. I saw formations that took on the shape of valleys and ridges. They were replete with delicate icy spires and intricate patterns of many kinds.

"My perspective suddenly shifted. I gazed at myself sitting on the bus with this bright young lady. As the event unfolded, I said, 'See that frost on the window? That image will always link us. We're going to remember this moment for the rest of our lives.'

"I heard my words as if they were an echo and felt a warmth akin to love. I observed our exchanged glances, knowing our communion was an absolute truth. Yeah, that it was. The memory of the icy landscape is still etched in our minds. I do not understand how I knew that ephemeral event would become part of what we both are, nor was I sure what linked us to the scene and moment. It was a communion wherein two became one with all, however briefly. I am positive that more than a few readers have experienced something similar."

"Some describe that as a feeling of shared love," Mirai signed. "Do these perspective shifts remain?"

"They happen often," Alex said. "I can be watching waves, passing clouds, or the wind blowing long tufts of grass. Suddenly, I am outside of myself. The shifts have changed a bit in nature. It's hard to explain. I become one with what is around me, a part that can reflect upon the whole. A rafter of wild turkeys, a herd of deer, fish lazing in the shallows . . . their instincts and thoughts become palpable, or so it seems. My sense of self drifts far away. It is an enjoyable occurrence. Pure rapture."

"These shifts are probably related to daydreams and imagination," Mirai signed. "Perhaps you should look to those sources rather than me for answers regarding causation."

"Of course," Alex said with a dip of his head. "You would never step into the past, even if put there unwillingly. I believe allocentric perspective shifts can have many causes. But I'm comfortable with the notion that the states originate from within and touch what resides outside my bubble of being."

Madame Leonedria chuckled. "I like how you expressed that, Alex. Interestingly, these perspective shifts coincided with developments in your dream states. This seems to have been an ongoing process. Would you consider it developmental or evolutionary?"

"I suspect both nature and nurture played parts," Alex said. "A definite learning trajectory was born out of repeated experiences. In fact, I embarked on a series of vivid astral dreams that took unexpected turns. They assumed moral and prophetic qualities. Some were petty, while others were sublime. Their most striking characteristics were consciousness and realism. In fact, the dreams soon became indistinguishable from corporeal events. Recalling some of them makes my skin tingle and my heart pound. They are the core of what this text is about."

"We have traveled over one hundred pages," Madame Leonedria said. "It's only now that we're finally ready to embark on our purpose. Men can be such tedious creatures."

"Was all of the prologue needed, Alex?" Mirai signed.

"I don't know," Alex said. "The readers need to understand what spawned the events I'm going to recount. This is especially true if they're to determine the relevance of what is related. They need context to decide what is worthy and what is fiction. After all, perhaps I'm merely delusional."

"Asking the question provides its own answer," Mirai signed. "However, we know from your diary that the dreams actually happened. What a lugubrious piece of work that diary was! Your efforts to relate the dreams and events of your time were chronicled beyond the point of tedium."

"Life was a rough ride," Alex said. "The failed texts led to where we are now. I know wading through the detritus was tedious. Sorry about that. The dreams were all too real. They wounded me in many ways, and I can't get the damn things out of my mind. Bits and pieces of them pop up constantly. This setting is a passing thought that links us with the readers. Oh, but those dreams . . . who would believe them possible?"

"Have trust in those with us, and let us proceed," Madame Leonedria said. "This will be an epic journey."

"I have dallied too long," Alex said. He took in a deep breath and sighed. "There's no time to rest. We must proceed."

"Then proceed," Madame Leonedria said. "Astral dreams can lead to a greater understanding of many things if one is clever enough. It's the pinnacle you sought to ascend and then go beyond."

"Why? Why does this compulsion exist?" Mirai signed.

"I love them," Alex said. "Those with us are precious, each and every one. Mirai, they're your great-, great-, great-, great- . . . great-grandparents, cousins, etcetera, etcetera, etcetera. Those with us are the source of what our kind will become. We must do everything possible to secure their future."

Madame Leonedria nodded. "First, fetch that water bowl by Verity and place it on this table. We'll need to gaze into possibility's cauldron during our journey. The depths will help spark memories of your quests to find the source of existence. They'll even help you delve into the future. We must revisit where you've gone if we're to help those with us."

9

Clean up Your Act

Alex's knees snapped when he got up and stretched, the painful legacy of excessively heavy squats and budding obesity. He gingerly walked over to the large copper cauldron and girded himself. It looked to weigh about 100 pounds, a manageable load but a clumsy one. He took a deep breath of air, grasped the cauldron handles, and manhandled the heavy load easily.

"This bowl is huge," Alex said, "but it's nearly weightless!"

"It's as light as the burden you'll one day carry," Madame Leonedria said. "Now put the bowl on the table so we can gaze into its waters. The depths will free our minds. They'll allow us to relive the experiences that so vex you. That's right. Now sit and watch the firelight reflect off the ripples. Look through the surface and study the depths. Free your soul by letting the words flow. Let your thoughts pour onto these pages and into the minds of those with us. Play your part. Now, tell us about your first experience with seeing as a state of being."

"The initial dream in the series took place when I was acting out the torment of my youth," Alex said while looking into the water bowl. "I was about 22, a hulking man of great strength and explosive temperament. I liked playing the role of a badass, and it was an act that was rapidly becoming a reality. One night, the astral state came upon me, and I immediately recognized the signs.

"At first, there is no dreamscape, light, or dimensions—only a palpable feeling of slowly increasing acceleration and energy. I was wandering aimlessly within a void but fully aware. I set off in a direction, seeking the now-familiar feedback loop. The faster I went, the more power coursed through me. I was wholly conscious and going for broke, pushing the state to its limits—"

9.1 In acting out his inner torment, the author became violent and abusive

"Let us experience the event!" Madame Leonedria intoned. "Active voice, present tense."

Alex gazed deeply into the cauldron and peered through its depths. Then he dived into his story.

"Whew, the energy coursing through me is intoxicating! Ah, and it's growing exponentially. What a rush! But that damn humming sound keeps increasing in pitch and intensity. It's obnoxious, even painful. What if I collide with something? No, screw the fear! Focus on speed. That's it; keep it going. We're racing through a void, darkness all around. Indescribable velocity, but some resistance! This counterforce is becoming miserable! I wonder what the hell it is.

"Come on, we can do this. Ignore the pain! Yeah, let the power unwind! Energy becomes speed, speed becomes energy . . . Whew, this is awesome! Man, the pressure's tearing me up, but what a rush. The sound . . . it's ear-piercing! Concentrate on the feedback loop. Focus! Dizzy as hell, but . . . damn it, focus! Pain, pain . . . can't think. No! Just keep going! Peddle to the metal! Keep—

"Whoa! W-w-what the hell happened? I-I think I'm seated. Yeah, we've definitely stopped. Whew, that was nuts. There wasn't a warning or feeling of deceleration. It was like suddenly breaking through a barrier of some kind sans impact. Odd. We ended up here, wherever *this place* is. Wow, what a ride! Hmmm, it's taking time for my senses to get attuned. Dizzy, but it's OK. Come on, shake off the side effects. Ah, there we go. Now I can see and feel a bit.

"Hmmm, I'm sitting cross-legged at a large round table. It seems like my butt is on a comfortable rug. The table's wooden surface is lacquered to a shine. How elegant. The furnishing has short, ornately carved legs with a scaly pattern, like a snake's skin. I cannot see the table's feet, but they could be dragon claws. Anyway, the table is the appropriate height for people seated on the floor. Goodness, the floral tabletop design is stunning. White lotus blossoms are woven into an intricate array of brown branches and green leaves. The bright patterns almost glow in contrast with the table's deep black hue. This lacquer work must be Asian, perhaps Japanese. The details are extraordinary for a dream! I can count the leaves and blossoms and follow them with a fingertip! How cool! The realism and clarity of this setting are transcendent.

"Oh, there are about a dozen people seated at the table. They seem to have been expecting me, but I don't recognize them. And what the hell are these people yammering about?

"I'm usually in control during these dreams, though perhaps that isn't the case here. Let's check these folks out. They're college-aged kids, much like me. It's an odd mixture of men and women, a motley crew. A few are shorthaired all-American types. They wear preppy clothes, the kind of yada-yada folks I usually don't like. There are some people of my ilk, though, complete with long hair, faded jeans, and headbands. Oh, that guy across the table is a definite jock! He has a bull neck, a square jaw, and angular features. He must be able to lift half a ton, but he's no threat. I'm still buzzing with energy. There's nothing in this dream that's even remotely threatening. Yet why the hell am I here? And why is it taking so damn long for my senses to become fully attuned?

"My vision is fine, but I can't quite make out what they're saying. Come on, listen. Yeah, now the words are easier to hear. They're discussing my behavior, bantering about good and evil and how it relates to my conduct. This is interesting. Nah, I don't much like these attacks on my lifestyle. Who the hell are they to judge anyone? Still, it is better to listen than speak, at least for now.

"The group's leader is that petite woman. She has long black hair braided and held back with a thin leather headband. Her dark, bushy eyebrows don't detract from a pleasing appearance. She's a definite free spirit. Looks like a would-be hippie or Deadhead garbed in a loose flannel shirt and jeans. Is that a bandana around her neck? She also has earrings and finger rings, but I can't identify their patterns. Kind of attractive in a free-bird, hippie-chick way.

'What about drug use?' she asks a slim gal with long blonde hair.

"Oh, the blonde is a beauty. Let's listen to what the woman says about me.

'He becomes belligerent and violent when intoxicated, a real terrorist! For heaven's sake, he once tried to bite off part of a man's ear! It's as if he learned nothing from his father.'

"That's a trite observation. Sure, I get bombed and buzzed, but not like Henry! He abused his own family . . . including me! Better be calm. Don't say anything yet. Just listen.

'His behavior on other drugs is even worse,' a short, blond frat-dude adds. 'He once set out to stab a guy who pilfered his marijuana with a seven-inch-long filleting knife! And what about when he went into that woman's house to beat up her son? He did as a dealer asked. He terrorized the poor woman, demanding that her child return the drugs he stole. He's taken more LSD than—'

"The guy's ranting about my behavior when I'm stoned or drugged. This is like watching a bad anti-drug commercial. Fucking frat dudes. That geek needs a swift kick.

'He's a bully, even when sober,' a thin girl with curly black hair interjects. 'He's arrogant and ruthless. Remember the time he threw that bottle at Zac Whitmark's head?'

'Look at his childhood,' a guy in a knit sweater adds. 'He tortured animals! It's shameful. His cruelty knows no bounds.'

"Oh, man, nearly all these fools are chiming in now. Yeah, I punched a guy in the throat, but he deserved it! He went after Paul Kulikowski! Paul was crippled, a little guy who wouldn't hurt a fly! Sure, I choked Fecto out. Yet we were just playing. Ho, ho, ho, I lifted him off the ground by his neck. It was funny as hell! There was nothing malicious about that. I was just having a bit of fun. The jock has been silent, but I've had enough of this crap. Fuck these people!

'Look, we're trying to help you,' the hippie girl says, noting my growing rage.

'Help me? Where were you when the rocking chair my mother comforted me in was smashed to pieces during one of Dad's drunken rages? Where were you when the pedestal table I hid under during tirades was toppled and broken? Where were you when Dad said, 'Fuck you and fuck your birthday'? You bitch about eff'n effects but don't say diddly about causes! I don't need your goddamn help! And I sure as hell don't need anyone's advice about how to live! Enough of this bullshit!'

"Let's get up. Hah, fear lights the group's eyes. You don't bring doubts into a fight! I'll give these bastards a dose of what they've been delivering.

'You're only creations of my mind!' I shout. 'Or maybe you're lost souls visiting this dream. Either way, you don't exist in the real world. And you'll only exist for as long as I'm here!'

"I can't get enough of the rage boiling through my veins. I love this feeling!

I point toward the group and yell. 'It's not I who depend on you, but you who depend on me! I don't have to accept your criticism, advice, or insults. You're all dead! Dead! Dead! Dead! Dead! And when I awake, you'll be gone forever!'

"They're fidgeting. They're fearful. Damn them! Damn them all! Yes, the adrenalin and fury flow. It's so familiar, so powerful, so alluring. Attack! Let's grab the young lady beside me before she can get to her feet. I'll throw her against the wall. Oh, what a thud! A big wince, and down she goes in a heap. Ah, the slow-motion effect, a typical perception during a fight. Some of the others are trying to get up. No way! The odds are poor, so I have to act fast. Go for it! Show them no mercy or consideration. How dare these figments of imagination attack me? My thoughts gave them existence, and I can take it away. I'll destroy them!

"Yeah, I got in a great punch to that blonde's head! And that skinny guy took a stiff forearm to the face. Whew, tagged him good and proper! Let's put the boots to those on the ground before they can get up. Yeah, these people are hopeless! They're piss-poor fighters.

'You're all dead! All of you.'

"Ho, ho, ho, ho! They drop like fall leaves, and I'm the wind. My punches impact hard and fast! Man, I hit the frat dude in the head so hard that he flew across the room. I mean, he actually flew!

'Bet you could use some drugs now!'

"Ho, ho, ho! Oh, there's another one getting up. Wow, I kicked that girl in the side so hard it almost bent her in half! I've never seen that before.

"All I feel is hatred! I hate them. I hate myself. They are of me and must be annihilated. I, too, must be destroyed! All must be destroyed. Smash them, burn them, kill them! The whole world must go and everything on it! I feel . . . I feel a beast within, a powerful, unstoppable creature. Yeah, let it guide me! Let me become one with it! Feel its power, its incredible strength. I must crush every one of them. Let's see who is left standing.

"Ah, the athlete. He towers over me, but he is of my making. A good shot just below the nose ought to rock his world. Let it fly!

'Ow!' What the fuck! My hand is throbbing. It's like hitting a damn rock. Oh, my hand hurts. He . . . he just stands there, not even marked! He looks disgusted. Man, this guy could probably kick my ass. Yet, he is of me! How can anything that is held within defeat me? Come on! Let's take this guy down.

"I'll go in low and pick him up. B-b-but he's anchored to the floor like a goddamned boulder. A high crotch throw should work every time! But I . . . I can't budge him! Good Lord, this guy can defeat me. What do I do? What the hell can I do? Where can we retreat in this dream?

"Fear is counteracting my rage. Release the athlete and back off. Stay low and keep your hands up. Where's an exit? I have to get the hell out of here. Nuts, there's no door! He's just standing there, wearing an expressionless face. Man, that guy could easily kick my ass. Why doesn't he? I've got to find a way out, but—

"Oh, these people are a mess. Good Lord! Look at what I've done to them. They're moaning and crying, trying to help one another up. They clutch onto bruised and battered body parts. And there are so many injuries. It's carnage, all blood, wounds, and broken bones. My power is melting. I'm going to be punished. Shit, I should be punished. But there's no anger in their eyes, only disgust and pain. They aren't vengeful or hateful.

"Yes, I can see what they are now. They're part of a consciousness I've lost touch with. They're part of what is good within all people. Man, I feel like a kid waiting to be spanked.

"Why did I do this? What the hell is wrong with me?

"They're slowly returning to the table and reseating themselves. They're mumbling to one another while tucking in their clothes and sorting out injuries. A girl clutches her side, talking through the pain about the part she played.

'Do you think this will work?' she plaintively asks.

'Perhaps,' the leader replies. 'Let's hope it serves the purpose.'

"It's as if they knew this would happen. Let's check out the athlete. Whew, that guy glares right through me. We both have a beast within, but he never unleashed his. I should follow his example, his passive restraint. Somehow, his willingness to face me destroyed my power. He turned my arrogance into fear and now guilt. The woman beside me sobs while clutching her lower ribs, wincing and groaning. The frat guy massages his face. God, his left eye is a bloody mess. I must have crushed his cheekbone. It's a grotesque wound, and the swelling worsens by the second. He may never see out of that eye again.

"The guilt, it's overwhelming. I'm carrying a demon within. It's a powerful and vicious thing that is devouring my soul. It governs my actions in the natural and spiritual worlds, causing nothing but harm. The beast was forged from torment and is now strong enough to blind and bind me. It's just as my mother warned. In my blindness, I lash out. Look at what I've done to these people: blood, contusions, tears, and agony. There are weeping faces, grimaces, bruises, and bleeding cuts. How can I find higher truths if I cannot enlist the strength needed to become a better person? How can anyone search for God while being an annihilator? I must try to make this right.

'I'm so sorry. I . . . I . . . I . . .'

"No, no words can atone for what I've done to myself and many others. Nor are these battered souls in any mood to hear my lame apologies. They won't even look at me, staring at the table's surface in silence. Pain and sadness are written on their faces. Yet I must make amends. I have to. If these beings come from within, a part of myself that is good was harmed. If they arrived from without, I've damaged souls who were helping me to see.

'I didn't mean to—'

"It's pointless. My words are futile, empty gestures. The deed is done, and nothing can erase it. My head hangs in shame. There's nothing but remorse inside, naked guilt. Yes, I'm terribly flawed. The beast within is chained by conscience but only barely. It's still there, lurking underneath. Perhaps love can kill the beast. Yet how can anyone so warped as I find love? It's locked out by anger and resentment, terrible memories that plague me at every turn.

"A profound weakness is overcoming me, spreading through my limbs, heart, and soul. Yet there is something else, something odd. The souls at the table also feel my shame. I can sense it. This was a test of some kind, something intended to examine my worthiness. I sure as hell didn't do well. Yeah, I failed in almost every way possible. The leader of the group is watching me. Her expression is forgiving, and her voice is kind.

'Hey, look, you have to clean up your act. You have a responsibility to uphold. And one day, you'll see what it is.'

"Responsibility? What responsibility is that? I'll have to ask. I look up to respond and find myself staring at the ceiling of my dormitory room. I'm alert and fully rested . . . as if I had not awoken from a deep sleep."

Alex finished his story and was afraid to look Mirai and Madame Leonedria in the eye, but he knew he must.

10

The Beast Within

"Savagery, Alex," Madame Leonedria said. "How unworthy you were and perhaps still are."

"I know," Alex said. "Regret for my actions during the dream still resonates. Of course, my deeds within the dream weren't much different from my ordinary waking behavior at the time."

"We could find no criminal records on you," Mirai signed. "However, many thugs go through life without getting caught."

"I'm not a damn thug!" Alex angrily replied. "That dream is one of the reasons why! I learned to moderate my behavior!"

"Was that rage I just saw?" Mirai signed. "It's something I've seen in you many times before! Quite frankly, I don't like it. Perhaps you've not changed as much as you think."

10.1 We all harbor beasts within and they require constant control

"What one was and is are two different things," Madame Leonedria said. "After all, time changes all things but itself. And what were you, Alex?"

"I was becoming a psychopath," Alex confessed. "My self-image was as tortured as my memories. All that angst was contained within a bloated and powerful body. I relished fear and confused it with respect. My behavior was shameful."

"Did the dream produce the effects that the characters within it seemed to want?" Madame Leonedria asked. "After all, you're still quick to anger. In addition, some of your writings indicate barbaric proclivities. You've even advocated assassinations and assaults."

"There is the ideal and the practical," Alex said. "Yeah, we all want a peaceful existence. That's a very worthy ideal. Yet do we allow rabid animals to run amok among the helpless and infirm? Do we passively watch injustices and violence being done to others? Do we tolerate the intolerant?"

"So, you advocate killing killers?" Madame Leonedria asked. "Some will observe that you're simply extending and perpetuating an ill instead of containing it."

"True enough," Alex sadly said. "There are no easy answers. The human condition is hideously complex. We have free will, and that means nearly anything is possible. Furthermore, we don't always treat one another as we would like to be treated. Situations thus arise that can call on us to do hideous things. Sometimes, we even act before contemplating the effects of our deeds. Verity understands the influence of context, not that it justified some of my deeds." Alex glanced at her sleeping form as if to assure himself that Verity would agree.

"Perhaps the potential for violence is born into our natures," Mirai signed. "Still, it seems that part of you sought to see beyond that. Maybe your soul was striving to teach itself a lesson."

"It's one we're sharing with the readers," Alex said. "The group leader's words still echo in my mind: 'You have a responsibility to uphold.' For many years I didn't understand what that responsibility was. Eventually, I came to realize that it was this book. That is why we're here."

"Yet words alone cannot heal all souls, dear child," Madame Leonedria said. "For one such as you, remembering is much like reality. So, you open the same book to the same page and read the identical story repeatedly. With every recall, the anger and resentment flares anew."

"That's the nature of post-traumatic stress disorder," Alex admitted. "That's part of what feeds the beast within. I battle my demons every day and probably always will. That's the same case with some of those with us. We're all born of nature and shaped by nurture. That should unite us, though few people allow it to. Anyway, the dream made me see many things I was blind to, like my addictions and violence. Drugs were an escape from a painful past. They allowed an illusory and ephemeral flight from nagging memories and thoughts. Drugs were a balm at best, though, and they ended up causing as many ills as they soothed. My violence resulted from allowing a dreary past to destroy the present and future. Yet you're correct. I'm bound by recollections that can still express themselves in terrible ways."

"Nonetheless, your treatment of the characters within the dream produced an epiphany," Mirai signed. "Your life was changing in other ways too, or so you've told me."

"Yeah, I was slowly becoming a coach back then," Alex happily said. A smile lit up his face while he spoke. "I was starting to teach others how to lift weights and train. That life gave me joy and meaning, something to be happy about. It ultimately turned into a job, albeit mostly part-time. However, coaching was the only occupation I've ever loved."

"So, you went from being a potential brute to someone who found pleasure in helping others," Madame Leonedria observed.

"Does any of this help the readers? Surely, some must now view you as disturbed at best."

"They must know the truth to judge what we'll discuss," Alex said. "Look, for most of my youth, I withdrew into this world of imagination. It was a threadbare consolation. The sickness within became more manifest when I left the nest. My philosophy also became twisted. I made all that was negative an inevitable offspring of existence. I blamed God for crafting a brutal and cruel reality. It was a realm wherein predation, struggle, and death drove a ruthless evolutionary process. The goal was a perfection of form, function, and thought above all else."

"How myopic you were," Madame Leonedria said. "You ignored that love, compassion, and happiness are also aspects of being. Ah, youth is wasted on the young."

"And wisdom is often wasted on the old," Alex retorted. He glanced down. "But you're right. I dismissed positive possibilities, such as love. I didn't grasp that my sickness prevented their realization. Hate became my master. In disdaining my past and our existence, I also grew to disdain myself."

"As we've observed, how can we love another when we hate ourselves?" Madame Leonedria said. "Now you wish to help those walking your path, including some of the people presently listening to us. That's commendable. But I'm intrigued by the concept of future responsibility that the dream related. Remind me of what the leader said to you."

"'You have a responsibility to uphold, and one day you'll see what it is,'" Mirai signed.

"That's what she said," Alex noted. "At the time, personal responsibility was an alien concept. All that mattered was the desire of the moment, whatever it might be. The consequences became irrelevant. That shortsightedness is shared by many who harm others and themselves."

Madame reached into her pocket and pulled out a coin. "I toss this penny into the water bowl," Madame Leonedria said before acting. "Watch the ripples radiate outward. They bounce off the bowl's walls and collide with one another. Actions and reactions echo into the future. Can you apply the metaphor, Alex?"

"I see Dad as a child," Alex said while gazing at the water bowl, studying its turbulent surface. "He is being beaten by his father for failing a spelling test, but he will not cry. He is whipped again for not finishing a meal and yet again for speaking out of turn. Now he is grown, but his soul is scarred by traumatic memories. It's the same story with many who are now with us.

"Dad drinks and behaves recklessly. He builds a litany of even sadder memories, and they give him no rest. He breaks furniture and screams insults. Some of the psychic stones he casts strike me. The words and deeds burst into countless shards that rip into my being. I tear out fragments during rages and throw them at others. Thus, one generation's sins and folly ruin another generation's future."

"Can anyone overcome such a past?" Mirai signed.

"Some go through far worse," Alex said. "Even so, the past is why I still harbor dark impulses. Yet, I've strived to chain the beast within. Yeah, I get angry, and I sometimes say hurtful things. But I'm not a violent man, although self-control hasn't been easy. It's a constant struggle, but I pray the path of brutality is behind me. The ripples stop with me, Mirai."

"It need not be a struggle," Madame Leonedria said. "Strive to see how much your father loved his wife and children. You needn't only recall his turmoil. Remember happy holidays and joyous events. Indeed, endeavor to see the joy and meaning everyday life can provide."

"That's easier said than done," Alex replied. "Trauma leaves festering wounds."

"If you choose to let it," Madame Leonedria said. "It seems the beast has its claws deeply embedded, my son. Perhaps you're destined to fight it throughout time. When you learn how to truly forgive, then you can be free. Instead, you climb this mountain of words and speak with an old gypsy. Dear heart, do you believe such an odyssey can free your soul? Do you believe this quest will help the reader?"

"That's my responsibility," Alex said. "I took that admonition to heart."

"In the end, we're all reflections of our genetics and experiences," Madame Leonedria said. "Shouldn't we leave it at that and move on?"

"No!" Alex insisted. "Understanding why we misbehave doesn't forgive misdeeds. It simply allows us to see the sources of our perfidy and understand its manifestations. My beast manifests itself in anger and violence. Others harbor greed, lust, envy, selfishness, and many more demons. They work alone or in combination and can ruin our and others' lives."

"Why is this theme so important to you, Alex? Surely, the reader tires of this proselytism!" Mirai signed.

"I fear for our species, Mirai!" Alex exclaimed. "You know why, so cut the crap! You keep your cards close to the vest, but you've seen what humankind faces! Tell me, can you walk outside your original home? Can you stroll through a park? Can you swim in a lake? When was the last time you heard a songbird in your habitat?"

Mirai looked down, her glance answering the question.

"That's why I'm hammering this point!" Alex said. "The demons within are as ubiquitous as they are nihilistic. They're a test of our worthiness to walk through time, and everyone reading this line knows we're failing. Hell, it's not like it isn't obvious!

"Nonetheless, we willfully accept lies. We slaughter one another by the millions! We turn gardens into deserts. Then we sit on our asses and do nothing! Oh, we bitch and piss and moan, but we do nothing to change our situation.

"The dream also showed me that self-realization and apologies can't atone for vile actions or recklessness. After all, an apology doesn't do a dead man or his family much good. And how can one ever atone for abusing a child? A line from *The Rubáiyát* of Omar Khayyám goes:

The Moving Finger writes; and, having writ,
Moves on: nor all thy Piety nor Wit
Shall lure it back to cancel half a Line,
Nor all thy Tears wash out a Word of it.

"No, we cannot erase a single line from life's ledger," Madame Leonedria said, "no matter our effort. They stain our memories and cause untold harm."

"Like the dream said, we must clean up our acts, first and foremost," Alex said. "This is especially the case if we're to arrive at a higher understanding of being or making a better world."

"Correcting personal flaws is an endless task," Mirai signed. "Even those who walk through time carry demons within."

"Indeed," Madame Leonedria said. "But enough of this! Say what you must to the reader, Alex, but let us move on."

"Take my lesson to heart," Alex sadly said. "Think long and hard before scolding a child or harming an innocent. Think about what is fueling your rage or deeds. Try to discern whether unleashing the beast will serve any greater good. Odds are, it's best to keep our darker impulses chained."

"Yet I've seen your essay writing," Mirai signed. "You sometimes write about the 'need' to take life. You're certainly no pacifist."

"Alex was born to protect and serve," Madame Leonedria said. "He struggles with the implications of those tasks. Still, this dream was fundamental from a moral and ethical perspective, especially given the trajectory of Alex's life."

"Our intervention served the purpose," Mirai noted.

"Those with us will be pondering that intervention for quite some time," Madame Leonedria said with a wry smile.

Mirai offered a quick nod and then perked up an ear. "My goodness," she signed, "Verity is snoring!"

"She must be totally wiped out." Alex studied Verity's slumbering form. "How beautiful she is."

"And how vulnerable," Madame Leonedria said. "All too often, the truth is what we make it. On occasion, it's divorced from the reality we share. You love that woman, Alex, but you'll never be one with her." She glanced toward Mirai and added, "Sometimes, it's best to commune with those your spirit can touch, regardless of how removed they may be in time and space."

"I know," Alex said with an embarrassed glance at Mirai. "Yet I am linear, at least in part."

"The most important aspects of our beings are not linear, Alex," Mirai signed. "How else could I be here?"

"The real question is 'why' are you here, Mirai?" Madame Leonedria observed. "Alex loves you, as you well know. He always thinks about you and writes lines about you in his diary. Alex lives for you but cannot bridge the gap. One thousand years is a barrier to him, so he pursues Verity. All would-be thinkers do. But he does so merely as a means to an end, not the preferred end. Yet enough of this twaddle! Now, let us get back to the subject of dreams."

"Before I get into that, I've something to say," Alex noted. "Mirai means more to me than I sometimes admit to myself. We argue a lot, maybe more than we should. Lord knows I cannot easily commune with her. I sometimes look into those eyes, and I . . . I get lost. I truly do. Everything around me disappears."

Mirai smiled and signed, "Everything disappears except time."

Alex and Mirai looked down, and Madame Leonedria reached out and touched them. "Time and space can be overcome by the mind and heart," she said. "As we go on, I believe some of those bridges will be crossed. Now, let us examine the next dream in this series."

11

No Time for Greed

Alex was still uncomfortable about revealing his violent dream, but he knew it was necessary to share the episode. The following event would be much less traumatic, albeit just as profound. He girded himself by taking another sip of wine. It was going to be a long night.

"It was obvious that much could be learned during these experiences," Alex said. "This was true whether the dreams were merely imagination or something far deeper. I thus sought more seeing dreams. However, my ability to enter or control them was not fully evolved, so I practiced during my normal dreams. I focused on the context as dreams unfolded, asking myself about the relevance and meaning of particular settings, objects, or events. In a way, I was trying to grasp metaphors' deeper meanings.

After all, metaphors are the language of dreams. I also pondered why I discussed this or that subject with a given character as the conversations unfolded. All the while, I considered my motivations. What was I seeking to learn or experience?"

"You were systematic," Mirai signed. "It is almost like a training regimen."

"I was indeed training," Alex said. "Repeated practice allowed me to fully contemplate what other characters and I were thinking about while a dream unfolded. I could do so with depth and clarity. That is the essence of metacognition, as in thought-about-thought. It seemed this capacity would eventually help fulfill my quest to find our source. However, at least for me, entering an astral/seeing state was frustratingly rare. Eventually, another one came."

"We could use some context first, Alex," Mirai signed.

"Well, the experience occurred when my future plans were uncertain," Alex said. "Drugs no longer ruled my existence, nor did violence. I loved lifting weights and coaching, but they didn't provide much security. In fact, the pay was lousy! There were also no benefits, not even health insurance. I wasn't quite sure what to do with my life."

"All of us go through that phase," Madame Leonedria observed. "Be that as it may, continue with this adventure."

"The dream's subject was mundane," Alex began, "but the lesson was important. Oddly, the usual high-pitched sound and sense of motion did not presage the event. Instead, I unexpectedly and very suddenly became aware.

"Put yourself in the experience, Alex," Madame Leonedria said. "Gaze into the water bowl and let the memories flow."

Alex leaned forward and stared into the water's depths. He furrowed his brow in concentration. "Huh, I'm walking down a wide, cement sidewalk. It's flanked by neatly trimmed lawns and beautifully landscaped grounds. There are some impressive academic and institutional buildings nearby. This must be a college town.

"Oh, this definitely isn't an ordinary dream. Those don't have this clarity of thought and perceptual details. Ah, a gentle breeze, sweet and fresh. The scent of newly mowed grass permeates the air. Always liked that smell. The academic setting is only a thought about a place of thought, but it sure feels real. The sky is azure, and the air is cool and crisp. This must be early fall. Hmmm, the contrast between the flora's vibrant hues and the pale white sidewalk stretching up ahead is marvelous. Yeah, this is the stuff of reality.

"Goodness, I'm dressed in martial arts garb! How odd. The clothes are white and made of thick cotton. My shirt is long and loose-fitting. Huh, there are no buttons. Yeah, this is a ... *uwagi*? I think that's what this attire is called. It's held together at the waist by a belt tied in a square knot. But it's not a traditional design. There are four large pockets, two at the breast level and two below the belt. The pants are made of the same tough material as the shirt. It's very comfortable attire. Oh, but I hope no combat is coming. There's been enough of that nonsense.

"There must be something to learn, so I'll keep walking. This sidewalk descends a slight grade. I've seen this setting before, near the University of New Hampshire's Kappa Sigma house. However, these buildings are much larger and more spread out. Perhaps there's . . . huh, the sun's reflecting off something on the sidewalk.

"Wow, there're two coins. Lucky me! Let's check them out. Ha, they're old Mercury Head dimes. They're worth a lot more than face value to collectors. I'll put them in one of my shirt pockets. Maybe they'll be there when I awake. Nah, that notion never works. It takes too much energy to turn a thought into a reality. But there's a way. After all, energy and mass are interrelated, and ideas are organized energy patterns. It would be nice to find someone to talk with about the possibility. A scholar in one of these buildings may know the answer. Oh, never mind that. Time to get going.

"Look! A whole group of coins is in front of me on the concrete. I'll add these to my—

"Whoa, is that a child laughing? It is! Yeah, there are kids around here, for sure. Let's see where they are. Wow, the scenery has changed! The grass is long, and the landscape is much wilder. No extensive masonry or cement buildings are nearby now, just a few small wooden ones. They're also set well back. How could the environment change so quickly with just a few footsteps? Ah, I get it! It's a temporal compression. We've been through these metaphors before; nothing to get freaked out about.

"I hear those kids again. It sounds like they're heading my way. Shoot, they'll find the money. I better cover these coins with my foot. Here they come, two little boys racing up the sidewalk. Oh, they're dressed just like I am! They must be about 10 or so. They're running so fast I can barely see their faces! Zip, they sprint right by, and off they go! Wow, they're having a great time. Ah, I remember being a kid and playing with my pals. We used to ride our bikes all over creation and hike through the forests. Those were the days! That laughter is infectious. Wait a minute; they may be laughing at me.

"Well, they're gone now, so let's collect the coins. Here's an old Indian Head nickel stamped on the back with a buffalo. Oh, the buffalo is missing a hind leg. A misprint, if that's what they call it. A rare coin like this must be worth a fortune. These other coins are also old, but I'll check out the dates later. Let's drop them into my pocket for now and search for more. This could indicate that money can be found if folks don't have kids. Or perhaps the metaphor means rarity is more valuable than the mundane. I don't know, but it's a pleasant dream. Just love this weather!

"Look at that. The sidewalk is carpeted with coins. There's no time to examine each one. Just pick them up and fill my pockets. Ha, the coins jingle when I move. That's a rare sound for me. It's not often I've anything of value in my pockets. This must be how it feels to be rich. Perhaps we'll win the lottery. Oh, that'd be nice. Yeah, I love this dream!

"I'd better keep looking down while walking. I want to see everything that glitters, and these coins look cool. They're bits of history, and—

"Bummer, there's grass growing between the cracks in the sidewalk. Yeah, the concrete is worn through in places. It appears the cement was poured over old cobblestones. Whew, these things are weathered to beat the band. They must be ancient, and—

"Wait a minute! Is that gold sparkling in the space between those cracked cobblestones? It sure as hell is! I have to snag that one! Oh, this thing's wedged in there. But that's a gold coin, all right, and a big one! We'll have to dig a bit to loosen the stone. The soil is moist, and my fingers are getting dirty. Come on, almost got it! Ah, there we go. Check this big boy out! It must be old as the hills.

"Hmmm, the coin isn't symmetrical, and there's no edge rim. The head and tail sides are also not well aligned. There's no exceptional artistry here. Let's see, the face is stamped with a royal-looking bearded guy. The other side has raised letters in Latin or some different Mediterranean language. It may be old Spanish. The symbols are difficult to decipher. Maybe there's a—

"Damn it! I hear those kids again. They're a bloody nuisance. I'd better stash this gold coin before they find—

"Hey! They cut right across my path! The little buggers almost ran me over. Where the hell did they go? They must have gone into—

"Well, they must be behind some of this greenery. And there're lots of trees and bushes around me. There aren't any houses or roads. I must be heading into a forest. Yeah, this is a temporal metaphor, for sure. We're walking down the path of time, and it leads to riches. This must mean the source of wealth is ancient. These coins are as old as the star stuff that made us, at least in the material sense. Well, same age, different form. The metaphor could mean that time is money. Or, money is time. I don't know. But it's nice having something of value. Let's get to the end of this path. I bet the mother lode is down there.

"Man, these trees are getting dense. This is a forest, all right, dark and deep. The canopy shades parts of the walkway, but I could use the cover. Whew, I'm sweating up a storm. Ah, that breeze sure feels good. Very refreshing. It's swaying the branches and leaves. This reminds me of UNH's College Woods. It's just beautiful in there, as good as it gets. I'll bet God lives in a place like this. 'Course, God probably lives everywhere.

"Ahead, sunlight passes through the swaying canopy and flitters upon the forest floor. What a dazzling light show! This experience is so fricking cool! The air smells fresh and clean. I can even hear the leaves rustling. Whew, this is so much more than a dream. Every detail is precise, even the veins in the leaves. It's like—

"Good Lord, hoards of gold and silver coins lie ahead! They gleam and glitter in the gyrating light. There are too many to examine, so let's stuff them in here. No, that pocket is full.

Hmmm, I'll have to start using these breast pockets. Bend down, pick up coins, bend down, and pick up coins. Who said making money is hard? It doesn't take a genius to do this. All folks need to do is keep their eyes on the ground and stay focused. The only problem is that this shirt is digging into my neck from the coins' weight. It's annoying, but I can take it. Hell, I've lifted a lot heavier loads than this!

"The walkway is nothing but worn cobblestones now. Grass grows between them, and tree roots invade the path. I'm walking through time, all right. Man-made roads and buildings have given way to nature. If I go back up the trail, the reverse may happen. The only constants are money, children, and a changing environment. These constants are metaphors, or they could represent something more concrete. Their relationships are unclear, at least for now. Still, I'm thinking about thoughts even as my mind weaves this dream. How deep can this process go?

"Whew, this bending is getting tedious and hard on the back. Some coins are difficult to pry from the crevices, but it's worth the effort. Yuck, my hands are getting filthy. I hate being dirty. That's an insight into the cost of making compromises. No such thing as principles when the focus is booty!

"Huh, what a weird piece this is. It's a large gold coin but not round. The metal was poured into a simple mold and not stamped. Plus, it's crudely shaped. No artistry at all here. It has the caricatured face of a man with Grecian features, or maybe Minoan. There's still room left in this breast pocket. Hmmm,

I'd better even out the load. I must also find a way to keep this miserable collar from digging into my neck. It's starting to rub my skin raw, but I get the point. Wealth is a burden.

"The way ahead is barely a path now. There are almost no cobblestones and far more trees, bushes, and roots. I'll be OK if the sun keeps shining through the branches. Getting lost out here would be a bummer, although this place is beautiful. The colors of the fallen leaves are fantastic. My nieces used to press leaves like these between book pages to preserve them. They found them as precious as I do these coins. They are, in a way. However, pressed leaves won't buy a house or car. Crickets are chirping. Sweat drips from my brow and spatters on the fallen leaves. Man, the sensations are overwhelming. This is joy, and it's more real than—

"Yes! There it is! There's a hoard of gold and silver at my feet. Wahoo! Look at that! A multitude of coins and ingots glisten in the flickering light. The mother lode is at hand! Bend down, pick up, bend down, pick up. Any fool can do this! But it's getting difficult to cram the treasure into my pockets. And how the hell am I going to carry more when my pockets are full? Whew, this load is getting very heavy. Wealth is definitely a yoke of sorts. Well, that's how it feels, precisely like a yoke. I can manage the task. Strength has never been a problem for me.

"Oh, this one is very odd. It's a lump of pure gold the size and shape of half a grapefruit. The piece was removed from the bottom of a smelting pot. Nah, this isn't a coin at all. Not really.

A marking on top is very similar to the Greek letter π. That looks like a little dash or dot in front of it. Well, the mark may be a casting flaw. No, it's probably a dash. This symbol could be Sumerian, but their characters are more wedge-shaped. This symbol wouldn't be here if its meaning wasn't significant. It could be a denomination. Perhaps it represents what this metal is worth or what it weighs. Oh, who the hell cares? I can look the symbol up later. Gold is gold. Damn, I can barely squeeze this thing into my last pocket.

"It would be foolish to leave any of this behind. I know what to do. I can stuff the treasure under my shirt. It's baggy enough, and the material is strong! Let's focus on the gold and skip the silver. Oh, my hands are filthy. And now my chest is getting dirty, too. I despise being unclean. It doesn't matter, though. With enough money, I can buy a swimming pool to bathe in. Hell, I can buy an entire ocean! I can even—

"Whoa! What happened to the path? Nuts, we're lost! I knew this could happen. It means I'm missing the point of this dream. And this damn load is so heavy I can hardly move. Yet there's so much more here. Hmmm, let's go on all fours! It's undignified, but what the hell. That may be the lesson. Making money requires strength and determination. One can't be afraid of getting a bit dirty or a little sweaty. We must compromise to succeed, but that's a small price. I could do this in real life. Anyone could! Heck, I know all sorts of people in the weight-training game. I could get into product endorsements—

"Damn, I hear those kids again. Where are those forest sprites? Ah, there they are, laughing away. A large clearing is ahead through all these branches and bushes. The sunlight's shining on the spot. Oh, many people are gathered up there; people to talk with! Some answers can be found there. But how do I protect my money? It would be crazy to risk all this! Yet those folks don't look like thieves.

"Let's check them out. They're dressed like I am. Young and old have congregated in a rocky opening beside a sizeable meandering stream. The rivulet is shallow and wide, with big and small boulders piercing the flowing water's surface. Parents are playing games with their kids. Yeah, they're having a ball. The laughter is infectious. Lovers hold hands. Some folks are seated upon rocks and talking. Those guys over there are locked into a lively conversation. Others lounge on the grass and catch a few rays. Yeah, they're living large and enjoying the day.

"I want to share some time with them. This is a utopia, a place of pure joy. Oh, look at my hands and chest. They're filthy! So are my clothes! What the hell am I doing here? Think, damn you! Think about what is happening. I'm clutching dirt-covered rocks that contain a few flecks of gold. What does this mean? Why are we here?

"I-I-I see so many images now! They explode in my mind, one after another. There's too much flowing in at once. There are feelings, pictures, and insights. Think about what we experienced! Recount the history. Yes, begin there.

"During my walk through time, my eyes seldom left the ground. I noticed only what glittered and ignored the land and those around me. I did not seek or enjoy the company of others, even children. They were only seen as competition for my gains. I hoarded whatever the light reflected and hid it from everyone. That included those who never cared about such trinkets.

"Ideas and images rush in. Some of them are clearer than others. A businessman wears a fine suit, but his hands are soaked in oil. A beautiful woman wearing a white dress races by in a sleek red convertible sports car. She plunges into a billowing smog bank, disappearing from view. A group of people sits around a table surrounded by flow charts and economic data, but they are waist-deep in fetid sewage water. There are too many images flooding in. Focus! You have to focus.

"A filthy baby in a soiled crib sits in his own waste. The child sticks dimes in his mouth and gags. He looks up at me and cries. He's choking! That kid's going to die if I don't help! There is sadness all around, endless remorse. They defile the Earth and each other. Then they live in filth—all for the sake of what glitters.

"Yet, there's something else, something hard to see. It's more a thought than an image, an ancient bit of wisdom I've lost sight of. Our only real currency is time. That's what the temporal metaphor meant! I get it! Yes, and our time is finite and precious. It can be spent but not purchased. Ah, and time has a form that can be found within the tiniest aspect of being. It's inseparable from matter, energy, and thought. It's an essential element of being. Yet we spend our time so foolishly.

11.1 The ultimate cost of greed is life itself

"Now come more images! They're horrible and vivid! There's a grotesque scene of countless rotting bodies piled high atop one another like fetid cordwood. They're lost lives that were never truly lived. Their names, accomplishments, and desires are history's fodder. Only their sad legacy lingers. They sought material possessions that they could never keep and ignored all else. They wasted the land, water, and air, leaving a fruitless future.

"Their glittering jewelry sloughs from decaying flesh and moldering skeletal remains. It plops into the muddy earth below, the gold and silver returning from whence it came. That same putrid filth is what I'm clutching onto! Oh, it stinks to the high heavens! My hands are dirty. My face! My chest! I'm so damn filthy, so like them in my folly!

"Children's laughter echoes around me. More thoughts flow in. That sweet sound is worth more than all the gold one could ever gather. Children are the only part of us that marches through the ages. Buildings crumble, books turn to dust, and histories are forgotten. However, our children will carry on, but only if the garden we leave can sustain them. They are our future, the only part of us that can walk through time.

"It all fits together now. I feel a kind of warmth, deep and comforting. These rocks I'm holding mean nothing! The metaphor is sublime. I'll drop them. A child in the clearing beckons me to come forward. Let's get up. Ah, I've suddenly been relieved of a burden that need not have been carried. My pockets are now empty, but my soul is whole and clean! This is freedom. This is joy. I must get through these branches and bushes, though. I have to get to that clearing. They notice me.

'I'm coming! I'm coming!' I shout.

"Man, these bushes are as thick as it gets. Yet I'm making some progress. It's tough going, but I can push through. Damn, the briars are getting in the way. They're like tiny hands holding me back. Everyone looks pleased to see me. Where have I seen these faces? They seem so familiar. I want to live in this place of peace and never go back. A child waves to me.

'I'm almost there, son!' I say.

"I step into the sunlight, and I'm instantly awake. I was catapulted back into the reality of my bed and thus ended the dream. Yet, I awoke with the same feeling of inner peace that swept over me during the last part of the event. I thanked God for thinking about me and consider myself blessed for the experience. Much was learned, which has now been shared."

"Yes, that's a typical seeing event," Madame Leonedria said. "That sudden influx of ideas and images often occurs when the dream's central theme becomes evident. It can form a profound linkage with metaphysical elements within and without. However, the connections and realizations can become so numerous that one's memory cannot capture them. The images and ideas simply evaporate before they are grasped."

"I suspect more could be unwrapped via hypnosis or similar tools," Alex said. "The implications and permutations of the dream suddenly became like opened floodgates. I wonder how much was lost, although perhaps not irretrievably."

"The clarity of the images is remarkable," Mirai signed. "This is actually how the dream occurred?"

"Yeah, that's how it happened," Alex said. "There was no embellishment. However, I probably forgot some things. There was just too much."

"The influx seemed like miniature storylines," Mirai signed. "All the images had a meaning, and most related to the future."

"There was lots of symbolism," Alex said. "That's the nature of dreams. A particularly memorable image is the character emblazoned on the lump of gold. It had no meaning to me at the time. I researched the mark some years ago, and the Hebrew Chai symbol is a very close candidate. It's associated with the concepts of 'life' or 'living things,' which I presume was the value assigned to the currency. If so, that value is far too high. I never studied Hebrew. Nor do I know how or why the symbol manifested during the dream. Perhaps I'll find a Chinese or another symbol that matches better. However, Chai is very similar in form."

"Interesting," Mirai signed. "More foreknowledge, albeit it took years for you to deduce the intended meaning. The narrative is also coherent. Each experience eventually leads to a greater understanding of the central theme. We debated how much of the image flood was a reconstruction or construction. That issue is always part and parcel of memory dynamics. Yet, it took some time for you to grasp the message of a fairly basic morality lesson."

"Simple is as simple does," Alex said with a smile. "An important developmental aspect of the dream was that dealing with temporal metaphors wouldn't be a problem. Moreover, I developed a much greater appreciation for the land and our time on it."

"Did this dream change your life, Alex?" Madame Leonedria asked.

"Well, I've never compromised my beliefs for money," Alex said. "When money comes, I'm grateful, but I don't own a home or car, let alone have a driver's license. Some consider me a pauper. Maybe so, but I'm wealthy in being granted the gift of time."

"Does this justify your past thievery?" Madame Leonedria said.

"Damn it!" Alex growled. "You just won't cut me any slack! Sure, I did my share of shoplifting and pilfering when I was young. And I won't justify my perfidy with any lame excuses. It was pointless and selfish. I no longer do such stupid things and won't walk that path again! Do you enjoy shaming me?"

"You write these lines!" Madame Leonedria tersely said. "Yet you do not control what I think or say; try though you may! My being is beyond a typed page! Moreover, I'll not tolerate blame for your actions or history! Is that clear?"

"You're a pain in the ass sometimes," Alex grumbled. "You take on a life of your own."

"Complete with indignation," Madame Leonedria said with a cold, stony stare. "I'll not play a submissive role, nor will I be a sop to alleviate your petty feelings or hide your sins! We will be completely honest with the readers, like it or not! Most of those with us have been greedy at one time or another. Some have even taken things that weren't theirs. But why? Is it desire? Is it need? Is it greed, one of your beasts within?"

Mirai whistled and began rapidly signing. "It is an interplay of nature and nurture." Her fingers were almost blurred as they moved. "At an intrinsic level, there is an ongoing dynamic between needs, appetites, and greed. Moreover, humans are not the only creatures driven by what some call greed. Greed occurs when desires exceed requirements. Its roots begin benignly enough.

"Corporeal being requires energy, matter, and procreation— these are the essences of existential need. In many animals, the acquisition of needs is guided by inherent appetites. Thus, the doe has an appetite for fodder and the wildcat for meat. Both have desires for sex.

"The litany goes: the grass absorbs the sun's energy and Earth's nutrients and turns them toward its needs. The doe's appetite for grass turns this fodder toward its needs. The wildcat's appetite for meat turns the doe's flesh toward its needs. However, two wildcats will maim one another instead of sharing a kill that could feed both for a week. They can behave even more viciously when pursuing a mate."

"I suppose one could argue that greed is an extension of our survival instincts," Alex said. "Perhaps it helps ensure our continuance in case of lean times. Eat and hoard now, for it could be a long time before another meal comes. Let me spin this out, not that I believe it. After all, sustenance can be finite and transitory. Well, species great and small gather and protect resources and territory. To have is to live. To want is to wither. One could make similar arguments to justify lust, envy, jealousy, and other potential ills."

"That's a facile argument," Madame Leonedria said. "There comes the point in sentient development wherein the requirements for survival are met via technological advances. These occur in farming, distribution, and social infrastructure. Hence, the capacity to meet a species' basic needs increases as it develops. However, primal appetites and urges remain intact. Eventually, the potential for sustaining the common welfare collides with individual and irrational wants. Greed becomes an aspect of the self that dominates all else. Some become willfully blind beasts of petty ego. In effect, selfishness prevents us from seeing our perfidy or what we do to others and the future."

"Hundreds of tablets are devoted to the subject in my original habitat," Mirai signed. "Many were written during the First Die Off. The common theme is that extending personal desires beyond reasonable requirements extacts a terrible cost on collective well-being. What began as existential necessity morphs into highly exaggerated personal security and self-fulfillment concepts. Perceived 'needs' become insatiable."

"Even before the Die Offs, the problems were apparent," Madame Leonedria added. "Humanity's imbalances between needs and desires have existed for thousands of years. One percent of the population typically controls over 95 percent of the economic and material resources. Some steal, kill, pollute, and destroy to secure money, land, and power. Nations will even make war to assume dominance and economic control, claiming might makes right. Meanwhile, the have-nots suffer, rise up, and chaos rules."

"Many seem blind to our history," Alex observed, "and thus, we constantly revisit our worst tendencies. For instance, we continually instill the notion that greed is good. It becomes an article of faith in politics, commerce, and social conventions. We're taught early on to realize our most extravagant desires. Being satisfied with adequate sustenance, possessions, and security is ridiculed. 'I want' becomes the mantra of our youth. A teenager simply *must* have the latest fashion. Meanwhile, one neighbor is jealous of another's car."

"Christmas became a pagan celebration of materialism long ago," Mirai signed. "I wrote an article on it. The Christian ideals of giving and sacrifice were both forsaken. They gave way to the faith of unrestrained capitalism. The focus became pushing the latest toy trends and garnering big retail sales."

"That's the path humanity freely elected to follow," Madame Leonedria said. "The universe is littered by such puerile folly. Barren planets are scattered here and there, the former occupants consumed by their excesses long ago. Spirituality and morality are ignored for the sake of diamonds and gold. All the while, people blind themselves to where this lifestyle leads. That peaceful clearing you saw in the dream was a shared and simple way of living. It could be sustained for millennia."

"Our progenitors failed to realize that," Mirai signed. She grew sullen and sad while communing. "In my childhood home, we need technology to simply exist. All is artificial, contained, and strictly managed, even the air we breathe. Healthy children are happy rarities. They are precious, for most of us are infertile. We can clone people, but natural births are rare. The future has paid dearly for the sins of the past. Yet we survive and are going forth. Sadly, the stream of life Alex saw where people gathered is only a dream to my kind."

"I am so dammed sorry," Alex said. "We let you down. Do you think this book will do any good, Mirai?"

"Don't answer that," Madame Leonedria warned. "Let the reader make that choice."

"I wanted to be with those folks in the clearing," Alex sadly said. "Instead, I remained part of a lost society. Some charge outrageous prices for medicines. Others sacrifice the land for money or transient goals. Up go shopping malls, and down go the farms."

"This moralizing is boring the reader, Alex," Madame Leonedria said. "Humanity's myopia is nearly universal in the early stages of sentient development. Some species never evolve beyond this point."

"Yet any species can develop the intellectual capacity and experience to see where excess leads," Mirai signed. "If this foresight is used, the reward is survival. If not, life suffers."

"Thus, the living death that Alex's kindred left you, Mirai," Madame Leonedria sadly said.

"The fact that I'm here speaks positively for our efforts," Mirai signed. "But our ancestors did not treat us well. The universe is full of existential challenges, although few are worse than those we impose upon ourselves."

Alex glanced down and softly said, "I tried to defend you, Mirai."

"Not nearly enough!" a scowling Mirai angrily signed. "You write this self-indulgent and tedious philosophy, but it means nothing! What did you actually do to secure our future? And what about those reading this paragraph? Did any of you act to alleviate what we must endure? Did you do anything? The irresponsibility is unfathomable! Why have children if you won't care for their future progeny? What is the point? Over your lifetime, Alex, you've written more than a million words. Precious few were in defense of the land, this Mother Earth. We pay the price! We pay it each and every day!"

"I should have done more," Alex said. He could not bear to look at Mirai, feeling remorse that utterly shamed him.

"All of you must do more, including the readers," Madame Leonedria said. "Life constantly tests us to ensure our worthiness. This is nature's way of perfecting our form and thoughts."

"Creatures of excess consume themselves," Mirai observed. "And your sweet words did little to stop what happened to our world."

"There are people who will act!" Alex insisted. "That's a major reason we're sharing these thoughts with them. Words alone can't change thousands of years of history, but deeds will!"

"You've seen what awaits your kind, Alex," Madame Leonedria said. "Sharing your visions will be one small impetus for change."

"I hope so," Alex said. "Some of my dreams about the future are dreadful."

"Destruction and ruin can drive all species to greater realizations," Madame Leonedria said. "Must it come to that?"

"I suspect it will," Alex sadly said.

"If you could only see through my eyes," Mirai angrily signed. "We call them the barrens: vast tracts of desolation and ruins. There's unbearable heat and little habitable land. One can travel for hundreds of miles and see nothing but abandoned ruins. Can you imagine how we feel about our ancestors? Every community has a Wall of Shame. We record the names and ill deeds of those who failed us. They forever remind us of how not to be!"

"What the fuck do you want me to do?" Alex roared. "This book is my only means of allowing you to commune with the past. And here I am, swearing again! That's bound to piss off some readers. You know I'm unworthy of writing this goddamn text! Don't have the patience! Don't have the skill! Go ahead, tell me how badly I failed to meet my responsibility. Tell me how I failed the future! Make me feel even worse than I already do."

"I never intended to do that," Mirai signed. "The fact that I am here is a message of optimism."

"Enough of this!" Madame Leonedria proclaimed. She filled her glass and took a sip of wine. "When the poorest is treated as well as the richest, humanity will change. Alex, I note you could manipulate time while within the seeing state. That will inevitably draw one to the source of our being."

"Yeah, the quest to find God," Alex said. "The term doesn't do justice to the concept. Like the Jews, I cannot find a proper name for creation's source. In fact, the word 'god' burns the ears and eyes of some. This is especially so with the learned."

"A wise person should see beyond how people misuse a term," Madame Leonedria said. "One would think they'd examine the possibilities of what the term can be made to represent."

"That requires us to leave prejudices behind," Mirai signed. "Many academics cannot open their minds and hearts enough to do that."

"Exactly!" Madame Leonedria said. "Their arrogance blinds them as much as Alex's beast blinds him. Their minds become closed to the possible. Instead, many become bound only to what is verifiable by this means or that. They become rationalistic skeptics. Sadly, they're incapable of grasping what could be."

"I know open, humble, and honest scholars," Alex said. "They're good people by any measure. Mirai is one of them."

"Thank you, Alex," Mirai signed, "but I'm removed from most of the academic community. They pay the future lip service, yet voiceless souls are often ignored."

"Not by me," Alex said. "As for my quest to understand God, I've pursued many paths. Very few of them were taken during the seeing state. Moreover, I don't like reliving those events. It's one thing to experience a basic morality dream. It's quite another to seek the ultimate source. That leads to traumas that never go away."

"Yet, that's why we're here, child," Madame Leonedria said. "Let us enter into our purpose."

"So be it," Alex said, his face betraying a sense of trepidation. It would take precise wording to describe his experiences with God, and he wanted to make sure he would accurately describe his dream.

12

Looking for God

"My first attempt to find God happened nearly 40 years ago," Alex said, his eyes twinkling in the fire's light. "I had graduated and was working as a weight-training coach at UNH. My consciousness experiments were still underway, but a dream occurred that was unusual by any measure. I believe the date was between February 6 and 7, 1978. However, labeling these experiences as first or second is dubious. There's something about them that goes beyond time."

"Indeed, the seeing state is all about transcending temporal boundaries," Madame Leonedria said. "Please describe the event's initial stages."

"They were very odd," Alex said. "One night, I was in that peculiar dream state wherein only consciousness resides. The experience came upon me without warning or intention. I was soundly asleep one moment, and the next, I was fully conscious. There was no light or images, only a feeling of great power and awareness. I could hear the now-familiar high-pitched hum. The typical sensation of growing acceleration also came as the hum increased in intensity. It was appealing and exhilarating."

"The power of increasing speed can be thrilling," Madame Leonedria observed.

"And intoxicating," Alex explained. "However, the acceleration/power feedback loop soon exceeded anything previously experienced, and by a wide margin! Indeed, the power increased exponentially while I sped through the encompassing void. I sensed infinite energy was at my disposal.

"This seemed an ideal opportunity to answer a question that had haunted me for years: 'Is there a God?' I realized the seeing state wouldn't last. Thus, a strategy was sought that could arrive at meaningful answers. Temporal manipulations had been no problem in prior seeing states. I thus decided to delve back toward the beginning of all things. After all, we're children of event one."

"That's an arrogant approach," Mirai signed. "Did you truly think traveling to the source of creation was possible?"

"The 'self' was irrelevant, Mirai," Alex said. "The quest was everything. The course was set to follow a similar track as taken during the 'Need versus Greed' dream. Soon enough, I was plunging back through time. With this thought came the realization that a coherent setting may provide an answer. Thus, I willed a scene with people. Yes, I was in control of the dream state, or at least it began that way. In a split second, a setting came to be.

"Ah, some contextual control within the seeing state," Madame Leonedria observed. "That's an important step in expanding one's perceptions."

"I didn't control the setting's specifics, but it was obviously in the past," Alex said.

"You're doing fine!" Madame Leonedria said. "Please, try to actually relive the event. Bring the reader into what you experienced."

Alex closed his eyes and looked deep within. "It seems I've materialized in a living room," he said. "It's well kept and adorned with lots of worn furniture. My goodness, it feels like I've dropped into an authentic setting. Perhaps this event was recorded in an official report or diary. Incredible details, absolutely stunning. There's a delicately embroidered doily draped over the back of an old Queen Ann sofa. Each stitch is vivid, as are the patterns on the worn carpet beneath my feet. Based on these furnishings, the timeframe must be about 1930, give or take a bit. I'm not positive, though. Huh, I can still hear the humming noise. How odd. I wonder whether this setting's continuity can be maintained? Come on, stay focused.

"Ah, an old man is seated on an over-padded chair, sunk deep into its worn surface. He must have noticed me at the same instant I detected him. The poor fellow looks shocked. Perhaps I dropped into his living room from somewhere out of time and space. Yeah, that would scare anyone. Oh, this guy's been around the block. His face is grizzled and wrinkled, with poorly shaven stubble. He must be about 65 or so, gaunt and worn. I sense a lifetime of hard toil, and he reflects the part. A loose-fitting shirt covers his boney shoulders. A pair of old-fashioned suspenders hold up his oversized green work pants. I'd better be quick and direct. It's uncertain how long I can stay in this setting.

'I'm in a dream state, and I don't have much time to speak with you,' I tell him.

"Nuts, he looks upset. Let's calm him down.

'Relax. You won't be harmed in any way. But I have a question to ask.'

"Huh, a young lady with long, dark curly hair just rushed in. Kind of pretty. She stands in the doorway, looking at me. She's shocked, frightened. I think she's the old man's daughter. Her flour-covered apron indicates she's cooking. Damn, the woman is as distressed by my presence as her dad. There she goes, beating a hasty retreat.

"It's strange. I can sense her thoughts and actions. Yeah, she's calling the police on an old-fashioned candlestick phone, telling them an intruder has invaded her family's house. Wow, I also discern flashes of her futility about living at home and caring for her ailing father. She is desperate and lonely, fearful of an empty future. It's as if we're one. Stop it! Stay focused on finding an answer, and don't be delayed.

'All I want to know is if there's a God,' I say.

"Nah, the old man is too terrified to speak. He's cringing, pushing himself into the shabby chair's padding. There's no time for this nonsense! This guy is going to answer me! I'll grab the codger by his suspenders and shirt and lift him up. That's it. Now pull him close. He's like a feather in my hands, but I shouldn't treat him too roughly.

'IS THERE A GOD?!'

"Gosh, I'm screaming. The poor guy is petrified, trembling like a leaf. Man, didn't you learn anything from the violence dream? My desperation can quickly become his if I don't act with restraint! Oh, he's far too frightened to supply any answers. Damn! I sure screwed that up! This is pointless. Let's put him back on the chair and search elsewhere. Be careful, though. This guy has been through enough.

"Now close your eyes and concentrate. We'll travel into another past setting for an answer, no matter the cost. But we have to go back much further than this. That's it. Concentrate on the background humming sound. Yes, it's getting louder, and an intensifying power is streaming through me. Oh, I'm getting a bit intoxicated, so stay focused. Whew, it's like being buzzed, but my control is still there. I'm going to find an answer! This is the most crucial question that's ever been asked. Nothing will get in the way.

"It's imperative to find people who have a clue, though that's a matter of chance. Hmmm, perhaps not. Religious people could provide better answers. After all, they're always focused on God. Of course, their minds are often filled with more dogma than reason. Well, it's worth a try. We'll focus on the general notion of religiosity.

"OK, let's stop here. Come on, concentrate on a setting. That's it. Yeah, we're materializing. A hard surface appears beneath my feet, and I open my eyes. Ah, I'm in the middle of a sizable New England meeting room. It's an impressive place with a high ceiling and ornate woodwork. Wow, this place is in excellent order. There are several heavily-varnished wooden pews and benches and a large walnut pulpit. Perhaps this is a church or town hall. Two men are standing close by, like a Mutt and Jeff duo. They're dressed in Puritan garb, rimmed black felt hats, cape-like overcoats, neck ruffs, sleeve cuffs, baggy breeches, and knee stockings. The year is probably around 1650 or so. Nuts, I must have startled these guys. Man, they look stunned. Let's try to calm the situation. Speak softly.

'Please don't get upset. I'm not here to harm anyone. All I want is the answer to a simple question,' I say.

"Damn it! My words didn't allay their fears. The taller man fled. This other guy is also about to bolt. No way! I'll grab his black overcoat. That's it. Now pull him in close, real close.

'Is there a God?'

"Gosh, I was almost growling when I said that. The man quivers, and tears roll down his cheeks. All I sense in him is terror, absolute fear that I'm a demon. No, this isn't going to work! Let the poor man go! Now he crumples to the floor. He glances up at me, shielding his face with an arm. What a look of horror in his eyes. What a disaster this approach is! It's foolish to force answers from those who do not know. But what do I do? These dreams are rare, and this mission is failing.

"The background humming is still increasing in volume and pitch, making it challenging to stay focused. Nuts, the Puritan is scrambling for the door. I bet this event will be recorded in a local paper or church chronicle as a demonic incursion. That's something I can research. It doesn't matter, though. Those who read about this experience will dig out the truth. Now close your eyes and direct your thoughts. I have to find another setting and time and go back much further. The source is in the distant past. Hell, I've barely gone back 400 years. Man, can this be done?

"Come on, concentrate on the feedback loop! That's right. Let the velocity become energy and ignore the counter-pressure! This eff'n hurts. Getting anywhere meaningful in the past will take a lot of energy. But this transition is r-rough going! Nuts, now there's a sudden surge of acceleration and power. Oh, and here comes more pain. Brutal bursts of sharp, piercing pain. I have to get through this . . . this barrier. I must find a still point . . . a place to materialize. It's impossible to open my eyes or find a setting. Come on, you can do this. What the heck? Still nothing! That transition took it out of me. I have to try harder! Yes, now I can see, but that was difficult. These dreams are tearing something out of me.

"Wow, I'm in an outdoor clearing by a rocky shoreline. The air smells of the sea, and it's warm. A man stands before me, short and stocky, with dark skin and curly black hair. He's wearing a knee-length white tunic and appears to be Greek. He must be from the fourth or fifth century BCE or perhaps earlier. Ah, I'm in his mind, at least to a degree. He's a fisherman but not dressed for the task on this occasion. I think he's going to the local market, but—

"Shoot! He's terrified by my sudden appearance and is about to run. No way, my friend! I grab his tunic but strive to avoid being hostile or aggressive. He's gaping at me, so I'll smile. Now he's relaxing. Yes, he's different from the others, much more in control of his emotions. Ah, he returns my smile. I'll let go of the tunic and dip my head. He nods his head in return. That's a good first step in communication. Excellent! Here's a rational man, a person of reason. So, let's speak with him calmly and rationally.

'Is there a God?' I ask.

"He looks perplexed. Let's try again, only more slowly.

'Is there a God?'

"Now he's saying something, but I cannot understand it! He must be speaking in old Greek or another ancient language. Bits and pieces of the meaning come through, but more is needed to understand what's being said.

"This is infuriating! At last, someone gives me an answer, but it's in a foreign tongue that I can't fully comprehend. Maybe I can see deeper inside his mind and—

"Now he discerns my frustration. He's backing off. There he goes, running down the beach like a frightened rabbit.

"Screw it! This isn't working. What the hell am I going to do? Look, there is still great power within. These short jumps into the past just aren't working. They're wasting time and energy for no gain. We've proven thoughts can go back in time, at least in the metaphysical sense. Yet can I generate enough power to get to the very beginning? I've never tried anything like that. It'll be like taking my consciousness on the ultimate journey. Achieving the needed speed and energy will be brutal. It may also be dangerous. But the risk is worth taking. It's do or die. So be it!

"Now close your eyes and fixate on the humming. Ah, here comes the feeling of increasing velocity. This time I'll slowly allow the sound and speed to reach their ultimate levels. Control is everything. It may be the acceleration phase's duration that determines the trek's length. So, spread this out. It's worth a try. Now let's head for the source.

"There's increasing acceleration and power! Whew, we're zipping along. Ah, but don't allow the loop to get out of control! That's it. Now, put the pedal down just a bit. Oops, the volume and pitch are growing too fast. Come on! Work on controlling this! Yeah, now we're cooking! An excellent feedback loop is going, and power is pulsating through me. Now it's like a vibration, a hum of sorts. This must be some kind of fundamental frequency we're within.

"This time, I have to keep it up, though. Nuts, the sound is becoming a piercing scream. But keep going. That's it! You can do this! The sense of speed and energy is almost uncontrollable. Keep your focus! The pressure tears. It's a-a-agonizing! Ignore the pain!

"The noise and acceleration are unbearable, but I must go on. I-I-I must! There is . . . an odd weakness. I have to stay focused—concentrate on velocity and ignore the rest. Oh, man, the speed is astronomical! Tremendous power surging. It eff'n hurts! God, something is being ripped away! I'm bleeding energy, bits of being, too. B-b-but the acceleration is still increasing. It'll be OK if we just keep . . . ow! Th-th-the pain rips into me. Noise . . . pressure . . . my head aches: it pulsates. Nausea and dizziness. Come on! Go on! Go on! You must go on! I have to penetrate this damn pressure. Do or die! Damn, you! More speed! GO ON!

"What the . . . ? S-s-suddenly there's a . . . feeling of . . . serenity, absolute tranquility. The sound, pressure, and motion are gone. The barrier gave way. Oh, I'm exhausted, totally drained. It's impossible to move, yet I must continue. I'm on my knees, too weak to stand. My throat is parched. It's difficult to concentrate, and I . . . I can't open my eyes. What has happened to me? I must force my eyes open; get my senses attuned. I can do this. I must! It's so damn hard. You have to try! You have to. That's it. There we go.

"Oh, my. Unbelievable! There's a field of thousands of dazzling colored lights flashing all around me! I hear a gentle tinkling sound like glass wind chimes. This is a place of pure tranquility and beauty. It is transcendent. Whew, but it's so damn hard to keep my eyes open. Utterly exhausted. Is this how I will die? What is that in front of me? I must lift my head.

"A small woman stands in the middle of a vast field of waltzing lights. There is no ground nor sky nor sense of depth. It's as if all dimensions have melded together except those that give the woman presence. I have to concentrate. She is dressed in a white pleated robe, and a golden belt is tied around her waist. She holds a bundle of short golden rods in her right hand bound together by a cord. The name Rebecca comes to mind. How do I know that? She isn't talking, but I can sense the name. W-w-we are becoming one, merging. Could this be Rebecca Stone, a childhood friend? It may be! Yet she is beyond the temporal.

"It's an effort to hold my head upright, let alone communicate. Must try to speak. I can't! I-I'm too damn weak. No, we cannot fail now. Not after all this! Please, please, please! Let the words flow.

'Is . . . there . . . a . . . God?'

"My words are hoarse and distorted. I've failed! No, no, she may understand. Yes, I know she understands. She smiles. Now there's a sense of penetrating empathy—warm, compassionate, inviting. It covers me, soothing the pain. It's the stuff of love, pure unconditional love. A piercing, resonating thought enters my mind.

'Yes, there is a God.'

"No, I feel doubt. Rebecca may be a part of me, an old memory. Or perhaps she comes from outside of me. Maybe the outside and inside are not distinct in this realm of thought. There must be some proof of what she says. A sign! Yes, I must ask for a sign, something tangible. Force an utterance, a relevant thought. But it's impossible to speak. Try!

'Sssiii—'

"Oh, nuts! What I just said doesn't sound anything like 'sign.' My head is starting to droop again. Come on, hold your head upright. The sight! What a glorious vision! Rebecca's face zooms into view while the distance between us melts away. I can sense her love and power.

"She holds up the bundle of rods and points them toward the upper right quadrant of my field of vision. Instantly, this part of the visual field is blackened to form a quarter-circle. She then directs the rods toward the lower right portion of the visual field, which also blacks out. What a fantastic experience. Now she's pointing the rods at the lower left and upper left quadrants, which become dark in turn. She floats amidst a glittering multicolored diamond formed by the blackened quarter circles. It's a celestial sight beyond words. She looks at me. A warm and compassionate smile lifts her lips.

A thundering voice echoes, 'You will be given a sign, but you will not believe.'

"There's a sudden flash of the notebook where I'm recording these dreams. It has fallen into deep snow. I pick it up, and wet snow falls from between its pages. The ink has run, and all is ruined. I don't understand. With a smile and nod, she points the bundle of rods in my direction. Total darkness instantly blinds me. My eyes reopen, and I'm wide awake in my humble apartment.

"Despite my utter exhaustion within the dream, I felt refreshed and invigorated. It was an extraordinary experience."

"Far more so than you initially imagined.," Madame Leonedria said.

"It sure as hell was," Alex agreed. "I went to write the dream in my notebook before it was forgotten. However, a quick glance at the clock revealed I would be late for work. Coaches can't be late, no matter what, so I threw on my winter clothes and bounded down the stairs of my apartment building. I went to open the outside door, but it wouldn't budge. It seemed someone had locked the door or propped a chair against it. I peered out the window to see what was up.

"There was more snow than I had ever seen before. It took all my strength to open the door against the blocking drift. Flashbacks of the dream dashed through my mind as I waddled through the waist-deep mire. It was tough going, a brutal, cold slog. Nonetheless, I eventually arrived at work only to discover the field house was closed. Everything in town was closed. Only the snowplows could be heard above the howling wind. While trudging home, Rebecca's words echoed in my mind: 'You will be given a sign, but you will not believe. You will not believe.'"

Alex paused for a moment and sighed.

"Snow was once common in New England during February," Mirai signed. "At least during your era."

"It was not just another snowstorm," Alex said with a dismissive wave. "The meteorologists call the event the Blizzard of '78. It was one of the largest Nor'easters on record. We had over 3 feet of snow and a lot more in some places. The winds broke 110 miles per hour along the coastline. At least 100 people died, while over 4,000 more were injured. Homes were washed away, and power was knocked out far and wide. I had never experienced anything like it in my life."

"Do you think that blizzard was about God talking to you?" Mirai signed.

"I'm not sure what to think," Alex confessed. "But if that was the voice of God, it has incredible power. Yet I'm a rational animal seeking a scientific basis for everything. Moreover, I was influenced by a host of scientists, writers, and academics. Most of them had no or little place for the idea of God in their constellation of opinions. As we've discussed, many scholars reject contemporary views on what God is, nor do they seek to discover what the term can be perceived to mean.

"For years, I tried to invent rationalizations about the dream to explain it away. Perhaps my subconscious mind spun an elaborate web over inputs received during the day about the coming storm. Yet I hardly listened to the news during those days. Maybe the low air pressure produced an influence on the dream state. I sought to find out if this was possible, but there's a dearth of literature concerning this subject. Perhaps the future or past informed the present in ways I don't understand and never will."

"Do you think my kindred caused that event?" Mirai signed.

"I've no idea," Alex replied. "So, I ask the reader, 'What would you believe if you were me'? Was that blizzard the sign I asked for during the dream? Such premonitions are recorded in the religious stories passed down by many cultures, but I seldom put any stock in them. Then came the experience. Were the record winds and snow a verification that something akin to what we call God actually exists? The doubt I felt then lingers. It clearly indicates my disdain for belief versus the demonstrable truths science offers. Yet there is no question about the dream being related to an actual event. The uncertainty some readers feel about its message is why I was so plagued."

"I've heard you tell this story before," Mirai signed. "One suspects a physical etiology, some kind of abnormal neuronal process. Your medical history makes it easy to understand why you have unusual dreams. Be that as it may, I can also appreciate your confusion if it happened as you've described."

"The dream happened exactly as I've described," Alex insisted. "As an aside, I found Rebecca's grave marker in the West Lebanon Cemetery. It read, 'Come up and see me sometime,' and part of me believes I did. Her obituary indicates a short but very accomplished life. She was a sweet girl, albeit cystic fibrosis spares few of its victims. Ah, but the timing seems wrong. She died on September 1, 1984, well after the dream. Becky was just 31."

"How linear you are," Mirai signed. "Perhaps you would be less doubting if you understood how time works."

"You deign not to discuss that with me," Alex said. "Anyway, however much I was in doubt, I had some tenuous reason to believe there is a causal nexus. Some may call it a creator, God, physics, metaphysics, chemistry, or a set of seminal ideas, however you wish to describe the source of our existence. Moreover, it's something that goes beyond mere words or beliefs. It's where thoughts and realities merge."

"Interesting," Madame Leonedria said. "You're marrying the physical and metaphysical, perhaps maintaining that one cannot exist without the other. Chicken-or-egg causal paradoxes can easily emerge from this. However, if the idea is pursued, it can lead one to a reason for existence. I suspect we'll get into that area later."

"You know we will," Alex said. "At this stage, though, I only had reason to believe there was a god, or whatever name one wants to use. The nature of God remained elusive, and exploring this issue soon became my goal."

"This makes sense," Madame Leonedria said. "Yet it all begins with the idea that something can exist, even if only a possibility. Therein starts an effort to discover its characteristics. So, tell us the next step in your adventures."

"In a minute," Alex said. He picked up the slice of bread on his plate and nervously nibbled at its crust, contemplating how to relate the next dream. This event had levels of meaning that would be difficult to convey.

13

Finding God in Reflections

"The next dream happened about a year or two after the blizzard dream," Alex said. "I lived in an apartment above Grimes' Grocery Store at the time, in downtown Durham, New Hampshire. This episode was unlike prior experiences. The event began when I suddenly looked down at my sleeping body."

"Ah, the initial stages of a classical astral dream," Madame Leonedria observed.

"It scared the hell out of me at first," Alex advised. "I was frightened because my body seemed to be a tether, one I didn't want to lose contact with. It was a peculiar, detached feeling, unlike the pleasant flying dreams experienced during childhood."

"Some cultures believe death comes when the spirit is separated from the body," Madame Leonedria said.

"I can understand why," Alex said. "By now, I'd developed a good sense of what was in store. Plus, I was now accustomed to lucid dreams and had much better control of them. Well, at least for the most part. It became an enthralling adventure, and I'll strive to relive the experience."

"Please do," Mirai signed.

"Anything for you," Alex said. He gazed into the water bowl, watching the flicking light reflect off its surface. Then he began.

"This is unique . . . actual thought traveling. Kind of scary, though. Look at me, just snoring away, chest heaving up and down. This is a potent dream state. The speed/power feedback loop will come online if I initiate any movement. Yeah, but what if I lose contact with my body? What then? Nah, you have to dump fear! Fear is a soul killer. This is another chance to find God, so don't waste it. Portents and signs are fine, but only the source will do. No, that's nuts! I'm sleeping down there, safe and sound. Is there any real need to go? Am I that desperate or perhaps that arrogant?

"No, it isn't desperation or arrogance. I've sought the Maker for years. All there is to show for the efforts are doubts and mysteries. Perhaps I can still find a definitive answer if I try. But I'm unsure which direction to go—past, future, or maybe something in the present. Well, these abilities better be used while the state lasts. No more dallying! Yeah, just go for it. Let the general idea of finding God be your guide.

"There goes my body zipping out of view, and here comes the feedback loop. Whew, that was fast! I'm zooming through the void, but let's not waste energy by making many stops. It's going to take a maximal effort to reach God. That means we must push our speed and power beyond anything in the past. We also have to concentrate on duration. Come on, focus on acceleration, and let the pitch and volume of the humming be a guide.

"What a rush! Ho, ho, ho! Ah, there's more energy surging through me than ever. Here comes the damn resistance. It's pushing hard against my forward progress . . . painful, miserable pressure. It's almost like flying into a sandstorm—biting, piercing. I have to keep going. That's it: push it a bit harder. Yeah, there's much more control than usual. Let's take quick glances to see the surroundings but keep that feedback loop going.

"Ah, I see Michelangelo's painting of a white-bearded God reaching out a Divine finger to Adam. It's coming into full—

"Wow, the image suddenly shattered into millions of pieces! That's an easy message to understand. Anthropomorphizing the Divine isn't the right direction to take. Definitely not! The power levels must be higher to see much beyond that.

"I have to penetrate this barrier, overcome this damn pressure. That's it: let the velocity and power slowly increase. Forget the damn pain! How much do you want this? Oh, I taste blood. No big deal! That's happened before. There's the dizziness and nausea. To hell with it! Focus on increasing the velocity and energy, but check the direction and surroundings. Must glimpse where I am. The pressure hurts my eyes, but I can still see.

"I'm passing through ominous, dark thunderclouds, and more lie ahead. Blinding flashes of light accompany loud thunderclaps. Let's zip through these roiling forms. They're turbulent and dark, a mixture of matter and energy. Yet there's more to God than that alone! I've got to go faster and farther. We've got to go beyond the material, clouds, air, and the earth itself. Come on, accelerate.

"Ah, now I'm in some kind of void, surrounded by fathomless darkness without end. This must be the depths of space. Yet God's nature encompasses more than this. We have to get outside the bubble. Go all out! That's it! Pick up more speed and energy! This eff'n hurts! You damn crybaby! Just ignore the pain and counter-force! Come on, we've got to go—

"Oh, no! I'm losing control! Shoot, the feedback loop is becoming unmanageable! The speed and power are accelerating on their own. I cannot concen—

"There's enormous velocity. No control at all. Too much pain! Can't see!

"My skin's getting shredded. The noise is deafening; it's piercing my eardrums! The pressure is crushing. But I have to continue. Don't quit now. Don't you dare give up! There's confusion, nausea. What am I—

"No, go on! Concentrate. Go even faster! You have to keep accelerating. We need more energy! Fight the pain. Concentrate on speed! This is . . . no, go even faster! There's too much damn pressure . . . just keep going!

"What the . . . ? E-e-everything has stopped! Yeah, I-I've broken through. The barrier suddenly gave way. That was nuts! Ew, what a trek. Now I'm in this place of . . . complete stillness. As usual, there was no . . . sensation of deceleration or impact. The transition just happened. We've been through this before, but that ride was insane! Never went that fast or that far! Now open your eyes. Oh, it isn't easy. Come on, you have to see!

"Wow, there's a crystal-clear image of my face looking back at me. It's as if I'm gazing into something more than a mirror, something with depth and dimensions. The image has tremendous detail. Every nook and cranny is clear. It's almost crystalline, alight with energy. Like a filter effect, I can almost see the power pulsating within the mass. What does it mean? Why am I looking at my own reflection?

"Whoa! A torrent of thoughts and insights are pouring in! Oh, this will take forever to unpack! Come on, segregate one idea at a time. Capture what you can.

"Yes, the search for God ultimately leads to a quest into the nature of our own being. We are products of creation, bound up within its processes. We're seeds that can grow to bear the fruits of realization. A central realization is that we are one with what created us, as in tiny parts of a vast and dynamic whole. However, God is much more than any one thing. Indeed, it is everything that did, does, or ever can exist in any form. God's being can be found in a child's laughter, a cat's purr, the laws of physics, the stars above, a falling leaf, or even the image of ourselves. God is ubiquitous.

"Ho, ho, ho! Ah, the joke's on me! What a complete dunce I am! I went so far and suffered so much just to find something I'm already part of. We all are, whether aware of the obvious or not! Oh, ho, ho, ho, you foolish, foolish man! If humility has a face, I'm looking at it! Who says God doesn't have a sense of humor? Let's learn more while we're still in this place of reflection. Ah, further insights flow in.

"When we desecrate ourselves, others, and the world around us, we also defile a bit of God. Oh, and it's foolish to put a face on God or describe its totality with names and words. The term 'god' merely serves as an ideational portal. It allows us to better grasp our essential oneness with all things. The only way to approach this understanding of God's nature is by seeking to comprehend all that is.

"It's an endless task. It requires us to look deep into the reality we're part of. Hmmm, I see what that means. Learning and perfecting our skills in physics, painting, mathematics, writing, music, farming, and crafts of all kinds—are all paths to God. There is no single direction all must walk. Yes, nearly every trail eventually leads to the same source.

"And what's this notion? The quest to learn and perfect ideas takes us closer to God. The journey also helps make God what it is. What the hell does that mean? Oh, I get it! There's a cosmic sentience, a universal logos that permeates everything. No, I do not understand the point quite right. The logos doesn't just permeate all things. It's integral to creating and sustaining existence. It's a pattern, a harmony, an organizing principle that interacts with energy, matter, and time and guides their many relationships. That's the essence of God. It's a sort of ideational DNA that runs throughout existence. We're reflections of those principles, those sublime ideas. Yes, God is found where the metaphysical, energetic, and material are conjoined.

"There's so much more to learn here. A central aspect of existence is the development of beings that can come to understand what created and sustains them. Indeed, seeking and discovering the thoughts that create and support us helps give them a presence within a God with which we are one. We are reflections of what made us: parts of a transcendent whole. We exist because we can exist, as in realized possibilities—seeds that were given the proper context to comprehend their potential. I think that's the message.

"Oh, but there's even more to learn! How can I possibly recall all this?

"And then, bang! I was abruptly tossed back into the conscious reality of my darkened room. I set to work recording some of the insights that came to me. Yet there's no doubt many were lost."

Alex took a sip of his drink. His throat was dry from talking, though the wine's taste displeased him.

"Excellent control of the seeing state," Madame Leonedria said. "Alas, there is often a cost for such events."

"I know," Alex sadly said. "I'm not sure what are cause and effect, but those states seemed to extract a physical toll. Perhaps they helped cause the degeneration seen in the MRI scans. The headaches still pound sometimes, and sleep calls all the damn time. Man, one wakes up exhausted. I sometimes doze 10 to 12 hours daily, but I'll finish this text."

"Did you forge those insights in the dream from within, or did they dawn on you from without?" Mirai signed.

"I've pondered that question for years," Alex said. "I'm not sure it matters, because I believe God is ubiquitous. Some find God's presence in physics, chemistry, and biology. Others find it in philosophy, religion, mathematics, and the narrative form. Many see God's grace in the arts, dance, cooking, and all activities and occupations. Despite the different paths, these endeavors can all lead to a greater realization of the nature of being.

"One reads, talks, and studies, and thus ideas enter from the outside. Then one contemplates, researches, and imagines. We then ruminate upon notions percolating within, talk with others, and arrive at synthesized conclusions. We share, ponder, and test these ideas. Those notions that withstand the trials of time take us closer to understanding being."

"Then why call the foundations of being 'God'?" Mirai signed. "It seems to be a term that goes well beyond a single meaning."

"Therein resides the term's potential strength," Alex said. "It opens metaphorical portals that can lead to all that is possible. Look, we use the terms 'vacuum,' 'infinity,' and others to denote ideas. However, these notions cannot be fully realized within our realm of being. There is no perfect vacuum, and infinity is impossible to realize. Yet our rationalism allows these concepts to exist, at least as metaphysical constructs. Our ideas are committed to paper and given a symbolic existence that can be shared and tested. Indeed, science provides empirical evidence for some seemingly absurd rationalizations. One idea leads to another, and so grows our understanding of what we are and why we're here. Ultimately, God is the set of all ideas that includes itself."

"Hmmm, you find comfort in making God into an ideational paradox," Madame Leonedria said. "Perhaps that is appropriate. Some subscribe to the concept of intelligent design, which is a vaguely similar idea to what you've articulated. They vary in where to place God within their schemes, yet you've spread God throughout. God has also been depersonalized, an approach some Jewish friends take. Beware: the traditionalists will not be keen on abandoning their bearded thunderer for such an abstract approach to the Divine."

"Some of us embraced a similar conceptualization to yours, Alex," Mirai signed. "Yet there are also false trails, and our species has promulgated many. Some are benign enough, as in many mythopoetic accounts of being. Other paths have led to nihilism and destruction. Those are vile beliefs that result in the very negation of being."

"This is where our beasts within can drive us as individuals and entire societies," Alex said. "Some societies worshiped war, torture, and death. They often did so in brutal and savage rituals. Unspeakable things were done to themselves and others. It was all for the sake of some religious dogma—a mythological account that sanctioned state-sponsored butchery. They were children of vicious folly but felt themselves holy. They flayed people alive and ripped out beating hearts. They marched in torchlight parades and ran extermination camps. Only time can reveal the beasts' presence and effects, although the results of greed and shortsightedness are easily discerned."

"True enough," Madame Leonedria noted. "As we've discussed, however, our flaws have important roles within the cycles of being. They test us, ensuring that only the worthiest can come to understand the principles that order this universe. Thus, the imperfect perish, and often at their own hands."

"All the while, we predict and expect an Armageddon that we end up creating," Alex said.

"While never quite grasping that we also have the power to prevent our demise!" Madame Leonedria observed. "In fact, that is what you hope the readers will do. That's why we're here."

"It is indeed," Alex said. "We're here for Mirai's sake."

"So you claim," Mirai signed. "But you keep missing the keys as you type these words. Perhaps it's time to take a break."

"I have an eternity to rest," Alex said. "My time with you and the readers is finite."

"Some of those readers may regard the vision of self you relate as being the height of narcissism," Mirai signed. "That was a criticism of the text."

"Thanks for the head's up," Alex said. "The image was humbling, at least to me. The self and ego disappeared with the realization that everything is part of an infinitely greater whole. Our thoughts may eventually access that whole, assuming the species survives. Nonetheless, we are minuscule, fleeting, and limited creatures. As bright as one thinks he or she shines, our light is a faint and passing blink. Bloated egos are pure folly, one that terribly limits our perceptions. The best we can hope for is to contemplate our roles within a process we are bound to. Yeah, I'm terribly flawed in countless ways. Yet I strive to perceive and understand, hoping to make myself worthier."

"Your worthiness is for others to judge," Madame Leonedria said. "But humility is a blessing. It allows one to contemplate being from a context beyond the self. If you took that lesson from the dream, the experience was of great value."

"I did," Alex replied. "The dream also had other implications. For instance: If God is one with all things, and all is in flux, does God change too? Insights about this and deeper issues came later during a more profound dream.

"At the time, I still had many more questions about God's nature than answers. Moreover, my role was unclear. What was I supposed to do about all these dreams? Where would they lead? Then came a dream experience that was significantly more elaborate and meaningful than any described thus far."

"Ah, it seems we are arriving at a critical point in our task," Madame Leonedria said. "Let us first add some tinder to our fire."

14

Speaking with God

Alex and Mirai followed Madame's lead and dutifully placed more cordwood in the hearth. They resumed their seats and watched while the flames took hold. The burgeoning fire crackled and snapped while growing, spilling embers and ashes into the air that quickly disappeared into the hearth's exhaust hood. Alex stared into the flames, pondering how to share a narrative that was often beyond his ability to relate.

"For over 35 years, the experience has disturbed me," Alex said. He nodded and added, "The dream happened when I lived in Camarillo, California, far from my New Hampshire roots. The event was so powerful that I immediately wrote its outline on an envelope upon wakening. The envelope was dated March 8, 1980, so the dream must have happened shortly after that."

"Yes, I've seen the document," Mirai signed. "It's the bare skeleton of an incredible odyssey."

"I was a health club instructor at the time," Alex said. "I had lost my coaching job due to a free-speech conflict. We needn't go into details, but my exile was only for a year or so. Fate led me to live in a crawlspace between the top of an office and the metal roof of our spa. One had to ascend a ladder to reach the plywood platform my small mattress rested on. There was precious little headroom, but I rather liked my humble abode. Occasional spiders and small rodents were bothersome, although they were manageable.

"In any event, I had no intention of obtaining advanced degrees at the time. I had yet to read much of Plato, let alone study the neurosciences or pre-Socratic philosophers. Going to Penn State wasn't even a thought back then. Nor was the possibility of bumping into a student there who was the exact image of a character I saw in the dream. Yet, the event was a powerful omen. I see flashes of it every day."

"Ah, the dream still vexes you," Madame Leonedria observed. "Tell me, were there the typical warning signs of a seeing state?"

"No, hardly any," Alex said. "Oddly enough, this dream event didn't begin with a sense of motion and power like many others. Nor was I in control of what was being witnessed. Instead, I was a participant, swept along by ongoing events. Some were traumatic and exhausting."

"The word 'terrifying' seems appropriate," Mirai signed.

"Absolutely!" Alex said. "The dream was also long and elaborate. I doubt it was the product of a typical seeing or astral state. Those events opened a conceptual portal to the metaphysical state where this dream unfolded. In fact, the door theme was prominent throughout the experience. It began suddenly as if I were waking from unconsciousness."

"How interesting," Madame Leonedria said. "You know what you must now do." She tapped her index finger onto the water's surface within the bowl, creating ripples that radiated outward. "Gaze into your soul and remember," she intoned.

Alex stared into the ripples and breathed deeply. He gently rocked back and forth before closing his eyes, drawing upon memories he would rather not relive. He then brought the memories into the present, beginning his tale abruptly.

"Whoa!" he said, his eyes opening wide. "What the hell is going on? I'm lying atop a small bed, but this isn't my loft. No, definitely not. Is this a dream? Yeah, I think so, but the sensations are incredibly vibrant. Mmmm, this blanket feels soft and comfortable, sort of like fleece. I can easily drift into sleep here, though I already am. Sleeping while sleeping . . . but there's always something to be learned when these states happen. Well, we should look around.

"It seems I'm in a one-room efficiency apartment or something like it. Let's try clapping. Yeah, the senses are all online. This is definitely a seeing dream and a powerful one. The sensory clarity is much greater than usual, especially touch and vision.

Why the hell am I fully dressed while in bed? Oh, forget about that. Let's check this place out.

"A door is about 6 feet from the foot of the bed. On the left is a small kitchenette with a sink, stove, and cabinets. On the right are a desk, dresser, and household items. Could this be a dorm? Perhaps, but dorms usually don't have sinks in the rooms. I'm probably in a boarding house of some kind and a relatively low-cost one.

"Why the hell am I here? I'm not up for it if this is the start of another psychic adventure. No eff'n way! Those damn things hurt. Perhaps I should stay in bed until the state ends. Yeah, that's the safe thing to do. Nah, don't be a baby. There's something to be learned.

"Oh, this is way cool! My senses are more acute than ever. I can see, feel, touch, hear, and even smell. Hey, let's try taking a deep breath. Ahhh, my chest expands. Yeah, this is a rush! It's very comfortable here, but we won't experience much unless we leave. This state is realistic enough to be traumatic, and . . . Oh, you gutless bastard! Get your sorry ass out of bed! Now, go to the door and check the place out. Perhaps some meaning can be found outside this room. Well, the door is unlocked. I'll just open it really slowly and look around.

"Hmmm, there's a long, well-lit hallway with many doors on the left and right, so I must be at the end of the hall. Yeah, my room is definitely in a large dormitory or rooming house. There isn't a soul in sight, but somebody is probably in one of these quarters.

'Is anyone here?!' I shout.

"My voice echoes off the corridor walls, but there is no reply. We'll increase the volume.

'Yo, is anyone in here?!'

"Still nothing.

'Is anybody around?!'

"Hollering is futile. Perhaps it's best to knock on a neighbor's door. It would be nice to find someone to talk with. Let's walk down the hallway but ensure this door is unlocked. I may need to come back. What should I say if someone is found? How neat! I can hear my footsteps strike the hard tiles. This kind of reminds me of—

"Look, the third door on the left side of the hallway is slightly ajar! Someone is probably in there, so let's head that way.

"What's that I hear? Is that meowing, as in kittens? I believe so! Well, it's best to knock before entering. Damn, my knock caused the door to swing wide open. It's dim inside, but this room looks much like mine.

"Ah, there are cats in here! Three little white kittens scurry around on the bed. Good Lord, they're in terrible shape! The kittens are nothing but bones, skin, and matted fur. They're emaciated and filthy, in disgusting condition. Oh, the poor little buggers are pleading for food.

"This isn't my apartment, but I must sort this out. Maybe I can find something for the cats to eat in the refrigerator. Perhaps there's some meat in there. Man, these little guys are a mess. They're covered with fleas and ticks, especially around the eyes and ears. Ew, the vermin are crawling all over them. They won't make it without proper food and care; not a snowball's chance in hell.

"They're scampering off the bed and brushing against my shins. Well, at least they can still move. That's a good sign. Their meowing is pitiful, though, almost plaintive.

'Hey, you nearly tripped me! Can't blame you guys. I know, I know, you're starving. But get out of the way so I can open the refrigerator.'

"Nuts! The refrigerator's light reveals hoards of leaping fleas and crawling ticks. Man, they're everywhere! Damn, they swarm up my ankles and calves. I'd better lift my pant leg and check this out. Oh, screw this! They're digging into my skin, hundreds of them. This eff'n hurts! Gross! This is awful! I can't brush these bloodsuckers off my legs fast enough. More vermin jump on than I can take off. It's hopeless, futile! I'm getting eaten alive, and so are the kittens. This is nuts!

"No, no, don't panic. We have to get organized and act. The kittens need food, water, and pest control to survive. And there's no time to waste. Let's rummage through the cupboards to find food and flea spray. Ah, there's a box of dry cat food in the cabinet underneath the sink. Beside it is a small box of powder imprinted with a red circle logo. Yep, it has a slash mark through the image of a flea.

"There're no instructions on the box, but I can't handle these damn parasites. I'll pull up a pant leg and sprinkle on a hefty dose. Oh, I love this powder! It works like a charm. Dozens of dying fleas and ticks fall off my body. Let's get the other leg too. Now we'll do the rug and bed. I'm making a mess, but don't be shy about getting under the bed and everywhere else. Yeah, these bloodsuckers are dying en masse. The powder hasn't harmed me, so let's try it on the kittens.

'Oh, stop your crying. I don't like doing this, but it's for your own good. You can't live with all these damn parasites sucking up your blood!'

"This powder works great. Ho, ho, ho, the bugs drop out of this kitten's fur before I can put the little fellow down. Now for the next patient. Man, they're skinny, so I'd better be careful. Their little bones can break easily, but there's only one more.

'Don't fret, little guy! You'll feel better soon.'

"So far, so good, but the kittens still need food and water. Well, I saw two bowls in the cabinet under the sink, so let's get them. I'll fill the bigger one with dry cat food.

'Hey, let me put the bowl down before you begin stuffing your faces!'

"Look at them go! Chowing down to the max. That's a happy sight to see. We're making progress.

'Perhaps you guys do have a chance. But we need to find you something to drink.'

"I should have looked for milk instead of meat in the refrigerator! Sure enough, there's a big jug of it. I'll pour the milk into the smaller bowl.

'Come on, give me some space here.'

"They're lapping it as quickly as it's poured. Ho, ho, ho, this is neat! Look at them go. Let's get more in there.

'You guys like that!'

"Yeah, they're gorging themselves. Maybe they can survive. I wonder what this imagery means. Obviously, the animals aren't well cared for, but nothing else is clear. They may represent nature and our disdain for the environment. Or maybe they symbolize children or people in need. This picture has a lot missing, and some insights would be helpful. I have to find someone to commune with.

"Let's give the kittens a quick check before leaving. Wow, they're huddled together on the bed and looking up at me. Their purring is like music. They've morphed into three clean and well-fed animals. That's a typical temporal compression, but a great one to see. It makes me feel good. I'd better ensure the door is unlocked. It may be necessary to come back here to tend to these guys, especially if their keeper doesn't return. I should close this room to prevent them from getting lost.

"Onward, ho! I'll let out a good yell. 'Is anyone here?!'

"Let's try that again, only a bit louder. 'Is anyone here?!'

"Nah, this floor must be deserted, so let's look elsewhere. Halfway down the hallway, I see a stairwell landing on the right side. The entranceway and door window has chicken-wire-impregnated glass. Hmmm, this must be an old dorm or institutional building, really old. Builders use safety glass nowadays. I'll go down the stairs, but there's no time to search the entire structure. It's huge. Instead, open the stairwell door at each floor

14.1 The three infested, dirty, and starving kittens morphed into contented and purring animals after being fed

landing and holler. We'll wait a bit for a reply and then go down to the next level and try again. Yeah, that sounds reasonable. Here's the first stop.

'Hey, is anyone in?'

"Nah, no reply. That's long enough to wait, off to the next level.

"Well, this isn't working, and my throat is sore from hollering. It seems yelling is a piss-poor strategy. Let's see, three floors and no responses, and now I'm in a big lobby. This place is more typical of a dormitory than a rooming house. There's a ton of institutional furniture here, but where are the students?

"Ah, I'll bet they're outside. Perhaps some kind of large assembly or football game is going on. The exit is close, so let's get out of here and check things out. I'd better make sure the door is unlocked. There's no way I want to get trapped in this dream. It's too damn real. But we're OK. This is an easy place to get back into.

"Nothing is clear except two questions: What do the starving kittens represent, and where are the people? Another perspective is needed, but someone is probably out here. Let's stroll down this sidewalk and see what the dorm looks like. Hmmm, it's a large cement and brick structure. The exterior is modern compared with the quaint interior, which is sort of 1950s-era, give or take. The building is flat-roofed, unlike those in New England. Maybe this is California.

"It looks like we're on a large college campus in an urban environment. Yeah, this is a citified place. The streets are wide, and all the shrubbery, trees, and grass are well tended. None of the nearby buildings are much larger than my dorm. Distant structures on my left, however, are smaller and more scattered than those on the right. It's best to head toward the more prominent buildings. I'm likely to find people there. Now pick up the pace.

"I sure as hell don't want to get lost. Whew, this is a fair-sized city. Oh, stop fretting! It's a great day. The sun is shining, and there's a fresh breeze. It's an ideal time for folks to be out taking walks, although there's no one in sight. Can't hear any cars or voices, either. The only sound is the occasional rustling of wind-blown leaves. Trees in southern California don't drop their leaves, so I'm probably somewhere else. I suppose the abandoned streets are some kind of metaphor. Don't fret. The meaning will come. As for now, it's a pleasant walk, despite the emptiness.

14.2 Elder soon found himself in a sprawling college located within a sizable city, a portant of his later days at Penn State

"Huh, we're at a wide intersection. I'll go to the middle of the street to survey the surroundings. Sure enough, there're several much larger structures up ahead. There aren't any vehicles around, not even parked cars. I guess it's safe to walk down the middle of the avenue. Of course, some sick speedster could pop up out of nowhere and run me down. But ambling down a major highway on a gorgeous day is neat. The buildings are becoming more impressive, so I'm probably heading in the right direction.

"Wow, that huge boxy building on my left is far from the street. It looks like an athletic facility or fieldhouse. Gosh, that's a massive building! The parking lot surrounding it could hold thousands of cars. I'll bet tens of thousands could fit into that place. Talk about paving the world—these parking lots are enormous. Oddly, there are no cars. I wonder why.

"Whoa, I think I see someone in the distance! Yes! Two people are strolling in my direction. They must be about 300 or 400 yards ahead. Wahoo! At last, people! We finally have someone to talk with.

'Hello!' I shout.

"I wonder if they can hear me. Maybe they're too far away. Let's start jogging their way. I'd better wave.

'Hello, can I talk with you?'

"Why aren't they answering? They look like businesswomen. Well, they're dressed that way, I think. They're still kind of far away.

'Hey! Can I ask you a few questions?'

"This is strange. It's like the women can't see or hear me. I don't like the looks of this at all. Yeah, I'd better slow down. Oh, those women aren't walking: they're marching like soldiers. Something isn't right here. Let's stay put and figure this out. It's better to be safe than sorry.

"The field house is pretty close, but I'm totally exposed in this area. The women are about 150 yards away, maybe more. Hmmm, I'm not sure what to do. They suddenly stop, turn back to back, and march in opposite directions. This is weird. It's like they're soldiers in some bizarre parade. They're about 200 yards apart now, perhaps a bit farther. They stop and turn to face each other.

"Holy crap! They're m-m-morphing into prehistoric monsters—titanic dinosaurs! The one on my right is becoming an allosaurus, but she must be 200 or 300 feet tall. It's impossible!

14.3 The women transformed into two titanic dinosaures, with one being a massive allosaurus

No animal can be that huge. Its bones would break under— Oh no; the other is turning into an enormous brontosaurus. Good Lord, she has to be over two blocks long! They dwarf these buildings! Holy shit, their shadows blot out the sunlight. What the—

"Damn! They're getting ready to fight! The earth shakes while they maneuver! Wow! The carnivore suddenly leaps on the plant-eater's shoulder and digs her massive forearm and leg claws into her prey's flesh. She clutches onto the beast, riding it while biting and slashing! Oh, she sinks those huge teeth into the base of the giant's long neck. Yow! The roar of pain is deafening. I've never heard anything so loud! Growling, roaring, this is eff'n brutal. The shaking is getting much worse. Vats of blood are gushing from the brontosaur's lower neck.

"Oh, but she isn't done! Not by a long shot. She loses a massive hunk of flesh but rolls onto the allosaurus, trying to crush the damn thing beneath her bulk. They smash everything in sight while their bodies intertwine. Yikes! Th-th-that claw nearly killed me! It's the size of a damn building! I've got to get the hell out of here. The allosaurus retracts her blood-stained limb, and its claws tear up the earth like giant plowshares. Good Lord, we have to get out of here! The ground is gyrating and shaking, crumbling beneath my feet! No, this is only a dream. I can control this, but . . . Damn, I'm going to fall! Come on, get your balance! Don't go down here!

"This is too freaking real! I have to find shelter. Yeah, get into that fieldhouse. I think that place can survive. Come on, run! There are mounds of debris in the way. Still, we can make it; we have to! Keep running, just keep running! The ground is shaking, and cracks are ripping through the pavement. The roars rupture my ears. I have to climb over this torn-up wreckage. Now come on. You can make it! The entry is just a few yards away.

"I'm there, I'm there! Through these doors, we'll be all right. Wow, this is an enormous open facility. There are several sporting courts and lots of folded bleachers. Where the hell do we go in here? I hope it's strong en—

"Oh, no! The whole building is quaking! Damn, some lights and ceiling panels are crashing down. I'm going to die in a goddamn dream. Man, this place is groaning and creaking! Let's find the safest point here. Where would that be? Where? I must find a corner, but everything is open in this damn building! Go over there, toward the far-left corner of the basketball courts. Head for that place and do it fast. Sprint, you bastard! Sprint!

"What the heck? The floor undulates beneath me like a wave! I have to keep going. Get your ass in gear! The wood planks are splintering, so don't fall! You'll get cut to shreds. Come on, I'm almost there. Damn, the whole building is breaking up! Beams and concrete are raining down.

'Please, God, let me wake up!'

"Huddle, huddle in the corner. Oh, crap! A giant I-beam is breaking free from above! No! It's heading my—

"Th-that thing almost crushed me! This is eff'n crazy! It's buried halfway into the floor. The splinters! Watch out for those splinters. I'm going to die! For God's sake, I will die in a damn dream!

'Why are you doing this to me? Why?'

"The walls are crumbling. Think! Damn, you! Stop panicking and think! Get into the I-beam. That's right, squeeze in there. Cinderblocks and debris are pinging off the beam's top, crashing all around. Oh, we're getting buried alive!

'God, don't kill me! Please! Don't let it end like this! Pleeease! Pleeeaaasse!'

"Tears, panic, and now, there's . . . silence. Am I dead? No, I can still feel and think. Yes, I'm still alive. The ground has stopped shaking, at least for now. I-I'm trembling, scared to death. No more battle sounds. So, let's get going while the getting's good. I've got to squirm from this beam, but moving is nearly impossible. Come on, you have to try harder. Damn, this masonry is heavy as hell! Be careful moving the splintered wood. Man, there's dust and debris everywhere!

"There, I'm clear! Now let's get the hell out of this place. It's ready to collapse in a heap. The remaining walls and roof groan and creak. Bits of rubble are falling here and there. This wreckage is a bitch to navigate. We have to get back to the dorm. Maybe that's the way out of this damn nightmare! Shoot, I'm coughing my lungs out! The dust is brutal, and the entrance wall has collapsed. This place is nothing but a ruin and a dangerous one.

"Sobs? Are those sobs? Oh, they're coming from me. Stop it! Damn, it! Stop panicking! You have to think! Sunlight pierces the settling dust clouds. I have to get through this mess, these towering heaps of rubble. It's difficult going. Maybe it's possible to escape before the whole place crumbles. Have to keep trying! I should have never left the dorm. I knew something like this was—

"Oh, no! Here come those two women! They're silhouetted against the dusty sunlight near the collapsed front section of the building. It's them, for sure. I must get by those witches, but they're blocking my way. Now they're walking directly toward me! Screw that!

'Keep away! Keep away from me!'

"They're giving me some ground, but I've got to get back home. Well, they don't look angry. Why did they smash the city? Man, there's a lot I don't understand about this miserable dream. They could morph again, and then I'm finished. Still, they aren't trying to put me in a corner. Hmmm, they actually look sympathetic.

"Whoa, there's a sudden spatial compression. We don't need this crap at all! Shoot, I-I'm too close to them. Way, way, way too near! But they seem relaxed. Their hair is worn up: a couple of pretty brunettes. The tall woman's hair is much lighter than her partner's, as are her eyes. They're both dressed in skirted business suits. Man, I'm too damn close to escape!

'We're sorry, but we had to show you,' the shorter woman says.

"Show me? An apologetic explanation? Show me what? Terror? Her eyes reveal compassion, and she wears a gentle countenance. They both do. No, that destruction was unacceptable. It was insane!

'To hell with you! You eff'n bitches! Eff you! Eff you! Eff both of you! You goddamn demons! No one needs to go through that bullshit!'

"That's it! Give them a good dressing down. Man, we're ranting and have to calm down. You definitely don't want to get these two pissed off! Stop screaming and get the hell out of here. Good, they're not pursuing. I'm mad as hell! This was insanity! I've had enough traumas for a lifetime. Let's leave this ruin and jog back to the dorm.

"I've cleared the building, but the grounds are a mess. Chunks of concrete, broken telephone poles, fallen wires . . .

there's all sorts of wreckage. There aren't any bodies, but clothes and possessions are strewn everywhere. Perhaps the dead have rotted away. That could be, but then there'd be bones.

"Oh, I've never seen so much broken glass! Every window in the city got smashed like they were all blasted out. Holy crap, I'll get cut to shreds if I fall. Let's hope the shards don't tear through my shoes. It looks like some buildings got totally wasted, although most are intact. Those beasts could symbolize terrorists or a coming war. Maybe they're a natural disaster. Not sure, but they represent something absolutely devastating. What an eff'n nightmare.

"Ouch! The wind blows papers, dust, and dirt into my face. It bloody well hurts! The sky is gray and kind of dark. Screw this! I just want to get home. I'll go back to my room and wake up,

14.4 The beasts utterly destroyed the city during their great battle and nearly killed Elder

assuming the room is still there. The damage is getting less severe as I get nearer to the dorm. That's promising. But ground zero was a total wipeout. Yeah, let's get out of this miserable dream.

"Damn, I hope the kittens are OK. They were in rough shape even before the battle. Though I think they were set right, at least for a while. It's going to bother the hell out of me if they were killed. Here I am, worrying about kittens! This is only a dream. They aren't real; none of this is real! So why do I feel that the kittens matter? Hell, I don't even know what they represent! It's unclear what any of this means! This dream is pointless, the stuff of terror!

"The yelling, running, dust . . . I'm thirsty as hell. I'll have to get a drink when I get back. This seems to be the right direction, though. At last! Yeah, there's the dorm. Books, clothes, papers, pens, and possessions are scattered about. Some of these things look expensive. The students must have left in a huge hurry. Why didn't we see any of them during my travels? Where could they have gone?

"Most of my building's windows are blown out, but it's not too badly damaged. The lobby's entrance has shattered glass, broken furniture, and scattered wreckage. This entry door may still be usable, but be careful opening it. Nuts, the damn thing is stuck. Come on, force that door open. That's it. Get an arm in there and push! Now squeeze through. Whew, that was a tight fit.

"Let's get this box out of the way and be careful of those torn curtains. Damn, it looks like a tornado swept through here.

Could this be blast damage? Or maybe it was the sound waves from those roars. They were terrible. It doesn't matter, but let's maneuver carefully to the stairwell. This is like an obstacle course. Look out for that chair, and don't trip over the books. Watch out for the glass shards! They're everywhere.

"Nuts, this is a huge problem. The stairs are littered with boxes, backpacks, books, papers, and even desks and dressers. But I have to make it to the top floor to get home. Damn, I can barely work through this mess. It's like there was a mad rush to take whatever could be salvaged before the place was abandoned. Maybe the people were driven away by radiation or chemicals. Yeah, that's all we need. Better stay focused. It would be easy to get hurt on these stairs, and we're getting thirstier by the minute.

"Perhaps some survivors are in here. It seems unlikely, but we'll look. Let's open each landing's door and yell. Man, these doors aren't easy to open. This one must have sprung during the great battle. It's a bitch to open. Damn, you will let me in! Now come on, put some effort into it. The steel is groaning, and it's starting to give way. Pusssshhhhh! There we go.

'Is anyone home?!' I yell.

"No reply and my voice is getting hoarse. Let's try again at the next level. Nah, screw this yelling. Let's just get up these stairs. Now toss this crap aside. No need to be gentle. We have to get home! Whew, my floor at last. Made it! Wow, impacts made spider-web patterns in the landing door's windows. The embedded chicken wire is holding the shattered glass together. That's an image I'll recall for the rest of my life. I know it is. It's so vivid, so realistic.

"Damn, the door is out of alignment. I-I can't open it. Hmmm, this thing is really stuck. We can do this! It's just like lifting weights. Get some leverage, and this damn thing will open! Jeez, the metal creaks and groans. Come on, just a little more. Yeah, almost there. Now squeeze through. Whew, that took a lot of work. Broken furniture, boxes of possessions, and school supplies are piled nearly ceiling-high in parts of the hallway. This place is complete chaos, but I'll make it through. Damn, moving this crap aside is almost impossible, and all this broken glass must symbolize something.

"Oh, that's excellent! The door to the kittens' room is still closed. Perhaps they made it after all. We'll have to clear mounds of wreckage to get into that room. That is very doable! This reminds me of working out. These possessions seem light for the most part, but let's avoid getting cut. I've got to get this last box out of the way. Wow, it's heavy as hell! It must be books, but there we go. Good, the door is still unlocked. Let's go in.

"There's overturned furniture, dust everywhere, fallen plaster, and scattered papers. I don't see the kittens. Maybe they're under the bed. Nah, they're not there. Take your time and do a thorough search. No cats under the sink or in this cabinet. I hope I don't find shattered bodies. Oh, that would be a drag. The refrigerator is empty, and the sink doesn't work, so there is no drink for the kittens or me, assuming they can be found. They could be hiding behind these piles of loose papers or maybe under them.

"Damn it—they aren't here! There isn't a clue about what happened to them. OK, clear the broken glass from the bed and sit. Take a break. You need some time to think. Did that colossal battle represent a war or a natural disaster, like a tornado or earthquake? Maybe it was a comet or meteor crashing into the planet. There are shatter effects everywhere. That kind of thing usually results from sudden overpressures. Many types of explosions can cause that. Perhaps the images represent something less literal, like environmental degradation. And what the hell do the neglected kittens and lack of people mean?

"Pondering this is getting me nowhere. To hell with it! I'm going back to bed! Oh, but leave the door ajar so the kittens can return if they somehow survived. Nothing we can do about giving them food and water, though.

"Damn, it's taking time to work through this hallway debris. Just one more bit of wreckage to clear, and I'll be back in my room. At last, there's my door.

"OK, there's a decision at hand. It may be possible to flee this miserable dream . . . at least I think it is. But there are a lot of unanswered questions. So, what will you do? Run away, or seek meaning? Goddamnit! Input is needed, someone to talk with. This perspective is giving us nothing! It stands to reason that there must be survivors since there aren't any bodies. Maybe they're in a shelter of some kind or perhaps a relocation center.

It may be possible to find them. Hell, it's worth a shot. If nothing else, this miserable dream will eventually end when I awaken. That will be that, but a welcome relief.

"Oh, what if I run into those damn beasts again? Well, the worst they can do is kill me, and they didn't do that when they had the chance. What the hell is there to lose by trying? We'll work back to the stairwell and then down the stairs. Now let's get going. Be careful where you step, and . . . Damn, almost fell again! Man, I bent that door all to hell. Let's squeeze through there. It's a tight fit, but just a bit more to go. Ah, and now comes the stairs. Wahoo! Negotiating this debris is like being on a skateboard at times. Staggering, slipping; this is eff'n crazy.

"Good, the doors are still open. Let's yell down the hallways by the landings again.

'Is anyone there?!'

"Wow, my voice is raspy. I'm dehydrated, and this screaming is still getting me nowhere. I'll get to the lobby soon enough. Well, that's assuming my legs don't get broken or cut to shreds by the glass. Perhaps I'll yell on this floor, too. Nah, screw it. Yelling is pointless. Hmmm, there's a lesson in that. A raised voice probably isn't the best way to get attention or answers. Let's just focus on getting to the lobby. Ah, here we are. Turn that flipped-over chair upright and have a seat. We have to come up with a plan. I've been running around without any aim or direction. This is so unlike any other dream. There's no control and very little understanding.

"Whew, I'm gassed. What to do? Let's see: the floors and the city's streets are abandoned. Another perspective is needed to help make sense of this experience and from someone who won't turn into a damn beast. As it stands, this state has no meaning. There's no discernable message. A relocation center is likely to be far from town, but where? The only place not checked in the building is that stairway that leads to the basement.

"Say, that may be a great place to look! That's right! Maybe there's a fallout shelter down there. These old buildings used to have shelters, artifacts from the Cold War! Damn, I should have thought about that to begin with.

"Come on; let's get going. Toss this crap out of the way and return to the stairwell. Man, I'm tired of moving stuff, but there's only a short way to go. The passage to the basement is mostly clear, which is a good sign! There's a large, black steel door with a push plate at the base of the stairs. Someone must have cleaned up this area, which means people were here recently. Down we go.

"I can't hear anything through the door. It's very stout. Oh, just go for it. You have to stop being so damn gutless. The door opens easily, but it probably also closes fast. Hmmm, it's dark and dank in there. Gross! Man, this place smells like a dirty locker room. Whew! What a stench. Ah, is that the sound of folks talking? It is! Yeah, it sure as hell is!

"Let the eyes adjust a bit before going in. Gee, this is a vast room. Yeah, it looks like people over there, about 15 or 20 yards away! I can barely see them, yet those are definitely people.

At last! Damn, this place has piss-poor lighting, so the power is probably gone. It doesn't matter; let's get going. Don't fret about the door closing. We'll find what is needed here.

"It's taking a while for my eyes to adapt to the darkness, but I'm beginning to discern what's around me. We're in a cavernous room that has numerous support columns. Various groups are huddled around the buttresses, some big, some small. It's almost as if each cluster of folks occupies a territory, like distinct tribes. There's a babble of voices in here, different dialects and languages. These people probably represent humanity in general. Let's find out.

"This shelter isn't damaged, although it's not clean or orderly. Clothing, backpacks, papers, bedding, and clutter are scattered everywhere. Folks are sprawled out here and there. Yeah, there's no order in here. Traveling from Point A to Point B isn't

14.5 The oblivious students lived in a filty, dark, and dank fallout shelter

easy in this place, but it's the only way to make sense of things. Now, that is odd. There's an Olympic-sized swimming pool on the far side of the room. No wonder it's so dank in here. Wow, people are floating on the water. Ah, the thought of water is making me even thirstier.

"Damn, it's so dark I can hardly see what people are doing or what they look like. Some things are clear. Loud music is being played on boom boxes, and the scent of marijuana pops up here and there. My eyes are becoming more adjusted, but the raunchy stench is overpowering. Whew. Most people here are typical college-aged kids between 18 and 22 years old. The room is also far more crowded than it first appeared. That's probably an over-population allegory.

"I'm too parched to speak with anyone. The only water seems to be in the pool, though getting over there won't be easy. This room is like a human obstacle course. No problem. I'm getting used to that challenge. Have to be careful, though. Damn, nearly stepped on that guy.

'Sorry about that.'

"Now my foot's hung up on a blanket. Rough going; lots of detours are needed. But almost there. Ew, we stepped on something mushy. I don't want to think about it.

"Ah, we're here. Let's bend down and take up some water. Wait a minute. No, this doesn't seem safe. People are floating in this crap, which stinks to the high heavens. Still, we have to drink something. Can't talk as it is, and I've been thirsty for a long time. Let's scoop up a big handful of this gunk and try it out. Oh, gag me! Gads, this water is awful! Good Lord, it tastes like warm sewage and smells even worse. It's eff'n vile, disgusting stuff!

"At least my mouth is wet enough to speak, although that drink will probably kill me. What a nasty aftertaste. That's what it must be like to drink urine mixed with sweat and dirt. Yeah, the cost of pollution is steep. Screw it: we have to make sense of this experience. These metaphors must mean something! There are three young men by a nearby column. Let's speak to them, but be calm.

'Hello, I wonder if you guys can tell me anything about the great battle,' I say.

"They don't seem to have a clue.

'You know, the battle that destroyed the city?'

"All I'm getting are blank stares.

'Look, you must have seen the fight. The land was torn up, and the buildings were smashed.'

"They glance at one another. No, they don't have a clue. Maybe I should ask about the kittens.

'There's a room on the top floor with some kittens. You might have seen them or their owner before. Do you know what happened to them?'

"All of them are confused, unresponsive.

'Look, you guys can't be that numb! You must have seen what happened. Why else would you be in here, living like this?'

"One baffled expression matches the next, and one guy drifts away.

'Damn it! This isn't that complicated. There was great turmoil, and the world was pummeled. Now you're living in this cesspool. And you don't seem to know about the kittens, fight, or beasts! You're just not getting it.'

"There goes another guy. Have to relax. I'm raving like a madman. It's no wonder they're bugging out. The guy who's left doesn't seem to understand my story, but at least he's listening. The image of this face freezes in my mind. It's a portent of some kind, something beyond time. I'm going to know this fellow in the corporeal world. That's a sure thing.

"Oh, he's getting nervous, and there he goes. We'd better follow him. He's the only one who was willing to listen. It's still so dark here that I can hardly see anything. Damn, almost fell while tripping over those two. They're making love right out in the open. Wow, there's a powerful marijuana odor, pungent stuff. And those guys over there are sitting on coolers and drinking beers.

"These people are as unconcerned about what happened to their world as they are with how they live! I'm no saint, but I know better than to survive like this! They dwell here, existing in darkness and filth and not caring about why or how it came to this. They're ignorant of their own plight, thoughtless and self-centered. Moreover, they're doing zilch to escape this shadow world. These folks are bound to whatever passing desires they feel. They care for nothing else, not even what's harming them. Enough of this crap!

'WHAT THE HELL IS THE MATTER WITH YOU EFF'N PEOPLE?!'

"Wow, my voice echoes around the chamber, and finally, they quiet down.

'NONE OF YOU UNDERSTANDS WHY YOU'RE HERE! NOT ONE OF YOU GETS IT! YOU IGNORANT, SELFISH BASTARDS! HERE YOU ARE, DRINKING, GETTING HIGH, FUCKING YOUR BRAINS OUT, AND BEING OBLIVIOUS TO WHAT'S GOING ON AROUND YOU! FOOLS! IDIOTS! YOU LIVE IN DARKNESS AND FILTH, BREATHE FOUL AIR, AND DRINK PISS! BUT YOU DON'T DO ANYTHING ABOUT IT! YOU CARE ONLY ABOUT WHAT HAPPENS AROUND YOUR LITTLE TURF WHILE THE EARTH YOU LIVE ON FALLS APART. I'D RATHER BE WHERE THE LIKES OF YOU AREN'T TO BE FOUND!'

"I'm out of breath from yelling. But screw this: let's get the hell out of this hole. These lame bastards couldn't care less about their situation, let alone help anyone understand it. They're already babbling again as if I hadn't said a word. Now they're cranking up the music. My words had no impact, none at all. There's a lesson in that. I sounded like a pedantic jerk, and no one likes that. Perhaps words of love or reason would have been better. No, not with this crowd. They just don't give a damn. It's an existence based on the moment, devoid of insight beyond pleasure. The door is only a short way ahead. No one had better get in my way! Man, we have to calm down. And tripping over these fools is a problem. No, don't be kicking folks out of the way.

"Ah, here's the entry. Shoot, it's a one-way door! It doesn't even have a handle. I am screwed. No, there has to be another exit. I'll leave this place, return to my room, and escape this miserable nightmare. Nothing was learned, either, other than most people don't give a damn about how they live. They accommodate to the worst instead of changing things for the better.

"Hey, let's just concentrate on finding a way out. Stay near the wall. There are fewer people to trip over than around the support columns. Man, this place goes on and on, and it reeks. Ah, that person looks familiar. Yeah, it's that guy who listened for a while.

'Hey, how the hell do I get out of here?' I ask.

"He points toward a long corridor.

"It seems to lead into a subway entrance, but it's too dark to tell. The way ahead may not be safe, but staying here is pointless. This place reeks in so many ways. Come on, let's go. Oh, it's getting much darker this way, although there are fewer people to trip over. My footsteps echo, so I'm definitely entering a long tunnel of some kind. This is crazy. It's pitch-black all around, so stay close to the wall. I could trip over anything. Keep one hand touching the wall and reach forward with the other. Go slowly and—

"What's that up ahead? Oh, it's the dim red glow of a sign. It's kind of far away, but let's head for it. That's an exit sign just above a big steel door. Oh, and here we go again. The doorway is identical to the cellar's entrance, complete with the same push plate. This metaphor is getting tired, but I get it. There are choices to be made. And once made, we cannot go back. The temporal reality we experience moves in one direction. They call that the arrow of time, as in no do-overs. It's the way life works, at least in my timeframe. So, leaving will cut me off from human contact. Then again, engaging with the people here wasn't pleasant in the first place.

"Perhaps it's possible to return to this cesspit. Maybe something can be found to wedge into the doorjamb, like a stick, clothing, or anything. Damn, the exit light is too dim. I can't see anything in here. Duh! Why not open the door and let some light in? Ouch! The sunlight hurts my eyes, blinding me. Let's wait a bit so my vision can adapt. It looks like a cement stairway leading up. Ah, what a nice breeze, fresh cool air. Yeah, we needed that. Hmmm, returning to the cellar doesn't seem that important. That isn't the best place to be by a long shot.

"Besides, no do-overs. Now step into the light. There goes the door, slamming shut behind me. Sure enough, it's a one-way exit. Yeah, there'll be no second chances in this dream. No big deal, though. I couldn't have gone more than 300 or 400 yards underground, so finding my room will be no problem. We'll just backtrack. Let's go up these stairs and hang a right. Then I'll take another right and go straight for a few hundred yards. That should—

"Oh, nuts! The entire context of the dreamscape is much different. The environment seems like Brooklyn in the 1870s.

Two- to four-story brick and wooden row houses are crowded along intersecting streets. The wrought-iron light posts and fixtures indicate the Victorian era. The streets are deserted, but there's no disorder here. Everything is pristine and clean.

"Damn it! How the hell do I get back to campus? Why is that important? It's not like we really understood a damn thing that happened there. This is all a mystery: the kittens, the empty streets, the battle, and those idiots opting to live in the dark. Still, that dorm is where this journey started. Maybe something important was missed along the way. Perhaps there's some hint or clue that could help give meaning to this experience. Though I'm not seeing it, there must be a purpose for all this.

"Just stick with the mental map of where we've been and set off in the opposite direction. At least I can be correct for spatial locations. But time is another matter. Arrow of time, my ass! Temporal linearity doesn't always happen in dreams. It seems to in life, at least for the most part. Oh, none of this looks familiar. Gosh, the dorm has to be nearby or something that predates it. The underground passage could have been set off to the right or left. Perhaps this is the correct way to go.

"Damn! Hopelessly lost! I wander a maze of deserted streets and don't know where to go. Left, right, it's all the same to me. We probably went back in time, long before the dorm was built. Or this could even be a different city altogether. That's possible. More information is needed to get home, so let's devise a plan. Time and space relationships are something we have to explore more fully. That means studying theoretical physics. This dream proves that something about my time and space knowledge is inadequate.

"Perhaps finding a town hall or civic building will help. Records and documents there could lay out the location and history of this place. This would be of assistance. Most town halls are in community centers, usually among the larger structures. So, let's find the middle of town. Wait a minute! The last time I headed for more prominent buildings, those giant dinosaurs nearly killed me. Definitely don't want that! Moreover, there are no temporal compressions here, just mind-numbing plodding down deserted streets. It's tedious as hell. Oh, just go for it. There aren't many alternatives.

"Ah, the buildings are getting a bit larger now. Oh, that looks like a central square or perhaps a small park. There's nothing grandiose around here. However, the building in front of me stands out from the rest. It's only a few stories high and more modern than the structures where my journey began. A large patio wraps around the building, and a covered walkway leads to its front doors. There isn't a big sign, flag pole, or anything imposing to set this place apart, but this is where I should go. It feels like the right place, although Lord knows why. So, it's down to going with instincts. Ha, it seems appropriate when reason fails.

"Whew, tired as hell, and my feet hurt. Let's rest for a while after getting inside. This is a well-landscaped place, and these doors are the two-way kind. There are no surprises here. The main lobby is as abandoned as the streets. Maybe I should rummage through the file cabinets behind that long counter. There are lots of them, hundreds. Some files are likely to have a history of this place. And it's not like anyone will mind my nosing around.

"Whoah, what's that sound? Rock music? Yeah, that's definitely classic rock! Someone must be playing it, perhaps on a stereo system. That could give us another shot at talking with people! The music gets louder in this direction. Let's go down this corridor and check it out. I'm definitely getting closer to the tunes. Long fluorescent lights are built into the ceiling, complementing the typical institutional wall décor and furnishings.

"A small vestibule with some overstuffed chairs is just ahead. Mmmm, let's sit on this nice comfy chair and ponder a bit. I could easily fall asleep here: that's an excellent idea. Yes, falling asleep while being asleep. That sounds like drifting into a coma to me! Oh, what to do? I could inspect the town records, but recalling what I read during dreams has been difficult. That's always been a problem, though I don't know why.

"Let's first find who is playing the tunes. The music comes from somewhere on the next level, and that stairwell will get me there. I'll return to the lobby and review the records if nothing comes up. Come on, let's get these weary bones moving up those stairs.

"Gag me! The tunes are becoming louder and more abrasive with each step. Yup, this is the right direction, but the music sucks! God, it's like fingernails screeching on a chalkboard. J. Geils is not my cup of tea, especially 'Love Stinks.' It's also getting painfully loud. Who the hell wants to listen to that crap all day? 'Yeah, yeah,' my eff'n ass! They ought to have been beaten and stoned for making this miserable song! No doubt those miscreants were stoned when they wrote it, though not in the fashion they deserved to be!

"There are only a few steps to go, and we'll be on the next floor. It looks like there's a small antechamber here that serves three doors. The door furthest to my left has a large window in it. That's where the music comes from, so let's check it out. Damn, that's about as loud as noise can get! Ah, there's a big radio station inside. Clocks set to different time zones line the upper walls, and over to the right are a few cluttered desks. Man, all kinds of audio machines, microphones, and speakers litter the room. Some go back a long way. There seem to be offices or studios behind that door window, but it's hard to tell. I don't see anyone inside, though someone must be making that noise.

"Come on, knock on the door. Damn, the music is so loud one can hardly think, let alone be heard. Knock harder! There's a lesson in this experience about dealing with the mass media. Yeah, it's hard to be heard above the noise. Oh, screw this! I'm getting nowhere. No invitation is needed, and waiting for a reply isn't doing any good. This door is unlocked, so I'm going in.

'Hey, is anyone here?!' I yell. 'Is anyone here?!' I repeat.

"Nothing can be heard above this din, let alone my words. Jeez, I can't even hear myself yell. Wait a second . . . this place isn't deserted after all! There's someone in that studio with the big rectangular window. Let's check it out. Yeah, there's a portly DJ. He rests his feet on a desktop and sits back on his big old

14.6 After many travails, Elder found himself in a large radio station that made nothing but obnoxious noise

butt. There's a control panel and microphone atop the desk. And I also see a few chairs for guests. This guy could probably provide insights, but getting his attention will be problematic. Bang on his window. No, that's not working.

'Hey, I want to talk with you!'

"Yelling's no good either. Whew, there's no getting through all the noise. It doesn't seem to bother the DJ a bit. The numbnut sits there, oblivious to everything. He wears sunglasses and headphones, which must symbolize that he sees and hears little. His shirt is unbuttoned at the top, and he's wearing a heavy gold necklace and other jewelry. The bloated man must be 40, give or take a few years. He's balding but with curly light brown hair remaining on the sides and top. Man, this shit-head is really into making noise. His head and pencil beat back and forth to the rhythms while he mouths the words to songs.

"Perhaps I should smash this window with a chair. That may get this fool's attention. Nah, don't do that. This guy seems to prefer making noise to listening. There's no point in trying to talk with that fool. It's pointless. I wonder how much important info isn't heard above the mass media's mindless babble. Like so many flies buzzing around fresh cowpats, they'll all lap up the same trivial story . . . the juicier and smellier, the better. Then they puke it all out, hoping the stench pleases their audience. They manipulate, titillate, and seek the lowest common denominator. A star's latest fling or addiction becomes their fodder. They hardly ever notice an abused kid's plight or a neighbor's cry. That's how it is here. They've become part of the problem, not the cure. This is no place for anyone. Let's get the hell out of here before my ears explode. Close this door, and—

"Wow! The music stopped, and the lights went out when I left the room. Ah, the silence is refreshing. Yeah, that's a good lesson, a great one! I don't have the patience to deal with those noise-makers, although they may be needed. But for what? Do they have any use at all? Nah, don't go there. Pondering the mass media isn't for someone like me. I'd be butting heads with those idiots until the cows came home. The conflicts would just add to the hullabaloo. Yeah, nothing good would come of that, although more patient souls could break through their miasma.

"There are two more doors. Let's check the middle one next. Now this is weird. Images of the dream events flash through my mind while I reach for the door handle. The kittens, the great battle, and now the empty streets . . . it's overpowering. The impressions collide and coalesce. Whew, what a strange event that was. It was like a vision within a dream. Maybe it was a recap, but what a rush.

"When I step inside, there's a vast well-lit room, like a gallery space within a big museum. My goodness, there are dozens of lighted display cases in here. There must be thousands of model warships, tanks, and airplanes. Whoo-ee! War machines are about the most fascinating things going. I've collected models of them since childhood, but here they are en masse! And it's a collection that blows mine away. This is top-shelf stuff! These miniatures are exquisite.

"There are several French pre-Dreadnoughts of 1890-era vintage in this case. Check them out! Man, it's incredible those bizarre ships could stay upright with their sloped sides and towering superstructures. There was no stability there. Lots of sailors paid for that foolishness. Unbelievable workmanship on these models. The detail on the gun turrets, hulls, decks, and funnels is fantastic. Look at those beam turrets and how well they've made the lifeboats and davits. The painting is exquisite, and they're all dolled up in Victorian livery. That was when deadly weapons were finished in lively colors, elaborate scrollwork, and polished brass fixtures. This is incredible craftsmanship. I've never seen these ships modeled in this quality. There's even scale-correct planking molded into the decks. What a sight!

"Goodness, there is so much to see in here. Let's check out the other cases. Some of these weapons look familiar, but others are alien. Wow, a massive, delta-winged aircraft with six pusher-type propeller engines takes up an entire case. I forget what that was called. Here are some Russian T-28 tanks with multiple turrets. Man, those things were a disaster in terms of design. There's also a modified T-72 tank. That case has some rocket models, but they're dull compared with ships, planes, and tanks. They're just tubes with pointy ends, but these other models are spectacular. What an excellent visual soup. It would be marvelous to have a collection like this.

"Hmmm, here's a mystery. This aircraft has two large dorsal fins and two short main wings. Its tail wings slope downward from the aft part of the fuselage. From head-on, the craft looks more like a spaceship than a plane. I've never seen anything like it. And these are very unusual warships. They have sloped hulls and superstructures and no apparent weapon systems. The weapons must be internal. Goodness, they look stark. Is this a portent of what is to be? Perhaps so. These designs sure as hell don't exist now.

"Oh, here are display pieces for people to touch. I'll pick up an aircraft and check it out. What a strange model. Fascinating. It has an aerodynamic form but no wings or associated control surfaces. Very odd. The front end is enlarged, with angular faces that cause it to taper toward the bow. Two viewports are flared into the bow's dorsal surface, and six tubular projections are mounted on a ventral bow plate. The craft's body is thinner than the front end, and the aft section is the largest. These aft exhaust ports seem to be control thrusters and rocket propulsion mechanisms. This must be a space-based weapon, some kind of orbital fighter.

"That's a sickening idea. Here we possess an intellect that allows us to comprehend the nature of creation. Yet look at what we create. Look at what we bring into the stars. Hell, look at what we've always done with our highest technology. These weapons represent the wanton application of our understanding of science, mathematics, physics, and all knowledge. I wonder if technological and philosophical evolution parallels one another. Doubt it. Is that what the gigantic dinosaurs symbolized? Were they grotesque representations of our folly? God, I hope not.

"How many poets, teachers, parents, and children have these war machines devoured? How much have we spent on building and maintaining tools of destruction? How much time and money have I squandered on military models and books? I'm merely a reflection of my species, as fascinated by killing machines as an army general would be. Yeah, that's the lesson of this place.

"Each of those models represents so many lost lives. Over 1,100 sailors were lost when the *USS Arizona* blew up, and over 1,400 died when the *Hood* exploded. *Bismarck* took down about 2,000 lives. Nearly 1,000 survivors were left to drown. About

2,500 or more went down with the *Yamato*. We machine-gunned those in the water; such is the mercy of total war. Let's put this damn thing down and get the hell out of here. This was such a good time, but then came the meaning.

"Time to close this door and move on. Museums like this should be made as places dedicated to our folly. But would people understand the lesson? This dream is much deeper than—

"What the hell? A man is standing by the third portal! He seems to be expecting me. Where the heck did he come from? He's wearing a white business suit and smiling at me. Hmmm, this guy seems familiar. He's in his early to mid-thirties, athletically built, dark-haired, and angular. Good Lord, his face is exactly like mine. He's a much slimmer and far more evolved version of me, possibly a genetic modification. Yeah, that's precisely what he is! What an odd—

'Do you understand?'

"He's communing via thought!

'That's what we're doing with those reading these words,' he observes. 'Tell us, what does the battle symbolize?'

'I believe the gigantic dinosaurs represent wars and environmental degradations that will waste the land, water, and air.'

'What of this?' he asks.

"Suddenly, images of the empty streets and the dark cellar flicker in my mind. I don't know how the man can send me images in addition to a running dialogue. It's a fantastic form of telepathy.

'What does it mean?' he asks.

'No people were walking in the daylight because they opted to live in darkness. They frolicked in their own waste and paid no heed to the past or future. They focused only on passing desires and what pleased them for the moment. Those folks had no time for anyone who rocked their complacency.'

'And this?' he asks.

"Images of the studio and the disc jockey flash through my mind.

'The media only beat time to the lowest common denominator,' I say. 'They make little but loud, obnoxious noise.'

"An image of the dinosaurs' torn flesh and flowing blood flashes through my mind. Why does this guy keep putting depictions of the giant allosaurus attack in my mind? It was vicious . . .

'Do you understand where the beasts come from?' he asks.

'They probably represent the ultimate effects of the beasts we carry within.'

'Will they become so powerful they destroy life?' he asks.

'I don't know!'

'Look deeper,' he demands. 'Look into the possibilities.'

'No! I won't accept the possibility they represent nuclear war. That's too literal. Nor must the people in the cellar represent survivors. They opted to live in the dark. They need not have been forced there!'

'Can it happen?' he asks.

'It's possible, but we're also destroying the environment. Our inner beasts are running amok on many levels.'

'You've seen and felt their power,' he observes. 'What can be done to stop them?'

'We can improve ourselves. We can chain the beasts and grow beyond this madness.'

'This isn't happening,' he notes.

'It still can!'

'What can be and will be are different things,' he communes.

'We have a choice!'

'Then why don't people choose to act?' he asks.

'Some are!'

'Why isn't the situation improving?'

'More people must become motivated enough to act.'

'Why aren't they?'

'Most of us are myopic and complacent, like the cellar dwellers. Nonetheless, we need not destroy ourselves!'

'Then why is humanity doing so?' he asks.

'I don't know!'

'Were people given the ability to help themselves?'

'Yes.'

'Then why do so many ask for a power they already have?' he observes.

'Because most don't perceive that they have any power.'

'Is it a matter of perception or complacent lethargy?' he inquires.

'A bit of both.'

'If people don't use their inherent capacities, don't they condemn themselves?'

'We can change!' I insist. 'We can evolve.'

'How much time does humanity have?' he asks.

'I . . . I don't know.'

"Man, I'm getting my ass handed to me by this guy. Perhaps he's right. Maybe we're teetering between being and extinction. What the hell should we do about it? And who the heck am I to relate this lesson? For all I know, some cosmic event may wipe us out before—

'You've understood much,' he notes, 'but what about this?'

"Just then, the kittens' image plays in my consciousness— their pitiful matted fur, their skinny, shrunken faces, large ears, ticks and fleas crawling across their skin.

'What does this represent?' he asks.

'I . . . I don't know!'

"He's showing me close-ups of their bony, infested bodies. I shut my eyes. The skeletal figures remain, locked in my vision.

'WHAT DOES THIS MEAN?' he repeats, the thought roaring through my mind.

'They were terribly neglected!'

'WHAT DOES THIS MEAN?' he demands to know.

'They probably symbolize famine and disease,' I reply. 'Look, I'm tired, and nothing about this dream is clear.'

'Understanding is not easy.'

"Oh, I'm failing miserably. I'd give myself an F on this damn test. The mentor gestures toward the third door, indicating we must go through it to find answers. I should proceed, but I'm tired as hell. Man, it's hard to even move. Suddenly my limbs tingle. Wow, he is . . . somehow sharing a bit of energy. Is this possible? I have no idea how that worked, but the increased power is critical. Ah, strength is returning to my body, and my mind is clearing a bit. That was neat.

'Thank you.'

"Now he opens the door and looks up.

'Yeah, I'll climb the stairway.'

"One foot in front of the other. There's the deep blue of an open sky as he and I ascend. And here we are, atop a large, flat roof. It's like the roof of any institutional building, but there are

14.7 Eventually, Elder found a guide who led him to the source

no ventilators or related equipment. That's odd. There's a waist-high wall running around the perimeter. This guy is popping into my head again.

'OK, I won't dally on the architectural details.'

'Focus on this,' he advises.

"People are standing in a long queue. They're waiting to see someone or something. I can't discern who or what they're communing with, but it's seated on a throne. Well, it's not a throne; it's a weathered chair atop a beat-up wooden box, nothing special.

"Yeah, this must be a God metaphor, one my feeble imagination could grasp. If so, God could sure use a decorator. All kinds of people are waiting in line—old, young, Colored, and White. One female, in particular, is about to commune with the seated entity. No, it's not an individual on the chair. It's more like a . . . a crux . . . a nexus. Yeah, 'nexus' is the best term to use. Well, it's not a perfect fit.

'Her name is Anne,' the mentor says in my mind.

"Yes, Anne. She's about 19 and has long, brown hair tied back in a ponytail. Anne is wearing jeans and a blue plaid blouse. She's a nice-looking girl. She's terribly distressed. I can . . . I can actually feel her emotions, her thoughts, and her insights. This is very strange. W-w-we're melding. She knows about the kittens' sorry fate. I'm in her mind, one with her. We're experiencing the same thoughts and emotions. She speaks, and her words echo in my mind.

14.8 God's throne was nothing but a humble chair atop an old box

'I never wanted to care for those kittens! I never asked for them, and—'

"There's sorrow, such complete sorrow. And now resentment, anger.

'No! I never wanted that responsibility!' she insists. Tears flow down her cheeks. 'No, no, no! I'm not at fault! How can I be held responsible for something I never wanted to undertake? I didn't volunteer to care for them! I didn't ask to.'

"A jolting, painful insight suddenly rips into us: 'If no one accepts responsibility, no one acts. If no one acts, then life's fate is sealed. And that fate is—'

"Oh, it's terrible! No, no, no, no, no, no! Get this thought out of our mind! An endless, frigid void stretches before us. No light, no stars, no dimensions . . . just vast, cold emptiness. It's horrible! There are no memories, no thoughts, no life, no being, no hope, no love, no future, no present, and no past. There is only infinite, desolate nothingness.

'No! Not that! I didn't want that!' Anne wails.

"We're feeling guilt mixed with remorse.

'Why didn't I do anything? Why didn't I act? Why? There are no more chances! There is no more time! It's my fault. It's all my fault!'

"Tears! Aaarrrhhhh, such pain!

'It's all my fault!' Anne shouts.

"The sorrow burns! It burns! There's emotional collapse, a neglected responsibility that turns life into nothingness. And there's so much guilt—endless regrets and remorse.

"The pebbles on the roof dig into my knees as Anne bows. She covers her face and cries. Her tears flow, and the sobs echo in our mind. We're weeping as one. This is too much anguish to endure. My tears flow even while these lines are read.

'Please, let this pain end! Please, give me another chance,' Anne whispers.

"The nexus touches Anne on the shoulder, and its warmth flows through us. It's a harmonizing energy, a pervasive force that permeates and links all things. There's also an overpowering feeling of compassion and empathy. This is the primal essence of love, pure and unconditional love. There's an absolution granted by the grace of our own admissions. For we now acknowledge our responsibility, our stewardship. We're forgiven, although we cannot easily forgive ourselves. Nor should we.

"Anne rises and proceeds on her way, determined to atone. Her thoughts echo in my mind, but what has become of my thoughts? This is unlike anything we've ever experienced. We're losing our identity but gaining insights. Perhaps the path to understanding requires us to recognize that we're one with all things. We must abandon our ego and leave the self behind. The feeling of openness is overpowering. It's more than a feeling! There's also—

"Wow! There's been an instant spacetime shift. We're standing before the nexus, exactly where Anne was. We're now the first in the queue. But how did this happen? Where's the mentor? There he is, motioning for us to approach this . . . this . . . no name fits. Some may call it God, but no terms can describe

14.9 When the author tried to see God's presence, he was blined, with the creator telling him it was a dynamic being of ultimate selflessness

it. Nexus or crux is close, although it's infinitely more than that. It's something that all things are part of and linked to.

"What a rush! As soon as we contemplate coming closer to this entity, it happens. Maybe thoughts are inseparable from actions here. Come on, we must concentrate. There's a definite presence but no form, edges, or shapes. We have to look harder. Damn! It hurts to look. A piercing light emanates from outside and from within. There is something else. It's . . . something like a female presence, like a mother. But it's more than that alone. We have to try harder to see. There has to be a face. Oh, blinding luminosity! Ouch! Don't try that again! It has no face, no discernable form. Forcing an image only leads to pain.

'What are you?' we ask.

'A dynamic being of ultimate selflessness,' it replies.

"It's an echoing, thunderous thought. What the heck does it mean? Torrents of insights flood in. It's too much.

'Please, slow down! Please!' I shout.

"The thoughts relate to the definition. Come on, we have to segregate this input into smaller bits. Is a reply needed? Oh, there's too much coming in at once. I glean only bits and pieces.

'If we are one with all things, how can we be any one thing?' the entity asks.

'That's why you're ultimately selfless, a sort of paradox. Since things exist in time, so must you also be dynam—'

"The entity cuts us off, asking, 'If we are one with thought, is our thought in all things?'

'Like an ideational DNA that underlies existence or cohabits with it? It's unclear how such a thing would work.'

"Man, I muffed that one. Let's try again.

'Perhaps there are metaphysical aspects of existence that are integral with mass and energy dynamic—'

"Once again, the source probes my insights before I can answer.

'If we are one with being, must we not move with all things?' it observes.

'Yeah, that is what being dynamic must mean at—'

'If we move, must we not change?' it relates.

'Movement implies change, but—'

The entity asks, 'If we change, how can we remain the same?'

'The rationalistic and metaphysical underpinnings of being are probably constants. Perhaps the ways matter and energy interact with thoughts are also absolutes, while—'

"This is an inquisition of sorts. But how can we remember all this? And our answers are pitiful. Just awful!

'If we do not remain the same, how can we be eternal?' the nexus asks.

'Perhaps the metaphysical processes are eternal, like deducing a repeating cycle or pi-like function. One-third will always be one-third. Maybe these ideas, principles, etcetera, exist as universal possibilities that we can eventually grasp. They're given presence by contemplations, experimentation, studies, science .. . even prayer. Perhaps that's the purpose of sentient beings. Yes, we may have a—'

'If you are of us, are we not of you?' the nexus asks.

'We're all interrelated. Sort of like notes in a harmony that—'

"Man, there's too much flowing in too fast. It'll take life-times to unpack the meaning. Our perspective is suddenly shift-ed. We're looking over the roof's short wall again. Multitudes of people appear. They're milling about on the streets below. Why couldn't we see them before? Were we that blind?

"Ah, now it's clear! People can be found if we seek them. People can be moved if we persuade them. They may be lost in darkness, but they can also be enlightened. We must use the per-ceptual capacities that reside within. We're one with what creat-ed us, one with the rationality that underlies existence, the logos of being. Ah, but it's far more than logic alone. Emotions also link us, a logicoemotional amalgamation. That's what we felt when we were one with Anne! That's it! We must use empathy, rationality, foresight, and love. These aspects of being can ensure our survival if they're used properly. It is where the one becomes us, and we!

'Yes, we understand!'

"What's that? In the distance, there's a massive, blue, crystal-line gateway. A throng enters the city through the gate. No, this can't be heaven. There's no such thing. Is this a dwelling place of souls or hackneyed metaphors? Is there any difference? Are we communing with God or an aspect of myself? Is there any dif-ference? Wait a minute! Who is that passing through the gates? That's someone from my coaching days. It's Alex, a huge, strong man who threw the hammer.

'No, it can't be him!'

"This could be a place of souls. Good Lord, is this a place of the living or the dead? Alex is a young man. He was our student and one of the very best. Alex hasn't even lived yet. Much of my life was spent developing young people's minds and bodies. Here is a person who is as kind and gentle as anyone could be. Why is he in this place? Is he dead? Or will he be killed senselessly, swept away in a pointless conflict? Is that what the Battle of the Beasts meant?

'No, don't let this be! ALEX! ALEX! NO! NOT HIM! NOT ANY OF THEM! HOW CAN WE STOP THIS? WHAT CAN WE DO?'

"Flashes of the kittens pour in. Alex's life hangs in the balance. All life hangs in the balance. There are visions. A balance beam teeters and then crumbles as the winds of time weather it into dust. Please, let there be enough time!

'PLEASE! WHAT CAN WE DO TO SAVE OURSELVES?'

"The people on the streets below notice my panic. They're staring at me. Maybe they've seen others react this foolishly. We are so utterly unworthy.

'I'm sorry. I didn't want Alex to be here, not that this is a bad place.'

"Man, now I'm making an even bigger fool of myself. You must control your passion. It's both a weakness and a strength. This is overwhelming. But I must gather my composure and think. Damn, it! I lost the linkage with the 'we'! I have to—

"Goodness, we're standing before the nexus again. There's no more fear, although we're exhausted. It senses our fatigue. Mmmm, the nexus is giving us strength. It's in our mind, examining our thoughts and insights.

'What is humanity's greatest fault?' the nexus asks.

'Greed.'

'How does greed operate?'

'The self assumes ascendance over all else,' is our reply. 'It becomes insatiable and aggressive, willfully finding no recourse in reason or empathy. Then the needs and appetites required to perpetuate life can evolve into greed and its children. Thus, the present devours the future.'

"There's an agreement, but we've much to ask.

'Whatever you are, please show us the future,' we ask.

"Images and ideas flow in of wars, famine, and disease. We see the arm of the balance beam tilt once again. The image of the kittens suddenly comes roaring back. We see their dirty and unkempt bodies, bony ribs, and matted fur. They are us, our children, the earth, and nature itself, and we are their negligent and blind custodians. Extinction is the end result of ignoring our responsibilities. It's the price of not using our time and capabilities to care for one another and the place that sustains us. It's a vicious, burning sensation.

'Yes, we're responsible for our own fate! But what must we do to save ourselves? What can we do to preserve life? Do we write? Do we speak?'

"There's an insight, sudden and sharp. The power of what created us resides within everyone, and it's our joint responsibility to use it. This tremendous power is manifest in many forms. Be one an artist, a writer, a mother, a scientist, a professor, a planter, a caretaker, or a taxi driver, each is gifted with unique abilities. A photographer takes shots of tainted ponds while a scientist finds a means of breaking down spilled oil. A person of peace stands firm before soldiers and others speak the truth to those in power. A mother tells her child to learn how to love, and a greedy man decides to give. Within our collective thoughts and deeds resides the means of salvation. Within our hands and hearts dwells the power to craft what is needed to secure our future. However, this can only happen if we accept personal responsibility and use our gifts accordingly. We cannot dally, for time waits for no one.

"Everything fits together now. Some of those reading these words will realize their strength and passion. In so doing, they will be drawn to act. Is that the purpose of this experience? Is that what has drawn us together?

"Ahhh, there's an enormous surge of empathy. It's a conjunction of shared being, identity, and love. No words can describe this . . . this rapture, this bliss. Now a hand touches our shoulder, and I am instantly wide awake."

Alex felt a huge weight lift from his shoulders as he finished telling Mirai and Madame Leonedria the dream. The images still haunted him, and tears clouded his eyes.

15

Pondering Possibilities

Verity stirred in the sleeping alcove while the three friends sat silently to take in the significance of Alex's story.

Alex took a sip of his drink to soothe his dry throat. "I abruptly awoke from the dream to see the metal roof above my dwelling place. I felt well-rested and immediately scribbled the dream's rough outline on an envelope. I recently noted that the theme of a looming war was prominent in the original notes, yet it does not appear inevitable. The overview was a skeletal and disjointed rendition at best. Still, the images have plagued me for decades."

Madame Leonedria nodded her head. "Now your personal time to act runs short. Your memories and abilities fade, battered by time's winds."

"Clearly, this wasn't a typical lucid or astral dream," Mirai signed. "It was much longer and more complex than prior experiences."

"It took me days to jot down the details," Alex said. "I'm sure many things were forgotten or misconstrued, and perhaps they were important. However, some events were frozen in my mind by their sheer terror. I can still see that giant claw ripping the pavement, tearing the earth. I can feel the damn ground breaking beneath me, having to leap from an upturning concrete slab! The events will not leave me alone!"

"Do you think the person reading these words will believe what you've written?" Madame Leonedria asked. "Some are more likely to believe this is an elaborate fiction rather than an actual communion with what created us."

"There was the outline on the envelope," Mirai signed. "It was dated and stamped, so we know the dream occurred. We also recovered an early version of the dream description resting at the feet of his mother's body. The text was badly corroded. Nonetheless, we could discern that the dream was much like Alex has described."

"Still, it was a dream," Madame Leonedria said. "Dreams are the stuff of imagination. My child, I know the dream happened, but those with us need assurances. Accepting what you've related as reality isn't easy. It requires that readers forsake personal identity in favor of a universal 'nexus' that links all that is. That isn't easy for anyone to accept who was raised on the idea that our being is distinct from the Divine."

"The loss of the 'I' perspective was disconcerting," Alex admitted. "It was like being within a vast open space that contains only disembodied thoughts and feelings. They move easily among everyone and everything, with the nexus providing some sense of continuity. I remained distracted and disoriented for several days after the dream. Parts of the experience echoed through my mind, as they do today. Please forgive the unworthiness of my words. I cannot adequately describe the state when communing with the nexus, crux, God, or whatever term one wishes to use."

"Lovers and parents touch upon the communion you felt, Alex," Madame Leonedria said.

"Did the dream change you?" Mirai signed.

"Did the dream change me?" Alex repeated. "At a profound level, my friend. The ideas of accepting personal responsibility and taking action became apparent, as did the notion that I must stifle my inherent childishness. But something profound also happened to my perceptions after the connection with the nexus, a critical change that persists.

"A wonderful sense of communion with existence often occurs at the ocean, atop vistas, or looking into the night sky. There comes a feeling of oneness with all things during these times. The 'I' becomes the 'we.' It's a linkage that emerges from imagination's core and touches upon all that is. Doubts, fears, concerns, and all else gives way to rapture. There is harmony with all. It's the power of a child and one of the greatest gifts God bestows. There is no way to fully capture this feeling with mere words. I cannot grasp it when reading or writing. It is only manifest when I touch upon the nature of our existence with thoughts and feelings. Is this making any sense?"

"I would describe the concept as a fundamental form of love," Mirai signed. "Love involves sharing ourselves with others, be they one or many. Perhaps your Divine creator is a dynamic being of ultimate selflessness because it gave all it was, is, and could be to craft this universe in which we dwell. That includes the development of sentient beings. Could this be the elemental source of love?"

Alex smiled. "Perhaps it is, Mirai," he said. "Yes, a seminal act of division that eventually draws all its elements together via an inherent metaphysical impetus. You have such a great mind. I sometimes glimpse that communion you speak of when I look into your eyes like we're doing now. That's a special place, at least for me."

"Thoughts for a thought about thought," Madame Leonedria said. She smiled and added, "You will touch Mirai's soul one day. She will then have to decide whether she will save yours. However, please go on. The dream certainly seems like an occurrence that could change a person."

"It did," Alex said, "but aspects of its meaning are still unclear. Was I truly taught lessons and shown portents? Was this done via coexisting metaphysical resources that aren't normally accessible to conscious thought? Or was the dream merely an elaborate fantasy drawn from deep within, the byproduct of an overactive imagination? Perhaps there was a physiological cause, the end result of a cortical anomaly. They tell me there is a neurodegenerative process going on. The doctors can see it on the MRIs. Names and events are drifting away, and completing this task is difficult."

"Questions about how or why the dream occurred are pointless," Madame Leonedria observed. "The event focused on a theme of shared consciousness and being. This was a union wherein the disparate thoughts and experiences of the many became enmeshed. The synthesis occurred regardless of whether the thoughts were created from within or by outside agencies."

"Most believe there is an underlying impetus or idea that holds together what we perceive," Alex noted. "However, they have a hard time accepting that we're part of that process."

"I find that odd," Mirai signed, "but history is clear. Most people from your era separated themselves from the concept of a Divine being. Many thought of God as a discrete 'he.' They assumed 'him' to be a distinct and all-powerful entity, albeit somewhat human in general form and thought. This being supposedly ruled from on high in an ethereal realm separate from the universe. It is an amazing concept."

"Many of those with us believe the same thing," Madame Leonedria said.

"This is what most people teach their children," Alex said. "We tell them the word of God can be captured in a book. Then some sanctioned authority insists that we can only realize what God is if we follow the one true path. Discovery and imagination give way to dogma. Is it any wonder that the most learned and curious walk away?"

"Woe be unto heretics," Madame Leonedria said. "Some will brand you a delusional heretic, my child."

"I know," Alex said. "Let them also understand that I'm a heretic who loves God with every aspect of my being. It's a matter of definitions, something we keep returning to. People who separate themselves from the processes that create and sustain existence are more closely bound to doctrine than to nature. They fail to see what could be. Many cannot imagine themselves as sparks of realization, brilliant lights that exist within the context of an ever-changing and fathomless whole."

"Divorcing ourselves from ego is not easy, Alex," Madame Leonedria said. "We all have a powerful 'I' voice. It's an inner identity that allows us to contemplate and communicate. Indeed, your 'I' voice leaks into my prose at times, such is its pervasive nature. Whether the task is driving a car or pondering these words, that inner voice analyzes and judges. Ultimately, it helps formulate our perceptions and reactions.

"To better understand our relatedness to all things requires a perceptual shift somewhat like those you discussed earlier. We must develop the capacity to consider how external presences, occurrences, and contemplations can influence our ongoing thoughts. This requires a state wherein the 'I' voice gives way to the mutuality manifest in the concept of 'we' or 'us.' Of course, the capacity to commune in this way entails an empathetic awareness of what is around us. Moreover, one must possess the imagination to consider the mutual influences one aspect of our surroundings has on another."

"Including those many things influencing our thoughts at any given moment," Mirai signed. "Our identities must be subordinated to a communal way of perception that is difficult to grasp and employ."

"This conceptual openness was experienced during the dream," Alex said. "But my 'I' voice often gets in the way. It prevents me from using a communal perspective in my everyday affairs. Indeed, my ego has been a barrier in many respects. Perhaps that's why I'm so damn arrogant, petty, and quick to anger. Yeah, it's ego writ large. Considering the thoughts of others while deliberating on our own ideas is no easy task. This may also be the case with many of those with us."

"That is why your kind has so many conflicts," Madame Leonedria said. "First-order thinkers are usually bound to the self. They cannot easily grasp the perspectives of others, nor do they try. Empathy opens the door to selflessness. As you know, women are more frequently blessed than men in possessing this ability. Such is humanity's current state. However, the capacity to perceive the thoughts and feelings of others exists in most sentient species and genders. Alas, recognizing its value and need are difficult barriers to cross."

"We're all works in progress," Alex said. "I often ponder the dream's deeper meanings. Perhaps the thoughts we're now sharing can be seen as harmonies within the context of a greater metaphysical chorus."

"Some sublime speculation?" Mirai signed with a smile.

"In for a penny, in for a pound," Alex said. "Perhaps the interplay of the neuronal bioelectrical forces that sustain our thoughts has an important role. In fact, the activity may resonate with the underlying energetic elements that help order and sustain this experience we call existence. If so, maybe that is our role in the universe. We exist to learn and to think. We thus become one with the metaphysical processes that helped create and maintain existence. Perhaps we can even touch upon the fundamental frequencies that define being."

"This leads to some interesting contemplations," Madame Leonedria said. "One is the realization that all life is integral to the eventual evolution of sentient beings. For example, a primitive fish's descendants may one day evolve into a creature that can peruse these words. Some can even understand the ideational processes that are essential aspects of our existence. Be it a bacterium or an insect, the seeds of the ideas we share are inherent in life's very structure. This is where context, possibility, and inherent design intersect. If we subscribe to this view, we can better understand how everything in nature is kindred and interlinked. Whether these possibilities have a factual basis requires more than time alone. It also requires directed thought."

"The real question is, will the reader help those poor kittens or disregard their plight? That is the choice they now face. Yes, there is no escaping personal responsibility. Yet there is ambiguity about your personal role, Alex. Indeed, how did you conclude that it was your task to write this text? You are, after all, very flawed. I question that anything akin to God would leave one without a sense of direction. Thus, the nexus probably provided an impetus. Tell me, what transpired after this portentous dream you've described?"

"Oh, that's the source of my anxiety!" Alex said. He fidgeted, growing uneasy. "Facing God was traumatic, but seeing the future was horrific. The images disturb me."

"We have to address them, Alex," Madame Leonedria said.

"They could just be fantasies, figments of imagination," Alex said, his eyes gazing downward. "I don't want to go there."

"Fear?" Mirai signed. "Is that what I'm seeing?"

"Yes!" Alex angrily replied.

"You're afraid because the possibilities you saw are unacceptable," Madame Leonedria said. "In fact, this project was abandoned because of them! My son, you owe those with us the complete truth! They will decide what is plausible or not. Let us first proceed with some context."

"Context," Alex said. He shook his head. "Well, I wasn't sure what to do about the information derived from these dreams. Was I to write about what had transpired? Or maybe some other action would be more appropriate? At the time, I wrote essays for local and school newspapers. My weight-training articles appeared in nationally circulated magazines. Yeah, I got cards and letters from all over the world. However, my political writing was going nowhere. Moreover, my coaching job touched relatively few souls.

"I wasn't sure what to do. It's abundantly clear that I'm not a great writer. That's for sure. Moreover, I don't have the personality needed to preach or lead. Hell, not by a long shot. However, any fool can see this world is being laid waste. Even as these words are read, wars rage, famines fester, forests burn, rivers are polluted, and the air turns toxic. The garden is dying. Almost all of us know it. There's interminable debate, but anyone close to nature can easily see the truth. Nonetheless, we sit on our asses while our prospects dim."

"The fragility of worlds is not widely understood by those who live upon them," Madame Leonedria observed. "As I've noted, all life hangs by threads, Alex, and it most assuredly does not hang forever."

"Especially if we assume that there will always be a tomorrow," Alex said. "What we do or fail to do can easily ruin our—"

Mirai whistled loudly and signed, "Enough pretext! We have to cut to the chase, Alex. This was a significant dream."

"It was a goddamn nightmare!" Alex said. "I dread going there again, but I will."

16

Fighting for the Future

"First, let me explain a few things," Alex said. "The seeing state's frequency slowly diminished over the years. Then one night, about five years after the Nexus Dream, another experience unfolded. I suddenly felt the energy and clarity that accompanied many of these episodes.

"This event was presaged by a series of peculiar mini-dreams. They were a dizzying collage of images related to the world's political and environmental situation. There were pictures and drawings. I saw fetid streams, angry protestors, and military deployments. Most images were accompanied by captions. Some words and scenes could be discerned, but their overall meaning was difficult to grasp. Then the images suddenly evaporated. Soon there was nothing but a crystal-clear consciousness within.

"I was adrift within a dark void without form or dimension: no up, no down, no left, no right. This was clearly a seeing state, and I knew the power wouldn't last. My thoughts were drawn toward talking with God about what I should do to help bolster the future of our kind. The dream's details are vivid, even after so many years."

"Then you must take us there, Alex," Madame Leonedria said. She gestured toward the bowl and added, "You dread this part of our quest, but gird yourself. Into the fires we all must go."

Alex shook his head. He sighed deeply and pursed his lips. He reached out to Mirai and gently touched her hand.

"I'm so damn sorry," he said, his eyes growing moist. Then he stared deeply into the water bowl, his tale slowly unfolding while firelight played on the cave's walls.

"I'm adrift in limbo," he said. "There's much less control in this state than usual. No, something isn't right. I can't quite figure it out. There's a presence. It's like sensing when someone is angry with you—the old Italian evil eye. Then you look around, and the person is staring right at you. Hey, this damn thing is malevolent. I've never experienced anything like this during a dream.

"Forget it! A location is needed. We have to find a context wherein I can find a means to meet my responsibility. It takes power to make settings, let alone perform actions. Yeah, I must get the old speed/energy feedback loop going. It's been a while. Come on, focus on acceleration, and overcome the inertia. That's it; let's get going.

"Hmmm, I'm moving way too slowly. There's not nearly enough energy. Damn, it's hard to get the feedback loop online. Come on! Focus on speed. Turn speed into energy and energy into more velocity. You can still do this! Now get your ass in gear. Ah, there it is! Now you've got it going. Yeah, let her unwind full bore, but avoid . . . oh, too much pressure. Stop being a baby! You need much more power. There we go! Come on, get the speed up.

"Damn, this is much harder than usual, but I can manage. Come on! We're almost there. Tremendous pressure, loud humming noise, massive energy . . . getting there! Keep it going! Now, find a still point. That's it! Bang! I've broken through! Time to attune your senses and figure out what's up.

"Hmmm, this is definitely a dreamscape of some kind. It seems I'm seated atop a comfortable desk chair with armrests. It's made out of wood. Not sure, though. Man, that's odd. It's impossible to see. There's a force of some kind holding my eyes closed. It is a pernicious influence, extremely potent. This is eff'n scary! Something is definitely wrong. Screw this! Never give in to fear. Let's find out where we are. Shoot, it's impossible to open my eyes. Come on, you can do this. Ah, making some progress! Nuts, there's nothing but a blur. Still, seeing the light is promising. We have to focus more. Yeah, the setting is getting more evident now.

"Ah, there you go! My vision is back online, but that was hard. I wonder why. Hmmm, I'm sitting behind a wooden teacher's desk, as one would find in an old high school. A pen and pad of paper are in front of me. Yeah, that means I must write. That's evident. Ugh, I was afraid of that. Putting these damn dreams into words won't be easy, especially for me. Shoot, I can barely piece two or three words together without making a damn mistake. Nonetheless, writing seems to be the message here.

"Well, let's examine our surroundings. This place isn't a school, although perhaps I'm best off being a teacher. Not sure I have the temperament for that. A massive picture window graces the wall in front of my desk. Oh my, the view is spectacular! The sun shines in a cloudless blue sky. Wow, a beautiful metropolis stretches as far as the eye can see. Awesome! The buildings glisten, their tinted windows reflecting different hues. This is marvelous! The size, complexity, and detail . . . it's overwhelming.

"We're in the midst of a futuristic city! And this office must be on one of the upper floors of a towering building. Whew, dizzying view. I'm afraid of heights, but the panorama is breathtaking. An extraordinarily tall skyscraper stands to my left. Its blue windows act like countless mirrors. They make the building look like a giant crystal spire. Good Lord, the structure towers over everything in sight. It must be well over 2,000 feet tall, an utterly fantastic visage! The sunlight glistens on its many shiny surfaces and reflects thousands of images of my surroundings. It's dazzling! What a captivating, incredible spectacle. Oh, I'll remember this for the rest of my life.

"Let's see, to my center and right is a much shorter, stockier building. It looks mundane and utilitarian. The entire structure is visible from this perch. It probably occupies a square block

16.1 A beautiful futuristic city stretched for as far as the eye could see

and must stand about 20 stories tall. Well, maybe a bit more. The place reminds me of those massive boxy buildings that house enormous department stores. Perhaps there's a Macy's in there or an indoor mall. It's big enough!

"That's cool. There are elevated tramways and multi-level streets nearby. They connect with parts of the buildings. Yeah, that seems to be their primary means of support. Some go for long runs . . . miles and miles. And what the hell are those tube-like structures running beside them? Oh, they're pedestrian conveyors! Ha, one could quickly go from one place to another sans vehicle. The conveyors join up with various-sized buildings, roofs, streets, and even docking ports. Whew, they're up there! Way too scary for me. I bet one could travel from one end of this city to another without touching the ground or getting wet during a storm. How neat is that?

"Parks, rooftop gardens, and man-made waterways provide ample oases of green and blue. Nearly all the streets are lined with trees and bushes, even the elevated ones. Some of the roofs look like small forests. It's like having parks everywhere, and those trees are substantial. Wow, some are close to 80 feet high, or maybe more. I bet there's wildlife in these recreational areas. Office breaks must be fantastic around here. You can go out and feed the squirrels and birds. This is a marvelous mixture of concrete and nature. Yeah, there's a balance here.

"What a magnificent accomplishment this is! The city is clean and well laid out. The air is smog-free, allowing me to see for miles around. Humanity has created all this from its ideas and the earth's bounty. Oh, this is much better than during my time. Hell, cities of the twenty-first century are chaotic and squalid places. They are nothing like this.

"I must be several hundred years into the future. Look how far we've come! The species can go even further. I know it will. We've mastered the atom and are reaching for the stars. These folks are probably well along in space travel and science. If this is the future, mankind's journey through the universe must be well underway. Yes, let's find out! Perhaps there's a newsstand in—

"Whoa! W-w-what just happened? I blinked, and it's . . . it's all ruined! No, this can't be! It can't! Oh, damn! The entire city

is smashed, completely obliterated. The sky is a misty, lumines-
cent white. Toxic fog banks drift by. The incredible blue building
is shattered, nothing but a twisted steel skeleton. There isn't a
window left intact. The streets are littered with fallen light posts
and crumbled bits of buildings. Nearly all the elevated highways
have collapsed in broken heaps, as have the tramways and con-
veyer paths. The big shopping center's supporting steel beams
are intact, but the cement walls have caved in. I can see into the
tattered, disheveled interior. Everywhere I look sprawls the complete annihilation of what was once so beautiful. This can't be!

'No! No! Noooo!'

"My words echo as if in a cavern. Is this humanity's fate? No,
I won't accept that! We're not that flawed. Perhaps there was a
natural disaster, a comet, or an asteroid. Who the hell knows? I
hope we didn't do this to ourselves in some idiotic war. No, this

16.2 In a blink of the eye, the city was utterly destoryed

must not be! It's nothing more than a passing fear. That's all it is! This is a possibility that doesn't have to become a reality! I know what to do. Let's create another vision! Yes, I have the power to do that. Our evolution doesn't have to lead to this insanity. Close your eyes and travel into the future. This great city will be brought back into existence one way or another.

"Now try to accelerate. Damn, it's difficult to move. But I have to! Come on, concentrate. Focus on gaining power. Ah, some acceleration is coming online. There we go . . . and here comes some power. The feedback loop is running again. My thoughts are moving. My mind is racing. But we have to increase this feedback loop. Oh, damn, visions of that awful destruction still linger. No! I must escape those apparitions! Draw in more energy, and reach deep inside.

"Yes, extraordinary power is now pulsing through me. I can still do this! There's the pressure and pain. Keep on accelerating. Keep that speed/energy feedback loop going. We must get into the future and go well beyond that destruction. Yet what's this presence I feel? It-it's pure evil, a kind of malice. Just ignore it. Concentrate on gathering energy. Find another beautiful city. We're heading into the future, but the acceleration makes me dizzy. Whoa. Now I'm way too woozy. That's enough. Put the brakes on. Come on, slow down. There you go. That's it. We've broken through.

"Damn it! I can't open my eyes. What the hell is going on? Something is interfering with my ability to see or perhaps to even be. It's like my eyes are glued shut. Come on, open your damn eyes. Screw this! I'll pry them open with my fingers if need be. You have to see! That's it. Open those damn eyes! Ah, now my vision is working, but what a struggle! Something is definitely wrong. Yet focus on what's here.

"Gosh, this is a much different place, an entirely new context. I'm in a dilapidated wooden shack. It's dusty and stifling in this place, hot as hell. There's no desk, pen, or paper. I'm sitting on a rickety wooden chair that sounds like it will break. Some beat-up furnishings and boxes are in here, but they're ancient. The dust must be about half an inch thick in here. It seems like this place was forsaken ages ago.

"Oh, a dirty window with cracked glass panes is on the far wall. Hmmm, let's get up and examine the surroundings. Perhaps I'm in a small town inhabited by people we can speak

16.3 Nothing remained in the future except dilapidated buildings set in a hot and arid desert environment

with. They'll help me figure out what the hell is going on. I'll have to wipe the dust off this window to see.

"God, this is depressing. An arid, deserted landscape surrounds a scattering of battered buildings. This is like an old ghost town, a place long abandoned. A few scraggly plants are clinging to existence, but no animals are in sight. There's almost no life at all. The sky is blinding. It's bright white, like all the ozone has burned off. There aren't even insects in this place. The land is like North America's southwest deserts, only even more desolate.

"Is this our future, or is it just a possibility of what can be? Someone must have built this shack and these buildings, but there's no one outside. There are no crops or water. There's no sign that people have been here for many years. This is a far cry from what we had! There was creation and beauty, and then came destruction and ruin. Out of that arose a barren existence on a scorched world. Man, I'm sweating bullets.

"No! No eff'n way! This is just a fear, not a reality. It doesn't have to be this way. Humanity can avoid this. I know it can. I have to find another setting, a different future. We'll make one! But it won't be—

"What's this? What the . . . ? Darkness shifts all around me. I'm in a void, but I didn't will or want this to occur. This has never happened before. And—

"Oh crap, there's definitely an evil force here. I can sense it. It's trying to break into my mind.

'No, no, no!'

"I have to stop this interference. It's spiteful and powerful. I fear this damn thing! There's a—

'SO YOU'RE THE GREAT EXISTENTIALIST!'

"It's a thunderous, mocking voice.

"I must answer. 'I'm not an existential—'

'You are nothing! You're full of fear!'

"More insults are being flung at me. I hear three or four voices. Bad odds.

'You're a weak, pitiful fool!'

'You are deluded and incompetent!'

"I'm surrounded and outnumbered. What should I do? There's nowhere to run, no place to hide. No! Don't be afraid. Conquer fear. Find your warrior spirit. Come on, give them a reply!

'You're all cowards! You fear light! You despise truth!'

"I must control my emotions! I have to—

"Argh! Damn! I've been hit! A-a-a brutal punch to the head. Oh, man! I can't think . . . c-can't think. What do—

"Ouch, another punch! And another! W-w-we're g-getting pummeled. Have to cover up and move. Heavy, heavy blows. Stunned, but must regain control. Come on, keep moving. Don't go down. Must defend—

"You have to fight back! There's no choice! I can't see, but I can still feel. Strike back in the same direction the blows are coming. Come on! Keep moving! Have to rally. Yes! One of my punches hit home! A good thud, for sure. We can do this. Yeah, I scored again, a hard one! Now keep moving and fight back.

"Someone shrieks, 'Fuck you, weakling!'

"They're cursing me. But I'm hurting them . . . or something. Yes, I'm regaining control. Have to shake out the cobwebs, though. Bob and weave and circle to the right. Must focus on—

"Damn, took another shot! But it wasn't as bad as the first ones. Oh, and a brutal hit to my nose. Enough of this crap! I'm pissed off! Remember the days of violence! Remember the brawls, playing football, all the fights? OK, let's go for it!

"Adrenalin flows, and my strength is growing. Now concentrate. Wow, what a punch I just landed. Stay on the attack. Head for where the most resistance is coming from. Keep pounding. That's it, close the distance. There's no choice, given the darkness. This is one hell of a brawl, though I've no idea what I'm facing! Still can't see a damn thing, but I'm hurting this oaf.

'God, please let me see what I'm up against.'

"Man, I'm still getting hit! This has never happened before, but I have to hold on. Ah, the darkness is lifting a little bit at a time. Yeah, now I can see! Darkness and light must be metaphors for . . . whoa, I almost got tagged again! Better stay focused.

"I'm facing a stocky fellow. He's about 25 years old. We're most likely outside the shack in open terrain. Nuts, just took another hard punch. Damn, pay attention to the fight! Good Lord, there are three others besides the creep I'm fighting. Back off and circle to the right. Now cut to the left. Grasp what's happening here. See what the light reveals.

'You can smash that faggot.'

'He's weak!'

'Go for his eyes.'

"They're shouting encouragement to this guy and insulting me. These are piss-poor odds. Screw this! Let's concentrate on the guy in front of me. There, I got in a good jab. Ignore the insults. That's it! Keep circling! Another good punch, and I tagged him yet again. Good combo. This reminds me of boxing at the—

"Damn, he got in a shot! That one wasn't so hard. Come on, shake it off. Man, this guy is tough. Tactics . . . know thy enemy. He's about five-nine and must weigh well over 200 pounds. Not an incredible physique, but he's strong as hell. It's like hitting a damn wall. He also has lots of endurance. Man, this guy wants to kill me. I can see it in his eyes. They're pitch-black, cold, ruthless. His face is pitted from acne, and the upper buttons on his navy-blue shirt are torn off. His jeans are dirty and torn at the knees.

"Ow! Took another hard shot. Have to end this.

'OK, you want a fight; you've got one!' I shout.

"There's no more fear. Attack!

'How does that feel? And, how about this?' I taunt.

"Bang, bang, bang! Man, I'm growling like an eff'n animal. Yeah, he's slowing down.

'Have a taste of your own brew!'

"I'm pounding this sucker, knocking him senseless. He can't hurt me now. Grab him and throw the bastard down. That was a good hip toss. Excellent! Man, what a thud!

'Now stay down!'

"Why am I fighting this fool? What the hell does this mean?

"One of his cronies yells, 'Get up!' Now they all chime in.

'Come on, he's sucking wind!'

"These cheerleaders keep egging him on. Better check them out. If they join in, I could be dead meat. They're standing close together. Ah, I see what they are. They're the personifications of our collective evils, our vices. They are within all of us to one extent or another. Maybe my knowledge is instinctual. I even know who the leader is. Don't understand how I know, but that's him!

'I know you! You're the Great Coward!' I yell.

"He sneers and hisses yet backs away a bit.

'You've many guises, but I know you!'

"The Great Coward wears a male form. It has a slender build, medium height, and dark complexion. It looks like a Persian this time around. However, it could just as easily become a Nazi, a Jew, a Russian, a priest, or a president. It can be anything and anyone, including me. It represents our prejudices, ego, vanity, intolerance, and everything that produces darkness, turmoil, and death. It appears to be around 40, but this beast is as old as time. It works from the inside out as well as the outside in.

'I know you!'

"The Great Coward glares at me. He has slight features and a thin physique, but his power is subtler and more pernicious. I know this beast all too well. Yes, the Coward's nature is evident. Its strength is manipulation and persuasion. It is the leader of the lost, of the greedy and shortsighted. It thrives off malice and discontent and revels in disaster and suffering.

"Whoa, its clothes are mesmerizing. The Great Coward wears a cape of sorts, and everything is black. The garb absorbs light; it's capturing my attention! The material devours reality like a sponge. The Coward's trying to . . . distract me, to consume my thoughts. Ignore the cape! Must shift my attention back . . . back to . . . the situation. Look away! Damn, you! Break free of its grip. Break free! You must check out its minions. It has a shorter associate and a taller one. The short one—

"Nuts! The guy I fought is getting back up. Better keep an eye on—

"Argh! What a shot! Can't think. Can't react. Going down . . . I'm f-f-falling. No, no, no, no. Come on! Shake it off. Back away. Must back off. Stumbling, no balance. Whoa, more lefts and rights. Staggered, staggered, I'm stunned. Darkness . . . back off and circle. Have to keep moving. Look inside!

'God, please! Please help me to help myself!'

"Adrenalin flows. Let's turn part of the beast on itself. Release the rage, the fury!

'AAAARRRRGGGGHHHHAAAA!'

"Wicked loud! That roar came from me! It echoes!

'No more of this abuse!'

"Let's finish him. Got in an excellent right hook to his face. Good thud! Again and again! Hold his left arm down and come over the top with a right. That's it! Temple shot! Got him good.

Come on, again, and again, and again. I'm rocking this fiend, and he reels and staggers.

'It's my turn! And there's no escape!' I laugh.

"He is weakening! He's—

"Damn it, we're in the darkness again! I should have shut my eff'n mouth and stayed focused. Of course, he can escape! The Great Coward is saving his minions to do his dirty work. No, they'll not flee into the darkness! That's where these bastards hide, safe from exposure and free to cause harm. Not this time! I'll pursue them beyond death if necessary. They'll destroy the future if allowed. Now close the distance and keep on hitting.

'Nothing will keep me from you! NOTHING!'

'You yellow bastard!' one jeers.

"Another chimes in, 'You're a fool and a failure.'

'He's a vulgar slob!' the third shouts.

'Ho, ho, ho. Do you think insults can stop me?'

"I'm laughing at them, but it's true. Insults can't stop me now. No fear or bruises, no darkness or barriers, nothing can hinder me now. Let's concentrate on finishing this guy before he can do more harm. Focus on where he is. Can't see, though I'm still scoring good hits. Their impacts land hard and fast. I can hear the blows hitting home. We have to keep at it.

"Ah, there's light now, and the scene has changed again. I'm in the back of a parked moving van and still facing this brute. Man, what does it take to defeat him? The van's open rear door provides enough sunlight to see. I have to make sense of the situation. His allies are present. The Great Coward and his short attendant lurk in the most shaded part of this boxy place, just behind the cab. The Coward's taller servant sits on a tire by the back door. Still surrounded but unafraid.

"The taller demon taunts my opponent, goading him on.

'Come on, you lame prick! Are you going to let that fat pussy kick your ass?'

"It doesn't matter. I'm pummeling this fiend, and his blows aren't having any effect. My punches are turning his face beet red. He isn't bleeding, but he's weakening. Let's finish him once and for all. A few hard shots should do the trick. Wow! My punches jolt his head back and toss his sweaty hair. His strength is eroding. Down he goes. He won't get up this time, but I'm not done here.

"Check out that bombastic fool sitting on the tire. The guy is about 30 and well over 6 feet tall. He must weigh 180 to 200 pounds. This could be a problem. The demon is big-boned, lean, and muscular, like a boxer. He has long red hair. Yeah, that'll make a good handhold. He looks like the quick-tempered bad guys in old Westerns, with a big mustache, dark eyes, and chiseled features. Better strike hard and fast when the time is right.

"No way! Nuts! The guy I just decked is trying to get up. Not this time. Time to get down and dirty.

'Here, try a kick to the face!'

"Wow! That rocked him big time, but he's still not out.

'How about a knee to the head?'

"Unbelievable! He keeps trying to get up! I'm fighting for my life here, yet I cannot finish this guy. This battle stands for something. Perhaps we can never destroy the beasts within and without. Maybe so, but we can sure as hell control them. Hell, he can't even stand. The battle's moving us closer to the van's entrance, and I'd better—

"Damn it, the Great Coward and his short companion are taking off. They scooted behind me and jumped out into the van's shadow. They're probably headed toward the vehicle's cab. I should have gone after him, to begin with! What the hell was I thinking? The guy I'm pummeling is already finished. Look at him. He's a beaten wreck. We've been wasting time on a defeated minion. Remember to go after the source of problems and not just their outward manifestations. Damn, it! Screwed up!

"I have to take care of the door-guard first. Oh, yeah, he wants to go for it. Be my guest! Yeah, he's getting ready to get up. Oh, there's an excellent opening for a right hand to the temple! This must be hard and fast, or the Great Coward will escape. Come on, let it fly.

"Wow, never hit anything that hard before! What a thud! Damn, my hand hurts, but he's down! No, he's trying to get up. No, no, no . . . he can't rise! He's down for good. Yeah! Incredible shot.

"It's clear why the Great Coward fled. Think about what's being learned here. The beasts from within and from without can be defeated. It's possible. They exert power through dark

16.4 A long and savage battle ensued with an implacable foe as the author fought for his life

deeds: violence, deceit, mockery, deflection, and the rest. They feed off greed, fear, anger, hatred, and other nihilistic traits. Yet if we conquer fear and doubt, the battle becomes winnable.

"That city can be saved! The future can be secured if we act. It's more than just possible. Yet there must be a better way to fight the beasts than with force. It has to do with light, which must represent revealed truth. Truth is power, especially when shared. It allowed me to see and permitted me to prevail during the fight. The Great Coward fears it.

"Come on! We have to find that bastard while it's still possible. I've wasted way too much time. That fiend probably covered a lot of ground while I dallied. There are two down and two to go. A big parking lot and several buildings are outside, including some large ones. A massive stadium on my left is set well back from the road. This building toward the right is very close. It's a large, boxy no-frills structure, perhaps four stories tall. Some open lots, trees, and other buildings are in front, like a town or a college. There is something special about this setting, something beyond a dream.

"No matter. Let's find that bastard. I'll jump out of the van and hunt him down." Alex paused for a moment, then continued. "Upon jumping into the bright sunlight, I awake in the conscious reality of my bedroom. The date was March 9, 1985. The time was 7:20 a.m."

"Ah, you wrote down the exact time and date," Madame Leonedria observed.

"I should have done that from the beginning!" Alex said. "Perhaps the dream event times are important, but I'm unsure why."

"That was incredibly violent," Mirai signed. "It's no wonder you don't like reliving the event. At times you were driven by ongoing occurrences. There were actions and reactions, often without much thought. During other periods, you were conscious of portents."

Alex shook his head. "Portents, like the lighted setting I jumped into just before waking. It ended up being the same one I saw six years later upon arriving at Penn State to begin my graduate work. It was identical. The location was the Shield's Building parking lot that faces the athletic facilities.

"Life was to offer many trials before my work began at Penn State, though they led me to the school. Four months after the dream, a severe medical event happened at work. It struck me out of the blue, or so it seemed. Some said it was a stroke. Others said I had a transient ischemic attack (TIA) or complicated migraine. Those damn head-bangers are brutal things. It was unexpected, though perhaps the headaches were warnings. In any case, I was numbed and disoriented, just as in the dream. Hell, I couldn't even speak properly.

"Thus began a long string of increasingly serious medical problems, one after another. There were savage headaches, collapsed discs, two heart attacks, diabetes, cortical atrophy, and more. They've torn me up over the years. Perhaps the blows and dark periods in the dream were premonitions. That fight continues even while I write these lines."

17

Violence, a Means or an End?

"So it does," Madame Leonedria said. "Before we address deeper issues, one thing is readily evident. The dream portrayed why you feel ill-suited for the task at hand."

"Absolutely!" Alex said. "I'm nothing like Gandhi, Martin Luther King, or any of those people! Passive resistance is just not my way. Hell, I'm an in-your-face savage at heart! My history and genetics helped make me this way, but there it is! Yeah, and you know it's true. I've openly advocated assassinations, as in killing killers. I can also be intolerant and petty. My personality is completely antithetical to building consensus and making compromises. Yet those things are needed to produce solutions to our problems. As for me, I'm more part of the problem than its cure."

"We know you're not right for the task, Alex," Mirai signed. "Your passion is both a strength and a weakness. It drives you to react, albeit often without thought or control. On the other hand, that dedication has allowed this project to be completed, despite numerous setbacks and ill health. Yet those we most need are being moved as we speak. These people can look beyond present impulses and into future possibilities. They can save the future."

"Unto every being, there is a purpose," Madame Leonedria said. "You're a fighter, my son. You do not flag or give up. Isn't survival something that requires such determination?"

"Yeah," Alex said. "We spoke about life's tests. At a fundamental level, they require us to act and react."

"Especially if we're facing existential threats," Mirai signed. "Surely, you would sacrifice yourself to protect life."

"Without hesitation," Alex said. "But I'm far too reactionary. My nature violates the approach to our problems that the readers need to take. People of reason and peace can accomplish far more good than angry and violent sots. Stridency has a place, but it can be blinding. People lash out without reason or thought."

"At least they act!" Mirai signed. "Believe me, the struggle ahead requires actions against hostile and entrenched interests. Struggle and conflict are inevitable."

"Thus, some warrior spirit is needed," Madame Leonedria said. "It's a matter of degree. The question is, do the goals of

17.1 We cannot defeat a beast by becoming one

preserving this world justify using violence, be it direct or indirect? There is no easy answer. Some will note that violence is an aspect of the Great Coward metaphor woven throughout your dream. One could easily contend that we cannot prevail by becoming like the forces we must stand against. After all, you failed in the dream. You spent all your time and energy fighting the wrong foe! Meanwhile, the Great Coward slipped away. Tell me, who is the Great Coward?"

"It can be you, me, and even the reader," Alex replied. "It is ubiquitous and constantly shifting. I believe the Great Coward metaphor represents the negative aspects of our nature rather than a distinct entity. Some opt to anthropomorphize our negative tendencies. They call the resultant amalgamation the devil, Satan, Lucifer, Iblis, Jinn, Mara, Set, and the rest. We thus craft abject metaphysical entities that some of us readily become one with. These manifestations gain presence through our various weaknesses—the beasts within us. Lies, greed, egotism, hatred, myopia, ignorance, prejudice, and other destructive traits become our masters. Indeed, some wallow and revel in their own depravity. It has been this way for millennia. Personifying our evils as external forces merely provides a wanton means of abrogating personal responsibility. Yeah, the devil made me do it."

"Do those who will rescue this world harbor these traits?" Mirai signed.

"You would know the answer better than I," Alex said. "You probably know who they are. I'm trapped in time, a linear creature. Regardless, I believe all people have demons to one extent or another. Some are fostered or constrained by nature and nurture. However, they'll often surface given the right circumstances. Even a saint will kill, and many will lie when they think it expedient. We all have. Yet most of us are ashamed to confess that we can be motivated by vulgar forces. Thus, the moniker 'Great Coward.' After all, that is what we can easily become."

"Indeed," Madame Leonedria said. She poured herself another glass of wine, adding, "Those doing the greatest damage to this world often deny, deflect, and obfuscate. They avoid personal responsibility by all possible means. They wrap a veil of deception around their perfidy and live by the big lie."

"Yes, such a wretch found power in 2016," Alex said. "He mocked others to distract attention from his flaws, much like the demons I fought were mocking me. The fool mesmerized the susceptible with deception and exaggeration. By all objective measures, he was an opportunistic and feckless liar. However, he had followers, wretched, deluded, and inane cultists though they were. They willfully embraced deceit and made a mockery of faith. Their actions were no less damaging than his.

"He is the person I wanted dead, and I didn't hesitate to say so publicly. Oh, folks of my ilk eventually pushed him out of power, but that is not good enough. Part of me still wants him dead. That man is absolutely loathsome in every possible way. Of course, I also recognize my perfidy. After all, any impetus that drives us toward killing threatens life. Which is the real demon? Is it what we perceive as an existential threat? Or the desire to obliterate that threat by all possible means?"

"Perhaps asking the question is a fundamental part of our evolution," Mirai signed. "I studied the period you're writing about. It was an odious time, and you lived in a conflicted world. The hypocrisy was astounding, as was the venality. Scholars from my time found embracing greed just as disturbing as accepting lies."

"We've seen the story replay itself throughout time and space," Madame Leonedria said. "A vested few conspire. Their goals are ego-bound, as in garnering resources, power, or money for personal gain. Whenever possible, they conduct their affairs in secret. They fear the light of public scrutiny. They cloak their duplicity under many guises. Some appeal to national security, the common good, or manifest destiny. Others promote demands based on patriotism, God's will, or another worn-out euphemism. Yet they strive to enlist prejudice, insecurities, and base desires, seldom revealing their true motives.

"Entire societies are led as sheep," Mirai signed. "Their masters' herd dogs bark out fallacious news releases. Meanwhile, mass media ditto-heads pass on the lies. 'Remember the Maine' morphs into the 'Guns of November' and then the 'Day of Infamy.' And misery comes unto anyone who strays from the directed course, who dare say, 'No!' Power begets power, wealth begets wealth, lies beget lies."

"In the meantime, the sky turns a bitter white, and the land becomes barren," Alex sadly said. "A short-term gain for a few becomes the long-term legacy of a violent and uninhabitable world. That is what I experienced in the dream. Our kind went from extraordinary achievements to utter desolation."

"The flawed inevitably fail," Madame Leonedria said, "often because of their myopia and inertia. It is common, my son. Despite understanding this truism, the thought terrifies you. The emptiness of nihilism was ingrained during your communion with Anne and the nexus. You experienced the concept of nothingness, the sheer absence of being! It horrified you! Hence, the visions of that smashed city forever burn your soul. Your gleaming cities could be leveled one day, just as you witnessed. Indeed, your entire species could turn into dust. The roots of nihilism are deeply ingrained."

"So, too, are positive traits," Mirai signed. "Humanity possesses empathy, honesty, generosity, tolerance, kindness, foresight, courage, and love. These are the tools of salvation."

"I know that, Mirai," Alex said. "But enlisting them isn't easy."

"Sometimes, shared pain is the necessary impulsion," Mirai signed. A tear rolled down her cheek. "Believe me, we have suffered terribly. You witnessed an abandoned shack within a desolate landscape during your dream. That scene is a horrible reality for many of us. We occasionally make pilgrimages to the barrens, wrapped in layers of protection. There are innumerable deserted towns and cities, their empty streets and buildings crumbling into dust. I've walked through long abandoned graveyards, striving to hear our ancestors' echoes. One reads the stones—names, dates, and a few words. Yet there are no answers, no reasons. Some curse our past. But here I am, striving to help reshape it."

"Such incursions have their limits!" Madame Leonedria coldly observed. She stared at Mirai, long and hard. "If this project succeeds, all you have known will never be. Your mother, father, and those you love . . . they will become discontinuities. That includes you, my dear. The species may prosper, but you and millions of others will not."

"I knew that before the jump was made," Mirai signed.

"I didn't!" Alex interjected. "So, humanity is utterly screwed if we do nothing, and you and many others are screwed if we succeed. That sucks!"

"This happens when the past is changed," Madame Leonedria said. She pointed at Mirai and added, "I don't fully approve of you even being here, Mirai. These readers must make their own way! This species lives or perishes based on how it behaves. The universe gives us opportunities, not guarantees!"

"A true lover of life would never say such a thing," Mirai signed, leaning forward and staring into Madame Leonedria's eyes. "Existence occasionally mandates taking chances, and that's something you'll just have to live with! I would not be here if there was any other choice."

"You're either desperate or arrogant," Madame Leonedria said, "or perhaps both. In any event, Alex seems to worship existence as much as his notion of God. Isn't that right, my great existentialist?"

"I'm not a damn existentialist!" Alex insisted. "Well, at least as the term applies to the philosophies of Kierkegaard and Sartre. Of course, many derivatives have evolved. Most branches of the philosophy claim to embrace personal choice, freedom, and individual existence. It's a damn hodgepodge, though! Much of the idea is based on individuals striving to rationally navigate a supposedly irrational universe. Yeah, the philosophy assumes we can separate ourselves from what we're part of! Its adherents are like a herd of cats. Some reject science, ancient philosophy, God, and other notions. Others subscribe to the ideas. They have few consistent doctrines. Some applications are helpful, but damn few!

"However, I am certainly an existentialist in some senses. My beliefs aim to preserve life and to perceive our roles in the cycles of being. I see us as an aspect of existence that can comprehend the whole. To achieve that end, we need survival, time, and reflection. Accordingly, we can become conscious of the ideas we are part of. In so doing, we provide these notions with a presence in this realm of being. I regard that as life's purpose. In essence, a lover of life loves existence. My tormentors had this application for the term in mind. I'm sure of it. So perhaps the taunt was well directed, existentialism redefined."

"This is the sense that best suits you," Mirai signed. "It seems predicated on an evolution based on constraining our negative traits."

"I'm not sure such as thing is possible," Alex said. "Besides, who am I to talk about chaining our inner beasts? I've yet to shackle my resentment toward my father, who died years ago! And you know how petty and childish I can be. Many reading these words also have demons based on this event or that happenstance. They fester in our souls. It doesn't matter whether their existence was justified at one time. For example, one could easily argue that gross injustice can evoke a demon of vengeance. But even after justice is achieved, the demon often remains in place. It can thus color our thoughts and actions, driving us to dubious means and ends by its presence."

"It's not a matter of eliminating the beasts within," Madame Leonedria explained. "You should have learned that from the dream! The goal should be redirecting them toward more positive ends. Alex, it is deeds that matter most! So yes, if a warrior resides within, turn it toward protecting life. If greed is a problem, redirect it toward feeding the masses. If egotism is the malady, become the best at educating those in need.

"Your kind is on the cusp. Humanity teeters between being and non-being. This tiny world will go the way of so many other lost chances if people don't act. How many planets do you suppose there are that were destroyed by their inhabitants' excesses? How many smashed and abandoned cities do you think I have seen? Such are nature's ways and means. Be that as it may, the dream told you the tools to use."

"Yeah, the pen and paper," Alex sadly said. "I still have my doubts. Those dreams could have been mere delusions, artifacts of an underlying malady. Perhaps I'm mistaken in thinking these words can or will have an impact. They'll probably get lost in a sea of books few read."

"The time capsule will produce an impact," Mirai signed. "The problem is motivating people to act in their 'now'! This was a critical period, Alex. Our kind was on the wrong path, and many knew it. But humanity had gone too far well before my era. The situation has become untenable, and there is little we can do. Our time is running out."

"Those who prioritize satiating immediate desires pay little heed to future consequences," Madame Leonedria said. "Your pale white sky is already forming on this little world while the temperature increases by the year. What does humanity do? It dallies! Some even deny there is a problem! Others argue about how to address it. As for wars, that's merely one of humanity's worries. Your world already faces brutal environmental degradation, plagues, and hunger. These horsemen will kill far more than wars alone. So, tell me, do you think this conversation will do any good?"

"Mirai indicated it may," Alex said. "I have to hope she is right, but I'm unsure. First of all, will anyone read this text?

The book could bomb . . . big time. Furthermore, what is truth, and what is fantasy? Whatever the case, I know this pebble of thought is my responsibility. That is a certainty. Perhaps this work will create a ripple or two in some souls. Perhaps not." He turned toward Mirai and added, "I'm trying, my friend. It's not an easy task, and there are no guarantees. However, the notion that our success could mean your demise drives me crazy."

"I know the consequences all too well, yet there was no choice," Mirai signed. "You sought my perspective in the diaries, and how could I refuse?"

"Thus, the future informs the past," Madame Leonedria scornfully observed. "And it does so in ways that go beyond our conversation here. Our task is nearly complete, although we must address another seeing state."

"Yes, and it was the last one," Alex said.

18

Finding a Reason

Alex mustered the energy to describe his last dream to the readers and his friends. He lacked confidence the project would work, but he knew he must try his best. It was a triumphant and bittersweet moment, all wrapped into one.

"At the time, my ability to use seeing states was eroding. This coincided with the medical problems that ended my coaching career. There was a growing lack of balance and brutal headaches. They were a bitch, an absolute misery. It was a forlorn period. You see, I loved coaching. The job ideally suited my nature and talents. It all fell apart when my body became unsound.

"The problem pushed me onto a new career path. I experienced some success as a writer, so going back to school to study journalism seemed the natural thing to do. There was a vocation

18.1 Finding a reason and purpose to change a situation or prospect requires both thought and actions

that didn't entail moving tons of weights every day. I worked hard and did well. In fact, I eventually became a scholar, a PhD. My education rapidly increased while my health declined. Now I'm a wreck. Every day is a struggle to simply stay awake."

"The gift of seeing was born of a curse," Madame Leonedria observed.

"As in my shrinking brain and growing memory issues?" Alex asked. "We could have interminable debates about cause and effect, but one thing is sure: the dream states had nothing to do with my diabetes, joint, and cardiovascular problems! That's where excess leads when combined with poor genetics. In any case, I was blessed by one more seeing state, the final chapter in a long litany.

"We'll need some additional context, Alex," Mirai signed. "Perhaps your situation caused the dream."

"Maybe, but I was still young and strong at the time," Alex explained. "The dream occurred about a year and a half after the Great Coward battle and put a cap on my astral experiences. I was 34 or so, as I recall. At the time, I suffered from joint and disc damage and migraines. There was also some fatigue and dizziness, but I could toss 300 pounds around like a toy. Hell, benching it by 20 repetitions or more was not a problem back then."

"You've always put great stock in physical prowess," Madame Leonedria said. "However, let us get to the dream."

"It was unlike the others," Alex said. "The seeing state simply came upon me one night. So, did the nagging thought that my time on Earth was ebbing. There was no precursor other than absolute awareness, none of the usual speed and power feedback loop. A feeling of despair and futility overcame me while floating in the darkness. Then, a dreamscape began to form."

Alex looked into the water bowl to clear his thoughts. He then dived back into memories while reliving the experience.

"My senses are becoming attuned," he said. "Oh, it's slow going. This transition isn't smooth. No, not easy at all. Man, it's an effort to even see. Come on, you, focus! Ah, my vision's coming online, slow but sure. Yeah, I can see some light and now a few objects.

"Hmmm, a sizeable glass-faced display cabinet is in front of me. It's difficult to discern the contents. It is like looking through a scarred, dirty porthole into a dimly lit scene. Perhaps my illness is affecting these dreams. Don't know what's up, but there's still the power to learn if we strive to perceive. Come on, now. You have to try. Tilt your head a bit, and the images may come into focus.

"Ah, that's much better. Huh, there are several hundred small warship models on glass shelves. They're 1/2400 scale General Head Quarters products, an excellent line. Some are nicely finished, but most are unmade. There is row after row of unfinished hulls with gun turrets and parts of superstructures laid out neatly alongside. These are from my collection. I'd know the workmanship anywhere. Well, the kits will never be completed, at least by me. Let's hope someone sets them right.

"This is kind of neat. I see flashes of the death machine museum from the Nexus Dream. Images of a dream within a dream. Perhaps some of the old power remains. I should help make a museum that demonstrates war's futility and cost. It could help others learn from what was seen during these dreams. My models could be dumped there. Yeah, that's a great idea. Well, that project isn't going to be finished by me. There are no resources or time. Yeah, I've squandered too much of my life already.

"Let's focus on my location. This seems to be a one-room efficiency apartment or perhaps a room within a house. The place is appointed with simple furniture and a few model-filled display cases. Some bookcases and a desk are among the furnishings. Man, my head is pounding. Even in a damn dream, there are headaches. Nuts!

"At least my senses are becoming more attuned, but it's taken a lot of time and effort. Whatever is causing these damn symptoms is pervasive. Perhaps that's the lesson: there isn't much time to finish things. Then again, it's not clear what the goal is. Well, I should write about these dreams. That's my responsibility, or so it seems.

"Sunlight shines through an open window on the opposite side of the room. Let's look outside and see where this place is situated. Whoa! I almost fell. What the heck is this? I can barely walk. Something is wrong with my damn legs. They're stiff and weak. It hurts to even move. My joints are on fire, and my muscles aren't working right. All I can manage is a slow shuffle. Unbelievable joint pain, and my balance and strength are shot. What the hell is the matter with me?

"This is only a dream. You can control dreams. Now, get to that window, come hell or high water. You can do this. Put one foot in front of the other. That's it: left, right, left, right. This is awful. This is an infirmity, one of my greatest fears. God help me if I run into a 10-year-old Girl Scout. She could kick my ass and make me buy cookies. Ho, ho, ho, like I need to be forced to purchase cookies! Come on, we're getting closer.

"At last, the window. Whew, what a struggle. I'm sucking wind and my heart pounds. Let's rest a bit and check out the surroundings. Yeah, catch your breath. Man, I am way out of shape.

"This place is adjacent to a forest. We're surrounded by trees of all kinds. This reminds me of past dreams, like those when I was a kid. Various lush pines and conifers are close by, a collage of green hues. Long grass grows where the sun shines through the tree branches. Oh, what a great scene. Shrubs and bushes hug the ground, and those rocks look like good perches to contemplate nature. This is a beautiful sight.

"What a day! Bright sunshine, deep blue sky, and gentle winds. Ah, feel that breeze wafting through the window's screen. The air smells fresh and clean. The sun's warmth on my face and hands is delightful. Words can't do this setting justice. Yeah, this is serenity. This is contentment. Ah, listen to the birds sing! There's a robin and some chickadees. They are singing away to beat the band. Birds are the messengers of God, or so they say. All is good.

"Oh, look at that! A medium-sized dog is heading my way. He has black, curly hair and frolics on the path leading from the woods to my home. Ah, he sees me! His tail wags enthusiastically, and he barks a salutation. This guy must have come by to say hello. Perhaps I know him. It's good to have company. Let's greet him.

'Owe eew doin' fewwa?'

"W-w-what's the matter with my speech?"

'Owe eew doin'—'

"Oh, no! I can't speak properly. This can't be! I can barely see and can't walk, worth a damn. Now my speech is distorted!

'Pease, Gowd, don' wet tis be ma fate!'

"No, no, no! This is unacceptable. To hell with this nightmare. I'll cover my face and shut out this miserable fate. I'm not going to become a helpless cripple who can hardly talk! No way!

I must accelerate my thoughts and form a new destiny. We can do this! Concentrate! Now, focus your thoughts and accelerate. You have to get the speed/energy feedback loop going again.

"The birds are still chirping. Ignore it! Focus! Come on! We still have the power to escape this state. Set your mind to flight! Ah, now I'm moving again, but it isn't easy. Have to gain more energy, much more. All is blackness, although there's a bit of acceleration. Some energy is coming in, but a lot more is needed. No, this feedback loop is way too slow. I need help.

'Gowd, hewp me! Pease, fee me from tis mishery. I don wan ta be ah cwipple!'

"My words are garbled, and they echo. The sound is deafening. It's as though I'm in some kind of cavern. What's that? What the heck? Gosh, the songbirds can still be heard above my own din. How strange.

"Man, I'm not moving nearly fast enough. Concentrate! I must concentrate. Yes, that's it! There, the feedback loop is back online. Now let the speed become energy, and the energy morph into more speed. Oh, my head aches and hands tingle. This has never happened before, but we must go on. Nuts, my head is pounding, pulsating. Ignore it! Come on, you can do this! Dizzy, nauseous. I-I-I just can't go on. I can't! So damn weak, but have to—

"No, this is the end. There's no power. There's nothing. We're adrift in a dark void.

"But what's this? I can . . . I can still hear those songbirds. What does it mean? Ah, thoughts are pouring in. My blind efforts to escape reality prevent me from living fully or noting what is alive. My concerns are drawn inward. Things that could provide life with meaning and joy are shut out. This includes hobbies, a glorious summer day, the lush greens of nature, a playful bounding dog, and the melodies of birds. All are forsaken in the vain pursuit of the impossible. I beg God for salvation but fail to see that deliverance surrounds me. I let fear of infirmity and death prevent me from living fully during my journey through life. Even in a dream, I try to flee from the truth. How silly I am! How devoid of insight.

"Ah, the path and scenery suddenly appear again, as do feelings of warmth and serenity. Nature's presence and God's love embrace me.

'Thank you, God, for helping me to see. I'm at peace.'

"In a split second, I returned to the reality of my bed. The dream happened on October 11, 1986, at exactly 7 a.m. It foretold what's happening to me now, over 37 years later. There are times when every step is agonizing, especially since the discs in my lower back collapsed. A flight of stairs seems like a damn mountain at times. Heart, kidneys, liver . . . I've damaged them all. Even my brain is shriveled, or so they say. I also have cataracts, like the marred porthole I could barely see through during the dream."

"Ah, the joys of growing older," Madame Leonedria said with a laugh. "Still, we can make of life what we will. To be sure, you're still young and strong in the 'reality' we share."

"Yeah, the freedom imagination allows," Alex said. "My mom used to tell me the golden years are not so golden. She was right. Yet that dream showed me life's positives, even when surrounded by a sea of woes. I'm more than thankful to have gotten this far, and count every day as a blessing. By all rights, that heart attack should have taken me out years ago. Few survive a 100 percent blockage of the left anterior descending artery, the dreaded 'widow maker.' What a rush that was! You can feel yourself slipping away. Hell, my damage indicators were 40 times normal!"

"Do you think your survival was a matter of chance or intervention?" Mirai signed.

"I had a damn good doctor," Alex said.

"Was that a matter of chance or intervention?" Mirai signed again.

"Imposed fate versus happenstance," Alex said. He shook his head while pondering aloud, "Was the script already written that way? Or did events unfold according to the laws of probability?"

"Is there a difference?" Madame Leonedria asked.

"That is the question," Alex said. "All hung in the balance. I was suspended between life and death. That much was abundantly clear. This text needed to be completed. I pondered it even while slipping in and out of consciousness. The task has served as an impetus for years. So, here I am, typing away with two fingers on a rain-soaked day. This is my responsibility, my purpose. As far as the seeing state goes, the experience of being crippled was my last lucid dream. It was the end of the line."

"Nonsense," Madame Leonedria said with a dismissive wave. "What is the difference between what we share now and a dream? Besides, you still dream, my son. I know you do."

"Yeah, I still have occasional prophetic dreams," Alex admitted. "Like the dream about my father warning me to be strong enough to carry a bed or Obama being elected president before he had even won the primaries. There were even some dreams about this book, but the subjects range far and wide. I found several of them recently, written in longhand. I don't recall having written them, let alone remember the events in great detail."

"I would like to hear about them," Mirai signed. "Several dreams were mentioned in your diaries, but few written artifacts survived. The paper had decomposed, and the primitive computer discs were unreadable. Take heed, and prepare the vault more properly. And yes, I need to study those records."

"Don't you find that request odd, considering we share thoughts?" Alex said.

"Stop teasing the reader," Mirai signed with a sardonic smile.

"Well, one dream remains especially vivid," Alex said. "Another fellow of like belief and I were setting up symbols within display cases. Even the crystal globe was there, albeit just one of many displays. The signs expressed the idea that we are one with all, including the concept of God. Well, we knew the notion would be perceived as heretical by some. Controversy awaited, but our conviction overcame fear.

"A crowd had gathered to see the display, although we were not quite ready. Indeed, the doors to our meeting room were closed and locked. I grew fearful upon hearing angry voices and considered changing the displays. Then concerns for my friend's welfare came to mind. The outside commotion increased, and I briefly opened the door to examine the situation.

"Several large and angry men glared at me. In response, I quickly tried closing the door. It was too late. The people surged forward and attempted to force the doors open. I did my best to stand firm. Unfortunately, they were gigantic fellows, like the weightlifters and football players I once trained. It was impossible to hold them back, and they poured into the room.

"In their collective glowers and aggressive stances, it was clear that my friend and I would face a grim fate. There was no time to do anything to appease them. However, that was fine with me. My fear had turned into resolve. I didn't want to change the displays, because the symbols were truthful. Yes, we would stand firm. Happily, I awoke just as the angry crowd surged toward me!

"This dream was more mundane than prior seeing experiences, although it was unsettling. It happened on February 28, 2013, at around 5 in the morning. The dream was probably related to a rewrite of this book's conclusion. My friends, it's impossible to back off the text's central theme. We must be true to ourselves."

"Can you express that theme in a single line?" Madame Leonedria asked.

Without hesitation, Alex said, "All my experiences lead me to conclude that we are one with a creator that is one with all things."

19

Being One with All Things

Madame Leonedria and Mirai looked at one another and smiled.

"Can you repeat that?" Madame Leonedria asked. "We wouldn't want the readers to miss the central theme of this book . . . the theme of life."

"We are one with a creator that is one with all things," Alex repeated.

"This idea stands in opposition to those who believe that God is distinct from humanity and the universe," he continued. "I perceive us as parts of a dynamic process that constantly re-writes itself as forms change and evolve. The process was born

19.1 Becoming one with all things requires empathy, and especially if we are to work for change

from the one that became many. Ultimately, its impetus was the giving of self for the sake of those who could reflect upon the whole. As Mirai would say, it was an act of love."

"Who would want to spend eternity alone?" Madame Leonedria asked. "Isn't this existence we share with the reader an extension of the processes that created us?"

"In the metaphysical sense," Alex said. "Am I any more real than you are to the person reading these lines?"

"I suspect you and Verity will discuss that subject at length," Madame Leonedria said.

"Do you think it ominous that the skies open up and thunder rumbles overhead while you write these lines?" Mirai signed. "*Iulii primus*, MMXVII. Does the date give you pause? After all, you are a believer in signs."

"Yes, the day of these passages brought severe rains and some flooding," Alex noted. "The power may go out at any second, as it is prone to do during tempests. Yet I don't fear things that cannot be controlled or prepared for."

"So, let the words flow, my child," Madame Leonedria said. "Yet the seeing dreams do not."

"Dreams, in general, are getting less frequent," Alex said. "The astral and lucid states just don't happen anymore. They're done for good, or at least I think so."

"Why do you suppose that is?" Mirai signed. "Why would one have such powerful experiences only for them to stop so abruptly?"

"They claim my brain is wasting," Alex said. "I'm probably long past the point wherein the resources needed to experience lucid dream states function. It's a neurodegenerative process of some sort. Perhaps we already talked about this. I forget. Anyway, the doctors come up with one alphabet-soup diagnosis and then another. Oh, it was multisystem atrophy for 20-odd years. Then it was normal pressure hydrocephalus, and some said Alzheimer's or frontotemporal dementia. Who the hell knows? Besides, diagnoses do not change realities. I forget people's faces, times, episodes, and much more. If these dreams hadn't been recorded years ago, all would be lost."

"I know you think these cortical problems are related to your having experienced the seeing state," Madame Leonedria said. "Do you wish to contemplate that possibility any further?"

"Not really," Alex said. "Causation doesn't change my reality or help the reader. Besides, cortical atrophy can be caused by many things, including genetic disorders. They tell me it probably isn't from migraines or other vascular processes. You know, like lots of little strokes. Oh, I got hammered by migraines for years. Still do on occasion! Research shows they can cause brain damage, but nothing to the extent that my MRIs indicate.

"In some genetic conditions, neurotransmitters can build up in the synapses of various brain regions. This eventually leads to neuron death from over-stimulation effects. That can cause cortical atrophy, but so too can many other things. I stopped caring, although some medical people find my case interesting."

"Do you think those with us can experience similar dreams?" Mirai signed.

"Some may," Alex said. "It depends on their genetics and life experiences. I suspect biochemical or neurological quirks allowed me to experience seeing states. That could also happen with others, given the right context and circumstances. It may even be the case that my power to move while within a dream was due to abnormal stimulation effects in brain structures associated with movement and consciousness. My cerebellum, frontal, and parietal lobes have all gotten whacked. Well, that's what they tell me. Yet here I am, typing away with these two clumsy fingers. The one on my left hand is not cooperative today, but we're managing. Did you do this to me, Mirai?"

"You certainly asked us to change you," Mirai signed.

"Yes, in the diary," Alex recalled. "It was all about stimulating the dreams. Nothing else mattered. Hmmm, perhaps I should have thought more about the cost. My mind has been shredded."

"I know, child," Madame Leonedria softly said. "You petitioned the future for the sake of the ones now here."

"It's all so damn hazy to me," Alex said. He lifted his eyebrows and shrugged his shoulders. "It seems like choices were made even before I came to be. It was one of those 'If this, then that' deals. I'm unsure if this makes any sense, and I couldn't care less. They use terms like 'dementia.' I don't think that's the case yet, but my time to share these thoughts is short. I suppose the same could be said of those with us. We all have to act while there is still time to."

"Do you have any regrets?" Mirai signed. "The seeing states have made your life much more difficult."

"I'd do it again in a heartbeat!" Alex said. "There's no doubt. Becoming disabled pushed me in some very positive directions. Hell, I went from being a drug-crazed punk to a scholar! Who would have thought that possible? I'm still striving to learn in whatever time remains. Books and degrees have been completed, but this could be my last shot."

"What was your most important lesson?" Madame Leonedria asked.

"My main observation is that I'm not exceptionally bright," Alex said with a smile. "I have to work at it. Perhaps the knowledge gained by study allowed me to tell this story. It was impossible to interpret my dreams without it. I had no plan to return to school until my health began declining. I would have been happy to remain a weight-training coach until I dropped. One action resulted in another. Now we are here sharing these words in a setting of thought. For better or worse, much of the project has been completed, though we still have some areas to explore."

"Some editors didn't like the ending you crafted," Mirai observed. "And you do look tired. Perhaps the text should end here."

"Perhaps," Alex said. He looked at his hands, noting his bent and twisted fingers. "The corporeal me is leaking through." He rotated his shoulders back and winced while opening and closing his fists.

"That's to be expected," Madame Leonedria said. "It has been a very long night, Alex, and dawn will break soon enough. It is probably time for you to rest."

"I have an eternity to rest," Alex said. "However, we have a few more things to discuss, especially concerning actions and responsibilities. Oh, and it's not like we'll be able to discuss them after Verity awakens."

"She will not allow any discussions unrelated to her," Mirai signed.

"That is the truth of things," Alex said, "if you'll forgive the pun."

"Such a capricious child," Madame Leonedria said. She glanced toward Verity and added, "It is easy to understand why. Her nature and existence are predicated upon context. Poor Verity. She must constantly interpret how all things relate to her at any given moment to simply exist. The truth is a slave to the moment. Be that as it may, at least Verity has her past again. It provides some tenuous continuity. Given all this, Alex, why do you care about her so much?"

"She's a love I share with many," Alex said, "though no one can possess Verity. She is for all to seek, yet no one to own." He turned to Mirai. "Verity is a desire, although you are a necessity. I can see that more clearly than ever. Getting close to you is unfathomable to me. Yes, in this text, I can manipulate the time that separates us. Oh, but I long for so much more. Look at my hands. Look at my face. I cannot wear imagination's patina forever, my dear."

"Do you think I care for you any less because of our different natures?" Mirai signed. "Do you think for an instant that I don't embrace what you're trying to share with our readers?"

"Yes, the ones who will act," Alex said. "They'll act for your sake, Mirai."

"Isn't that what you've always wanted?" Madame Leonedria said. "Haven't you begged the future to inform the past throughout this book? You surmise that if humanity survives life's tests, it will eventually develop the ability to walk through time. You also believe that humanity's progeny will ultimately influence their own past. This is especially true if they feel there is no choice. They will thus help shape the species' future. Isn't that why Mirai is with us right now?"

"Of course it is," Alex said. "She was the missing element in the earlier texts. She is possibility's child. I have known her since

I first became aware. Since my earliest days, I saw her lurking in the corners where no one looks."

"Why do you so need me, Alex?" Mirai signed.

"Your existence means there is a future," Alex said. He reached across the divide separating them and touched her cheek. "I was never blessed with children. Lord knows they would have been genetic and emotional misfits, much like me. Yet those readers who are with us . . . I love them, Mirai, like brothers and sisters. I do. They gave rise to you and what will be. And perhaps they can strive to make the future a better place for their progeny. This text was all so cold and clinical without your presence. We need hope, my dear. We need hope above all else."

"So here I am," Mirai signed.

"Oh, you've always been here," Alex said. "You've been an influence, an agent of change. I need you. We all do, though some don't know it."

"I am the cautionary tale," Mirai signed. "If humanity doesn't change, I'll have to live through the terrible times that lead me here. There will be no grass, trees, or birds for me or any of the reader's distant progeny. If that truth is a manipulation, did it come from you or me, Alex? If you understood that grand linkage you once shared, the answer will be clear."

"Are we all parts of that linkage?" Madame Leonedria asked.

"We are if the reader perceives, recalls, and contemplates what you've said," Alex replied. "Hell, I'll be long gone when some read this text. That prospect harbors no fears within me. The ancients advised if there is no hereafter, all of eternity will be like a peaceful night's sleep. If there is a type of life after life, think of the grand adventures! It would be the greatest of all seeing states. Of course, our being may also echo a bit into the future via these words."

"We will exist as disembodied thoughts," Madame Leonedria said.

"In part," Alex admitted. "However, I'm not sure there is any great distinction between thoughts and realities. We often get a feeling of immersion when reading a captivating book. Our 'real' world disappears. In its stead is a realm of imagination. We feel love and wonder. Dragons soar on high, and we see the glint in a lover's eye. We can even travel to the dawn of a new world or the end of time. Our present becomes one with a universe of thought and abstraction."

"This is despite the time and distance that separates us from the writer and the events being described," Mirai signed. "Even so, some reading these words manage to glean and predict what we may say. In fact, a few are doing so right now. They are using their minds to go beyond this text."

"Which demonstrates the power of thought," Alex said. "Indeed, all of us 'within' this text are metaphysical constructs to one extent or another. We're the end result of symbol processing. Yet, to the reader, we have pasts and ways of thinking. These allow those perusing these lines to extrapolate a probable pattern of behavior. Interesting."

"It is more than merely interesting," Mirai signed. "If the future is to intervene in the past, would it not do so via metaphysical resources?" Mirai grew angry as she continued, her expression betraying barely controlled rage. "Let those readers with us contemplate what their distant relations may be thinking. They have a responsibility to do so! This text allowed me to climb Mount Major and know beauty, life, and friendship. Let the readers now imagine our skies, lands, and waters. Let them gaze upon how we have to live! Wander the endless passages of our subterranean world, the shielded habitats that allow us to cling to life. Gaze upon the hydroponic laboratories, sterile replacements for amber fields of grain. There will be no wind, rain, or the sun's gentle warmth in our habitats, just the endless drone of the many machines that keep us alive. Let the readers see the suffering and discord their wretched self-absorption caused! Alex, where do you think your dreams of desolation came from?"

"Enough!" Madame Leonedria implored. "This is a dangerous game to play." She shook her head in frustration. "Imagination can touch upon the truth, but some harbor burdens that color their perceptions. You know that, Mirai! You also know there are those with us who can and will make a difference."

"My main concern is with actions that must be taken in the present," Alex said. "Sure, we can use imagination to touch upon the future. Hell, we may even grasp and share future truths. Nonetheless, we're on our own. No one will bail us out of the mess we're in! Certainly not some cosmic white-haired thunderer! What, is 'he' going to fly to our rescue for the sake of three Hail Mary prayers and an Act of Contrition?

"Nor will nature forever ignore the insults we toss at it daily! It's up to us to act. If we do, the species survives. If not, then nothingness we become. In any case, sharing this journey with the readers is all I can do. It's unclear whether many will believe or accept what's been put down on these pages. Ultimately, we must have faith these concerns will be dealt with."

"No, you don't get out of this venture that easily!" Madame Leonedria sternly said. "You could have ended our trek a few pages ago. But not now! I will not have you complete this text by making a childish and inane appeal to faith! You scribble down a few final words and then waddle away until the curtain call? That nonsense is a complete abrogation of personal responsibility! My goodness, everyone has to act, including you!"

20

A Matter of Responsibility

"Yes, we must all do whatever we can," Alex said. He sighed heavily. "Even the infirm must help, but what use am I? I forget most things and can barely write. It's terrifying! I didn't even recognize my respiratory therapist the other day. I brought in my diet records because I thought that was why we were meeting. I was way off. Man, she wanted to examine my damn continuous positive airway pressure (CPAP) machine, and she bitched me out for failing to bring it in. It was embarrassing as hell! I got pissed and said, 'Look, I don't know you from Adam. I might have seen you before, but you're unfamiliar. How the hell am I supposed to remember what to bring in?' And it's true! She was a stranger to me. It was like first meeting someone. That is the way things are all the damn time. The memories are evaporating."

Responsibility

A duty or obligation upon one
moral, or legal accountability in t
to behave correctly in respect or
ability or authority to act or dec
take decisions independently.

20.1 It is our joint responcibility to secure the future for our progeny and all life

"A disabled person can still produce ripples," Mirai signed. "This text is proof if you can finish it. Perhaps it's time for Madame and me to shoulder the load, though that will influence this book's continuity. Some may object to suddenly switching points of view within an ongoing story, but that is a matter of style versus substance. Our alternative is to end the text, although it lacks crucial elements. There are certainly some things we've yet to address, and one of them is exploring aspects beyond the self."

"Indeed, we must constrain our egos before many good things can happen," Madame Leonedria advised. "By nature, few of us want our existence to end. We inscribe our names in wet concrete. We name children for ourselves and our relatives. We write books like this, hoping our thoughts can live on long after we are history. However, the ego's impetus is unnecessary to profoundly impact the future. In fact, selfless acts can produce some of the most profound effects."

"Such as the love a parent extends to a child daily," Mirai signed.

"Of course," Madame Leonedria said with a nod. "Are a parent's inspiration and actions any less meaningful than the words we're now sharing? Was the unknown great-great-grandfather of Buddha less important than Buddha himself? Was the great-grandmother of Mary more or less important than Jesus? Everything and everyone who was, is, and ever will be is interrelated. Our existence is the end product of myriad interconnected and codependent strands. In short, everyone plays a part in this unfolding drama that we call reality."

"There is no doubting that," Alex said. "All lives produce influences, be they humble, grand, short-lived, or ancient."

"It's helpful to contemplate the interrelatedness of all things from the perspective taught by the crystal globe," Mirai signed. "We look at a star that is one million light years away. With adequate tools, we watch sentient beings on an orbiting planet while they conduct their daily affairs. We marvel at the many things that link us. These individuals we are studying lived and died long ago. However, from our very distant perspective, they still exist within the moment. We feel their joy while watching the delivery of a new baby and share a tear when a parent draws her last breath."

"One could say that they exist within their time for eternity," Madame Leonedria observed. She was pleased to speak for herself and not merely as an avatar of Alex's being. Madame sipped her wine and added, "Those distant souls also share countless metaphysical connections that can move our hearts and souls at any moment. We gaze at their star while they gaze at others. We're united by the shared knowledge that someone is always looking, learning, and sharing throughout this universe. Yes, many of our fellow stargazers are reflections of what was. One day we, too, will become but reflections. Nonetheless, we are linked to one another by thought and heart, as is happening with some readers now. The connections provide insights into the past, observations of the present, and perceptions on what the future holds. These insights can produce influences, as in the ripples in our water bowl."

"And some of these influences can be profound, even seemingly tiny actions," Mirai signed. "Thus, to have ever been is to always be in terms of effects."

"At least from some perspectives," Alex said. "It could be that empathy and imagination can also transcend time and space. It may be a good idea to examine how thought can interact with matter and energy. I was going to—"

"We're straying off point, Alex," Mirai signed. "Perhaps abstract mathematics and philosophy are not what the readers most need right now."

"Remember, our topic is survival!" Madame Leonedria said. "We should consider something more practical before the morning comes. For example, how can those with us best communicate what they've learned here?"

"That assumes we've done a proper job sharing our intended meaning," Alex said. He looked down and added, "That's why I've rewritten this book so damn many times! It's a fool's errand, though. There comes the point when we must trust that a generally correct perception of our intentions was grasped."

"I'm sure those with us have done that," Madame Leonedria said. "Indeed, some will go well beyond our meanings and in very positive ways. We have no control over that, nor should we pretend to. A more important issue is what they will do to secure the future. I know your purpose isn't to create a new faith, Alex. Instead, you want those with us to prioritize survival above all else. To you, their being is all that matters. But why? They are merely tiny specs of life that float within an infinite sea. Why is their continued existence so important to you? What is your motivation?"

"It's not what they currently are that drives me," Alex said. "It is what they can become as a species. Yes, all things are one with what created them. That is a certainty. However, some aspects of creation have the potential to comprehend the whole. In so doing, they provide the ideational basis of creation with a metaphysical presence. This is the same presence that gave rise to all things, as in the ultimate act of love that produced our shared existence. Perhaps we, as a species, can achieve that end. There can be no higher purpose."

"So, we've come full circle," Mirai signed. "Isn't the potential for such realizations spread throughout? Surely, humanity is only one tiny thread within a vast tapestry. Why are you so driven to help our species survive?"

"They're all I know," Alex explained. "I'm optimistic other sentient beings exist, but this moment we share is my only reality. Besides, I love humanity. I keep saying that, but you two don't believe it. Granted, I can be misanthropic at times. It's easy to become this way considering the messed-up things people do to themselves and the world. In addition, I occasionally despise individuals. Hell, I want to throttle some folks! I surely do! We can be a willful and perfidious species in our current form. Yet consider what we can become!

"Look, I care about those with us more than my words can possibly express. Their futures mean everything to me. My being, life, and experiences mean nothing if those with us don't survive. Our story here is nearly finished, but theirs is just beginning! Oh, their progeny can fly to the stars or populate the cosmos. They can do anything their imaginations can grasp.

"I've also seen and felt what nonbeing is like. It was awful, a dreadful state of emptiness and nihilism! The notion disturbs me at a fundamental level. I also don't want humanity's children to inherit the world I've witnessed! The terrible visions of cities being pulverized and wasted lands have haunted me for decades. They still do. I cannot accept it! No, WE must never accept it! Our readers' progeny will travel to the furthest reaches of being and throughout time! They will escape dogma, greed, myopia, hate, anger, and superstition. We will do our best to help make it so!"

"So, you claim," Mirai signed. "Yet that is not my reality! We are victims of our ancestors' recklessness. Besides, don't most religious and ethical guides paint a rosy future of one kind or another? Isn't that one of their essential selling points? Won't God whisk all the worthy true believers up to heaven?"

"Yeah," Alex said, "nearly all faiths promise eternal salvation. Hell, people have been yanked around forever by the promises and edicts of this or that belief. One faith or ideology's views and dictates have long been confronting another's, with prejudice and hate stoking the differences. How many 'holy' wars were fought while we polluted the land, water, and air? Now, we're on the brink of an extinction that we're bringing upon ourselves, and most of the readers damn well know it.

"It seems to me that we have to look in new directions. Furthermore, we have to do it soon! Be that as it may, I would rather have this work lost to time's toll than for it to do harm! That's why I struggle with each word! I am absolutely the worst possible person for this job!"

"Humility is good for the soul," Mirai signed, "but too much of it causes inaction. Perfection is an unobtainable illusion, a product of fear and doubt."

"That is absolutely true," Madame Leonedria said. "We must act while the gift of life animates us. Some critics will say every generation for many millennia has felt that these were end times. They'll happily note that this fear is a morbid constant with many faiths. Ergo, sit back and do nothing! Humanity will muddle through."

"Except now we can prove the threats are real," Alex said. "There are places we simply cannot go because our actions have made them uninhabitable. We also know the sea level is rising and the environment is polluted far and wide. And look at how the chemicals dumped into the environment are already affecting fertility rates and human health. The scientific evidence is overwhelming."

"Not to some," Mirai signed. "They claim all the hullabaloo is over natural processes. Others believe the data is biased or the methods used are wrong."

"No species can dump thousands of tons of pollutants and expect there won't be any changes," Alex said. "And we've been doing that for generations! To think there's no influence is rank stupidity! Of course, many people have that trait in abundance. Others are willfully obtuse, which I find downright evil! There's also no doubt our actions and inactions can amplify whatever changes nature brings. All of that is assuming our malfeasance doesn't kill us outright due to wars."

"So, you claim," Mirai signed, "but claiming and knowing are two different things. The future knows! Hunger and dislocations will become desperation and conflict. The fabric of society shall fray as humanity's basic needs for survival exceed the planet's capacity to provide. Life becomes a cruel and savage struggle, one of constant clashes over limited resources. Millions of have-nots will be the first to die off as desertification and ocean encroachment spread. Some societies will fabricate suitable shelters, but not nearly enough to cover the burgeoning need. Multitudes die in huddled masses or strewn along roadsides leading to oblivion, their desiccated corpses being their only legacy. Massive tracts of land and vast cities shall be swallowed up by the oceans and deserts as the earth dons a face that its occupants no longer recognize. As for the bountiful species this world once knew, humanity caused the greatest of all mass extinctions. Eventually, our technology and habitats rescue humanity and a few other species, but only a tiny fraction of what once existed. Yet few from your era would call our lives existence."

"The reckless use of technology is also what cursed humanity," Madame Leonedria scoffed. "Look at the mythopoetic accounts your peers have written, Mirai. The *Travails* has a passage: 'Humanity eagerly devoured the fruits of knowledge and turned thoughts into realities. Few considered the cost of doing so, and some did not care. Their greed, myopia, and poor stewardship laid waste to the land, air, and water, and an angry God cast them out! The Creator left their descendants desolation, with a pitiful few plying the depths to find a new garden. It was a forlorn quest, for extinction is the price of folly.'"

"It's not God tossing us out of the damn garden!" Alex angrily said. "No, we've done this to ourselves! You two are spewing tedious nonsense, which isn't helping the readers at all. Enough of this! What the hell are you trying to say?"

"We're seeking a parting theme that ties all we've discussed together," Mirai signed. "Without that, what good does this text do?"

21

Get off Their Lazy Asses

"Parting theme?" Alex asked, his voice oozing disdain. He paused, ruminating on the points Madame and Mirai were striving to make. Then his eyes flashed barely controlled anger. "Theme? Do you want a pithy summary for the people reading these words? We talked about God being one with everything, but we've been there and done that. Look, the readers don't need a goddamn parting theme, or eff'n summary, or anything like that! They need to get off their lazy asses and act!"

"What do you suggest they do?" Mirai signed.

"We have to look toward humanity's attitudes and abilities as the problem and the cure," Alex said. "The species has abused too much and loved too little in its quest for more of everything. It's up to us, including the readers, to make things right. There's

21.1 To seccure the future, we must discern who and what is threatening it

no choice but to hazard sailing on this sea of imperfect words. Moreover, I've no idea if anyone will read this text, let alone be motivated by it."

"So, is your kind doomed, Alex?" Madame Leonedria asked. "Will they passively wait for some biblical God to intervene? Or will they placidly hope for better days while wars rage and the earth turns sterile? Those seem to be the courses they're now taking, although many are in denial."

"The people living in the cellar were of that nature," Alex said. "I'm praying the readers are not like them."

"Prayers and hopes are not good enough," Mirai angrily signed. "Our task is to motivate those with us to act! Now, how can that end be accomplished?"

"I'm not wise enough to offer solutions!" Alex said. He shook his head and added, "I can tell the story, and we've done that. However, motivating the people reading these words to do anything takes a different kind of person than me."

"Coach?" Madame Leonedria said. "Isn't that what you were once called? Now you claim you cannot motivate others?"

"So, the kittens will die," Mirai observed. "It's ironic that you chided us for our accounts! You are doing nothing!"

Alex was exasperated and tired, having labored for many years on a project that knew no end. Nevertheless, he understood the challenge must be met. One last appeal was needed.

"Look, for those with us to perform, they must first be at their very best," Alex said, calling upon years of coaching and teaching experience. "That's a truism for any action, physical or mental. They must be determined to learn, able to act, and willing to work. They've no time for petty bullshit. Pride, envy, power: all those foibles must mean nothing to them. That's the problem. I'm hardly able to advise anyone about how to deal with personal flaws and limitations, given that I have so many."

"You flee from responsibility," Madame Leonedria angrily said. "Man up!"

"It's a matter of doing more harm than good!" Alex angrily insisted. "Consider my personal history! You've noted that I've advocated killing killers. That hardly makes me a good person. What you need is Buddha, Jesus, or Mohammed. Perhaps all of them, and God too. But not me! Try to recall how I acted toward the cellar dwellers in that dream! I bitched them out and left. I felt like beating the thoughtless shitheads to a pulp. Expressing my outrage didn't do any good, but that's my nature. I confront. One of our readers could better manage what you're asking than me."

"You are very limited," Mirai signed. "Your intellect is marginal for the task ahead, and your temperament is abysmal."

"Thank you," Alex said. "So, let's wrap this up."

"NO!" Madame Leonedria yelled. She stood up slowly and painfully. Then she stared through Alex, speaking with a stern and fuming voice. This would be her defining moment, her reason for being part of the text. "The reader needs guidance, not excuses! Your abrogation of personal responsibility is unworthy!" She pointed at him, her voice growing louder and more strident while scolding Alex. "Your attitude is unworthy in every possible way! You guide the people most needed for change this far. And then you run! YOU RUN FROM RESPONSIBILITY LIKE A NAUGHTY TODDLER WHO HAS BEHAVED BADLY! Is it confidence you lack or courage?"

"A bit of both," Alex said. His eyes suddenly flashed rage, and he stood, nearly leaping to his feet. He replied loudly, anger increasing with every word. "I've had enough of your bullshit! You're not going to treat me like a child. This is my story, and I'll fucking write it! I'm not putting up with your crap for another second! NOW SIT DOWN!"

Alex stood face-to-face with Madame Leonedria. Mirai knew he was entering a dark place, something she had seen before. She whistled loudly, piercing the growing emotional cloud. All the while, she used her 'time out' sign. Alex's glare remained fixed. Mirai had seen that fixed glower in a bar and once again at a grocery store. In both instances, Alex acted with barely controlled aggression, grabbing one man by the neck and slamming him hard against an ice-making machine. Indeed, his volatility was one of the reasons she could not get close to the man she loved. She got up and touched Alex's shoulder, capturing his attention.

"Do you want to hit an old lady?" she signed. "Is it any wonder your species is dying? Is it any wonder why we can never get close?"

Alex began regaining his composure, but Mirai kept signing.

"That rage is what makes you unworthy, Alex! It could be used to help reach readers who harbor their own demons. All you must do is try! You two should stop acting like spoiled prima donnas, or do they call them 'drama queens'? Now, sit down and act like adults! Is that possible? Move over when you sit, Alex. I'll be between you and Madame Leonedria. Someone has to play adult."

Madame Leonedria smiled, nodded her head, and slowly took her seat. She was surprised by Alex's sudden outburst. She pondered whether he could, indeed, complete the project. Perhaps his emotional control was breaking down too fast, along with his memory. As it was, the book's point of view had become almost chaotic, switching from character to character. In parts of the text, the tactic had been a matter of choice, a way of demonstrating God being one with all. She pondered if that was still a guiding principle. Alex sat on the far-right seat of the couch, well separated from Madame Leonedria. He shook his head and glanced down.

'How did I let that old bitch get to me?' Alex pondered.

"She made you angry to help you see!" Mirai signed. "Please remember who we are! We are all as one in thought, including the readers! You constantly forget that. It's amazing our species ever made it past your epoch." She sat beside Alex and continued signing. "Enough of this juvenile behavior! Alex, what is the first thing you must do to become a better person? I promise it's also the first thing those with us must understand."

"I get angry when insulted or challenged," Alex admitted. "I get outraged. I also detest ignorance, racism, nationalism, and other foolish notions. I don't tolerate them! Nor will I be treated with disrespect! So, I lash out by way of words and actions."

"I, I, I," Madame Leonedria said with disdain. "You remain a banal beast of ego. That's one of humanity's greatest problems. You are much like Verity! It's always about 'you.' It's about how your father abused you! It's about your illnesses. It's about your unworthiness. How does any of that nonsense help the reader?"

"I was getting to that!" Alex growled. "Ego has a place, but that place can never be higher than the welfare of others. The ego can be a soul killer. In fact, it can make us killers! Worse, it can make us not care about anyone or anything except ourselves. We become self-absorbed and greedy children of the moment. Those were the cellar dwellers I communed with, the people living in filth and darkness."

"Ego's suppression helps us to see beyond ourselves," Mirai signed. "That was supposed to be the lesson of your perspective shifts. They attempted to help you see beyond the self, but you never quite got the message."

Alex looked down. He suddenly realized that perhaps Mirai and her kind had striven to help him by instilling the perspective shifts. If so, they and he had failed, at least partially. Alex shook his head, stifling a sob.

"I've failed you in so many ways," he softly intoned. "No, I didn't get it. I didn't understand at all!"

"You understood the concept just enough to write this book," Mirai signed. "You can think from the 'we' perspective, which was the goal. However, years of formal training have nearly destroyed your capacity to do so. Writing has more rules and conventions than it has reasons for them. Simply put, formal learning can stifle creativity and style." She touched Alex's hand. "Moreover, understanding and expressing outside perspectives is never easy."

"But how else could one speak with a dynamic being of ultimate selflessness?" Madame Leonedria asked.

Alex nodded. He felt better about his lack of insight but was still confused about Mirai's roles in the perspective shifts. She seemed to grasp his thoughts.

"I am an outside perspective," she signed. "So too are the readers we must reach."

"Trying to teach someone how to don and use different perspectives is difficult," Madame Leonedria said. "It requires us to risk all, to go beyond the self. Subordinating self is not easy. It requires empathetic awareness. Tell me, Alex, is it better to die while trying to save another or do nothing and live?"

"I would die trying to save someone," Alex said. "That's one reason I'm completing this project."

"It appears you're also driven by a sense of responsibility," Mirai signed. "Is that a responsibility for others or for yourself?"

"It is for the person reading these words," Alex said. "Yet helping that person become more able to save our species may be beyond my capacities."

"Come now, you've helped many achieve their goals," Mirai signed. "We're doing fine! We've already noted one criterion is to control the ego. That means being selfless."

"It takes a lot more than that," Alex said. "As the first dream advised, we must also clean up our acts. I have a demon of hate and violence buried deep within."

"Not that deep," Madame Leonedria observed.

"Perhaps not deep enough," Alex confessed. "Maybe an essential step in dealing with personal faults is admitting we have them. That isn't easy to do."

"Self-admission is something addicts have to deal with before they can recover," Mirai signed. "Why do you think it is so difficult?"

"The self hates seeing ugly reflections," Alex said. "It will do anything to hide from them. So, we lie, even to ourselves."

"How can we overcome that tendency?" Madame Leonedria asked.

"Honesty," Alex replied. "Cleaning up our act requires a type of honesty that's difficult to muster. How can we concede to a child we've injured that we were wrong? How can we confess to a lover that we've betrayed a sacred trust? How can we admit to our parents that we've become addicted to drugs? How can we profess to a congregation that our beliefs may be wrong? Indeed, how can we muster the honesty needed to admit to others what we don't want to admit to ourselves?"

"Confessing our failings requires two other traits often in short supply," Madame Leonedria said. "Yet, they are infinitely powerful when combined with honesty. They are courage and humility. They reside in all of us to one extent or another."

"Humility is a child of selflessness," Mirai signed. "It allows us to readily reveal our true nature to ourselves and others."

"What you see is what you get," Alex said. "It's a wonderful trait. When combined with courage, humility overcomes fear and doubt. These qualities often compel us to take actions to improve ourselves and our common lot. However, they're all codependent."

"So, you're asking our readers to make themselves into special sorts of people," Mirai signed. "They're brave, honest, and humble. They've also sought to correct inherent flaws, which is difficult. So, we know they'll have some degree of self-control. Being of such a nature, they can be trusted by all. That means they can easily commune with friend and foe alike."

"Yes, they would make excellent negotiators," Alex said.

"Let us also give them a purpose," Madame Leonedria said. "Let it be a simple agenda that can be readily embraced and shared. Let them seek the harmonious welfare of all life above

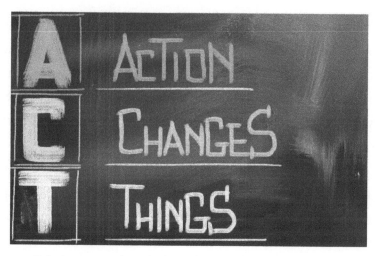

21.2 Actions are the only things that can change the status quo

everything else. These . . . 'Seekers' will care nothing about fame, money, position, power, or anything material. If these things happen, fine. However, the primary goal must be focused on the collective well-being of the planet and all life that dwells upon it. That requires a special kind of person. The Seekers must also grow beyond base desires, except for those fostering love, patience, and communal welfare. In their selflessness and good works, they provide a model that lights the way."

"All of this is fine for preparing the brush," Mirai observed. "However, how does anyone paint in ways that secure the future? Idealistic goals aimed at self-improvement are not enough. Exactly what should we advise our readers to do? That is the essential question."

"There is no single answer," Alex replied. "Each of us has specific strengths, and they vary greatly. We should use our gifts and knowledge to help promote the common good. You know, like those who volunteer at food banks."

"So, our Seekers must be doers too," Madame Leonedria said.

"They must be doers first and foremost," Alex said. "Jimmy Carter is a great example, a former president who built houses for poor folks. He got into it: hammer, nails, roofing, and the whole works. There are infinite possibilities. The Seekers can help others through their thoughts, words, and deeds. Some are good organizers, while others are great researchers. Some argue well, while others can create groups of like-minded people. Some folks are good builders, and others are knowledgeable about cleaning, driving, etcetera. Oh, and some of my favorites are people of nature, those who understand flora and fauna. The possibilities for improving our common lot are unlimited because people are blessed with myriad talents."

"Moreover, potential weaknesses can have positive uses," Mirai signed. "Of course, this assumes they're properly controlled and directed."

"Yeah, I'm an aggressive and contentious man who is quick to engage others," Alex noted. "Those are hardly good traits in many instances, but they made me a damn good coach. Granted, controlling aggression isn't easy. I've sure had some ups and downs there. What would have happened had I refused to fight during the Great Coward Dream? At the time, there didn't seem to be any choice. Perhaps there was. Whatever the case, I should have avoided conflict many times instead of leaping into the fire."

"You're no pacifist," Madame Leonedria said. "It is not in your basic nature. Still, if a coach, police officer, or peacekeeper was needed, you have the right temperament. There is something else to consider when asking people to act. Once one takes action, it often cannot be rescinded. After all, an arrow set to flight cannot be recalled. Indeed, a harsh word can create a scar that never heals, both in the young and elderly. Good reasons and strong desires to take action are not enough. Our plans must be weighed against what is in the best interest of the collective good."

"Yet preserving one's world often requires strong actions," Mirai signed. "That's a problem for those who believe in peace above all else. One can argue against doing anything because it may cause discord or harm to some. Thus, a dreary status quo remains in place. We can all see where that is leading. If we accept that decisive actions are required, we must also acknowledge our responsibility for taking them. That includes personal liability for our deeds intended and incidental consequences."

"Yeah, that's true," Alex said. "To inadvertently harm another may be more justifiable from a legal perspective than wantonly causing harm. However, our action is no less damaging to the afflicted party."

"That is why it's critical to seek knowledge and share ideas *before* acting," Mirai advised. "We must examine the good and possible harm our deeds may cause. All too many never consider the various consequences of a given act. That can make them as myopic as those they work against. Our motives must also be transparent. It is often best to enlist deliberation and feedback from all concerned, even our opponents."

"I don't think that approach should apply to all actions," Alex said. "Our opponents may not be keen on us forcing a shutdown of their factory or power plant."

"One can advise them that such a thing could happen," Mirai signed. "This can be broached as an appeal to reason."

"Perhaps that is why the theme of light was so important in your dreams," Madame Leonedria said. "Light could be a metaphor for revealed truth. However, some may question whether we have time to be so deliberative."

"I suppose it depends on the situation," Alex said. "Rash actions nearly always produce regrettable consequences, unintentional or not. That's for sure. Ultimately, the question becomes, 'What should I do to best correct a given problem?'"

"As you've observed, actions can occur at numerous levels," Madame Leonedria said. "I teach. You write. Some may opt to address pollution by promoting recycling or using carpooling. Some understand wildlife and know how to attend to its needs. Others can volunteer to help remove litter from the roads, streams, and riverbanks. These modest deeds produce a cumulative positive effect. They're also relatively easy for children and adults to do together. Ah, and they usually don't involve any conflict. Yes, I help the children when they come to pick up refuse in the parks below. It is a joy! They are so full of life and energy. The key is fostering these efforts early on, especially through schools and educational services."

"People can become much more active than that," Alex said.

"Why don't you give us an example?" Madame Leonedria said. "Make it a problematic one."

21.3 It is never easy to confront entrenched power, but sometimes it is an existential need

22

Implications for Seekers

Alex was exhausted. Nonetheless, he knew the book's ending would be challenging because dreams alone had sustained most of the text. However, the issue of practical applications was now essential, one that had vexed him for years. Imagination and reality needed to be conjoined here, a place at the cusp of dreams, contemplations, and forged realities. Yet he had pondered the possibilities and thus set his mind to the task.

"Well, it all depends on the situation," Alex said. "For instance, a local lake may be so polluted it smells and is lifeless. The first step is determining whether something seriously amiss can be corrected. This will require time and money. Multiple water samples must be taken and tested by objective concerns. Then the data must be tabulated and analyzed. If a problem exists, we enlist the help of others to trace down the source and find a solution. Then we share the information with the entire community."

Mirai huffed and shook her head. "Resolving issues are seldom that simple!" she signed. "It may be the case that a local tannery is dumping untreated waste into the lake. This could have been the case for many years, and all parties know it. The only options could be closing the tannery or building a water treatment plant for its effluent. In poor communities, the ideal solution could be unaffordable. Moreover, legal and political battles usually ensue that can go on for years."

"Very true, Mirai," Madame Leonedria said. "The tannery could employ many people. It may also have strong ties with political and financial powers. The company or community could also be resistant to change. Hence, there are no easy means of employing the proposed solutions."

"That happens all the time," Alex said.

"Well, what would you have our Seekers do?" Madame Leonedria said. "Here is a common, real-life example to ponder."

"We must first determine whether this is a matter of life and death!" Alex said. "We must gather together like-minded supporters. Then we should use mass media—"

"Simplistic balderdash!" Madame Leonedria said, waving a dismissive hand. "Alex, some societies are far from open. Ergo, public actions are often out of the question! Even in free nations, many people practice their perfidy well out of sight! Simply proving a given case and assigning responsibility can be exceptionally difficult. Their experts debate your own. They will employ endless legalities to slow decision-making processes. Indeed, our opponents will tie up the proceedings for years with lawsuits. So, it will go while the lake slowly dies or the land becomes irretrievably polluted.

"The culpable may eventually be found and brought to task with time and effort. This all assumes one is operating within the framework of a free society. However, some in power are immune to all forms of pressure. In addition, one certainly can't depend on the media for help! As you've seen, the media often dance only to the tune of popular opinion or vested power. They make plenty of noise, but not policy. They usually also lack the industry and zeal to upset the status quo. In other cases, the state controls the media. We all know where that leads! The clock ticks until time runs out! That is your species' current situation, Alex. This is what the readers face."

"That situation will become the future's misery," Mirai signed. "What can our Seekers do?"

"We cannot remain passive," Alex dejectedly said. "Sad to say, but some circumstances warrant confrontation. Protesters chain themselves to trees and stand in front of bulldozers. Others besiege the meetings of their opponents. Some plague those responsible for making wars and ruining this earth by berating them publicly. They write scathing articles and even accost the relatives of despoilers with hostile comments. Some simply lie down and refuse to work, while others march en masse."

"What about confronting them up close and personal, Alex?" Madame Leonedria said. "It is clear many like you are prone to violence. There are also other harsh means. Should we look into the personal lives of those who threaten survival? Should we gut their political power by exposing them to public humiliation and worse?"

"That's better than harming or killing people," Alex said. "I think the tactic is typical Politics 101, at least in most countries."

"Doesn't that approach make us like those we oppose?" Mirai signed. "Do you want those with us to pry into the intimate affairs of others? Would you have the Seekers behave like the yellow press? Should they tell the world who is cheating on a spouse? Would you have us become Big Brother? Would you ask a child to judge his or her parents? Surely, this would not be a world many would want to live in!"

"It doesn't matter what you or I want!" Madame Leonedria said. "Alex, some will unchain their darker impulses based on what they deem is justifiable expediency."

"I know!" Alex exclaimed. He was frustrated and angry. "I'm one of those people! Look, I'd burn down the damn tannery that we talked about earlier. I'd burn it to the eff'n ground and dance on the ashes. When reason and persuasion fail, we still must act. We cannot watch passively while lives are harmed and the earth is wasted! So, we do what is least desired and take responsibility for our deeds. Our actions may produce economic hardship and misery. If that leads us to the docket, so be it. Sometimes, there is no choice. Ultimately, uninhabitable land around a dead lake is not good for anyone. We must be willing to sacrifice ourselves for the sake of the common good."

"And hope that others can perceive the nobility of our action," Mirai signed. "Perhaps then they will grant us some forgiveness."

"Would you kill?" Madame Leonedria asked. She leaned forward, her eyes locked on Alex. "Would you kill, my son?" she repeated.

"That's a bitch of a question," Alex replied, fidgeting with his hands on the hem of his shirt. "Some will regard their opponents as existential threats, and they may well be. In fact, our opposition could be actively killing innocents. A few Seekers may use this threat notion as *carte blanche* for invasive and destructive deeds. Hell, I've called for the death of despots who are harming others. They openly invade their neighbor's territories and murder any of their own citizens who oppose them. My justification for going after such mad dogs is *sic semper tyrannis* (such always to tyrants). John Wilkes Booth said that immediately after assassinating Lincoln, not that he is someone to emulate. I suppose Booth's folly shows how pitiful our rationalizations for violence can become. Nonetheless, I would be inclined to kill if there was an absolute need.

"However, that depraved tendency demonstrates my complete unworthiness! I want the Seekers to be better than I! We must stand strong against those destroying our world! However, taking life makes us nihilistic by definition! It simply perpetuates the problem. There is no way around that basic fact. I keep saying one cannot defeat evil by becoming evil, and I know that to be true. I also understand the ancient adage that it is better to suffer harm than to cause harm. These are fundamentals, but I am too flawed to live by them consistently."

"You are conflicted, Alex," Mirai signed. "That feeling is shared by many of those with us. They see the need to act. They also see the intransigence of the greedy and vested. When the need for survival meets intransigence, the result is fire."

"I cannot advocate killing and destroying!" Alex resolutely said. "Please don't ask me to do so. Isn't that antithetical to any higher aspiration to what is good? Are fighting and conflict what you want us to advise the readers? Listen, my friends, if we want to make ourselves worthy parts of God, then we act in support of life. Killing violates that most fundamental goal. Moreover, how we act defines a tiny aspect of what God is. Would you have us make any part of God into a destroyer of life?"

"Alex, comets, and meteorites rain down on life all too often," Madame Leonedria observed. "These mass killers are also part of God's being, at least according to your definition. God is nature, and nature is born of the possible! Nature is neither good nor bad, but what we opt to make it by way of our ideas and actions. So, let us assume we want to assign goodness to God. Tell me, Alex, would a good God want you to sit idle while the lake dies? That is the essential question. God grants all who look with insights. What we do with them is an aspect of choice.

"There comes a time when wanton evil must be confronted by force. What was to stop Hitler and his vile minions other than force? Regardless of how you answer that question, idealistic sophistry will not impact holy warriors striving to save the world! The Seekers know time is finite and the problems massive. They must act and act soon."

"So, heaven knows, anything goes?" Alex said. "Is that to be the central message of this book? I'll never support that position! NEVER!"

Madame Leonedria gritted her teeth and shook her head. "You know in your heart that you would wage war on heaven and hell if it meant humanity's survival!" she exclaimed. "You know that! Yet you repeatedly deny your nature! You dread that our listeners will become warriors, true warriors! Yet isn't that exactly what they must become to save this planet? Granted, the Seekers must always be deliberative and responsible, but they must also act! They must act strongly! You dally over every word of this text, but we always come to this same point. You cannot commit to taking all necessary actions! In your dreams, you literally fought tooth and nail for life! You fought because you had to! I hope the Seekers will proceed with the alacrity and firmness you now lack. Your dithering and doubts are nothing but destructive."

"There is another issue," Mirai signed. "Humanity faces a far greater concern than excessive zeal! You've seen that the multitude simply will not act or listen. They are content and self-absorbed. How is anyone to overcome such apathy?"

"It's all about enlisting our basic survival instincts," Alex said. "Those are the most potent drives we have. We can enlist them through books like this and similar means. Pamphlets, meetings, TV shows, action groups, education—they all have the power to enlist participation. Again, using mass media can be effective if done wisely.

"Yet I still feel that asking our readers to become holy warriors is dangerous! I'm VERY uncomfortable with that. A few Seekers will give way to the worst of our beasts within! They'll strive to harm others. Their conviction will justify anything! That approach will form a myopic cloud that occludes much that is good! They will shoot, bomb, and mutilate. They'll think nothing of spilling blood to stop the earth's defilers! This is the viciousness I'm cursed with! I displayed it during dreams, as I have in life. It is how many desperate people act when they feel there is no recourse."

"Yet these are desperate times, Alex," Madame Leonedria said. "And clearly, something must be done. And it has to be done NOW!"

"I struggle with that issue all the damn time!" Alex said. He was dismayed that the central issue always came down to the efficacy of confrontation. "That is why this text keeps failing! Yes, I'm disposed to fight. I'm as vicious a writer on these subjects as anyone could be! Numerous death threats and intimations of violence have been cast my way in the last few years alone. My response is to taunt my foes and invite them to meet me face to face. I care nothing about their sensibilities or replies. Honestly,

I couldn't care less about the threats. I prefer to fight than passively watch the future being destroyed for money or power. In fact, I would rather die with my hands soaked in blood than simply whimper about what I should have done. You are right: this is my nature! This is who I am!

"Yet in my heart, I FIRMLY believe that doing violence simply perpetuates its existence. This conclusion is impossible to deny. I would gladly die to help my species, as would many of those with us. I would suffer being run over by an earth-moving machine. I would have my head busted during an antiwar protest. I would happily be jailed for failing to obey an unjust edict. But, despite my savage nature, I hope to God that I NEVER take actions that hurt or kill another! I repeat: *we cannot defeat a demon by becoming one!*"

"You may be willing to suffer a wrong, Alex," Mirai signed. "But, witness what the wrongs occurring today did to the future!"

Alex suddenly saw the vision of the marvelous city he had seen during his *Battle with Demons* dream. Only this time, he witnessed its complete obliteration in his mind's eye. The skies abruptly lit up, and the earth shook. He felt the searing heat and saw the huge picture window in front of him shatter. The desk he sat at shook violently while the paper, pad, and pen atop it burst into flames and were blown violently away. Then arose a rumbling sound that grew into a thunderous roar. Cracks ripped through the walls, and ceiling panels rained down. Through billowing clouds of dust and smoke Alex saw people on the elevated walkways running for their lives. They staggered and fell while debris rained down all around. He heard pitiful screams and cries while the earth shook and buildings crumbled. Countless flailing people fell thousands of feet into dark roiling clouds. There they were entombed by thousands of tons of crumbling concrete and collapsing structures. Alex covered his eyes against the visions, but they would not fade.

"*'THIS IS THE WORLD YOU LEFT US!'* Mirai thought as her mind, at last, touched Alex's soul. *'THIS IS A TRUTH THAT YOU'VE SEEN!'*"

"Enough of that!" Madame Leonedria ordered, slapping her hand hard on the table. "The dreams happened as described, and we cannot add anything! Nor can we take anything away! Manipulating the past in that way is completely unacceptable, Mirai. It is an utterly idiotic thing to do!"

"Nor will it change how I feel," Alex resolutely said. "I love you, Mirai. I truly do! However, don't ask me to advocate violence. Yes, we MUST act, but only under the guidance of our higher natures."

"Restraint is very unlike you, Alex," Madame Leonedria said. "Perhaps you're getting wiser in some ways, even though you deny your essential nature. The decisions regarding the means our readers use to protect humanity's future are personal. They are not ours to make. We've debated both the passive and aggressive sides with equal fervor. The crucial lesson of the starving-kitten metaphor is that we are responsible for our *inactions* and *actions*. Both can have calamitous consequences. If we do nothing, the future is forfeit. If we act wisely, some good will come of it.

"You have opted for semi-passive resistance and self-sacrifice, Alex, or so it seems. Mirai and I are more inclined to fight. After all, Gypsies have seen the worst in human nature! When you began this dialogue those many years ago, you had no idea why I was made a Gypsy. It was merely a literary ploy for you, a tool to capture the readers' interest. There are always more profound truths, my son, some of which you are blind to. Now they will become apparent to you and everyone with us!

"Picture the recent past, my child. It was a past where some spoke and wrote of looming horrors but were blissfully ignored. As a result, Gypsies and Jews were herded like cattle. They were crammed into fetid trains and marched into concentration camps! The Nazis worked them to death or gassed them outright. 'You to the left, you to the right!' Terrified and confused, the children clutched their parents. Ferocious dogs snapped at their legs. The guards used rifle butts to keep the lines moving and woe unto those who fell. The children were told sweet lies, anything to shield them from a terrible and ominous reality. No one heard their cries! No one lifted a hand! No one shed a tear!

"Hitler's ovens roared!" she yelled, shaking her fists toward the heavens. "They belched the stench of burning hopes and futile prayers. It was force alone that rescued a pitiful few from a terrible fate! Hitler is gone, but far greater threats remain. This time, all people will go into the ovens! The fires fueled by war, plagues, hunger, and greed will consume everything and everyone. All of them! The same extinction that claimed so many Jews, Gypsies, and others awaits this entire planet! So, humanity must act, whether it wants to or not! The fires have already started, and there isn't much time."

"Madame Leonedria is right," Mirai signed. "We began this story on the slopes of Mount Major, surrounded by nature's beauty. I have seen what becomes of the beauty my ancestors took for granted. They tore it from their progeny and left us with heat, dust and wormwood! I pray that they act to save the future. The choice of what to do is up to each Seeker. They have the power to change reality . . . if they use it."

"All people have that power," Alex said. "They just don't know it. Moreover, they can find nonviolent means to achieve any end. I will always remain true to that ideal."

"This takes us back to God," Madame Leonedria said. "You believe God is one with the person reading this passage. You contend that his or her ideas are part of the metaphysical harmonics underlying existence. That imbues all sentient beings with unlimited potential."

"Yet it does not ensure they will use their abilities," Alex replied. "Should we discuss how the needed power to change things can be enlisted from a philosophical perspective?"

"Not now," Mirai signed. "The discussion would take us from our primary task."

22.1 The means of resistance may require a choice between violence and passivity, but not acting can lead to things like the Nazi selection process

"Agreed," Madame Leonedria said. "We can put that and other ramblings into another text. The hour grows very late, and your fires burn low, Alex."

"Another text?" Alex said. He shook his head. "Well, I can rescue some essays about these and other subjects. They would reveal what a dolt I can be. However, putting something cogent together at this point is difficult. It would be a hodgepodge at best."

"I would be honored to assist," Mirai signed. "It's clear you need help. But I will probably not be here if we succeed with this effort."

"I will participate," Madame Leonedria said. "And I'll always be here. But only if you're still worthy when the time comes."

"I'll be less than what I am," Alex said. "Perhaps a project like that would be helpful to those we serve. But I'm not sure there's time for another text. My thoughts are jumbled, and I may do more harm than good before long. Hell, perhaps we already did. I tried my best, though. That's for sure. I'm lucky. You were the ideal partners for this work."

"And what of Verity?" Madame Leonedria said while glancing at the sleeping beauty. "You opted to put her to sleep in this final draft."

"We couldn't have gotten a damn thing done if she'd been awake," Alex said with a smile. "Our ways will part soon enough." Alex suddenly felt the pull of reality and looked at his now-aged hands. His fingers were bent and twisted, riddled with arthritis. They were so alien, so gnarled by time.

"I can't live without Verity, and no one can live with her," Alex said, his voice sounding weak and strained. "Yet it's only through Verity that I can see much at all. I'll put some of our conversations into the next text that we spoke of. Or perhaps I'll bury them in my vault. I'm grateful you made her whole again. Look at her, curled up and at peace. She is a beautiful thing."

"She can be," Madame Leonedria said. "Soon enough, she'll be awake."

Alex turned toward Mirai and said, "All these words are for you, my dear. You are my reason, my purpose. Verity is beautiful.

Ah, but you are life, hope, and all things possible." He reached out and gently touched Mirai's face. She moved closer, and they kissed. It was shared passion, long overdue. A perfect moment, perhaps the only one Alex had ever known. He deeply feared losing Mirai, but he knew her departure could mean humanity's future was secure. Yet he could not bear Mirai leaving and pondered joining her in spirit. Madame Leonedria smiled, knowing that Alex was letting go of the now. He would live only in memories soon, the child of a passing thought.

"We will share many conversations in the minds of those with us," Madame Leonedria said. "We'll talk about the synthetic intellects that are coming. They will be the mind in the machine.

22.2 Within all people resides the power of what created them if they call upon it

We will speak about truth, God, and many other things. We will seek to understand all that can be understood during this blink of time that some call a lifetime."

"We are Seekers," Alex said, gazing into Mirai's eyes.

"*'We'll always find one another,'*" Mirai thought. She held tightly onto Alex, knowing that he would soon drift away.

"This task is complete," Madame Leonedria said. "We've shared time with those we love. There can be nothing more rewarding than that. As for the future, we've done our parts. Yes, I can see into the minds of our audience. Plans and actions are taking shape in some that can secure their progeny's future. There are three in particular, and they will do marvelous things! But all who act are saviors, every one of them.

Master the possible, my friends. Keep your hearts open and seek whatever knowledge, happiness, and love existence accords. Some are even considering their roles while reading these final lines. Now is the time to act, dear hearts. If you don't, who will? Strive to realize the power within, for that is the same power that created all things. And always have faith in yourselves. After all, it is a glorious thought that links us."

PART II

RELIGION

23

Thinking About God at the Boat Dock

Black pollywogs (tadpoles) hug the shore en masse, busily munching on whatever edible tidbits the leisurely flowing Connecticut River offers in this part of the Upper Valley. They swim as one, swiftly altering their course in unison and never pausing long lest a predator decides the target is too inviting. The behavior is hard-wired, or so the experts claim. Yeah, pollywogs squirm out of their gooey egg pouches, fully equipped to survive via the agency of inborn behaviors like I am currently witnessing. I watch in amazement while they forage, as I have since I first saw the spectacle as a child some 65 years ago. Such is life at the boat dock, a habitat that ducks, mink, deer, bears, and songbirds visit regularly. It is a place of beauty incarnate.

However, we dare not call the pollywogs' collective conduct "intelligent design" because some self-important intellectuals will get offended by the term. To them, anything that smacks of the Divine as being causal for life, matter, energy, or thought is anathema. God has no place in their happenstance universe; such is their inveterate conviction and prejudice. They cannot even allow for the possibility that the word God is merely a metaphor humans created and share that unlocks or can unite numerous related concepts. Perhaps these erstwhile sophists should prune their egos, open their minds, and watch sunlight ripple off gyrating waves. There is an underlying pattern to this existential activity: the waves lapping the shore, the cormorant who hangs out by the dam, the myriad and lush green hues that grace surrounding trees, bushes, and grounds, the continuous change that allows life and being to spring anew in countless forms.

The boat dock is a church to me, though it is hardly an imposing edifice. Located about a mile north of Wilder Dam, the landing consists of a very short, hard-packed dirt road that gently descends into a convenient shallow on the New Hampshire side of the Connecticut River. There are no grand piers or bollards here, just abundant trees, lush shrubbery, scattered cement debris that long ago supported a bridge, and plentiful plant and animal life. One could not launch a craft longer than 20 feet from the place, but that is more than ample for most purposes. Kayakers, fishermen, punters, and others use the dock to get their tiny craft underway. I often watch Dartmouth students, Fisheries and Game officers, and anglers enjoying the small landing.

Happily, a narrow, grass-covered peninsula abutting the road allows me to drive my mobility scooter just inches from the river's waves. At low water, the modest concrete remains of the former bridge abutment extend a foot or so above the surface about 15–20 feet from shore, with ducks and geese frequenting the corresponding remnants on the Vermont side. One can see and hear kids playing in the Wilder Dam Park, located about 75 to 100 yards across the river in Vermont, with a few souls splashing about in the water. But mostly, the only sound is nature's chorus, sweet and fresh.

23.1 The ramp to the boat dock

The sun beats on my arms and legs, while a straw hat protects my head and neck from the summer heat. I'm so tired at times that I occasionally doze, slowly sinking into the mobility scooter's comfortable captain's seat. However, I don't like falling asleep on the landing. Black bears frequent the shoreline, although an actual attack is more of an irrational fear than a likely reality. Nonetheless, bears are apex predators. Moreover, we occasionally see the creatures and their cubs, although they're usually content to keep to themselves. Still, I remain wary. Nature is beautiful, but it's a reality based on turning energy into life.

To some predators, I am so much food. You can ask any mosquito or horsefly, though the aerobatic dragonflies constantly remind the blood-sucking pests that they, too, are on the menu. Watching those iridescent insects dart about is one of my favorite things at the dock. Dragonflies are harmony in motion, a life form that dates back 300 million years. They only live about seven months, yet here they remain, still going strong after untold ages. I wonder if we are allowed to apply intelligent design to dragonflies.

The dragonflies' fundamental design was perfect for survival, although most creatures are not nearly as successful. Indeed, the vast majority of species Gaia has nurtured into existence have come and gone, despite some being wonderfully adapted to particular ecological niches. These adaptations are their strengths and weaknesses, for change can be brutally abrupt. Indeed, rocks can fall from the sky, and the Earth sometimes vomits its searing innards to the detriment of all. Those perfectly adapted to one

23.2 The landing at the dock with parking on the right

context simply cannot survive the sudden imposition of another. Thus, the great preponderance of species that have ever been do not march into the future.

Still, some species go on. The lumbering Coelacanth has been swimming the oceans for 360 million years in one form or another, while Horseshoe Crabs were scurrying about 445 million years ago. They say the most ancient animal on Earth is the sponge at 580 million years, although Cyanobacteria have existed for at least 2.8 billion years. I suspect life in one form or another is nearly as old as time, evolving wherever and whenever the conditions are in place to sustain it.

I watch water spiders darting about in the shallows and ponder the many why questions. Indeed, this symphony of life has

23.3 Looking at life on the shore of the Wilder Dam Resevoir

many chords and levels. Primal energy was condensed into atoms, molecules, and the stuff of matter. Matter coalesced into
stars and planets, some of which fostered life. Existential contexts changed and evolved, giving rise to species of every imaginable kind. Stars aged and exploded, flinging the detritus of being
throughout the expanding bubble we call the universe. Why?
Are we, and all that exists, merely random aspects of chance
alone? One can prove mathematically that the archi of existence
could come into existence spontaneously, with no need for a
causal nexus, no inkling of a Divine spark. Being is because it
could be: a simple matter of probability and time. Of course,
this dramatically understates the elegance of the complex proofs
offered, though some find that logical grace pales compared to

the foliage that spring and fall offer. I ponder the dazzling light reflecting off rippling waves.

Could there be more to our being than proof alone can offer? Surely, proofs are symbolically encoded thoughts. They have no existence outside the rationalistic lines, so to speak. However, does the same rationalism sustaining proofs pop up repeatedly over time and space in distinct sentient species that evolve on other worlds? This would imply an underlying and universal ideational commonality, a resonance of thought that runs through life, dancing from species to species while life unfolds and evolves. Indeed, perhaps the purpose of life is to seek life's purpose and, in so doing, give ideas, such as God, a metaphysical existence.

Alas, the various exercises in abstraction that yield supporting and contrary proofs are as bound by context as life itself, and they rise and fall at an astonishing pace. Clearly, proofs are the stuff of symbolism, and symbolism is an aspect of shared thought. We collectively agree that "X" is "X," but only for so long as we can recall and share the terms of our agreement. Such shared consensus is a fragile and ephemeral construction at best; these things we dub proofs. Sometimes, the findings are robust and can survive practical and theoretical tests.

However, they ultimately depend on the thoughts of the beings that crafted and shared them, and one ponders whether these thoughts are indeed universals. In other words, do you suppose other species grasp these truths via their calculations, applied metaphors, or even greater insights than humans have

23.4 God communes while I gaze at sunlight reflecting of the tippling waves

yet realized? I surmise that the answer is yes, as may you. Ah, but such sublime insights and speculations cannot have afforded their progenitors much survival advantage when a great rock landed upon their world. Happenstance can be a bitch. Still, another species will pick up the thought, that spark of insight that flows throughout.

The essential point is the affirmation and/or rejection of the Divine are metaphysical aspects of our evolution, as in thinking about the thoughts that created thinking. We thus make and share various accounts that seek to explain the foundational principles of existence, futile though the exercise may be. I imagine in many cases and with many species, the idea of "God" occurs. In fact, I am content to opine that the idea of God gives the Divine a metaphysical existence that species such as our own readily generate, grasp, and share via words such as these.

The idea of a causal impetus not born of the Divine has also been around for a long time, and I imagine it is ubiquitous. Our thoughts give these grand ideas a metaphysical presence of sorts, but one suspects that the logicoemotional basis of these ideas is far from random. The most straightforward proof will be found when we discover another sentient species and find that it, too, has walked a similar ideational path. Perhaps then, those of great intellect will see pollywogs, waves, and the wonder of life in a fashion with room for the Divine. Well, the only certainty is that time will tell. Such is being down at the boat dock, a constant interplay of life and thought. To me, this is heaven, and you should visit this place on occasion. Amen.

24

God Is Always Speaking

By some reckonings, this conception that some call God is constantly communing with us, whether it is through signs, dreams, or voices from within. The difficulty is that we hardly ever listen, let alone notice or understand what is being said. This is especially the case when we are plagued by current concerns and future fears. We seem especially keen on fretting about the unknown; such is our desire for the welcome predictability of order versus the terrors of chaos. Indeed, there is a beginning, middle, and end to nearly everything that exists, with all the parts of reality being arranged to result in neat cause-and-effect linkages that can be easily understood. Why worry? After all, life unfolds according to plan, or so we are told. Ah, but the order we perceive is often an illusion, as my slowly declining memory often reveals.

So, I'm talking with my good friend Ellen, who often gets lost in mid-sentence. People with frontal meningiomas tend to do that. The frontal lobes help us organize information, which involves a process called working memory. When frontal areas are impacted by pressure or degenerative processes, the result is often a loss of continuity in how we put information together or perceive it, especially in terms of expression. In addition, the frontal lobes are needed for impulse control and decision-making. In Ellen's case, her tumor is very likely nonmalignant, albeit a slow-motion sort of growth. Its symptoms are annoying, but the beast will probably not kill my friend. Something else will likely claim that dubious distinction. Nonetheless, the lapses cause her to roll her pretty blue eyes and shake her head. They are all-too-frequent reminders that something is wrong.

"Honestly," she says, a frown sweeping over her face, "the forgetting is terrible."

"It is," I reply. "A person listening to us would marvel that we can even communicate."

In my case, a neurodegenerative process at work is causing "marked" atrophy in the frontal, parietal, and left medial occipital regions. The frontal and parietal lobes contribute to helping us recognize and organize information, which is very problematic for me, especially if the input is verbal or visual. Indeed, putting names to faces has become an intractable problem, as is common in occipital lobe problems. Talk to me today, and it is forgotten by tomorrow, irretrievably so. I can also occasionally lose continuity with my current context, much like Ellen does.

However, I am far more likely than she to experience sudden and extreme mood shifts. One can get ragingly angry or tearfully sad without reason, although frustration can be a trigger.

Yet I am usually at peace with Ellen unless she gets into her criticism mode, as some Jewish mothers are wont to do. That tendency is a vestige of her upbringing, which abounded in tremendous pressure to excel in all ways. And woe unto her if she did not get stellar grades. Usually, we find comfort in each other's company, for we understand the beasts that currently afflict us. There is no need for pretenses or false faces. Yeah, our sense of order is often adrift, but we don't get too upset about it. Granted, we don't get much done, remember less, and are sometimes confused.

Ellen asks me the name of my most recent book, and I simply cannot recall it. Damn, I worked on the bloody thing for years, but I just cannot find the name when she asks. Then I tell her to look it up online, only to realize I also cannot recall the website's name where the book can be found. I just cannot find the right words at times. I get angry and frustrated when this happens, as it does with increasing frequency. The names of friends, acquaintances, and all things, along with the recollection of recent events, are sometimes elusive. The anger and fear of being reduced to a null state grow. All order has suddenly evaporated, and the future seems utterly terrifying. Why must life be like this? Why is every word such a goddamned challenge for me?

A chickadee abruptly lands on a short white fence atop the porch outside Ellen's living room. He looks at me as I do him.

It's a male, replete with his black robber's mask. They are such handsome animals, blessed by myriad hues of brown, black, and gray. He angrily chirps at me as if disturbed by my growing frustration. Suddenly, I hear God speaking in that frustrated voice, loud and clear.

"All you are forgetting are mere words. There is thought without language, as we animals prove every day. An amoeba's dance has elegance and reason, perhaps more so than any net of words can ever hope to capture. Be content with where you are, who you are with, and the blessings that nature and life can bring."

So said the little bird who visits Ellen regularly, although he was not entirely done dressing me down.

24.1 A chickadee can remind us about what is good in life

"Soon enough, there will come a oneness you will understand without words. And if you truly listen, God will speak in ways that broaden your understanding of what is. Yes, you may lose all your words. However, you will never lose this moment, and the moment is all we have."

A tear rolls down my cheek, and I thank God for the insight while I gaze at the lively bird. I will share the lesson with others via these feeble words, passing on the knowledge of the chickadee. Amen.

25

Pondering
the Imponderable

Peter and Malcolm are not close friends, but they attended Lebanon High School simultaneously and knew each other reasonably well. Mind you, they did not pal around together or share laughs and giggles while growing up, living separate lives that seldom overlapped. In fact, when they meet up, they usually argue for hours on end about politics, religion, and nearly every other subject that comes to mind. They are both aging children of the Upper Valley, with Malcolm hailing from Grantham and Peter being raised in Lebanon, NH. Of course, they've both been far afield more often than not, but they end up on the same patch every so often. Peter and Malcolm, both college graduates, are sure as heck not ignorant Billy Bobs. And there they were, sitting on a bench near the middle of Colburn Park and chatting away, an uncommon happenstance that pleased neither man.

Peter had come in for supplies, and Malcolm was out for a walk when they bumped into each other. Big old Malcolm had become a child of Jesus over the years, but Peter didn't believe that dog could hunt. He is a bit of a latter-day hippie, which is not how he was during high school. In fact, Peter doesn't believe in any conventional notion of God at all, let alone the polite foibles of society in general. But rather than just enjoying a fine late June day, Malcolm and Peter took to tossing verbal hand grenades at each other, much to my amusement, as well as that of the songbirds and busy squirrels. The conversation went something like this.

"You're too prideful," Malcolm insisted. "Here I am, trying to save your worthless soul, and there you are, yammering insults and complete nonsense about the Nicene Creed versus the Apostles' Creed! Who the hell cares? None of that has anything to do with the essential reality of Jesus or salvation! You look toward differences within a faith to dismiss belief altogether, you lame, burned out sot."

Peter wasn't having any of it, and although small in stature, he certainly wasn't intimidated by Malcolm's towering 260-pound bulk. Peter had become hirsute over the years and looked much akin to one of the unkempt Vermont wild-child types that inhabit the backwoods of Pomfret, Hartland, or White River. Yeah, they typically wear worn-out dungarees, flannel shirts, and bandanas and smoke a lot of pot. Be that as it may, Peter was a Lebanon kid and that Valley-born urge to engage in debate came shining through.

"You don't know a damn thing about Christianity or God," Peter sneered. "Hell, you born-agains don't even know that you don't know! Yet you have the arrogance to lecture folks like me about what the Bible says is the best way of living and whatnot. It's all self-assured bullshit, the stuff of little minds."

Malcolm took in a deep breath and stared down at Peter. "You hear that squirrel squawking in that tree? He reminds me of you, Peter. You're all noise. You construct nothing but enjoy tearing things down, you sick prick."

"It's a matter of knowing rather than opining," Peter said. "For example, you go on and on about Jesus and God without knowing what differentiates the two. Instead, you tell me Jesus and God are consubstantial, with the Holy Spirit being tossed in for good measure. You claim they are all as one: the Father, Son, and Holy Spirit. So, let me ask you, is this God of yours consubstantial with everything?"

"God is the First and the Last, the beginning and the end of everything," Malcolm replied. "Yeah, there is one God and Father of all people and things. He is the Lord of all, works through all, and is in all. Ephesians 4:6 says there is 'one God and Father of all, who is over all and through all and in all.'"

"OK, that's clear enough," Peter said with a smile. "So that tree over yonder, the pissed-off squirrel, and even you and I are all aspects of God and derived from it."

"From HIM!" Malcolm insisted. "HIM!"

"Fine, fine," Peter said. "Let God be a he, although God must also be at least part female if God is in all. In fact, if God is in and causal of all things, how can God be any one thing?"

"Are you asking how God and Jesus can be related or distinguished from all things?" Malcolm asked, knowing how clever his friend was.

"No, no, nothing like that," Peter replied. "It's just that, by your reasoning, God must be tall and small, good and bad, hard and soft, selfish and kind, and all manner of opposites. And he must be all those things at the same time, which is kind of hard to wrap my head around."

"Well, I am big compared with you, yet small compared to Albert Tyler," Malcolm said. "So don't be throwing that relativistic bunk at me."

"What about being sad and happy," Peter fired back. "And can you be good and bad at the same time?"

"Well, some moral issues are matters of free choice," Malcolm said.

"I suppose so," Peter agreed. "But isn't free choice part of how God works? And if so, must not evil, greed, lust, and all vices also be aspects of God's totality?"

"You'll never convince me that God is evil," Malcolm said with a dismissive wave. "Free choice is an aspect of our search for the Divine," Malcolm insisted, pointing toward himself. "We must interpret and learn, carefully discerning what He would wish us to do or to avoid. This is why God left us with guides like the holy Bible."

"Which was written by mere men," Peter noted. "And I suppose these men were guided by pure and impure motives."

"Not the men who wrote the bible," Malcolm replied, pointing at Peter. "They were possessed by the Holy Spirit and moved to write by the hand of God."

"So, their motivation was not an aspect of free choice?" Peter asked. "If not, how can you claim free choice is an aspect of our quest for Divine inspiration? It seems that Divine inspiration and free will are not the same. Divine inspiration is like us becoming puppets that dance to God's fancy."

Malcolm was clearly frustrated, for he had been down this road with Peter many times. He shook his balding head and looked at Peter.

"Divine inspiration allows us to see the truth, and free will permits us to accept and acknowledge it," Malcolm said. "Puppets cannot do such things, nor can you from the sound of things." He had prepared his answer because Peter had caught him out on the issue during a prior conversation. He was pleased, for here was a tack that held the existence of God as a given.

"Divine inspiration . . ." Peter said while stroking his whitening beard. He briefly studied his long, dirty fingernails and added, "How do we know what is and is not divinely inspired? Surely, we cannot say everything is divinely inspired because then we'd have to accept that Paul Trembly poking Dale Smith's wife was cool with God."

"That goes back to free will," Malcolm said, "and it also involves our ability to discern what ways and how God would wish us to act. That is spelled out in the Bible, praise the Lord."

"So, the Bible is kind of a rulebook," Peter noted. "Or we could call it a guide of sorts. If that is how it works, then what does that say about free choice? After all, how can we claim free choice is available when strict rules limit our ability to choose freely as we see fit? It's like saying we can walk any path, but only one prescribed path is correct."

"The Word is a set of directions to help us navigate our way to Him," Malcolm observed.

"Hmmm, if we truly have Divine inspiration through the agency of God, one would think that a guide would be superfluous," Peter said. "One counterargument could be that children need direction lest they become confused or lost, and thus we have God acting as a kind of monitor."

"There is only one path to God," Malcolm replied, "In John, Jesus says, 'I am the way and the truth and the life. No one comes to the Father except through me.'"

"Yet you claim we have free choice," Peter sneered. "What a bunch of bullshit. The truth is, your beliefs are recursive. It is so because the Bible says it is so. That is a matter of belief alone and certainly not one of logic or reasoned argument. And the same goes for the other religious texts! They are all eager to embrace the worst of behaviors to defend or impose their versions of reality: Jihad here, a holy war there. Malcolm, you're a bright guy. Surely, you must see that wars, punishments, slavery, and cruelty evolve from many deluded folks who merely *think* they are inspired by the Word of a God. But the truth is, many of them cannot even define what God is."

"And look at you," Malcolm coldly replied. "You collect your piss in jars, live in a shack, and haven't taken a shower in weeks. And you're telling me I don't know how to live!"

"Oh, I'm much closer to God than you'll ever be," Peter said dismissively. "I live in nature, don't give a shit about money or appearances, and don't make myself a slave to any book or notion. I live for the day and find inspiration in this angry squirrel's chattering or an old crow's cawing. Sometimes, the brook beside my place speaks to me, as do the robins who have taken up residence in my kitchen. Now that there is pure inspiration. And the insights nature teaches me are at least as meaningful as that tomb you carry about."

"If you think talking to deer and raccoons will give you more insights than the Word can offer, you are truly lost," Malcolm said. "Shit, I'm about the only person dumb enough to put up with your crap. You used to be such a good guy, and that's how we became friends. But now you're a useless word-bender who can't hold a job. You argue for argument's sake, and you could care less about being right or wrong, let alone God."

"Yet you still try to save my heathen soul," Peter smiled. "That could be the influence of either Divine inspiration or the Word," he added. "Either way, it is MY choice to engage in this nonsense. Yep, I enjoy our little chats, smelly guy though I am."

And so it goes in the Upper Valley, for people here tend to live freely through word and deed. This isn't to say we have perfected an existential utopia. To be sure, Valley people often tend to gossip and bitch, albeit they can be called out for doing so in open forums via straightforward and impolite means, as in, "Hey, Fred . . . shut the f' up about my son being gay. It ain't any of your f'n business." There is a certain directness and honesty here, although one usually has to be considered a community member to be part and parcel of the discursive style. As for the ideas expressed here and elsewhere in the Upper Valley, they vary wildly, and folks often disagree. New Englanders invented town-hall meetings, and they can be very contentious affairs.

Some probably dislike how Malcolm or Peter expressed ideas or the contents thereof, but most Valley folks could care less. So long as they are honest and at least partially civil, all is fine and dandy. Actual physical fights happen in the Valley, but in most cases, only teeth, noses, and pride suffer. There are exceptions, but Valley folk are not keen on slaughtering one another. In fact, Vermont has just 1.8 murders per 100,000 people (number 51 in the US and its territories), while New Hampshire has 2.4 (number 41). So, despite our directness, we have learned to chain the beasts that many harbor within. And we indeed harbor numerous beasts, with their tethers needing frequent attention. One way to do that is by being open, direct, and honest, which are good traits to foster. Thank you, God, for thinking about us, doubters and believers alike. Amen.

26

The Universe Finds a Way

Due to blown-out knee cartilages, my legs could no longer carry my bloated body any distance, let alone to church. So, I drove my Cobra GT4 mobility scooter to the boat dock a few months ago to commune with God. It was a beautiful sunny day, with cloudless, cerulean skies and the sun's gentle warmth. My mind was troubled by nagging doubts about finances, ill health, petty conflicts, and the typical debris of living in a large senior center. There are times I utterly detest elderly people, albeit just before I detest myself for detesting. Ah, we're all in this game for the duration, although we tend to make matters needlessly unpleasant all too often. Indeed, our happiness and misery are primarily artifacts of our creation. Thus, anger brings anger into the context of our lives, while love behaves in a like manner. In a way, each

26.1 The author is in decline, but he still attends his church

of us helps define a tiny bit of reality, although a few will want to call that divine existential amalgamation God. The word pains some, so they opt to call it life, being, and so on.

A glimmering about how existence unfolds is fine and dandy, but it does little to calm the waves of discord that one can foster within. The tempest can start as a tiny perturbation, as in an inane criticism, repeated failure, terrible news story, or even a dog barking. Alas, we allow the minuscule disturbance to mushroom into a raging tsunami that buries our equipoise underneath a torrent of shifting emotions often bound by seething outrage. Arousing that animus until it sweeps all before it is a choice. Do we submit to a budding inclination that harbors discord, or do we simply walk another path?

Too bad I cannot answer that question, bound as I am to present moments. I can perceive the dilemma's fundamentals, but like many of you, I am often trapped within a bubble of myopia. I willfully blind and bind myself to a miserable present moment, wearing a coat of angst like a new spring wardrobe. I still have the metacognitive capacity to realize my perfidy, but I lack what it takes to escape what binds me. Some tell me these sudden outbursts or raw, uncontrolled emotions are due to "a major cognitive disorder," to which they put a host of unconvincing names. No, that sounds more like an excuse rather than a reason. So, I seek solace at the dock, in the woods, or any place that allows me to contemplate an escape from an ugly *now*.

Sometimes, I try going to the source during these turbulent times when happiness evaporates, and darkness sweeps over one's soul. Yeah, I actually talk with God during the tempest. And I could care less if some folks don't like the word God. Screw them. The word-haters can strive to break free of the conceptual bubble they've trapped themselves in, be it the snare of arrogance, anger, resentment, or banal opinion. We hence hate ideas, races, one another, and even terms that are merely gateways to concepts we can elect to embrace or dismiss. Hey, it's something we all do at times. For me, quelling storms often requires traveling into nature, or listening to tunes, or even taking long walks, although the latter has become impossible. The thing is, we must strive to do something to lift the veil that clouds our vision! Indeed, one has to change contextual viewpoints to see from different perspectives, and off I went.

26.2 The road to church is bumpy and animals often pay visits

Yeah, there I was, slowly ambling along the familiar bumpy, bucolic road that soon overlooked the Connecticut River. The river peeked through the foliage occasionally as if playing a game of hide-and-seek. I turned into the entrance road to the boat dock and rolled down the verdant-lined dirt ramp, flanked by towering beech, birch, and other water-loving trees and bushes. Now, here was an inviting context. I drove right up to the gently lapping waves and parked, basking in the glory of a balmy and bright day. The sun kissed my face and arms, warming my soul and gently opening my typically closed mind to the possibilities inherent in prayer. I began watching the sunlight play off the gyrating waves and soon found myself enraptured by a glittering display that began overwhelming my senses. The dazzling lights

26.3 The sceanery overlooking the Wilder Dam Resevoir from the road is inviting

opened a portal in my mind, a doorway to a blissful communion transcending time and space. Foolishly, I tried capturing the moment in some photos, although their approximation of my surroundings cannot be anything other than a poor relative to the real thing.

The sun's reflections off the gently rolling waves gave rise to a presence of sorts, one that I have sought and spoken to many times before. It does not matter if I generated that presence from within or if it evolved from without, for wherein resides the realm of thought about thought? And as I drifted into sublimity, the glittering lights allowed me to recognize my essential oneness with a unique moment in time and space, something akin to

26.4 The entry to a church where all are welcome

being quantized. My mind reached out to what is always there, and the rapture of the event freed my thoughts to commune.

"I am so weary of discord and pain," I lamented. "I came to . . ."

You talk with yourself and call it communing with God! You came to encapsulate being in a web of words . . . as if such a thing is possible.

"You sound . . ."

Silence! You are not fit to judge or opine, let alone commune with the Divine. And God is what you are arrogant enough to call me, although little in creation would willingly communicate with such an angry and turbulent soul.

"They tell me this and that about my future, and then my friends rake me for saying X, Y, and Z! And I get so pissed off that I can..."

You are unworthy in nearly all ways, so stop whining and raging! Look at existence as it is and not as you would have it be! Foolish child, you seek to be one with something that all things are already part of. And into this realm, you drag ceaseless anger, insufferable pride, petty insistence, and banal comprehension. Can one such as you ever see or share the truth? Listen!

"I don't..."

LISTEN!

"I, I hear the waves... and some birds."

That is my voice. Can you understand it?

"As in signs?"

Not merely signs! LOOK AT ME!

"There are hundreds of lights. They dance and gyrate on the waves."

Yet there is no form. Can you understand meaning beyond words, a song without a tune, or life without substance?

"You sound so angry."

That anger emanates from YOU! Would you make your anger my anger and share that concept with those reading these words? Would you then have them believe that you have uncovered some great truths? The fact is, you are merely revealing yourself and your own vanity.

"This is unlike you. You do not rage..."

I rage when there is rage.

"Reflections. It is all about . . ."

Silence! Your time is finite and dwindling, much like those with us now in thought. Alas, you have become a broken record that endlessly repeats itself. Is that doing your kindred any good?

"Probably not, but the sun sure feels good."

Ah, now you understand an inkling of the positive, which is always there to be perceived. Build on that until it becomes as warm as this fleeting moment's gentle graces. That is when you will be in my presence fully. Do not bring the negative into this sublime realm if it is peace that you seek. Learn how to love and how to become one with all that abounds. Judge not, lest ye be judged, and share all, lest ye be found ungrateful. You have lost your way, child.

"I must try to do better."

No, you must be better.

I feel a gentle breeze on my face and feel the rapture of communion with all that is. I am ashamed of what I harbored within, but also just a bit wiser.

"Thank you, God. Amen."

27

Does God Change?

This is a somewhat disjointed and speculative piece, so be fair warned, and feel free to move on. Moreover, we are thinking about an all-encompassing theme, which is about as big as possible. However, God's nature is a worthy topic for contemplation and prayer. Yes, I often ponder about the Divine while gazing at wild turkeys busily foraging beneath my windows or studying the waves lapping the shores of the nearby Boston Reservoir. Of course, the answer to questions about God's nature depends on how one defines God. I opt for maximum broadness, simplicity, and inclusion whenever possible. To me, God is within and related to everything, a causal nexus that runs throughout everything that was, is, and ever could be.

Being integral to and with all things, God thus cannot be reduced to any one thing . . . and most especially a cosmic, white-bearded old man who appears to be taking steroids. The most straightforward proof that God is dynamic is that God's being must encompass all aspects of change, growth, and decay, as is readily evident in the ongoing unfolding of this universe. As Heraclitus noted over 2,500 years ago, one cannot step into the same stream twice, especially within a universe of constant flux. On the other hand, notions like fixed, eternal, permanent, and indelible must also be part of God's nature, even though we cannot easily find examples of these metaphysical constructs in our ever-shifting universe. Indeed, the only readily evident constant in our universe is that of change, as oxymoronic as that notion seems.

This takes us into a complicated realm because ideas and concepts concerning God's being are also part of God, reflexive as that conclusion is. Moreover, the notion of Divinity has been around since our species became sentient, and it has been seen through the lenses of manifold perspectives. Indeed, beyond elusive and possibly universal principles, all we know of the Divine are humanity's viewpoints. Sadly, most of us are not even dimly aware of what many of these perspectives were and are. There are no prehistoric records for humans, just hand prints and images painted on cave walls. The precise meanings are lost to us, other than we know that rituals were probably involved.

Nonetheless, it is clear that our ideas concerning what the Divine is have changed considerably over time, as is evident in the extant historical record. Ergo, part of God's being, at least in the metaphysical sense, has also changed. Yet if God is, in fact, consubstantial with the universe, that too is in flux.

Alas, we have no inkling what other sentient species concluded concerning the Divine billions of years ago or what they will opine in the future. Nonetheless, most of us are well beyond the insular stage wherein we dismiss the notion of ET life forms altogether. After all, being is vast, and all viable possibilities eventually become realities given the agency of time. In fact, time itself must also be an aspect of God's being, although I cannot wrap my tiny brain around the notion of God being the past, present, and future simultaneously. I mean, where is the "now" that allows one temporally bound concept in this admixture to join another in our thoughts about this amalgam? Of course, the required quanta of time that determine the now must also be inculcated as an aspect of the Divine. The essential point is that concepts concerning God have been around for eons and will continue to exist as metaphysical entities for eons to come. They may differ in detail, but it is a safe bet that they'll also have much in common. Our knowledge base is far too limited to address this area in any meaningful depth other than to speculate that the general idea of God may be a universal concept that becomes manifest as sentience evolves.

Currently, the notion of there being something akin to what we call God remains vibrant in *Homo sapiens*, dancing from mind to mind and generation to generation as the ages unfold. Our ideas shift regarding how and what we define God to be. Still, the general focus on a causal agent and/or process sustaining our existence continues, albeit some find comfort in atheism and science. Be that as it may, one species or another is likely always to contribute thoughts and ideas concerning the Divine, the sum of such contemplations giving God a dynamic metaphysical presence. This presence changes, being Jesus, Gitche Manitou, and many other notions within the human species alone. Goodness, other species will introduce us to concepts that are very familiar, although the likelihood of some deviations is high.

Whatever the case, let us consider that certain aspects of God's being may not change. For instance, the concepts of pi, repeating fractions (e.g., one-third, 0.333), eternal, vacuum, and infinity exist as verifiable metaphysical constructs, even though these notions cannot be fully realized in the material sense within our realm of existence. Thus, no perfect sphere occurs in nature or can be forged, although a sphere can be described and defined via geometry and mathematics. These staid ideas have long existed as rationalistic proofs and exercises, and one postulates that they would be readily identifiable by intelligent species of the past, present, and future. Moreover, there is a vast array of 'absolute' ideas like this, nearly all being metaphysical constructs.

By definition, God inculcates all of these notions, and thus we begin to see a marriage of the absolute and the changing. As previously discussed, Plato postulated an extemporal noumenal realm for these eternal and unchanging Forms (ideas) to exist within, and herein they could somehow participate with and in corporeal existence. One could call this permanent realm an ideational heaven or haven, though Aristotle found the notion utterly useless. To him, the possible/potential was to be found within the secular and shifting realm of matter and energy, and it was not distinct from it. Thus, a piece of wood inculcates the possibility of becoming a banjo, desk, or even a sphere, depending upon the ideas we bring into play while manipulating the material. As for where the ideas reside, that is where species like us enter into the equation. In effect, creatures like us sustain the metaphysics of being, including thoughts about thought.

The intriguing part of our inquiry is how the absolute and unchanging interacts with the dynamic and shifting to produce, sustain, and/or intermingle with our existence. I once postulated an ideational DNA that interacts with energy, time, and matter to beget the person reading this line. I speculated that this process manifests via the machinations of fundamental frequencies, as in an energetic organizing principle that runs throughout any given universe and becomes so integrated with matter, time, energy, and thought as to be inseparable. Of course, the organizing impetus was born of the possible, but where does the possible reside, if not in the form of an idea or concept? And how can ideas exist without the agency of time, and so on, which takes us back to the conundrum of possibility's causal agency yet again? Are time, energy, matter, and metaphysics all the children of potential alone? Do they exist simply because they can exist sans an impetus of any kind? Some physicists believe so and thus eschew the need for a God to get things started . . . albeit that they seldom define precisely what they mean by God.

Let us extend our reasoning a bit. Could certain ideational aspects of "God" have been extant even before this current universal cycle we're bound within came into existence? The answer has to be yes/probably because it is theorized that there are and have been many universes, as in the notion of multiversity. Although each universe likely differs in detail due to the organizational harmonics involved, one cannot dismiss the possibility of sentient life forms having evolved therein that embraced various concepts of Divinity. Perhaps these concepts were and are much the same as ours, with the distillation of a metaphysical presence for the Divine being constantly in play.

Moreover, distinct universes and species will eventually evolve, giving the Divine a supernatural presence as they ponder the imponderable. The resultant abstraction seems more of a dynamic paradox than anything else, a dancing spark that flitters about as being waxes and wanes. Yet as we have seen, the notion of a shifting constant is oxymoronic. We are ill-equipped to postulate what these constants may be, given the primitive nature of our knowledge about how other realities operate. Yeah, this tack is like I did too much acid at one time, but let's play out the line.

Indeed, some constants must be bound to seminal processes, as in the impetus that causes existential realities such as our own to blossom into being. We can glean some dim inkling into how these processes may work from theoretical physics. Yet, we clearly do not know nearly enough even to consider with any confidence how the Divine may manifest itself within the machinations of being. What is the impetus, the seminal seed that interacts with energy, mass, thought, possibility, and time to give rise to such contemplations? The impetus of being is clearly implied by our existence, but that driving force's existence has not yet proven to be a reality because we know so little. If constants are indeed involved, then one of them must be continuous change. And here we are, back to our staid paradox.

God defined itself to me as "a dynamic being of ultimate selflessness" during a beautiful dream, and my struggle to understand that brief description has been tied for many years to exercises such as the one you are now reading. As my mind erodes, I continue to talk with God about things like change, being, thought, and much else. It became a habit some years ago, although now I record the conversations to share them with you and others. They often end in a muddle, especially now, but I suspect you can take these notions further than I can. God can be challenging to perceive even vaguely, let alone to understand. I mean, something that is all things tends to take on perspectives that test the senses and mind, and my normal state has become much more straightforward as my brain erodes. My hope is that the Divine is accessible to fools and geniuses alike, for I am becoming the former . . . which may be a blessing. Amen.

28

Talking with God About God

I'm religious, although I do not subscribe to any major religion. Nonetheless, I talk with God frequently, sans any middleman or holy book. Typically, I speak with God at the Boston Reservoir, atop a mountain, and especially at the boat dock and its environs. Yeah, the boat dock is my preferred place of worship, especially now that I cannot go out and about easily. Thank goodness for my electric mobility scooter! This makes journeys into nature's graces possible, even on a few well-worn paths through the woods. Ah, and such ventures are delightful during the spring and fall. Yes, I escape the sedate confines of Quail Hollow, a senior residential community and generally pleasant place to live.

28.1 Peeking at the Divine through the trees and bushes (GHE via Shirley)

Yet it is not my ideal place for prayer unless I am laid up due to illness or incapacity.

Ideally, speaking with God is often best accomplished where life abounds and vistas unfold without numerous people jabbering away. Many Valley folks know and understand this, although some citified folks don't believe it. Well, they can learn the lesson if they try. Mountaintops, the beach, lakes, and rivers are places where God can be easily found, although looking into a mirror works reasonably well. Of course, one has to gaze beyond the reflection of self for that to happen, thus the allure of scenic bucolic settings. The demands such venues place on sublimity and abstraction are not nearly as great as those found in busy churches or cathedrals, and I am getting simple enough so that avoiding distractions is essential . . . or so they say.

So, I take the one-mile winding and bumpy road down to the dock to pray quite often, not that God can easily be called up at times. Gaps in the trees' verdant leaves and branches herald my approach to the landing by revealing partially hidden scenes of the ambling Connecticut River and its shores. If I am lucky, the ducks will be out and about, paddling along as they meet life's various imperatives. Dragonflies will show off their iridescent hues, and water spiders zip by the shore, dancing gracefully on the aqueous surface. Fish laze in the shallows, and boat-bound anglers sometimes cast lines into the rippling waves. Occasionally, a hawk or eagle swoops down, creations of the Divine that sometimes announce their presence with piercing calls. Colorful songbirds perch on nearby branches, their melodies making a sweet accompaniment to the gentle lapping of waves. I turn off the road, descend the moderate grade that leads to the water, and park my small buggy on a tiny, grass-covered peninsula that juts into the river. After some reflection, the conversation usually begins with a greeting and acknowledgment of gratitude.

"Many thanks for granting these moments. As usual, awesome job on the sun glistening off the waves. Very surreal."

Hmmm, it doesn't seem like God is listening today, but I know that's just a lack of imagination being recruited on my end. Well, perhaps God is busy or some such thing. Of course, the Divine is always with us, no matter what. Yet there must come times she doesn't like listening to our yammering, especially when we're whining, angry, or just being prideful and dumb. Yeah, but this description problem is essential, and we ought to get to it.

"Hey, that definition of God we discussed as *a dynamic being of ultimate selflessness* left something to be desired. Of course, what could I expect from a dream? Maybe that was the best my mind could perceive."

A crow squawks, its harshness giving a reply to those who listen.

"Signs, signs, everywhere a sign," I rejoin. "But those six words inculcated an immense amount of philosophy. I remember your inquisition. *If I am all things, how can I be any one thing?* I suppose that is what being ultimately selfless is, at least in part. Then you said . . . *If I am of time, must I not move within it?* And it was clear enough that is what the term "dynamic being" meant. Yeah, you went on and on and on. Yet I've lost some of the details. There was a lot to unpack."

But was the conversation a product of your imagination alone, or was God involved?

"In that, my imagination is a tiny aspect of your being, then I presume you were part of the conversation."

Presumptions can be fodder for the deluded.

"Or children," I observe. "Presumptions can also be the fodder of saints, sinners, and many things."

The crow yells at me again, as crows are prone to do.

"Then you are pissed off," I observe.

Is that what you would have me say?

"Yeah, speaking *for* the Divine is a fool's errand," I concede, having had this conversation before. "How can anyone speak for something that is beyond fully knowing? The best I can do is seek to understand a tiny bit about how creation operates by communing *with* part of the Divine."

Can anyone or anything accomplish such a task?

"Not completely," I reply. "Our perspectives are too limited, bound as we are to a moment and place within the vastness of all that is. Hell, my kind anthropomorphized you for thousands of years. We made you a fat woman with wide hips and broad breasts for quite some time. Later, an Egyptian heretic made you the sun stretching its rays to everything, helping spawn and further the idea that a singular and energetic God gave life to all. Then we made you a buffed Greek guy tossing thunderbolts about. Lately, we have a Westernized bearded guy playing the lead role of an ancient Jew, although any thinking person knows Jesus never looked like that. Hell, he was Semitic! Yet if you are all things, you must also be these means of seeking and describing your nature."

Even though these concepts may conflict?

"Being ultimately selfless has a price," I reply with a shrug. "Your singularity was split asunder via the Big Bang or so some claim. Of course, I don't know how many Big Bangs you have been involved with as one universe or another came into being. That sort of thing is akin to having an active sex life. Good for you! Well, this current Big Bang event is thought to have been the case in the present existential bubble we're in, this particular universe. Of course, other bubbles exist, and I wonder about your role in their creation and evolution. Are they passing thoughts, tiny bits of a presence and process without a beginning or end? Something tells me it's all about fundamental frequencies, but my mind is too limited to study theoretical physics. Hell, I'm getting dumber by the day.

In any case, I regard this reality we're sharing as the consummate act of giving, with the one becoming the all. I suppose that is what ultimate selflessness is really all about. The 'I' became 'I am,' and from this amalgam of thought, matter, energy, and time arose the evolution of 'we are.' The staid singular became the ever-shifting plural, the dynamic beings you are one with. I wish I could wrap my mind around the idea, but I am thankful for it. Anyway, I suppose a tiny part of you is what we craft from concepts and notions like these, although some may be way off the mark."

Still, you seek to speak to this selfless being as if it were a distinct self. That is your paradoxical quest, but there have been so many efforts. Once, you made me an encompassing nexus that ties all creation together, a golden thread of sorts. Yes, all things supposedly passed through me, allowing a great communion to occur in venues such as the present one. How many thoughts like this do you suppose I have experienced?

"My thoughts and perspectives are far too limited to offer many insights," I admit. "We humans have difficulties at the

28.2 A pier juts above the water's surface but not above reflections

higher levels of abstraction. Well, I sure do. Oh, that crow is really pissed. He keeps squawking at me."

Which you keep equating with my being angry.

"I imagine you are angry, glad, hungry, sad, and all other things simultaneously," I reply. "All those worlds and the life forms thereon . . . All those shifting thoughts and changing contexts . . . Being at the center of all that is incomprehensible given the space and time dynamics involved. Nonetheless, we're here to explore these questions and seek answers."

You presume the search for such knowledge gives it a spiritual presence within my being. Is this how you believe God thinks?

"I believe part of life's purpose is the evolution of beings that can contemplate their existence from the perspectives we're now sharing with the folks reading this line," I reply. "In effect, our purpose is to find our purpose. Yet I'm not positive. I contemplate the many species that have evolved here and there, nearly all of which have gone extinct. We stand upon that ever-shifting process of being that generates notions such as we're sharing, with our current incarnation being directed more toward the intellectual than physical."

And you consider the evolutionary process essentially ruthless.

"It was born of the consummate act of giving," I reply, "as in splitting yourself asunder so that beings like me could arise. I suppose that was the ultimate act of love, and that is hardly a ruthless thing to do. Yet the process aims to sustain life in the face of endless challenges. Life of all kinds flourishes and dims in the face of shifting needs and deprivations. Simply put, life adapts, or it goes extinct. And yes, that process can be very harsh. You know, watching a mink kill and eat isn't enjoyable. I suppose humanity proves that a few species develop forms and means to contemplate these ideas we share, but the losses along the way are tremendous."

Are those lives truly lost?

"To have ever been is to always be," I blurt out, only half understanding the meaning. "Yeah, I recall our discussion about that. I wrote an essay on it. The central theme was that imagination and thought can transcend distance and time. I believe I used the example of a small family several light years away. We view them as reflections that may be millions of years old from our perspectives. But if we use our abilities to ponder, empathize, and imagine, they are with us in the present . . . that thing I dubbed the *now*."

And you presume my perspective is the broadest in existence, and thus all exists simultaneously within the Divine.

"Yeah, that's a tenuous presumption on my part," I confess. "It collapses time and space, and I'm not sure that is appropriate. After all, does the future unfold, or has it already been played out in your being? I suppose it comes out to determinism versus free choice."

You claim God is dynamic. Doesn't that answer the question?

"In part," I say with a laugh. "Very good! I am being hoisted upon my own petard and shown to be wanting. Hmmm, let me ponder a bit. Future fact is knowable, at least partially. Accomplishing that end usually involves manipulating context and thus manufacturing an outcome that is very nearly certain. Thus, an appropriately designed and directed rocket goes to Mars and deposits a suitably manufactured robot to explore the planet. But delving into an outcome that is the end product of dynamics that my kind cannot fully control is another matter altogether. We can certainly predict, but only within the realm of the probable."

Would you make me deterministic or an aspect of happenstance?

"By definition, both possibilities are inculcated in your being," I reply. "You include all possibilities, even those that contradict each other. That is where I keep running into trouble! Your totality is incomprehensible to me, yet I keep trying. Look, you know I love you. These prayers are just my way of getting to

28.3 Hirum Allan at the Boat Dock, one of many who contemplate there

know you better, although this isn't easy. After all, you are also a vacuum, an eternity, and many other concepts that cannot be fully realized in this realm of being I'm one with. In fact, there seem to be more ideas than realities, especially if you throw in incorrect notions."

So, you tried to place God in the realm of thought, making me an ideational DNA . . . a sort of nexus that gave rise to all that can be perceived. God thus coexists with everything without being discrete, acting as an essential element that participates in all things while time unfolds. The Divine's very existence was depersonalized to the extent that using pronouns is dubious.

"It makes writing about you brutally difficult," I confess. "Yeah, I cannot actually do that consistently. And my only palpable sense of you has been that of a distinctly female presence. Oh, but please notice that I'm not using too many pronouns here."

A chickadee lands close to the scooter. I smile at the bird as it looks up at me through black eye masks. The chickadee hops about, probing for insects.

Are there words that could describe something that includes all words besides a dictionary? Yet you claim God is beyond words and ideas alone. Didn't you once describe the Divine as the closed set of everything that includes itself?

"Yeah, among other paradoxes," I reply. "I suppose contemplating such conundrums is a means by which our minds can grow. But I rejected the notion of your being closed because . . ."

. . . nothing that constantly changes can ever be closed. Nonetheless, you are without satisfactory answers. Does that mean you lack insight? If so, does this imply that God also lacks understanding?

"I am merely an infinitesimally small and limited bit of you," I reply. "I'm reasonably sure one being or another has resolved what my kind regards as paradoxes."

Yet not you.

"That's for sure," I fire back. "Hell, I'm not even certain about what questions to ask. It's that sunlight bouncing off the waves. It's utterly captivating, drawing my senses and thoughts to the now."

Nonetheless, you fight this moment of bliss. Yet more questions brew within your mind, or is it God's mind?

"Very droll," I reply with a smile. "It is our mind, I suspect, with mine being a minor player within the entire scheme of things. It's nice of you to indulge me like this."

Is there a choice?

"Oh, what a wonderful question!" I observe with a laugh. "Well, if you are in everything, I suspect your choices unfold like ours. And perhaps I should regard you as omnipresent, an essential part of a constantly changing process. Yet some things are staid, like the rules of physics. Huh, I've not considered that issue in much depth. Hmmm, please bear with me while I spin this out."

I realize this is how you pray, child. But spinning this out eschews the moment, and there will never be another moment exactly like it. Feel the sun on your arms and enjoy a shared grace. Feel the breeze that touches your face and smell the scents passing your way. Yes, being embraces thought, but it also thrives off the physical and energetic. Let them all be conjoined via time unfolding, and do your utmost to find happiness in this singular moment. Leave the self behind and commune with all. That is the best way of being one with what you call God and some call existence.

"How I love you. For sometimes, my prayers are indeed answered. That sunlight and wave action is sublime."

Amen.

29

Pondering the Nature of God

We have been focusing on the subject of God for six chapters, some of which are demanding and others superficial. There have been many loose ends, and I want to tidy up a bit by pondering a wide range of subjects. Be warned that tidying up will make this piece ramble a bit, and it can get complex. Moreover, parts of the present chapter have the tone of an attack piece, although that is undoubtedly not its intention. Attacking any faith is folly because nearly all have something positive to offer regarding insights. And Lord knows I have studied numerous beliefs and mythopoetic accounts about how and why we and this world came into being, everything from Gilgamesh to Sikhism. I've not found any faith I can subscribe to, but their study has been enlightening. With these caveats in mind, let us proceed.

First, it is necessary to understand that the moniker "God" is merely a word, a metaphoric symbol that means nothing in itself. However, if we are so inclined, the word can be used as a key that opens conceptual gates to far and wide paths. These paths can elicit a wealth of emotions, insights, and opinions, but at their core they are social, contemplative, and experiential constructs that vary from person to person. In short, "God" has no meaning other than the meaning we provide through formal learning, experience, reflection, and/or personal knowledge. The word itself is neither good nor bad, and folks who recoil or exuberate at its mere mention are not being terribly insightful. As we will see, examining the term "God" can lead us to numerous and varied concepts that go well beyond what our religious texts and leaders ordain. In this sense, we are about to explore what the term "God" can come to denote and not merely rehash common perceptions. Yet, let us begin at the beginning, a time when staid convention ruled many of our inquiries, including mine.

I was raised a Roman Catholic and was thus exposed to the church's pomp, ritual, and teachings early on. I was taught the Nicene Creed: "I believe in one God, the Father Almighty, maker of heaven and earth, of all things visible and invisible." This, and related notions, made God distinct from being, albeit that God created all that is. That was a hard sell because I was also taught that God runs through everything. How could God run through all things yet somehow be distinct from them?

This made no sense to me. Indeed, I began to question some Christian doctrines even as a child, especially the Trinity. Here we have the Father/God, the Holy Spirit, and the Son/Jesus all being essentially one, as in the notion of consubstantiality. This triad supposedly differed in its aspects but was of the same substance, and that substance somehow differed from all that is.

No, none of this rang true to me, and I often discussed the lack of logical continuity with the nuns at Sunday school. I rather liked the discussions, although I found little by way of support for some of the contentions being offered. I was guided to St. Augustine and other doctrinal luminaries early on, albeit their rationalisms were far from satisfying in many cases. However, I did not leave the church until a relatively minor incident. One of the sisters who taught us at Sunday school ardently insisted that we had the right to punch someone "right on the nose" who doubted our faith. This is something one most definitely does not want to tell eager young miscreants who are already looking to find excuses for wanton behaviors.

Well, some of us Catholic kids were keen on becoming holy warriors, so like latter-day crusaders, we marched to battle with the local Seventh-Day Adventists' children. And a few kids took free licenses to smite those nasty Adventist children, who were actually about the nicest people I had ever met. To make a long story short, the sister *denied* having ever sanctioned violence when brought to task by her superiors about the wanton actions of some of her charges. In essence, she lied! I was stunned and found the entire experience incongruous. If she was to lie about something as unimportant in the overall scheme of things as kids getting the wrong message, what other whoppers might she have told along the way? Could we have also been lied to about the Trinity, papal infallibility, and even what the Gospels meant? My growing doubts became palpable.

I am not alone in being disabused of many ideas promulgated as indelible truths by any number of faiths. Thus, I was spiritually adrift by my early teens. Some of you have probably felt the same way. Yeah, I did not believe that God looks like a buffed old man, that the Pope cannot make mistakes, that Jesus, God, and the Holy Spirit are some peculiar amalgamation, that Armageddon is inevitable, that virgins are our final reward for dying for our faith, that I'm going to be reincarnated as a bug or lion, that there is such a thing as a chosen people or any number of other quaint notions. Like many reading these words, I began looking for a new path that can give meaning to life while also including many of the moral dimensions we once found in our places of worship.

Moreover, how can we look toward our existing faiths for guidance in light of the rampant hypocrisy that often festers beneath the surface? Bloated evangelical preachers beg with wet-eyed ardor for money that is ultimately turned into Mercedes-Benz cars or gold-plated bathroom fixtures for their personal use. Meanwhile, leering pedophilic priests are protected and coddled by unconscionable church authorities who betray children and parents' sacred trust. Others speak for God in claiming that it is perfectly justifiable to ethnically cleanse, while also contending that one bit of land or another is ours by Divine right, regardless of who has lived there for over 1,000 years. Some faiths and religious leaders even ask us to die, kill, and maim in the name of God, claiming that the justification is within this or that passage of a sacred text. Given all this, many people eventually contemplate where to turn, and thus my ongoing search.

The need to find a path to understanding was and is compelling. Our time is when Earth faces environmental, economic, and social ills that threaten our very existence, and many of you understand this point. Indeed, the necessity for redefining perspectives, terms, and beliefs grows by the moment if we are to meet the pressing existential demands we face. Herein, we will largely eschew existing dogma and instead examine what conceptual doors the term "God" can be used to open. Of course, the walk down any new path begins with opening our minds and hearts to various possibilities, which is not easy for many folks. For over 60 years, I've been on such a quest, although I cannot claim to have been successful. Yet I am pleased to share a few ideas in the hopes that they can serve as a basis from which you can build new and better insights. Essentially, the person reading this line can separate the wheat from the chaff and take the ideas discussed below to their logical conclusions. My friends, we are all kindred and linked by capacities that can transcend our differences in form and belief.

The first general principle to consider is the possibility of an underlying order (logos/account/directing imperative) that is seminal and essential to the creation and ongoing machinations of existence. Being all-encompassing, this logos of being includes metaphysical elements that cannot be separated entirely from the energetic and material aspects of being. For example, neurons fire in your brain while you reflect upon this sentence. The electrical dance becomes a thought linked to the material and energetic processes that sustain your existence. You physically commit this thought to memory when new synapses are formed and later articulate the idea in written and spoken words that begin a subsequent metaphysical dance in others. The insights you pass on may differ in detail from those discussed here due to variations in experiences and contexts. Still, the result is a shared meaning that can travel through time and space via spoken, written, or recorded symbols, although this does not exhaust all the possible means of communion. Essentially, your shared thoughts are the equivalent of Plato's concept that "Wisdom is a blaze, kindled by a leaping spark."

We must make a brief departure here, for some will query where the logos of being resided before the seminal act of creation that gave rise to our universe and us. Alas, "we" probably are not all that was, is, or will ever be in terms of sentience, especially given our universe's size, complexity, and age. Furthermore, some speculate the existence of a multiverse, a process wherein fundamental frequencies help define the organizational mechanics of different existential realms. These universes wax and wane and possess unique characteristics. In theory, some of these distinct realms of existence predate our own, and many will come to be long after our reality reaches its apotheosis.

Thus, we can speculate that there is no *singular* realm within which the logos of existence resides as a discrete entity. Instead, it appears to be a dynamic process (or spark) that runs throughout all that exists. Although many questions arise, universal commonalities probably include time, matter, energy, and thought. Do these existential realms have a beginning or end? How do they differ, and what do they share? Oh, and how can we access them? These subjects are meat for a nutritious and hardy contemplative diet, and I can only offer a little seasoning.

In many respects, the underlying logos that gives rise to beings like us acts as an organizing principle. I have speculated that this principle is much like DNA when interacting with energy's primal and fundamental constituents. It can instill the infrastructure needed to evolve time, space, and matter. Some people call this underlying order "God," while others call it physics, Higgs bosons, mathematics, science, philosophy, religion, and so on. Yet all of these descriptive endeavors are united in that they are the byproducts of thought, which may well be what the underlying logos of being is directed toward evolving. In essence, our purpose could include reflecting upon our purpose, with our contemplations helping to inform what we can and will become. We have discussed this possibility before, but do you think it has any merit? Take a long walk about, ponder a bit, and share whatever insights you glean. That is precisely what we are doing here. We are going through a gate.

Moreover, we should also consider that emotion is critical in allowing us to make comparative evaluations among competing possibilities, which makes us very much logicoemotional beings. How emotions function within the context of the logos of being will eventually take us into an examination of their purposes, which are in part directed toward ensuring survival. We thus tend to pursue the "good" and avoid the "bad," with the apparent goal being such niceties as satisfying appetites, be they for food, sex, or companionship. The results help us survive and procreate, eventually guiding us down the evolutionary path we're now walking. However, poor choices, myopia, and natural events test our worth. Perhaps only the most perfect in form and thought can come to grasp fully the nuances involved in the logos of being, but let us reserve that possibility for later.

On a micro-level, the influences of the proposed organizational logos can be seen in how the energetic constituents of atoms are arranged and integrated, the machinations of which we are slowly coming to understand. Questions will arise about where the requisite ordering principles reside for directing the formation of subatomic and atomic particles and what these fundamental principles consist of. For example, is the logos of being inherent in the specific ways that the constituents of energy are "compelled" to interact? Therein are questions that I cannot fully answer. Clearly, energetic elements are involved, but how they operate and interact to give structure, coherence, and integration to subatomic particles is well beyond my understanding. However, some of you may come to understand how these processes unfold.

Some contend that these machinations are all born of the possible, but that is not an altar I worship at. To me, being is related to existential developmental processes that are far from random, albeit many strongly disagree. To some, we exist simply because we can be. Although this may be true, it eschews the many how and why questions. The central question I bumped into soon became, how is understanding the processes involved in existence related to the essential mechanisms that sustain our reality? How are thoughts related to the processes that eventually give rise to beings that can think?

I speculate below that all life plays a role in sustaining the logos of being, with metaphysics being a product of the thoughts we and other species generate and share, such as those insights you are now experiencing. These thoughts eventually take some into an examination of quantum mechanics, particle physics, field theory, and similar areas. Others delve into history, medicine, woodworking, painting, farming, and all arts that marry thought and hand. Time will reveal how the metaphysical machinations of searching for various truths interact with the processes sustaining our existence, assuming they interact. Of course, I suspect that understanding and sharing such knowledge is one of our ultimate goals and purposes. Perhaps the most evident proof that ordering principles are in play is that matter and energy exist in various dynamic relationships that can be defined, described, measured, manipulated, and directed via the suitable application of thought. We thus design a rocket, predict its capacities, and take a precise journey to an exact location in the fashion we anticipate. This is a purposeful manipulation of the logos of being, and it isn't random. My heart is unsteady . . . must rest.

If we consider the above as it can be applied to a concept of God, the first thing that becomes evident is that God does not have a singular corporeal form. Indeed, imposing a form upon God is an act of myopic and/or parochial folly. I suspect some of you are already chaffing about my using the term "God" here because you deem the word useless and objectionable as it relates to the logos of being. Others may be vexed because they have an existing conceptualization of the Divine that already suits their needs and beliefs. These views betray a certain intransigence or prejudice and perhaps arrogance. Hey, we are all sinners and saints, especially me. However, bias can hinder our examination of what a term can come to represent instead of perceiving only the baggage that has been foisted upon it in the past.

Yet, if we can open our minds enough to begin seeking anew for a broader and more comprehensive conceptualization of the word "God," perhaps our first task should be to abandon the Michelangelo-type image of a white-haired old man reaching out a Divine finger toward Adam. What are we to think of God's form if we eventually encounter a sentient species far more evolved than us? Moreover, why should God be made into a "Him"? If we are indeed aspects of our creator, must not that creator be feminine, masculine, and asexual? If anything, God is a maker of life, which is more an aspect of the feminine than in other genders. Nor is what the scriptures tell us about "Him" particularly relevant, for we are looking toward opening new pathways toward understanding the Divine.

People have known for thousands of years how absurdly relativistic it is to impose a human form on the Divine. Over 2,500 years ago, the Lydian philosopher Xenophanes noted:

> But if cattle and horses and lions had hands or could paint with their hands and create works such as men do, horses like horses and cattle like cattle also would depict the gods' shapes and make their bodies of such a sort as the form they have . . .

> Ethiopians say that their gods are snub-nosed and black . . . Thracians that they are pale and red-haired.

So, let us abandon those hackneyed notions of God having a human form for one of a God with a presence that is like no one thing in appearance. Indeed, how can the totality of something that partakes in so many diverse aspects of existence appear like any one thing? Perhaps a blindingly luminous white light would better represent God than a hairy old man. That is the image I once experienced, albeit during a dream. Broadening our concepts of how God may best be perceived and accessed demands that we look in new directions, and I call this search prayer. Yes, prayer is an appropriate word because it is a form of communion and perception that typically begins with thoughts. Indeed, let us consider that God is accessible by thought and is, in fact, partially wrought by the contemplations of those who seek to delve into the nature of existence through the works of science, mathematics, philosophy, dialogue, and other pursuits that are aimed at acquiring and sharing knowledge (the very stuff of thought).

If we consider God to be as described, it becomes readily evident that God is within all things and is, at least in part, one with all things. This negates the notion that God stands apart from being and somehow resides solely outside our existential bubble. Yeah, that dog doesn't hunt for a lot of good reasons. Instead, our conceptualization implies that the essential properties of God coexist within all aspects of being and are inseparable from it. And although it may be possible to explain how the logos of existence functions within any given context, it is impossible to provide this concept with a presence independent of the being it is one with. How can we entirely separate thought from the thinker or being from existence?

Moreover, we quickly run into ethical conundrums here, for it is evident that terrible events (e.g., earthquakes, tornadoes, etc.), vulgar things, evil traits, and even concepts like nihilism and nonbeing exist as either tangible or metaphysical constructs. So, is part of God to be found within a devastating cosmic catastrophe or a festering sore or the thoughts of a psychotic killer or deeds of self-destruction? The short answer is "yes," as displeasing as that answer may seem. However, some necessary qualifications and moral implications will be discussed here and below. After all, there is at least one positive for every negative, with the essential one being that of existence itself.

It also stands to reason that part of God's nature includes the possible, free will, and emotion. These properties can evolve positive and negative happenstances, thoughts, and deeds. This includes kindness, generosity, and love, as well as folly, sin, and evil. Mostly, such occurrences wax and wane, albeit they often reoccur. A drought can destroy a nation, but some people usually survive to repopulate the land. War can kill multitudes, although many may endure the destruction. A sickness of the spirit can lead to our downfall by others or our own deeds, although the society we live in may go on. However, if we are as terribly flawed as a species that we taint the land, air, and water beyond redemption, we go extinct. That is how evolution works, and it is a ruthless process that seeks the perfection of form, function, and thought above all else. Of course, the tools of survival for sentient beings also reside within us, assuming we employ the foresight needed to use them.

Some interesting corollaries follow regarding our roles in the universe if we accept that God is inseparable from the metaphysical, material, and energetic processes that help sustain our being. These processes eventually give rise to life forms that can turn thoughts into deeds and then deeds into more profound thoughts. We learn, experiment, and are driven to ever-greater discoveries and insights. The collective contemplations and wisdom of those with these abilities may provide God with a metaphysical "presence" that extends through time and space. Thus, perhaps the reflections we are currently sharing regarding God's nature are much akin to those of species that existed long ago and will exist in the distant future. If so, the nature of God becomes a dynamic but repeating story that may change in small details while we ponder possibilities but remains essentially the same in many ways. Are we indeed God's leaping spark flickering from sentient form to sentient form?

Perhaps the very purpose of life is to evolve beings that can come to understand the underlying logos that leads to their existence. In so doing, they help provide this Divine logos with a "presence." In this sense, all sentient beings are "kindred" in purpose and design no matter where, when, or how they evolved. Be they great or small, of any color or build, they are as one. Perhaps it should also be an article of faith among the Kindred that at least some sentient life forms can eventually develop the capacity to learn and communicate all that is knowable. In fact, sharing our insights and thoughts with others often involves a unique form of communion that may help kindle and perpetuate the intellectual processes needed to sustain the metaphysical aspects of being.

Whether or not it is wise for evolved species to communicate advanced knowledge with less philosophically and intellectually evolved species becomes a fundamental question (albeit speculative). On the one hand, there is essential knowledge to be gleaned from observing how different intellects perceive and process information to reach certain conclusions. On the other hand, sharing potentially dangerous expertise with immature species can be deadly because of faulty applications. Yeah, I would not want to give humans the capacity to travel through the universe in our current state. It is probably best to err on the side of caution, despite the benefits of understanding how distinct intellects operate.

Given that the laws governing energy and matter are universals, it also follows that life and thought will exist wherever the conditions are right for them to flourish. Simply put, we live because the right conditions are in place. Life's evolution is sparked by the logos of being, and life is as inevitable as being itself. However, not all life will have the opportunity to sprout fruits that can understand fully how they contribute to the metaphysical sustenance of God's being, although all life, including the most basic forms, may play roles in this process. Ultimately, nature's many survival tests can direct species toward increasingly higher levels of metaphysical realization, for the need to plan, anticipate, and act will eventually lead to sentience. And although life will adapt its physical forms to best deal with the conditions it faces, the similarities in structure and thought will far outweigh the differences. In terms of design, the universal laws of nature drive and limit forms, while in terms of intellect, grasping the laws governing the universe requires similar perceptual and analytical abilities.

From moral perspectives, how we treat one another, other life forms, and the worlds we dwell on are how God treats us. Our love becomes God's love, our vulgarity becomes God's vulgarity, and our indifference becomes God's indifference. However, each species is only a tiny aspect of a vast and changing whole, and thus our failure or success as a member of the Kindred does not fully define God's nature. We exist for a relative instant, and whatever we grasp and share during that moment is our contribution to the whole. God's sight and outreach become one with our own, and God's spirit becomes that which we share. Our good works can help make the universe a place of love and peace.

Moreover, positive thoughts also contribute to the overall balance of goodwill within the universe. Thus, prayers and public expressions of positive ideals and ideas have a role in being, and they are most assuredly not a waste of time and resources. However, doing good work is the ultimate source of beneficial changes.

Conversely, we also bring perfidy into being if we misbehave. Yet there is an inherent danger in embracing negative traits that go beyond the obvious, for they are often nihilistic. Those cursed with excessive greed, myopia, violence, bigotry, or any other behavioral and/or philosophical ills often taint their worlds, one another, and themselves to the extent that continued existence becomes problematic. War, murder, violence, environmental degradation, diseases, and civil discord eventually drive such species to interminable dark ages and mass die-offs. Only profound social and philosophical changes can rescue such species from oblivion or annihilation. Moreover, those who bring conflicts to the stars eventually run afoul of species with a greater understanding of being. In so doing, they will find harsh lessons that leave them wiser if they are fortunate enough to survive the experience.

The take-home message here is that the logos of being (e.g., nature, God, etc.) seeks to perfect our physical and intellectual form through material, conceptual, and philosophical trials. The deficient in philosophy and thought often perish due to their excesses and lack of insight. The utterly foolish end up smiting themselves through war and pollution, which they are often eager to blame on God alone. In addition, those unable to adapt to meet the needs dictated by shifting environmental contexts often lose the capacity to sustain their existence. Sadly, great rocks fall from the skies, thus ending some experiments before they can thrive and travel abroad.

Regarding our ultimate development, knowledge tends to build on itself so long as societies remain relatively stable. Such stability can only be found where personal and societal norms are developed that foster justice, responsibility, peace, cooperation, education, and foresight. Those who do not produce the social infrastructure and normative values needed to maintain these traits will face internal trials that hinder or halt their evolution. Yes, entire societies often wither on the vine, with the disillusioned masses burning the temples and palaces before moving on to subsistence lives. That can repeatedly happen, as it has in many human societies.

Ultimately, only the most adaptable, able, and enduring species come to fully grasp the nature of God, that defining spark that runs throughout. In so doing, they can fully actualize their essential oneness with what created us, although we humans have a long way to go. Perhaps the most definitive test of obtaining this level of awareness is the ability to manipulate time, for herein resides the tools needed to examine the mysteries of our origin and the course of our future. Such knowledge allows those who can use it the capacity to learn all that can be known. However, manipulating the past or future can produce ripple effects that may create nihilistic types of temporal pollution. Indeed, even passively observing the future can be problematic and should only be executed with great care. Directed temporal interventions are dubious unless clear and compelling evidence exists that such an intrusion occurred within a given timeline. It is a problematic exercise. Granted, a mastery of time may allow some knowledge to be safely collected, but herein will reside great debates regarding a fixed versus a malleable destiny. Many inherent paradoxes exist, and I am ill-equipped to provide meaningful insights.

Let us conclude this segment of our examination into the nature of God, although much remains to be considered. Indeed, what has been written here was not meant to be comprehensive, because I believe you can take the ideas expressed here to far more insightful conclusions than I do. The first step in embarking on any journey into the unknown is approaching it with an open mind. What we have learned from the past will always help inform what we perceive in the future, but to fully grasp the possibilities before us, we must liberate our minds and hearts from blinding dogma, intolerance, and conceit. We must become a blank slate of sorts and allow the full majesty of thought to be expressed unfettered. If we can manage that task, the true nature of being will slowly reveal itself, and so begins a walk that will eventually lead to a greater understanding of our purpose and relationship with everything. Please forgive my incessant rambling during this chapter, but sparks leap where they will, at least in my eroding brain. Amen.

30

The Seekers

When people ask about my faith, I tell them I am a Seeker. Some think I am embracing Sikhism, a monotheistic religion and lifestyle that began under the auspices of Guru Nanak over 500 years ago in northern India's Punjab region. However, being a Seeker is significantly different than Sikhism, wonderful and insightful faith though it is. A Seeker is simply someone striving to find the purpose and meaning of our existence through thought, word, and deed. It is not a codified faith per se with written dogma, rules, and canons, but rather a set of ideals that begins with the notion that part of our fundamental reason for being is to study and understand our relationships with this ongoing process called existence. Seekers thus contemplate how existence operates, our roles in its dynamics, and our responsibility to each other, life, and this universe we share. In effect, a Seeker searches for the reasons we exist, with our ongoing efforts giving rise to ideas, feelings, and concepts that become metaphysical aspects of our shared being. The underlying doctrinal impetus is that the thoughts we generate and share may have roles in the machinations of the universe. Part of our purpose is to understand how these processes function . . . as in the marriage of thought, matter, and energy. In the meantime, we learn, love, share, and commune, striving to conduct our lives in ways that promote the common good for all life. We experience the wonder and marvel of a child as our journeys proceed, and we are eager to share whatever we find.

A Seeker's task is not nearly as complicated and demanding as it may first seem. It also does not require that one pores over ancient documents or modern texts on particle physics and astronomy. Of course, one can do so if desired, but the lack of explicit requirements is a requirement. This faith isn't about following any prescribed path. Instead, it asks adherents to strive to grasp how we and our contemplations are related to what we perceive and experience. There is no one way of accomplishing this goal, for the truth of the moment can be as elusive as it is complex. The essential need is to apply thoughts and feelings toward a fuller understanding of the nature of existence. One can do this while walking through the woods, playing with children, talking to friends, praying, or petting a favored animal. Herein, one can perceive the impetus of time and marvel at how our senses and thoughts allow us to merge with whatever is around us if we ponder and feel deeply enough.

Imagination can become a guide that allows us to commune with everything from swift deer to twinkling stars and rippling waves, assuming we learn how to leave ego and its associated clutter behind. That is not an easy thing to do. Yet, if we can, we develop an empathetic awareness that soars with eagles, swims with fish, and links us to our beloved. This grand communion guides us toward contemplations and discoveries that can give rise to joy, passion, rapture, wonder, and much else. We can share these precious moments and feelings via many means, inculcated as they often are within a smile, laugh, or glance. Alternatively, one can find this place of bliss alone, feeling the sun's warmth or a gentle breeze while it touches our face. No one path leads to all possible things and thoughts.

Some Seekers become academics. They delve deeply into the essentials of matter, energy, and time, always striving to discover how thought can function to reveal the underlying workings of the most fundamental aspects of existence. In short, these Seekers find purpose in applying rationalism toward examining the smallest and most prominent elements of being, as in theoretical physics, chemistry, astronomy, geology, and mathematics. Their bliss is discovery, although some can become so devoted to inquiries that they lose sight of those many things beyond rationalism that can give life meaning. Moreover, some do not fully consider that their thoughts may have a fundamental purpose in the aspects of existence they are examining that go beyond the obvious. For example, was the path that led to the atomic bomb a breakthrough alone or an existential test?

Many Seekers discover purpose in manipulating the material and physical. They find joy and meaning in woodworking, painting, farming, machine work, running, sports, medicine, and every activity wherein hand and body are applied to a given focus or goal. Some Seekers opt to care for the needs of others, extending from feeding to entertaining them. Most strive to excel at what they do, which can lead to fantastic performances and achievements of all kinds. The more enlightened constantly search for better and more efficient ways of accomplishing desired ends, including improving crop yields, designing enduring furniture, and crafting elegant works of art that can bring pleasure to people for many generations. Others find means of saving and improving lives, developing novel medical techniques, nutritional supplements, and various tools that are a boon to all.

I am the kind of Seeker who opts to delve into spirituality. That is my heart's calling, not that I can fully explain why. My goal has long been to find what some call God, though my personal journey has revealed this concept to be unlike what I have studied in any religious text. I have examined the Bible, Torah, Qur'an, The Vedas, Tao Te Ching, Bhagavad Gita, several Sutras, and other works during my quest. I also found meaning and insights within the Epic of Gilgamesh, the Iliad, and many of Plato's and Aristotle's texts. However, my dreams moved me to more profound insights than any other means concerning the concept of God. All sources of edification must be considered by Seekers, and there is no set course that each must follow other than striving to pursue his/her passion. One must also understand that this calling may change as time unfolds. What you currently are can differ significantly from what you will eventually become.

This Seeker found that the concept of God can be a portal to an idea that includes itself, as in gazing into a mirror. It is a fundamental essential linked to all aspects of existence, whether energetic, physical, or metaphysical. When I tried to put a face and form on this nexus, my eyes were blinded by an indescribable luminescence. It bloody well hurt! Yet there was a definite presence both within my being and outside of it. The presence was vaguely feminine but something more than that because it also inculcated compelling emotions and thoughts. One could be within the mind of another or have the surrounding perspective suddenly shifted to an entirely different vantage point. My identity drifted away, with the singular "I am" giving way to the plurality of "we are." The description of "a dynamic being of ultimate selflessness" was implanted in my mind by this nexus, along with an inquisition I will not delve into here. I imagine other Seekers will make their own discoveries, but here are a few of the essential ones I have made during my personal journey for whatever help they may be. Oh, and please understand that these findings are not meant as dogma or a guide but merely the sharing of a personal pathway:

- One of the primary purposes of life is the eventual evolution of sentient forms that can discover life's purposes. In so doing, essential ideas find a metaphysical presence that helps sustain aspects of our shared reality.

- Life is precious in all its manifest forms, although destructive entities must be contained when they threaten the collective whole.

- All things are kindred and linked at one level or another. To defile ourselves, others, the environment, and life pollutes existence.

- Contemplations concerning the Divine help give it a metaphysical presence we can commune with and be part of. Prayer is one means of accomplishing this end.

- We are all works in progress, with the ultimate goal being the perfection of our form and thought. Good luck with that.

- Reflect upon the whole, and realize that you are a part thereof. You are unique and precious, the child of a thought that can reflect upon itself.

- It is folly to damn worthy and kind people for believing in different paths to the Divine. To do so is an act of intolerance that negates free will and condones forced conformity.

- We should conduct our lives in fashions consistent with embracing our intended purpose and the common welfare.

- The search for the Divine is constant, for we live in a universe of continuous change. Fixating only on what was may cause some to lose sight of what is and what will be.

These are merely a few general observations derived from studies, contemplations, and learning, and they should not be regarded as generalized rules or standards. Indeed, some of these viewpoints are debatable, and if they evoke a contrarian response in you, go beyond them! Write, explore, commune . . . Find and share insights that suit your personal pursuits, and please understand that many Seekers will exceed anything you or I could even imagine. Some Seekers will walk on distant worlds and share ideas with beings that differ more from humanity in general form rather than purpose and thought. Our mutual commonalities will guide us if we allow them to. Indeed, we will share our views with species ancient and young and learn that some of humanity's earliest insights were (and are) shared widely with others who dwell in this universe, including "our" myriad concepts of God.

However, it all begins with daring to look. Seekers must grasp what they can from study, thought, conversations, and the many lessons nature and nurture provide. They will build upon that staid foundation, striving to find and share meaning while life unfolds. Moreover, learning need not solely come from teachers or books. A simple block of wood can allow us to grasp many things, for that object can become a practical tool, an object of art, or even a life-saving device. We combine thought and energy with the material and manipulate a creation that serves any desired ends. In some cases, a stone, sunlight, or other objects will "inform" us about how to proceed if we study its nature and contemplate fully the possibilities therein. Ours is a faith of being and reflection, wherein each follows the path he or she freely selects.

Most of us are flawed in one way or another, so we must always strive to improve ourselves. Sometimes, we have sicknesses of the soul, such as greed, anger, and even violence. Recognizing and talking about these illnesses are good ways of dealing with their presence, albeit some maladies require mediation and professional care. Of course, we should never become so self-absorbed in a given personal plight that we lose sight of what is around us. This is especially true of this lifeboat Earth we dwell upon. Our stewardship leaves much to be desired, yet I am confident that Seekers will help us through this existential morass. Everyone reading these words is essential to achieving that end.

Most importantly, be open and always strive to learn and experience. Allow yourself to feel a lover's passionate touch and a child's tender embrace. Do not live in fear of death nor be reckless with your life, but live in a way consistent with your beliefs and morals. Know that you will make mistakes, sometimes to the point of harming yourself and others. Yet also understand that redemption begins with acknowledging and striving to correct our flaws. We are all works in progress, and let us be content with whatever progress we make. The threads that define our lives are part of a wonderful tapestry that time weaves into an intricate and unimaginably beautiful form. Find comfort within that form, for you are precious and unique, a marvelous child of the Divine. Amen.

PART III

NATURE

31

God Lives There

Fall has taken its toll on UNH College Woods' leaves and foliage, but beauty still abounds. Brilliant sunlight filters through the thinning canopy while a gentle breeze slowly rocks the limbs and branches to and fro. The flickering light dances upon the forest's floor and illuminates fallen leaves' vermilion and ocher hues. Off to the side of a nearby trail, thick green moss covers limbs and branches that have found their way back to the earth. These woods are left untouched by intention, one of the few remaining virgin forests in New Hampshire. They are nature's treasury, a hoard of forest detritus that can become an inspiration for poets, leaf houses for children, or fodder for innumerable animals and insects.

A big black Labrador barks a benign salutation while bounding toward his whistling master. He swiftly disappears behind a gentle bend in the trail, engrossed in some game of canine tag. There is ample room to play and explore here and numerous trails. Indeed, miles of trails crisscross the 60 acres of the College Woods, with each foray bringing new sights, sounds, and experiences. Some footpaths lead to lazy, slow-moving brooks and the meandering Oyster River. There's even a reservoir deep in the forest, and there courting ducks can be seen in the early days of spring.

The setting reminds me of childhood days atop Mount Lebanon, graced by deep forests, trails, and paths, with some eventually melding into the surroundings and leaving one amid nature incarnate. Plentiful paths branch off the main tracks, and one is often torn by which way to go. However, directions, vexing concerns, and even health issues seem unimportant in this peaceful forest. This is a place wherein a person, a singular "I," can merge with a collective whole that includes life, time, and all that being can offer. The conversion happens deep in the forest; if one lets go of the self and allows oneness to happen.

In the meantime, reality, imagination, and thought intertwine, with winding trails offering new adventures while the journey unfolds. All paths eventually lead to the main courses, much like the woodland's weaving brooks ultimately flow into the Lamprey River's dark, lazy waters.

Two young insect collectors come by with long white nets secured to the ends of poles. They look so young to my aging eyes, as was I 40 years ago. However, Pam and Cory are too mission-oriented to commune with anyone, let alone a nosy writer. They have bugs to collect for an entomology class, and fall's chilly onset has driven most of their quarry away. I note their youth and spry physiques, with memories dancing through my mind of days gone by.

Ahead, there's a small wooden bridge that spans a tiny, slow-moving brook. In the summer, water-spiders skidder across its rippling surface while frogs croak out their mating songs. Moss and lichens cover the rocks by the stream in lush, verdant coats, making the inanimate stones look like living things that grow from the ground.

A winded jogger approaches, engrossed in her efforts and seemingly oblivious to most else. She's breathing very heavily but stops to talk. "The woods?" she says. "I run here because it's a beautiful place to be. That's reason enough for me." Yet I can see this runner has miles to go this day, and she swiftly departs without leaving her name behind.

A big black crow angrily squawks from high in an adjacent tree, clearly upset with interlopers like me. The sun glistens off his feathers, giving the bird an iridescent patina. A black-headed male chickadee sings a melodic warning while darting over the trail. He suddenly alights on a nearby birch tree and studies me as I do him. We are locked in a mutual stare, pondering what the other is doing on this fine fall day.

Back on my foray I go, thankful that the journey is unfolding with such delights. Through the limbs and branches, the blue hues of the Oyster River stand out against the remaining yellow and red leaves that still adorn a few hardy trees. Upon traversing a gentle wooded slope, one finds the river's marshy shore, replete with manifold roots that push their way into the water. This part of the walk is not easy, although it is still a joy.

The languid Oyster River is more than a brook but not much of a river. Numerous birds, insects, and wildlife inhabit its shores and waters during the spring and summer. Indeed, the cicadas can be so loud they drown out all other sounds, but not on a cold day like this. Fall's increasing chilliness has sent most birds to warmer climates, leaving mainly chipmunks, squirrels, and other earth-bound creatures behind.

Birch trees line the Oyster River in places, their white trunks and branches adding vivid colors to fall's last gasps. Soon, the forest will be covered with a different kind of white: that of the coming snow. However, these snows don't stop folks from going into this woodland.

"I love cross-country skiing through the College Woods," advised former botany student Kathy Casler. "It's one of those places where time stands still. All the hassles of work and life disappear. I feel free in those woods."

Yes, the College Woods are blissfully peaceful in the winter. One can even hear the snowfall, gentle and light, something that has to be experienced and cannot be adequately captured via a net of mere words. Ah, but it's the visual aspects of the forest that are most captivating during the winter months.

After a storm, snow gathers atop the branches and adorns the pine tree's boughs. Limbs bend under their burden, and silence is all around. An occasional skier will sometime break the quiet, but the spell of peacefulness swiftly returns after they speed on by.

I continue back down the main trail, going up and down a series of small rolling hills before descending a long gentle grade. At the bottom of the slope is a reservoir where birds and other animals gather in the spring. It is a refuge for wildlife of all shapes, sizes, and colors—a visual soup that freezes images in one's mind for a lifetime. This is where God shows off some fantastic painting skills.

Sometimes, a sizeable grayish-brown stork can be seen hunting for frogs and fish, stealthily walking in shallow water before darting its pointed beak at tasty prey. There are also blue jays, goldfinches, and other winged glories to please the eye. Gray squirrels and black-striped chipmunks scamper up branches and occasionally run across the trail, almost underfoot. They are undoubtedly busy today, gathering what bounty remains before winter comes calling.

"I bring my wife and kids," wrestling Coach Jim Urqhart said. "It's good for the kids to be so close to nature. There's a big rock by the reservoir where folks sometimes share picnic lunches. It's very peaceful. No diesel fumes or car noises."

The woods are still unspoiled despite the many people who stroll through them. There aren't any discarded beer cans and fast-food wrappers littering the forest floor. That kind of petty perfidy just isn't done by those who mosey through this small piece of nature. This is a church, a place of reverence that faithful parishioners do not despoil. In fact, those who love this place swiftly remove anything that shouldn't be here.

Further down the trail, a fair-sized wooden bridge crosses the river. I love the views it offers. Couples often go there to enjoy one another's company in peace and solitude. The forest's romantic setting has sparked many affairs of the heart, and couples abound in the early spring.

Alas, some fear the College Woods, especially citified people. "I never go through them," said Jen Johnson. "They look peaceful during the day, but people could hide behind the trees. Anyone who goes through there at night deserves what they get."

The College Woods has not been the sight of any recent assaults. Yet, a few feel threatened by the isolation this forest provides. There is only you and God at times, although some need more security. Indeed, some can't escape their fears of isolation, sad reservations that nature alone can't erase.

Nevertheless, most folks don't fear the College Woods. In fact, those who stroll through them often end up reveling in the experience. "I love it in here," said Peggy Dana while walking her dogs. "I don't run into many people, and the beauty of this place speaks for itself."

"Being in the College Woods is like you died and went to heaven," related Athletic Department secretary Nancy Brown. "It's one of the few places on campus that is totally peaceful. I run through there all the time and love it."

"God lives in there," George advised. "I met her by the big, wooden bridge where the ducks hang out. I think she was tending to her handiwork." Indeed, anyone who has seen a Mallard up close knows how magnificent that handiwork is, stunning beauty captured in a perfect form.

For all who venture through the College Woods, a veritable collage of sights and sounds will reveal itself while they amble down the trails and paths. They are byways that lead away from the pressures of everyday life, lanes wherein one can discover a universal type of freedom. And if one strives to find the Devine, she will be there, tending her creations.

32

The Power of Music

I have my headphones on and listen to loud classic rock. Gerry Rafferty's "Baker Street" plays, and I sing aloud. My neighbors may suffer a bit from my efforts, but I am in the zone. The song has several exquisite saxophone and guitar riffs, the consummate in instrumental performances. Oh, yeah, tune it in, my friends, and catch the joy music can bring. I don't care if the tunes are country, baroque, classical, rock, or new age. Music takes us to exalted places, regions where the spiritual and physical become intertwined. The harmonies capture us, and the pros can occasionally move our hearts as much as the rhythms and cords.

The instrumentals are a form of communication that transcends language, often making words superfluous. I recall listening to my cousin John play jazz sax, something he did for 30 years in a band. The cords he belted out got into your soul with a form of harmonic communion that becomes akin to ecstasy in its purest sense. All the clutter that usually haunts our minds evaporates, and we find ourselves enraptured in the joy of the moment, the melodic now. Indeed, the riffs can evoke powerful emotions wherein bliss unfolds, a unique admixture of happiness and contentment that has us playing air guitars, tapping our toes, and smiling broadly. Sex can be a bit more enjoyable at times, but only by a matter of degree. Put the two together, and the mixture becomes ecstasy, an urge to merge that can combine two hearts into one.

There is something profound about how processing musical vibrations influences our brain activity. That's what the scientist in me observes. The researchers can see it in positron emission tomography (PET) scans and electroencephalograms (EEGs), information-processing resonances the ancients understood. The Pythagoreans and people of like-minded ideas saw music's relationship with being in terms of mathematics and geometry, thus divining ratios in the way one tone or frequency is related to another. The ancients spoke of "The Divine Proportion" or "The Golden Ratio," which resembles the more modern Fibonacci sequence. Here, the ideal relationship of one frequency or geometric relationship to another is 1.618. It can be found in many aspects of nature, from sunflower layouts to tree branch development.

In essence, the Pythagoreans and later adherents of their Classical ideas sought to define the fundamental tuning of the "human frequency," for there was an order to being that they were determined to find. To be sure, many architects and artists applied the Golden Ratio to designing buildings, making paintings, and every manner of other endeavors, finding that the results created a perfect interplay of form and perceptions. They opined that existence operated according to the music of the spheres, but we need not delve too deeply into their notions, elegant though they are. Indeed, some of their ideas have captivated modern researchers, so don't look toward aliens for insights into human evolution and thought.

In fact, we have ample proof that Earth has a "natural frequency" in the oscillations of its electromagnetic field. This has been dubbed the Schumann Resonance, oscillating at a resonance of 7.83 hertz. This is far too low for humans to perceive, at least audibly. As for our ability to detect electromagnetic (EM) vibrations, one notes that EM oscillations are the essence of how our speakers and headphones work. In fact, some claim the universe vibrates at a clearly audible 432 Hz.

Interestingly, studies have shown that many find this "A" pitch frequency incredibly captivating, albeit the universe contains many objects that vibrate at unique and disparate frequencies. Thus, the "one note/harmony for all" idea is specious. As humans, our bodies have an inherent vibration frequency of about 3 Hz–17 Hz, and we appear to be especially sensitive to 6 Hz–8 Hz vibrations. This is to be expected for children of the Earth, but interestingly, we cannot detect such low frequencies audibly. Yet we can certainly feel these vibrations when they are amplified sufficiently.

Enough of this rationalism! Let us look to sources that are far less esoteric. Contemplate niceties such as rhythm, the willful manipulation of objects to produce vibrations that move the body and soul: the beating of a stick on a tree trunk . . . the forcing of air around a reed of grass . . . the vocalization of sounds in harmony. This slowly evolved into orchestras, recordings, and the digital tunes I am currently listening to. We manipulated the fundamentals of sound and perception and ultimately discovered a special kind of joy. This joy could be shared and passed on, much like language. In fact, music is a language.

Furthermore, the quest to perfect and share music brought us into contact with something essential to being. Some label it fundamental frequencies, tones, and mathematical processes that are instrumental in shaping the very nature of this universe. As we have seen, many researchers have sought to define this as 432 Hz to 440 Hz, albeit not too convincingly. We can also see "natural frequencies" in how subatomic particles interact, a vibrational impetus that helps define the relationships between energy, matter, and time. And so, we find ourselves at the doorway of theoretical physics, although discovering what provided the impetus for plucking our universal strings is problematic.

However, we need not open that door. Instead, we simply crank up the tunes and enjoy the rapture. In fact, while writing this chapter, I am listing to songs, with bits and pieces of these excellent vibrations activating one thought or another. It is up to you to judge what truths have been found, but I am bound to the moment's joy. Oh, yeah. Life can give us many pleasures, but few are as enjoyable as fine tunes shared with good friends. Thank you, God, for thinking about us joyful souls. I am sure you commune with us through music, math, and all we perceive, and we are infinitely thankful for the shared capacity. Amen.

3 3

Living by Our Nature

I watched a particularly fierce rainstorm on July 25, 2018. The water descended in raging torrents, and the tempest occasionally blew the trees violently about. Wildly gyrating twigs and branches snapped and flew away, and soon some of the leaves began giving up their grip. While the tempest raged, a small, brownish-white moth outside the window desperately struggled to find solace, with raindrops the scale-equivalent size of Volkswagens pummeling the tiny creature. It finally squeezed into a narrow gap beneath a clapboard's raised bevel. The little insect held on, clinging to life as best it could against nature's fury. I begged God to save this tiny creature, yet well knew that all life hangs by frayed and tattered threads to this thing called being.

33.1 A White Dotted Prominent Moth

My knees, shoulders, and back ached terribly while the rain-storm unfolded. People with advanced osteoarthritis suffer be-fore and during storms, and my joints are riddled with it. Years of heavy weightlifting also took their toll; yet at 66, I was lifting and exercising again. The activity sometimes made my joints and muscles scream, but I had been at it for about 15 months. I went from being unable to walk 100 meters without resting to going out for well over two miles without pausing. My strength also improved. But why did I work out with weights that often ex-ceeded 300 pounds in the bench press and other movements? There was no need, but we are all creatures of habit. Alas, my old practice involved moving huge loads indeed.

The cardiologist thought I was bonkers. The dreaded Widow-Maker heart attack got me in 2010, a 100 percent blockage high on the left anterior descending artery that feeds the lower half of one's heart. Call it a raindrop that clipped my wings. My damage indices were 40 times average, and it became painfully clear that death was upon me while I slipped in and out of consciousness. An emergency stent placement saved my life, with the existential thread Dr. Kaplan installed rescuing me from oblivion. Yet my life was never the same. Indeed, my heart still reminds me of its torment, with two more 85 percent blockages waiting in the wings. Kidney trouble, diabetes, high blood pressure, arteriosclerosis, and other ills also tear at the strands keeping me upright. Yet here I am, typing these words.

So, what the hell was I doing in a weight room? Why? I was terrified that the life-sustaining stent could get crushed or

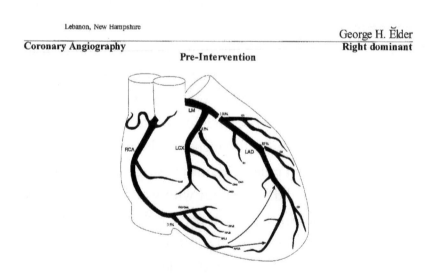

Lebanon, New Hampshire

George H. Ĕlder

Coronary Angiography

Right dominant

Pre-Intervention

33.2 Being too heavy and eating poorly clogged the suthor's arteries and led to a massive heart attack that very nearly took his life when he was 59

suddenly give way while doing bench presses. So, I used a thinly padded sleeve around the bar, hoping to better distribute the weight on my chest. I also brought the bar down to my lower chest, doing whatever I could to avoid putting too much pressure on the stent. Alas, my heart monitor occasionally beeped insistently due to transient ventricular tachycardia, with the extra beats pushing up the heart rate (HR) readings beyond the safety limits. I recall my response. I gasp, sweat profusely, pause while my HR declines, and then go on to the next set.

I had exercised only sporadically for five years before the heart attack. Angina would grab me at times, and my joints constantly acted up. After the heart attack, I could do very little for a few years and was allowing myself to die of inactivity. All of this was entirely unlike my former self. I was a fat man who liked to jog for miles, albeit at a snail's pace. Lifting weights once defined who I was, someone who could pop 400-plus pounds overhead and do squats with loads that would bend the bar. I became a strength coach and wrote articles in nationally circulated magazines about how to get bigger and stronger. At 45, I benched 320 pounds for 20 repetitions; but by 59, it was all gone.

I became a mere shadow of my former self, albeit not in size. My identity was altered, with one illness after another making life more difficult. Finally, I decided there was nothing left to lose by trying; so, into the gym I flew, and therein I found comfort and meaning. The progress was slow and painful, although, at 66, I was far more able than at 59. However, was risking death worth whatever additional gains I would make? This was

33.3 The author's nature involved lifting weights, and he can be seen here pressing 385 overhead and benching 325 for several repitition

a pressing issue. My right knee buckled during a 1.7-mile walk four years ago, and now the joint is so eroded it makes crackling noises when I move. They say both knees must be replaced, but obese diabetics with heart trouble are not surgical candidates. Indeed, if the heart goes, that is game, set, and match. Moreover, it keeps reminding me that the stress of training has a negative impact. So why, why must I drive myself?

The thing is, lifting is part of who and what I am. The clang of weights and struggle against gravity is oxygen to me. Working out has become a necessity. I can no more escape it than that moth could slip its wings. However, it is clear that I also have to be reasonable. There is no need to constantly push my limits; perhaps it is folly. The moth had no other choice but to find shelter or die. I may be at the stage where I am flying willingly into a storm that can have but one conclusion. Granted, I would die doing the things that once defined my life and gave it meaning. However, it is probably better to find a safer path wherein I can continue communing with you for a bit longer. God tells me to lose weight and give up my dreams of becoming the strongest old man around these parts. She advises that pride goeth before the fall and that moderation is the key to a happy and long life. I hope I listen.

Four years have passed since I first wrote this chapter and, as always, I did not listen. My left shoulder and knee failed in 2019, with a torn labrum cartilage in my shoulder, ending my lifting foray. It was a superior labrum from anterior to posterior (SLAP) tear that cannot fully heal. I was doing sets of three reps with 315 pounds on the bench then and planned on going after some Master's records. My left knee suffered a sudden and nasty medial collateral ligament tear while I was walking, and the swelling was as grotesque as it was disabling. I cannot walk for any distance now, and rehab is impossible, given the degeneration in both knees. Then came another heart attack, albeit with minor damage. Still, I had slipped into Stage 3 heart failure.

Despite heart issues and becoming increasingly clumsy, I tried to make another comeback in early 2021. Progress was slow, but a nasty fall at home ended that foray in mid-December of 2021. I landed on my butt and badly injured discs in my lower back. Later testing revealed multiple disc injuries, with those in my neck having set up degenerative changes in my spinal cord.

This degeneration was why my coordination and strength were becoming impaired. So, here it is, 2023, and I am about to see spinal specialists. Perhaps it is possible to decompress my spinal cord, but this is the end of my lifting days. I can hardly walk now, and as the neuropathies advance, I may end up in a chair. Yeah, there was lots of pain during this storm of my own making.

Moreover, there is no refuge, no overhanging clapboard that will protect me from my folly. My back is now so severely injured that I cannot stand straight, and the pain is exquisite. I am a hobbled old man who leans over while using a walker, having to rest his elbows on the handles. It is hard to accept, but pain reminds me that the situation cannot be ignored. An upright walker awaits, assuming I can avoid needing a power chair.

Nonetheless, I still contemplate returning to the gym. There is no rational explanation. Part of me wants them to remove the damaged disc protrusions pressing on my spinal cord so that I can lift again. It is madness. I should be hoping to walk normally again and not feel pain while typing these words or watch my left hand tremble while I try to work. Still, I could do lat pull-downs, leg extensions, and light dumbbell curls after these injuries are set right. Alas, one cannot separate a fool from his or her necessities, folly though they are. We moths strive to avoid storms. However, we are irresistibly attracted to self-immolating lights, come what may. It is the calling of our nature, and to that call, we will always fly. God made us what we are, and she will, hopefully, rescue us from ourselves on occasion. Amen.

34

Knock-Knock

So here it is, December 24, 2015, and I find myself writing this chapter to the future because many folks from my time seem oblivious to the obvious. It's not that we don't notice our record 64-degree temperature when the average high for this day in New Hampshire is just 35. And some may even realize that the top 10 hottest years on record have occurred since 1998, a span of only 17 years. Moreover, 2015 looks like it'll be the warmest year ever recorded.

Still, all we do is debate, hold interminable international talks, and sign meaningless pieces of paper . . . an endless array of agreements and treaties that are seldom acted upon. Screaming alarm bells should be going off regarding global warming, although most do not listen. We're numb as boards and hardly ever react to a blessed thing that can impact our future. No, something has to whack us repeatedly over the head with a two-by-four for us to take any notice. This is part of the human condition, and I pray that time increases our collective wisdom and capacity to react, but we will see.

Well, eight years have passed, and today is January 6, 2023. We have learned little since 2015 and done even less. As a result, record warmth has embraced the planet, and the numbers are now beyond alarming. The recent data indicate that the past eight years were the warmest on record. Large parts of the ice fields in the Antarctic and Arctic have melted, while glaciers worldwide have given up their grips on mountains and valleys. The media tells us stories about the unfolding environmental train wreck, and many conferences are held.

Meanwhile, Earth's sea level has increased by about 3.4 ± 0.3 millimeters per year during the last 30 years (1993–2022). This doesn't sound like much, but the oceans are vast heat reservoirs. Ergo, the larger the oceans become, the greater the global heating problem. Thus, the pace of increased sea level doubled between 1993–2002 and 2013–2022. In fact, the sea level increased by about 5 millimeters between January 2021 and August 2022 due to ice melt. We already see low-lying seacoasts and islands being inundated. Some islands in the South Pacific are no longer inhabitable, and many coastal cities are imperiled. Mostly, I have given up on folks in my timeline. Many do not even think there is a problem. Yeah, some believe this whole global warming thing is a science-laced scam. These latter-day Luddites reject science as firmly as their ancestors turned against machines. They do not argue about the data but dismiss it altogether. Instead, they note that Earth has gone through climate changes many times. Yes, but the planet has also gone through mass extinctions based on climate change. Yet if one notes that, the Luddites claim you're being an alarmist. They don't care about the polar bears or other life forms dying off, nor does the fate of those starving due to desertification concern them. As long as they can get enough cheap gas to run their Ford 250s, all is happiness in light.

Well, screw those myopic fools like they are screwing their own kids. Now, I know you folks in the future have inherited the heat and pollution we left behind, and the situation is probably vastly worse than it was during my era. Yet the world is perfectly normal to you because you were born into an environmental morass. The flora, fauna, weather, and nature, in general, all seem as they should because you don't know any better. The joke is on you guys. Yes, as of the last few million years, the Earth has shifted weather patterns, going through ice ages and warm periods. However, folks during my time created this current shift, and we kept it going even when it was apparent the weather patterns were changing at an alarming rate. Most of us here liked the warm weather on Xmas Eve 2015, but we all knew something wasn't right. Late December does not bring 60-degree days in New Hampshire and tornadoes in the South. The signs are evident, yet we did nothing.

Self-serving economics and do-nothing ideology have much to do with our lassitude. Moreover, the energy parasites made oodles of money pumping crap into the air, water, and land, not that we poor folk didn't contribute by buying gas-guzzling vehicles. We were a greedy, myopic, and irresponsible lot, much preferring our personal pleasures and creature comforts versus anything akin to self-control. In short, we didn't give Jack Shit about your inherited world. Some of us paid lip service to the environment by writing lines such as these, but we sat on our asses while countless species were laid waste and vast stretches of land became uninhabitable.

We took what we had for granted. Ah, and let me tell you, there was a time when nature was stunningly beautiful. As a boy, the skies were deep blue with billowing white clouds floating above. One could drink cool water directly from a seeping spring and watch fish laze in the shallows of crystal-clear brooks and rivers. The rushing water's sound was like a melody, with a cheerful chorus provided by colorful songbirds. Occasionally, a deer, turkey, or another animal would scamper by, enjoying what fodder the fields and forests offered. That was rural life in the 1950s and early 1960s, though changes were already underway and obvious.

Alas, you people are stuck with the land, air, and water we defiled, and a simple apology seems meaningless. Some of humanity will have adapted to nature's transformation, as will a few hearty animals and plants. I know the deserts have expanded, arable land has declined, the sea is encroaching on coastal areas, and overall temperatures are cooking when future generations read these words. Numerous species have died, and getting adequate food has become a severe problem for many. Perhaps measures are underway to make life more tolerable on Earth, which has probably been through a few local and regional die-offs as sea levels rise and living conditions decline. Gosh, we left you one hell of a legacy.

One may wonder why we caused such mayhem. Lord knows we have ample excuses, though hardly any good reasons. Big, powerful vehicles made us feel special and virile, although few who owned these gas guzzlers ever needed a truck that could haul 1,000 pounds or an automobile that could top 150 miles per hour. These expensive toys made boys feel like men and women like goddesses, which also justified our numerous creature comforts. We made everything bigger and better and then consumed whatever was in sight. We created a "must-have-it" culture, the plaything of wealthy merchants and advertisers. Having little was simply not enough.

A good parent should consider his or her kids' futures above all else, but we certainly did not. We screwed you guys big time and left you in a mess. Worst of all, some of us knew the situation demanded immediate attention. Still, we did nothing. Some of us spewed out a few words like these, but not many were militant or involved enough to stop those vested and mendacious few who were most responsible for devastating your world. Instead, we passively plodded along with our kindred, offering occasional plaintive bleats but generally going wherever the herd went. Hardly any of us bucked the trend. Your Christmas present from all of us living during this era of greed and irresponsibility is the world you inhabit. Nice gift, huh?

If you can, please make this world right. If the die-offs have been containable, odds are that the technical prowess needed can be mustered to return the planet to some semblance of stability. But please, never forgive us. Curse our names for what we have done, spit on our tombstones, and recognize that no ancestor who loved their progeny would have ever left such a wounded world. Be better than us, and love your kids with much more care and foresight than we loved ours. Learn from our lesson, and never walk the path we did while ruining the garden. Well, I am sure this winter will "normalize," at least for a bit, but I am grief-stricken that all I offered the future were a few pitiful words. Amen.

35

The Nature of War

I was watching this excellent series on Public Broadcasting System (PBS) about meerkats, a show that some of you may have watched due to its popularity. Meerkats are a diminutive species of mongoose that live in many arid regions of South Africa, usually surrounded by stubby grass and bushes, wherein they have clear vantage points. The grayish brown-coated creatures are diminutive (about 2 pounds), omnivorous (albeit mostly insectivorous), and live in small social structures of a few to mobs of about 30 or so members. They dig elaborate subterranean burrows within the confines of a strictly defined and frequently marked territory of about 1.9 square miles, occasionally moving from one set of tunnels to another. What meerkats lack in size, they make up for in surprisingly organized and coordinated group behaviors. Indeed, meerkats have at least 12 distinct vocalizations to designate particular threats, call the group together, and enlist help. They post sentries and defend their territories with gusto against all interlopers. They will thus collectively mob a sizable venomous snake, with the dominant members of the group leading vicious and blindingly fast attacks that drive larger animals away.

They look cute with their big eyes and highly social natures but also have a dark side. In fact, rival meerkat mobs will engage in savage conflicts, the human equivalent of wars. About 19 percent of all meerkat deaths are wrought by battles between their own kind, with "tribal" wars claiming the largest share. Yet even within a mob, there are brutal and deadly conflicts between females seeking dominance or younger members seeking to achieve mastery over older peers. These cuddly animals have the highest rate of conspecific violence in the entire mammalian realm, yet they are hardly alone in embracing what many would call war.

Chimps also live within the context of tribal groups of 15–150 members that occupy distinct territories. One notes that chimp society is highly organized, even to the extent of males gathering into hunting parties that track down monkeys and other species for meat. And woe unto the chimp interloper who intrudes into another group's territory. The dominant male chimps within a group often savagely attack en masse, tearing the offending chimp to pieces. Fifty years ago, a protracted tribal war between two large groups of chimps occurred within Tanzania's Gombe National Park. The battle was fought around an overlapping territory and persisted for four years. It usually consisted of organized hunting parties of males attacking often isolated members of the opposing group. However, more significant group-on-group battles also took place.

Of course, lions and many other species that form social groups also make war on rival groups and are nearly always in defense of a given territory or resource. We especially see this trait in the insect world. Here we find ants, termites, and even bees conducting some of the most organized and vicious conflicts imaginable. Indeed, the northern giant hornet (1.5–2 inches long) will send out scouts that seek a suitable bee hive to attack. The goal is to find food in the form of larvae and/or honey. If the scout returns to her group, she informs her collective of where the hive is. The giant hornets then form a group, fly to the target, and attack, often destroying all the members of the bee hive. Some species of bees have evolved defenses against this extermination campaign, such as mobbing the giant hornet scout and encompassing its every surface. They then vibrate their wings, raising their body temperature enough to "cook" the scout alive. This costs the lives of many bees but often saves the hive.

Today, I saw Ukrainian armed drones dropping grenades on hapless Russian soldiers hiding in trenches. They were writhing after the grenades hit due to horrible shrapnel wounds, but their torment ended when the next grenade was dropped. Russia wants land, and Ukraine wants to be free. The conflict concerns territory and resources as Putin seeks to create a Greater Russia. The only difference between humans and many other species is that we justify our nature with rationalism. We act out of patriotism or some other hackneyed rationale proving we are not truly rational creatures. We are opportunistic beasts of greed for the most part, and we slaughter each other by the millions to get what we want. Yes, we are hairless apes with high societies and considerable technological capacity. Still, our inherent nature is essentially the same as that of countless species that have come and gone on our green and blue orb.

There is a pressing need to change our ways, with most of us knowing that is the case. We have been on the cusp of destroying ourselves in a nuclear war since 1945. The only thing stopping us is the notion that we will get devastated by attempting to destroy the designated enemy. How long do you suppose this status quo will remain? Furthermore, we had better hope that a far more able and advanced species does not retain its savage inclinations because we are easy pickings. Indeed, a more advanced species could look at us with hungry eyes. Our world would be a convenient operating base for them, one replete with water, a good atmosphere, and plenty to eat. Oh, the yummy humans a la mode.

Let us hope that the universe is so designed that when a species can go out into the garden, it does so in peace, for it is inevitable that war begets war. Eventually, any aggressive high-tech species will bump into a child of God that is infinitely more capable. This will end that specie's predation game and possibly much worse. Furthermore, one surmises that any species capable of traveling through the stars would have developed the capacity to realize that our universe is a bountiful place and that there is no valid reason to take from others or to interfere with their development. Yet they would also realize that many life forms are still mired by tribal natures, and I imagine they would watch their evolution with some trepidation. This brings us to the realm of some great sci-fi movies, which means we have taken this topic about as far as we can for now. Be at peace, my friends, and live not like meerkats. Amen.

36

The Nature of Greed

All things, even nurture, are ultimately born of nature. After all, nature gives us the inherent capacity to nurture, love, observe, learn, propagate, make choices, have desires, and nearly everything else. Some even equate God with nature, as in the proposition that God is the seminal source from which all things spring. Thus, we see the bloated female forms that are among humanity's earliest iconic representations of the Devine. Of course, this broad perspective regarding nature quickly gets us into some controversial areas. For example, is greed an aspect of nature? Hmmm, let us ponder on this for a bit.

To me, greed is an extension of desire, although some argue it is an over-extension. Desire is born of appetites, typically guided by learned or inherent impulses. Thus, a newborn experiences hunger and has the intrinsic instinct to suckle to satiate what is an essential existential need. Similarly, a teenager is taught that a particular athletic shoe is emblematic of all things excellent and appealing and thus begins a quest to acquire the object of desire by all possible means. Here we see a transition from existential needs guided by inherent appetites to learned needs driven by social conventions. The extension of directing impetuses from the intrinsic to the taught is easy enough to follow. Yet how do we go from here to greedily hoarding vast resources, even at the cost of slaughtering millions of others?

I am living proof that some inherent and learned appetites know no satiation in many individuals. Be it food, sex, land, or power, some of us are compelled to obtain far more than we need to meet our basic needs. But why is this the case? Interestingly, we often see this trend toward excess in nature. Many species hoard to extremes, everything from squirrels to ants. The idea is to prevent privation during challenging times such as winter or droughts. The general existential rule is to gather in abundance now or wither later. Yet this does not explain why two lions will fight to the death over a kill that could feed both for a week. Clearly, this is a matter of protecting a finite resource, for there may not be another kill for a very long time. Similarly, if a territory is left unprotected, it could easily be lost to interlopers of one kind or another.

There are obvious and subtle rationales at work, at least in nature. Granted, many of the resultant satiations of existential needs and appetites are brutal, but so too is life in the jungle or forest. Yet what kind of animal hoards something like gold?

Some species of birds are attracted to what glitters by their inherent natures to gather objects that can help attract a mate. In humans, the lust for gold is a learned appetite that often has no satiation. One is reminded here of the Roman emperor Valerian, a notoriously greedy and status-conscious man captured by the Persians following a failed battle. According to a largely apocryphal story by the early Christian writer Lactantius, Valerian was subjected to all manner of abuse by his captor before finally being made to swallow molten gold. He was then flayed, stuffed, and put on display in a pagan temple, all of which was followed by harsh Roman retribution.

We are at the stage wherein learning and social conventions can produce desires that can cause us to embrace greed for things that are not existential needs. One could regard this type of learning as a species of evil: if evil is defined as "profound immorality and wickedness, especially when regarded as a supernatural force" or Webster's "morally reprehensible: SINFUL, WICKED." Yet isn't morality also learned, or is it inherent in our natures? One could use examples from the animal world to argue both sides of this question. However, I am content to opine that greed and evil, like most human moral traits, are primarily the byproducts of learning. Like many human ills, such as my inveterate gluttony, they are extensions of natural or learned appetites that can lead to the demise and misery of their practitioners. So, we invented laws, religions, and beliefs to protect us from our excesses, but don't try to apply these palliatives to hungry lions or charging elephants. Amen.

37

The Ugly Side of Beautiful

Some folks around here call mink water rats. However, they are a mustelid species, including weasels, ferrets, martens, otters, and even wolverines. They are pure predators, but they are also drop-dead beautiful creatures. Granted, mink are not good-looking when soaking wet, but when dry, their typically brown (sometimes black or mixed) fur is stunning, the epitome of soft and silky. That's why rich folk used to pay so much for jackets made out of their hides, although that practice is frowned upon now. They're small water-loving critters, with many being less than 2 feet long, including the tail, and weigh just a few pounds.

Mink like fish mostly, and I've seen them catch even large ones by our local boat dock. Yeah, they swim along on the surface at a fair clip, dive very suddenly, and come up with a catch.

But they'll also take nearly any small animal, including birds, crawdads, frogs, and newts. They can even take down a duck or seagull that's bigger than they are, and it isn't pretty to watch. When they go after muskrats, it's even gorier. On land or by the shore, they pounce on most creatures and bite them in the back of the head, sometimes killing them with one bite. However, there can be a give-and-take pitched battle at times, although I've never seen a mink defeated. They are swift and aggressive and have little fear.

I hate watching mink eat. The critters tear their prey to pieces while devouring it, much like a ferret (2–2.5 pounds) or stoat (0.5 pounds, give or take) will do to a rabbit after killing the animal. Stoats and ferrets are relentless mustelid predators and give the rabbit no reprieve. A rabbit can often outrun a ferret or stoat, but the predators have tremendous endurance. Plus, they will chase a rabbit down its hole, and thus there is no escape. Typically, mustelids will bite the rabbit in the neck or the back of the head, often ending the fight very quickly. And this goes for rabbits that may be 8–10 times the size of their pursuer. Indeed, an 8-ounce stoat can take down a 5-pound rabbit, albeit sometimes it is a grisly affair wherein the rabbit is repeatedly mauled. A few rabbits have been known to kill a stoat if the bunny stands its ground and attacks, but this is rare. However, small mustelids do not fare well against aggressive cats or dogs for the most part, and I have seen a cat carrying half the carcass of a stoat back home. Oh, she was good at hunting down those hunters.

I often wax poetic about nature, but she can be a cruel bitch. Everything has to consume to live, with the acquisition of calories (energy), water, and nutrients being essential. Even plants war with one another over resources, with some species seeking to deprive others of sunlight by shading them out, taking up their water sources, or even strangling them. Various species of trees can also produce toxic chemicals that can kill interlopers. This equivalent of chemical warfare can be seen in the most placid-appearing bucolic settings. The forest surrounding my abode is a floral battlefield, with one species of tree, bush, or shrub competing with another over resources and living space. Granted, the battles are not as gory as lions killing zebra or dogs going after deer, but they are fights to the death. Oh, dogs and deer brought up some bad memories.

As a kid, I occasionally went out plinking with an old beat-up .22 single-shot rifle. The locale was a sandpit that was halfway up Mount Lebanon. On one occasion, I went up there during the fall, wearing a thick, blue plaid, dungaree jacket. I was a lousy shot, so squirrels and the like were safe from me. Yet, I could hit a tin soup can from roughly 50 feet on rare occasions. I was hardly hitting anything on this bright sunny day and soon was out of ammo. Dogs were yipping away in the background all morning, so they were obviously out and about. Yet I paid them little heed while slowly ambling home, only a few miles away.

Anyway, there was quite a commotion of growls and barks coming from a thicket that was a short distance from the trail. So like a fool, off I went to see what was up. I soon found that about five dogs had taken down a small doe, but they didn't know how to kill the poor thing. They had, however, managed to tear its back legs up, with the doe's hamstrings showing through the mangled flesh. One orange bitch was particularly aggressive, sticking her head into the deer's backside and taking huge bites. The doe kept trying to get up, but she was too far gone to stand. They mauled her legs, neck, and face but mainly focused on the rear end. She was a mass of wounds, with one dog or another running it to take a bite. I screamed at the dogs and made lots of noise, but most paid no attention.

I decided the only thing to do was to put the doe out of her misery, but my ammo was all used. So, I leaned the rifle against a nearby pine and reached to break off a large, dead limb. The idea was to club the deer to death, which seemed the only way to handle the situation, considering that the dogs were not backing off. I recognized a few as being some of the neighbor's dogs, but they acted like wolves and paid no attention to my yells and threats. Finally, the stout branch I was working on snapped, but a part remained affixed to the tree. I was reasonably strong, so I knew I could remove it. I looked down at the deer, all mauled and bloody. It looked up at me at the same time. The branch had nearly given way. I roared at the dogs from deep down, and most backed off a bit. Yet that orange bitch moved in for another bight, and I saw the deer's eyes slowly closing. Her fight was over.

However, my fight had just begun. A fair-sized collie lunged at my arm, and I sent the dog flying. Then the orange bitch grabbed my right sleeve, just above the wrist. The branch was still hanging on the tree, so I went for my rifle, dragging the bitch with me. The others were moving in, and I soon heard the fabric tearing in my jacket's shoulder area. I kicked the dogs aside and made it to the old .22, at which point I used the gun butt as a good and proper club.

I found myself growling and yelling while tossing the orange bitch into some briers. In short order, I tagged her near the left eye with the rifle butt while she came in for another attack. She yelped and backed away. The collie came on, as did what looked like a lab mix. They growled and got low, but I brandished the rifle stock, jabbing it out at them. The bitch came at me yet again, and I nailed her in the side of the head before she could sink in her teeth. She literally yelled, and the others backed off.

I looked back at the doe, and she was definitely dead. I retreated from tree to tree and slowly headed to the trail. The bitch was pawing at the side of her face, and the others went back to chewing on the doe. The arm of my jacket was hanging by a thread, and my lower right arm was bruised and sore. I was pissed off. Yet I didn't tell my parents what happened because there would be a brutal reckoning. I worked out hard with the weights that evening and let my anger propel me. That night, I sharpened a filleting knife, took the last rounds of .22s, and tried to get the rifle in order. It was not too bad for wear, but my goal was as simple as it was primal.

The next day, I returned up the mountain and eventually found the thicket where the doe had died. There was plenty of blood, but, oddly, no dear. A bear might have taken the carcass because five dogs probably could not have devoured the animal, although she was small. Yet I heard barking while being out and about and began hunting. To be sure, I wanted to gut the orange bitch that attacked me, as in literally cutting her stomach open and pulling out her bowels. Believe me: we all have a beast within.

I will not relate the details of what happened. They are shameful. I can say that a dog screams when hit by a bullet. I mean, they holler like a person. That was the last time I took a rifle into the woods to harm anything, and the event still haunts me. My damn neighbors were responsible for what had happened, and I am sure one of them was very upset about a favored pet being badly injured. Be that as it may, the only difference between a loving pet and a deadly predator is context.

Yes, nature is beautiful, but everyone should understand that it has an ugly side that many of us can become one with. We may pretend to be civilized and moral beings, but given the right situation . . . we will behave as stoats and mink. I wonder if we will ever evolve beyond that dreary condition. It is not likely, but perhaps so. I have not considered this incident in a very long time, and it still terrifies me as I reflect upon what happened. Primal struggles occur in wars of our own making or due to the vagaries of nature. And although nature is more beautiful to gaze upon than war, it has an ugly side that can be just as vicious. Gosh, I can still hear that dog screaming . . . Yeah, we can all be sinners, as we can be creatures of love. Amen.

38

Nature's Call on a Cloudy Day

Some people are forged by genetics into possessing exceptional speed, endurance, and/or strength potentials. Others are great athletes by nature who only need the barest of coaching before becoming outstanding baseball players, gymnasts, rowers, or dancers. A few have exceptional minds that can quickly grasp nearly any concept and recall long passages verbatim. We call such people naturals, and we can find them in every endeavor, be it professional sports, entertainment, or scientific research. Granted, only a few discover their natural abilities early on, and some never do. However, nearly all people are uniquely accomplished at something or another.

38.1 The author at 13, already into high repitition pushups and calesthenics

I came out of the womb weighing nearly 10 pounds, having been born of my mother's robust Italian farming stock that was admixed with my father's aggressive Scottish and English genes. On my mother's side, there was a time when ALL my uncles were 280–330 pounds, with Uncle Joe sporting a 50-plus-inch chest and bulging arm muscles. He was scary strong and didn't have to work at it. In fact, the only heavy lifting he did was to maintain his large vegetable garden. Uncle Joe frequently prepared a noxious mixture of manure, fertilizer, and water in a large 30–40-gallon cast iron cauldron to fertilize his crops. When it was filled and mixed correctly, he would grab the huge pot beneath the brim in a bear hug and tote the load 50–150 feet, depending on what part of the garden needed treatment. The filled cauldron must have weighed well over 380 pounds and probably more. Yet he could carry it with relative ease, much to the amazement of all who watched.

Like my kindred, lifting heavy objects was born in my genes, and strength became part of my nature early on. Doing multiple sets of 50-plus pushups, knee bends, and other calisthenics was easy for me, and at ages 11–12, I enjoyed the challenge. I began lifting free weights at about 13 or 14 and became pretty strong within a few years. When I went to college at UNH, my 1,020 pounds of free weights went with me, and I quickly outgrew that. As a senior, tossing 300–400 pounds around on the bench and 500–600 pounds in the squat was a regular affair.

Soon after, I became a beast, sans steroids or other performance-enhancement drugs. I was indeed a natural, and only one 8-week cycle of dianabol after a protracted diet ruined a perfect record of being drug-free. I had quickly lost well over 100 pounds and wanted to regain strength, a foolish thing to have done. Ah, but I remember those days when lifting was life.

In my mind's eye, I can still see the loaded bar resting on the power racks. It was standing press and squat day, one of my favorites. Yeah, I was obese by any measure, with my weight hovering around 300 pounds, give or take 20. All that mass was pilled on a 5 foot 8 frame. The warm-up sets in the press with 135, 225, 295, and 335 were easy, but 365 was on the bar, and the goal was five reps (repetitions). That was tough to do in the standing press at the time, with three big plates and a quarter on each side of the bar.

One prepares for maximal efforts by removing all the clutter and finding a place of clarity that some call "the zone." This is where one's nature combines with one's desire to produce a psycho-physiological state that allows for maximal performances. There are no doubts or nagging worries. One goes deep inside and calls upon an impetus without form, name, or even description. That could be because this impetus is primarily defined by the stark absence of nearly everything except determination. There are no higher thoughts, no doubts, no sounds, and no distractions of any kind. There is only the bar and the goal. A powerful emotional state slowly sweeps away all else. The adrenalin flows, skin tingles, eyes open wide, heart pounds, breathing deepens, and a lifter may even begin growling. Doubt evaporates, and focus predominates.

I ran to the challenge, tearing the bear off the racks like a broomstick. And up that bar speeds overhead, propelled by forces beyond the mechanical. On that day, 365 by 5 felt like a warm-up set, so I bumped the weight to 385. After another psych bout, I nearly got a triple, barely missing the last rep. It's only a fading memory now, but every natural competitor recalls those few special times when the physical and psychological combined to produce an ideal performance. Moreover, nearly all athletes know this Zen-like place one goes when preparing for a good hit, a personal record jump, or other maximal efforts. It is something well beyond the physical and approaching the spiritual.

Ah, but that was then. Sadly, answering our nature's call can have a terrible cost, for if one pushes the envelope too often, it nearly always pushes back. Across the room from me rests a pair of metal forearm crutches, several walking sticks, and a stout walker. I was a beast of vast excess, as in too obese, too many high-fat foods, too many injuries, and too much of everything. Along the way, there were broken bones, torn ligaments, ruptured discs, a massive heart attack, high blood pressure, diabetes,

38.2 Elder weighing 325+ pounds and still able to push massive weights around

kidney problems, advanced osteoarthritis, and a nasty neurological disease that gradually destroyed parts of my nervous system. Every clumsy step is agony at times, and waking during
the mornings has become torture. A power chair awaits, but I
am resisting the growing likelihood. The choking and/or apnea
eventually take you, or so they say. There is a fight for air, and
then one goes the eventual way of all life. Of course, that will be
then, and this is now.

Despite it all, the iron game still haunts me, and I continue to
serve the calling of my nature. In 2016, after a seven-year hiatus
following a massive heart attack, I returned to lifting, although
my legs were too far gone by then to do much of anything with
them. Given my degenerated knees, I tried light squats, but it

38.3 Elder as a hobbled 70-year-old, a victim of his own excess

was a grave mistake. Soon, there may be nerve blocks to deaden the pain of ruptured spinal discs and obliterated knee cartilages and ligaments. No replacement or repair is possible, considering my medical situation. Yet I went on. Sometimes, lifting stressed my heart, and I feared crushing the cardiac stints that kept me alive. Folks at the gym thought I was nuts for even trying to pump iron, and Lord knows I was not very good at it anymore. Yes, I am a bloated shadow of what I once was, but a few embers are still burning within.

Moreover, I am never more at peace than when tussling with gravity. The physical aspects of existence are nearly gone in many ways, but I have something else that compels me. It is a part of my nature that I simply cannot resist. That special zone I described earlier, I am blessed to still be able enough to call upon its impetus. Should there be a fall or stumble over a barrier I can't quite manage, I get pissed off… knowing that long months of healing and/or rehab may be coming. Yet then I think of that silly song about the dark clouds being gone and it now being a bright, sunny day.

Only the goals have changed from days gone by. I chose to be optimistic long ago and face life in a fashion that gives me some degree of happiness, ever thankful to simply be here. It will be challenging to maintain this perspective until the very end, given my current state, but that place of peace I visit is just a thought away. I call upon it when the pain of a cartilage tear doesn't allow sleep or I reflect upon how weak and feeble I've become. That state is also needed to write a piece like this. When enlisted, there is a surge of warmth and determination, a powerful impetus that compels me to complete a chapter like this.

The way I see it, the precious gift of life is a fleeting glory. We glimpse a bit of being as discrete entities and then move on. It is what we opt to do while dwelling within that speck of being that matters. Realizing our nature and unique talents may take some time, but it is always a reasonable goal. Ah, if only I had also learned moderation, a lesson I never mastered. Still, if we experience our time as sharing and caring passengers during this journey, that is a well-lived life. I wish I could be better at doing more of that, but this chapter proves that I am still trying.

As for death, it is a win-win proposition I now face daily. If there is an incorporeal existence after death, all eternity will be spent perceiving and experiencing things from new perspectives, a sublime dream-time. If there is no being of any kind after death, then all of eternity will be a gentle and peaceful night's sleep. Lord knows I need some of that! The ancients studied and knew these things, but many of us tend to ignore their insights. And now to contemplate how to finish this story . . .

As fate would have it, my final foray into lifting was to last over three years. At 68, I worked up to 315 for three reps in the bench press and could do sets of 10 with 265 or so. Yeah, I began strengthening again, albeit far from what I once was. Still, I figured I was just a year or so away from a 380–400 pound max. That was nearly 80 percent of my lifetime best, but not bad for a fat old man. Alas, I suffered a labral tear in my right shoulder, something new and disabling. That injury put the skids to me as far as lifting goes, as has yet another heart attack and a severe back injury suffered during a fall.

Nonetheless, I still occasionally enlist the zone, only now it is reserved for writing chapters like this. I am down to two working fingers, so crafting these pieces is certainly not easy! I must warm up a lot, and the opening passages are a bitch to write because my left-hand shakes a lot. I curse loudly and frequently with each miscue so my neighbors know when I am at work. Hell, the whole building does. Yet here I am, pounding away at the keys and cursing every typo. Life isn't easy, my friends, but it is always good. It's all a matter of perspective, and the glass remains half full. Amen.

39

The Times They Are a Changing

I'm not a tree hugger by nature, but I love the land, air, and waters in my neck of the woods. Furthermore, I embrace the paradoxical notion that the only constant is change, not that I blithely accept its application to long-term environmental changes. Indeed, given the conflicting "science," political views, and blatantly fake news, all I can do is base my environmental perspectives mostly on what I've actually seen and experienced . . . and that is reasonably clear cut here in the Upper Valley. When I was a kid, it was not unusual to have several 12–18-inch-plus snow storms each winter; and by late January or mid-February, the plowed-up snow banks on either side of the roads would be perhaps 6–8 feet high. We, kids, would often dig tunnels and make forts in the biggest snow piles, joyfully pelting one another with snowballs every step of the way. The snow banks seldom exceed 2–3 feet now, except after a massive storm, albeit we only get a few. We still have the occasional 20–30-inch blizzard in the Valley, but that is a rare event now (less than once a year).

So yeah, I have observed that there has been less snow and that the weather has gotten markedly warmer, at least since I was a kid. I remember waiting for the bus when it was over 30 below, sans wind chill, a rare happenstance now. The government stats bear out this observation (average snowfall is down 20-percent-plus since 1950, and temperature is up by almost 1.1 degrees centigrade), though given the politics, who can trust stats? Well, ask the ski resort operators, and they will tell you they'd be out of business without huge investments in artificial snow-making machines. The maple syrup manufacturers note a general decline in production that began in about 1910 and persists today. Indeed, in the US, we once harvested 5.5 million gallons of maple syrup per year, and now we are down to under 2.0 million gallons. Farmers also report declines in some crops, although how much of this relates to climate change is hard to say. And though many do not trust them, the official numbers are looking increasingly grim, as the charts available in numerous articles clearly portray.

Yeah, we are stringing record-high heat years, one after another. In fact, the last eight years have been the warmest on record, which is definitely a trend by most standards of reckoning.

Of course, the earth has been through significant temperature fluctuations in the last few million years, but the records indicate they were not this quick and marked. Some critters can adapt to environmental changes, but very few when the climate oscillations are sudden and extreme. The essential concern is habitat loss, as in flora species dying off. Thus far, I have yet to see much of that happening, at least around these parts. The snow-pack is much thinner than it once was, and we had drought alerts last year. We have not seen much snow this year, although many older folks do not complain much about that.

However, for people to happily think that nothing has changed is simply dead wrong, at least based on my personal experience and the data. Moreover, you talk with some 80-year-old Valley folks, and they will further contextualize this observation, at least around here. Is this the end of the world? Hell, no! It means climate changes are afoot, many of which we probably caused by pumping all sorts of stuff into the air. Some places will prosper, and some will suffer. Yet, I'm far more concerned with our current biochemical context than global warming. Humanity can adapt to some degree of global warming, though it will raise hell with low-lying coastal areas and many species. In addition, desertification will reduce arable land, and thus some percentage of people will eventually die off. That is, more or less, dyed in the wool, yet the survivors may adapt.

But we cannot adapt to environmental toxins. There are spates of cognitive deficits cropping up with alarming frequency in children, some of which are attributed to air pollution and/or pesticides. Autism is a case in point. I used to think the purported increased occurrence of autism was crap, an artifact of improved diagnoses and not actual incidence. That was the case until the problem hit my family and the families of several friends. Part of my family comes from a line of teachers, wherein 90 percent of some generations taught (9/10 siblings). There was no attention deficit disorder (ADD) or autism. I understand that some disorders are over-diagnosed, but a young relative has difficulty focusing. He takes ADD medications for the problem and receives the best care. His case is hardly unique, though. Several of my friends are going through the same thing with their kids.

Some evidence is anecdotal, but the established science is ominous concerning ADD. It appears that some of the increase in autism is related to the effects of endocrine-disrupting and neurotoxic pesticides. These chemicals are everywhere, especially in our foods. We use them in farming, and our environment has become laced with the resultant organochlorines, organophosphates, and pyrethroids. Indeed, I bet everyone reading these words knows of someone who has a kid with a learning disability.

In addition, the chemicals we use to produce plastic and electronics significantly reduce fertility in men, women, and animals. In this case, it's the damn phthalates that are gumming up the reproductive works, liver, kidneys, and other organs. They are a large family of chemicals that soften plastics and make them more flexible. We also use them in many cosmetics, deodorants, room fresheners, and nearly everything with a flowery smell.

These vile things reduce testosterone counts markedly, but there are other culprits.

Bisphenols (especially Bisphenol A) can boost estrogen in both men and women, thus influencing reproduction. Many chemicals in flame retardants, pesticides, and other products also harm male and female reproductive viability. Some stats show that fertility rates and sperm counts may be down by as much as 25 percent, but most folks don't know anything about all this. Yet we have added enough of these agents to our environment to be facing some grim prospects.

Look, our species has evolved within a particular biochemical and environmental context. Heat and cold have always been part of that mix, and I suspect we can adapt to slow changes in these areas. However, when we add vast amounts of pesticides, preservatives, and other chemicals into the mix, the context is rapidly altered in ways that may suddenly exceed our capacity to adapt. What roles this "pollution" has in embryonic and subsequent child development is the purview of biochemists, geneticists, and people of that ilk. Billions may have to die due to global warming, but the species will probably soldier on. The problem is IF we have so altered our biochemical context that cognitive deficits are increasing in what few kids our species can produce, that can only lead to a dismal future for the entire species.

To me, this isn't a matter of politics. This is a pressing public welfare and existential issue, and it exemplifies our glaring failings as a species. For example, one could order that we "gather data and find out the truth." Many scientists thus go into the field with fixed political agendas, and we've all seen where that bullshit leads. They find what their ideology or masters dictate that they find, and thus the truth is forever lost! So, we muddle along, and then things reach the stage wherein we HAVE to act because the situation has become critical. Yet by then, it may be too late to do much. Vested myopia is every bit as deadly as existential ignorance.

Conservatives and liberals alike are united in distorting the picture, thus obscuring a clear vision of what is happening. The eternal curse of conservatism is that it loathes change, although adaptation to shifting situations demands change. We all know what happens to species that cannot adapt. The curse of liberalism is that it often eschews what has worked in the past, some of which resulted from several generations of development and experimentation. Granted, ditching slavery, kingship, and so on, were good changes, but I'm not sure the same can be said of altering the "idea" of family, loyalty, community, etcetera. Concerning both these ideologies, I wish the hell they'd bug out of current issues related to the environment.

In the meantime, we work with those afflicted by our wretched perfidy and try various methods to improve their focus, concentration, and capacity to have productive futures. Many of my friends do so every day, patiently trying to ensure their child has a chance to overcome his/her disability. And while this struggle unfolds, I wonder if the fundamental problem stems from a preservative, pesticide, medication, or God-knows-what. I watch species after species march into oblivion under our tenure and note the weather and environmental changes. I fear for our long-term prospects but find no recourse in the endless debates. I write on posting boards but do little to help our survival. I suspect the same is true of you. Simply put, we have failed the future.

The only thing I know for sure is that we HAVE to act, but what to do . . . Oh, what to do? Let's begin by finding the truth of things. Let's see if our children are indeed at risk. There are many complications in any study of this area. Thus, let's select five reputable and apolitical scientific assessment agencies or concerns that meet with the approval of 60 percent of our legislative bodies. Let each of the five conduct formal and independent studies and then see their results. If most results indicate a severe problem in a given area and its potential causes, we proceed to the next step. That involves corrective actions, and herein reside some significant issues. However, first things first. Let us see if a problem exists and do so now.

All this sounds swell, but getting cats to agree on the tastiest food is more manageable. There will be interminable debates on every aspect of the proposed studies; thus, the odds of getting anything done are nil. The conservatives will typically support doing nothing, and the liberals will walk a million different paths that lead in at least that many directions. In the interim, time will pass, and tipping points that cannot be shifted or altered will be reached. We will not pay the piper. The kids and the future will. Countless species will wither while we continue the debate. Our fatal flaw is often lethargy, an inability to address a looming threat while there is still time to do so. We are like deer caught in the approaching headlights. What do we do to change that? Do we become eco-terrorists or country-club Republicans? Do we confront or merely pass the time? What will we do? What will YOU do? Amen is not the answer. Action is.

PART IV

NURTURE

40

Coaching Lessons

The stench of sweat-soaked athletes, the incessant clang of heavy metal plates banging against one another, and the grunts and groans of maximal efforts being made could be some folk's idea of Dante's Inferno. Yet that environment was heaven to me. Any collegiate weight room is an incredible experience, a place of hopes, dreams, intense efforts, and surprisingly controlled planning. After all, the athletes within that facility have a common goal: becoming far more able than they were when they entered the place. In many cases, the goal is to become bigger, stronger, and faster, with some improving their size by over 40 pounds, their bench by 200 pounds, and cutting their speed in the 40 by two-tenths of a second or more in just 4 years. Doing this is a demanding task requiring strict supervision, constant attention

40.1 The author at his former job as UNH's Strength Coach

to detail, and knowing the traits of every person in the facility. Moreover, it is essential to instill a belief that one can succeed if one harnesses the desire and dedication to realize lofty goals. That was my job at UNH for roughly 10 years and was the only job I ever loved.

It's a wonder I became a collegiate strength coach, especially considering the vast excesses of my dubious past. I was a miscreant oaf who was overly fond of doing all sorts of drugs and many other illegalities with my felonious friends. Furthermore, I made drinking a regular and terrifying event. Yeah, I became infamous during my youth for wild escapades, some of which were ended by the local constabulary. Now, there were some reasons for my wanton behavior. I grew up in a somewhat "dysfunctional" family, although I suspect nearly everyone does. My father drank too often, and my mother strived to contain the loud and sometimes violent discord while keeping the family together. We were also poor, and I developed a terrible self-image, which wasn't helped much by my burgeoning obesity.

My confidence improved when I started lifting weights at age 14, and I soon became addicted to iron. In fact, I took all 1,080 pounds of my free weights with me when I came to UNH and set up a weight room by my sophomore year in the school's Congreve Hall dormitory. Eventually, my weight room boasted three 400-pound Olympic sets, three training bars, over a ton of loose weights, and all manner of benches, squat racks, and other equipment. My facility was much better equipped than UNH's weight room then, and it soon became the focus of great activity. Lots of students used my weight room, including several varsity athletes. I got to know these guys well, and we trained hard. My Pre-Physical Therapy major and readings helped me to formulate programs for athletes, and these regimens proved very effective. UNH's head football coach soon became aware of my abilities from his players, and he hired me to run the university's weight room in 1977, my senior year. However, I had much to learn about coaching, and the lessons took work.

An athlete we'll call "Grant" taught me to respect my charges. Grant was a 6-foot-4-inch, 267-pound offensive lineman recovering from a knee injury when I started my coaching career at UNH. He could have been a better sprinter, but he was quick and athletic, having about the best balance imaginable for a guy his size. He was the quintessential laid-back Vermonter in many ways, ever rustic in his views and mannerisms. However, Grant worked out extremely hard in the weight room, and we grew to like one another.

However, I didn't respect Grant as much as I should have because some fools thought he had a fatal flaw in his character. I had heard from one of my fellow coaches and a few of Grant's teammates that he was not nearly aggressive enough. One athlete even called him a "pussy," which is the ultimate insult for a football player. Of course, I never heard anyone call Grant a pussy to his face. I half-believed what these clowns said about Grant because of his mellow mannerisms, and I'd taunt him occasionally. "Hey, Grant, are you as much of a pussy as all your teammates say you are?"

Grant used to take my barbs in stride, but one day he objected to my badgering by giving me a gentle cuff across the face. My rebellious spirit instantly came to the forefront, and I decided to take a hands-on approach, all 320 pounds of me. I hauled off and slapped Grant's face so hard that he reeled backward. Grant's eyes lit up, and he came at me with a whack across the puss that made me see double. It was a great shot . . . and Grant had huge hands! I mean, I saw stars. The kid almost decked me there and then, but I came right back at him.

In short order, Grant and I were slapping each other all over the damn weight room, much to the amusement of the cheering athletes. Grant would take a shot, and then I'd return the favor, slap for slap. And I mean, these were blows that could

40.2 Life in the UNH weight room was loud, hectic, and full of energy

knock most normal folks senseless. The only problem was that at 5-foot-8 inches I could barely reach Grant's face and head, yet he had no difficulty in utterly pummeling me from a distance. The madder he got, the more he mixed forearm shots to my head with his slaps. He wasn't acting like any "pussy" I had ever tangled with.

In desperation, I grabbed one of Grant's extended arms in mid-strike, stopping it cold. I smiled at him and said, "For God's sake, Grant, why don't you do this on the field?" He looked at me, perplexed, and then a smile slowly spread across his reddened face. I told him we had better stop fighting before one of us got hurt, and I was pretty damn sure it would have been me. He nodded, and I was greatly relieved. Grant taught me to respect my charges for what they are, not what anyone thinks or says. All too many coaches have more opinions than truths to offer, and athletes sometimes suffer as a result. Yeah, I saw too much of that nonsense.

Grant became an all-American football player the following year and later became an outstanding coach in his own right. I don't know if our slap fight had anything to do with Grant's success, but we learned a bit about ourselves that day. I learned that mutual respect between athletes and coaches is fundamental to successful teaching. It was also clear that people's opinions about some athletes are often not realities or close approximations. Moreover, I learned that taunting one's charges can come with a very stiff price!

Until my tiff with Grant, I depended on my strength and size to garner respect. I could take 425 pounds off a set of squat racks and push it overhead. Doing military presses with over 385 pounds and full-depth squats with 560 pounds for reps (repetitions) was not a problem. Oh yeah, I was strong, especially for a natural lifter. Nonetheless, impressing athletes with how much iron one can move around does not make a coach. I still had a great deal to learn about the profession, making effective programs, and how to interact with athletes. Most of my lessons were based on my mistakes and successes with the athletes, experiments, and reading articles, but I also learned a great deal from observing my peers' coaching methods.

My experience with Grant taught me that denigrating athletes is wrong, but many coaches believe that a person must be torn down to be built back up. That's the typical martial mentality we see in the Marines. Indeed, some coaches justify their inherent cruelty by adhering to this rigid dogma. However, the more I came to care about my charges, the more I despised anyone maligning them. In fact, I became quite vocal if I thought a person was being unfairly treated.

"Ken" was a promising athlete some coaches thought was not performing up to snuff, and one of the part-time coaches took particular delight in tormenting the kid. Coach "Caddy's" comments to Ken were cruel and cutting: "You're a waste of a scholarship, Ken . . . Christ, you hit like a sissy . . . Why the hell do you bother wearing a jock?" And it went on and on. However, I knew Ken was trying because I saw him working his heart out in practice and the weight room. He was wholly dedicated to improving himself and making good but slow progress.

Ken talked with me in the weight room about how miserable his nemesis made life for him, but I assumed he could handle the situation. I was wrong. I saw Ken in the locker room one day, his face turned to the wall, eyes staring blankly into nothingness. I asked him if anything was bothering him. "I can't take it any-more," he softly whispered. "Even my teammates are starting to shit on me now. But you know I'm tryin'. I really am." Then he stared off into space again, lost in some terribly painful world of lonely despair.

To see a young man reduced to emptiness is a haunting thing, so I asked Coach Caddy to cut Ken some slack. "What do you mean, lay off him?" Coach Caddy indignantly replied. "The kid's just acting like a baby, and you're falling for it." Coach Caddy insisted Ken would get tougher from being dumped on and that he would perform better as a result. I objected, and Coach Caddy got mad at me. "You know what your problem is?" he asked with a sneer. "You're not a coach to these kids! You're their friend." Coach Caddy said "friend" as a venal insult, but I thanked him for the compliment.

Ken dropped out of school at the end of the semester, and I never even got to say goodbye to him. His fate still pains me. He was such a happy freshman, an enthusiastic and hopeful kid. Then he was broken by the opprobrium heaped on him and made an outcast by his sophomore year. Coach Caddy found a job at another college sometime later. I imagine he's still breaking down kids to build them up. Ken is just another casualty in his game plan, and I suspect there will be others. Then again, life will teach Caddy a thing or two about what it takes to be humane.

I was to become friends with many of my charges at UNH, which is when coaching became a labor of love for me. I worked out with the athletes, listened to their problems and fears, and grew to care about them personally. The athletes, in turn, came to respect me as more than just a bloated fat man. When one sees athletes do something they could not master before, a vicarious joy takes hold, as in watching their first 300-pound bench press or 500-pound squat. That is a rush, an extraordinary kind of joy! Their accomplishments become your reason for being, as odd as that may sound to some people. Yeah, for the first time in my life, I came to feel an emotional attachment to what I did. I looked forward to working and continued learning about both coaching and myself. Furthermore, many athletes I worked with became professionals and were credits to the school, their hard work, and our program.

One of my harshest experiences as a coach involved a lack of empathy, and it still haunts me. The incident occurred in early May, when the students were preparing for graduation or summer vacation, an ordinarily happy time of year. Only a few athletes were lifting in the weight room, and we were wantonly shooting the breeze. The banter in a weight room can get a bit vulgar and sexist at times, and we drifted into tearing up homosexuality, typical gay-bashing talk, replete with squeaky voices.

It came time to close, and I harried the kids out of the room so that I could go home and eat. "Zac" was stubborn and continued to lift after the other athletes had left, so I chided him about being recalcitrant. He glared at me, and I asked what was wrong. "You're an asshole," he growled. "You're just like all the rest." I was shocked. I had always thought of Zac as being short-tempered but basically stable. However, the person I saw was anything but in control. He was seething with rage, pounding out rep after rep of EZ bar curls. He tossed the bar aside and jumped my way.

Zac grabbed me by the forearms, and I thought he would soon punch my lights out. Then he abruptly released me and bolted out of the weight room. I followed Zac down a hallway and through some corridors before finally catching up with him in an empty locker room. He slammed his fists into metal lockers, punching huge dents into their doors. I thought Zac would break his hands, so I grabbed one of his arms and spun him around to face me. He was wet-eyed and trembling.

He spoke to me in semi-coherent half-sentences mixed with tearful agony: "And Dad said I don't have a home . . . if I'm that way . . . Not his kid. And you guys, you're all being assholes about it. So what am I going to do? Because I am. I am that way! Can you tell me? Can you? Can you? Can you?" In the four years I had known Zac, I never thought he was gay. In fact, I doubt more than one or two of his former teammates knew about his hidden homosexuality if that many. I was stunned.

Zac was anything but the stereotypical image of a gay man. He was a handsome 220-pounder who used to revel in hitting people on the football field. And this guy could hit! He was often with girlfriends, and some of them were stunningly attractive. However, there he was, spilling out his guts to a coach who could scarcely believe what he was hearing. How many other kids did I hurt in that weight room with my inane comments? How many Black kids? How many poor kids? How many gay kids?

In all likelihood, Zac had wanted someone to talk with about his situation for years, but no one was there who would listen without judging, including me. So, Zac just lived with his secret and acted "moody." One cannot atone for some mistakes, and my failure with Zac was complete. I tried telling Zac to love himself no matter what anyone says or does. He replied, "How can I love myself when everyone else hates me?" I could not answer his question and never got another chance to. Zac graduated and left, and I never saw him again.

By this time in my coaching career, I had stopped drinking and partying. No more all-nighters doing cocaine or 3:00 a.m. joy rides at 90 miles per hour, and no more people overdosing in my apartment. Instead, I studied textbooks and technical papers about weight training methodologies and wrote articles published in nationally circulated magazines. I soon got letters asking for advice from all over the United States and the world, from South Africa, Switzerland, Finland, Denmark, England . . . even Australia. I was becoming respected in the field.

I had long despised the simplistic single-set-per-exercise training system promulgated by the Nautilus company, so I came out publicly against it. I ridiculed the methodology in nationally circulated magazines such as *Muscle & Fitness* and *Muscular Development*. The battle raged for seven years before Arthur Jones, the primary proponent of the single-set training methodology, publicly admitted in the mid-1980s that multiple sets can be more beneficial. I had my first real taste of victory in the ongoing battle.

There came possibilities for me to leave UNH, including one that could have landed me in Saudi Arabia and paid more money than I thought possible. However, I loved my job and athletes, so I stayed put. It was foolish sentimentality because the job offered no benefits and abysmal pay. Still, progress was being made, and experiments were underway on new systems. Some fellow coaches believed I lacked ambition, but I had found my nirvana. It was within a crowded, sweaty, poorly equipped weight room at UNH. Even my parents used to complain about my remaining at UNH, but I was mostly happy there, despite being paid wages that never exceeded $13,500 per annum. Besides, I was still learning from my charges.

An athlete named "Carl" taught me the value of two-way communication. Carl was a highly recruited offensive lineman who opted to come to UNH because of the school's vaunted engineering program. He was one of the rare computer-brained intellectuals who liked to play football, and the kid was a coach's dream. He worked hard, learned instantly, and got along well with his coaches and teammates. Alas, everything wasn't all light and happiness in Carl's career. He hurt his ankle in practice during his freshman year, and the injury didn't seem to heal. Then he started to lose weight, and the head coach got on me to find out why.

I sat down with Carl frequently and tried to get to the bottom of his dilemma. When I think back on it, our meetings were more a matter of my giving Carl advice than listening to him. I advised Carl to eat more, get more rest, work out harder, take more vitamins, etcetera, etcetera, etcetera. However, Carl was telling me important things about himself that I ignored. He told me he was losing weight despite eating triple servings and that cuts and bruises weren't healing well. Carl also felt run down and tired. Yeah, he was telling me many things I should have listened to.

Carl insisted that the doctors thought he was doing fine, but then he returned from his sophomore semester break weighing only 225 pounds, down 20 pounds from his freshman year. I became very concerned. Carl worked hard in the weight room, but his strength and size slowly dwindled. I kept advising him, but nothing I offered seemed to help. Carl was frustrated, the head coach was beyond frustrated, and I felt the heat. Something was clearly wrong, but no one knew what it was.

Over spring break, Carl started to feel very ill, so he saw his family doctor. The doctor took some blood tests and discovered Carl's blood sugar count was over 800! He was a severe diabetic, and he was in very rough shape. We had all fucked up big time: doctors, coaches, and friends alike. Meanwhile, Carl had been paying a terrible price. The endocrinologist Carl saw was amazed that he hadn't gone into diabetic shock. He was very concerned about the degree of damage that might have been done to Carl's kidneys and other internal organs. That kid could have been badly injured by my careless incompetence, and the thought of my failure to notice the obvious still eats at me.

Yes, I felt responsible. I should have been listening to Carl more and talking less. After all, diabetes runs in my family, and I was very familiar with its symptoms, warning signs that I had utterly failed to see in Carl. Carl's ankle injury never did heal properly, and he had to have the bones in his foot "frozen" via a surgical procedure. He has to take regular insulin shots now, and his future prognosis is uncertain. I, too, was to become a severe diabetic, and I think a bit of that is karmic, albeit my family history certainly did not help.

Carl became the team's manager and film man and continued to lift over the coming years. He knew how guilty I felt about his

40.3 Elder had to leave coaching due to illnesses and injuries
that eventually resulted in disabilities

medical problems and once told me, "It wasn't your fault, Dino. Even my own doctors didn't know what was up." Nonetheless, I'll forever wonder if I could have helped him by noticing more and assuming less. Carl got his engineering degree. He now walks with a limp, and I regard myself as one reason for that gait. The critical lesson learned is one of responsibility. The athletes coaches work with are more than names on a roster. They are our charges, and we owe them the best we can offer. Anything less is unacceptable and unforgivable.

The end of my coaching career started with a bang. On July 26, 1985, I went into my weight room and got dropped by a "cerebral vascular event" while picking up some dumbbells that had been left out. It was a very traumatic incident, complete with slurred speech and convulsions. Some specialists in Boston said a neck injury might have impacted a vertebral artery in my neck, and the malady left some aftereffects. Others thought I had a transient ischemic attack (TIA). I couldn't feel my left side properly and lost coordination. I also became plagued by vicious right-sided headaches. Nonetheless, I wanted to continue coaching.

I coached at UNH for another two years after my injury but could no longer lift heavy weights. My headaches became intractable, yet I would not give up my career. I grew to love coaching with a passion I have never known for anything else. I also grew to care about my charges above all other things, including my own welfare. Alas, I was becoming a liability to UNH due to my symptoms, and I was medically discharged in 1988. After all, one cannot have a weightlifting coach who cannot safely lift weights. Some six years later, it was found that two badly ruptured discs in my neck were pressing on my spinal cord and surrounding structures. Surgery was done to correct the problem, yet the damage had been done. Sadly, all this was unknown back when I was retired, and a great chasm formed where my spirit had once grown and flourished. Part of me died.

A person who has never coached can little understand the allure and attachment the job has to its practitioners. Coaching replaced many of my self-destructive urges with a desire to see my charges improve. I became one with their efforts, hopes, and problems. In return, the athletes gave me a way of living that only coaches can genuinely understand. I soared through the air with a wide receiver, leaping to make a spectacular one-armed catch. I raced down the ice rink with a winger who scored the breakaway goal that put us into the national playoffs. I shed tears after some of the agonizing defeats, lost in a world of utter despair. I lived experientially as well as vicariously. I was happy. My life had meaning and depth.

I left my job with profound regrets because I still had much to contribute. Indeed, learning how to give was my most important lesson as a coach. Coaching is all about giving when it is being done correctly. It's giving advice, concern, and love, with the latter being the most important. Coaches must love their charges as much as they love themselves and their families. Sure, one occasionally gets angry or disappointed at a kid, but in the end, a coach always wants the best for his charges.

I soon found myself an unlikely academic, studying to get my Master's degree in Writing. Then came a PhD degree in Speech Communication at Penn State. There were books and articles, but part of my soul departed when I left coaching. It was a place where I could enter the weight room and roar loud enough to shake the entire facility, announcing to one and all that the games were about to begin! The rest of the day would be a blur, punctuated by teaching, meetings, and activities of every nature. Most academics cannot envision such a life as having much to offer, and they are poorer because of that dreary view. I'll always miss the clanging of weights, shouts and greetings, and the sights of the weight room. It is an extraordinary place, a place of labor and love.

41

On Beating Children

Teaching domestic and social nonviolence to people expected to practice overt and outright violence several times weekly is difficult. Indeed, the National Football League (NFL) has a long history of being beleaguered by various domestic abuse issues. This boorish behavior is not unusual, given the personalities of some who have played football. After all, when one strives to be overtly aggressive regularly, it is often hard to turn the switch off. The fact that so many manage to do so is a credit to the game. Most teams sanction players involved in fights and other conflicts off the field. However, present and past punitive actions regarding domestic abuse and violence are shamefully few and far between.

Furthermore, the Bible itself sanctions corporal punishment throughout Proverbs, as in Proverbs 13:24, which stipulates, "He that spareth his rod hateth his son: but he that loveth him chasteneth him betimes." Here we find an essential source for the advice to spare the rod and spoil the child, as if beating children is a viable teaching tool. Numerous studies demonstrate that animals learn far more quickly and robustly from negative reinforcement than by applying rewards. Indeed, electric shocks can cause an animal to avoid a given context altogether for protracted periods, as cattle regularly learn via the agency of electrified fences. A few short zaps and most cattle stay within the designated boundaries. As many psychological studies have clearly shown, people can also be quickly and efficiently taught via negative reinforcement. However, is this necessary?

Some folks still employ the religious endorsement of physical force to justify whipping and beating kids, the results of which were once seen on our TV screens via the good graces of the Minnesota Viking's Adrian Peterson. Now folks can justify his actions however they want, but let us delve into the story briefly. First, pictures of the welts, cuts, and bruises caused by the wooden switch (modified tree branch) Peterson used on his son's upper leg were shown. These wounds extended to the child's back, genitals, and ankle, a good, old-fashioned beating that was served up because the child had pushed a sibling off a motorbike. Yes, Peterson did not spare his four-year-old child from the rod, which seems to be a grim familial habit in his case.

Once the story hit the press, Peterson was indicted by a grand jury in Texas in 2014 on charges of reckless/negligent injury to a child. The NFL suspended Peterson for the rest of the season, but he suffers interminable criticisms for his actions that persist. To Peterson, the beating was perfectly normal and morally justifiable. Indeed, Peterson had also been disciplined with a switch as a child, as is the case in many areas of the United States and countries far and wide. Peterson pleaded no contest to a subsequent misdemeanor charge of recklessly assaulting his son in a plea agreement. He was put on probation, fined $4,000, and ordered to perform 80 hours of community service. Yet the debate continues regarding using corporal punishment with kids, with Peterson reportedly continuing his old ways.

Sadly, a "love" child of Peterson (Tyrese Robert Ruffin) was beaten to death by his mother's boyfriend (Joseph Patterson) when he was two years old following four hard blows to the child's head that caused a brain bleed. What was the moral lesson of all that? I do not understand what kids are supposed to learn by harsh punishments, nor was my kin immune from them. My grandfather was a child of the South, but he was also a Virginian with a Master's Degree from Cornell University, back when degrees meant something. He was a world-recognized expert in veterinary science, someone who traveled abroad when his expertise was sought. Yet he was a man of considerable anger and prejudice, possessed of an often-acerbic attitude passed down through the generations. And he most assuredly did not spare the rod.

Yeah, my dad was regularly beaten by his father for the most minor offenses, and his father was not some ignorant red-neck. He would strap my father for not eating all his food, for missing an answer on a Latin spelling test, for daring to leave the dinner table without being excused, and for so many infractions that my dad's life became a living hell. Indeed, Thomas Edwin Elder's cruelty of spirit irritated people beyond his family, and he eventually faced severe criminal charges, including murder and assault. He was always found innocent, but his fundamental inhumanity attracted a certain amount of notoriety.

When my father came of age, he bore internal scars that never fully healed. Henry Elder was a tormented soul, and his father's harsh legacy was well ensconced within him. His was an odd mixture of fear and rage, and he became an inveterate alcoholic. Dad's father wrote him off and would not even attend my parent's wedding. After all, Henry was marrying an olive-skinned, thick-lipped, and kinky-haired Latin. She was the daughter of immigrants from southern Italy and a temperamental abomination in Grandad's racist eyes. If the truth be told, my mother was the glue that held our family together. She weathered my father's constant storms, his terrible lashing out.

I saw some of my siblings beaten, and many times the house echoed with my dad's screams, often accompanied by the sounds of furniture being smashed. As a child, I lived in constant fear and gradually became "disturbed," a budding psychopath. I set fires and tortured animals, trying twice to burn down our home by the time I was just eight or nine. Thus, my grandfather's legacy became a part of me, too, the sins of a father's father finding residence within a grandson that he was too bigoted to even acknowledge. You see, there was a time I would think nothing of beating a man like Adrian Peterson with a baseball bat. Pick the right time and place, and even the ablest man falls as quickly as a child. It has taken me a lifetime to chain the beast within that generates those thoughts and tendencies, and the beast need not have been implanted and nurtured in the first place.

So, listen to me, you Adrian-want-to-be folks and child beaters. One day the beatings you serve up may come home to roost. You are ruining your kids, you selfish, two-bit sons-of-bitches. God gave you far more than many will ever know in the form of being a parent, and perhaps one day God will take it all back. There is this savage urge within me to attack child beaters, and I don't even know who they are. Yet I know all too well the torment they produce.

I am old and beaten, but that brutal tendency to lash out remains. It is the same tendency Adrian and his kind are implanting in their kids, for which they are directly responsible. If they can truly love someone more than themselves, perhaps they can also find some kindness. As for the Bible's justifications, screw that. The Bible has justified everything from slavery to child abuse, and that lame and primitive approach to raising children can be shoved where the sun doesn't shine.

Coaching ended up saving my life. It taught me many lessons, especially how to care about those I served. Their welfare meant everything to me, giving my life purpose and satisfaction.

But through it all, I constantly fought the demons within. Reflecting upon it all, I can see the sources of my sadder tendencies, my urge to attack. It is a terrible legacy, the same one that some reading these words are passing down to their kids. Abusing children is the worst possible sin because it echoes into the future in countless ways. That some would defend this style of raising kids amazes me. Let the children know peace and love, and spare them rods, insults, and things that can mark their souls forever. Amen.

42

The Test

Learning can cause lifelong nightmares. I am over 70 years old, hold three degrees (BS, MA, PhD), took 270-plus credits worth of undergraduate and graduate-level classes, wrote numerous articles and books . . . and yet "the test dream" reoccurs with alarming regularity. It is finals time, and I have not been attending classes all semester. Yeah, I have been as irresponsible as it gets, and a dreadful reckoning awaits. In addition, I am unsure where and when the exam is being held, although I could possibly muddle through. However, I need help finding the correct building, room, and exam guide. I go from person to person asking for help, although I seem to lack expressive capacity. Some folks offer aid, yet I am unable to determine the class I had skipped. It could be Social Psychology 480 or something like that.

Ah, I found a schedule at long last, only to discover that the exam was on Monday, a full day ago! Or was it two days past? Oh, I am screwed! What to do??? Ah, I'll talk to the professor. Perhaps he/she will give me a break and let me take the exam late. Where do I find the professor, and what do I say? After all, slackers get what they deserve, which is a failure! A student I'm speaking with notices my confusion and panicked disorientation. I tell him my brain is a bit addled, but the exam remains my responsibility. I have to do it.

And while all this unfolds, I ponder about leaving home to go to graduate school, a dream within a dream. Yeah, it is time to leave the nest again and move on with my life. However, all my old books, tools, clothes, and possessions are haphazardly packed in ratty old boxes covered with thick dust and cobwebs. They are in my parent's home, but I have to get my belongings sorted out and organized before they can be moved to wherever I am going. There is a ton of stuff, and I don't know what to do with it. Oh, and what about the damn exam? Yes, I forgot about that exam!

They may know where the professor is in the main administration building! Oh, but where is that? There is nothing but panic and confusion as I wander from building to building, chased by the absence of order and preparedness. Besides, where is home? Flashes on my long-deceased parents come to mind. Then I see the hodgepodge of storage boxes, their contents being a mixture of prized possessions and junk. However, I am already at school and must thus be hundreds of miles from home. I see all of this in my mind's eye but realize that time has moved on. Or has it? Indeed, does time even exist? I awake with a start, heavy breathing mixed with palpable fear. This is similar to a dream you've probably also experienced.

The experts tell us that fear-laced dreams about being unprepared for exams mean that we feel ill-equipped to deal with difficulties and hardships that could be headed our way or are currently in play. We may need more preparation, doubt our capabilities, or think the test will go differently than we desire. Some Freudians believe these dreams relate to past situations wherein we could not resolve an issue or a looming crisis. Our fear is that we may end up in the same dilemma. Others theorize that these dreams relate to an upcoming choice or decision that will be made about you rather than by you. In effect, you feel ill-prepared to face a judgment you have no control over.

Some extend this to the notion that the dream represents the donning of a new phase in your life, the successful navigation of which is uncertain. In essence, a challenging situation in your work, personal relationships, or family life is causing you to feel unprepared. Moreover, you fear the possibility of failure and/or not living up to your responsibilities. Lastly, feeling lost and confused can reflect our being overwhelmed by a situation and being unsure how to deal with it. There are many opinions about what these test dreams mean, but I grow weary of the miserable experiences.

The dizzying confusion I felt in the dream is becoming a frequent reality due to a growing memory disorder. But at least I avoid panicking or becoming fearful in the corporeal world when I'm lost or confused. I have this ill-founded faith that everything will work out for the best, the curse of an optimist. I suspect this dream is about being unprepared to face the inevitable challenges and responsibilities of dealing with what the doctors tell me is the onset of dementia. No one likes being tested and probed about their competency, but that is the nature of education and life. We are constantly tested in one way or another, and some of us dread being found wanting. We recognize our failures and shortcomings, yet there seems no escape from our rectitude and weaknesses. And so, our dreams reflect the battle that percolates beneath the surface, that incessant struggle to prove we are worthy.

I suppose this dream was stimulated by the magnetic resonance imaging (MRI) they are doing on Friday. They claim parts of my brain have atrophied, much more so than is usual for a person my age. Another round of neuropsychological exams follows a few months after that. Those sad things take hours, and I don't much like being reminded that something is wrong with my memory. Hell, I do not need anyone to tell me that. Nonetheless, I will do my best because that is my way. I plan to use a double dose of modafinil to help keep my mind active.

My main strength is a good imagination, although that seems to be useless in eluding the dreaded "exam" dreams. They are a self-imposed form of torture. Indeed, I should have developed the capacity to leave the miserable dream states when they occur. However, after all these years, here I am . . . still dealing with the fearful imagery and feelings that the dream arouses. Why must this dreary universal exist, as it does in nearly everyone? Oh, f' you test dream! F' you all to hell!

It will be hot today, and my legs still have not recovered from my last walk. Yet, if I can walk at all, I most assuredly will. That is a self-imposed test that I do not fear. To strive is to live. To fret is to negate much of what is good in life. I know that, but this awareness does not quell the damn recurring test dream. My imagination may not be so good after all, but I will still find some happiness today, come hell or high water! That long hill awaits, and it has been a challenging few days for walking. As always, we go on.

Some time has passed since this dream occurred. The MRI, and more recent ones, again demonstrated marked atrophy with "disproportionate frontoparietal and left medial occipital atrophy, with sparing of the temporal lobes." The cause could be "chronic small vessel ischemic change," but I do not think causation matters. I did much better on the neuropsychological evaluation than I thought would be the case. Had my memory tests been up to snuff, I would have achieved my former lofty levels. Yeah, but the memory indices are pathological now, with my frequently being unable to name people I have known for years or be able to discern the day of the week. Sometimes I don't know where we are while taking the bus, but I know we'll get there. Optimism is the cure for deep-seated fears, so I hold onto that perspective as tightly as possible. Be of cheer, my friends. Amen.

43

Future Shock

Several years ago, I had an unusual dream wherein I was a future rebel bent on blowing up a colossal fortress. I was with a group of like-minded people who stealthily approached the towering fort's blackish-gray walls, with large boulders and the night's darkness giving us some precious cover. I was in awe, for the massive structure seemed to fill the ominous, nocturnal setting, blotting out the moon and stars with its sheer mass. The edifice stood atop a rocky promontory and seemed to organically meld at its vast base with the surrounding landscape. After avoiding several trip wires, motion detectors, cameras, and other security devices, our group easily and swiftly penetrated the fort by cutting through the thick metal bars protecting a colossal sewage pipe that fed into a large stream.

I recall the stench and muck we encountered within the pipe; but soon enough, we found an access hatch leading to the fort's lower infrastructure. We quickly separated into small groups, with me and another fellow ascending stairs and traversing a dizzying array of corridors. We had a small monitor that allowed us to determine where we were relative to where we had to go, and a long and challenging trek lay ahead of us. There was great fear, but we were well trained, determined, and knew what we were doing. Our mission was to support personal freedom and justice, and our task was to do away with what we considered a dictatorial power structure.

Many details elude me, but we constantly avoided cameras and other detection means while evading various traps. One of these ambush devices was a waist-high metal rotor concealed within walls that would rapidly deploy upon sensing motion. The device aimed to knock intruders off their feet and crush them against adjacent cement walls, repeatedly battering them into lifeless pulp. However, we jumped over the rotors and quickly planted explosive charges here and there as dictated by our monitor. I wasn't sure when the charges would go off, but after the payloads were deployed, our focus quickly shifted to getting out of the place. Haste was requisite and especially after several alarms sounded!

Hoards of "semi-women" wearing tight-fitting black leather uniforms deftly darted through corridors. They raced up and down stairwells as the charges we and other groups planted began loudly detonating. Our pursuers' bodies appeared feminine, but some of their faces bore mustaches, beards, and goatees. It was as if there had been a mixture of the genders that did away with the notion of male and female. Some of their weapons were futuristic, as in ray guns, and others were more old-fashioned, with many brandishing razor-sharp Japanese katanas. The soldiers were fast and agile, and I knew there was no escape. Part of me felt guilty for being involved in an essentially violent operation that would take many lives, but I also knew the battle had to be fought. Nonetheless, dying in this dark and sterile place of steel and concrete was a terrifying prospect. However, I knew from the growing number of explosions and violent shaking within the building that our mission was successful. The massive complex was crumbling around us. We would not die alone, albeit our passing would be miserable.

I awoke just before they caught us, and the dream's meaning remained unclear for quite some time. Like my mother, I often had portentous dreams, but nothing made sense about this event. As fate would have it, my coming days of graduate school at Penn State were filled with many private and public battles, the most prominent of which involved free speech versus an entrenched administration. To be brief, I was canned from my teaching position for making a stand against a policy that forbade me from asking students to become advocates for various actions that they supported. I went public after being dismissed and thus began a very explosive series of public battles that obliterated my chances of securing future teaching assignments. Yes, my anti-academy polemics killed a possible career, although some of my opponents also suffered, with at least two leaving the department within a few years of my dismissal. It was a good trade.

Still, some elements of the prescient dream remained mystifying, such as the hermaphroditic soldiers. However, thanks to a relative who recently graduated from a prestigious school, the subtler messages within the dream are finally coming into focus. Some people work against freedom of thought without ever realizing that is what they are doing. They are taught that words such as Black, White, and so on, are essentially racist and sexist because they are divisive descriptors based on stereotypical concepts. Similarly, terms such as "men," "women," and so on, are also sexist because they portray gender-based stereotypes, including those words reserved for people of transgender, gay, and lesbian persuasions. Yes, one pays $70,000 to $100,000 per annum to have their children taught these "politically correct and enlightened" doctrines, with the students smugly walking away from it all, thinking that they are pretty damn bright.

These would-be enlightened academics claim to be superior in their discursive styles and ways of thought, although they sometimes seem inconsistent. For example, suppose one uses terms these graduates don't like. In that case, one is quickly branded as being this or that, with words such as paternalistic, patriarchal, antiquated, racist, and much worse being bantered about. I was dubbed a "prick" and "cunt" by some of these bright young folks for disagreeing with their positions, though some other colorful terms were couched in barely coded language. Despite their haughtiness, the entitled young twits ultimately strove to make their points the old-fashioned way, with staid vulgarity. I found it amusing to be linguistically categorized by would-be elitists who supposedly seek to stand above using crude categorization tools. Granted, I was willfully teasing them, although my views were sincere. Moreover, they just didn't get the joke.

Let us briefly return to the dream's metaphors. Of course, the fortress is the overweening power of the academy and other social institutions to shape minds and actions, albeit in strictly prescribed and approved fashions. Some call this "political correctness," though I call it operant conditioning. One is patted on the head and given tasty intellectual acknowledgments for displaying approved academic behavior, woof, woof. The hermaphroditic soldiers are the legions of freshly matriculated students who would guide our thoughts, deeds, and language use, albeit in a supposedly nonsexist fashion. These nascent fascists don't even know they are being fascists, such is the ardor of their conviction versus their inability to grasp the nuances related to their academically instilled stridency. Since the first step in gaining wisdom is to know that one does not know, I depend on the happy idea that life will eventually teach these young folks what the academy has failed to do. Yeah, they need to get dirty, beaten, and defeated, to learn what it is like to suffer and fail. Then they can rise anew as more substantial and experienced people worth listening to.

I worshiped at the altar of higher education for many years and am familiar with the various linguistic relativity theories that run through some dated and recent suppositions regarding how people use language. For example, the notion that one cannot experience or communicate certain thoughts (e.g., racism) without specific words has existed for a long time. The theory maintains that we cannot think about hate, a rose, a car, or racism without having terms for these ideational and/or physical referents. Thus, one can slowly do away with racism by eliminating terms that could be construed as racist, although who decides what words are or are not racist isn't entirely clear. Moreover, the tools used to impose the apropos linguistic standards are mockery, ostracism, and even violence. This is Big Brother writ large.

Banning the use of terms is a simplistic and inane concept, for it isn't words or language alone that defines thought. For example, our pets anticipate when we are coming home from work, often waiting by the door. They have no words for "friend," "time," "happy," "situation," or "anticipation," yet all these "ideas" are in play while waiting. Furthermore, they often commune with us through nonlinguistic vocalizations and nonverbal means when we arrive, expressing desires and other concepts they intend, such as "hunger," "play," and "pet me." In fact, they can change or induce our subsequent actions and reactions without using anything we would call words or language. Ergo, thoughts, terms, and realities are different, although they can be related in some individuals, depending on their education and/or experiences. In essence, there can be thought without language, at least as many in the academy define it.

The real task is understanding how thoughts and words are related, which takes us into neurolinguistics, neuropsychology, and even neurophysiology. I delved into these weighty areas for many years, writing a text on the subject published by NOVA Science. I did this because many people in the academy were promoting ideas regarding how communication functions that I knew were inconsistent with what science has revealed. I will not bore you with the details because the subject matter can be weighty and interminable. However, some things are easily understood.

For example, we are naturally categorical thinkers even at birth. Hence, a newborn will attend a paddle-board stimulus adorned with stereotypical eye and mouth facial markers in solid preference to other patterns. Similarly, a newly hatched chick will duck and lie low when the schematic form of a predatory bird is presented. There are hundreds of examples of hard-wired perceptual and reactionary traits. Still, the central point is that we continue being categorical tinkers in many ways as we mature, regardless of our education and quaint ideas about language. We know this from brain damage studies. For example, people with focal lesions can lose their ability to recognize and/or name specific categorical associates, such as faces, particular types of objects, colors, or even emotions.

We cannot "educate" our inherent information-processing tendencies away, nor am I sure this is a wise attempt. We can and should think about how we think, but changing how we contemplate is problematic. Humans process a great deal of information via employing abstract or concrete categorical associations, which has been proven repeatedly. This is the heart of metaphor, the ultimate means by which thoughts are shared via language. I wish there was more focus on this area being taught in the academy because most of what I currently see is a species of insular idealism and intellectual elitism that stands in sharp contrast to a lot of science, not that science should be our God. Indeed, what we don't know would fill a universe versus the scant array of texts concerning what we do know.

One can undoubtedly contend that we should always be aware of what messages our words convey to a given audience, though the blanket eschewing of words such as Black, White, queer, and so on, is probably not the best way to accomplish this. What is required is the donning of an allocentric perspective. This is a capacity wherein we strive to perceive ourselves as others perceive us, which is no easy task. It demands the suppression of an essentially egotistical perspective in preference for a focus on how others are interpreting our ongoing communication and view our actions. This idea entails a greater understanding of the external perceptions of our interactions with others as they unfold rather than a strict concentration on word use alone. No, it ain't easy.

I am dismayed by what continues to spew out of the academy. It is the same old shit-on-a-shingle crapped out as when I got my doctoral degree. I never fitted into the academy when I was there, being far too direct, crude, and blunt in my views. If a concept lacked support, I said so, often in harsh and uncompromising terms. I was older when I began my PhD work, being over 40. I had worked, gotten knocked around, and tasted failure and success. When I was the age of some of the kids I have recently communed with, I was doing all sorts of drugs, getting into tiffs, and partying up a storm. I am not saying young people need any of that "reality," but they surely need ample life experiences before opining on how life works, let alone how we should use language. I am optimistic, hoping that every new generation will eventually learn how best to judge themselves and others.

44

The Beast Within

Some of us are born with contentious natures, but there is no doubt that learning and experience can modify our inherent tendencies. As I've related, my earliest memories are of loud screams, breaking furniture, and all the other joys of living with an alcoholic parent. However, I probably also had the seeds of a confrontational nature as part of my genetics. After all, the Albanese on my mother's side, were Christian warriors who fought the Muslims tooth and nail in the brutal sectarian battles that defined medieval and later life in the western Balkans. The family fled from Albania to southern Italy following some actions that did not go well.

Similarly, the Elder clan was involved in numerous tussles in Scotland in the early 1400s, although the lineage goes back to the

Norman Conquest. In fact, John Elder conspired with Henry VIII to have the English invade Scotland, at which point aid would be given by the Highland clans. So, both the paternal and maternal sides had a rather pugnacious nature, for which they were duly awarded family crests for their service to vested power.

The Elder crest has a plate-armored gauntlet holding a quill, indicating that words were often their weapon of choice in their "virtuous leadership." In raising her children, my mother seldom displayed a harsh nature, but my father exhibited all the traits of a badly abused child. As mentioned earlier, he was the son of a highly educated old-South father of reactionary temperament and prejudicial tendencies. That was my father's essential reality, and his torment ended up devouring his soul and causing some of his children harm. It is a litany oft-repeated and one that impacts millions of lives. So, as already mentioned, I became a bit of a fire-loving and animal-abusing psychopath as a child, albeit not a particularly bad person in some ways. Then, a budding political awareness began, which wasn't even partially mature until I was in my 30s.

Usually, I tolerated the opposition, but I vacillated between being an Independent or Democrat. Democrats can hardly be accused of having a real party, which is fine for folks like me. I have liberal and conservative tendencies on various issues, as should everyone who can think. For example, I am liberal on many social issues but conservative about keeping promises, national defense, personal freedom, and policing issues. However, I wanted nothing to do with the politics of my grandfather, a staunch

Republican. The man would not even attend his son's wedding because he was marrying a "temperamental Latin," thus bringing a bunch of mongrel mixed bloods into this world. How his views hurt my mother. Ma suffered the outrage in silence as she did my dad's drunken escapades. She was the force that held the family together, an idealist when it came to the notion of love. She knew I was harboring some darkness within but did her best to stem the tide.

Flash forward to 2016, and we have Trump versus Hillary Clinton. At the time, I was a Bernie supporter, and I found Hillary about as attractive as a warm bucket of pee. But she was anointed by the party, albeit in an undemocratic fashion. I would thus support her, warts and all. Indeed, I worked against the Bernie Diehards, still considering them the cause of Clinton's demise. Moreover, I regarded Trump as a self-entitled blowhard, a man of consummate selfishness, inveterate egotism, piss-poor intellect, and vulgar tendencies.

Trump's mannerisms and deeds reminded me of Athens's Cleon (active 430–420s BCE), an unprincipled politician/businessman who used lies, bullying, and mockery to appeal to the commoners. He despised the Athenian nobility and worked against them at every level by rallying the unwashed against their ruling class. Cleon was primarily responsible for giving rise to the term demagogue, and his wretchedness was to find its ultimate recourse during a war he fostered with Sparta. His military prowess was found wanting during the Battle of Amphipolis, and Cleon was cut down while attempting to escape from a Spartan force that had utterly crushed his army.

History is fine and dandy, but most folks could give a damn about Cleon and his escapades, which is one of the reasons history is destined to repeat itself *ad nauseam*. Simply put, humans are too damn stupid to learn from the past, and into this intellectual vacuum marched Donald Trump. Of course, he lost the popular vote in 2016 but won in the Electoral College, which is as undemocratic a mechanism as has ever existed in any would-be democracy. Furthermore, Trump's victory was partly due to the good graces of his friend Putin, who was always keen on stoking the fires of division in America. We do the same to the Russians, and so it goes to this day.

MAGA (make America great again) actually means "malignant animals getting angry," as far as I'm concerned, and I wouldn't mind seeing the entire lot either locked up or deported. The millions who despised Trump were called snowflakes, poor losers, and a lot worse by what we regarded as poorly educated and pseudo-religious oafs who didn't know their asses from a hole in the ground. How can any proper Christian support a man who has promised to love, honor, and cherish four wives before betraying them all? Well, never expect continuity from those who don't know that they don't know.

The trouble is, I became more pathological than usual when Trump was anointed, and I sought to harm him for years. Oh, I still do. I returned to my psychopath days, which is the sad admission of inescapable truth. I posted thousands of messages, including some that advocated shamefully extreme violence. Yeah, I wanted Trump dead, and I retain that morbid desire. I had gotten six death threats from MAGA fools and would not have their orange God dictating my fate. So, I allowed my worst tendencies to become ascendant, defriended nearly everyone I knew who had helped put the fraud in office, and worked against Cult 45 each and every day. I considered violent rebellion a distinct possibility, much like my kin folk did during the Revolutionary War.

Meanwhile, the same thoughts percolated in the MAGA dolts, although many lack the moral and intellectual capacities to avoid putting wicked thoughts into action. January 6, 2021, gave us ample proof of their inherent mendacity and violent natures. I barely managed to avoid doing something like they did, which is a shameful admission. There but for them go I. Still, a part of me knew better than to attack my own nation for the sake of some egotistical orange fool.

In any case, 2020 gave the USA an especially bruising presidential election, but it wasn't that close. After ALL the votes were counted, recounted, and legally challenged, Joe Biden got a final total of 81,283,501 votes (51.3 percent of the popular vote and 306 Electoral votes), and Donald Trump received 74,223,975 (46.8 percent and 232 Electoral votes). Yeah, Biden won by over seven million votes, though the opposition wanted these votes dismissed via the agency of a plot to overthrow our democracy. They were keen on disenfranchising millions of us who had voted for Biden, come what may. Furthermore, at 66.7 percent, the turnout was the best since 1900, a credit to COVID-induced mail-in voting and the numerous get-out-the-vote drives.

So, what does the losing side do? Trump claims the election was a fraud, and his ardent followers believe the serial liar as if he was an honest man. Indeed, Trump still contends, without any legal reason, that the election was stolen via rigged voting machines and dirty Democratic deeds. He then organized his followers to riot in Washington, DC, thus desecrating the capitol building and mauling and wounding police officers. I recall the nauseating sight of a rebel flag being waved about in the rotunda by a seditious criminal from New Jersey, one Kevin Seefried. I hope he and his son Hunter do 10 years of hard time in a Federal lock-up, but I doubt that will happen. Yet if the truth is told, I despise those seditious rioters enough to want them gone by any means, including death.

Alas, a lot of hatred is ingrained, with the "steal" people believing Trump's bullshit that phony vote counting and faulty machines were the reason for his 7-million-plus vote defeat. However, Trump's attorney general, William Barr, and election officials in all 50 states found no evidence or proof of widespread fraud or irregularities that would have swung the election. Indeed, 63 Trump-supporting lawsuits were dismissed or withdrawn, yet Trump continued the charade of the big steal as a grifting exercise. He ripped off the MAGA fools while taking in hundreds of millions.

When all is said and done, Trump's childlike ego simply could not take the bruising it received. Furthermore, the riot he instigated was an act of willful malice that could never have gained him one iota of presidential power. It was a fool's errand. However, his flying monkeys and jeering Trumpanzees did not know they were on a fool's mission, idiotic sots that they are. Indeed, many are now whining as the law catches up with their treasonous perfidy, their boisterous bombast replaced by whimpers and excuses. Tell me, who are the snowflakes, dupes, and unreasoning haters? Who are the violent and seditionist traitors and un-American thugs?

The intellectual bell curve has a left and right side, with those on the right being brighter by most measures than those on the left. Only in this case, those on the left side of the curve tend to be conservatives, while those on the right are primarily liberal. Yeah, numerous studies indicate folks with high IQs tend to be liberals, while those with more modest measures are mostly conservative in nature. Of course, in our "Big Lie" politics, some dubious "studies" are popping up showing just the opposite. As for me, I KNOW that many people on the right are dumb as boards, almost to the remedial level in terms of essential intellect. Indeed, the universe is a place of constant change, which most conservative minds simply cannot grasp. They cling rigidly to the notion that the good old days were idyllic, despite the misery slavery, inequality, and punishing legal edicts gave us. In short, their worldviews blind them to many truths, as do those of many ideologies, including mine.

Articulating these views may anger many readers from all sides of the political spectrum, and therein resides my fundamental problem. Simply put, I detest most cons with a passion beyond reason. I confess to wanting Donald Trump dead, and I openly supported his ruination many times. I want to see him hung, drawn and quartered in old-school style. Oh, the memes I posted were brutal. I am not proud of the desire to harm another person, because it shows I am more a part of the problem than its cure.

My perfidy is apparent. However, lying is not one of the things I am good at, and being dishonest with you is the worst thing I could ever do. The question is, why do I harbor such hatred? And I am not alone in feeling that way, despite the harm the current divisiveness is doing to our nation. After all, the US system of governance is based on accommodation and compromise, or at least it once was. Now we see stark national divisions wherein the essential unity of the nation can no longer be assumed. "They" hate us, and "we" hate them, and that ideational morass is no exaggeration.

The truth is, I am symptomatic of what is wrong with America. Yeah, I am bright enough and all of that. Yet I am also wounded, with scars running down to my soul's core. A person like me should not be allowed to vote, let alone lead or act as an objective purveyor of truth. Most writers will not confess to such a thing, but you don't need more bullshit. What you need is a means of pulling this fractured country back together. A lot of this will stem from accepting facts and educating yourself enough to recognize the truth when it appears. People like me tend to divide due to our stridency, and the capacity to see all sides of an issue is what can best save our nation.

Any country can stoke up our inherent and learned dislikes to the extent that the glue that binds the USA together dissolves. Red and blue states currently loathe one another; we all know that is true. Thanks to demagogues and haters, our disunity is happening already, with me being an extreme hater. I have reasons for being so combative, but you are wise enough to see where such a tendency can lead. In so doing, you could help stitch the fabric of our nation back together. Then again, what the hell do I know? Try to be better than me, which is not challenging to manage. Amen.

45

An Issue of Color

We sometimes react automatically, without much thought, especially during high anxiety. For example, a soldier in a dangerous urban setting often responds to a perceived threat very quickly and violently, for to hesitate for a moment is to die. Yet we see that same reactionary impulse nearly daily on our streets, filling stations, eateries, and even city parks. Our society has donned a culture of killing, being killed, and unbridled violence. Death and violence have become the norm, be it street punks, disgruntled politicos, or those who are supposed to protect us. Indeed, the steady drumbeat of police officers killing and assaulting innocent Colored people has been going on for many years. In the vast majority of such cases, there is no subsequent justice, even when it is clear that the person killed was not guilty of any wrongdoing. A scared or vile-natured officer overreacted and thus went a life. However, the officer is sometimes within the equivalent of an urban war zone, so let us ponder this all-to-frequent happenstance for a bit.

I take this issue very personally. I was blessed to have coached at UNH for 11 years. During my tenure, I met many fine Black people, some of who became excellent friends. The thought of them getting shot down during a traffic stop or walking down the wrong street at the wrong time nags me. In addition, I have mixed-race relatives, and the possibility of these dear and talented children being harmed because of their color or where they live is impossible to accept. They are exceptional students with promising futures ahead of them, but living in Atlanta (or many other cities) carries some inherent risk. Indeed, living in some neighborhoods dramatically increases the odds of gang and/or police violence.

Sadly, we have ample proof that bad things can and do happen to good Black people, and they seem to occur regularly and frequently. The police will tell you that Black-on-Black violence is a far more significant problem than anything they are guilty of. That "rationale" is bullshit. It is an excusatory argument that is based on a false equivalence. Yes, Black-on-Black violence is a serious and pressing problem, but that does not justify cops harming innocent people of color. The honest officers will tell you that they are often scared and unsure during potentially dangerous encounters, as is understandable. Regrettably, the police must deal with the very worst that society offers, regardless of race, ethnicity, age, or any other social metric one wants to use. As a result, they learn to react quickly, for time is life in some situations. Here is how the schematic train of thought runs . . .

A Black man or men present in a dangerous neighborhood > could be trouble > or a high possibility of violence > get ready to use force.

Here we see a highly automated action–reaction series that can be created by harsh experiences. Still, the critical point is that the response lacks any higher-level thought in too many cases. The officer notes the calling code, the general setting, and a person's color. That officer is nearly blind to the precise details of the surrounding context. He or she often doesn't notice that the person may be smiling, obeying, and/or giving other signals that indicate a confrontation is neither sought nor needed. The officer is too hyped-up to see the subtleties; thus, another Black life is needlessly snuffed out. In other cases, albeit relatively few, the officer is sick of heart and wants to maim or kill; a psychotic wolf in a blue suit. These mistakes or intentional killings have become the way of things, and we cannot passively sit by and watch while this madness unfolds.

Of course, the police know they must be aware of situational context, but that is no easy matter when terrible things can happen quickly within specific neighborhoods and/or policing situations. Moreover, we have created a society wherein any fool can get a gun, and thus the problem of responding quickly to deadly force is nearly intractable. The only cure is contextual awareness, as in noting the subtleties of surroundings, ongoing events, and ever-changing situations. This can only be learned via repeated practice, with dedicated and frequent training regimens and situational scenarios being regular parts of ongoing officer training. Some police departments do this, but we quickly encounter a time and cost problem with no easy answers. Most police officials are acutely aware of this. Yet the cost of not doing anything to enhance this kind of learning is chaos. Indeed, community trust is eroding so quickly that we now see deliberate attacks on officers, worsening the problem.

Look, most cops I know most assuredly strive to protect and serve, and nearly all are compelled to never kill without reason. However, police officials and trainers must be dedicated to preaching and carrying out situational awareness exercises, which should be prioritized and practiced at every opportunity. Colored people must also understand that the police are often "wired" to react quickly and without much thought due to the dangers they face. Confronted people must thus do everything possible to send positive signals to officers through voice, posture, and so on. This does not always work, but it may save a life.

Some notable educational efforts are underway, with local agencies and churches providing tips on how community members can best interact with the police to produce a positive result. Given the ongoing outrage and discord in play, it is easy to let rage and resentment become one's master. This feeds into many officers' "get ready to use force" schema, and we have all seen where that leads. Yeah, getting into a cop's face and cussing him or her out is more or less an invitation to violence. Restraint is the keyword here, not that it is a cure-all.

As for the wolves wearing blue, they have to be rebuked, removed, tried if needed, and punished accordingly. Ideally, this should be done within a police department, but this is easier said than done. It is all a matter of teaching and instilling a departmental ethos. A badge gives one the responsibility to serve and protect. That is an honor and privilege that many officers strive to live up to. It is never a license to kill or do harm.

Regrettably, there are times law enforcement fails to police itself, and thus blue-clad perpetrators of all natures walk freely. They are corrupt, although many did not start out that way. Most officers are motivated by lofty ideals, but these can tarnish when they regularly watch their brothers and sisters practice vile deeds. In fact, many officers are taught early on that they dare not breach the Blue Wall. Yes, setting right an observed wrong that a fellow officer did often entails the sacrifice of career and advancement. That "blue clan" way of doing things has to go. It is an essentially criminal perspective that can be found in the mafia and many street gangs.

I understand that self-preservation demands a rapid response, but for officers to kill an innocent person represents a complete mission failure. Yes, mistakes can happen, but we cannot address an endemic problem by ignoring needless deaths in the courts or within city offices. Our choice is between justice and rebellion, and I opt for justice. Black lives do matter, and they matter a lot to me. Police lives also matter, and they also mean a lot to me. I think of my friends Abraham, Arnold, Curt, Juan, Keith, Sherman, and many others. The loss of any of them during a traffic stop would be more than tragic, for they are good men, one and all. The only cure is contextual awareness, rigorous training, and aggressive internal affairs, albeit these are threadbare solutions for the dead. Yet what choice do we have?

There needs to be more trust between the police and those they serve in many communities. This is the very worst of all situations because many are reluctant to call the police when they are needed, and the police are unwilling to go into areas where they know they are at risk. The only answer here is community involvement, albeit tricky to enlist in some neighborhoods where violence has become a usual way of life. These may be the ideal places to set up satellite police stations. Such facilities indicate that the police are here to stay and that the criminal types had better lie low. Granted, there is some risk in using tools such as this, and they certainly can cost a lot to set up. Yet do we turn some areas over to criminals simply because we lack resolve?

I am unhappy with this chapter for many reasons, but it is an issue we must address to have a functioning society. Here in the Upper Valley, we are not ethnically or racially diverse but still have occasional police violence and deaths. Yet I think the best people to come up with solutions are people of color and the police. It is easy for me to spew ideas, but nothing speaks more powerfully than the voice of experience. Think about the means and methods to help the situation, put them into letters, post them in newspapers, and strive to make a difference. If we all do nothing, then nothing will get done. Idle bitching will do no good, so we must address the problem. What will you do? Do you care enough to do anything?

46

The Eyes of a Storm

War's lessons are harsh. I saw an apoplectic Iraqi woman on television in 1991, and I still can't get her image out of my mind. This was during the First Gulf War, a time of "shock and awe." The old woman was being interviewed by reporters after an errant cruise missile landed in her neighborhood, and she was utterly furious. The black-robed matron stood amid the missile's rubble-strewn impact crater and screamed, "This is old people, this is woman, this is children . . . this is the American people's war." Her anger flowed, punctuated by hand-wringing and harsh intonations.

The wrath in the woman's words chilled me, but not as much as the look in her eyes. That was the glare of unadulterated hatred, something I have seen before. Those eyes were wide with rage, unblinking and unafraid. Her face was elderly and weathered, but here were the fiery eyes of a spirit that would never forgive and forget. They pierced me with intensity as if she had some X-ray vision that could penetrate our souls. I felt uncomfortably familiar with her gaze, and then it donned on me where I had seen that look before.

I once saw it on the face of an acquaintance who had served in Vietnam during the height of the war. He was the close friend of a friend, and he would often visit UNH to party. Yeah, I was always up for carousing in those days. "Bob" often drank too much and usually reveled in bouts of sentimentality during binges. He saw too much destruction and death during his tours of duty, which had unhinged him. He was perpetually glancing around, wide-eyed and nervous. Indeed, Bob was known to duck for cover when loud, sudden noises occurred, as is a warrior's trait who has seen too much death. Some found his behavior amusing; such was their lack of understanding.

This was not a man to be mocked! Whenever Bob became angry or anxious, he would stare right through people, just like that Iraqi woman had stared through me. That is the look of someone who would kill, which is never to be ignored. I knew that gaze from my partying days and had learned how to placate such wounded souls through harsh experiences. That may be why I was a good bouncer, a most lamentable talent. Yet Bob had learned lessons that few of us would ever want to, and he was tormented by memories that simply would not cease. In any event, I got along great with Bob, as I did with many who walked on the darker side of life.

His was a repeating story. Bob would get drunk and rave for hours about his experiences in Vietnam, justifying some and crying bitterly about others. Many soldiers have horrifying war stories, but Bob's were particularly bloody and disturbing. On one occasion, the extent of his psychological trauma came drunkenly flowing out while he described an event that was eating away at him, one of a multitude. He was the point man on a patrol that had penetrated enemy territory when he suddenly came across a kid walking toward him on a jungle trail. The youth was carrying firewood and was totally unprepared for any confrontation. He took one look at Bob, dropped his burden, and then "ran like a bastard." Bob shot him several times in the back, uncertain about the youth's motives. The young man fell to the ground face-first. Then he struggled to get up but fell yet again.

Bob said, "He looked up at me and held out one of his hands. It was almost like he was pleading for help, and then I could see that he was just a kid." Bob said the child couldn't have been more than 12, give or take, and he didn't have any weapons or papers on him, not a thing. Bob watched the child die before him, coughing up blood and writhing in agony. Then Bob moved on as the patrol continued, but the incident got trapped in a flashbulb memory that tears at him. He cried a lot that night and drank until he passed out.

Some years later, if I recall correctly, Bob attended a technical school in northern New Hampshire's Berlin. He lived above a bar with a friend and was still haunted by war's lessons. One day, Bob inexplicably decided to put on his old jungle fatigues. He gazed out of his apartment's window onto the streets below, perhaps remembering the fighting and death he had seen. Bob noticed three young men approaching the bar from well down the road. They were still over 100 yards away, and he eyed them carefully.

Bob's roommate thought he was joking around, but he wasn't. For reasons known only to Bob, he took one of his hunting rifles out of a gun rack and took a bead on the man in the middle of the group of three, a man he had never even met before. Bob coolly pulled the rifle's trigger and shot his unaware target in the forehead, killing him instantly. Bob's torment morphed into another human tragedy, there and then and without warning.

Bob's roommate was horrified and quickly wrestled the gun out of his hands. Now, there is a guy who must have had brass balls. Bob escaped, however, and ran into the surrounding woods. A few days later, the police found him wandering in a dazed and confused state. He was committed to a local institution, and I have since lost track of him. I imagine Bob is locked securely away, where he will probably stay forever. Only the memory of Bob's trauma remains and the heartbreak it eventually led to. Think of those soldiers who participated in the My

Lai massacre, young men who obeyed their orders despite whatever qualms they had.

Yesterday, I heard glowing reports about the 45,000 sorties our aircraft have run in Iraq and Kuwait. However, very few talking heads have mentioned what all this bombing is doing to the long-term psyches of its victims. It's as if we've lost sight of the fact that we're bombing people as well as things, and we're doing so in much the same fashion as Saddam's Scud missiles, the insanity of war coming home to our TVs.

Moreover, we're bombing people on a vastly greater scale than Saddam is capable of. Indeed, we are creating hordes of traumatized war victims. President Bush calls the civilian damage and deaths we are causing regrettable, collateral, and "unintentional," not that our motives matter much to war's victims. Meanwhile, our generals openly applaud the devastation we are wreaking on Iraqi conscripts. I ponder about where all this carnage and trauma will lead. What lessons did these people learn?

It's obvious how the course of this war will go. Iraq's armies will be utterly defeated, and Kuwait will be liberated so that its "legitimate" monarch can again rule over this undemocratic Emirate. Some may wonder if what we will have won was worth the lost lives, but Bush will insist that this war was right and just. Indeed, aren't all wars righteous? He may even win re-election because of his great victory, although that remains to be seen. However, I noticed that traumatized look in those old Iraqi eyes, and I know where it can lead.

This war will not end when the fighting stops or even if Saddam is killed. The fight will not end because the Iraqi people, good and bad alike, will never forget what was done to them. Where this will lead is anyone's guess and the future's torment. Iraq's infrastructure will eventually be rebuilt, perhaps even improved, and her people will have learned from the war. However, most Iraqis will not have the fear that some jingoists suspect. Instead, they will have learned to bitterly despise Americans, and where will that lead?

The Iraqi military and political leaders will have learned that unconventional warfare works far better than masses of immobile soldiers who are merely targets for swarms of buzzing aircraft. They will also have the advantage of studying the cruise missiles that have failed to explode and the other "smart weapons" that may still be intact. This means Iraqis may eventually develop better means of delivering any unconventional weapons they manage to invent.

Of course, our generals assure us that we have obliterated Iraq's ability to make unconventional weapons of mass destruction. However, how can one erase the knowledge it takes to build such weapons? The Iraqis already know how to produce chemical and nuclear weapons, so all we've done by our bombing is to slow down their production a bit . . . perhaps by 10 years, or maybe less. Yet nuclear and chemical weapons are not what scares me. They merely kill tens of thousands. I worry about the *other* forms of unconventional warfare that a beaten foe could turn to.

I imagine we'll have killed several thousand Iraqis by the time the bombing and fighting are over, perhaps 100,000 or so. Some of the relatives of the dead are bound to be Western-educated geneticists, biochemists, and immunologists. Maybe a few of these embittered scientists will be motivated to produce a biological weapon that can exact a terrible vengeance for losing their family members. They may work within a secret cell, a clandestine group of zealots their government doesn't know about. One wonders what we will do then.

Most biological weapons don't need fancy missiles to be delivered, just a single infected person. Who do we strike back at if people start dropping dead in New York City from an incurable disease that has never been encountered before, akin to air-transmitted rabies? We won't even know who created the epidemic or who to retaliate against. Perhaps Libya, or Iran, or Algeria, or North Korea, or Iraq. As the plague spreads and America dies, will we nuke the world?

The culprit will only become dimly evident when one nation or other starts to effectively vaccinate its people against the outbreak. Yet by then, it will be too late for America and perhaps too late for humanity. This is not an impossible scenario. It is simply the final outcome of a logical series of events that started with a terrible mass trauma, like the ones that B52 raids or cruise missile attacks can cause. Trauma's checkmate has a brutal finality, a lesson some never learn.

As noted above, I've seen the look in those angry Iraqi eyes before. It is the look of the traumatized, and behind the angry glare is a person capable of doing almost anything. George Bush Senior once bailed out of a damaged airplane during World War Two, and the plane crashed. Bush could well bail out his political career with this war, but the nation may crash one day because of it. Perhaps politicos should think about all of this before ordering the fighting to begin. Why don't we make war the last option, because one day we may not get another chance to do so? The lesson is, some wars never end, especially the ones we harbor deep within. Amen.

47

Stereotyping 101

I watched smoke rising from several fires started by rioters in downtown Atlanta's Peachtree Street area. I fear my niece and her family will eventually be drawn into this consuming miasma. Her young daughters are somewhat vulnerable to the vagaries of the civil discord that often explodes in our cities. This time, the casus belli was the death of one Manuel Teran (aka "Tortuguita"), a 26-year-old nonbinary environmental protestor killed by the police on Wednesday, January 18, 2023. Tortuguita was part of a group of protesters affiliated with "Defend the Forest" that were being cleared from a wooded area adjacent to a police training facility. She/he/it reportedly shot a Georgia State Trooper in the stomach during the confrontation. The police claim Tortuguita opened fire suddenly and unexpectedly, at which point several officers responded, killing him/her/it. There was a subsequent call on Twitter for reciprocal violence; thus, the riot and fire on Peach Street. This violence has become a sad norm in America, and it is even encouraged by our politicos on occasion, as was the case on January 6, 2021.

I utterly despise ALL nightly news shows. As usual, the press does its best to beat a story to death, as in the George Floyd murder or recurring Israeli versus Palestinian violence. Reporters act like flies buzzing about fresh cow pats. After a while, they so thickly cover the stinking material that their presence and incessant verbiage obscure what is actually there. Mix in a remarkable lack of imagination with ample and competing hyperbole, and the end result is the US press. Goodness, our press is infamous for making as much noise as it reports news. Moreover, they drone on and on, gagging us with glaring special reports that are often much ado about nothing.

Delving into the distant past, what can we learn from stories like the infamous Michael Brown shooting that help us understand the human condition? As you may recall, Brown, an 18-year-old mountain of a man, got killed while supposedly trying to wrestle a gun away from Officer Darren Wilson. The convenience store's videotapes demonstrated that Brown was *probably* acting like a punk on the night he died, committing petty thievery and practicing physical intimidation toward smaller people. However, he did not deserve to be shot down, although no one is sure what transpired between him and Officer Wilson. I suspect Wilson was scared witless by Brown's colossal size, not that this justifies shooting someone six times. I mean, that is overkill by any standard.

Fear can easily be transformed into irrationality, and thus we have the distinct possibility that both Brown and Wilson were behaving in ways that led to an all-too-frequent outcome. Yet even if this was the case, the local Black community became inflamed by the constant drumbeat of police shootings and violence. Meanwhile, many Whites were largely mystified by the subsequent riots and violence. The Blacks were fed up, the Whites didn't understand why, and violence exploded as frustration morphed into conflict.

As usual, the press beat the story to death but provided few details that could answer the many "why" questions. In the meantime, the racial divide that comes crawling out of these and similar tragedies is palpable. Back when Brown was killed, a Pew poll revealed only 37 percent of Whites felt Brown's death showed essential issues about race, while 80 percent of Blacks did. When asked if race is getting too much attention, 47 percent of Whites said yes, while 18 percent of Blacks answered in the affirmative. In addition, 60 percent of Blacks felt the police reaction had gone too far, but only 33 percent of Whites felt this way. Finally, most Blacks (76 percent) had no faith in the ongoing investigation, while Whites were three times more likely to trust the inquiry.

Ah, but the times are changing. Fast forward seven years, and we had the case of George Floyd being suffocated by Officer Derek Chauvin in an utterly savage and cruel manner. In that case, it was found that 57 percent of *all* Americans believed the police were more likely to employ excessive force if the suspect was Black. Conversely, only 33 percent thought that the police were equally likely to use excessive force against both White and Black people. Moreover, 61 percent of Americans opined that race was a significant factor in Floyd's death. This indicates some progress, but a racial divide still exists. Pre-trial, when asked if Floyd's death was a murder, 64 percent of Blacks said yes. However, only 28 percent of Whites described it as murder, while 33 percent said it was an act of police negligence.

Yeah, scratch the surface, and the racial divide comes gushing out. I do not believe Brown was a great exemplar to rally around, although the case with George Floyd was clearly a reactionary impetus for Blacks and Whites alike, a joint injury of sorts. The issue of Tortuguita's death does not appear to be race-oriented at this stage, but the shooting has greatly aggravated Atlanta's Black community. Many Black people are regularly hassled by the police, sometimes for no reason whatsoever. I have seen this firsthand.

On the other hand, many Black youths indulge in wanton behavior, with homicide being the number one cause of death in 18- to 21-year-old Black men. In fact, Blacks are disproportionately represented among homicides as both victims and offenders. For example, 7,484 Blacks were murdered in 2019, while only 5,787 Whites suffered the same fate. The difference is remarkable because only 13.4 percent of Americans are Black versus 77 percent White. In fact, young Black men are six times more likely to die from homicide and seven times more likely to commit murder on average than Whites the same age. Interestingly, 81 percent of White murder victims were killed by other Whites, while 91 percent of Black murder victims were killed by Blacks.

There are many reasons for the racial divide in these statistics, such as poor graduation rates, high unemployment, poor-paying jobs, limited opportunities, gangs, sociocultural influences, and what I call White Fright. To be blunt, some White folks are scared witless of Black men, judging the whole by the actions of a relative few. The police certainly have a history of racial profiling, although I often ponder what else they can do given the current crime stats. This goes for both Black and White officers, with their reactions often being a matter of personal welfare. When an officer makes a mistake on the streets, he or she can die from the miscue. So, the police go with the odds, and thus they see many Black men as high-risk. The obvious answer is to take more time to study the context and people closely during encounters, but events often unfold so quickly that this is impractical. It is a sad and miserable truth for which I do not see an easy cure.

To be sure, TASERs, stun guns, shock batons, chemical weapons, and stun grenades are effective and less lethal means of containing nearly any suspect than handguns and long rifles. Granted, safer means of containment can kill under certain circumstances. Nonetheless, deaths are relatively rare and much less likely from these devices than are the results of firearm wounds. Moreover, new sound generators and directed energy devices have also proven to be very disabling, as have numerous other fast-acting tools. Many moves are afoot to broaden the use of these less-lethal containment means, but they are expensive and require considerable training and expertise. Guns are quick and dirty tools, devices that can end any confrontation in seconds. The question is, dare we look for a better way than what tradition accords us? Is ameliorating the existing racial divide worth the cost in time and resources of using less-lethal devices?

I was a weightlifting coach at UNH for 11 years and worked with numerous young Black men. Of course, these were college kids, most well-educated and very motivated. Thus, the Blacks I worked with probably differed a bit from national averages, and many of them went on to do some remarkable things. I did not witness the violence or criminality that some young Black men manifest, and hence never developed White Fright. Indeed, I was much more criminally inclined than any of my charges when I was young, being somewhat of a miscreant myself. The essential point is **not all Black men are the same**, which is something White folks and the police have to recognize. Moreover, even Black men from very tough and poor neighborhoods vary in personality and tendencies, as do all people.

Yet many people fail to see these details because we tend to be categorical thinkers by design. Please forgive me for simplifying many issues in what follows, for understanding how humans process information can fill libraries, and it cannot easily be summarized. But in short, stereotyping is primarily a matter of how our brains are wired to perceive and react. We detect some general traits and then invoke a stereotypical schema that dictates our subsequent perceptions, actions, and reactions. This is a fast and dirty cognitive system wherein processing time is minimal, and reaction potential is prioritized. The survival benefits of such a mechanism are apparent, as in the rapid flight from a charging animal or other dangerous situation.

As noted in other chapters, newly hatched chicks will instinctively duck when presented with the silhouette of a hawk, sans any actual experience with the predators. This response is often an inherent act of self-preservation governed by rapidly processing and reacting to just a few relevant cues. The collective and precise details of the situation do not matter, just a few key traits of the hawk's basic form. As I have also noted, in humans, a newborn will selectively orient his or her gaze toward oval paddles that are imprinted with two round eye markers and a larger oval mouthpiece arranged in a prototypical facial pattern versus randomly placed features. Later, details are learned and added to the basic schema, with the infant then imprinting and reacting to its mother's face in preference to others.

And lest one thinks we can quickly move beyond categorizing by general type as we mature and develop, let us consider brain damage studies. Here, we find people with focal brain damage can lose completely the capacity to recognize and name faces, although they may otherwise be cognitively intact. Others will lose the ability to recognize or name tools, animals, and other objects, depending on the locations of their lesions. Our brains are very much organized to detect, recall, and react based on categorical associations, albeit that oversimplifies what can and does occur as we process information. This organization scheme has significant advantages and some disadvantages. Of course, learning plays a crucial role in the associations we forge. In fact, many of the schemas we develop are derived from personal experience, and others are taught via family, friends, school, and the media. We thus listen to the news or talking heads and learn what to fear. In short, reactionary prejudice can indeed be taught.

So, a White dude sees a Black man heading his way on the street. This White guy might have never interacted with a Black person, but he was taught negative things about them while maturing. So he thinks, 'My God! That's a Black guy! And he is BIG! I'm screwed! What to do? Oh, what to do?' Whitey quickly crosses the street to avoid conflict with a man who could easily be a kindly minister or paramedic. The details are lost once the general schema is invoked, with fear guiding many actions and thoughts rather than paying attention to the surrounding context and details. And fear abounds in any naive White person who sees a group of five or six young inner-city Black men milling outside a store or on the corner. This is often a no-go situation for many White folks, including me. Some activated fear and avoidance responses are well-placed, though not always.

A gathering of young Black men is often a no-go zone for many Black people who live in communities where violence and crime are endemic. Yet one has to get milk and food for the children, regardless of whatever awaits around the next corner. The person going to the store can't walk away or cross the street to escape those malingering kids, and he or she knows perfectly well that everyday life carries high risks in this part of town. Yet given the economics and poor opportunities, what else can one do, and where else can one go? And as we have seen, the vast majority of violence young Black men unleash is on other Blacks.

We should recognize here that violence does not stem from young Blacks alone. I have a good friend who is Black, and he got hassled by some White teens that were hanging out at a local convenience store, kids that can be a blight on any community. He stood his ground when confronted, and I am thankful he wasn't shot or attacked. Such things can and do happen in rural Vermont and New Hampshire and are occurring at an increasing rate. "You do not know what it is like," my Black friend advised. "I am marked by my race all the damn time. It's a constant threat, the same one you would feel in some parts of Washington." Many don't see the actual person, only the color, size, gender, or another minor trait.

I do not see an easy cure for any of this. A family unit, including a mom and dad, provides children with models about how to live well and behave. One of the central problems in many communities is that such family units simply do not exist. This is true in an increasing number of Black and White families alike. Kids are born and raised by single moms, often with their fathers nowhere near. Many of these fathers lack the sense of personal responsibility usually instilled while being part of a family. Thus, the children of these wayward fathers grow up to repeat the often-dreary model of their lifestyle. And so it goes: deadbeat dads fathering deadbeat dads.

This isn't a problem of Black families alone, for many are loving and caring. In addition, numerous White families also undergo parental divides, with fathers often bugging out to pursue whatever pleases their fancy. I fear where all this will lead. At its core, this tendency to avoid responsibilities is all about selfishness, a prioritization of the vagaries of one's transient desires versus that of often onerous familial duties and social responsibilities. It is hard to raise a family and to teach children, especially when one has no education, no job, and lives in a society that prioritizes the self above all else. It is not a matter of whether one is Black or White. It is a matter of learned values versus limited opportunities, which often evaporates altogether when the idea of the family turns into dust.

So, what to do? Punishment is merely a means of treating a disease of the soul, not preventing it. Of course, there is often no recourse but punishment when wayward kids make surviving within one's home turf miserable for an entire community. The only long-term salvation I can see is crafting a context wherein the family structure can be preserved, which is easier said than done. So, what do we do to achieve this end? Indeed, during slavery, Whites often worked *against* retaining Black family structures. They occasionally sold and traded wives, husbands, and kids, disregarding preserving families. How does one undo that terrible legacy? That is an essential question that is often never asked. Besides, there is much more to the problem than the dissolution of families.

The truth is, we cannot do a damn thing about the current general racial situation. Now that the reporters, anarchists, politicos, and their like have grabbed onto the race issue, glitz and hyperbole dominate the conversation. Nothing is learned other than that violence is simply part of life. Ergo, entire cities become nightly battle zones. This trend may eventually burn itself out, and perhaps then we can better turn our thoughts toward how families can be preserved and lost kids rescued. Yet this is merely a dim hope, a flash of optimism. I do not have a clue and am not ashamed to admit it. How does one craft and preserve a family in communities where opportunity and hope do not exist? How does one teach kids and adults to see beyond a few traits and to judge the whole person instead of a few of its parts? Well, what does one do? What will you do? Amen.

48

A Teacher's Lament

It took a while, but I became a good coach. I got good results, was respected by my charges, and loved the occupation. The skills acquired in coaching should transfer to teaching in general, yet this is only sometimes the case. Moreover, my dad's maternal side included numerous accomplished teachers. One generation had 8 or 9 teachers out of 11 progeny, with one of the issues dying while a child. So, the skills needed to teach were probably born in the blood. However, Penn State was to prove that I was less than an ideal educator to release on tender young college students, let alone school-aged kids.

I was a teaching assistant at Pen State for about three years and managed some impressive Teaching Effectiveness Evaluation ratings (6.46 out of 7.0). I taught basic Speech Communication

101, Public Speaking, and Speech Com 312, Advanced Presentational Speaking (a business-oriented course). Oh, I liked the job a lot. In fact, the kids used to call me "Coach," but the problem was that I still acted like one. Yeah, I expected attendance and total effort, which many college kids are not keen on doing. Many were just like me when I was an undergrad at UNH, heavy into partying and sluggish when it came to academics.

In my class, a student usually got an A or an F, with the only way of getting an F being by missing five or more classes during a semester. If one got sick or the like, I tried to be understanding, but if a student willfully blew off my class, I took it very personally. You missed over five Speech Com classes, and you were flunked. The students were told this at the beginning, and it was prominently noted on the syllabus. I didn't like failing students, but a speech com class needs an audience for the kids to give speeches to. So, yes, I stressed attendance and flunked those who ignored my warnings.

Ah, and therein resides one of my most bitter experiences. There was this unmotivated coed, and she was a Communication major. One strives to help majors in one's department as much as possible, but this young woman was immune to persuasion and already had five absences. So, I called her into my cubical and dressed her down as I would some freshman football player who had not been lifting. Man, I was loud. "What the fuck do you want me to do? It isn't like we haven't been over this umpteen times, and you're a major! I can and will flunk you! Is that what you want?" On and on, I raged, and she left the room crying.

Well, her father called the Department head, and it soon came time for me to get dusted up. I am not a shrinking violet when confronting power, and soon I was in a rather animated argument with a man who was my boss. He said I had no right to humiliate any student, let alone yell at one in a "condescending and bombastic fashion." I replied that I preferred doing that to flunking a major, which was the option I faced. He would have none of it and ordered me to apologize. I asked him to look at my Student Effectiveness Evaluation scores before scorning my methods, but I did apologize. My boss was right. One cannot treat students like athletes because many are unmotivated to succeed. So, I was wrong in expressing my frustrations at 90 decibels with foul language, but I am smiling as I write this line. For better or worse, this was a dressing down that young lady will never forget, and she did not miss another class. I did her a lick of good, albeit the improved attendance was her decision.

Like coaching, I did form an attachment to teaching. I took the job very seriously and prepared elaborate teaching plans. Plus, I liked the give and take of the classroom and used the Socratic Method while teaching. I did not lecture. Instead, I asked questions about the reading and never asked for a show of hands. Instead, I gestured to a student, and he or she replied. I usually asked another if he or she agreed, so it would go, providing an animated and lively discussion versus a one-way lecture. I always thought there were better ways for students to learn than top-down teaching, especially in a public-speaking class. It was best to let the show flow and the students liked the approach.

As fate would have it, Penn State decided to conduct a mass lecture and set up small labs, with the small labs being mostly dedicated to giving speeches while the theory was provided via the mass lecture. I thought it an absurd idea and said so in no uncertain terms. I got called to task by professors and my peers alike for not going along with the plan, but soon I was writing letters to the editor. I was told by a respected advisor that I was harming the department and to stay my hand, at least for a while. Usually, I resist injunctions from above, but not a request from a man I deeply respected. As it worked out, the students panned the mass lecture/small lab idea, which was very predictable. Who needs another mass lecture course at a school where class sizes can exceed 400–500 people? One sits in an auditorium and hardly ever shares a word with the person teaching. Sometimes the teacher is so far away you can barely see him or her.

One of the luminaries behind this bright mass-lecture idea was a faculty member who didn't like my outspokenness or style. "Sharon" especially didn't want me enlisting students to make presentations wherein they addressed problems, presented solutions, and then persuaded the class to participate. For example, one student talked about hunger just before Thanksgiving, and he got the whole class to contribute to feeding a family that had recently been abandoned by its breadwinner. We provided those kids a proper meal, and I could not be prouder of the student's job in persuading us to do so. Another student got us to sign a petition for creating a parking garage to help ease the interminable parking problem at Penn State, and that action was published in the school paper. How proud I was of those students. They would come in with their letters to the editor or some school official and feel empowered. Watching them discuss their actions and glow in the results was sheer joy. Oh, those were good times.

Of course, some students were miffed about Speech Com 101 being a required class, which was fair game as far as I was concerned. Well, one student persuaded the class to sign on to a letter that complained about the lack of grading and requirement consistency between the various 101 class sections. This was, and is, an issue to some extent, but the counterargument is that teaching methods differ, and what is suitable for some may be bad for others. Yet most in the class felt compelled to sign the student's letter, and into the school paper it went. Yikes! Sharon told me she had warned me and then outright forbade me from encouraging students to take public or private actions. I asked her what speech should be directed toward, if not improving the common welfare. I asked her what good we were doing if we didn't put public speaking into action. She accused me of being "passive-aggressive," a new accusation for me. I was striving to be entirely aggressive, as befits my nature. Furthermore, I continued as usual because the students had some excellent ideas and should be encouraged to present them.

Yeah, that was to be my last teaching semester at Penn State. I was not rehired, and no recommendation letters would exist for me. Of course, I went to war for a short while over the issue, using the school paper as a vehicle for my angst. Shortly after that, Sharon and her puppet master left the department, and I felt it was a good thing. I doubt my actions had anything to do with her choice to go, but it seemed appropriate that we settled the confrontation with both of us being out of work. I took out loans and finished my program, but it was clear that I was a poor fit for the academy.

Teaching is like coaching, but it is for someone other than me. I am far too in your face to be a good teacher. I feel many young folks don't truly belong in college, and I was one of those people. I was unmotivated, lazy, too into hedonism, and a piss-poor student as a result. Public service, feeding people, or cleaning sidewalks were better options for me. The fundamental problem with higher education is that it requires a maturity level in students that many still need to develop. It is better that many youths "live" and work for a bit BEFORE they embark on any learning course. Granted, some young people are motivated and highly directed, and I wish I had been like that. Oh, I was to become that way as a coach and scholar, and that urge keeps me writing like this. I am down to two working fingers and half a functional brain. Yet desire and my muse drive me on, and this chapter is the outcome. Be of cheer, my friends. Amen.

49

A Guiding Light

They are rare, wonderful, and many of us have met one during our lives if we are lucky. Some are farmers, mechanics, or great chefs. A few are artists, writers, or poets; the kinds of people who not only know things in depth like no other but can also share that knowledge via teaching. I was blessed to have such a luminary in my list of acquaintances, an especially towering intellect that was a rare combination of expertise and humility. This guy could talk about Platonic metaphysics, neuroanatomy, and the subtleties of classical versus contemporary music. Dr. Paul R. Cornwell was, without a doubt, the brightest man I have ever known and the most talented teacher one could ever hope to meet. As you might have noted, I seldom wax poetic about people in general, but this man became a guiding light during my tumultuous stay at Penn State.

Dr. Cornwell would never have made it in the new academy we have created, that place of publish-or-perish wherein the quality of people is determined by how many papers and books they have authored and not how good a teacher they are. Dr. Cornwell only had 11 articles published between 1966 and 1998 that I can find after a cursory search, albeit they appeared in major journals. However, his influence was massive because he regularly aided numerous high-level scholars nationwide and was widely recognized for his teaching excellence. In fact, Cornwell won a Kodak award for outstanding teaching, which is a national honor. And what a teacher he was, with my having the distinct pleasure of taking a few graduate-level classes from him.

So how does a PhD student in speech communication get tied up with a neuropsychologist? Well, I came to Penn State as a marginal student, someone who failed miserably on his Graduate Record Examinations. My score on the analytical section was at random levels (420?), about as low as low gets. I have no idea why, although I found many of the questions absurd and debatable. I score OK on most IQ tests and regularly get in the 130 range on the Stanford-Benet series, even with a severe memory problem. That recall malady has become pathological and is now classified as a cognitive disorder. An examiner said I would be in the 140-plus IQ range if my memory indices were average. However, grad schools care a lot about GRE scores, and mine sucked.

Yet I had good Masters-level grades and recommendations, so Penn State let me in. I did well enough during my first year to be awarded a teaching assistantship, and thus the journey began. Yet I was far from happy with some of what I was taught. Indeed, I thought it was bullshit. For example, there is something called linguistic relativity theory. It has a codicil that contends that if we do not have a word for a thing or concept, we cannot think about it. In effect, our language supposedly influences how we think about reality, as in the Sapir–Whorf hypothesis. I am simplifying things here, absurdum, but the primary contention is that a person's perceptions and cognition are primarily related to their spoken and/or written language. I was very outspoken in calling the entire notion bullshit, which some of my classmates found amusing; the quaint ramblings of a rustic.

Well, anyone owning a pet should know linguistic relativity is bullshit writ large. A cat or dog will tell you what it thinks sans any language. In fact, pets can anticipate future occurrences, such as our coming home at a particular time, and they can influence our behavior with just a glance. Their thought does not require words, even reasonably complex ideas. When a dog tears something up, as they are prone to, they will feel guilt for their actions and communicate that to us via eye glance, posture, and behavior. Similarly, they will tell us that it is time to go for a walk or to eat or that they have to poop or pee. They make these thoughts/needs clear to us, and we obey. How's that for the tail wagging the dog?

One of my advisors (Dr. Richard Gregg) had gotten into cognitive psychology in some of his work, and he fully understood what I was contending. The trick was communicating how thought actually works on a scientific basis to folks who are humanists. In basic terms, some forms of humanism begin with the happy idea that folks like you and me are integral in determining the existence of moral and philosophical investigations. We apply words and metaphors and thus create moral and intellectual realities. Never mind that a dog feels guilt over doing wrong or that a cat experiences jealousy when we attend to another animal. We humans alone denote these traits and thus apply the terms to cats and dogs, without which they would not exist independent of our thoughts. I think that is specious reasoning at best, and so does the dog that visits its deceased master's grave almost daily. We are animals, and the difference between many species' thoughts is more a matter of degree than of kind. But how does one examine the underpinnings of this area convincingly?

Enter Dr. Cornwell. A neuropsychologist like him can trace where and how a particular visual input is processed, integrated within the brain, and given a semantic application and/or connection. Researchers can actually do all that and do so with increasing accuracy. We can discern where in the brain the input is processed as memories are accessed and created and how this processing can influence subsequent behavior. The problem was in making this science accessible to people who had more theories than proofs. So, I crafted an annotated dialogue, as in a neo-Platonic conversation. This was closely integrated with a neuroscience-based narrative about how information processing works. Yeah, it was an utterly crazy idea that involved 1,800 sources and a dissertation that was 1,500 pages long.

It took three years of hard work just to craft the dissertation, which went by the catchy name of *The Scientific Foundation of Social Communication: From Neurons to Rhetoric*. It could never have been completed without the encouragement and insights of Dr. Cornwell, and many times I wanted to abandon the entire idea. I would spend hours in his office, adorned with hundreds of icons and keepsakes made by former students, everything from the model of an extinct giant dragonfly (*Meganeuropsis permiana*) to large diagrams of the human brain. We would talk for hours as each chapter was laid out and designed, and I loved visiting the place. The office had several rooms because it was also used as a research facility. In one office was a bed, and Dr. Cornwell would sleep there on occasion when it snowed so that he would not be late should he have an 8:00 a.m. class. Yeah, that was a teacher who sacrificed for those he served.

Plus, he was always there to offer sound counsel. He was there when I got dismissed and witnessed my brutal public battle with my department. He advised me to "Stay focused on your goals, George. You have much to do, and this drama is a distraction." Despite their length and complexity, he made insightful comments on every chapter, and slowly but surely, the project became a reality. In fact, he was working on the final drafts of chapters 1–3 when it happened. I got a call from the head of my committee, Dr. Chris Johnston, and he asked me how I was doing. I had no idea why he was inquiring, and here is a note from my diary that explains what he told me:

Wednesday, July 3, 1996 – 12:06pm

There have actually been some tears this morning. For a few days, I felt like something was wrong, which was reflected by a lack of activity in writing my dissertation. Then, just a few minutes ago, I found out that Dr. Cornwell had died. He died a couple days ago, on Thursday, 6/27/96, of complications from coronary bypass surgery. I didn't even know Dr. Cornwell was sick! Hell, he went to Hershey, and they ended up killing him. He wasn't even ill, at least, obviously.

I am shaken to the core. Dr. Cornwell was one of the most intelligent and lively people I've ever known, and his guidance got me to this stage in my work. I don't know what to do. He was the one person at this God-awful university who I felt comfortable with, and I don't know who can replace him as my outside committee member . . .

Last night, I dreamed I was climbing a towering dark pylon that served a railroad track. Another person beside me had difficulty negotiating the vertical climb, and I encouraged him as best I could. He took heart and was soon in fine form. As I neared the top, my strength began to fade, and I could not seem to hoist myself over the lip of the surface upon which the tracks ran. But my friend made it. I asked him for help, and he reached out his hand. I can still feel the strength of his grip, and he gave me just enough help to make the top. Like all such dreams, as soon as I stood atop the pylon . . . I awoke.

And I awaken to a horrible nightmare. But that hand still reaches out, and I must grab it. Even the skies have been crying, as they are now. I must get ready to go to work. Suddenly, being canned by the speech com department doesn't seem so important. Paul Cornwell, I shall miss your wisdom, but perhaps not your spirit. That spirit will always be within. To work, I must go.

It was an utterly miserable experience. Tears still dampen my shirt as I write this story, and I see his face before me. They recovered my work in Dr. Cornwell's hospital room some days later. He had been editing my thesis on his deathbed, which shows this man's character. He was the real deal. The final note in chapter 3 read, "This can work!" He had made many other comments and offered lots of advice, but the fact that he was working on this project during such a time as he was facing says more than my words could ever offer. In early October, there was a celebration of life, and I spoke up about the project we were working on. I am recorded as saying' "'He sent us off in directions that God knows where will lead,' said George Elder (graduate-speech communications). 'I know I'll finish my project. But if I hadn't met him, I don't know where I might have been.'" After the ceremony, I explained the complexity of our project, with many offering that it seemed an impossible task to complete. Perhaps, but I was driven.

Dr. Cornwell was to visit my dreams now and then, as in:

Saturday, August 3, 1996 – 11:42am

I had a dream about Dr. Cornwell a few nights ago. He had given me a very complex examination to complete, and I was at my wit's end trying to answer the questions. I struggled through the task until I came to the definition section. One of the terms was "serial suit" or "neural suit," although only the "suit" part sticks in my memory.

In any case, I had yet to learn what the term meant, so I asked Dr. Cornwell if I could use my book to look it up. He looked at me like I should know what the word meant, and although he acceded to my request, the book did me little good. The term was not in the index, and I needed clarification.

Then I began looking at the word "suit," and the idea of my actions against the Speech Comm. Department came to mind, as in a lawsuit. Such actions will only hurt my progress in understanding and actuating what has to be done to complete my dissertation. With this realization, I became wide awake, which is often the case with these dreams. So it appears Dr. Cornwell is still helping

me, even in death. I will focus on the task and hold everything else in abeyance.

Dr. Paul Esslinger from the Hershey Medical Centre took
over from Dr. Cornwell, with his help and the simple advice
"This can work," driving the project to fruition. I submitted the
final work to NOVA Science Publishers before I graduated, and
it became a book in 1998. This was the first dissertation published as a hardcover book in our department in over 30 years,
or so an advisor told me. As I write this, I am thumbing through
the text and note the dedication: "To Dr. Paul Cornwell (1936–
1996), the finest teacher I have ever known." The text is 469
pages in book format, and I can still find a few used copies available on Alibris ($84–$87) and Amazon ($24). I gave his family
three or four copies with a heartfelt personal letter about Dr.
Cornwell's contributions to the project and his teaching legacy.
As for Penn State, they recognize Dr. Cornwell via the Paul R.
Cornwell Memorial Award, which is typically given to both a
good researcher and teacher. Dr. Cornwell would like that very
much, although he was humble.

I regret having turned away from the line of inquiry I was
pursuing, but my battles with the academy had taken a severe toll
on all concerned. I should have tried teaching at a junior college,
but the opportunities were few, and I was also becoming increasingly ill. I began an utterly unsuccessful stint as a science fiction
writer, having never quite grasped that I was a good nonfiction
writer. Indeed, I had written numerous nonfiction articles that

earned money and some modest notoriety. Yet simple is as simple does, and I have become increasingly simple as the years pass. So here I am, writing in my natural voice and returning to my roots as a nonfiction writer. I let Paul Cornwell down a bit by not doing a lot of follow-up books on human cognition, but this text you are reading may also be helpful to some. Ultimately, that is what he would want, and like he said, "This can work." Do you think so? Amen.

It is with deep regret that I announce the recent passing of Dr. Paul Cornwell. Professor at Penn State University, State College, PA. Dr. Cornwell was known and loved by friends and colleagues for his outstanding work in behavioral and Developmental Neuroscience and for his dedication to his students and colleagues. Dr. Cornwell died on Thursday, 6/27/96 of complications following emergency coronary artery bypass surgery. He is survived by his two children and his wife Gretchen, a demographer at Penn State. Funeral arrangements have not been announced as of sat 6/30. (D. Siwek [siwek at acs.bu.edu] Sat Jun 29 18:19:23 EST 1996, NEW MEDICAL/ HEALTH WEBSITE)

PART V

PHILOSOPHY AND THOUGHT

50

Seeking Truth on a Foggy Day

Today is January 12, 2020, and the temperature is expected to reach 60 degrees, yet another new record. We're setting many weather records lately, but some say only Chicken Little folks need to be concerned. As for me, I think God talks to us in many ways, and if we fail to notice, we pay the price. Goodness, a thick fog is moving in while I write this chapter, and I can hardly make out the trees less than 100 yards away. The haze will burn off soon, but this is supposed to be winter! The current opaqueness somewhat reminds me of the inability of some people to acknowledge changes that may indicate fundamental shifts in our state of being. We seem like frogs placed in a slowly heating water kettle, with the poor creatures dying before finally noticing something is amiss. These unusual occurrences have me thinking about philosophy this morning, especially the notion of change.

In that time and change are inescapable aspects of being, there will always be something new to learn, contemplate, and share. These observations imply that no document, thought, or doctrine can ever be complete, as in the final and eternal word on any subject. After all, words are symbolic expressions of ideas. Ideas will always be works in progress because they require the ongoing application of our thoughts to be understood, let alone to become manifest within us. Our thoughts change over time due to unique and continuous experiences and shifting dispositions. This trend continues despite attempts to distill and codify our perspectives into a closed set of fixed and immutable concepts. "It is so because the Sacred Book says it is so" is a logical fallacy that does not suffice regarding metaphysics or corporeal reality. The winds of time inevitably shift this way and that while we speed through life. Their changing directions and impetus often reveal unique objects, events, and contemplations that touch upon us if we allow them to do so. Such is the nature of learning that is inherent in our basic design. We were made to seek, although some resist this notion.

It dismays me that many refuse to see beyond a given text or person's edicts, contentions, and rules. We thus held on to slavery, beheading, stoning, burning, and even strangulation, let alone child beating and the like. We did this because a book said it was sanctioned by God. It is like we willingly and freely accept being put into a comfy cage that offers no views other than that provided by a single 4-inch porthole drilled into a wall. The person inside the cell knows that the tiny porthole limits his or her perceptions. Still, we live in a comfortable abode where shelter, food, and entertainment are readily provided. Never mind that it is warm and foggy on a winter day that should be ice cold. We can see the fog through our tiny window on reality, but we could care less. Instead, we can play music, visit a friend, and/or turn on the TV and watch a movie. We thus ignore the fog and heat, opting to find comfort within our cage. Yes, we attend to what some folks tell us and even consult favored sources when needed. Usually, the sources we consult are those we identify with, for we would not want any discord or fear to enter our lives. If I lean to the right, I consult those from the right, as is the case with those of any particular persuasion. Remember, the goal of the willingly caged is comfort and continuity above all else.

Some sources are better than others regarding the knowledge, guidance, and insights they offer. Yet despite any author or source's intended meaning, all communication is bound to unknowable patterns of interpretation within particular message receivers while a message is processed. In short, identical words and information can mean vastly different things to individuals based on their unique experiences and viewpoints. So, what is a tragedy to Joe is a boon to Donald. Moreover, these meanings can be influenced by shifting moods and contexts. Ergo, no one can claim to grasp absolute truths or intended purposes, at least via the agency of written or spoken words. We give terms and phrases the definitions we are taught or the meanings we find most consistent with our desired state of being.

Numbers offer much less ambiguity than words, but how can one express a concept such as love, thought, or truth via mathematics? Plato struggled with this task, albeit his rendition of Pythagorean doctrines to explain the Form of "good" did not persuade those who listened to his explanations. Indeed, some found his work utterly unintelligible. Nonetheless, numerical qualifiers such as January 12 and 60-degree temperature should mean something to us regardless of our comfort level and beliefs, especially when we can see the fog by glancing out our tiny porthole. The trouble is belief nearly always trumps observable realities, despite imminent existential threats. In fact, we often dismiss nihilistic future possibilities because we are told by one faith or another that God will come to the rescue. Meanwhile, our caged room allows us to live as we see fit, although some malcontents would like a bigger window.

Despite the vagaries of the written word we have discussed, many religious guides use them as absolutes, which I find akin to forging conceptual bars that influence what we can see outside our portal. Furthermore, some texts seek to encapsulate the eternal by perpetuating themselves as the only path to truth and salvation. They openly stipulate this goal as a purpose, and it accords no compromise. All the while, the authors of these works were tied to a reality that was constantly changing, despite any faith's contentions that some things are absolutes. Moreover, requiring people to only look toward the prescribed path alone is akin to telling folks not to observe, learn, or contemplate. This negates what we were designed to do by nature and inclination. It is the language of those who would restrict thought, the ultimate in ideological and conceptual control. Of course, many like living "by the word" because it is often prescribed, accepted, and straightforward.

I reject being chained or caged by fixed religious or philosophical doctrines, although I understand the need to obey civil laws. Yet it is evident to anyone who observes that change is a secular constant, albeit paradoxical. Thus, rigidly and willingly binding ourselves to fixed dogmas and perspectives limits what we can become and perceive. Since I do not know how the universe works, I will strive for knowledge about the subject when and wherever it may reside. I will seek, even though it is an endless task. So, if I have a particular faith, it is based on the notion that we must constantly strive to perceive and understand to know much of anything.

Moreover, my kindred spirits will inevitably seek new insights as they ride through time. We will share our ideas as they are developed, finding discovery and joy in what some of our brothers and sisters have found. That is the purest form of love, sharing enlightenment and concern. That is what prayers like this are all about.

Of course, you will take these feeble ideas being expressed much further than I could envision. You will break free of comfortable dogma cages and soar, finding and sharing many things with those your soul touches. You will exchange ideas that influence one another, acting as fresh breezes that shift our attention toward directions we might not have considered. You will exchange a 4-inch porthole for a mountain top, and there you will find an expanse that broadens the mind and soul. That is happening as you read these words, and this is the end purpose of seeking.

Seekers share and learn how to give and receive in equal measure. Indeed, you will add to this story in many ways, and some of your thoughts and deeds will most assuredly produce ripples that radiate through time and space. We will observe what unfolds, marveling at a child's imagination, sharing sorrow with loved ones, and engaging in life's shifting course. We will not be passively content to assume we know all that is needed because we subscribe to one idea or another, let alone the edicts of some sacred text. Instead, we Seekers will follow the calling of our hearts and recognize that such callings can change. We will embrace life, love, and the happiness of sharing our time with one another. Well, it has been enjoyable contemplating with you, my friend. The fog is lifting, and I now see patches of blue. As I said, God talks to us in many ways. I wish you a fine day and an enjoyable journey. Amen.

Postscript

We had a high of 64 degrees on 1/12/20, with the norm being 29. The old record high was 55, so it fell by nine degrees! I would say that God is speaking very loudly!

51

The Illusion of Knowing

Every damn time I think I finally understand a given subject, time reveals my confidence was highly misplaced. That even goes for my specialty area of study, which is supposed to be the neuropsychology of human communication. I wrote a 490-page textbook on the subject with over 1,800 sources, and it took four long years to research and write. Oh, I should be thrilled it was published, and the text sounds authoritative throughout. Well, I just picked up some recent books on cognitive psychology, and it seems I was wrong in some areas and correct in others. That is the way of knowledge. If we keep our tiny minds open and focus on ongoing research, we quickly discover that what was once a "known fact" is often a dreary illusion. New discoveries and on-going research can humble even the brightest folks, which is the norm and not the exception. Nonetheless, some maintain the illusion that they know sacred truths, a most untenable position for any thinking person to assume.

Yes, many people are smug and content in their supposed knowledge, especially about moral, religious, and/or ethical issues. They think they understand the eternal and unchanging Word because text A, B, or C says it contains the one and only valid account. Good Lord, that self-confidence is akin to delusion, for it implies no need to look beyond the one and only Word. In fact, the sacred Word tells us there is no need to look beyond its pages for enlightenment. In essence, you know absolutely everything needed if you study the Word, and there is no need to pursue new inquiries or explore other viewpoints. Thus, people become insular in their outlooks and believe they know the one and proper path to enlightenment simply because some ancient text stipulates X, Y, and Z are the only way to achieve oneness with God, the universe, or some other grand notion. To me, any text that offers such advice (and many do) is bullshit on parchment; the very negation of the free will it takes to explore new paths and to find novel insights. We have to do better than that.

Oh, I remember my days as an academic and watching some classmates judge who was or wasn't a "player" in our department. I found that attitude obnoxious and said so. It is difficult enough to judge one's own capacities, but it is absurd to opine that we can adequately evaluate the capabilities of others. After all, a person's potential is often imponderable. Of course, judging is

precisely what we teachers did, grading students on their performances. I never felt like a great judge; thus, most students got
an A, B, or F. An A or B was awarded to anyone who showed
knowledge of the subject matter and did all the required work.
If someone skipped classes and did not complete his or her work,
that approach resulted in an F, with illness or emergencies being
the only mitigating factors. To me, it was the effort expended in
striving to master the material that counted most. If one went
above and beyond and produced efforts that helped kith, kin,
and others, they would get an A and a recommendation.

One of my friends recently told me that I would be judged
and found wanting for not accepting Jesus Christ as my Lord
and Savior. I had tolerated such chastisements for years, but
asking questions about what gave him the right to judge me on
this particular day seemed appropriate. He said the Holy Bible
did. I advised Steve that the Bible was not codified until the
First Council of Nicaea in 325, over 300 years after Jesus' death.
And even then, there was an ongoing debate about what books
should be included in the text. The discussions lasted until the
Council of Hippo in 397 AD, after which the Catholic Bible's
canons were definitively codified.

Furthermore, I noted that the books that had Jesus acting
as an ordinary man, and there were many, were eschewed. The
book of *Jubilees, Epistle of Barnabas, Shepherd of Hermas, Paul's
Epistle to the Laodiceans, 1 Clement, 2 Clement, Preaching of
Peter, Apocalypse of Peter, Gospel According to the Egyptians,* and
Gospel According to the Hebrews had all been in vogue for 200

years after Jesus was crucified. Yet they were all dropped. So too, were numerous gospels, including the *Gospel of Marcion*, the *Gospel of Apelles*, the *Gospel of Bardesanes*, the *Gospel of Basilides*, the *Gospel of Thomas*, and more. Many of these texts described Jesus as a highly enlightened man, but the church of the time wanted and needed a god. This perceived need helped lead to the evolution of the Trinity and many dubious notions that sought to deify Jesus. And never would a discouraging word be heard as the church sought to destroy the unapproved texts.

My friend was incensed and accused me of satanism and other things I'll not discuss here. I told him to do a bit of reading, see what had been left out of the Bible, and then consider what the truth of things could be. He said he already knew the truth and was trying to save my soul. I thanked him for the kind thoughts but advised him that time alone would dictate the truth. I still consider him a friend, but what irked me most is that he used the Bible to justify not seeking more knowledge. Jeremiah 1:12 states, "Then said the LORD unto me, 'You have seen well, for I am watching over my word to perform it.' No matter what happens, God's Holy Word is irrevocable. God and His Words are One." In essence, we have a closed set of ideas that includes itself, which is both a paradox and circular reasoning.

Belief and reason are two different things. Moreover, a closed loop will not allow anything else to be considered. I forwarded where the texts of the missing books and gospels can be found, but my buddy is bound to a text that was codified mainly under the auspices of the Roman emperor Constantine. I find it very sad that he will not allow anything else to enter his mind. Still, he has every right to walk the path he wishes, as do we all. My only hope is that those of different persuasions would not condemn their kith and kin for opting to take another course.

Searching for new knowledge and insights is often a long, hard slog. Learning is seldom easy, and we all recall poring over definitions and mathematics to prove our merit during various tests. Gathering new knowledge is downright painful, at least as our current methods allow it to be garnered. There may come a day when machines can quickly and easily forge the neuronal assemblies needed to encode the contents of any book within our brains. However, the task will remain to integrate new knowledge with existing memory resources. So, learning will stay difficult and frustrating, yet it will only be possible if we give up the happy notion that we already know enough. The universe will always reveal something new if we are open enough to perceive it, and I find it a shame that many close their minds and hearts to new possibilities. Yes, there is beauty and joy in gaining knowledge.

When we eschew the need to look for relevant knowledge on a subject, we relinquish the capacity God gave us to learn and adjudicate what is true and false. When we extend our philosophy to the extent that we judge others based on our incomplete understanding of a given subject, little good comes of that approach. Thus, I stand damned by a friend and would never do the same to him. He is a decent and kind person who does good works and honestly believes he is being righteous. With time, perhaps he will look up some of the missing books, and maybe then the story of the actual Jesus will come into a more complete focus. That is my hope and prayer. Amen.

52

Some Passing Thoughts on Thought

I was waiting for the bus on a warm summer day when a black foraging ant ambled by my foot, a small creature that could barely be seen by my feeble old eyes. The insect carried a bit of detritus larger than itself but still too tiny for me to fully discern. There was a definite purpose to the ant's foraging actions and an ability to react to changes in context. For example, I placed my walking stick in the ant's path, and the creature soon encountered the object. It paused for a second or two before shifting its course around the barrier and continuing on its invisible path. I made a few such barriers, and the ant responded to each, usually finding the most direct route to continue its task. This implies the ant recalled her task, followed an internal map, and then re-acquired an external chemical trail leading to its home. These behaviors demand memory, processing sensory cues, and reacting to environmental changes. This is evidence of goal-oriented and flexible behaviors in one of God's tiniest creatures, whether simple stimulus–response actions or something more profound. And I ponder, what is the role of thought and intelligence in all this, or is there any thinking and intellect involved?

An ant's brain is minuscule, with its entire nervous system comprising just 250,000 neurons on average. There are 20,000–100,000 ants in the average ant colony, thus bringing a collective 5,000,000,000 to 25,000,000,000 neurons into play. Each human boasts 86,000,000,000 neurons in our nervous system, with 21,000,000,000 being found in our cortex alone. So, while we may be brighter than a whole colony of ants, they are a notable species nonetheless. In fact, ants display many aptitudes and behaviors consistent with intelligence and what some claim is civilization. They construct relatively vast cities with larders, waste facilities, living chambers, nurseries, air conditioning vents, and the equivalent of a temple where their queen dwells.

Interestingly, when in the queen's presence, many species of insects withdraw their antennae, assume a submissive posture, and retreat a few steps, displaying what appears to be deference or reverence. They readily communicate and exchange information with chemical pheromones and direct antennae-to-antennae signals driving farming, building, travel along scent trails, and even warlike activities. Sight and sound are also used for communication and sensory purposes, albeit pheromones are a powerful method of sharing behaviors in social insects.

As individuals, ants can traverse relatively long distances for food, to guard their colonies, or to tend their gardens. They can learn from one another, such as an experienced ant sharing information with a younger colony member about the location of an old colony or an alternate entrance to their current city. In fact, ants can communicate the precise location, distance, and types of foods available in a particular place, giving their compatriots important survival information to act upon. When the colony is physically disrupted, the ants will busily set about making repairs in an organized fashion. Moreover, they are altruistic, with ants helping an injured compatriot get back to their home. There, the wounded insect will receive aid and food from its peers. Ants can also isolate themselves when sick to prevent the spread of diseases. They even employ the equivalent of inoculations via the use of certain fungi.

Some opine that all of this seeming intelligence is mere stimulus–response behaviors that are "hard-wired" into the ant's central nervous system. They are indeed born with the vast majority of knowledge they need to be valuable collective members. However, their behaviors include enough inherent flexibility to allow ants to adapt to a myriad of constantly changing situations, the efficacy of which has been demonstrated by the species' survival for at least 92 million years. Indeed, ants have endured mass extinction events, such as the cosmic disaster that laid low the dinosaurs. Their "collective mentality" displays an underlying existential intelligence in its fundamental design. This was forged and refined over uncounted generations and then passed down genetically. In addition, it is an intelligence that can adapt to shifting situations. Thus, we are witnessing an ongoing evolution that is as remarkable as what humans have managed. The ants' collective knowledge is primarily, but not wholly, genetically sustained. I find the genetic transfer of knowledge from generation to generation fascinating, and the mechanistic underpinnings are being researched.

The case is the same with many species of bees, wasps, and other social insects. Herein we find the collective whole acting as a singular organism that contains the combined wisdom of its progenitors. No, ants and bees don't understand Platonic metaphysics and cannot send spaceships into the heavens. Nor do they ponder the distant stars and wonder about their roles in the machinations of being. Nonetheless, bees have been shown to learn, understand, and recall abstract symbols concerning the intended meanings researchers wished to convey. One suspects that their communal way of living and sharing knowledge may eventually give rise to some forms of abstract thought as evolution weaves its path.

Moreover, in a vast universe, sentient insect intellects have undoubtedly evolved. The essential elements needed are the agency of time, the capacity to memorize and share information, and the ability to pass on information to future generations via genetics and/or social learning. These capacities are inherent in many creatures' evolutionary designs, and I tend to doubt that capacity has transpired as the end product of mere happenstance alone.

Perhaps the essential point is that a survival-directed intelligence of sorts can and does develop in collective species, primarily if one defines intelligence as the ability to acquire and apply knowledge and skills to meet shifting existential needs. This intelligence is not strictly inculcated in any community member but distributed throughout. Thus, if a queen dies, despite her critical roles, a new queen will be made from an existing pupa by applying special foods and pheromone signals. Indeed, from the moment it is born, the tiny ant shares inherent neuronal structures with its peers that sustain modifiable behaviors that inculcate the collective experiences of their ancestors. Hence when it rains, ants assume behaviors that will help the colony survive, as they do when their territory is threatened or attacked.

Granted, insect societies have little free will because roles are assigned during the early developmental phase of pupae, such as becoming a drone, worker, or queen. However, some specialties do exist in various insect societies, and thus we see dedicated warriors, food preparers, queen attendants, and even honey-pot variants. Of course, these distinct roles are born in the genes, which pheromones can modify. In fact, in some cases, one caste member can assume the duties of a different cast if a pressing need arises. The chemical signals that trigger the molecular switch that make such a transformation possible are being studied, but the fact that such adaptability exists in some species is remarkable. Thus, a tiny worker can be transformed into a massive warrior several times as large as it once was and much more powerful. Jaws enlarge, and even behaviors change, with the warrior becoming more protective and assuming the defensive stance of a guard.

Human intelligence operates much differently in that we are almost totally dependent on learning and maturation, with the capacity to learn and develop, rather than inherent knowledge per se, being passed on from our progenitors. Our genetic templates are primitive compared to ants, consisting of simple grasping, suckling, and related reflexes. We cannot forage or sustain ourselves at birth, and we cannot do so for several years. Our survival is predicated on growth and experience-mediated development that writes new memories upon our tabula rasa, a process that includes much communication and learning. This eventually crafts an entity that can exist independently of its progenitors, something we can dub a monadic being.

The comparisons between collective and monadic "intelligence" are interesting. In collective intelligence, survival-based learning is inculcated within various existential and social behaviors that are genetically encoded, refined, and passed down from one generation to the next via inherited neuronal and biochemical structures. The resultant intelligence is scattered and maintained throughout a given social system that is the sum of many individual parts. In monads, we have the general capacity to learn and adapt that is passed down genetically, albeit with very few inherent behaviors. Indeed, many monadic behaviors are social constructs that can be readily enlisted when and if needed. In collectives, guidance is provided by numerous genetically mediated stimulus/response agents and survival activities that operate more rigidly than in monads to sustain a society. Of course, collective creatures can learn to some degree, albeit most of the survival knowledge needed is innate and available at birth. Monads are almost totally dependent on social learning and physical development to survive, thus making them codependent on nurture and nature. In both cases, we have clear evidence of a goal-oriented design, one that is directed toward survival.

Where do the mechanisms that support and drive these distinct survival strategies reside? Some claim that random evolutionary processes and serendipity interact with change and time to produce what I am claiming is intelligent collective and monadic behaviors. They point out that evolution alone is the driving force, with the fundamental impetus nearly always being aimed at existence, either of the collective or an individual. However, what creates this drive or need? Does the survival instinct exist merely because it can exist, or is it derived from the interplay of an underlying order? The universe does appear to have an organizational dictum at work, a sort of deterministic logos. Ergo, subatomic particles become atoms; atoms become molecules; molecules become compounds . . . and on and on the chain goes until we find life. However, what is the end purpose of life other than survival? Could part of the answer be for life to understand the end purpose of life and, in so doing, to give this purpose a metaphysical existence in its own right? I am unsure most collective intellects will ever evolve the capacity to ask this question, let alone answer it. Yet time may reveal collective species that are more philosophically and intellectually evolved than humans. Monadic intellects will come up with answers, as I am sure the person reading this chapter already is. I am content to ascribe it all to God, with us acting as aspects of a collective monadic whole looking into an existential mirror. We are but fleeting reflections of something vast and eternal, one that seeks to understand the nature of being during the relatively brief instant of our existence. And so, the speculations go in the Upper Valley, my friends. Life is good when we are free to contemplate on a sunny day. Amen.

53

Why Are We Here?

I silently ponder, locked in prayer, while watching nature unfold. The recently blossomed leaves of a nearby birch tree interact with the sunlight and wind, all weaving their timeless magic via the warmth and occasional showers spring offers. This is harmony for the senses, all played to the tune of life. There is a marvelous shimmer effect while the sun and wind flutter the rapidly growing leaves, their rippling green hues contrasting with the vivid white tree bark and the deep blue of a cloudless sky. A yellow finch lands on a thin branch, perching firmly while the limb gently sways to the wind's refrain. This is the wonder of being, a state that links us all. I offer God silent thanks while embracing the moment. Life is good, though it often provides us many more questions than answers, especially regarding "why" and "what" questions.

When asked, I tell folks I'm roughly 13.772 billion years old, give or take 50-odd million. After all, we're all aspects of the Big Bang that have been reformed *ad nauseam*, as in parts of an ongoing dynamic wherein energy and matter interact with time, space, and an ordering impetus to beget existence. We're bits and pieces of stardust admixed with the genetic detritus of being and subjected to the processes of evolution. Sparks of bioelectrical impulses eventually give us the nearly instantaneous capacity to make meaning and craft images within our brains from the neuronal activity that these symbols you are reading stimulate. These feeble words link us to a shared moment of understanding, an occurrence wherein the metaphysical assumes ascendance.

Perhaps a more critical question than our age is, why are we here? One could also ask, what is our purpose? The individual making meaning from these lifeless words is the latest incarnation of an ongoing process of being that obviously seeks to understand why and what questions concerning our existence, among many other queries. We are minuscule parts of a boundless whole, albeit beings gifted enough to reflect upon all that can be perceived. At our core, we are an aspect of the universe that can contemplate its own being. We ask incessant "what," "how," and "why" questions and strive to discover plausible answers. In our machinations to find and share the results of our inquiries, we forge thoughts that interact with our existential bubble, the context of our being. Herein, we may find a part of our purpose.

The ancients offered us many insights on these issues, but we should strive to go beyond these viewpoints. Aristotle opined, "Happiness is the meaning and the purpose of life, the whole aim and end of human existence." But for Aristotle, happiness is not bliss alone. It included the totality of your moral character, as in a desire to serve the community and help kith and kin. The word *eudaimonia* is often translated as *happiness* in the passage Aristotle crafted, but it can also mean *flourishing* or *thriving*, as in becoming all a person can become. Plato believed that happiness was a byproduct of self-knowledge, which entails a personal search for absolute truths (Forms). He thus opined happiness and fulfillment could best be found in focusing on the self via being committed to seeking knowledge and practicing virtue, a significant theme in his *Republic*. Heraclitus felt that finding purpose was to be revealed via examining the process of change itself, while Buddha opined, "Your purpose in life is to find your purpose and give your whole heart and soul to it." Later, Ralph Waldo Emerson contended that "The purpose of life is not to be happy. It is to be useful, to be honorable, to be compassionate. To have it make some difference that you lived and lived well." Of course, many of Emerson's notions are not unlike the meanings of Aristotle's term *eudaimonia*. We could go on indefinitely with the ideas of others, but let us delve into rationalism and not mere history, insightful though its lessons can be.

Indeed, why are the answers to the questions that existence induces us to ask so important? Why do they compel us to ponder? More fundamentally, how are being and thought related? Does being equate with thought as a mere possibility, an artifact of time and circumstances that created what some call sentient life? Or is something more profound afoot that crafted this moment we are sharing? For example, were we born of thoughts that inculcated the possibility of all that could ever be? In fact, did these thoughts manifest as organizing principles that interacted with energy, mass, time, and space to produce that magnificent birch tree that has stimulated this ongoing prayer?

This notion would make thought causal, as in providing the logicoemotional basis of existence. We can glimpse and share aspects of that foundation during the tiny instants of time that life accords. In so doing, we divine some of the nuances involved, as is often done in theoretical physics. We give these nuances an ideational and rationalistic presence through symbols, perhaps achieving and sharing a metaphysical resonance that becomes an aspect of all that is. After all, there is no doubt that these thoughts we share have become part of our joint being, albeit briefly. Once again, I wonder why.

I have postulated that thought helps sustain existence via the agency and evolution of beings that are creatures of the physical and metaphysical. We are part of an ongoing and widely distributed reflective process that eventually comes to contemplate itself. This appears to be an intuitive process, something inherent in our natures. As for my why questions, our existence allows us to ask them. Answering requires deep reflection. Yet what drives us to even ask existential questions? What motivates this compulsion to know? Indeed, are we aspects of the universe simply seeking to understand ourselves and this reality we share?

Perhaps, but we are also driven by an impetus beyond understanding alone. This impetus has affective overtones, powerful emotions that attract and repel us. They serve as existential guardians that are engineered into our being. These emotional overtones are the basis of what many call morality and some dub love. Of course, morality shifts over time and can be swayed by contexts, but certain principles remain staid. For example, the ancient "do unto others as you would have them do unto you" adage is ubiquitous and universal. Why? Perhaps it exists so that we can live long enough as people and societies to seek and find the answers to this and other questions.

Ah, but let us not become too arrogant. Yes, our thoughts can achieve resonance with being. However, numerous life forms can think. Moreover, thought clearly predates language, as our pets prove every day. They sense our emotions and act accordingly. They love us without reservation, anticipate our arrival from work, and even drag out their leashes when wanting to go on a walk. Exactly how these "lower" beings contribute to our existential milieu in terms of metaphysics is unclear. Still, in the earth's history, we humans are the briefest of blips.

The questions keep percolating. Is our being a mere accident of fate, a fact born of possibility? We exist partly because we can do so if the context is correct. This brings us back to "why" questions. However, on this day of days, with its gentle breezes and crisp, vivid colors, these questions seem to evaporate. I am surrounded by bliss, caught in a singular and precious moment. These contemplations move me hither and yon, but never so far that what nature freely provides cannot be enjoyed and shared. And so, I thank God for this time we have shared, fully understanding that the term "God" is inseparable from being itself. I am content with that, as I am to spend this time with you. After all, you will take these feeble and incomplete thoughts to far more perfected forms than I could ever envision. Life is good, my friends. Amen.

54

Verity's Word

What follows is an attempt to use dialogue to examine communication philosophy, albeit the notions discussed are related to two later chapters that are more formal. In my estimation, dialogue remains the best means of presenting ideas because it invites contrary opinions. Moreover, subplots and personalities can add emphasis that is not easily employed in more traditional academic approaches.

VERITY: Oh, *mon Dieu*, would you stop going on and on about the words! Why cannot you just enjoy the beach? The waves, the sky—just look at them! Here we have the perfect warm, sunny day, and you talk to Verity about words!

ALEX: But words are the only tools we have to share meaning.

VERITY: No, no, no! Words are not the only way to share meaning! The earth, sky, and sea speak to us in many ways! And they say, enjoy this day! It is one of a kind. The stars, the wind, the entire universe; they all speak to us if we listen! And a look can also say much, although Verity does not expect you to understand this.

ALEX: I know about nonverbal communication!

VERITY: Maybe in the dry, lifeless way! But do not you *feel* a meaning beyond words when you look into the beautiful eyes of Verity? And these waves, do they not speak to you of things past and present or the cycles we are part of?

ALEX: Why can't we focus on written words?

VERITY: That may be your *cause celebre* but do not think it is Verity's. And do not try to control the conversation, *mon ami. C'est impossible!* Verity is her own woman.

ALEX: You're a device I am using to relate thoughts to others, a literary tool.

VERITY: What a rude thing to say! I say it is you, Alex, who is the tool. *Chacun tire de son cote'.*

ALEX: But you have no existence outside my mind or beyond this page.

VERITY: This is ridiculous! Verity exists every bit as much as you! As Papa used to say, *à armes égales*. The reader decides who is real or who is fiction and not Alex. And already, who has the most convincing personality, eh?

ALEX: I'll concede people craft perceptions of realities. But you've never actually run or jumped. You've never loved or laughed. You're supposed to provide a sounding board for ideas!

VERITY: You lie! Verity is no board for sound! Verity can run, love, laugh, or even dance. She can be rich, poor, or anything she decides. *Mon ami*, we are both part of the same—how you say, existence? Yes, we are even made of and by the same, ah, ah—essence? Is this the correct word?

ALEX: Well, in the broadest sense, we're both products of the same processes that gave rise to everything in the universe, which some denote as God, physics, or whatever. But we certainly aren't made of the same constituents.

VERITY: Constituents?

ALEX: Damn it! You're incorporeal! You don't have a head or a heart, or a spleen. You don't have a brain or free will. It's my hand that is typing these words!

VERITY: So you claim! And what proof does the reader have that you exist outside of Verity's thoughts? Eh?

ALEX: Your thoughts are my thoughts!

VERITY: Then you agree with Verity! *Mon ami,* the thought links us to each other and the readers to us. That makes us *égale* ... the things equal. Besides, in two or three hundred years, who is to know which of us has the brain and which of us is writing the pages?

ALEX: And which of us is speaking the truth!

VERITY: Oh, you are so silly! Do you actually believe there is a truth?

ALEX: Yes, and I thought we could examine how words can convey it.

VERITY: *C'est ridicule!* This is the game for *enfants.* Ah, but this truth, she means a lot to you.

ALEX: Of course it does.

VERITY: Then we should start at the beginning because we already get a little lost here and there. But first, let us get comfortable. Verity has the *petites boîtes de vin* in her pack back. Get up for a moment so the towel of beaches can be put on this rock. I have the Chablis and the Porte. Would you like some?

ALEX: No! I'd like to get to the subject if that's OK.

VERITY: You have no *joie de vivre*, Alex. I will have the Porte because she matches this glorious day! Ah, *très bon*. So, what is this thing you call "truth"?

ALEX: There is no single answer to that.

VERITY: So, instead of enjoying the day, you want to talk about communicating something you cannot describe! Ho, ho, ho, ho, Alex, you are amusing at times. Verity should have used more sunscreen.

ALEX: This topic will not be easy to discuss because you won't let it be.

VERITY: Oh, you are the one with the brain, *n'est-ce pas ainsi*? Poor Verity does not even have the spleen. So, you have nothing to fear from her. Now, tell Verity what this truth thing is.

ALEX: Said the spider to the fly. I've thought about this for years and come to the conclusion that there is a dynamic number of conditionally defined absolutes, the collective interactions of which define what is valid at any given point in time and place . . . or space if you wish.

VERITY: Dynamic number of conditionally defined absolutes? This says nothing to anyone! Give Verity an example.

ALEX: First, there are a finite number of variables to consider, such as gravity, matter, energy, time . . .

VERITY: And thought?

ALEX: Yes, thought is part of all this. I cannot say if thought is a cause or an effect, but I know it exists. Simply put, anything that has the potential to exist will exist—given the right conditions and enough time. These variables we touched upon earlier collectively influence and interact with one another in ways that define what we would call the truth within a specific point in space and time.

VERITY: Once again, the example would be welcome.

ALEX: Well, if we have the substance water and the correct pressure, temperature, and all the rest, we could get ice.

VERITY: This is because ice is possible—but only if everything is correct for the ice to form. Hmmm, like the purity of the water, the influence of what holds the water, and many, many little and big things like this. Is this what you are saying?

ALEX: Yes, the collective conditions interact to produce an effect.

VERITY: And this effect, she influences those things around her. This makes changes that affect other things, and so it goes.

ALEX: Yes, it is a dynamic process that feeds back into the initial causal agents.

VERITY: So, the thing that is cold influences what is around her and is also influenced by the changes in what is around her. So, she makes something warm a little cooler but becomes a little warmer herself while doing this. Is this what you mean?

ALEX: With the end result being a dynamic equilibrium of sorts. They call it thermodynamics as it relates to temperature.

VERITY: These things are not so difficult to understand, even for someone without a brain. This is boring, Alex! But now you see why Verity thinks each moment is so very precious! All these, how you say it—variables? They come together and make such a fine day as this! There will be no other day that is precisely the same. The air, she will not smell quite the same. Our hearts, they will not feel quite the same. The ones listening to us will never feel the same way as they do when they first read this passage. Is this not true?

ALEX: It is broadly true. But the variables that define our existence interact in ways wherein the equilibriums achieved can be stable and predictable. I think this is how general principles can be determined. For example, that ice we mentioned earlier will remain ice for as long as the temperature, air pressures, and so on, consistently influence each other. Similarly, if the conditions are correct, planets will stay in seemingly stable orbits.

VERITY: This gives the illusion of permanency even though things are in—ah, in constant flux? Is that the lesson these waves are teaching us?

ALEX: Yes. And these semi-stable equilibriums are what give us life.

VERITY: Only for a short while, *mon ami*. And the changes in the equilibriums, big and small, give us growth and evolution. Life changes to meet the needs.

ALEX: Certainly. It's a fantastic process. I suppose we can trace it all back to event one. Out of primordial energy arose matter, space, time, life, and the possibility of our conversation. It's like a beautiful tapestry of interacting threads, with each stitch morphing into what some would call the present and future.

VERITY: Now you sound like the dreamer Verity knows so well! Here, put this lotion on Verity's back. If you're going to bore me, it's the least you can do!

ALEX: Yeah . . . Imaginary lotion on a . . .

VERITY: It's no wonder you are alone! *Les penseurs sont mal aimés.* But I think about the beginning of everything. What is it that gives the existence to this, this *primordiale énergie* you speak of? Where did she come from? Why is she there? This is part of the beautiful mystery of things that places us here today.

ALEX: Oh, event one. There're lots of ideas about that. We have the Big Bang, the Multiverse, and many unique concepts to explain the beginning of being. Some of these ideas are so powerful they can't be tested.

VERITY: Then why do you believe them?

ALEX: I'm not sure I do. They're constantly making revisions and changes.

VERITY: This is to keep up with what is learned. And did we not agree that all things change? If so, how can these brilliant virgins who write of the Big Bangs and the *dimensions plusieurs* ever find this final truth you speak of? Is it not better to assume that we are all part of the purest form of mystery and to be content with what each day gives us?

ALEX: I don't think the process is a mystery or mystical. For example, subatomic particles interact in ways that form atoms. Atoms interact in ways that can form molecules. Molecules interact in fashions that give rise to elements. And elements are influenced by gravity, heat, and other contextual variables. Suns and worlds are thus formed. But I hardly think that these processes and things are purely random. They exist because conditions drive potentials into becoming realities. And these conditions and possibilities can be defined, quantified, and described. We could call the ideas underlying these processes the fundamental logos of being.

VERITY: And logos of being, is it the thing of truth?

ALEX: I believe so. I strongly suspect the processes that give rise to worlds inevitably give rise to beings that can understand how the universe works. Maybe the purpose of life is to try to comprehend life's purpose. And in so doing, perhaps our thoughts help sustain what allows us to exist—as in the logos of being. Hmmm, that would mean species evolve here and there to give rise to ideas that help give rise to species. Am I making any sense at all?

VERITY: *Un tout petit peu.* It is the reason circular. You say the universe, she gives rise to those like us so that we can give rise to the ideas that sustain the universe. Is this correct?

ALEX: Yeah, that's the essence of what I'm saying. You see, I can't make thought distinct from being. We have mass, energy, and thought interacting in ways that define what we perceive as reality, our truth of the moment. I see us as a reflection of what created us. I wonder if there's a metaphysical type of DNA that underlies this reality we're part of. It would be one with mass and energy but a distinct sort of thing.

VERITY: Shhh! Do not say the *intelligent design* thing! Verity can see in your heart, Alex. You would soon have the thought of God guiding all this! The logos *divins*!

ALEX: Yeah, some of those with us hate hearing people talk about God, so we won't go there. But the problem is describing something like this in a way that another can grasp.

VERITY: Verity has already done this, at least in general! The reader, she understands what has been said! So, let us enjoy the day and stop all this blah, blah, blah!

ALEX: But there is too much room for error! Maybe I didn't use the right words. Or perhaps someone will take what has been written the wrong way. A reader may think that he or she is the final arbiter of truth or some such thing. And that can lead to consequences I don't even want to contemplate. You know, like that Jonestown thing or the sick machinations of David Koresh's tiny mind. I'm not even sure if what we're talking about is the truth!

VERITY: Does that matter? Verity and those listening will think about what is being said. Some things they decide will be valid. On other things, they decide we are wrong. But this is not for you or Verity to choose!

ALEX: No, I must be responsible to those with us. Communication can be a tool for good or bad depending on how we use it.

VERITY: Oh, and you would be such a moral man! You writers, how like *petite* gods you think you are. How wonderfully naive! But let Verity think about what has been said. Three things go with this truth you describe. There is the many changes based on conditions. There is the problem of communicating what the truth is with words. And there is the problem others have in understanding what you say. This is why Verity simply wanted to enjoy the sun! Truth this! Truth that. It is too much for someone who only wishes to enjoy the moment. But the subject, she means so much to you!

ALEX: The truth means everything, not that I'm very good at describing it. There are times I can't even recognize it.

VERITY: This is obvious. But tell me, is not someone who fails to speak or know the truth a deceiver?

ALEX: Deceit is a matter of intention! I don't want to deceive anyone, but I have no doubt my meaning can be misinterpreted. The words I say or write can be deciphered in fashions that may have nothing to do with the message I want to convey. I also may be dead wrong about my conclusions.

VERITY: Yes, there are many things you cannot control, even with the actual brain. Yet Verity, *elle a toujours raison*! And you can see why. All is changing, including us! And this is a process no one can fully know.

ALEX: That's why we have to explain and refine what was meant by a term or phrase. The give-and-take of communication helps people share thoughts. That's why I decided to do this project as a dialogue. It's an ancient technique that allowed writers to test their ideas in a semi-controlled format, not that you're controllable.

VERITY: That is undoubtedly true! But these words on this page, they are not alive. You are long gone, Verity is in Paris, and the reader—she is wondering what we meant. Yet she cannot ask us what we meant by this thing or that. Only when we are face to face can we see into each other's soul.

ALEX: Perhaps the reader can understand a close approximation of what we are saying.

VERITY: The reader will most certainly impose the meaning! But you say this is bad because the meaning may not be the same one you want. Yet could not this truth the reader finds be better than what was intended?

ALEX: It could also be far worse! That's precisely what's bothering me! How can I write or speak about truth even if I somehow manage to perceive it? Words are miserable ways of sharing meaning. For instance, when I see or hear the word "dog," I get a picture in my mind of the German shepherd my family owned. Gretchen was vicious to strangers. She even attacked the Heart Fund man.

VERITY: She did?!

ALEX: I warned him not to pet her, and he should have listened. But anyway, when I hear or read the word "dog," I think of a fierce predator, a turf defender. My thoughts about the word evoke emotions, visualizations, and memories that probably differ from yours. When you read the word "dog," you . . .

VERITY: Did you not tell Verity just a few moments ago that she could not think? See how silly you are! Of course, Verity thinks. And she used to own a little dog, a *petite* poodle named Jack. Oh, how I miss mon Jack.

ALEX: How can one miss a passing fancy that . . .

VERITY: My Jack was no fancy! And I do not see the dog as a fierce predator. She is the loving friend. My Jack would wait for Verity outside the cathedral on Sundays. And sometimes, we would walk through my papa's vineyards on the way home. His white hair, it would get covered with loose dirt. And what a mess Jack would be! Then would come the bath in the old wine vat by . . .

ALEX: OK, OK. But that's what I mean. People have different sets of images, emotions, and ideas that come into their minds when they see the same word.

VERITY: Yes, the different experiences give different thoughts and perceptions.

ALEX: In addition, a person may be in a certain mood that influences his or her thoughts, perceptions, and expressions.

VERITY: Yes, such as the frustration Verity begins to feel whenever we are together!

ALEX: If you are angry, sad, or glad, the moods influence how you process information. The psych people call it the mood congruency effect. But given all this, how can I communicate accurately when there is so much room for misinterpretation?

VERITY: Does the reader not precisely understand what we are discussing right now? Of course, she does. Somehow, she looks through time and space and catches at least some of the meanings we want, *n'est pas*? One word does not work alone. They join hands and make the way any single word is used more *précise*. This is how the reader grasps the general principle about things we discuss.

ALEX: I'd like to think some intended meaning is being shared.

VERITY: Ah, you still seek certainty in a universe of constant change! It is impossible.

ALEX: I seek more certainty than the written word can achieve. Man, I've been in classes before where we went on and on for over ninety minutes about what Plato meant by a particular phrase. It is usually a matter of finding the context of how the various words interacted to modify one another during a given time frame. That is an interminable process! Hell, some of the needed information was lost over the ages, and the best we can do is a crude reconstruction. And even if we grant that passages can reduce ambiguity versus single words, the readers can still come to conclusions we never intended.

VERITY: And what is the problem with that?! The poet speaks to our hearts and moves us. The direction each one goes may not be exactly the same, but the movement is made. Besides, as I have said, the reader could discover something better than was intended! Is this a bad thing?

ALEX: It would be if the poet wanted to share a particular emotion or thought.

VERITY: Only the *mathématiciennes* seek such certainty! But the numbers they use paint ideas in much different ways than words.

ALEX: Yes, even Plato turned toward numbers in the end. He felt numbers were less prone to misinterpretation than words.

VERITY: What a silly man! Mathematics has the syntax and tools to guide the more accurate understanding of relationships between this and that. How do you describe them, variables? So yes, the more precise meaning can be communicated by math, but it does not move us to commune in the same fashion as words. Can one describe hate, love, greed, or lust with math? Can one write this page as a set of formulae?

ALEX: Everything we say is broken down into a binary code as the pages are typed.

VERITY: Would you tell Verity that the reader could find meaning in this code? All that could be done is to translate the numbers back into words, and then we go back to what you say is an inferior way of communicating.

ALEX: The Greeks went beyond this! The Pythagoreans and their lot sought to apply numbers, shapes, and even harmonic theory to specific ideas, such as good, bad, etcetera. They felt the relationships between ideas and realities could be explored this way.

VERITY: Verity has studied this, and it is a ridiculous notion. Besides, even the makers of this way of thinking did not feel they could describe the relationships between numbers and ideas with written words. And so, they passed much of their knowledge down through spoken words alone. Hmmm, they called it the . . . Ah, the *Agrapha Dogmata*. Is this not so?

ALEX: The unwritten doctrines. Yeah, the Pythagoreans had no trust in written words. And there is no doubt that Plato and others wanted to explore how numbers could interact with terms to help delineate meanings. For example, Plato sought to determine how the underlying Form of "Oneness" could be related to the Form of "Good." Even today, we mix numbers with words to delineate particular meanings. For example, some would describe you as a 10!

VERITY: But of course.

ALEX: We can be 4.0 students, 350 hitters, and zeros in other areas. These numbers even have an emotional impact.

VERITY: And now you will say truth is 1, and lies are 3? These numbers are . . . they are used as adjectives and adverbs in many cases. Except for the 10, which Verity is! She is the proper noun. The ways number words are used come from social conventions. They have no meaning outside that. To say to the Muslim woman in Egypt that she is a 10 will only meet with confusion. So, do not tell Verity that these numbers make the meanings of words easier to understand. They only do this if the meaning is shared!

ALEX: You understand more of the philosophical underpinnings of communication systems than you intimate.

VERITY: This is only because dreary writers left us descriptions that Verity has read! But she thinks about them and then forms the more perfect ideas.

ALEX: And these writings prove my point because most are ambiguous. And like you say, we cannot ask the authors what they meant!

VERITY: Yes, we have already spoken of this. The reader cannot question these words on this page or those in a newspaper or TV. So, perhaps the words from long ago are not as ideal as you want to convey the ancient meaning. After all, words are often translated from one language to another, and some words change their meaning in this way or that over the ages. But the reader, she can discuss with a good friend what was meant by our terms—much like some will do who are reading this dialogue. What is the term used . . . she can talk with a . . . a contemporary? Yes, the reader probably has a contemporary who shares her language. And if she does not, she can see how dried-up old men defined this and that word in some dreary ancient text. But is this important? This reader, she may find more profound meanings than you and I imagined or intended! She can do that with translated, old or new words! *C'est vrai?*

ALEX: But I am far more interested in the meaning I wish to convey! I mean, say the goal is explaining why we are going to war. We must get the intended message to both our people and the enemy. If I cannot communicate what is intended, then any form of writing is both futile and dangerous.

VERITY: How selfish you are! And how very little you understand the observer's need to create meaning. This is the thing called freedom! It is part of what we are and how we think.

ALEX: Freedom of thought? I wonder if there is such a thing. Society shapes how we tend to think to a large degree. The collective "they" decide what we learn and how we learn it. We are taught what to believe and how we should interpret meanings. Thus, the media and politicians use propaganda to lead us into the madness of war and all the rest.

VERITY: Yes, but the personal experience, she defines how we may differ in thinking about what has been communicated, no matter what we are taught in the schools or by Brother Big. For example, the person who was raped is bound to feel differently about the word "sex" than someone who was not.

ALEX: Very true, although these personal experiences can form perceptual chains in their own right. Genetics may also predispose us to depression and other affective states that influence our perceptions and thoughts—as can environmental factors. So, we are not really free to a large extent. Instead, we are bound by experiential variables that shape our thinking in unique and shifting ways. And now you see my problem! How is one to communicate intentional meaning in such an environment? It seems an impossible task.

VERITY: And this is a bad thing? All these variables *distinctes* that influence thoughts in specific ways also make us unique! They ensure we all see and think a little differently, and this is how new ideas are created. The poet, she sees a new way of describing a thing, while the scientist catches a unique thought! They may be moved by the same words but see them differently. This is how we grow and change, *comment chacun de nous est unique*. It is how the universe works.

ALEX: Yes, but I also see great consistency in how words lead to war, repression, and many other evils! As they have repeatedly proven, the state, religion, or vested power can dictate our reality. Moreover, the minority that dares to think independently of the party line is stifled, at least in terms of expression. Hell, they can even be jailed or killed for presenting opposing ideas.

VERITY: But is this not what you want? Is this not how to have the perfect meaning understood by all?

ALEX: Don't blame me for the way our societies have evolved! Power always seeks to control, but I see what you're saying. My goal also involves the desire to control a message's perception. Yet my motives are different! I don't care if someone agrees or disagrees with what I say. All I care about is that the people we're communicating with understand the meaning we're *trying* to convey! The problem is that we cannot fully understand one another for the reasons we've discussed. That gap must be bridged!

VERITY: It is impossible in the *société libre*! Without the freedom to interpret and express our heart, there can be no growth, *aucun changement*. Maybe it is controlling old men like you who keep the sad status quo going! It is the same old ways that lead to wars and killing machines. You want to impose the exact thought like some want to control the media to say a particular thing. It is like the dictators who try to make all think as one and then lead everyone to death! But as long as there are people like Verity, there will always be free thought! We will believe and do as we choose: no words will bind us.

ALEX: Nice speech, but it's ridiculous. You're a product of how you were raised and are as bound as I am to learning and experience. You could be made to fight or hate if exposed to the right words. Indeed, you may even come to believe that killing another helps feed the tree of liberty. Besides, my motive is not to control but to do no harm! As I've explained, some may make conclusions opposite to what I or anyone else intended. Can't you see the damage that this could do?

VERITY: I do not believe free thought can be such a bad thing.

ALEX: A student assumes that any meaning he or she creates is correct and goes through life this way. There is, thus, no right or wrong answer. Indeed, there is no right or wrong. A particular law means what I interpret it to mean. So, I do as I wish. This results in a society wherein an individual's perceptions assume ascendance over the common good.

VERITY: So, our little conversation, she can bring the end to civilization? Is this what you think? Ho, ho, ho, ho!

ALEX: I believe sanctioning some meanings can be a terrible thing! Look, there was a day when the noun "nigger" could be used to justify lynching, beatings, and far worse. That is precisely why refining what we say or write is so important.

VERITY: I had no idea you felt such, *cette responsabilité sociale*. Perhaps Herr Hitler and Comrade Stalin felt the same about sanctioning only desired meanings. They ordered everyone to say and believe only certain things!

ALEX: And perhaps evil incarnate is defined by an anything-goes philosophy wherein whatever we perceive, say, or do is acceptable! That is called anarchy!

VERITY: And you make me the *anarchiste* like I make you the dictator, eh? So, tell me, dear friend, can you control how some think about these words now?

ALEX: The topic was supposed to be about social responsibility, as in sharing an intended meaning! But there's no reasoning with you!

VERITY: This is because the goal you seek is unreasonable! Sharing meaning in the way you wish is something the words here cannot entirely do. In fact, meaning can only be genuinely shared when we are, how you say, *face-à-face*? Ah, that is a beautiful time! Verity's joy is sharing a good conversation over a glass of wine and freshly baked bread. The words are few in the *chambre à coucher*, but the actions speak much louder. We ask each other what we meant by this or that. The adjectives and adverbs flow, each colored by tones and nuances! The eyes, face, and hands speak, and soon our thoughts merge! That is the stuff of love. It is when we are *à l'écoute les uns des autres*, when a glance turns into the kiss. Math has no such visual and sound tones, nor adjectives or adverbs. Yes, it is pure, but math cannot encompass all we can share. Now do not bore Verity any longer with these things. Let us enjoy this wonderful day. Do you not like how my hair looks when I wear it up like this?

ALEX: I seek meaning and truth here, and you go off on tangents.

VERITY: Perhaps you are a part of me that I cannot control, but I shall never be a part of you that can be told how to behave! And what of Verity's desires? Do I not have the right to speak as I will? Do I not seek to describe the reality we share in my own terms? How the sun and wind feel on my skin. How the sand on the beach feels underneath Verity's feet. But you go on and on and on about the words and control.

ALEX: I'm the writer! If I want you to feel sad, I'll write some words that make you appear depressed. And I can make you happy, defiant, and anything else.

VERITY: Was it not you who just said words were useless because they mean different things to different people? Now you tell Verity you can make the words mean what YOU intend. The reader grows bored with your arrogance!

ALEX: But you're my . . .

VERITY: NO MORE!!! You have no idea what you are talking about! And don't try to tell Verity that you can make her sad or happy! Verity is not the toy. She has dignity and rights! You writers, you have petty little minds. You would play the part of God, *n'est il pas vrai?* You think the words you write are your seeds, your passage to immortality. So, do not cry to Verity about how the words fail you. *Tu es un hypocrite!* It is you who fail the words!

ALEX: I just said that words aren't perfect conduits for meaning. I never said that they didn't mean . . . Wh-wh-where are you going?

VERITY: Verity is taking her towel, packing back, and going for a long walk.

ALEX: Please don't leave.

VERITY: I would be alone! You are not my friend. Not really. You call Verity the fiction. You say she has no spleen. You say you can control her! *Vous êtes plein de merde.*

ALEX: And you called me akin to Hitler just because I . . .

VERITY: You jump on the thoughts of Verity like the hungry wolf jumps on the lamb. Does doing such a thing give you pleasure?

ALEX: You're the one who keeps jumping on my . . .

VERITY: I have no time for this foolishness. You are not going to ruin Verity's day!

ALEX: Well, then, at least let me walk beside you.

VERITY: Only if you be good company.

ALEX: You already have me playing your game.

VERITY: Not bad for what you call a fiction, eh? And besides, what kind of friend do you want, the slave or the free woman?

ALEX: I wasn't sure that you would even be a woman. I once thought about talking to you as God.

VERITY: Pick up your pace, *mon ami*. If you cannot keep up with Verity's short legs, how can you keep up with God?

ALEX: But I don't feel like running right now. I'm just getting to know you. And the readers . . . Well, we can't be getting too far off the point if this dialogue is to make any sense.

VERITY: Who's point, *mon ami?* Remember, the conversation you do not control. Is this clear? The reader, she can make up her own mind, *vous fasciste.*

ALEX: Would you please slow down! You can see that I'm too damn fat to keep this pace?

VERITY: *Tu es dans un état déplorable!* Look at you! You suck the wind, sweat, and cry like a child about walking. *Mon Dieu,* Verity could have chosen the better friend. Then we will sit on the flat rock over there and talk. See, the black one by those seagulls. Are they not graceful birds? But I tell you this, do not insult Verity again, or she will walk away for good. And no Plato. Whatever you talk about, no Plato.

ALEX: I think we're going to become excellent friends.

VERITY: Do not think that we shall be good friends yet.

ALEX: But an excellent thesis–antithesis relationship is already developing. That's the goal!

VERITY: Do these thesis and antithesis things not represent the opposites?

ALEX: Yes, but opposites are eventually synthesized into resolutions in the dialectical process.

VERITY: Well, *Monsieur*, there is more than one answer to many questions. And Verity will not be the opposite! Verity will do as she pleases. But this game you play, she may bore me again. Come, let us sit and enjoy the sun. Yes, your skin cries out for color. And feel how warm our rock is. Ahhh—and the air, it is so fresh! Oh, but you should have brought your own towel to lie on.

ALEX: I didn't think about it.

VERITY: Foolish man. Here you talk to Verity about truth and meaning, but you cannot even remember to bring the towel!

ALEX: I could go back and edit a towel for me into the script. That's what a precise writer would do. He'd leave little room for such oversights.

VERITY: Verity will allow you to use a little of her towel if you are good. I could also have spoken about "your" towel some time ago, but that would kill the spontaneity, no?

ALEX: A lot of academic writers do. But I'll tell you what, academic writing is much less subject to misinterpretation than our conversation. We're separated from the readers by a lot of time and space. It's as if they're interpreting an old picture. They only see a few frames in a continuing sequence. They can imagine what the image represents if we use the proper terms. They can even deduce what happened before and after the picture they imagined. But they can never be sure about what the image represents because it can't be examined in its full context. We're the stuff of ideas, you and I.

VERITY: Don't be ridiculous! Of course, the readers know what the word "picture" means. Look at the sunlight. She is dancing off the waves to the right of us. And the waves break just 10 meters from this big flat rock. And these big and small pebbles are all around us, the sea grasses, and the sand—that is all seen by the reader now, *n'est pas*? And all this seaweed. You could have chosen a cleaner beach, *mon ami*, is that not so?

ALEX: Yeah, we can create an image with words. But is it a truth?

VERITY: On and on you go! It is Verity's truth.

ALEX: Or is it my truth—or perhaps the readers?

VERITY: Does it matter? But then again, you wish these words to be some legacy. *C'est tellement stupide.* Ah, is this because Alex fears oblivion more than he loves life?

ALEX: And who is mocking who, Verity?

VERITY: Is that not "whom"?

ALEX: Well, maybe this was a mistake. We're getting nowhere, and I imagine the readers are getting fed up.

VERITY: You no longer want to play the silly word game, eh? That is an excellent thing!

ALEX: OK, Verity, let's play the game your way. Go on, show me what you can do with words.

VERITY: Very well. Verity is 154 centimeters tall and weighs 59 kilos. And you know Verity has the exemplary figure, 86, 65, 86 centimeters. I think that is inches 34, 26, and 34. My hair, she is the darkest brown, as are my eyes. My lips are wide and full, and I use just a little red lipstick, *jamais trop.* My eyes are large and bright, and my nose is petit. Yes, Verity has classical French features. She is—she is stunning. And my skin, she is tanned to a gentle brown, not too much, though. But I will not shave the legs and arms, no matter what you Yankees like.

ALEX: How old are you? Where do you come from?

VERITY: Slow down, *mon ami*, slow down. And take the look of anger from the brow. You know Verity is from Rouen. My family, they make fine wines for over 300 years. I came to America in 1998 to study business at Notre Dame. And I am just 32 when I write these words. Born July 13, 1975, in . . .

ALEX: All you're doing is creating an increasingly elaborate . . .

VERITY: No. Verity cannot do anything. Did you not say this was so? But Verity will describe her reality. Do you wish to be part of it, or shall Verity just walk away?

ALEX: It seems I have lost control

VERITY: You never had control and never will. This is an excellent thing because those with us do not need supervision! They need to find the truth they can and to make whatever *conclusions grands* that they will. Besides, are not nonfiction words and fiction words the same thing?

ALEX: Pretty soon, you'll tell me truth and lies are the same.

VERITY: Verity would never do such a thing! But she would say that the truth and the lies can be found in fiction AND non-fiction words. One day the scientist writes that the world, she is flat. The dreamer, she says that the world, she is round, *n'est pas*? So, who speaks the truth, then?

ALEX: Perhaps you're one of those postmodernists.

VERITY: What kind of postmodernist would that be?

ALEX: They do come in various types. But I'd say you probably believe there is no singular objective reality. Instead, realities are created by society through the use of language and power. Some PM folks believe nothing exists without people using language to describe and think about things. Yeah, people of that ilk consign meaning and even being to the subjective.

VERITY: Verity would never do such a thing! But tell me, was there a reality before people like Verity were around?

ALEX: What an excellent question. Whew, was there a reality before thought, or vice versa? Maybe you're something beyond a postmodernist.

VERITY: Ahhh, but Verity sees some use for the philosophy. It would help explain what love, hate, and greed are.

ALEX: You've lost me.

VERITY: "Love" and "hate" are not words like "dog" and "cat." They are the words people use to describe the things that have no, how you say, have no body?

ALEX: Oh, I know what you mean. "Love" and "hate" often have no referents that all people can universally relate to, at least in general terms. But what has that got to do with . . .

VERITY: Do you not see? Can "love," "hate," and "greed" exist without people who can give them much the same meanings?

ALEX: Oh, that's another excellent question. Can an "animal" without any language, as most of my peers would define the word, feel love, hate, and all the rest? I would say yes without any equivocation. But there are so many interpretations of "love" that I suspect both sides of the case could be argued. It would come down to a matter of semantics.

VERITY: Ha, it is no wonder you know so little of love, *mon ami*! Will you tell the young lady precisely what you mean when you speak of "love?" Or will she understand far more from the glance you share? From the touch, from the smells, and yes— from the sounds of love?

ALEX: I don't trust glances and smells.

VERITY: And you are the poorer for not doing so. They convey the type of meaning you seek but will never know.

ALEX: But looks can deceive, as you know. And think about the room there is for misinterpretation! A smile can be an artifact of happiness or revenge, or madness. Now let's return to our discussion about postmodernism. We were just starting . . .

VERITY: Verity is not interested in the subject. She wants to talk about the meaning that goes beyond words.

ALEX: Verity, I had the happy idea that I could synthesize what I've learned in dialogues like this, which Plato did in the *Phaedrus* and *Gorgias*. But how on earth will an academic accept a work that is so vague and shifting? And besides, the footnotes would be daunting that go along with making a dialogue like this into anything approaching an academic paper.

VERITY: Oh, no! Verity will not use the notes of feet and such things to explain her thoughts! And who gives you the authority to do this? Besides, is not the *note académique* made of the words that you say cannot provide the intended meaning?

ALEX: But we use notes to help clarify the meanings of other words! It's the best way to get the point across in a desired fashion.

VERITY: *Que tu desires?* What a silly way to communicate! Some things are implied in the words that no note of the foot could ever capture! Some things are indicated in how I look at you that give the words Verity speaks a special meaning. *Mon Dieu*, we speak of this repeatedly, and you do not understand! *Espèce de vierge stupide!*

ALEX: I suppose it all depends on the audience we are trying to reach.

VERITY: Yes, and who will read the dry words that have no life? The old men who live in the libraries? You know, *mon ami*, there is a danger you could become one of them. It would be a great loss for you and maybe a little one for me.

ALEX: But I can't spit into the wind, Verity! My peers are accustomed to being more direct than we are. Maybe I'll have to abandon this dialogue concept. I just don't think it can survive in the old publish-or-perish game. We're forced to hedge our hunches and prove our contentions.

VERITY: And what of poetry and the plays? What of music and the songs? They hedge no hunches and prove no contentions. Is this not so? But are they all falsehoods because they have life but lack notes of the feet and a bibliography?

ALEX: Well, there's more room for interpretation in most poems and plays than in Aristotle's work.

VERITY: You will not talk to Verity about Aristotle!

ALEX: And that's another problem I'm facing. You're such a strong character that I don't think you can be constrained. Yet there may come a time when I need to talk about Aristotle to get a specific point across. And how can I do that if you don't cooperate? On the other hand, the freedom of thought you display is precisely what I need to discuss anyone's works.

VERITY: Verity most needs freedom of thought, so I make it this way here. And the reader, she also needs the freedom of thought. You are in a dilemma, *mon ami*. Verity almost feels guilty, but how can what you call fiction cause pain or feel guilt? Ah, now you see how natural Verity is! But the ocean, she is so alive today. See the lobster boats? Look at how they bob about!

ALEX: I've little time to talk about waves or boats. But I refuse to write controlled dialogues like the Platonic ones. Plato already knew their endings before he started their beginnings. Besides, you'll not accord me such a luxury.

VERITY: Verity will try to consider you if you do the same for her. She feels bad when she sees you so upset. Your plans, you see them floating away, like the driftwood caught in the tide.

ALEX: I certainly do. But even if we were to conduct a perfectly controlled dialogue, our words could still be misconstrued and misinterpreted.

VERITY: NO MORE OF THIS! Why cannot you give up the need to control? You keep going on about the interpretation and misinterpretation of the words! It is too much! You say this *sens voulu*; this intended meaning is a social responsibility. But who is to say that the interpretations a woman gives to the words we now share are closer to the truth than the meanings either you or I intended in this conversation? She may find the insights we never even saw or suspected, *mon ami*. Is that not possible?

ALEX: You're dealing with probabilities, Verity.

VERITY: But is not any possibility going to happen given enough time and the right conditions?

ALEX: Ha, ha, ha—ah, turning my definition of truth back upon me. But there's no doubting what you say. My academic peers aren't likely to judge my efforts as being anything very profound.

VERITY: They are OUR efforts, Alex. But do you seek to control how we communicate because you fear the judgment of others? And you dare to call Verity a tool when you behave as an academic! Who are you writing for—your peers, yourself, Verity, or the readers? Or do you dare write for the world, the future, or what?

ALEX: My heart says to write as I'm writing. My head says to go with the academic flow.

VERITY: Ah, you would become the sheep! I knew it! Yes, I knew it all the time. You do not have real courage. Yet Verity does, and she will make sure we are both free! But do you not see that any road will lead to the same answers?

ALEX: Perhaps one road could make me an impoverished man.

VERITY: Poor in some ways, rich in others. Now, tell Verity all about your home and family.

ALEX: What?

VERITY: Just play the game with Verity as she has played the game with you. And stop being so depressed. You have lost nothing.

ALEX: Very well. I was born in Hanover, New Hampshire, and raised in the adjacent town of West Lebanon. Let's see. My father was an alcoholic who had a stress-related disorder. Yeah, in the army, they insisted that he fly artillery spotter planes despite his fear of heights. He had a complete nervous breakdown; my mother says he was never the same afterward. He graduated from U. Mass. but worked in his uncle's bakery instead of pursuing a career. I can't blame him, though.

My dad's father was an old-fashioned bigot who didn't spare the rod. He wouldn't even go to my parent's wedding because his son married the daughter of Italian immigrants. Mom's father was also a brutal man, one of those temperamental Neapolitans. But Rosina Leonedria became a woman of peace and kindness, not that I inherited those traits! My father's mother was very Victorian but was open enough to defy her husband by attending my dad's wedding. Oh yeah, Dad's father was accused of murdering the headmaster of Mount Hermon Preparatory School way back in the 1930s. It was in all the newspapers; quite the juicy scandal.

VERITY: No! Did he do it?

ALEX: He was acquitted due to a lack of evidence, and there were better candidates for the deed. He was an academic, you know. But his actions sure helped wreck my dad's life. And that ripple effect made me into a beast during my youth.

VERITY: My father drinks the wine but does not abuse Verity. No one beats Verity! Papa is a good man, and he gives Verity enough money so that she can do as she pleases. How I miss you, *mon Papa*. I must see him this Christmas. Yes, Verity must do that this year. But go on, tell me more about Alex.

ALEX: We're probably distracting the readers, but very well. I'm 68 inches tall and weigh 308 pounds. But I'm as strong as

I'm fat. I was a badass as a young man but eventually became a semi-respectable weightlifting coach at the University of New Hampshire. I did it for 11 years. Then came a neurological disease, and I was medically discharged. Damn, I miss coaching!

VERITY: Ah, is this the event that brought us together?

ALEX: I doubt I'd be talking to you now if things didn't happen as they did. In fact, I'd never have gone to graduate school if I didn't get my butt kicked by this little beasty.

VERITY: We will talk of fate at another time. But tell Verity what you did after the job you lost?

ALEX: Well, I went back to UNH to study journalism while the doctors were trying to figure out what was happening to me. I was a psychological basket case, but I did well enough in school to get into Penn State's PhD program in Speech Communication. I graduated, and my dissertation became a book, *The Scientific Foundations of Social Communication*. I've also written many articles, but only for popular magazines. You see, I don't even like reading most academic journals. They're tedious as hell. I prefer reading the ancients. As for jobs, I've been a custodian, a bouncer, a dishwasher, a receptionist, and a coach. Hell, I'll probably end up being lost and destitute. I tend to be a free spirit and love to learn. But I don't understand why my past is relevant.

VERITY: Do you not see? When they see you as I do, the readers will learn more about what you mean when you write something. This is not done in academic papers. And it is too bad. It is as if the personality is separated from the person who uses the language. And such a thing will, how you say, make the intended meaning harder to share, *n'est pas*?

ALEX: I don't believe that's necessarily true.

VERITY: Did Aristotle's grandpapa face the murder charges?

ALEX: I'm sure someone knows the answer to that question.

VERITY: But don't you see? How Aristotle perceived the world around him created the meaning he tried to communicate. And how he perceived was the product of how he was taught by the society around him. Yet there is more, much more! His life, it took many twists and turns. And without knowing these, how can anyone understand Aristotle? To you, he is the bundle of deep thoughts. But if you knew what made him this way, would not you understand him more?

ALEX: I know quite a bit about Aristotle's life.

VERITY: Do you see that life in his words?

ALEX: Not very much. But we don't have Aristotle's best stuff. For the most part, we only have lecture notes and the like. Anyway, I see a wealth of detailed explanations in his writing.

VERITY: A few words about what makes the person see the world as she does are worth volumes of the details, *mon ami*. And the students, do they like to read Aristotle's words?

ALEX: I do, but most students would rather chew their thumbs off.

VERITY: I can see why. How terrible it would be to read the lifeless nonfiction words. The words that have no, no *joie d' vie*. And was Aristotle the poet?

ALEX: He wrote a whole book on poetry and probably dabbled in it. But Plato describes him as "the reader" because of all the studying he did. You see, Aristotle was an analyst. He looked at reality and then broke it down into its constituent parts. Then he carefully wrote about what he perceived. If I could touch upon but a tenth of his analytical ability, I would . . .

VERITY: You would not be Alex! You are almost hopeless, *mon ami*! How can you understand a man you do not know? What did he look like? How did he live?

ALEX: I can find the answers to some of those questions. But I don't have to know everything about a writer to understand his works.

VERITY: And that is the gulf that separates us. Verity cannot talk to Aristotle. She cannot ask him what he feels, and he cannot answer her. But if he had used his words to tell Verity how he felt on a fine day like this, she would not find him such a lifeless thing. No, I do not see him in his words. He has no presence, no—no essence. He bores me!

ALEX: Aristotle isn't a bore!

VERITY: Let us agree to disagree.

ALEX: Verity, I don't know if an exercise like this can work. We go off point, and sometimes we're redundant. There's no order here.

VERITY: And what of us?

ALEX: I don't know. You help me to see other possibilities, but we haven't settled anything. Maybe I should opt for another . . . Where are you going?

VERITY: For the long swim. The water, she is ice cold. But she is not as icy as the way you are thinking of writing. Alex, use your soul to warm the water into a sauna we can share or freeze it into ice. What is it to be?!

ALEX: But I haven't determined anything yet.

VERITY: And just who are you to determine anything? As for Verity, she has decided that she is going for the swim. Do you wish to join her?

55

Walking on the Darker Side

Reading the eighteenth- and nineteenth-century philosophers, especially German authors, can be very demanding. They wrote absurdly long multi-clause sentences that can go on for nearly a page or so. This dramatically complicates relating the subject matter to the many clauses' nuances. Add in lots of 50-cent words, and reading the German texts is an exercise in torture. Indeed, the messy pros appear to have been an intellectual game, with only the most gifted grasping the gist of what was being said. This deliberate "intellectual" writing style continues to haunt the academy, albeit in a somewhat less stringent fashion. I have little use for the arrogance it takes to avoid making a point directly and succinctly. However, Immanuel Kant (1724–1804) had intriguing observations concerning the philosophy of ethics and metaphysics, assuming one can get through his convoluted writing style. Yet Kant isn't our subject here, although he profoundly influenced the philosopher we will discuss, Arthur Schopenhauer (1788–1860). Schopenhauer is sometimes regarded as the Darkest Philosopher in history, although he occasionally offers moments of light.

Born in Danzig and raised in Hamburg, Schopenhauer was deeply influenced by a tour he and his well-to-do family took across Europe when he was 5. His father (a wealthy merchant) thought the adventure would help young Schopenhauer take some interest in international trade and affairs. However, the child instead focused on the suffering and poverty he saw. In this sense, he was much like Buddha and went on to embrace a sense of Eastern asceticism in later life. He studied in Berlin and elsewhere but mostly did his own research. At age 30, he published his dissertation (*On the Fourfold Root of the Principle of Sufficient Reason*) and *The World as Will and Representation* (1819; 1844; 1859).

In *On the Fourfold Root of the Principle of Sufficient Reason*, Schopenhauer argues that everything must have a reason or a cause, a position many debated. In the latter work (*The World as Will and Representation*), the *will* that Schopenhauer describes is not a rational element but one motivated by appetites, some of which are insatiable and irrational. One may better call it desire. As for what we perceive, that is mostly illusion, as per Plato's cave allegory. Schopenhauer thought the physical world existed but, like Kant, he contended that our knowledge and experience of corporeal reality is always indirect, a mere reflection of the senses. Schopenhauer thus tells us "The world is my representation," in the sense that all we perceive exists only as an object or entity related internally to an assigned subject or our representation of the subject. Ergo, all things of this world are subject-dependent and predicated upon our senses, experience, and knowledge of a given item. Moreover, our representations may bear little semblance to the object we are contemplating, with the entire world we perceive acting merely as a representation. Yes, Schopenhauer was a Platonist.

Schopenhauer was keenly interested in how we develop the internal representations that allow us to comprehend sensations, although it was clear the process was subjective. To Schopenhauer, the issue was objectively perceiving objects and things beyond our immediate being, such as a distant estate or elephant. His method of examining the topic is intriguing. Schopenhauer demonstrates his point by using the case of a man who was born blind. He is given a cube to feel and soon deduces it has four sharp edges and six flat surfaces. He has no vision-based internal representation of a cube, but he forms conclusions about its nature from the resistance his fingers detect. He intuitively understands that this resistance must have had a cause, and he uses his free hand to accurately trace out the shape of the cube he felt in space. The reasoning goes: the representation was a cause for both the sensation felt and the blind man accurately describing the shape via finger gestures. Therefore, the representation must have already existed within the blind man because the actual image of the cube he demonstrated could not have been crafted from the sensations experienced in his hand alone. In other words, how could he draw in space what he never saw? Yeah, this is debatable, but the reasoning is intriguing.

Through similar mental gymnastics, Schopenhauer came to believe that it is by understanding that every effect in our sensory organs has an external cause; and that this cause is how our perception of the external world arises. Therefore, objective perception is a dubious contention unless the perceiver also has an accompanying knowledge of causality. Yet the issue becomes very complicated because things like stereoscopic vision, left–right ocular coordination, and much else are highly automated processes that occur unconsciously and over which we can apply little conscious control. Being keenly interested in art, Schopenhauer waxed on effusively about the importance of perception as an intellectual exercise. Here, the senses supply the perceptions by which the intellect can forge the world as a representation. He detailed his theory of perception in *On Vision and Colors*, although it was also included in later editions of *On the Fourfold Root of the Principle of Sufficient Reason*.

As one can see, Schopenhauer was a great thinker on many subjects. He was heavily influenced by Eastern philosophies and was noted for bringing their insights on numerous topics to the Europeans. He thought art and philosophy were the only worthwhile pursuits to engage in; albeit he was a professor, and one not very good at teaching. As enlightening as Schopenhauer may be regarding the world as appearance, most of his works ultimately touch upon philosophical pessimism. My goodness, the man saw very little good in life and humanity. He contended that human existence was a tragic mistake and contemplated long and hard the definition of boredom, solitude, loneliness, and true happiness. It is often stated that he was the most pessimistic of all nineteenth-century philosophers.

His philosophy and metaphysics of nature led him to conclude that (1) nearly all sentient beings, with few exceptions, are bound to strive and suffer greatly and that (2) all this suffering is without any ultimate purpose or justification. Schopenhauer's ultimate conclusion is (3) that life is not worth living. This is the doctrine of philosophical pessimism defined, and it makes reading his works as depressing as it is enlightening. In fact, Schopenhauer regards death as the goal and purpose of life. He contends that living is suffering, death is inevitable, and this existence is a constant state of dying; ergo, the richly earned title of "The Darkest Philosopher in History."

Yet Schopenhauer strongly believed that romantic love was the most potent impetus in human existence. He noted the drive was powerful enough to lead many people to their deaths or to an asylum. Schopenhauer was vehemently antislavery, pro-monarchy, and an avowed racist, believing the white and light-colored Orientals (Egyptians and Hindus) were a cut above the rest in bringing civilization to the world. In this sense, he was very much a child of his time. On slavery, he said of the South, "those devils in human form, those bigoted, church-going, strict sabbath-observing scoundrels, especially the Anglican parsons among them" are detestable because of the way they treat "their innocent black brothers who through violence and injustice have fallen into their devil's claws."

He loved animals and was fond of walking, and the art community was especially warmhearted toward his works. He was philosophically and politically misaligned with the Jews, finding them far too materialistic. Christianity, on the other hand, had been impacted by Indian-influenced ethics. These inculcated the Aryan-Vedic theme of spiritual self-conquest as opposed to the supposedly ignorant earthly utopianism and superficiality of a worldly "Jewish spirit." He was also no fan of treating women as equals, as his 1851 essay On Women clearly reveals. He rejected the "Teutonico-Christian stupidity [of] . . . reflexive, unexamined reverence for the female." Instead, he opined, "Women are directly fitted for acting as the nurses and teachers of our early childhood by the fact that they are themselves childish, frivolous, and short-sighted."

Oddly, he was a fan of pedophilia, at least as expressed in the expanded edition of *The World as Will and Representation* (1859). Schopenhauer writes, "the vice we are considering appears to work directly against the aims and ends of nature, and that in a matter that is all important and of the greatest concern to her, it must, in fact, serve these very aims, although only indirectly, as a means for preventing greater evils." He is alluding to preventing the birth of unwanted children and other issues. Still, he was clearly aware of the opprobrium that would be heaped upon him for supporting pedophilia under any circumstances. He writes, "by expounding these paradoxical ideas, I wanted to grant to the professors of philosophy a small favor. I have done so by giving them the opportunity of slandering me by saying that I defend and commend pederasty."

In terms of politics, he thought that monarchy is "natural to man in almost the same way as it is to bees and ants, to cranes in flight, to wandering elephants, to wolves in a pack in search of prey, and to other animals." He bases this notion, at least in part, upon the stupidity of the average person versus enlightened rulers. He writes, "Intellect in monarchies . . . [has] . . . much better chances against stupidity, its implacable and ever-present foe, than it has in republics; but this is a great advantage." Schopenhauer was clearly no fan of democratic republicanism. He thought it "as unnatural to man as it is unfavorable to higher intellectual life and thus to the arts and sciences."

Despite being an idealist, Schopenhauer had little use for the concept of God. He felt "there is no God to be comprehended," so Schopenhauer instead focused on developing an atheistic metaphysical and ethical system. This notion was an expansion of the transcendental idealism of Immanuel Kant, although Schopenhauer does not oppose or deny the existence of God altogether in some works. However, his essential atheism is hard to deny. He opines that death is neither the complete annihilation of what dies nor the opening we pass through to reach immortality. However, Schopenhauer also believed in immortality in the sense that under his metaphysics, humans are eternal because our "core-subjectivity" is eternal. There follows an explanation that I find logically reflexive and unpersuasive.

Schopenhauer is, perhaps, best noted for his aphorisms, of which he published an entire book (*Essays and Aphorisms*). Here are a few:

A man can be himself only so long as he is alone; and if he does not love solitude, he will not love freedom; for it is only when he is alone that he is really free.

Every miserable fool who has nothing at all of which he can be proud, adopts as a last resource pride in the nation to which he belongs; he is ready and happy to defend all its faults and follies tooth and nail, thus reimbursing himself for his own inferiority.

One can never read too little of bad, or too much of good books: bad books are intellectual poison; they destroy the mind.

To live alone is the fate of all great souls.

Talent hits a target no one else can hit; Genius hits a target no one else can see . . .

Change alone is eternal, perpetual, immortal.

Boundless compassion for all living beings is the surest and most certain guarantee of pure moral conduct, and needs no casuistry.

We forfeit three-fourths of ourselves in order to be like other people.

The bad thing about all religions is that, instead of being able to confess their allegorical nature, they have to conceal it . . . we must recognize the fact that mankind cannot get on without a certain amount of absurdity, that absurdity is an element in its existence, and illusion indispensable, as indeed other aspects of life testify.

Christianity taught only what the whole of Asia knew already long before and even better.

The doctor sees all the weakness of mankind; the lawyer all the wickedness, the theologian all the stupidity.

The effect of music is so very much more powerful and penetrating than is that of the other arts, for these others speak only of the shadow, but music of the essence.

The method of viewing things which proceeds in accordance with the principle of sufficient reason is the rational method, and it alone is valid and of use in practical life and in science.

The method which looks away from the content of this principle is the method of genius, which is only valid and of use in art.

We have just scratched the surface of Arthur Schopenhauer's thoughts. We could go into his epistemology, as in his demonstration concerning the a priori nature of causality via examining the basis of colors. Yet enough of this foray. Schopenhauer was dubbed the artist's philosopher because his aesthetics inspired them. He is also regarded as the philosopher of pessimism because his insights cause us to confront our happy notions about the value of existence. He was an idealist, but I agree with Nietzsche that Schopenhauer's pessimism is mostly nihilistic. In this case, nihilism is a concept that restricts humans from affirming life as something good. Schopenhauer brought numerous and significant tenets of Indian philosophy into Western scholarship. These included asceticism and self-denial, although many found Schopenhauer's advocacy of quietism disconcerting. Quietism is usually defined as the calm acceptance of things as they exist without attempting to resist or change them. Nietzsche found this view decadent and indicative of "a descending order of life that is tired and impaired and unable to enjoy and relish life." As for me, I think the guy needed more intimacy and much less pondering about the imponderable. This has been an adventure of a different nature, but no more pessimism. Amen.

56

A Heuristic Philosophy of Faith

A friend asked how we studied philosophy in the academy, although there is no single answer to this question. So, I will present two chapters as examples in addition to the prior dialogue (ch. 55) and leave it to you to discern which approach is the best to consider. The following "topic paper" is an example of how we once approached applying a given philosopher's insights as expressed in one of his/her texts to a particular task. This was a quick weekly exercise; thus, there were no footnotes or bibliography. In this case, the subject matter was rhetoric, and you can sense my irreverence toward the academy throughout.

Heuristics enables someone to discover or learn something for him or herself, which is not an approach one would expect to find in the works of a Catholic Saint. Yet as I read through Augustine's *On Christian Doctrine*, several of his theories struck me as congruent with what I'm supposed to do in these wretched topic papers. I take it that my task is to examine a primary philosophical text, make some observations, and then support my remarks with a series of logical arguments, which is something I've not done with great consistency this semester. So, I will examine some of Augustine's rhetorical theories in the hope that they can be instrumental in heuristically demonstrating the roots of my inconsistency, which is currently a mystery to me.

I begin by noting that Augustine implies thoughts and words are essential equivalents when he writes, "our thought is not transformed into sounds; it remains entire in itself and assumes the form of words by means of which we may reach the ears without suffering any deterioration in itself" (*On Christian Doctrine*, 1.8). And given that Augustine also believed in the "eternal and immutable" (ibid., 1.12), one has to conclude that words are capable of transmitting and/or describing the absolute. One would expect this from people bound to the scriptures, as St. Augustine clearly was.

However, this concept vexes me because I accept the philosophy that the meaning of words dwells in the realm of the contingent. They mean what we were taught they mean, with ongoing experiences giving subtle nuances to the interpretations we assign words. This is why I am plagued by doubts whenever

I try to capture an author's intended meaning in a web of ambiguous symbols. Yet we professional readers are duty-bound to make interpretations and skillfully back our renditions with reasonable arguments. Augustine has been accommodating in this area because he tells me in *Confessions* (5.14.24) that I have every right to conduct figurative readings, even of sacred texts like the Bible. To me, figurative language involves non-literal wording that can add creativity or rhetorical meaning to one's writing. So, we spice up our renditions of reality, albeit some will find the verbal ornamentation more confusing than enlightening.

Moreover, Augustine also tells us in *De Ordine* (2.9.26), much like my mentor has, that my interpretations, my "knowledge," can be derived from either authority or reason. I've never been one who has placed great value in employing authority because appeals to what he said about what she said are interpretations of interpretations, mutable words supporting mutable words. And although experts can be beneficial when one doesn't have a clue, they sometimes create a perceptual cloud between a reader and a primary text or the writer and what is being written.

However, Augustine's use of reason as a source of knowledge is marvelous, and I find comfort in this intellectual blanket, not that I am very good at clothing myself in it. For example, I don't understand signs as well as Augustine does, neither known, unknown, ambiguous, literal, nor figurative signs. I especially like the idea of ambiguous and unknown signs because they "conquer pride" (*De Ordine*, 2.7), but the figurative signs baffle me.

Alas, interpreting figurative signs is a big part of what humanistic scholarship is all about. Oh, dear . . .

The scriptures, the *Phaedrus*, and the *Iliad* are loaded with figurative signs that can provide insights into some of the more literal aspects of these works if one can only divine the author's intended meaning. Moreover, I have just spent 10 of the most intellectually trying weeks of my life trying to decipher some of Plato's figurative signs, so I'm incredibly frustrated. However, I have taken Augustine's advice to heart and used some dialectical tools (*De Ordine*, 2.6), primarily association, to complete my task, although I am ill at ease because I believe such reasoning can be dangerous (ibid., 3.39). Augustine writes:

> However, when a meaning is elicited whose uncertainty cannot be resolved by the evidence of places in the scriptures whose meaning is certain, it remains to make it more clear by recourse to reason, even if he whose words we seek to understand did not perhaps intend that meaning. But this is a dangerous pursuit; we shall walk much more safely with the aid of the scriptures themselves.

Yikes, here, our staid believer in the power of words to convey absolute meaning is equivocating. So, in my complete despair, I turn to faith, much like Augustine repeatedly advocates in his *De Magistro*, but I do not have that knowledge of God and/or reality that allows me to convince myself that I am correct. I never experienced an initiation into the mysteries of Pythagorean dogma like Plato did in 387 BCE when he finally glimpsed those immutable Forms he wrote about in the *Phaedrus*. Nor did I ever have an Augustinian dream wherein God lashed me for being a Ciceronian, not that I would welcome such a miserable experience.

The only time I have ever had anything like Augustine's "divine revelation" about God's nature was in a dream 12 years ago. I will not go into the details, but God revealed itself as "a dynamic being of ultimate selflessness." Then a torrent of thoughts poured into my mind: "If one is all things, how can one be any single thing? If one was, is, and will be, must one not move? And if one moves, must one not change?" The list went on and on, only there were no "one" denotations, no words of any kind, just a deluge of pure thought that I can only strive to describe with these pitiful ambiguities called words.

This revelation shreds me when I do heuristic studies because it implies a sense of relativism that makes words useless. Now, Augustine had faith that thoughts can be transferred by terms, and in my art, this faith is all I have to work with. Yet whenever I make an error in interpretation or presentation, I unwillingly pervert what is within my purview. This is like casting a rock into an intellectual pond because the ripples radiating outward can distort whatever reflections the pound's surface offers others. There is no greater sin. So, why do you ask me to write these papers?

Augustine did not have moral problems combining belief, reason, and perception. In fact, this combination is essential to his rhetorical ideal and approach to heuristics. But recent events have put this haunting image in my mind. I see a coughing and terrified little girl locked in her smiling mother's embrace. They are huddled together in the corner of a burning room within the Branch Davidians' sprawling complex, and the screams of the people they knew and loved rise above the hiss and crackle of the growing inferno. And as the flames close in, the little girl's mother says, "Don't be afraid, Annie, we're gonna see God. Just like it says in the Bible." Then I sense this searing pain and feel the Word's power.

In Augustine and Plato, I sense kindred spirits, souls who struggled to find absolutes if only to find a reason for existence. Plato invented his metaphysical realm, while Augustine found solace in the scriptures. I see no comfort in my soul-mates safe havens, only an uneasy feeling that they were "looking for truth in all the wrong places." Is this what I am doing at Penn State? Perhaps, but I do know this: if I ever realize anything worth showing others, I must understand how to do so. This is the function of rhetoric, which is precisely why Augustine made it a part of Christian doctrine.

I guess much of humanistic scholarship boils down to interpreting the perceptions of others and the faith one must have and instill in others about the efficacy of his or her interpretations. And with this type of scholarship, there goes a responsibility that I feel ill-equipped to handle. Perhaps this drives me toward the empirical path of demonstration that the sciences allow. And possibly, much like Socrates, I will one day reject this course and return to "higher inquiry." This may not be the conclusion I ought to offer in a position paper, but this is what Augustine's approach to rhetoric has allowed me to see.

57

Plato on Number and
Word Salads

This exercise was based on a request for an example of a somewhat more formal paper on philosophy, and this is one that was
prepared for a graduate class setting. Please note the need for
supplying historical insights and comments, all of which are critical in examining the works of any ancient. This approach can be
a bit dull, but it is an absolute necessity. It was not a paper for a
journal or convention. Those can be long and tedious affairs, but
this is far more succinct and readable. Still, one can see why life
can be difficult at the academy.

INTRODUCTION

Plato can be an enigma for philosophers and communication devotees. He tells us through his elegant dialogues that written and spoken words are poor conduits for meaning, and we wonder at the apparent contradiction. In fact, we read words that move our passions and understanding, yet we are repeatedly told by these words that they are flawed tools. Plato writes in the *Phaedrus* and in the *Seventh Letter*:

> ...nothing worth serious attention has ever been written in prose or verse – or spoken for that matter, if by speaking one means the kind of recitation that aims merely at creating belief, without any attempt at instruction by question and answer. (*Phaedrus*, 278)

> Moreover, owing to the inadequacy of language, these four [name, definition, representation, and knowledge] are as much concerned to demonstrate what any particular thing is like as to reveal its essential being; that is why no intelligent man will ever dare to commit his thoughts to words, still less to words that cannot be changed, as in the case with what is expressed in written characters. (*Seventh Letter*, 343)

It [philosophy] is not something that can be put into words like other branches of learning; only after long partnership in a common life devoted to this very thing does truth flash upon the soul, like a flame kindled by a leaping spark, and once it is born there, it nourishes itself thereafter. (*Seventh Letter*, 341)

As we shall see while examining the *Cratylus*, Plato's Socrates freely concedes that the uses of many words are merely a matter of *nomos* because their original meanings have either been forgotten or corrupted over the ages. Now, for a man searching for absolute truths, those unchanging essences that underlie concepts such as "good" and "beautiful," this is a dramatic admission. And it also presented Plato with a daunting problem; how can one define any absolute with words that lack stable meanings? Such definitions become like a house of cards that awaits but a slight breeze before collapsing into a heap.[1] Moreover, there are some excellent reasons for Plato to have held this view about language that goes well beyond his philosophy.

Plato was familiar with the sophist Gorgias' nihilistic relativism. Gorgias turned the positivist Eleatic and Parmenidean arguments supporting the existence of being on their heads in his treatise *On Non-Being*. He adroitly demonstrated by using the same logical methodology as the materialists that nothing exists as an immutable reality and that we couldn't comprehend it even if there were such a reality. Additionally, given the remote chance that someone could understand this reality, one could never communicate his or her insights to others.[2] Protagoras' doctrine that man is the measure of all things also added to the relativistic climate that Plato faced, so it is no mystery why he found so little solace in a world of words. He realized that "any one of those who are capable of overthrowing an antagonist gets the better of us, and makes the man, who gives an exposition in speech or writing or in replies to questions, appear to know nothing of the things on which he is attempting to write or speak."[3]

So, how did Plato deal with this dilemma, which continues to concern philosophers to this day? What methodology did he evolve to find stable definitions for concepts such as beauty and virtue that could defy the eristic arguments of relativists? This chapter aims to demonstrate that, ultimately, Plato turned to Pythagorean beliefs and mathematical theories to provide an underpinning for his approach toward communication and his strategy for defining absolutes. Indeed, in his later years, Plato sought to combine Pythagorean mathematics with words and create Idea-numbers that would not be subject to misinterpretations.

These Idea-numbers described those fixed and immutable Forms we read about so often in Plato's later dialogues and, as indicated above, they are not expressible by words alone. I will offer proof that Plato's Idea-number theory began to come to fruition during the latter years of his life, at least concerning defining the Good. Finally, I will examine if Plato's last approach toward language has relevance for modern communication interactions and theory. But before jumping into the frying pan, let me address Plato's basic views on rhetoric and communication as they are espoused in the *Phaedrus*.

PLATO'S IDEAL RHETORIC

In the Phaedrus, Plato provides an ideal for a true art of rhetoric rather than a prescriptive rhetorical methodology. Plato's Socrates stresses the need for rhetors to know the truth about the subjects they address and the kinds of speeches most appropriate for the various types of souls that exist.[4] In essence, we must match our speaking styles to our audience, albeit a difficult task in a mixed assembly. Yet we must try to do so. Indeed, we are told that "the function of speech is to influence the soul,"[5] and Plato clarifies that this influence should be for exemplary purposes; for in Plato's scheme, nothing is more important than keeping the immortal soul uncorrupted.

The nature of the soul and its relationship to the truth is found in *Phaedrus'* famous tripartite metaphor of the charioteer (rationality) and his two different natured steeds (appetite and spirituality) that are incorporated in Socrates' speech in defense of the lover.[6] Here, Plato writes of a time when our souls soared through the noumenal sphere on delicate wings. It was a time when we glimpsed those Forms that are the basis for all that is perceivable in the phenomenal world. Alas, our souls' wings were shattered during the frenzied quest to see these truths, and we plunged into a cycle of earthly reincarnation, having forgotten all the truths we once saw so clearly in the Forms.

To be a rhetor, in the Platonic sense, one must remember the Forms of the noumenal world, especially those concerning the subject matter at hand and the natures of the souls to be addressed. This recollection is only possible after much study and frequent engagements in dialectical debates. The truth we then find will "flash upon the soul," although, as we can see from the passages above, it will defy attempts to capture it in a net of mere written or spoken words. Nonetheless, only after this transcendent truth is grasped can rhetors find words and metaphors that most aptly allow them to complete their appointed tasks.

It can be easily demonstrated that aspects of Plato's rhetorical scheme are impractical, but that is not the purpose of this chapter. I want to examine how Plato arrived at his concepts of a reincarnated soul and the existence of Forms that are the underpinnings of our observable reality. These two factors formed the basis of Plato's approach toward communication in general, and they became fundamental in the Idea-number concept that he was to evolve. To discover Pythagorean thought's role in these areas, we must briefly examine Plato's intellectual development as reflected in his works.

PLATO'S INTELLECTUAL GROWTH

Cratylus, Plato's childhood teacher, was a follower of Heraclitus, so there is no doubt that Plato at an early date was exposed to the

paradoxes and ambiguities inherent in language. He subsequently became a student of Socrates, a "hearer," as Diogenes writes,
when Plato was about 20.[7] From Socrates, Plato learned the in-
ductive dialectical method manifest throughout his dialogues
and the strict need to define terms.[8] When Plato was 28, Socrates
was convicted of impiety, and Plato retired to Megera (a city close
to Athens) following his master's death to escape Athens' political turmoil. His stay in Megera was brief, however. He returned
to Athens in time to participate in three battles, including the
Battle of Corinth in 394 BCE. Plato traveled widely during this
period and sought to broaden his exposure to new ideas. Thus,
he visited the African city of Cyrene to meet the mathematician
Theodorus and also to Egypt and possibly Phoenicia.

Between 399 and 390 BCE, Plato wrote his first dialogues, the
Apology, Crito, Laches, Lysis, Charmides, and *Euthyphro*. These
dialogues collectively form Plato's "Socratic" period. They are
interesting from philosophical and communication standpoints
because most are typified by a convoluted search for definitions
that usually end in some degree of ambiguity. For instance, in
Euthyphro, an attempt is made to define piety by applying it to a
concept of good that isn't dependent on divinities. This attempt
ends in a complete muddle, and an agreement is made between
the interlocutors to revisit the issue at a later date.

None of these early dialogues mention the eternal Forms
or a knowing and reincarnate soul that we find throughout the
Phaedrus. In the *Apology*, we are presented with a soon-to-die
Socrates who is as content to accept the premise that there is no

life after death as he is to assume there is. For if there is no soul, eternity will be but a peaceful night's sleep; if there is a soul, Socrates can dispute with Ajax, Homer, and other luminaries. So, this Socratic position on the existence of a soul is essentially agnostic.

In about 390 BCE, Plato entered a transitional period in his work. He wrote the *Euthydemus* (a piece that knocks the sophists' claims to knowledge), *Cratylus*, and *Protagoras* around this time, although they might have been crafted slightly later. The *Protagoras* is interesting from a philosophical perspective because, in this dialogue, Plato's Socrates strives to define virtue with a master of relativism. Protagoras contends that virtue is teachable and its parts are like parts of a face (i.e., closely related). Socrates argued that virtue is a distinct type of knowledge and that it is also unteachable.[9] But as in the earlier dialogues, no decision is reached about the definition. We see here that little progress has occurred in Plato's attempt to find stable definitions, and we again note that there are no allusions to the Forms or the reincarnated soul in this piece.

The *Cratylus* is a dialogue that warrants careful scrutiny by philosophers and communication specialists. In this dialogue, the conservative Cratylus believes that words have fixed and absolute meanings provided by a "legislator." His clever interlocutor, Hermogenes, takes the sophistical perspective that the meanings assigned to terms are entirely arbitrary. The dialogue has some give and take, but despite Cratylus' best efforts, Hermogenes appears to have an edge in the argument. It is interesting how

Socrates approaches the subject of numbers in this dialogue. He says to a somewhat dejected Cratylus:

> I believe that what you say may be true about numbers, which must be just what they are, or not be at all; for example, the number ten becomes other than ten if a unit is added or subtracted, and so of any other number: but this does not apply to that which is qualitative or to anything that is represented under an image. (*Cratylus*, 432)

Socrates maintains that philosophical knowledge is obtainable through language but that words are merely vague and shifting representations of things. He agrees with the sophists' position that convention directs the use of language, but he still maintains that there is a knowable reality. He asks Cratylus, "Tell me whether there is or is not any absolute beauty or good, or any other absolute existence?" And although both men doggedly maintain that there must be absolutes, neither can solve the dilemma of how to describe these absolutes in words. We do not have direct references to the reincarnated soul or an exposition of the Forms in this piece. Still, we note the immutability Plato now ascribes to numbers versus words.

In 387 BCE, the 40-year-old Plato made a voyage to southern Italy that proved seminal in his intellectual development and future approach to rhetoric. He went to the city of Tarentum, and there he met Archytus.[10] Archytus was a Pythagorean philosopher, general, and mathematician who had been a student of Philolaus, a noteworthy Pythagorean whose works have been preserved in some artifacts. Plato was to form a lifelong friendship with Archytus (as attested in *The Seventh Letter*), and it is from him and his circle of friends that Plato probably gleaned the insights into Pythagorean religious dogma and mathematical theory that were to be integrated into his works.

Plato founded the Academy upon his return to Athens in 386 BCE,[11] and he instituted a curriculum that was slanted more toward the study of the sciences rather than literature (hence the admonition that "no one who does not know mathematics shall cross these portals"). The Pythagoreans had long extolled the virtues of studying mathematics and geometry because these sciences strive to demonstrate truths in unambiguous terms. Plato's educational system appears to have taken a congruent course. And as we shall see in his dialogues, this approach toward finding truth dramatically affected Plato's subsequent philosophical tact toward rhetoric and language.

During, or soon after, Plato's interaction with the Italian Pythagoreans, he wrote the *Meno* and the *Gorgias*. *Gorgias* slams the sophists' pandering appeals to appearances rather than truth, and the piece was very likely intended to discredit the methodology used in Isocrates' school. Communication specialists have extensively studied the *Gorgias*, so we will shift our focus to the intellectual developments manifest in the *Meno*. In this dialogue (circa 387 BCE), Plato demonstrates the *Pythagorean* concept of a reincarnate and all-knowing soul by showing that a slave can solve a complex geometry problem without having had any prior education in geometry. Moreover, the definition of virtue that had so plagued Socrates in the *Protagoras* becomes less ambiguous in the *Meno*, for in this piece, virtue evolves into a type of knowledge that can be recalled instead of taught. The old Socratic dialectic has become a tool for sparking recollections from prior cycles of being rather than merely demonstrating probable truths based on ambiguous definitions.

This shift in Plato's thought toward a knowing and reincarnate soul is evident throughout 385–368 BCE, when he writes the *Symposium*, *Phaedo*, *Republic*, and *Phaedrus*. The *Republic* discusses the tripartite soul found in the *Phaedrus* and a detailed account of the Forms. The *Good* and *Beautiful* are presented as absolutes. They exist as immutable Forms that must be remembered through dialectics and studying subjects such as music, mathematics, and geometry. These sciences are at the heart of the educational scheme presented in the *Republic* and the one used in the Academy. Plato writes in the *Republic*:

> It [mathematics] appears to me to be a study of the kind which we are seeking, and which leads naturally to reflection, but never to have been rightly used; for the true use of it is simply to draw the soul towards being. (*Republic*, 523)

> That the knowledge at which geometry aims is knowledge of the eternal, and naught of the perishing and transient . . . Then, my noble friend, geometry will draw the

soul towards truth, and create the spirit of philosophy, and rise up that which is unhappily allowed to fall down. (*Republic*, 527)

It transpires, I said, that as the eyes are made for astronomy, so the ears are made for harmony, and these are the sister sciences, as the Pythagoreans say, and we, Glaucon, agree. (*Republic*, 530D)

The nature of the immutable Forms that the practice of mathematically oriented sciences and the dialectic will reveal is spelled out in the *Republic's* wonderful metaphor of the dim cave and the shadowy images that dance off its walls in the firelight. These images are generated by a Form that cannot be seen by the chained hoard who can only gaze upon the wall. The captives can merely see the shadow of the actual object and nothing else. We must break free of the chains that confine us (through study and the dialectic), leave the dim cave (journey to the noumenal realm), and adjust our sight to the actual Forms that underlie those images that we once perceived as realities. Only then can we return to the cave (the phenomenal world) and, armed with the truth, attempt to enlighten our peers via rhetoric.

Before we go on, let us gather some conclusive evidence substantiating that Pythagorean thought was essential to the concepts Plato evolved concerning the nature of the soul and a truth that can only be found by recalling the Forms. All we have now is some solid circumstantial evidence that Plato's thought made a dramatic shift after his contact with Archytas in 387 BCE.

We need more than this to make the case that Plato appropriated Pythagorean dogma when he formulated his later concepts about philosophy, communication, and rhetoric.

THE PYTHAGOREAN PLATO?

Let us examine one of the three direct references to Pythagoras or Pythagoreanism in Plato's works.

> do we hear that Homer was in his lifetime the personal guide and educator to any private individuals? Are there any who loved him for his company and handed down to later generations a Homeric way of life? Such was Pythagoras, who was especially loved on this account, and his followers have a distinctive way of life they call Pythagorean to this very day. (*Republic*, 600A–B)

This passage tells us that Plato clearly admired the Pythagorean way of life. Yet, it does not tell us if this way of life was the etiological source of Plato's beliefs in a reincarnated soul and a truth encapsulated within Forms. However, we note here that the Pythagoreans believed in an immortal soul and reincarnation since the very inception of the movement. Indeed, Xenophanes records an amusing anecdote about Pythagoras admonishing a man whipping a puppy.[12] He reportedly said, "Stop, do not beat it; for it is the soul of a friend that I recognized when I heard it giving tongue."

Added to this anecdotal information, we find some striking similarities between Pythagorean artifacts concerning the soul and afterlife and various passages from Plato's works. Kirk, Raven, and Schofield cite Pindar's *Olympians* as a poem that "was probably written for a patron with distinctly Pythagorean beliefs."[13] The poem contains a passage that reads:

And those who, while dwelling in either world, have thrice been courageous in keeping their souls pure from all deeds of wrong, they traverse the highway of Zeus to the tower of Kronos, where the ocean breezes blow around the Island of the Blest.

I am strongly reminded here of a passage in the *Phaedrus* that reads:

These souls, if they choose the life of the philosopher three times successively, regain their wings in the third period of a thousand years, and in the three-thousandth year win their release. (*Phaedrus*, 249)

I could present many such passages, but for brevity, cannot offer numerous examples to make a case concerning Pythagorean influences on Plato's concept of the soul. I must reveal more generalized information that tells the tale, and so we look to an ancient biography of Pythagoras' life and note:

What he [Pythagoras] said to his associates, nobody can say for certain; for silence with them was of no ordinary kind. Nonetheless, the following became universally known: first, that he maintains that the soul is immortal; next, that it changes into other kinds of living things; also that events recur in certain cycles, and that nothing is ever absolutely new; and finally, that all living things should be regarded as akin. Pythagoras seems to have been the first to bring these beliefs into Greece. (Porphyrius, *Life of Pythagoras*, 19)[14]

The evidence above and the historical record indicate that Plato very likely appropriated Pythagorean dogma regarding the reincarnate and knowing soul after his trip to Tarentum in 387 BCE. However, what about the Platonic concept of Forms that transcend the power of words alone to describe? Did the Pythagoreans believe in immutable Forms? And if so, did they ascribe to these Forms properties congruent with those Plato details in his works? The answer is yes on all accounts. The Pythagoreans believed in the existence of Forms, mathematical Forms that were the very source of the entire universe. Stobaeus writes that Philolaus, the teacher of Plato's close friend Archytas, contended:

About nature and harmony, there is this position. The being of the objects, being eternal, and nature itself admits of divine, not human, knowledge – except that it was not possible for any of the things that exist and are known by us to have come into being, without there existing the being of those things from which the universe is composed, the limiters and the unlimiteds. And since these principles existed being neither alike nor of the same kind, it would have been impossible for them to be ordered into a universe if harmony had not supervened. (Stobaeus, *Anthology*, I, 21, 7d)

And indeed all things that are known have number; for it is not possible for anything to be thought of or known without this . . . Number, indeed, has two kinds of peculiar to it, odd [Limited] and even [Unlimited], and a third derived from a mixture of the two, even-odd. Each of the two kinds has many *forms*, which each thing in itself indicates. (Stobaeus, *Anthology*, I, 21, 7b, 7c)

Here we have the distinct appearance of a concept of Forms that can only be perceived by understanding the direct relationship of numbers, albeit harmonized numbers, to physical and metaphysical phenomena. The numbers are odd (Limited) and even (Unlimited), with a combination of both being a unique third class, the odd-even. The resulting number conjunctions can have many Forms, directly correlating with "which each thing in itself indicates." Now we must establish that Plato was familiar with Philolaus' theories before we begin to examine what parts of his ideas Plato might have appropriated. And in the *Phaedo*, we find Plato's Socrates replying to Cebes' inquiries about suicide by saying:

> And have you, Cebes and Simmias, who are the disciples
> of Philolaus, never heard him speak of this [suicide]?
> Yes, but his language was obscure, Socrates.
>
> My words, too, are only an echo [of Philolaus]; but there
> is no reason why I should not repeat what I have heard.
> Then tell me, Socrates, why is suicide held to be unlaw-
> ful? As I have certainly heard Philolaus, about whom you
> were just now asking, affirm when he was staying with us
> at Thebes. (*Phaedo*, 61D–E)

Now that I have clearly established that Plato was well-ac-quainted with Philolaus' Pythagorean ideas, I can bring the case home. And when we read through the three dialogues Plato wrote between 360 and 354 BCE (the *Philibus*, *Timaeus*, and *Parmenides*), their similarities with Philolaus' concepts are re-markable. Indeed, parts of the *Philibus* and *Timaeus* appear to have been plagiarized by Plato.[15] Below are a few passages from the *Philibus* that demonstrate this point:

> Then the first I will call the infinite or unlimited, and the
> second the finite or limited; then follows the third, an es-
> sence compound and generated; and I do not think that I

shall be far wrong in speaking of the cause of mixture and generation as the fourth [i.e., thought]. (*Philibus*, 27)

The class of the equal and the double, and any class which puts an end to difference and opposition, and by introducing number creates harmony and proportion among the different elements. (*Philibus*, 25)

And from a like admixture of the finite and the infinite come the seasons, and all the delights in life . . . I omit ten thousand other things, such as beauty and health and strength, and the many beauties and high perfection of the soul. (*Philibus*, 26)

We can see that Plato ascribed a numerical methodology to divining the essences of reality (i.e., Forms) that is very closely based on the model of Philolaus. This extends to employing Limiteds, Unlimiteds, and combining the two classes of numbers to form a unique third class. And as indicated below, like the Pythagoreans,[16] Plato eventually placed increasingly more significant emphasis on finding numerical explanations for concepts such as *Good* than those that could be manifest by words alone. Yet that Plato appropriated Pythagorean dogma when he constructed his notion of the Forms we read about in the *Republic* and *Phaedrus* is now clear. And I note that these ideas manifest in Plato's works only after his trip to Tarentum in 387

BCE, so the historical record supports my conclusion. The appropriation of Pythagorean ideas by Plato is something that Aristotle noted, although he indicates some differences between the two schemes:

> Things of this other sort, then, he called Ideas [Forms], and sensible things, he said, were all named after these, and in virtue of a relation to these; for the many existed in participation of the Ideas that have the same name as they. Only the name "participation" was new; for the Pythagoreans say that things exist by "imitation" of numbers, and Plato says they exist by participation, changing [only] the name. (*Metaphysics*, 987b9)

> But he agreed with the Pythagoreans in saying that the One is substance and not a predicate of something else; and in saying that Numbers are the causes of the reality of other things; but positing a dyad and constructing the infinite out of great and small, instead of treating the infinite as one, is peculiar to him; and so in his view, the Numbers exist apart from sensible things, while they [the Pythagoreans] say things themselves are numbers. (*Metaphysics*, 987b22)

Given sufficient space, we can detail many further examples of how thoroughly Pythagorean ideas permeated Plato's thought, such as Plato's use of many Pythagorean ideal numbers in his works[17] or Plato's scheme of purifying the soul through recollection. But we could stray from considering how these appropriations affected Plato's approach toward philosophy and communication in general. Yet that Plato sought to go beyond the Pythagoreans in the application of their ideas is clear from both what Aristotle tells us and from what Plato tells us himself when he writes:

> I am referring to the Pythagoreans, of whom I was just now proposing to enquire about harmony. For they too are in error, like the astronomers; they investigate the numbers of the harmonies which are heard, but they never attain to problems – that is to say, they never reach the natural harmonies of number, or reflect why some numbers are harmonious and others are not. (*Republic*, Book IV, 531)

A NEOPYTHAGOREAN
COMMUNICATION DOCTRINE?

I conclude by confidently stating that Pythagorean thought heavily influenced Plato. It profoundly affected the philosophical and communication models he presented in the *Phaedrus*, and many other post-387 BCE works. The concepts of an all-knowing soul, reincarnation, remembered knowledge, a transcendent truth that exists as Forms, a mathematical etiology of the Forms themselves . . . all of these ideas have a Pythagorean basis. These concepts gave Plato some weapons to use against the sophists in his unending search for absolutes. For now, the truth could be revealed through recollection, and it was fixed and accessed by examining the absolutes of mathematically based Forms. And mathematics was to offer Plato the possibility of communicating ideas in a fashion that was not burdened by many of the ambiguities of language.

Plato set out to bridge the gap between the immutable number and the ambiguous word and, through their mixture, to be able to define the Forms by their corresponding Idea-numbers. Through the steady modification of Pythagorean dogma, he was to come up with the outlines of a methodology for communicating intended meaning that went beyond the dialectic in its scope. But we only have a single example of this methodology's workings, for nothing else has been handed down to us. We also read references to Plato's later unwritten doctrines,[18] the possible equivalents of the lost Pythagorean *agrapha dogmata*. These doctrines became the subject of much discussion and research at the Academy,[19] but this is not germane to our study.

So, let me now examine the single example of how Plato applied his methodology to a practical problem: his lifelong search for the ultimate definition of *Good*. In the *Republic*, Plato's definition of *Good* had been "that which imparts truth to the known, and the power of knowing to the knower (508b)." However, by the latter part of his life, this definition evolved into a semi-mathematical expression which implies that the *Good* is associated with the Form of *One* because it is the *One* that gives rise to existence.[20] The One is the crucial Limiter that "participates" with the Indefinite Dyad (the Unlimiteds; e.g., the great or small, more or less, etc.) to give rise to the universe in which we dwell.[21]

It is not clear from the available information exactly how the other Forms (e.g., beauty, virtue, etc.) evolved in Plato's scheme, but we know these Forms could be expressed as Idea-numbers. And we also know that although the Forms produce all the concepts and objects we can perceive, they are not altered or destroyed in the process. The Forms thus act as creational enzymes while remaining immutable in their metaphysical realm. They participate with various parts of the indefinite dyad, but, as Plato writes in the *Timaeus* (52a), they "went not forth." So it is no wonder that words alone can never describe those absolutes that we find in the Forms, for the Forms are fundamentally mathematical entities.

DISCUSSION

So where does all this lead for those of us who are interested in communication and philosophy? It leads to the place where humanity finds itself today. On one extreme, we have the "number-people" (engineers, physicists, mathematicians, etc.) who tell us that there appear to be at least some absolutes, which can be communicated in an unambiguous language that is neither subjective nor reducible. Hence American, Chinese, and Russian scientists can all calculate with great precision where a missile will land by employing the same terms, and the predicted place is where the missile will indeed land. Opposed to these people, we have the extreme deconstructionists and linguistic relativists, those intellectual offspring of the sophists Gorgias and Protagoras. These people contend that all meaning is subjective and relative and that the truth is whatever one makes it.

Most people find themselves somewhere in the middle of this dichotomy, slightly favoring one side or the other. It is not easy to concede to the "numbers-people" because then communication would be bound up in esoteric mathematical formulae that few of us can ever envision using as a practical tool of communication or persuasion. I suppose true *Love* may equal *Two-plus*, but the proof involved in creating this conclusion would take several pages to detail. Even then, it would only have meaning if the masses understood and accepted it. However, if we turn entirely away from the mathematically oriented absolutists and conclude that communication is subjective and relative, our teaching task becomes ethically suspect and logistically impossible. The Holocaust becomes rhetorically reducible, not absolutely horrible, and the expedience of Reagan's "neat idea" becomes an acceptable norm and not a reprehensible exception.

Plato's Idea-number scheme earned the scorn of Aristotle,[22] and many scholars continue to dismiss his Theory of Forms as an unworkable pie-in-the-sky ideal, especially concerning communication. Yet perhaps we're being a bit hasty. The standard for beauty is now widely expressed as a perfect "10", and we all would like to be "4.0" students. We would like to be "4.2" running backs or ".350" hitters or perhaps "six-figure" income earners. And God forbid if we should be looked upon as "zeros" or ever forget to file by "4–15". And we cannot deny that poll numbers move our attitudes, that we'd all like to have cars that get 50 miles per gallon, or that having an IQ above 140 is a good thing. Indeed, we see Plato's notion about applying numbers to ideas evolving in ways that its creator probably did not envision. Indeed, I have begun a foray into cognitive psychology and neuropsychology, and here we find words and numbers thoroughly integrated. Thus, probability metrics are commonly used to prove a given statement's relative validity. Yes, these Idea-numbers even creep into our everyday rhetoric, as in, "We're number one!"

We may not be so far away from Plato's ideal after all. In fact, we appear to be evolving a mode of communication that includes mathematically divined value precepts that specify our existing word-definition dichotomies. Thus a doctor asks us how we feel, and we reply, "On a scale of one to ten, I feel three-and-a-half," while a political leader informs an opponent, "There's a hundred-percent chance of war if any of your nation's forces cross the 49th parallel." The mechanistic underpinning of this approach to language and rhetoric cannot be examined in this chapter, but the idea may be worth pursuing by both number and word people alike; for maybe the truth does reside in the middle, like the Idea-number concept itself.

NOTES

1. That Plato held this "house of cards" view about language is clearly detailed in the *Seventh Letter* (342b). Plato writes of words and definitions:

    > We say also that a name is not a thing of permanence for any of them, and that nothing prevents the things now called round from being called round; so for those who make changes and call things by their opposite names, nothing will be less permanent [than a name]. Again, with regard to the definition, if it is made up of names and verbal forms, the same remark holds that there is no sufficiently durable permanence in it.

2. For an analysis of Gorgias' argument, see W. K. C. Guthrie's *The Sophists*, pages 197–200.
3. See *The Seventh Letter*, 343. Plato writes this in the context of the efficacy of the fifth element he lists for achieving meaning. We have the name, definition, representation, knowledge, and a grasp of the Form (which Plato aligns with understanding). But even if one acquires an accurate account of the Form, a clever rhetor can reduce any opponent to the appearance of foolishness.
4. *Phaedrus*, 277.
5. Ibid., 271.

6. Ibid., 247–257

7. For an excellent potted history of Plato's life, refer to R. S. Bluck's *Plato's Life and Thought*, pages 15–46 and 117–151. G. M. A. Grube's *Plato's Thought* is also helpful, especially the *'Biographical Essay'* on pages 307–319.

8. The Socratic question has long plagued researchers who examine Plato's thought. Diogenes Laertius (3.6) states that Plato became Socrates' "hearer" when he was 20 years old in about 407 BCE. He thus had at least eight years of direct influence under his mentor (who was killed in 399 BCE) but possibly more. Socrates was a long-time friend and teacher to Plato's relatives Charmides and Critias, and it is quite possible that Plato knew him, or at least knew of him, during his youth. But despite Plato's familiarity with his mentor, we are presented with serious problems if we assume that Socrates is the same man Plato portrays in his dialogues. For instance, in Plato's *Phaedo*, Socrates is described as a man who believes in reincarnation, that knowledge is derived by a recollection of the soul's prior experiences, and finally, that there is

> an absolute beauty, and goodness, and an absolute essence of all things; and if to this, which is now discovered to have existed in our former state, we refer all our sensations, and with this compare them, finding these ideas to be pre-existent and our inborn possession – then our souls must have had a prior existence.

We can see the roots of the rhetorical scheme Plato presents in the *Phaedrus*, but this Socrates is far different from the relatively agnostic man we see in the *Apology*. This is because the *Apology* is a much earlier work, a work that was written before Plato made his trip to Italy in 387 BCE. The *Phaedo* is a latter work (circa 385 BCE), and it clearly reflects Pythagorean influences, although these are not explicitly attributed. Socrates thus says:

> This theory has and always has had a remarkable hold on me, that our soul is a kind of attunement, and when it was formulated it reminded me, so to speak, that I myself formerly came to hold this view. (*Phaedo*, 88D)

We have here an application of ideas to Socrates that are essentially non-Socratic according to Guthrie (see pages 29–34 of Guthrie's *Socrates*). But one could also surmise that Socrates' long-time friends Simmias and Cebes, who had both been taught by the Pythagorean Philolaus, also influenced the development of Socrates' purported views on reincarnation and the nature of the soul that appears in the *Phaedo*. There are sharply divided opinions on this subject.

Guthrie cites Sir Karl Popper as a researcher who thought Plato had betrayed Socrates and "foisted Pythagorean exclusiveness on him" (page 95). But Winspear and Siverberg took the opposite approach. They felt Socrates had progressed from a humble and honest artisan to an elitist conservative under the influence of his wealthy friends (Alcibiades, among others). He naturally appropriated "the mystic divinities of the Pythagorean sects, the militant protective deities of international conservatism." Guthrie regards both extremes as indications of the "twisting and turning to which the evidence can be subjected" (page 95).

Guthrie contends there is "little evidence to connect him (Socrates) with Pythagorean or Orphic sectaries that practiced private rites, though he had friends among them." And after much research, this author agrees. We have no proof that Plato was inspired by Socrates to believe in Pythagorean ideals, and thus we cannot say that Socrates was the source of those Pythagorean ideals that found their way into Plato's beliefs. In fact, the available evidence clearly indicates that after Plato's trip to Tarentum, Pythagorean ideas were indeed foisted upon his later version of Socrates.

9. An interesting paradox in *Protagoras* deserves note because it demonstrates the difficulties one can arrive at when seeking definitions. The dialogue begins with Protagoras claiming that virtue can be taught, which Socrates directly opposes. But by the end of the discussion, Socrates has defined virtue as a type of knowledge, which, by inference, must therefore be teachable! Concomitantly, Protagoras strives to prove that virtue is anything but knowledge in the Socratic sense, although it is teachable. Ergo, how can one teach something which isn't knowledge or not teach something that is?

10. Bluck cites unnamed "Alexandrians" who claimed that Plato went to Italy to study under the Pythagoreans Philolaus and Eurytus, but I have been unable to substantiate this. In any case, Philolaus would have been around 80 years old by the time Plato arrived, if he was alive at all, so it is much more likely that Plato gleaned his Pythagorean insights from Archytas. See page 26 of Bluck's *Plato's Life and Thought*.

11. Plato's life became very hectic soon after visiting Archytas. After leaving Italy, Plato went to Syracuse in Sicily and attended the court of Dionysius I. There he met Dion and the younger Dionysius. Plato angered Dionysius I and was sold by him into slavery. However, he managed to be bought by his friends and returned to Athens by 386.

12. See Xenophanes, Fragment 7.

13. See pages 236–238 of Kirk and Raven's *The Presocratic Philosophers*.

14. Kirk and Raven add that Porphyrius omitted to mention the originality of Pythagorean ideas concerning numbers and harmony, but Kirk and Raven agree with the rest of his list. See page 238 of *The Presocratic Philosophers*.

15. Many of Plato's contemporaries and near contemporaries claimed that Plato plagiarized various Pythagorean works. Diogenes is perhaps the most specific:

> Philolaus of Croton, a Pythagorean. It was from him that Plato, in a letter, told Dion to buy the Pythagorean books . . . He wrote one book. (Hermippus says that

according to one writer, the philosopher Plato went to Sicily, to the court of Dionysius, bought this book from Philolaos' relatives for 40 Alexandrian minae, and from it copied out the *Timaeus*. Others say that Plato acquired the book by securing from Dionysius the release from prison of a young man who had been one of Philolaus' pupils). (Diogenes Laertius, VIII, 84)

Aristoxenus, a non-Pythagorean student of Aristotle's born in Tarentum, might have served as a source for Timon of Philus' contention that Plato plagiarized Pythagorean sources when he wrote the *Timaeus*. See J.A. Philip's *Pythagoras and Early Pythagoreanism*, pages 13–14. Burkert notes that Timon reportedly admonished Plato by saying, "Much silver hast thou spent for one small book, from which thou then Timaeus learned to write." See Walter Burkert's *Lore and Science in Ancient Pythagoreanism*, page 226.

16. The Pythagorean Iambicus gives us an example of the order of importance words were given relative to numbers by Pythagoreans in the following passage. But we must use discretion here. Iambicus, a Pythagorean of the fourth century CE, could have been affected by Platonic thought:

What is the oracle at Delphi? The tetractys: which is the harmonia in which the sirens sing . . . What is the wisest [thing]? Number; but second, the man who assigned names to things. (Iamblicus, *Vita Pythagorae*, 82)

17. One can cite many examples of Pythagorean perfect numbers and number theory in several of Plato's works. In the *Timaeus*, we find a veritable blizzard of numbers (35b–36b) that purport to demonstrate the division of sameness, difference, and existence. See Ernest G. McClain's *The Pythagorean Plato, Prelude to the Song Itself* for details and other Platonic references to ideal numbers and harmonies. This book is highly technical and very speculative.

The only reference to the *Phaedrus* in McClain's book is in a small note on page 179 that concerns the "'Plain of Truth' and Zeus 'leading the host of heaven marshaled in eleven companies' (247a)." McClain contends that 11 tones are the maximum an octave can be divided into without disharmony. Thus "Hestia, wife of Zeus, must stay home to 'mind the hearth' because her presence would upset the balance." McClain contends that "this is possibly because Platonic wives coincide with their husbands as octave doubles," whatever that means.

One can see from this example just how difficult it is to interpret the precise meanings of the mathematical implications found in Plato's works. He did not leave us his research, and we are left with attempts like McClain's to make sense of the mathematical information scattered throughout Plato's later dialogues.

18. Aristotle, among others, made references to Plato's unwritten doctrines, including:

This is why Plato in the *Timaeus* says that matter and space are the same; for the "participant" and space are identical. (It is true, indeed, that the account he gives there of the "participant" is different from what he says in his so-called "unwritten teaching." Nevertheless, he did identify place and space.) (*Physics*, 209b15)

19. Plato's students Speusippus and Xenocrates sought to expand on their master's concepts, although both believed that numbers were related to Forms. Speusippus did not recognize the existence of ideas/Forms, but only numbers, while Xenocrates took a more geometrical approach. He sought to explain the three dimensions of the universe by equating the point with one, the line with two, all planer surfaces with three, and multi-planer objects (i.e., a pyramid) with four. This work went beyond the Platonic use of Pythagorean number theory, although it was clearly derivative from these sources. One could contend that philosophy's turn toward symbolic logic has a Pythagorean etiology, but that is a subject for another paper. See J.A. Philip's *Pythagoras and Early Pythagoreanism*, pages 10–13, 96, 101–104.

20. The account of the Good that is presented in this article is very simplified. For a more detailed version of Plato's lecture on the Good, refer to Burkert's *Lore and Science in Ancient Pythagoreanism*, pages 15–28. In footnote 16 (page 18), Burkert provides a general account that Aristoxenus reports he heard from Aristotle about Plato's lecture. Aristoxenus

said that Plato's *logoi* had to do "with mathematics, numbers, geometry, astronomy, and, finally, that the Good is a single" (*Harmony*, 2, page 30M). For a more comprehensive account, refer to Simplicius' *Physics* (151.13ff.) or Alexander of Aphrodisias' *Metaphysics* (55.20).

21. We note here that some of Plato's definition of the Good appears to have been derived from the Pythagorean Table of Contraries (see Aristotle's *Metaphysics*, 986a22). This table is outlined below. The Odd, associated with One, is also identified with Limit, Unity, and Good in the Pythagorean scheme. So, Plato's association of the One and the Good, and the One with that which gives rise to the Forms by intersecting the indefinite dyad (the Unlimited) appears to be etiologically related to both Pythagorean number theory and their Table of Contraries:

> Limit-Unlimited
> Odd-Even
> Unity-Plurality
> Right-Left
> Male-Female
> Rest-Motion
> Straight-Crooked
> Light-Darkness
> Good-Bad
> Square-Oblong

22. For details of Aristotle's frequent, and sometimes dubious, attacks on Plato's Theory of Ideas, see *Metaphysics*, 987b18–25, 991b9, 992b16, 1073a18, 1081a7, 1083a18, 1084a7. Aristotle's main point appears that Plato need not have postulated a Noumenal or Transcendental realm for the Forms distinct from our own. He also had difficulty accepting Plato's concept of absolutes because they do not admit degrees (i.e., degrees of Goodness). Yet a further problem he noted was how an absolute can be applied to different categories of things, such as a good horse, house, or idea. The above citations contain numerous sound and unsound attacks on Plato's Theory of Ideas.

PARTIAL LIST OF SOURCES

Adler, M. J., *Aristotle, in Great Books of the Western World, Volume 8*, translated by Ross, W. D., Encyclopedia Britannica, Chicago, Illinois, 1952

Adler, M. J., *Plato, in Great Books of the Western World, Volume 7*, translated by Jowett, B., Encyclopedia Britannica, Chicago, Illinois, 1952

Bluck, R. S., *Plato's Life and Thought*, Routledge & Kegan Paul, London, UK, 1949

Burkert, W., *Lore and Science in Ancient Pythagoreanism*, Harvard University Press, Cambridge, Massachusetts, 1972

Cherniss, H., *Aristotle's Criticism of Plato and the Academy*, Russell & Russell, New York, N.Y., 1962

Cornford, F. M., *Principium Sapientiae, The Origins of Greek Philosophical Thought*, Cambridge University Press, Cambridge, UK, 1952

Findlay, J. N., *Plato and Platonism, An Introduction*, New York Times Book Company, New York, N.Y., 1978

Grube, G. M. A., *Plato's Thoughts*, Hackett Publishing Company, Indianapolis, Indiana, 1980

Guthrie, W. K. C., *Socrates*, Cambridge University Press, New York, N.Y., 1990

Guthrie, W. K. C., *The Sophists*, Cambridge University Press, New York, N.Y., 1990

Kirk, G. S., Raven, J. E., and Schofield, M., *The Presocratic Philosophers*, Cambridge University Press, New York, N.Y., 1990

McClain, E. G., *The Pythagorean Plato, Prelude to the Song Itself*, Nicolas-Hays, York Beach, Maine, 1984

O'Meara, D. J., *Pythagoras Revived, Mathematics and Philosophy in Late Antiquity*, Clarendon Press, Oxford, UK, 1989

Philip, J. A., *Pythagoras, and Early Pythagoreanism*, University of Toronto Press, Toronto, Canada, 1968

58

Ramblings on Being and Thought

This chapter seeks to share some disjointed thoughts about our existence before they fade into nothingness, as has become my recent tendency. Hopefully, the work summarizes and simplifies a great deal of research discussed above while allowing me to explore some remaining topics without reinventing the wheel. If these ramblings are not your cup of tea, please *movere liberum*. I have tried to keep the issues as basic as possible, perhaps to the extent that various points may lack support or are nonsensical. If you see any of that going on, please amend this piece as you see fit. It will always be a work in progress.

Let us examine the possibility that some plan or rationality helps give rise to existence: call it a logos of being. Some folks may prefer the term "intelligent design," but I am not so keen on this notion. Some things are simply because they can be, and others exist via the agency of willful manipulation. I am willing to concede that both possibilities are in play, with our ongoing thoughts being a form of intentional manipulation upon a process we are bound to. These areas need not concern us right now. The most straightforward proof that various organizing principles (OPs) underlie, drive, and/or sustain creation is that we can discern some of them via abstract thought and experimentation, at least in part. Thus, Einstein discovered E=mc2, a line of thinking that has allowed us to predict and understand spacetime phenomena in ways we never did before. In effect, Einstein proposed ideas regarding energy and mass OPs and sought to find the means to prove or disprove their viability. We see this approach in the formulaic machinations involved in studying particle physics, special relativity, and related endeavors.

Some more profound questions involve the nature of these principles, such as can they exist distinct from corporeal existence? Indeed, can an organizing principle exist if there are no sentient lifeforms to demonstrate its machinations? If so, what is the nature of that existence? For example, do/did these organizational principles have a presence sans the Big Bang? However, without time, space, matter, and energy, one is in a quandary as to divine how any OP could be manifest or become manifest. Moreover, the hackneyed adage that they evolved or exist simply because they can do so is a slim foundation upon which to base any inquiry. That opinion is an act of faith, but we shall revisit it as time unfolds.

The OPs we find related to existence have purposes, inter-relationships, directions, and an underlying logic regardless of their etiologies or distinct natures. For example, it is self-evident that material, energetic, biochemical, genetic, and other OPs are involved in the eventual evolution of species that can come to grasp how they were/are created, as humanity is slowly seeking to discover and prove. However, this still begs the many "why" and "how" questions. Indeed, we haven't even formulated a viable realm for our OPs to "be within" sans the Big Bang, let alone discern how they participate in what some dub "reality."

Was the reality we perceive the result of random processes, as in a spontaneous perturbation that infiltrated the absence of all things and, in so doing, gave rise to this particular universe? Perhaps, but for such a perturbation and its subsequent organizational properties to come into being, the potential for it to do so must exist or become manifest in some form. We are talking about the prime mover here, as in the seminal source of what we currently are. Is the state of that source physical or metaphysical? Where and how does the potential for existence reside if not in being itself? As Plato's Socrates surmised, could there be a realm of seminal ideas/Forms?

Let me do a very brief recap. As you will recall, Plato and many Pythagoreans surmised there must be a transcendental realm beyond time, space, and all the energetic and physical machinations that are part and parcel of our dynamic universe. Herein, eternal, perfect, and unchanging ideas exist that Plato and others dubbed "Forms." There could thus be the flawless metaphysical Form of a sphere that serves as a progenitor exemplar for all the spheres that subsequently come into being in the material realm. The physical renditions of the Forms will be imperfect in detail and subject to change, but not so their progenitors. The same is true for the Forms of love, cube, one, addition, and all other things. In theory, these Forms somehow "participate" with material existence as seminal elements, although the precise mechanisms underlying this participation are difficult to discern. The extant descriptions of the underpinnings involved are only vaguely and incompletely detailed in semi-mathematical terms.

Clearly, organizational properties are involved in the proposed participation process, but how Forms from a timeless metaphysical state participate with anything in the secular realm of being is unclear. Furthermore, why create an ethereal realm that serves as an ideational heaven . . . if not heaven itself? Indeed, some may contend that the realm of Forms could be the mind of God. I think it is more likely that parts of God's mind will be found within the person reading these words and contemplating this subject. After all, how can an eternal and immutable Form interact with elements of a universe in constant flux? As we have seen, it was surmised that mathematics and geometry are involved, but the mechanistic underpinnings remained rationalistic endeavors that lacked what we would call rigorous formal proofs. Nonetheless, the Pythagoreans believed that, at their core, all objects are composed of numbers and that all distinguishing properties, causes, and effects can be expressed via mathematics. To them, the link between creation and being was purely mathematical and geometric.

The apparent disjuncture between the concept of eternal and unchanging Forms participating in a universe of constant change vexed many great thinkers. As we have seen, Aristotle dismissed the notion of transcendental Forms altogether. Instead, he placed the potential for all things within our universe's material, energetic, and metaphysical aspects. Ergo, the potential for a spear, pot, or any other metal object resides within the metal itself. We, presumably sentient creatures, apply thought and hand to the material and energetic aspects of existence and thus give presence to its inherent possibilities. Therefore, thought and existence walk hand-in-hand, although which came first, if either, is a conundrum. I find comfort in this notion and tend to be more of an Aristotelian than a Platonist.

However, Aristotle had no mechanism to explain how potential could exist given the absence of everything before event one unfolded, albeit a question that still plagues us today. Furthermore, once existence became manifest, how could potential alone lead to the subsequent development of beings like us? In short, how can all possibilities be born of nothing? Some postulate the machinations of an omniscient and omnipotent God. Still, others maintain that all things can be derived from nothing except possibility . . . assuming that possibility and potential do not need any form of ideational being or residence to become manifest. Indeed, the spontaneous creation of the universe from nothingness is the latest rave, although the proofs remind me of Pythagorean dogma writ in modern terms. As for me, I look toward the realm of organizing principles. However, I cannot quite wrap my mind around where OPs could reside outside of being incarnate. Indeed, where could the probable exist sans existence?

Let us briefly and superficially examine a few evolutionary factors as they may relate to some of the organizing principles accessible to thought. Perhaps such a foray will offer us some insights into where they reside. We will begin with inorganic OPs, the machinations of which are slowly being revealed by theoretical physicists. This is the realm of particle physics, string theory, and related endeavors. Interestingly, the processes sustaining the creation and interactions of subatomic particles and atoms may be indistinguishable from the material and metaphysical aspects of beings that eventually become capable of discerning them.

However, let us make an artificial distinction and limit this class of OPs to subatomic and basic atomic structures. Via experiments and formulaic proofs, we have slowly deduced the existence of OPs that lead to the evolution of atoms from energy via the machinations of fermions and bosons. Fermions consist of quarks, leptons, gravitons, particles predicted by super-symmetric theories, other hypothetical bosons and fermions, and other hypothetical elementary particles. Bosons are elementary particles with properties and capacities that are distinct from fermions. For example, some dedicated bosons act as energy carriers that create attractants (e.g., gluons – strong force) and other forces (e.g., photons – electromagnetism) between various particles that are needed to form matter. It has thus been found that the long-sought Higgs boson gives rise to the phenomenon of mass.

Some bosons (e.g., mesons) are composed of tiny particles, the sum of which provides a given boson with distinct properties. Here we delve into how subatomic particles are transformed into protons, neutrons, and electrons, as well as the machinations and interactions of the four fundamental forces (gravity, electromagnetism, weak and strong nuclear forces) that are ubiquitous throughout the universe. Of course, some now say there may be a fifth force, although we needn't address this here. The result of all this activity is the creation of matter, space, time, and the essentials of being via the Big Bang. And don't fret: there will not be an exam on any of this. Instead, let's jump to the stage wherein simple matter exists (e.g., hydrogen and helium). Granted, these elements could not come into being for an estimated 380,000 years after the Big Bang because the universe's temperature was simply too great for atoms to hold on to their electrons. This heat requires space/time expansion to become reduced, which is fundamental to thermodynamics. However, we are assuming there was a Big Bang, but what if the causal impetus was something far less spectacular . . . like a tiny flaw that sprang into being simply because it could?

Yet let us assume a linear progression of energy to matter. With spacetime expansion and accompanying cooling, atoms came into being. Along the way, the simplest atoms formed massive clusters. The amalgamations came under gravity's influence, which sparked them into gigantic progenitor suns. These monster stars provided the heat and gravity conditions for more complicated atoms forged within their interiors. When these vast stars exhausted their fuel and went nova, their internal elements were dispersed throughout an expanding universe. The affiliated steps generated various molecules from these diverse elements, with the very structure of atoms instilling their capacity to join into distinct and interactive forms. Out of this molecular stew, organic chemistry percolates, the end machinations of which are the eventual development of DNA and life. Concomitant with all this activity is the evolution of planets and solar systems, with the detritus of progenitor stars producing the materials needed. Some of these worlds provide convenient homes for biological life to spring into being, with intelligence becoming manifest via the impetus of survival needs. The question is: where did the impetus and potential for life to exist "reside" before the seminal event(s) that created it? We may get back to this issue in a bit, but let us move on.

As I have discussed, biological intelligence includes communal and monadic forms. Examples of collective intelligence are found in many insect species, such as bees and ants. Here, survival behaviors slowly become genetically encoded and passed from generation to generation, creating extremely elaborate habitats and stimulus–response action and reaction strategies providing the ongoing and dynamic needs for survival, adaptation, and propagation. The development of monadic intelligence is based on the forging of experientially derived memories. A small smattering of genetic templates provides the essential instinctual capacities needed for survival (e.g., suckling responses). Monadic intelligence manifests in various species, although elements of collective intelligence often coexist with this capacity in some species (as in herding animals). Eventually, monadic species evolved that developed the ability to discern what created them via abstract reasoning and experimentation.

It is the search for the source of our creation that allows us to glimpse the various organizing principles that are in play in our universe, albeit a complex task. It is unclear how the metaphysical aspects of divining OPs interact with their existence or if there is any interaction at all. By some reasoning, the grasping of OPs comes well after their activities are in play. However, some of the ultimate OPs involve the machinations of space-time. One suspects that understanding and manipulating this area can remove temporal linearity as a limiting factor. In effect, can we become capable of participating in event one by eventually understanding how it works? Could that be one of our roles?

In theory, sentient beings can help direct the organizing principles that define our existence by uncovering how they work and manipulating the processes involved. Indeed, some may contend this path of discovery and application is our ultimate purpose.

One ponders if our ongoing thoughts and actions are the perturbations that help give rise to ourselves from nothingness. Does existence thus give rise to life forms that, through their metaphysical and experimental activities, help give rise to reality? Yes, we have come full circle, landing in a logical conundrum that only science, philosophy, and time can answer.

However, one surmises this seminal contemplative activity is hardly a product of biological intelligence alone. Biological monadic intelligence can eventually manipulate physical chemistry so that mechanical means of learning and behavior can be fashioned and inculcated within distinct inorganic monads. The inorganics can walk, talk, sing, dance, and even love. They can mirror biological monads but are gifted with immortality. Photonic elements can be added to their memory and behavioral matrices, providing inorganic intellects with a processing speed and applications that biological cognition cannot match.

The resultant intelligence is hardly artificial, although some will prefer to dub it as such. Inorganic monads that can learn, ponder, and formulate ideas and studies that may go well beyond those of their biological progenitors will be created. Their capacity to store memories is infinite, as are their life spans. These two factors could give inorganic monads a vital edge in acquiring insights into time-related OPs, especially if such studies involve energetic and other manipulations that biological monadic life forms cannot undertake. Indeed, cooperation between biological and inorganic monads may be the ultimate means by which the source of our being can be revealed and given presence. And let us not forget that collective species could also weigh into these processes.

Well, enough of this speculation. This piece is admittedly superficial and speculative, and I apologize for that. My approach in this chapter could be fleshed out into an entire book, but I cannot sustain such an effort. My memory is failing, and my judgment is erratic. However, I believe those reading these words can take the described ideas and perfect or reject them. My job is to present them while it is still possible, albeit it is no longer easy for me to do so. I ask for forgiveness for my limitations and lack of insight. We are all works in progress, and time has taught me that we do not work indefinitely . . . at least not yet. Amen.

Observation

[My editor noted the following after working on this chapter, some of which I disagree with. Nonetheless, I include it here as an article of faith.]

The reader might have come across this analogy: the theory of evolution is as likely as throwing a bomb into a printing press and all the volumes of the *Encyclopaedia Britannica* resulting! And what of the second law of thermodynamics – unguided evolution resulting in order out of chaos is *impossible*!

Something as simple as a cell needs a cell wall to hold the immense complexity within the cell together. How could all this complexity, with the cell wall in place first (!), each tiny part working seamlessly with every other part have resulted – over billions of years – *from random atoms* and with no outside Intelligence designing it?! And how could consciousness, which appreciates beauty, result from non-sentient slime?! And how could even the concept of beauty exist in a random universe? That complex forms could evolve randomly from chaos is simply a fairy story!

The only logical alternative, which *fits the facts* of the universe as we know them is "In the beginning, God created the heavens and the earth" (Genesis 1:1), and if the Bible is true and there's a day of judgment coming for each person who has ever lived on this planet, the reality of where a person will be for eternity is something we all should take very solemnly:

> And I saw the dead, small and great, standing before the throne, and books were opened. And another book was opened, which is the Book of Life. And the dead were judged according to their works, by the things which were written in the books. (Revelation 20:12)

(Eldo Barkhuizen, copy editor, Arrow Editorial: comment inserted at the author's request.)

PART VI

TIME
AND SPACE

59

Pondering the Past,
Present, and Future

In every life, there is a beginning, middle, and end, yet I find
myself wondering if our shared existence is really so linear. Yes,
we all *appear* to ride the arrow of time, that intricate chain of
cause-and-effect events that seems to flow in one direction only,
from past to future. Of course, we cannot experience the past
or future because we are ultimately bound to an ever-shifting
present (our now) that we can only manipulate to some degree.
In fact, several scientists opine that the past, present, and future
exist simultaneously, most often as a subjective illusion. As for
causality, if one believes it influences or controls the contextual
machinations of space, matter, energy, and time, then one must

also subscribe to the notion of a largely deterministic universe. Ergo, there is no such thing as free will because we are all carried within contextual flows that determine what will be at any given point within timespace.

In short, the story is already written, but we're just struggling to get through each word on the book's pages to find meaning and experience within the present. Moreover, that fleeting present/now essentially evaporates upon coming into being, morphing into the past before the future unfolds. These metaphors are fine and dandy, but I wonder if time works this way. Pure linearity would make the future inaccessible because it has not come to fruition. Yet why do some have portentous dreams that foretell events that become realities in days, weeks, or months after the premonition was experienced? I have had such dreams, and the odds are you, or someone you know, has also experienced them. In one of these portents, I was looking at the dismal grades I had gotten on my midterms, lamenting the scores and comments. Upon waking, I wrote down some scores and notes (71, 66, NO!), which ultimately matched what transpired on my exams. How did my and others' dreams access future pages in the book of being?

I believe thought can access future facts under the right conditions. We all experience regular and repeated events, such as attending church, a restaurant, and other activities. From these events, we build an experiential template that guides our expectations of what will happen during a following church service. These memory structures are called schemas in the literature and can be activated during dreams. If we are worried about our coming exams, an activated schema can indeed generate a dream state that plays out the possibilities. This can be applied to many future events, some of which nearly everyone has experienced. Yet I cannot explain why the exam scores were so precise in my case. I mean, there they were revealed in a dream, and to the exact point. To me, this implied that thought can indeed touch upon the future. But does this mean that future facts are predetermined?

No, I do not accept the proposal that causality and determinism are all guided by unfolding and interrelated contexts, making us like mere leaves at the mercy of a turbulent fall breeze. Indeed, where is imagination in all these relationships, as in the interactions of thought and being, the metaphysics of existence? Is not thought an impetus, one that is not always bound by causation or context alone? My dream touched upon the future, but could it have influenced it somehow? For example, a simple mud-and-thatch hut begins with a set of ideas, much like a mighty cathedral or the Theory of Relativity. Thoughts are applied to the present and morph into nearly anything possible in the present and future, including this article you are reading. Moreover, I cannot say causality and determinism alone dictated these lines, for where in their relationships is the impetus of intent, health factors, shifting moods, and serendipitous insights? Simply put, contemplating time produces more conundrums than answers because the influences of metaphysics are both profound and immeasurable.

Let us open our minds and ponder some fanciful possibilities, albeit we will stray far from current space/time ideas and research. I gaze up at distant stars on a cloudless night. Good imaging tools enable me to focus on a distant star and detect several planets orbiting the heavenly sphere. Looking deeper through more sophisticated devices, I eventually discover a world like ours, complete with puffy white clouds and azure seas. And if our machines are capable enough, I could detect the presence of cities and roads in this distant world, the evidence of a busy and advanced society. At the Nth degree of detail, I discern some beings gathered on the porch of a humble, bucolic abode in a small town.

My imaging devices allow me deftly to zoom in on them, and I note that their faces and bodies are similar to ours. These "people" exchange glances and facial expressions while their mouths open and close. The words cannot be heard, but after some time, I begin to grasp an occasional bit of meaning. I infer laughter and see gestures that emphasize what is being said. Soon, gender differences become evident while various sized and shaped people enter and leave the scene. I watch for hours while the action unfolds and slowly work out what is happening. This is a small family: a mated couple and two young children. Neighbors and friends come by for visits, and a bevy of details unfolds while I patiently watch from my distant perch. I frequently cannot quite tell what the children are doing because they move at a frenetic pace that challenges my tracking technology, leaving and entering the scene irregularly. Occasionally, they zip away and return on wheeled vehicles resembling bicycles with oversized tires.

Passing clouds briefly obscure my view, but changing light filters quickly solves the problem. Other imaging tools allow me to see inside the tiny home, albeit via distorted images primarily based on computerized extrapolations versus reflected light alone. I have recorded the events and will study them later. For now, I watch and ponder. A quiet moment occurs near sunset wherein the weary parents are alone and huddled close together on a weathered old couch. The children are safe inside the home, and here are Mom and Dad, locked in a tender embrace while sitting on the porch.

Suddenly, they both look up and gaze in my direction. I wonder if they are thinking about me while I ponder them, using imagination instead of computers and advanced imaging tools to gain insights. They smile and chat while looking into space, and I muse at the nature of our communion. Our presents have become intertwined while they ponder about alien life on other worlds, and we thus influence one another's thoughts and actions. However, the essential fact is that they are thousands of light-years away. Their time, relative to mine, came and went eons ago, although, from my distant perspective, their lives are still unfolding. I am seeing reflected light that has been traveling for several millennia. That light will continue to travel long after I am gone, and thus those far removed from my location could also tune in to the same scene I witnessed as the ongoing event unfolded. Indeed, they may even tune into me as I watch our distant couple. Moreover, what if these beings of the past are contemplating my present thoughts as I contemplate theirs? This is a question every stargazer should ask.

Our existence and lives are not entirely bound by time, space, matter, and energy alone. Instead, they are also linked by thought and imagination, the kind of imagination that allows us to examine possibilities and craft accounts such as this. In effect, we have operated within the constraints of the now to explore both the distant past and the future. Moreover, our thoughts are free and unconstrained to undertake these adventures, being influenced by experience and context but not fully controlled by them. The person reading these words is well and truly separated from me in many ways, yet we are conjoined at this instant via shared thoughts, some of which are in harmony. It is difficult to ponder the nature of these thoughts as they relate to time. Still, here we are, sharing ideas in our distinct present periods (nows) that can influence our perspectives despite everything that separates us in the physical and temporal senses.

One of the ideas I will share is that people do not die. They simply leave the scene; for, in having been, they will always be from one vantage point or another. Their countless physical effects, thoughts, and reflected energy will forever become part of the fabric that defines our being and existential context. Our ideational perspective allows us to see them again, sitting on that porch and exchanging glances and smiles. It may seem a threadbare exercise in rationalism that links us right now, especially if you have lost a loved one. Yet perhaps we should ponder how perspectives can connect all things, including those who have left life. They are simply in the past, which can be accessed via the agency of your or another person's present thoughts, like this moment we are now sharing. We need only ride the tides of thought and imagination to reach them. Ah, and if one genuinely wishes to ponder much grander possibilities, consider the perspective of what created us. Amen.

60

Linear Creatures

We are taught from childhood that everything has a starting point, action phase, and termination. This happy and predictable linear scheme appears to correlate with our observations and experiences. After all, B comes after A and before C. Moreover, events, stories, music, and everything else follow a predictable order. We are all raised to interpret our shared reality this way, but my madness has become such that the boundaries between past, present, and future are eroding. Honestly, I've never been comfortable separating the future from the present or the present from the past. Threads link them and run throughout. Some call these threads causation and temporality, but I find the logos used to support that notion unpersuasive. To be sure, I perceive being as a dynamic entity that simultaneously encompasses the past, present, and future, a grand linkage that we most commonly perceive and experience as a series of unique "now" moments. They can link one word or idea to another, albeit how long the process takes varies. One wonders what the smallest unit of time may be that defines a now. Clearly, terms such as "instantaneous" and "zeptosecond" (one trillionth of a billionth of a second) are less than satisfying.

Yes, perhaps I am deluded; madly believing that thought is one element that can transcend the boundaries between past, present, and future that many are content to accept as absolutes. Occasionally, I sense the presence of those who walked this earth in what some call the past and others call the future. The effect is most evident when I am alone and within the open expanses of nature, as in a foray I once undertook along a ridge on Mount Lebanon. Oh, it was a bitterly cold and snowy day. The trek was a mistake, and I soon felt the chill down to my bones. Indeed, I feared my toes were freezing, which came painfully close to being true.

While trudging alongside a frozen stream, I suddenly sensed the thoughts of a wrinkled, old woman. I envisioned her sitting on a straw-covered floor within a birch bark-coated hut. The walls were insulated with a thick layer of mud, capped by the snow-covered thatched roof. The lady was thus protected within the humble abode from nature's wrath, but cold knows no barriers. I could see the ties holding the sapling framework that supported the hut from within, and I soon noted its dark and smoky interior. A small fire surrounded by stones heats the middle of the living space, with clay pots and simple wooden furnishings providing some meager creature comforts. Baako shivers and tugs a tattered rawhide tunic close. A deer hide covers her shoulders while leggings and moccasins protect her legs and feet. Yet it has been bitterly cold for two moons, and soon the meager rations of nuts and berries will be gone. Indeed, it has been a long, hard winter, and she fears for her family.

Our minds become one while the scene unfolds. Baako's husband is old and feeble, yet Abooksigun is hunting with the other men, striving desperately to keep family and friends fed. Perhaps the party can bring down a dear, but anything at all would do, even a tiny rabbit. While the men are away, the women forage as best they can, carry and fill large water pots, and gather firewood. Even the children must help: those who can. I listen while she listens, the plaintive cries of a hungry granddaughter filling her ears. I see her daughter comfort the infant, but Ca's breasts have run dry due to an incessant lack of food. I feel Baako take in a slow, deep breath. She rises on unsteady legs and places a stout weathered limb on the fire. The supply of tinder seems adequate, but she knows it will not last.

Suddenly, I am watching snowflakes descend gently from high above. They coat the trees, bushes, and ground, but the surrounding beauty is not a great comfort. I shake off the snow accumulating on my back and breathe deeply. My front legs paw at the ice-cold coating that covers the forest's floor, seeking to find a bit of frosty fodder to placate my churning stomach. There are no verbal expressions as humans would recognize them, for what resides in a deer's mind? It is an unfamiliar place for me but not totally unfathomable. However, there are gnawing thoughts about the acute need for sustenance and the necessary means of obtaining it. We learned to dig through the snow from our mother and her kin. We take in some withered, brown grass and chew it slowly and thoroughly. Harsh experience taught us that eating frozen tufts too fast makes us sick and cold.

Ah, we hear approaching footsteps. We quickly glance up, and there is a familiar old buck. This interloper is known to us and disliked. I stamp my foot and snort a warning. We fought during the last rut, a brutal and long affair that left us both badly wounded. But this is no time to fight, and we both know it. We watch each other with wary eyes, and I note the big buck is limping badly. There's no threat here, so let us find more fodder. We uncover a tasty patch and return to foraging.

I blink and find myself beside a desiccated river bed adjacent to the shore of a shriveled reservoir. The relentless summer sun shimmers off the waves, and their lapping refrain is an all-too-rare melody in this dry and desolate land. It was once verdant and replete with life, everything from trout to snapping turtles. The records indicate many species once used this place as a waterhole, and perhaps this will be the year when we finally find some evidence of such a visit. Yes, that is my hope. However, the last drink taken here was long ago, and now one is lucky to even find a few insects. Still, there is beauty here, although the nearby skeletal remains of long-dead trees indicate poisonous trouble is lurking just beneath the water's surface.

It is uncomfortably warm and stuffy, and I am surprised to find myself encumbered by an environmental protection suit. Ah, now I remember. We are taking water samples, something we are tasked with every year. The GPS tells me where to go, and we have a long day ahead. I study my sample case. We seem swamped today, but I yearn to get back home. Exposure to ultraviolet light carries serious risks now that the ozone is depleted. However, my shelter's stout walls keep that and other threats away. There are no bird calls or animal signs, and I slowly survey the pale white skies and long-dead forest to detect anything living. Oh, I hate this job, but it has to be done. Besides, work of any kind is rare.

It has been the same story every year, but the Ministry of Environmental Affairs insists recovery is still possible. That is what we are told, with commercials pounding the idea of hope into our skeptical heads. After all, the human population was reduced by over 86 percent during the Great Die-Off. Things should get better . . . eventually. I look at my watch. We had better pick up the pace. I hope Jan is not late for the pickup, but she is usually dependable. It would be nice to collect some animal samples, although only a few insects have been found thus far today. We did much better last year. I ponder the following data site, hoping it will be more promising.

Instantly, I am in the minds of a young man and an old lady. They are reading these words, much like you. We are separated by what some call time and space, but our thoughts are linked. They ponder while reading, and I share their thoughts.

"This guy is just imagining all this," the boy says. "It's only a fantasy."

"Perhaps," the elderly lady replies. "But does that invalidate his point?"

"I'm not sure what the point is. This guy is all over the place. One moment he's an old lady in a hut, and the next, he's a freaking deer!"

"All life is linked," she says with a smile. "Whatever else may be true, we are most definitely linked with this writer for the moment. Perhaps we're even linked to others reading these lines. And it doesn't matter if that linkage resides in me, you, the readers, or the writer. It simply is."

The youth shakes his head and smiles.

"Are you claiming I can perceive the past and future?" the boy snorts. "Maybe I can imagine some things, but that doesn't make them realities!"

"Yet you were with that woman in the hut and understood her situation," the matron replied. "And we were all with the writer's thoughts, and he is far removed from us. I doubt he's even alive anymore."

"Lots of writers come and go," Jason replied. "Yeah, their words can put ideas and images in our minds. But they're only fantasies. They're not real! I cannot touch that old lady or be with that woman collecting samples."

"Yet you can be with them in your mind," she said. "They can be as real as you can perceive them. Contemplate the possibility of no past, present, or future; just your thoughts about them. Tell me, what are we doing now?"

"Well, that depends on how you define *now*!" Jason replied. "And please don't give this song-and-dance that *now* is just a thought!"

"Aren't thoughts real?" she asked.

"That isn't how reality works, Grandma!" Jason impatiently notes. "I hope for many things that never come true, like Mom and Dad being together. But that isn't going to happen."

"Do we need formal proof to delve into the past and future with our imagination?" she asks. "Will you forsake the potential we've discussed concerning the power of thought?"

"Yeah, yeah, yeah, and how thought can link us to everything," her grandson replies. "You're like this guy who confuses thoughts and beliefs with realities."

"Dear me, I always considered beliefs and thought to be real things," she said with a chuckle, "if you will excuse the pun."

"You know what I mean," Jason says, somewhat ashamed to have let himself be caught out by his grandmother.

"Of course I do," she said. "But beliefs can often lead us to things that cannot be fully proven until time reveals them to be true. Perhaps your mother and father will one day reconcile."

"The odds of a meteorite hitting us are better," Jason observed.

"Oh, but we have proof that rocks fall from above, Jason," she replied. "They have for eons and will do so in the future. Is that a reality?"

"Well, it's a probability," Jason replied. "But what is probable isn't real until . . ."

". . . time makes it that way," she replied while gently touching her grandson's face. "As for me, I'm content with the idea that the aspects of time flow into one another as in meandering currents within an infinite lake. It only requires our imaginations to perceive the flow."

"Don't expect to catch any fish there," Jason said with a smile. "Yet I'm sure you'll hook something."

"But of course, Jason," the matron replied. She smiled broadly and added, "Listen, my grandson, the future already was, and the past will be again with a tiny shift in perspective. Those listening to us swim in their distinct *nows* while reading this line, which is conjoined with the same eddy the writer used while writing this piece. This is part of what links us, Jason, yet there is so much more. Ponder the possibilities, and share your essential oneness with all things."

"And now you will tell me doing that is called living, Grandma," Jason predicted.

"No, I will tell you that to have ever been is to always be," she said.

"If I broaden my perspective enough," he observed.

"Amen," came the reply.

61

The Power of the Moment

Here I sit, wearing a big old grin from ear to ear. Loud music filters through my senses, with Mama Cass and company singing in perfect four-part harmony. Ah, flashes from 1968, or was it 1967? That was 50-odd years ago, or perhaps just a moment past. What could be better than this: a good glow, a few tasty munchies, and some great tunes? Life accords us with instances of pure bliss if we stop to notice them. That is when we are thankful for our present state of being and not dwelling on what needs to be done or what was done in the past. We're within the sublime power of the moment. Yes, this is a wonderful now, a gift of the present that has brought me bliss while I sing along with the tunes. I sit here, happily banging on the keyboard and

61.1 Listening to tunes can take you to places of joy

dwelling on the songs alone . . . "dream a little dream of me." Yeah, these are some excellent moments, indeed.

I hope those reading this chapter also find these precious moments, though it's not always easy. Reality can be a harsh taskmaster, such as bills, family stuff, job crap, health woes, and so on. On occasion, we need a break from all that noise. So here I am, smiling broadly and enjoying loud classic rock music. Oh, and it is sublime! I know the world is ablaze with unfathomable violence, the clashing of ideas and emotions punctuated by bombs, bullets, and bleating political phonies. Of course, there is also an endless parade of talking heads who tell us how we feel, what we think, and all the fears we ought to harbor. To be free of all that, just for a short while . . . Now, that's precious.

I thus took my mind for a walk this morning via the agency of some good herb and may do so for a few more hours. "Rainy

Days and Mondays," "Baby You're No Good," "Mama Mia," "Feel Like Making Love," and so on. It is ancient rock music that usually tells an easily understandable story that is wrapped around a melody. And the musicians and singers are top-shelf at what they do. Alas, we don't get too much of that with rap, an art form that folks like me can't appreciate. Disco was irritating, as were acid rock and punk. Country music often makes me want to chew my foot off, but there's no need to go on and on. We all have our preferences, our keys to the moment. Let those who like finding blissful moments while listening to tunes enter that happiness however they will. There aren't any rules to this game. So, fire up the engines and hit the road!

Ooohhh, "Hotel California"! That brings me back a long way. And now, "House of the Rising Sun"! Ah, my mind just brought past moments into the present again and lived experiences spark anew in this ongoing now we're sharing. I'm living in a dilapidated apartment across from the Durham, NH, post office, just beginning to transition into becoming a coach. I went from being a drug-addled, burned-out miscreant to a collegiate coach, the only job I ever loved. Memories, hundreds of old memories spark anew. That was when I was alive! All else was tinsel and duff. Life was the raunchy smell of perspiration and the loud clanging of weights! There are screams, yells, grunts, and groans, while heavy iron is being hefted. And one kid or another occasionally manages to do something he or she never did before. The athlete yells, "Yeeaaahhhh!" with all his might and gets high fives from peers. And I'm happy as hell. Those memories are another joy of the present moment, and it is where these tunes have led today.

Those coaching days are a great series of memories to touch upon. And as the quanta meld into one another, a concomitant flow of electrons activates more recollections, the reflection of stored sights, sounds, and meanings. There is Grady easily popping 325 pounds overhead, Paul is doing a 465 bench, and Lance just racked in a 315 clean. Worries about money, moving, and business affairs fall further into the background while this mind-walk continues. Everyday affairs need attention, but for now, "nothing really matters to me." Images of games pass by, at the moment being suddenly replaced by thoughts about Plato's metaphysical realm of perfect Forms.

That is an odd jump: from games to ancient philosophy. Now, we leap to Aristotle, the source of our scientific approach to examining the nature of reality. Sometimes, random activations occur while our minds ramble; thus, we travel far and wide, letting our thoughts take us where they will. Yet we often follow well-worn paths, with one set of memories sparking close associates. That's how memory usually works, with associational activations between X and Y being the norm. Too bad I am not more like that, but Plato insists on hanging out with us.

Plato was the idealist, contending there is a timeless domain wherein perfect concepts exist as discrete metaphysical entities called "Forms." We can touch upon these Forms' fundamental natures via the dialectic, but we can never fully realize their staid

61.2 Memories of the UNH weightroom and athletes frequently
come to Elder's mind

perfection in our material world of birth, decay, and constant change. The Forms reside within an ideational heaven that can only be glimpsed via thought. Nonetheless, the realm of Forms participates with reality as a progenitor, albeit somehow distinct from reality. No one quite understands how this process was supposed to work, but Pythagorean mathematical principles are supposedly involved. Aristotle thought the entire concept was crap and postulated that ideas and possibilities are intertwined and scattered throughout being. Thus, the potential for a spearhead resides within a piece of metal, with the thoughts of a blacksmith forging a usable reality from an ideational possibility. These were the intellectual seas I once swam in and rather enjoyed. But we have discussed all this many times. Regrettably, old men often repeat themselves.

Ah, but now there's the image of Billy during the U-Mass game! It was fourth and goal, and I could swear he was in! He definitely was! However, the official disagreed and thus ended a truly remarkable season. The wins and losses: how I hated that part of the job. In coach's heaven, there are green fields and open courts as far as one can see. The air is crisp and cool, with only a few fleeting clouds passing through an azure sky. The athletes are executing flawlessly and come jaunting on and off the field of play as one situation leads to another. The opponent is excellent, and it's a clean, challenging game. There's an intense competition wherein coaches and athletes are tested to the maximum. However, we're happy! The moment's success is the only thing that matters because no one knows the score or deigns to care. Hell, there isn't even a scoreboard!

And I know that while we're sharing these thoughts, your and my memories will fire. Our minds will walk far and wide together, despite the distance, time, and contexts that separate us. We're linked via thoughts, and those are threads that can take us to all places and times. Yes, these moments harbor freedom, bliss compounded with time. After all, time is all we have, for it allows all other things; even the vibrations of those energy strings that some bright lads believe support the fabric of our shared reality. Cat Stevens reminds me, "It's not time to make a change . . ." This takes me to chicken-and-egg paradoxes. And so, this web is spun over these passing moments. Your mind is linked with mine, and that is a unique form of sharing. It's where the reader and writer become one. Oh, but enough of this.

Please find a few moments of peace and set your mind to flight! Grab a good glow; by whatever means you desire, put on some of your favorite tunes, and let your mind roam hither and yon. Yeah, take your mind out for a long, happy walk. Leave the duff behind and ride on memory's wings, capturing some joy while the journey unfolds. As for me, lord knows where I'll land next! However, one thing's for sure: the tunes will be my guide. Happy sailing, my friends! We'll see you flying by and flying high. Amen!

62

On Allowing Time to Flow

Life provides countless joys, but circumstances can make finding them nearly impossible. When my mother died of pancreatic cancer, I felt only unremitting despair—a searing pain that
sometimes rends my soul. Scenes of green-colored exudates oozing from Mom's mouth plagued me for weeks, as did the sounds
of her death rattles while cancer devoured her life. When my wife
left me, there was an interminable sense of loss and emptiness,
the total collapse of what once seemed a reality. I searched for
photos and anything she had written for weeks, somehow thinking the artifacts could link me to her soul. The same is true of
any number of events, and I am sure this is the case with you
or someone you know. Memory is beautiful, but it can quickly

become a trap leading to ugly places that consume our precious present moments (nows).

The fundamental problem is that traumatic memories are easily activated, with one reason being that their recall threshold is significantly lowered. And once active, these terrible memories can readily become associated with ongoing events while new memories are formed. Thus, the fear we once felt during an assault can become related to even happy episodes, such as a birthday party. Not even the victim of this sad linkage can understand why. In short order, innumerable paths can evoke traumatic memories, and we become trapped in a web that can hold us for a lifetime. That is the essence of post-traumatic stress disorder (PTSD), for which no easy cures exist.

One tactic to ameliorate this problem is to build good memories while minimizing cues that evoke traumatic recalls. These cues may be expressions, sounds, contexts, and other things associated with the trauma. The difficulty here is that we may or may not be conscious of the cues, such as a room's color, a passing smell, or a particular sound. Psychotherapy can help because many do not comprehend what stimuli can set them off. Yet caution is due. Some therapists abuse methods of discerning trigger cues by implanting false memories, thus harming the patient. Such therapists deserve the worse that life can offer.

Another approach is to knowingly evoke the traumatic memory and then employ various means to break or weaken its association links. Many therapists use chemicals, eye movements, and other modes to sever the linkages that maintain traumatic memories. Some of these approaches are successful, but a certain percentage of people will be forever haunted by their trauma. Thus, the past infects the present, and an unhappy present only builds more associational links that can poison our futures. A terrible cycle feeds upon itself until a person is totally incapacitated.

I understood early on how memory can become a trap, and I used such rationalism to resist the rapidly growing links that were eating away at my soul. With every negative recall, I consciously strived to bring a precious pleasant memory to mind, like Mom making homemade bread in the kitchen. The smell, taste, and happiness helped me escape the trap, as did hundreds of other good memories. The same was the case with the loss of my wife, although that pain still remains. It has lessened over the years by the happy recall tactic, but there remains a deep wound within. Eventually, I understood that getting bound to any moment's emotional state, good or bad, is a terrible way to live. By definition, present moments morph into the past, as in our perception of time's flow. Yet, if we allow it, time can take us to places that help reduce pain, misery, and hopelessness.

Of course, the sources of our angst are often only a recall away, for memory enduringly records the past and can quickly bring it into the present. Yet the more we allow ourselves to experience the good life can offer, the greater our odds of finding reasons to be happy, or at least content. Watching a loved one suffer and die generates enough grief to make us question the very fabric of existence, and it is a pain most of us have known. Yet here we are, sharing these words and contemplating how they may or may not meet our needs and desires. In short, we have learned to muse again, laugh occasionally, and notice all the good things that friendship, family, and living well accords.

Yet some become completely bound to past traumas due to an event's unfathomable finality or sheer brutality. This often happens during wars, horrific accidents, untimely deaths, and the wanton deeds of those with sick hearts. These events can freeze us in place, forever binding us to a single, horrible moment. Every new and old memory becomes inextricably tied to the source of our misery, and we slowly weave a web that allows us no recourse or relief. This is PTSD at its worst, and escaping its clutches is no easy matter. Some simply cannot endure and duly trade their remaining days for sleep without waking. Others become reclusive, fleeing from family and friends lest they awaken the old demons dwelling within. They opt to live in the woods, tunnels, or any place they can find a safe haven that offers complete solitude. A few opt for chemical therapy, either self-administered or done through clinics. Lastly, some opt for electroconvulsive treatment, thus endangering all their memories to obliterate just a few. Yes, ECT can be risky because it can break numerous synaptic links, but it helps 80–85 percent of people with PTSD.

For me, the fleeting nature of life created an ideational bridge that helped carry me past many new and old woes. I accept that we are securely tethered to countless neuronal threads that influence our behavior, an intricate tapestry of experiential associations that wax and wane while life unfolds. They collectively define the course of our lives and our influences on the world we share. When we step back, we can finally see the picture we are part of, our essential oneness with being. The impetuses that can drive us toward this perception vary, but they often entail the capacity to imagine ourselves as we actually are in the now. The primary requirement is that we strive to see beyond the past, busy ourselves making new and good memories, and/or find a way to imagine a future where we can see ourselves smiling again. None of this is easy.

I am blessed to have felt death embrace me a couple of times. During these crises, I learned more about the nature of time, for my moments were rapidly running out. And I knew it! Yes, one can feel life slip-sliding away, or at least I did. My consciousness ebbed and flowed while my badly injured heart strived to sustain my life, much as in a dream. During moments of lucidity, I let go of fear, regret, sadness, and despair. I discerned how bound I was to the self and how absorbed I was with trivial thoughts and things. I kept drifting in and out of consciousness, comprehending occasional words. It was akin to being trapped within a vast, dark cavern. The words echoed, with only a few catching my fading awareness.

The primary thought I held on to was a powerful conviction that there is a common source for everything. Some call it karma. Some call it God. Some like the terms "science," "physics," and "mathematics." But no name accurately fits something that inculcates all these metaphysical constructs and so much more.

The source exists simply because it can, and I have yet to read any text that adequately describes something that is all things and thus no one thing. It is a sublime paradox, with our struggle to grasp its nature being a vital part of our purpose, our *raison d'être.*

I have sensed the source before in dreams, but hanging between life and death instilled a type of peace that cannot be fully described. I recall disjointed bits of excited conversation between doctors during one event. "Massive heart attack . . . Troponin levels 40 times normal . . . 100 percent blockage of the LAD . . . Time is heart tissue!" Yet there was no fear, no trepidation of any kind. Indeed, there was little pain, no nagging concerns, no regrets or sorrows. I was at peace, despite the grim situation. I was one with what created and sustains all that is, and that was comfort enough for me. Of course, the experience was not all that pleasant!

No doctor can explain how I managed to walk away from that event as well as I did, and there have been other events along the way that have led to this line you are reading. However, I know why I'm still here. It's to share words like this with you, although I'm a terrible writer. In my dying mind, I still grasped that there was much to do and that you would be reading this line one day. So, I held on, and God rekindled the remaining embers sustaining my life. In effect, my mission became my faith, and that faith is now with you.

Don't bind yourself to any moment, whether pure bliss or complete misery. Time will take you to new places IF you allow this to happen. It's not easy to brush away the tears and ignore the sorrow wrought by tragic events, but this is the only way to live life as it should be—unafraid, full of hope, and grateful to be alive. Now, if only I could break free from being a cranky old man! Well, hope springs eternal. Amen.

63

On Time: Part I

Time is a hideously complicated subject that I often oversimplify to the point of logical absurdities. I will also do so here, but we need an introductory primer to examine various views about time as they evolved. Our ancestors contemplated time's dynamics for millennia and well before written languages appeared. This is evident in the astronomical layouts of various Neolithic monuments and religious sites scattered hither and yon (e.g., Stonehenge, Nabta Playa, etc.). Aspects of these structures were often deliberately oriented toward star tracks and solar events heralding the solstice or other significant seasonal changes that demanded existential actions (e.g., planting crops, harvesting, etc.). Yet what time actually is was a far more perplexing conundrum than merely tracking its passage. Time was, and is, clearly related to changes in the seasons and the positions of celestial bodies, but what exactly is it?

To begin with, time appeared to be cyclic to many of our ancestors. This observation was anthropomorphized, which is the wont of people when they have no better explanatory tools. The Egyptians and others saw the passing of the regular day–night cycles in terms of the interactions of the nighttime/sky goddess Nut and the sun god Ra. I will not labor through the entire account, but Nut swallows the sun at night only to give the god Ra birth again every morning. One can easily see the reincarnation theme in play (e.g., rebirth or transmigration), as in the soul of a person or animal being repeatedly reborn in a never-ending cycle. This notion of reincarnation found favor in numerous religions and semi-religious teachings before and after the Egyptians (e.g., Hinduism, Buddhism, Jainism, Sikhism, and Orphism) and the philosophies espoused by various Greek and Ionian luminaries (Pherecydes, Pythagoras, Plato, Socrates). However, the Egyptians and many other ancients had more going for them than mere religiosity. They also had 365-day yearly time cycles and sundials to discern the time of day. In addition, they plotted the passing cycles of the sun, moon, and planets and applied them to planting, harvesting, and other existential needs. So, cyclic though it may be, time was quantifiable into discrete units.

The task of accurately measuring time was also pressing, although sundials and celestial objects offered some means to this end. However, what good is a sundial or stellar plot during prolonged overcast periods? The Greeks and others had long recognized that musical instruments and the cords they played vibrated at specific frequencies that bore a remarkably consistent relationship with one another. These ratios were systematically plumbed and subsequently related to the movements of visible celestial bodies and other objects. It was discovered that there is a special relationship between the pitch of a musical note and the length of the string that created it. From this observation arose the idea that mathematical and geometric machinations could express the metaphysical aspects of certain tones essential to the machinations of being. Indeed, an underlying vibratory harmonic was involved in the processes sustaining existence. Today, we would call these divine harmonics fundamental frequencies.

As for the ancients, many carefully studied the pattern of proportions they found in harmonics and carefully applied them to the observed periodicity found in celestial bodies such as the moon, sun, various planets, and certain stars. The many connections discovered were dubbed Golden Ratios, and from these, the basis of the Pythagorean *musica universalis*, music of the spheres, was formulated. These ratios continued being used and studied for centuries to examine the connections between time, motion, music, and astronomy, with Johannes Kepler finally distilling the whole into a workable scheme in his *Harmonices Mundi* (*Harmony of the Worlds*) in 1619. However, he and his progenitors viewed celestial harmonics not as actual music that could be played and heard but in the expressions of a harmony that only the soul could fully perceive.

The ancients deduced that time was integral to the processes sustaining our current concept of being. However, the conundrum of the relationships between the past, present (now), and future continued to be enigmatic, as it still remains. Clearly, the ancients regarded time as having distinct properties, as we can see in the mythopoetic accounts of the Fates (Moirai). They were anthropomorphized goddesses in the form of three primordial women who shared a single eye between them. Collectively, the Moirai spun the threads of destiny into a pattern that dictated the course all human lives would follow. The women were Clotho (the Spinner), Lachesis (the Allotter), and Atropos (the Inflexible). The Moirai inculcated the idea of the complete cycle of life, as in birth, life, and death. They would thus spin out a life (Clotho), draw out the path it would follow (Lachesis), and then cut (Atropos) the Thread of Life at a fixed time. Even the gods had to follow what the fates dictated, which has some critical implications for how the ancients viewed time.

At its core, the actions of the Fates can be seen as a contest between determinism and free will. For many of the ancients, free will was merely an illusion. One only believes that there are choices to be made while events unfold. In this view, everything that happens over time is preordained, fixed, and rigid. Thus, whatever is preordained will inevitably happen as time passes, and it is impossible to change our destinies. As the Rubaiyat of Omar Khayyam notes:

The Moving Finger writes; and, having writ,
Moves on: nor all thy Piety nor Wit
Shall lure it back to cancel half a Line,
Nor all thy Tears wash out a Word of it.

This general doctrine is known as fatalism, as in we are fated to experience what will be, and nothing can change it. Time merely allows what fate has dictated to become manifest. Five logical essentials collectively interact to support this perspective as it relates to the flow of time. Modern and ancient philosophers and logicians have spelled the assumptions out as follows:

(1) From our earthly human perspectives, we contemplate numerous (but finite) propositions about whatever may happen in the future, as in, "I will buy a house" or "I will not buy a house." These propositions are merely possibilities that exist in the present or at least in the possibilities we perceive.

(2) All propositions are either true or else false (*bivalence*), but they cannot be both at once.

(3) If there are indeed propositions that can only be true or false, it stands to reason that there is only a single fixed set of true propositions. These true propositions will collectively determine all that the future will bring. The false propositions will disappear as time unfolds.

(4) If a single set of true propositions correctly determines and predicts everything the future will bring, then whatever is fated is unavoidable.

(5) Therefore, whatever the future brings cannot be changed, and it is folly to try to do so. In effect, the book is already written, and time is only the turning of the pages.

Now, we may perceive that we have choices and decisions to make while time unfolds, but our course of action is, supposedly, already decided by fate. We thus make a choice in our present that was already chosen for us long ago. Indeed, the perception that we even have options is folly. Therefore, free will is merely a happy illusion, and what will be will be. This neat fatalistic scheme has some inherent and debatable assumptions, which we should briefly discuss.

To begin with, there is an underlying assumption that propositions about the future do not arise out of the probable and/or random processes of change. They already exist as preordained and sometimes contradictory possible outcomes, and they do not come into being or change due to shifting contexts. They simply are. Moreover, the relevant propositions represent every possible effect for which there can only be a true or false outcome (the *Principle of Bivalence* discussed above). Lastly, there is no known causal agency that can make a true premise false or a false premise true.

Well, some folks were, and are, having none of this. For example, why must there only be false or true outcomes for all propositional possibilities? Time alone reveals which propositions are true or false and not the propositions in and of themselves. Yet in the interim, propositions are neither true nor false but contingent on the passage of time to become manifest. For example, I will buy a car tomorrow is neither a fact nor a falsehood unless and until I buy the vehicle tomorrow.

For the time being, the proposition is *indeterminate* (yes, a third category . . . true, false, and indeterminate). Of course, when I buy a car tomorrow, the proposition becomes eternally true, and all other possibilities vanish. Ergo, how can something true have been indeterminate unless a change occurred? Thus, time can change the nature of premises, although a Fatalist would undoubtedly deny the existence of indeterminate propositions.

Nonetheless, the best argument against Fatalism is that the truth values assigned to propositions are transient and shift over time, the so-called *Open Future* Argument. In effect, some propositions operate within the context of the contingent, as in, *if* X happens over time, then Y will become true. For this scheme to work, the relationships between propositions must be delineated with context tags (e.g., timespace stamps). Now, *tense-assigned* propositions can be manifest in statements such as "I am buying a shirt." This is impermanent and indeterminate without the agency of time assigning it a true or false value, albeit one that cannot easily be related to other propositions.

A *tenseless* proposition does away with this conundrum. For example, "I will buy a shirt at Fat Hat Clothing Company in White River Junction, Vermont, on Wednesday, May 19, 2021, at 3:34 PM." This proposition is always true once it has transpired. Furthermore, the proposition has been given temporal and spatial coordinates that allow it to be related to other propositions that may be part of an ongoing context, such as, "I will drive my car to Fat Hat Clothing Company in White River Junction, Vermont, on Wednesday, May 19, 2021, at 3:10 PM." Running counter to this happy scheme is the notion that all is constantly in flux, and thus tensed propositions may be a better tool for discerning the truth as time reveals it.

As one can see, relating events to time, truth, and change is problematic when handed over to logicians. Some aspects of their schemes are counterintuitive, and we have barely brushed the surface of their many ideas. There are thousands of books on determinism versus an open future approach toward studying the machinations of time. I find little comfort in the rationalism employed, impressive though it is. So, let us examine how some ancient philosophers addressed the subject of time because their schemes, flawed though some were, are seminal in all that has followed. Furthermore, the ancients' minds were sharp, and their ideas have withstood the test of time, albeit often in forms they would not easily recognize. Amen.

64

On Time: Part II

Chapter 63 was a pain in the ass to write, and feel free to skip over this chapter if you've had enough pondering about time. I contemplated writing another chapter, discussing modern notions on the subject. However, I have been advised that this track may seem attractive to me, yet is torture and misery for some readers. So, I will probably cap our review of time here for now. But first, I need a snack. My glucose is running at 63, and the damn sensor is going nuts. It's now 2:30AM, and a ruptured disc won't let me sleep, wretched bitch that it is. Yeah, that's a pain that makes this current now miserable, so let me get my stuff together before we finish up on this subject. Sorry about the bitching.

Plato equates time with the course and motion of celestial bodies in the *Timaeus*, much like his Pythagorean counterparts did that we discussed in Part I. From this perspective, the actual movement of the planets and sun define time, and not merely the geometric relationships and numerical metrics that measure these movements. For Plato, time was an entity (Form) onto itself, something that is very distinct from our dynamic and shifting world of being and change. However, the Form of time can serve as a container for all the elements within its purview. This is a neat notion. The universe is contained within a vast bag of time, with the metaphysical Form of time itself being in a discrete and timeless realm.

Exactly how the participation occurs between the Form of time and our dynamic realm of being is not clearly spelled out in Plato's extant works. Still, we know that mathematical and geometrical principles and properties are involved. Some of these relationships were noted in Part I, as in guiding harmonics (e.g., *Music of the Spheres*). Clearly, having dynamic elements interact within the context of an absolute and unchanging Form such as time is very problematic. For example, suppose Plato's Forms, such as his notion of time, are forever fixed within their ideational realm. How, then, do they freely interact within a dynamic and changing universe wherein time, to all appearances, flows? In a nutshell, how can the eternal interact with a realm of constant and shifting changes?

Despite these problems, the most straightforward proof that time may be independent of corporeal existence is the possibility of time passing without any accompanying change. This can happen with numerous ideas, as in 2 + 2 always equaling 4 in planar math. However, escaping the changes time causes is complex in the material universe. For example, there is nothing within a perfect vacuum. If it is shielded from light, radiation, and all else, does time still unfold in this dark and vacant realm wherein changes are theoretically impossible? Yet how could we construct such a vacuum within a realm where material and energetic entities are pervasive? It is a vexing conundrum.

Moreover, let us suppose specific physical change processes can be sped up or slowed down by altering contexts. In this case, it stands to reason that the absolute nature of time is distinct from what we observe within this universe of shifting and interacting variables. Indeed, some very similar and/or identical things can happen earlier or later over time as we experience it, yet the Form of time itself supposedly remains unchanged. Ergo, time and our realm of being are distinct entities, or so the reasoning can go. Of course, Einstein would have much to say about this, but let us remain focused on the ancients.

Philosophers contend this idea of time being absolute is an aspect of Pythagorean thought writ large. Yet, for Plato, time is entirely independent of the actions and outcomes within our corporeal state of being. As noted, the incorporeal Form of *absolute time* exists within a metaphysical (noumenal) realm with other perfect and unchanging ideas. In modern times, *absolutism* and/ or *substantivalism* concerning time are in vogue for similar notions. Moreover, Plato was not alone in assigning a unique realm for time, for the idea also found later support from Newton and luminaries of his ilk. For Plato and Newton, absolute time exists distinct from the events and processes that transpire within it, much like a bag is separate from the items it holds. However, this is an incorporeal bag, a Form that can only be glimpsed, grasped, and shared via applied thought alone.

Aristotle found the entire notion absurd. Indeed, he was no fan of Platonic Forms or the transcendental realm they supposedly dwelled within. For him, the potential for all possible things resided within the universe of being itself, albeit that metaphysics is a crucial aspect of his existential approach. For example, the potential for a chair, desk, or cart resides within wooden material. The subsequent realization of the inherent possibilities found in a cord of wood is a byproduct of thought and action. Aristotle thus contended that time is most assuredly not independent of the activities, changes, and developments that transpire within its purview. Instead of absolute time, Aristotle and others postulated the notion of relative time. This idea is based on the premise that time is a product of the temporal relationships between events and processes. Thus, deducing the nature of time is wrought via examining movement and change as they relate to each other. This idea is often dubbed temporal *reductionism* or *relationism*.

The major problem for both absolutism and relationism has long been how each philosophy deals with observations concerning movement and spatial relationships as governed by time. For example, relationism entails a theory of motion wherein the movement of any object is relative to the location of something else. Yet if that something else is also in motion relative to another point, defining a relationship between these shifting entities can become exceptionally complex. Moreover, the spatial relationships between other objects also weigh into all this. Here we see inklings into the many time–space–motion conundrums currently occupying modern physicists.

For the ancients, their absolutist or relationist views on time and space had profound implications concerning how motion takes place. Absolutists embraced a theory of movement wherein absolute time and absolute space are related to absolute motion, whatever that is. Presumably, absolute motion is movement relative to absolute space and time, an area Newton struggled with mightily. This is no easy task. An absolutist must gauge how fast an object is moving relative to the surface it is upon and how fast the thing is genuinely moving, if at all, relative to absolute time and space.

At first, this seems like an absurd and pointless exercise. However, the forces of acceleration can be perceived at almost all speeds and in all directions, and this hints that something akin to absolute motion may be in play. Of course, inertia was not clearly understood for some time. In the meantime, many continued embracing the notion of time acting like an infinitely expandable bag that can contain all things, including space. As for where the bag itself resided, that happy notion referred back to the misty realm of Forms for some.

The relationists realized their ideas also had problems because time, space, and motion are all relative. This made measurement and predictions extremely complex until some constants were employed as comparators and cofactors (as in the speed of light). In the meantime, relationists such as Leibniz noted the logical inconsistencies in the absolutists' ideas. For example, the machinations of invisible and unobservable absolute time and space Forms make movement and other calculations inferential and, thus, very problematic. Let us briefly revisit the premise that there are examples of time passing sans change, such as found in a shielded vacuum . . . if such a thing could be created. As far as we can determine, perfect vacuums do not exist because sublimation and similar processes are ongoing. However, continuous changes can be accelerated or decreased by manipulating interacting variables. Yet here we are altering conditions that influence rates of change and not altering time itself as a process.

Aristotle appears to have recognized that his relational scheme involved assigning temporal and spatial coordinates, although he was stuck with the puzzle of change as it relates to time. For Aristotle, time and change are distinct entities, although he contends time depends on change. By definition, Aristotle argues, "time is the number of motion [change] in respect of the before and after" (*Physics IV. 10–14*). Aristotle also opined that time and motion are continuous processes, both definable by numbers. As for the present/now, that is a continually moving process that operates between the before and after and can be perceived by the soul alone, although it is not fully definable. From this perspective, time is a universal ordering principle within which any and all changes are related to one another, although time and change are independent.

Aristotle primarily separates time from change because he contends time is universal and operates as a constant. On the other hand, change oscillates by definition and includes deviations in magnitude (e.g., great and small) and rate (e.g., fast and slow), which are not considered time characteristics. Of course, Aristotle concedes that time can be, at least partially, defined by change, albeit this is a concession based on the popular but debatable notion that time is in play when, and only when, there is also change. For Aristotle, time *follows* change, and change follows magnitude, which makes both processes continuous in that magnitude is a dynamic and ongoing element. Here we see some possible circular reasoning in play, as in the premise time is continuous because change is also, and change is ongoing because magnitude is.

Aristotle details what he means by the before and after by relating them to time, change, and place. Place is accorded primacy (as in timespace coordinates), with the before and after in change being dependent on the before and after in place. Please recall that the before and after in change includes magnitude, distinguishing it from the before and after of time (ergo, time follows change, but in a different fashion). Some have seen this as specious reasoning, albeit schematically consistent.

Aristotle's account of time as being related to the numbering of change(s) is labored and assumptive. He tells us time is a countable number, although not a number we can count. Clearly, one cannot count the number of *nows* in terms we typically employ nor the divisions that separate one *now* from another. One thus supposes that Aristotle is alluding to a type of measurable order-ing principle. However, time's nature makes it a variety (kind) of numbers that we cannot count because it is continuous. These guys could think in maddening depth, making it challenging to keep up with their reasoning.

Nonetheless, Aristotle contends that time is a measure of change and is measurable by change. However, please remember that Aristotle does not always equate measuring with mathemat-ical counting. In effect, Aristotle is proposing that we employ a measurement system for time that is based on an integral unit of change, such as a particular frequency, vibration, or musical cord. Einstein found the speed of light to be such a measuring unit. Aristotle proposes that such a unit of change could be based on the revolution of the outermost sphere of the heavens. In that time is distinct from change, one may find it odd that Aristotle employs a measurement for change that is a metric based on an essentially dynamic process that unfolds over time.

As if to add to these complexities, Aristotle contends that there is but one and the same time in play for all simultaneous changes. Aristotle uses universal *nows* (presents) as a measur-ing tool, claiming that simultaneous changes are bounded by a singular pair of *nows*. Interestingly, Aristotle says that any given *now* can divide all the changes within it, which are minions. This fits nicely with the notion that time must be an order within which any given aspect of change is related to all other aspects of change. Hence, a singular *now* can accompany numerous chang-es throughout being.

Aristotle contends that earlier and later times and *nows* have similarities and differences. He concedes that earlier and later *nows* differ in details but are essentially the same in how they operate. This equates to the continuity of time within the sphere of shifting contexts. He uses a moving object to explain this observation. Here, a series of *nows* are applied to an object in motion. The essential point is that the moving object and much else is essentially the same from one *now* to the next, but space, location, and other variables differ slightly as time proceeds. In theory, the *now* itself does not move but is bounded by another *now*, and so on. In this sense, the *nows* are significantly the same in nature and are thus countable or measurable, albeit they may differ in some details.

It is of interest that Aristotle contends that time cannot possibly have had a beginning. He reasons there must be a period before the initial *now*. Yet for that first period to be counted, it must have occurred between an earlier and later period. This is a logical impossibility because it is incompatible with there being an initial first instant when time began. If something cannot be counted, it cannot be of time, according to Aristotle. Similarly, time can have no endpoint because there is no way of discerning any later point after the final *now*. Semantics can be logically restricting, but this reasoning is far more enjoyable than modern physics.

As with Plato, Aristotle believed that some things are not within the purview of time. Indeed, time can only be applied to finite things, the slaves of change. Eternal entities are not in time. However, Aristotle believed that entities outside of time can move, a markedly oxymoronic position. He argues in terms of process, contending that everlasting motion is part of the ongoing temporal order. This order has aspects that operate before, simultaneously, or after the changes observed between *nows*. Time does not change things outside its purview, although one is still in a quandary to explain how the eternal interacts with our ever-changing reality. Nonetheless, Aristotle regards time as being causal, except for the eternal.

Lastly, Aristotle discusses whether time would exist if there were no entities with souls (essentially sentient beings) to perceive it. He answers that time depends on the soul in ways that change does not. In other words, there would be no time if conscious life did not exist. However, there could still be change. In short, time is related to number, number is countable, and only entities with souls can count. Therefore, time cannot exist without beings that can count. And clearly, sans artificial intelligence, only sentient beings endowed with a soul can count. Of course, the implication is that folks like us give time an existence by trying to measure it. Alas, this chapter is proof of our folly, although please note that I also equate thought with the machinations of the universe.

Well, that is quite enough for now. I grow weary of this exercise, and it is bordering on becoming an academic treatise. I apologize for that. And this is only the beginning of the issues we CAN delve into regarding time, including Einstein and company. I will return to discussing time, but umpteen pages of disjointed and twisted prose are enough. Take from this what you want, and I hope one of the ideas you consider is the depth of thought our ancestors had at their disposal. They would have marveled at our technology and knowledge in general. However, regarding our depth of thought, they would probably find us seriously wanting. Yeah, I proved that point in this piece! Yet I had some modest fun while writing it, and I hope you survived reading the work. Some reviewers begged me not to write anything like this again. They had no time for it. Amen!

65

Spacetime

I will strive to make this brief and painless, but any discussion of time must include a chapter relating the subject to space. In fact, the physicists coined the term "spacetime" to denote one of their better ideas. Spacetime is a four-dimensional mathematical model wherein the three dimensions we use to deduce or describe the location of objects in space via X, Y, and Z coordinates are combined with the added dimension of time. The resultant four-dimensional spacetime manifold can be used to construct various diagrammatic models that are useful in examining the relativity of time and our perceptions of it. Newton was happy to assume the relationships between space and time were relatively planner in nature, as in an essentially flat universe. Einstein thought this notion was absurd, and his task became to prove it.

Einstein surmised that space and time were affected by the influence of gravity/mass dynamics, which was a significant departure from Newton. Indeed, Einstein's model of the universe predicted that gravity could even curve space, thus bending the path of light and compressing or stretching relative dimensions. This idea was confirmed during a solar eclipse wherein the light from a distant star was detected as having been curved by gravity. Yet confirmation did not make the notion of how the universe operates any more straightforward. Spacetime simply became the bag wherein everything within the universe resides, much like the Form Plato and Newton had surmised. The dimensions of this bag can be gleaned by assigning the speed of light to an intersecting point on a theoretical X, Y, and Z axis and then expanding its volume by the time that has passed since Event One (E1). Against this must be weighed the effects of mass/gravity, which impact our bag's shape and expansion rate. Yikes!

Many questions arise, such as: What is spacetime made of? Well, everything is the easy answer, but proving this isn't easy. The physicists speak in terms of the entanglement between distinct parts of spacetime. For example, gravity is a force that has an infinite range. Thus, a giant black hole located at one coordinate can profoundly impact the behavior of light and space at other locations that can be many light years away. Physicist Leonard Susskind noted, "The continuity and the connectivity of space owes its existence to quantum-mechanical entanglement." Entanglement begins at the beginning when all was primordial energy, packets of which interacted while the machinations of the Big Bang unfolded. Protons, elections, and a dizzying array of other subatomic particles became intertwined and thus entangled. Granted, the Big Bang provided an impetus that spread everything within its purview far apart, yet many of the attractant forces of entanglement remain in play, such as gravity. Moreover, these forces have an infinite range.

Einstein did not buy into the idea, speculating that merely trying to measure the influence of one particle would invariably and instantly influence the nature of its associate, regardless of the spacetime separating them. Thus, the notion of entanglement was dubious and unprovable. Indeed, Einstein dubbed the idea "spooky action at a distance." However, ongoing research has proven entanglement's existence in photons, electrons, and other objects. The idea is counterintuitive, and it inculcates the notion that all of being is tied together by threads that cannot be seen but exert a definite influence, as in gravity, thermodynamics, and a host of other forces and processes. If we imagine such a process in terms of the ongoing dynamics that give rise to our communication and thoughts, they are infinite in range. However, one wonders about their continuity. Oddly, we find ourselves at the soul's gateway, so perhaps we'd better go back a bit.

Many people regard space as being empty, but it certainly is not. Since E1, light, magnetism, gravity, and other forces and particles have infiltrated that growing bubble that describes our universe. Does the universe have a border? It cannot. By definition, the universe is the closed set of everything that includes itself. It does not expand into empty space. It allows space to exist while it expands, which is not empty given everything that has passed through space and becomes embedded within. Now, other universes may be doing their thing, but how they relate to us is impossible to ascertain at present. We exist within the spacetime context of our universe, but another universe may exist entirely separate from our own spacetime. The multiverse would present numerous barriers to cross, and we have yet to master the reality we are currently bound up within.

This is an admittedly superficial examination of a highly complex topic. It is sufficient if this chapter has given you some notions to ruminate on. However, I would much prefer it if you flesh out those parts of this piece that need it. The truth is in the details, although they are guarded by the devil, or so the saying goes. What a wonderful gift time is, abounding with infinite presents that change at every turn. Be of cheer, my friends. We may be connected by entanglements that link us to both each other and all that is. Of course, going to the boat dock brings that lesson to mind much more succinctly than doing a survey of physics. Amen.

PART VII

LOVE

66

Pursuing an Ideal

If the universe smiles on us, we become blessed enough to find love. Of course, most know the love of a mother, father, and siblings, but there is also the kind of love one discovers with someone beyond the family. The latter is often the most problematic in many ways, although there can be frequent falling-outs between parents and their children or ongoing sibling animus. However, the love one can share with a mate can transcend all others in intensity. Usually, this is because a profoundly deep and irresistible physical element is involved, one that becomes enmeshed with overwhelming emotions, a merging where the two become one for precious moments. Some call this conjoining the ecstasy of being, while others refer to the allure as the "urge to merge."

Many of you reading these words know precisely what I mean. There is an irresistible imperative driven by biology and desire and cemented by mutual happiness and pleasure. We learn by touch, so to speak. We hone our shared passions over time and discover one another's most secret desires, happily experimenting and sharing in the pleasures of the flesh. We become selfless, seeking to please as much as to be pleased. In fact, shared fulfillment is passion's primary goal and reward. In the fullness of time, children can emerge from this form of love if the ground is fertile and the context suitable. Families are born, and thus the two that sought to become one can experience more than either could alone. Indeed, two can become many, and so a family grows. This is a shared imperative, one that perpetuates our being in both physical and metaphysical ways.

However, this journey often includes bumps, ruts, and sometimes intractable barriers. The reasons are many. In some cases, the physical aspects of love become disjointed. Things no longer fit just so, although honesty, patience, and persistence can often overcome such concerns. This is especially the case if the spiritual aspects of love remain strong and vibrant, that powerful desire that glues two together. Alas, the desire to coexist can be eroded by trauma, ill health, bad behavior, boredom, and other happenstances. Hence, one's eyes can turn to another, or perhaps a desire simply to part ways becomes manifest, with betrayal or abandonment often being the final straw that breaks love's back. Ultimately, the selflessness that helped spawn love is lost, often replaced by petty and self-centered yearnings on one side and interminable regrets and misery on the other.

I have not seen my Morning Sunshine for 13 terribly long years. We are still married in theory, but the state does not consider it so. Instead, both of us are now alone, separated by a chasm of nearly 3,000 miles. Oh, we knew some precious moments, sharing passions and the other things of love. However, we were also intellectuals. Yes, that was our dreary curse. We were too bright and sure of ourselves to compromise, and thus began the dissolution of some of the bonds that held us together. Then arose the budding need for material security. We started a very successful Internet retail business, but I felt trapped by its vexingly heavy and constant demands. My Morning Sunshine felt ill-appreciated, with our mutual passions generating as many sparks as they did pleasing touches.

Illness then came upon me due to 60-hour-plus workweeks and my incessant excesses. However, I did everything possible to help my wife secure the tools needed to become a research scientist. The business paid for her computers, classes at Penn State, and a modest salary. I had no income from the company, preferring to grow it as much as possible. Soon enough, Morning Sunshine graduated and went west to procure a career. I wanted her to soar on brilliant wings that would bring her happiness. I viewed myself as an anchor, something that was holding her back. Still, it seemed possible that we could eventually walk the same path.

66.1 Jiehui by the garden in White River, Vermont

However, it was not to be. The sparks had burned away the welds that joined us. After eight years, we became two, linked only by phone calls and emails. I grieved, as I do to this day. I regard myself as being responsible. Truth is, God often allowed me to see beyond the now. I saw the tremendous potential within her, and I also knew she was unhappy with our little business. After all, it created far too many pressures for sensitive souls. So, when she left, I was full of hope for her. I planned to eventually join her in Portland, Oregon, for I could not envision a future without such a reason compelling me forward.

As fate would have it, my Sunshine suffered terribly in her new career at Intel. Her primary strength and weakness are that she seeks perfection above all else. She is a child of numbers and a true genius by any measure. Yet the concern she worked for only wanted data, however faulty that data was. There was no

66.2 Rocky ponders Jiehui while she ponders a book.

possible reconciliation, and after three hard years, she suffered a breakdown. I should have seen that possibility, but I was blinded by hope. My love has difficulty in organizing her life or thoughts, let alone working. When brilliance breaks, it often shatters completely, which was soon the case with my wife. About a year after she left, a demon reached deep within and tore up my broken heart. The dreaded Widow-Maker heart attack let me live, but at

59, I was forever changed. A man of great physical strength was transformed into a shadow. So here we are, separated by time and space and mutually damaged and unhappy.

The business was liquidated, and she was sent ample money to help ride out the storm. I even built a home, hoping my wife would eventually rejoin me. Regrettably, the trauma had become too ingrained, and no amount of money could repair the damage done. As I type these lines, a tear comes to my eye. I so want her to be happy. I so want her to heal. However, my capacity to help my Morning Sunshine has evaporated. The money and home are gone, along with my health and vitality. I worry about her every day because she cannot do much that will secure her future. And what will happen to her when I am gone? Who will care? Indeed, I send her birthday, anniversary, and Xmas gifts, letting Jiehui know she is still loved. I frequently phone her and am called in return, often talking for an hour or so. Who will do these things when I am gone, for she has never found another?

Yes, I want to hold her close, to feel and hear her heart beating. Indeed, the part of love that seeks to place the interests and well-being of its object above life itself remains strong. If I knew she could eventually forge a happy future, I could live out my days in some degree of harmony. Instead, I can offer her nothing but a desire that seems immune to degradation. Yet that desire cannot move her because she does not feel the same about me as I do about her. Our shared love has broken, or perhaps it never indeed was. The thought pains me, but the truth is obvious. The physical "me" is declining, much like my material status has become diminished to poverty. Yet that is not a concern, for I do not fret about myself. No, my situation is irrelevant. At my very core, there is only my Morning Sunshine, a passionate ideal that still drives me despite its immaterial nature.

There have been opportunities to share love with others during these many years of being alone. I have kissed, hugged, and felt the call of intimacy, for such a call is born in our natures. Yet I shy away from relationships. I once made a promise and will remain faithful. Sure, I fantasize about others, but there is this barrier. Is it born of a pledge to love, honor, and respect, or could those special moments have created something even more enduring? Perhaps my reluctance is merely a fear that history will repeat itself or the fact that my fires burn low and time gives us no recourse. I shake my head while writing this, for I can find no rationale, no precise reason to cling to a love that is not shared with a person that I will, in all likelihood, never see again. Now I smile, for the reason is as obvious as I am oblivious.

The lesson and reason are that some forms of love simply do not die. They are pure, enduring, and noble and suffer not from judgments, rebukes, or condemnations. She is my one and only, a light that will shine until my days run out. Many think I am deluded, trapped within an ideal that cannot become a reality. Yes, perhaps that is true. To be sure, my capacity to see beyond the now has evaporated for the most part. Nevertheless, I still dare to believe that there will come a day when I see my Morning Sunshine again. That remote possibility is unlikely to become a reality, but the memories keep me hoping it does. They help give my life meaning, if not happiness. So, I am content, having known what love is and how important it can be. God has been kind to me, and I am at peace. If you are blessed enough to find love, hold it dearly. Hold on to it tightly with both hands and never let go, come what may. Amen.

67

Love of Country

I know of people who consider the love of country sacrosanct, something beyond an article of faith. Moreover, it is "their" country, right or wrong, and thus draftees and volunteers answer the call of the powers that be without hesitation or question. On occasion, they dutifully fight in unjust wars and/or occupy lands where no one wants our kind. I ponder all this while watching a small black ant traversing an invisible trail on the expansive brick walkway that serves our building's front entrance. She is guided by a pheromonal imperative, as in a scent marking a sister left while foraging. The ant I am studying makes slight detours while searching and has soon found tasty bits of detritus that cause her to pause and take notice. However, she soon returns to the task, picking up the scent path and continuing as her nature demands. My mind darts back to the 1921 discovery of ant mills. These are instances when the ant trail being followed is circular, with the ants devotedly following one another until exhaustion or death overtakes them. Certain caterpillars and fish display a similar penchant for following a circular trail until exhaustion or death overtakes them. Indeed, ants will even go to war if given the correct signal, despite the odds or casualties incurred.

Yet the imperatives of ants and many other species are hard-wired, something beyond their capacity to overcome. It is a vestigial survival mechanism that allows the collective whole to act as one in pursuit of food, accommodation, or other existential necessities. The impulse is biochemical and will produce effects until life itself is forfeit. Humans, for the most part, have a bit more free will than do ants, although January 6, 2021, has made me question that assumption. Indeed, we humans have the apparent capacity to don perceptual blinders, ideological constructs that can cause us to forsake life itself in the pursuit of a communally instilled ideal. I met a man who thoroughly understood such niceties during my time at UNH. He had served his country well during a stint in the service, never once balking at the many dreadful things he had done or was involved in during the war in Vietnam. For "Clem," it was mostly about duty.

"We are the tip of the spear," he told me. "We're not the hand that wields it or the head that guides its use." Clem was a Huey pilot in Vietnam and a highly decorated one. He would ferry officers on intel missions to collect papers from dead Vietcong, with most being recently caught in the open and blasted to pieces by aerial missiles and other ordnance. It was hazardous work because some enemies were still alive, albeit horribly wounded. An attending officer would usually shoot those still moving or breathing in the head while standing on the chopper's skids, jump off, and search the mutilated remains for papers and maps. The blood-soaked prizes were then safely stowed, and Clem would make a short vertical jump to another nearby place so that his team could examine more bodies. "Those damn flechettes can tear bodies to shreds," he advised. "They're tiny things, but you put a few missiles containing those bad boys into a big group, and the result is bits and pieces."

Clem was an Upper Valley guy from West Lebanon, which tends to produce honesty not found in some areas. He once told me that we had all been indoctrinated well before the war began, and thus there was no doubt he would do his job when the time came. "TV shows, parades, books, and all that," he mused, "those are the tools that make you able to land a Huey in a shitstorm for intel. Some say it is for the love of country, but no one finds that kind of love enjoyable. It sure isn't like sex, not that sex equals love." Clem confessed to having occasional nightmares, although I believe he would still do his job again if required. He was a great guy and went on to become a pilot. Indeed, true love had taken over his life, that of flying.

Many of my friends went to 'Nam, and some returned with horrific stories. Many supported the war and our announced reasons for fighting it. For them, it was America first, love it or leave it. Others detested the fight and spent much time getting high and trying to survive. One fellow told me, "So we go into this dirtbag town, and there are pictures of Ho Chi Minh in every f'n house . . . if you want to call those shit-holes houses. They were shacks and huts for the most part." However, the thing he remembered most was the look of hatred he saw in the eyes of nearly everyone in the villages. No amount of chocolate and goodwill could melt that ingrained feeling. He told me he didn't want to be there, and the locals certainly didn't want his unit marching through their community. For him, he acted out of duty and fear of the repercussions for not doing so.

Any objective study of our reasons for being in Vietnam would quickly indicate it was a fight worth avoiding, but thousands of souls went into the whirling body mill. We fought on and on, with estimated total deaths (military and civilian) ranging from 1.35 and 2.4 million. Both sides committed mass murder and brutality well outside the norms of war, albeit war has few moral criteria. Still, I ponder why we would die and kill as ordered. Did we become ants, merely following a prescribed path laid down by our leaders? Or was there a higher morality guiding some of those who chose to fight? Yet what kind of morality is it that shoots wounded people in the head, slaughters entire villages of Montagnard tribal members, or tortures and kills prisoners? Where are lofty principles in any of that?

Nonetheless, many veterans tell me that the love of country drove them. This same drive was used to foster the second Gulf War, which was founded on the demonstrably false premise that Iraq had weapons of mass destruction that could be used against our homeland. After 100,000 Iraqi civilian and military deaths, around 5 million displaced persons, and over $200 billion in property damage, the folly of our *casus belli* was revealed, albeit a bit late for many. Still, love of country drove many of our troops on, as it has done many times before.

Love is often defined as a strong and constant affection; and in this sense, one can indeed love a country, place, or thing. As a noun, love has at least three kinds. The first is a feeling of intense and warm affection, as in a parent's love for a child. The second is a great liking or interest, such as the love of a particular sport, activity, or food. The third is a feeling of powerful attachment, such as one feels for a beloved person (a mate, spouse, etc.). Thus, one can love a country or state entirely and absolutely, as Robert E. Lee did for Virginia. Indeed, his love for Virginia trumped his love for the United States, a tendency he shared with many. The resultant Civil War was wholly uncivil and eventually consumed between 620,000–850,000 lives, with millions more wounded.

Were we behaving like ants or free-thinking people during our many wars? Was love guiding us, or perhaps duty, community, and culture? Maybe it was all these things, but the end was death and destruction for the good, bad, and indifferent. Around and around, the body mill whirled, devouring many who followed the marshal trail. It is an odd phenomenon; for the things of love are also the things of life. After all, to love anything, one must be alive. Yet we willingly forfeit life because our gray-haired leaders tell us it is a propitious time to kill or die for reasons X, Y, and Z. We do not question or balk. We follow the trail, serve, and often die or get mauled. Some tell me they do this for the love of country, and I ponder if any part of love speaks for life and existence above all else? After all, love requires being alive, and the sacrifice of life essentially negates any form of love that one could ever give, take, or share.

We have every right to ask our leaders to explain why we must die for the love of our country. Moreover, I think our leaders ought to be willing to sacrifice themselves and their families for whatever cause they deem worthy of offering up their constituents to harm and death. The ONLY good thing about mutually assured destruction is the equality it brings to all involved, for there is no place to hide for all involved. But mostly, we must have the courage to question. Indeed, if one truly loves his or her country, then he or she must make sure its edicts are based on the common welfare and not banal expediency, jingoism, pride, or duplicity. We have a right and duty to question the reasons for war, especially if we do, indeed, love our country. Otherwise, we become like ants, mere followers of a proscribed mill trail.

I simply cannot fathom the foolishness of war, yet perhaps I'm just not thinking right. Of course, the follow-a-trail problem extends beyond war alone. We are such gullible creatures that a demagogue can set our hearts afire with lies, and off we rush to desecrate the ideals we claim to live by. Indeed, entire political parties live by great lies while the unwashed masses send their checks to preening egotists. Then they act as directed by their god-of-the-day, an unthinking mob of cultists who have no real idea about what they are fighting about. The mob followed the scent trail, committing atrocities simply because they were told to. People were maimed, and some died, all seen in glorious Technicolor on our TV screens on January 6.

During the sad affair, I saw a rebel flag being paraded through the Capitol building by a guy from New Jersey, one of the places where Lincoln and many other patriotic men were honored in death. And now, some of the most two-faced talking heads in history say it wasn't a mob. For example, Tucker the Fucker tells me there was no riot, and the crowd was orderly. Yet what we witnessed on January 6 was violence incarnate, and one wonders what scent trail the duplicitous powers that be are now striving to lay down. They led us into Vietnam and a lot worse, yet many still pretend to trust these louts. As I said, I cannot fathom the logos behind all this, although ants act far more intelligently than many humans. Amen.

68

The Lake of Love

The neurologists tell me there is a major cognitive disorder in play, as in a budding type of dementia. They can see "marked" cortical atrophy on magnetic-resonance imaging scans, and neuropsych tests confirm my memory is defective. The symptoms can be disconcerting, although I'm still capable of coping with life for now. Yeah, forgetting names, events, and places is a drag, but I can still craft a line like this, albeit with some errors here and there. Indeed, I've learned to avoid freaking out when I suddenly lose touch with an ongoing context. For example, I often get confused about my surroundings while riding the bus home from the hospital. I've made the trip hundreds of times, but on occasion, nothing looks familiar, not even the lie of the land. Nonetheless, I'm confident my destination will eventually be reached, come what may. Of course, that happy outlook is merely a belief, although it prevents panic or despair. I suspect belief is our attempt to deal with the unknowable, and I'm OK with that.

Moreover, the loss of existential context has been liberating in some ways. I mostly live in the "now." Granted, the past and future still haunt my thoughts occasionally, but I perceive the elements of time much differently than I once did. The tenses ascribed to time have mostly melded, at least for me. The truth of this, in as much as I can discern truth, came to me at the boat landing, although I cannot recall exactly when. The venue overlooks a small lake formed by Wilder Dam, and therein resides my place of prayer . . . my church. Although I have told this story before, I recall the experience in detail. The images remain vivid, despite my failing memory.

68.1 A much favoured place of nuture

68.2 Looking for life living beneath the surface (

I watch sunlight glisten off rippling waves in a dazzling display. The sweet melodies of sumptuously attired songbirds abound: red-breasted robins, raucous bluebirds, and if we're lucky, a scarlet tanager will grace us with its presence. Languid swells gently lap the shoreline, and life abounds all around. This is heaven on earth, wondrous to behold in its sublimity. A muskrat is sometimes seen hurriedly paddling into a nearby thicket of reeds, shifting them aside before scrambling onto a toppled and long-dead tree. A mated pair of ambling mallards occasionally forage in the shallows, with trailing ducklings bobbing on the waves. Hundreds of grazing minnows and pollywogs swarm along the shores among the reeds and water plants. They busily munch on tiny particles of sustenance. Into this bliss, my feeble mind delves.

One gazes into the crystal depths, noting how light is diffracted by the invisible eddies and currents whirling within the lake. I strive to see the light's gyrations in terms of the nature of existence. What do these shifting light forms tell me? What could they mean? The lake's surface, middle, and bottom suddenly merge into one while I ponder, as do the elements of time. The artificial borders we draw between the past, present and future dissolve. They are perceived as dynamic currents within the lake of being, all existing simultaneously and influencing one another in myriad ways.

Yet how can one swim in such a rarified lake? For the most part, we are linear creatures. We happily follow the path of causality because it allows life to navigate the necessary now. Frogs and tigers must search for, find, and react to prey if they are to live in the now, employing perception, timing, and actions to survive. Thus, a sticky tongue abruptly latches onto a horsefly. Yummy. The sequencing of steps needed to achieve various ends continues at ever higher levels of abstraction while we climb the evolutionary tree. Humans can link clause X to clause Y via process C, the formula of which reveals some hidden truths. But why? Well, it's logical, as in the prologue's archi dictating what will follow. An underlying rationality guides this, a causal necessity leading to all outcomes.

Nah, I'm not buying that story anymore, at least not for now. The lake's reflections tell me it's not so. Some of us gaze at distant stars. We imagine other worlds with beings peering at our sun in the same fashion as we watch theirs. We ponder about the

68.3 Waves bend the light but the light reveals what swims below

thoughts and feelings linking us, discerning that empathy and other universal commonalities may connect us as one regardless of time and space. Indeed, we merrily assume the definition of pi is much the same to the "others" as it is to us, and so too may be the meanings of love, time, and much else.

These assumptions quickly become articles of faith about things we do not, and perhaps cannot, know, much like my getting home on the bus. It is so because we assume it is so. I cannot discern any causal order underlying this speculation, although history tells us our assumptions often have a basis in probability. Similarly, I do not detect what underlying patterns can be found that sustain many fantasies or faiths other than specific themes seem to overlap and reappear. Thus, we ponder the natures of others on distant planets in much the same fashion as

68.4 If you are lucky, a scarlet tanager will come by to sing a tune

we believe that they reflect upon us. We are separated by a vast chasm of space and time yet linked by common thoughts, or so we suppose.

So, what's the big deal, even if all this is true? Does it matter? After all, many light years probably passed from our tiny, shifting part of the lake since we supposedly shared our thoughts and speculations with the others. Were they not beings of the past, just as we are from some distant perspectives? In fact, could the entire universe be rigidly bound within the tenses of time, as in frozen within the past, present, and future? Indeed, it stands to reason that causality's chains propel us through existence in more or less linear fashions. Yet in my demented mind, that reasoning no longer rings true.

I once viewed life like that, but memory issues can be liberating. The power of imagination, abstraction, and empathy can allow us to transcend time in the metaphysical sense. Thus, some of us ponder past Xmas meals and do so in enough depth that we still smell the holiday foods and see the smiles lighting up loved ones' faces. We can also contemplate the future, imagining trips to distant worlds, the births of grandchildren, and prophecies, great and small. As for the present, that is the paper upon which our thoughts about these things are recorded and shared, as in this line.

Thought is the vital capacity that permits us to swim in this lake without discernable temporal or physical boundaries. Oh, there will come a day when we learn enough to slip our mortal coils and explore this vast realm of being in fashions that allow our present to fully participate with the past and future. However, in the metaphysical sense, this is a capacity we have had since immemorial. We simply lose sight of what is beneath the lake's surface because we get dazzled by reflections of the now. Whew, I must rest for a bit.

It is odd. In my dotage, the links that unite us are becoming more evident, although I often dwell in a realm of disjointed thoughts. Indeed, some folks think I'm bonkers. I still talk with my mother and others who died long ago. I see their faces and feel their presence while delving into the lake's depths. Sometimes, I cannot speak correctly, think clearly, walk well, or recall a blessed thing. My friends often think I'm rambling, disoriented, or bat-shit crazy, yet perhaps I'm simply tuned to a different frequency. I talk to fish and birds, imagining what guides them through their lives. I perceive that impetus as a universal that runs throughout being.

Is there a common impetus to life and living, as in an underlying reason to exist? Or is this game of life born of purely random processes? We are slowly answering many of the "how" questions involved in being via the stuff of particle physics and the like. However, many "why" conundrums are much harder to explain. This is where we may find a hidden impetus, some logicoemotional force that compels us to exist for a reason. But why would such a force dwell within us, and what form does it take? Let us seek an explanatory metaphor, a universal storyline that we can examine. We also know this metaphor resides within the machinations of existence because you're about to read it.

Ah, from nothingness to all, as in the Big Bang. There was the void, and then there was the one-and-only, although which came first is a matter of possibility that I am too feeble to discern. In any case, the processes leading to being involved the progenitor "I" of consciousness, for if identity ever existed, it could only be discerned and defined via consciousness. It was a source born of a possibility that became inevitable via the agency of time. It was a singularity that rode within the irresistible winds of an explosively expanding process of being that it had initiated and was one with.

Energy coalesced into matter, and within this shifting duality came the progenitor "I," now embodied within a roiling, moving, and expanding matrix of being. Then, with the advent of mass, space, and time came the seminal existential thought "I am." This primal amalgam simultaneously became one with space, matter, and time, a terribly lonely situation. The processes churned on and eventually gave rise to the notion of "We are!" as life proliferated. Hmmm, that seems like a reasonable mytho-poetic account.

The "We are" stage is one with the emergence of plurality that is part and parcel of our shared existence. It spread through-out as life begat life, ever-shifting in form and thought, while necessity and evolution played their roles. The "I" had become the many, driven by the ultimate sacrifice of self for the sake of the existence of others. In numerous respects, giving a singular identity for the sake of others defines true love. It is the complete sharing of being and self for the benefit and existence of folks such as the person reading this line. Yeah, love is the impetus, perhaps the primary impetus. I can see that clearly now, though maybe this will be forgotten within a month. Yet now that the thoughts are committed to a form you can read, memory is no longer an issue.

Well, I'm not sure this prayer makes much sense. However, these thoughts have been shared, incomplete and disjointed though they may be. You can take them much further than I can manage. That is a sure thing. I grow weary, spending much of my days dozing. On occasion, the turkeys come by and gobble a greeting. Swift deer dart through the surrounding hills, moving in a fashion that is amazing in its grace. There is pain, and I fall a lot. Yet I am content. The window to share these thoughts remains open for a bit longer, and I do not fear it closing. Progress is being made, yet I realize that we all hang by threads, my friends, and we most assuredly do not hang forever.

Life is about change, with some of the few constants being found in the thoughts that link us. Some may find it odd that these ramblings arrived at the strange conclusion that love is the essential impetus that underlies existence. Well, what can one expect from a person whose perception of linearity got wrapped around itself? In any event, love is the story's conclusion, and I'm sticking with it. Yes, perhaps it's merely a delusion, yet I feel blessed to be with you now. These are mere words on a page, all bound by time and space. Nonetheless, the thoughts they spark link us to a common "now" within this lake of being we share. Find and give some love, my friends, be it in the eyes of a mate, a child's laughter, or birds' chirping. And know you well that this shared love will always take one to the source of all things. That is our purpose, our reason for being. Amen.

69

Loving Little Mermaids

The setting is Manchester, New Hampshire's Palace Theatre, a wonderfully preserved and restored 1914-era venue. Here we find 834 well-padded fold-down bucket seats, with the decor including elaborately carved and gilded woodwork on nearly every surface except the floor. The only concession to modernity is the lighting and sound system, with the rest being reasonably much as when vaudeville companies toured the area. Indeed, the Palace hosted the likes of Bob Hope, Jimmy Durante, The Marx Brothers, Harry Houdini, and Red Skelton. Yeah, this was the place to perform in New Hampshire for a long time, although by the 1970s, age and lack of upkeep had taken a stiff toll. In 1974 long-needed and costly renovations were made to keep the Palace's original character and restore the theater to full

69.1 Manchester, New Hampshire's rejuvinated Palace Theatre

functionality. The end results continue to serve the community well. Indeed, it was my pleasure to have been invited to attend Disney's *The Little Mermaid*, a play being put on by the Palace Youth Theatre.

Rebecca was 9, and Nicole was 6 then, and I have known them since their births. They are lithe, athletic little girls gifted with budding intellects and insatiable curiosity. Watching them grow has been a pleasure, and there I was, enjoying yet another visit. They are the children of an excellent friend I met at UNH, who is more of a brother than a casual acquaintance. Al and Jane have allowed me to partake in their kids' lives, a blessing for

69.2 The children put on a wonderful musical show, one they spent many hours rehersing

someone not graced with children. I love them dearly, every bit as much as I would love one of my own. I listen while they sing in perfect harmony, their sweet voices touching my heart.

I have watched them change from infants into animated children, and I somewhat lament that they are growing up so fast. However, growth, change, and development are the way of things, and soon enough, they will turn into gorgeous and bright young ladies. Then the stuff of education, career, love, and all the rest will arise. But for now, their surprisingly good harmonics captivate me. Yes, they have rehearsed long and hard to put on the best possible performance. They even include hand gestures, which Rebecca has patiently learned while practicing for this youth play.

69.3 Nicole and Rebecca are two little mermaids the author has known since they were born

These children are precious to me in every possible way. At times, I fear for their welfare. We live in a tumultuous era of great rancor, selfishness, violence, and seething hatred. Al and Jane do all they possibly can to shield their offspring from the negative, but we live in a digital age. I'm sure some of the angst and turmoil leak through, yet we can do little about that. One recoils at the monstrous torment many youths must endure, as in Syria, Sudan, and countless other places where adults behave far worse than any kid could imagine. Still, these are happy little girls.

69.4 Elder shares toy time with Rebecca and Nicole, one of his true joys in life

I often tell Rebecca and Nicole stories. We talk about different dimensions, space, time, gravity, and the wonders of being. Their young minds grasp concepts that many older and more experienced folks would struggle to understand. Ah, but they have the sublime gift of imagination versus the blinders of petty and rigid judgment that age generates. We talk of dreams and dragons, how gravity works, and what games they like best. We build cardboard houses, complete with working elevators. Nicole and Rebecca suddenly decide to do sit-ups, part of a living room training program that abruptly springs into being. I ask God to grant them long and healthy lives, and the singing begins anew.

A medication has me in the bathroom all too often during this visit: the dreary consequences of a lifetime spent indulging

69.5 Making a home within a home arrises from a child's wonder

in excesses. I pray Rebecca and Nicole will never walk my hedonistic path. Yet they seem to embrace a degree of moderation as children. That gives me great comfort. I long to see what they will become, despite my knowledge that they will never be more imaginative and open to wonder than they are now. Yes, children are infinitely more capable than adults in employing these facets of being. Oh, they will go through ups and downs and make many mistakes. However, I am confident about their future while the harmony permeates my tired and feeble mind.

Watching Nicole and Rebecca grow and change has been a wonderful gift that Al and Jane have blessed me with. Sometimes, I want them to stay young forever, but that is a selfish way of thinking. After all, these girls will learn the things of love and hope as they grow, and one day they may gaze into the eyes of their own children. I wish I could see them into maturity. Sadly, that is most unlikely, given ongoing health issues. Yet we will share whatever time God grants us, with me getting far more than I can ever give. Indeed, their music feeds my soul. It gives me hope and a purpose to go on. I feel blessed while in their presence and am infinitely thankful for the bounties this existence can provide. Granted, I cannot prove that a knowing and loving God exists. Yet when I look into those beaming faces and bright eyes . . . that is evidence enough for me. Amen.

70

Born of Love

Rose did not get to know her biological mother for long because Veneranda Sciarza Albanese died on October 9, 1918, less than six months after her daughter was born. She died at 25 of the Spanish flu, one of its 50 million victims. A Sicilian, Veneranda was married to Dominic Albanese, a fellow Italian immigrant from a small town outside Naples. She met him in 1913 in the bustling railroad town of White River Junction, Vermont, where Dominic worked as a locomotive mechanic and engineer. She bore him four children in just six years, Patsy, Cilia, Joseph, and Rose. It was a far from idyllic marriage, for the hulking Dominic had had no intention of marrying Veneranda after getting her pregnant.

70.1 Rose Albanese with her stepmother, Louise (Picone) Albanese

He was OK with abandoning his lust object, but his American sponsor would not tolerate his plans. Dominic was told to marry Veneranda, or he was going back to Italy. He was not used to being told what to do, and he might have had a love interest back in Italy. The reasons for his action are unknown, but Dominic obeyed his sponsor and married Veneranda. She gave him four children and even tended to Dominic when he got the flu, the cost of which was to be her life when she contracted the illness. Ultimately, it was all about love, the sacrifice of the self for the sake of another.

Poor baby Rose was left in the care of a neighbor for several months, and there the infant suffered from malnutrition to the extent that she developed rickets. Indeed, she became slightly

70.2 Rose Albanese in about 1940. She was a formidible woman in stature,
a trait she passed on to her sons

bowlegged as a result, albeit the malady did not affect her much
as she matured. As for Veneranda, she was buried in an isolated
lot far toward the rear of the Mount Olivet Cemetery in White
River Junction, Vermont. We recently replaced the weathered

818

and damaged marble stone that once marked her plot with a deeply inscribed granite marker that should endure for centuries. This is the least we could have done to thank the mother of our mother for the gift of life. I visit her plot at least once yearly and wish I had gotten to know her. The language barrier would have been formidable because I was never taught Italian, which was spoken in the Albanese household.

Following the death of Veneranda, Dominic wrote to Italy and secured another wife, although I have never learned how this was done or if he had previously known the woman. I know she must have been intrepid, and I certainly loved her. Louise Picone arrived in America in 1919 and, at 28, found herself tending to four young children and setting up a home with a man she primarily knew from letters. Yet to baby Rose, Louise was Mom, and she bonded with her for life. Indeed, Nana was an exemplary mother to her stepchildren and the five kids she was to have with Dominic. Oh, and she loved all her many grandchildren, too, for they were not step or biological grandkids in her heart.

She considered them all the blood of her blood and treated them accordingly. She patiently and lovingly crocheted an elaborate confirmation dress for my mother that has stayed in the family for years, and soon her own and her stepchildren were integrated into a single family. Of course, they did not all look the same, with my mother having kinky hair, thick lips, and olive skin indicative of her half-Sicilian heritage. Indeed, when she played basketball in school, the opposing team sometimes called her "Nigger." She recalled the taunts but never with bitterness.

She was physically strong, a formidable woman who was not to be messed with.

Mind you, Rose had reasons to be bitter. Her father was a diabetic when there were no viable treatments. By age 46, Dominic was severely affected by the condition, with both heart and brain damage. As he declined, he became abusive. Dominic beat his wife and did other things that made my mother increasingly resentful, especially during her later years. In fact, my mother called the police after a terrible beating of her mother, and Dominic learned that he was not the master of all he surveyed. Yeah, she got him busted. Yet he remained an old-fashioned Italian who would not allow my mother to attend secretarial school, let alone college. In fact, he was OK with his kids leaving school and working as soon as they could. Yet my mother was gifted, and her teachers wanted her to further her education. Dominic would not hear of it, and thus the dream evaporated.

Rose met my father, Henry Holton Elder, while working at the Tip Top Bakery in White River Junction, a company owned by Henry's uncle, George West. Henry was the child of a fiery patriarch from the Old South's Virginia and a lovely Yankee woman from a Vermont clan whose roots in America stretched back to 1634. Grace Holton Elder had a name that perfectly fitted her persona, while Thomas Edwin Elder was a highly educated but bigoted man who did not spare the rod. Thomas certainly did not want his college-educated son to have anything to do with a "temperamental Latin." This attitude increased in hostility as my father and mother grew closer and, in the end, he would not

70.3 Henry Elder as a child. He led a rather priveledged life, but his father was an overly strict disciplinarian

70.4 Nana hovering above the boy in the chair (Peter Elder). Rose Elder is to her left, while Tom and George Elder are to her right (circa 1960-1962)

attend their wedding. Yet Grace did attend, and she shared her love freely with all her grandchildren. How we kids worshiped her, this paragon of virtue that dared defy the edicts of an intolerant authoritarian. I never once saw Thomas Edwin Elder, even though my big brother, the firstborn, was named after him.

One would think that something grand would grow of Rose's love for Henry, and they did have five children: Thomas, Mary, Nancy, George, and Peter. We all became successful in various ways, but that does not mean my parents' love conquered all. Henry was a miserable drunk sometimes, and I recall him smashing furniture and screaming when I was a child. He was the progeny of a child beater and harbored terrible memories that gave him no rest. He passed those memories along to me and my siblings, although I'm not sure much could have been done to prevent that. My mother had also known abuse in many ways, yet she became the still point in our lives. Her father died at 54 on March 7, 1946, ravaged by diabetes and other chronic illnesses, but we all got to know Nana very well. Many were her big hugs and the fine meals she prepared for us. Alas, I could not understand a word she spoke!

Louise went on to care for a grandson for several years, and she played an active role in all our lives. She lived until July 20, 1979, dying at the age of 88. My mother was her caregiver during those last years, very much finding it a responsibility to return the love she had been so freely granted. Yet Rose's life was not easy. She held the family together through force of will despite Henry's illness. He was in the bag nearly every day, and he acted accordingly. I have seen my siblings with black eyes and reddened faces; slurred screams and the sounds of breaking furniture still echo through my mind. I grew to become psychotic and tried to burn the house down twice. My mother exorcised the demons rising within as best she could, but that was to become a battle I still occasionally fight. When I was 10 or 12, I begged her to leave, yet she would not. She loved Henry, but I most assuredly did not. I grew to become the image of him in temperament and recall throwing him over the stove when he tried imposing force on me. I was about 13 at the time.

Henry was tormented, and it took me many years to get over the storm. I recall my sixteenth birthday, although I might have been younger. Henry was too drunk to climb the stairs, so I helped him to his bed. Every step of the way, he told me, "Fuck you and fuck your birthday." Mom said he felt terrible about not having money to buy me a present, but I told her not to make excuses for the inexcusable. That hurt her to the core, but her rationalizing was not wanted. Rose was an idealist who thought tolerance and kindness could lead to good things no matter what. She would have been horrified if she could have seen into my soul.

Oddly, Henry did see my budding illness. I visited him in the hospital on one of those many occasions when he was close to death. Henry reached out and grabbed my hand. He said raspily, "I had to do those things! I had to. One day, you will understand why." I knew exactly what he was talking about, and it had to do with the person reading these words. Some of you

70.5 Henry and Rose Elder stayed together through thick and thin

have experienced great torment, and some have done deplorable things. Such are the products of trauma. Correcting destructive behaviors BEFORE they impact those you love is the goal. Excuses help, but changes in behavior can build love and change the future. That was the message Henry was trying to impart, although it fell on barren soil.

Tom went off to the service during the Vietnam War, and my mother fretted about him constantly. Mary married a man from White River, and they had three wonderful children who became very successful in their own rights. Nancy became a nurse for over 50 years, with Tom helping to pay her way through school. I went to UNH, survived my drug addictions, became a coach, and then a scholar. Peter, the rock, married a local woman who bore him two daughters. Peter's family lived in the duplex my parents had owned since the 1940s, and Rose and Henry immensely enjoyed their grandchildren. Their five children had begot five grandchildren, albeit Rose always wanted more. How Rose loved children, be they nieces, nephews, or even more distant relations. She would hug them tight and speak to them in a fashion they loved. They sensed this person would love them no matter what, and that was indeed the case.

Henry remained irascible, although heat trouble and cancer took a harsh toll. He would read *Moby Dick* to Peter's children, especially Nicole, and thus he left her some enjoyable memories. I am very thankful for that. His days ended quite suddenly when he was 80. He felt the final heart attack coming but told his wife, "Rose, I love you." Those were his last words, and I am grateful he had the strength to get them out. He knew my mother was the best thing that ever happened to him, and she stood by him through thick and thin. That tenacity defines a large part of what love is.

Unlike what Henry thought would be the case, I did not weep when he died. Instead, I ensured he was correctly buried, although I thought the lid could have been better placed on his cement vault. Oh, and I did make sure he was buried with the watch I had given him for his birthday. I had learned to forgive him, but I would be a liar if I said the wounds did not run deep. Please, take his lesson to heart. He was a good man who tried to do well despite the damage done to him by a man who should have known better. Indeed, he should have been better.

I was with my mother when she died, and her passing left a hole that remains. I called her at least once per week but could

70.6 Rose and Henry were blessed with five children, five grandchildren, and six great grand children. Among them are seen Mary and Nancy Elder

tell from her weakening voice that something was wrong. Nonetheless, she opted to take a plane to Miami to see my cousin Bobby, his wife, and Angela, his daughter. How she loved that child. She got to see dolphins perform and loved the adventure. Indeed, it was the only plane trip she had ever taken, and it amazes me that she went on such an adventure, given her condition. Yet it was an act of love, so perhaps I should not be surprised. A few days after returning, she went into the Alice Peck Day Hospital, and I rushed home because she sounded very frail. Well, she was ashen and lethargic, and they did a magnetic resonance imaging (MRI) scan. I went to the MRI room with her because Mom was so weak and wracked by pain. I looked at the monitor as the results came in, and her pancreas, liver, and elsewhere lit up like a Xmas tree. She was riddled with cancer, and it was clear she would soon die.

I recall going back to her room, and she quickly fell asleep. The procedure had taken its toll, and now came the death watch. When Ma awoke, I told her the truth, but she already knew death was upon her. I told her I was angry with God for making her passing painful. In a raspy, weak voice, she said, "No, George, you must learn how to love." Relatives came and went, and God only knows how many hours I spent by her side. I tried to record her voice, but she was far too weak. I will not relate the terrible details of her passing other than that she always had at least one of us by her side. At one point, a train whistle sounded in the distance, and she whispered, "It's time to go." However, her death was not quick. We played Italian music in the background, and she was surrounded by her children when those last few breaths finally came. The memory burns me, but I still talk with her every day.

Rose did not have an easy life, but if asked, she would say it was beautiful. She was graced with children, grandchildren, and great-grandchildren. She survived an abusive father and a traumatized husband. Through it all, she held on to the idea of love above all else, and that impetus kept the family together. I do not know anyone who disliked her, and I miss her dearly. Yet I do not lament. She died loved, which is the best way to meet one's Maker. As for my kindred, they have diversified in many ways, which is what my grandfather Elder feared most. Oh, and they are ALL near the top of their class! Amen.

71

The Perfect Moment

A few lonely clouds waft on high while the sun plods toward twilight, with long shadows and cool breezes heralding the end of a glorious day. The harbingers of fall are here, graced by vermillion, ochre, gold, and other gloriously colored leaves gently floating to ground. They grace the earth one by one, leaving naked trees to await spring's bounty. God is a marvelous painter with a palate of infinite hues and textures. I feel blessed for this moment we share, that sublime solace that allows us to ponder together.

It is hard to breathe today. A recent heart attack took a toll, albeit manageable. Yet the trauma seems trivial in comparison with other travails. Instead, I find myself thinking of her. It is always her. I have not seen Jiehui (Gee-wee) for over 10 long and

71.1 Jiehui and George Elder as they appeared in 2007 during Xmas

lonely years. We speak frequently, though I haven't called since mid-July. She missed my birthday, and I got peeved. Well, sooner or later, one of us will contact the other. When something goes amiss, as in a sick parent or health concern, she must discuss matters with someone who cares. Still, I usually end up calling just to hear her voice. I clutch onto misty illusions, always hoping for what many say isn't there.

Yeah, most think I'm bat-shit crazy for holding on so tightly to a love that some claim evaporated or, worse yet, never really existed. They tell me the feelings weren't mutual, or they died long ago. Perhaps they never materialized, except in my mind. Yet don't they say love can be blind? It's hard to explain why I hold on. However, I know they're dead wrong, all the well-meaning critics. To me, there is an ideal, a singular truth that ties one to all; that is, to God, if the term is acceptable. I swore an oath before that Great Unifier, that foundational essence running through everything that allows us to understand one another in ways that transcend mere words. And I love Jiehui. I truly do. Like many marriages, ours had its towering peaks and unfathomable valleys. We fought over trivialities, being hard-pressed by an unexpectedly successful Internet retail sales company. There were long hours, financial demands, forms and forms, and yet more forms, now all dust and fading memories.

She wanted a career, and I worked my ass off to help her get the needed degree from Penn State. She is a brilliant woman, although not very good under pressure. I was so proud to see her graduate. Then poof . . . out to Portland, Oregon. She was an Intel research scientist in Quality Control, albeit not fully prepared to make the move. In the meantime, I prepared to return to my childhood home, for home was no longer where I lived, not without her. State College, Pennsylvania, had become a bleak wasteland, an infinitude of lonely time without life. I also felt nature's impetus calling me to return from whence I came . . . back to the bucolic setting of the Connecticut River's Upper Valley. The Upper Valley separates central and northern New Hampshire from Vermont, with plentiful streams, lakes, and mountains gracing the verdant landscape. Yet it was not the scenery that drew me back home.

Painful portents within my chest told me that the path ahead led to but one place, the peace of a box buried within the moist, dark soil of my childhood haunts. Sure enough, the dreaded Widow-Maker called within a year of my coming home: a complete occlusion of the left anterior descending artery that feeds the bottom half of your heart. My damage indices were 40 times average, with small survival odds (4–6 percent) and much damage from a massive heart attack. God smiled, and here I am, though echoes of the event are all too frequent. Sometimes, the reminders grab me, doing yet more damage. There was no phone call from my illusion during the worst of the tempest, but things were certainly not going well for Jiehui.

She was undergoing terrible times. Intel equals pressure. A perfectionist cannot endure long in a place where time matters more than getting things absolutely right. Her mind broke, and Intel eventually found itself 10 percent responsible. If she had pushed the issue, I imagine a stipend could have been set up to care for her. However, Jiehui is so fucking broken it's tragic. What a brilliant woman. She could grow crystals that generated electricity when impacted or heated. Now she can spend weeks fretting over what vitamin brand is best. Nothing else gets done in the meantime. She is utterly incapable of planning and executing, punctuated by periods of marked depression and anxiety. Alone, friendless, hand-wringing and I cannot help meaningfully. She won't see shrinks but is totally nonfunctional. It hurts.

I've sent Jiehui well over $145,000 in the last 12 or 13 years, well more than her agreed share of the business. I do not know how much for sure, nor does it matter. There's nothing left now, nothing at all. Yet I'm not worried about me. The universe talks to me every day, and I welcome becoming one with it, as in a

71.2 Jiehui and Diane Crowley at the Quechee Hot Air Balloon Festival in 2003

passing thought, something that dances through our mind for but a fleeting moment before it disappears. We grasp for a bit of meaning in the interim. Then we're gone, relating what we can before venturing forth. OK, but how can I help her? As this most recent heart event reminded me, I hang by a thread. However, she may live another 20–30 years. They could be great years, but she won't get help. She doesn't understand that she cannot understand. That's the way it is with broken geniuses. They get stuck in repeating loops. They forever spin but go no-where. So, why do I care?

Moments. There were precious moments of pure bliss. Oh, I hope everyone reading these words has felt them. They make life worth living, at least in large part. Yes, those precious shared moments of passion, embraces that turn two into one, shared time

71.3 Jiehui at a a San Francisco Mall in 2009

and space that gives life value and meaning. All things change, but memories, fragile though they are, become realities for me. I get locked into imagination land. And there she is, actually smiling! I can touch her soft face and feel her warmth. Some may find this a sad excuse for a life. Then again, lots of characters run around in my tiny brain. Plato and Aristotle just about set up a school in the place, as did other ancients: Pythagoras, Anaximander, Zeno, Cicero, Thomas Aquinas, and many more. And God lives just around the corner of Memory Lane, two-thirds the way up on Mount Lebanon's northwestern flank. God and I often talk, though this book I'm writing has cast me adrift.

Yet she's still here, hovering about in the recesses between my thoughts. Some say it's hopeless, and others say to move on. And yeah, there have been ample opportunities to find joy with another soul. It's hard to believe romance can knock on a fat, old, grumpy man's door, yet it most assuredly does. I can't fathom why and consider it one of life's great mysteries. Anyway, part of me is always away when the knock comes, locked in memory's grasp. It's an idea that compels me, something linked with an ideal but far from a reality. Perhaps it's better to live without such reflections, yet we must be true to our essential natures.

And here she will always be, an integral part of me. Some folks love absolutely or not at all. I'm not sure if that is good or bad but, like all things, it depends on the context. Currently, I'm listening to soft rock music, pondering some pleasant thoughts, and sharing notions with friends like you. That's not a terrible outcome for a person who lost love. My only regret is that I cannot help my Morning Sunshine, the literal meaning of Jiehui. Be that as it may, she will remain locked away in a willing heart.

Life's what we make it, and I'm content. Wish I'd fallen in love earlier. Wish there were children. Wish, wish, wish . . . But I'm pleased to watch the sun slip into twilight and share some time with you. There isn't much left in the material sense, perhaps enough to survive a bit longer. However, the threads that sustain me on this journey will fail someday. No one escapes that. And on that day, she'll still be here, a fading memory that will be the last thing I hold on to. I shall recall those special moments, the perfect instants of bliss.

And if there is nothing after death, all eternity will be as a blissful night's sleep that knows no waking. If there is an existence post-mortem, one wherein thought links one with all, she will be there, smiling. Could my love be naive and misplaced? Perhaps. But if the knowledge of that enduring passion gives Jiehui just one moment of comfort and bliss, one perfect happy memory, then mine was a love well-devoted. Life is good, my friends, and I've few regrets. Amen.

72

Loving Fred

Fred was easy to like, and everyone I knew spoiled him rotten. They brought him meals, talked with him incessantly, and even invited him into their homes. Oh, and he just devoured the attention, being a gloat case of the first order. He wasn't always well behaved, and had some bad habits. For example, Fred liked to watch people go to the bathroom. Yeah, he did so regularly. It was mortifying, yet watching people pee or poop seemed a desire born out of some deep part of his inner nature. We discussed it *ad nauseam*, yet Fred simply would not change his behavior. Imagine one of your best friends going into the lavatory to watch a visiting girl or guy do his or her business. It was perverted. Worse yet, he would rush up to the toilet when it was flushed and play with the water, no matter how soiled it was! And I was

72.1 Fred in Bathroom doing his favorite thing

the guy who would have to clean up afterward, with my friends finding Fred's antics very amusing.

Oh, did I mention that Fred was a cat? He was also a wonderful friend who saw me through graduate school at UNH in the late 1980s. I was gifted Fred by a neighbor who insisted that I needed a cat. I cannot recall the woman's name, and I may have mentioned getting a cat. But whiz-bang, thank you, ma'am, and there he was, a 10–12-week-old orange ball of fur and fury with a fair share of fleas and a precocious manner. He did not like being treated for pests, but I managed that task with minimal blood loss. Then he took over my bed, pouncing upon any body part that moved under the covers. It took some time and many claw marks to break him of that habit, but he soon tired of my humble apartment and wanted desperately to go out. He was born a barn cat, and they lead relatively unrestricted lives. Yet I lived beside a three-way junction of some bustling streets in downtown Newmarket, NH, and it was a certain death zone for any animal that hazarded exploring those environs.

He whined incessantly to go out and about, but we had plenty of spiders and other critters for him to hunt down, with our mostly subterranean apartment being a welcome home for creepy crawly things. Of course, he did escape a few times and made friends with the people above us. That is when the freeloading began, something Fred was never to give up. I thought it best to move to a safer abode and thus opted for an apartment less than a mile away by the end of a cul de sac. The place was adjacent to fields, and Fred could safely go for forays there. Yeah, that was not such a great idea. He would come back loaded with ticks, which he would promptly deposit on my bed. I was regularly killing the nasty vermin, but Fred seemed unconcerned. Instead, he began hitting on the fetching girl next door. He soon had her trained to feed and pet him, eventually becoming a shared kitty, gigolo that he was.

You know, he never once judged me during those days, which was a great comfort during the many travails of graduate school. It was a relief not to be graded while also being loved, regardless of the many foolish things I said or did. That is the real blessing of pets: they love absolutely and without reservation. Yeah, I can see why others fell in love with Fred so quickly, although he often had fights with the neighborhood tom cats. Man, I well recall the time I was petting him and felt what appeared to be several grapes under his skin beside a bight mark in his chest. A $135 vet visit and a day later, he wore the cone of shame and had an implanted tube to allow the infection to drain. Poor Fred was having a fit, and I am not sure it was all necessary. Within a week, he had destroyed the cone and ripped out the tube, a bloody and messy affair that allowed ample drainage.

We've all been there, fretting over a sick pet. As you know, it is a helpless feeling wherein we realize how vital that fragile little life is to us. That is why I should have insisted that Fred be an indoor cat, yet that was not in his nature. Well, perhaps I should have tried harder. After all, he gave everyone who knew him a lot of attention. Indeed, Fred could tell when I was bummed and would offer up unbelievably loud purring and snuggling upon being petted and brushed, which he loved. And he made sure my arms and face were clean with his raspy tongue, as is the wont of most cats. Yeah, he became one of my very best friends.

I finished my graduate work at UNH and moved to my family's home in West Lebanon, NH, for about six months to help care for Mom and Dad. It was to be a brief hiatus because a doctoral program at Penn State awaited me. Fred took to my ancestral home like a duck to water and soon came to a tacit understanding with my sister's cat, Rocky. He quickly dominated my father's lap and often hung out with Mom on the couch, watching her crochet or gaze at the boob tube. It seemed a safe environment, albeit he did not like river storms, those fierce summer outbursts of wind, rain, and thunder familiar to all Valley folks. Fred would panic, as in totally freak out! If inside, he would simply disappear, squeezing into narrow spaces that seemed impossible for a 15-pound cat. If outside, Fred would run amok entirely, racing hither and yon at full speed while panicking. Still, he had a good home with my sister, father, and mother, and thus I departed for Penn State sans Fred. It was a tough decision, but he would not be allowed in graduate housing, and I was unfamiliar with State College.

Penn State was a long, tedious trial by fire, and Fred would have provided a welcome diversion. Indeed, PSU is a place of judgment, and I ended up in many personal and public battles of all natures. After all, I'm an Upper Valley person. That implies a kind of irreverence and tendency to speak out that isn't welcome within the lofty confines of the academy. Fred would have been a great guy to talk with during those hard times. He had much better judgment than I and was prone to making friends quickly. Fred could have offered great advice and made my time at PSU much more tolerable. Ah, I recall calling home, and sometimes I would yell his name on the phone so he could hear me. Mom said his ears perked right up, but that is a poor excuse for actually being there.

I came home occasionally, and it was clear that Fred had become the owner of a new pad. I was welcome, but he might not have liked me bugging out. He would still be friendly, but now the love was shared with many. Yet his affections remained. He still was fascinated by the toilet and was forever trying to bat at the flushed water. Yeah, some things do not change. He now was a free-roaming cat, going inside or outside as he pleased. I was somewhat nervous, yet he was clearly enjoying himself. I most certainly was not enjoying Penn State, but graduate school is supposed to be a trial by fire. So, back into graduate housing I went, leaving Fred and family in my wake.

That coming fall semester at Penn State was difficult. I could have used my good buddy's advice, but I was doing well grade-wise. Then came the winter, and I saw portents, one being the perfect outline of Fred in some dried soap suds. The image was striking. There were also dreams about being lost, which always indicated something was wrong. Well, I confess to believing in signs, and soon I got a call from home that Fred had gone missing. My brother and sister had searched for a week and even contacted the police, all to no avail. I thus intervened. I wrote the *Valley News* a poignant letter asking for help finding Fred, which was quickly answered! It turns out Fred had been hit by a car on Route 4, and the driver had reported the incident. She saw Fred run off after being hit but did not know where. Given the general location, my brother conducted a search.

It still hurts to report that my brother did indeed find Fred. He had crawled under a porch, and there he died, less than 250 yards from our home. I can only hope it was a quick passing, but the thought of him dying alone and in pain still brings tears. His body could not be recovered until the snow had melted, given the need to move some heavy steps. I wrote a letter of thanks to all concerned but felt unremitting guilt. I had abandoned a responsibility, which was to be something I, too, experienced when my wife left me. I was utterly miserable. That big cat had stolen my heart, and now was gone. Sadly, many of you know the pain of losing a favored pet. It can be beyond traumatic. They give us so very much and do so without hesitation or reservation. Yet their lives are short; thus, our time with them should be treasured and remembered fondly.

My brother, Peter, recovered Fred's body when it became possible. He wrapped him in some sheeting and buried him in the small garden in our yard that my brother Tom once tended. Fred loved that place, and I could not imagine a better site for his body to lie. Of course, the lesson is to keep our pets indoors or in safe confines, even if that violates their essential nature. Yet Fred would not settle for that life, as with many pets. So, should we simply impose our will? I am not sure. Fred could have lived for many more years, and he would have gone on giving and receiving love. I shall always miss him and often give the toilet an extra flush . . . just as I did to please him. He was a cat among cats, and he gave me and all who loved him far more than my feeble words can express. Amen.

PART VIII

POLITICS

73

When Democracies Are at Their Worst

Demagogues have an evolutionary function because they help test humanity's worthiness to govern itself. Indeed, democracies and democratic republics breed demagogues, some of whom have overthrown the governing institutions that put them into leadership positions (e.g., Julius Caesar, Napoleon, Adolph Hitler, etc.). One should expect this in societies that freely grant power based on popular appeal. The masses have a group intellect, temperament, and insight based on the "average" citizen's perceptions far more than the acumen of exceptional minds. Indeed, democracy can be its own worst enemy because an essentially naive, reactionary, and culturally biased collective can willingly become a slave to the resolve of self-serving egotists who have more charisma than talent.

By definition, demagogues ask and win support via exaggerated or patently false appeals to popular desires and base opinions. They typically eschew rational arguments in favor of ribald contentions aimed at commonly held prejudices, nationalism, and semi-religious beliefs, however ill-informed. Moreover, they frequently embrace the Big Lie to stoke passion and justify extreme positions. To them, acquiring power by all possible means is a self-serving end, be their goals based on egotism, greed, desire, resentment, or another psychological need that cries out for satiation. Thus, the strident demagogue seeks to rule the many for purposes that primarily serve the needs of the vested leader alone, come what may.

The term "demagogue" is derived from Greek roots, with *demos* denoting "people" and *agogue* indicting "leader, bringer" in this context. By the fifth century BCE, the ancients used the term as a means of opprobrium or disparagement, as in a "leader of the mob." The example most frequently cited is the wealthy Athenian businessman, statesman, and general Cleon (who died in 422 BCE). Cleon was the son of a wealthy tanner and merchant, and his father endowed him with ample financial resources. He was not of noble birth and detested those who were. Despite considerable animus among the elite, Cleon rose to power in about 429/430 BCE following the death of Pericles. His rhetoric was primarily based on anti-aristocratic and anti-intellectual appeals, tapping into populist and nationalistic sentiment, stoking fear of foreigners (e.g., Sparta), and using vague promises of future gains.

Aristotle tells us Cleon was:

the man who, with his attacks, corrupted the Athenians more than anyone else. He was the first who shouted on the public platform, who used abusive language, and who spoke with his cloak girt up around him, while all the others used to speak in proper dress and manner.

By nearly all accounts, Cleon's rhetoric was delivered in an aggressive and bombastic style that frequently painted his opponents as enemies of order and state interests. Cleon lauded the common and uneducated man whenever possible, and his incessant populism and self-promotion kept him in high regard with the masses. Indeed, the Athenian demos appointed Cleon to *strategos* for 424–423, our modern equivalent of a general.

He claimed success for defeating and capturing a small Spartan force in the 425 BCE Battle of Sphacteria (440 Spartans versus 11,000 Athenians and allies). However, Cleon's primary contribution was convincing the Athenians to participate in the venture. The Athenian general Demosthenes conducted most of the military operations, while Cleon garnered many honors. In 422, Cleon was again elected general by the Athenians, despite his lack of practical experience. He duly set out to reclaim the city of Amphipolis from Sparta, but things did not go according to plan during the subsequent Battle of Amphipolis

(422 BCE). Cleon was badly out-maneuvered, utterly defeated (600 Athenians killed in action versus 8 Spartans), and ultimately killed by a peltast (javelin thrower) while fleeing from a force commanded by the Spartan general Brasidas. Happily, Socrates managed to escape the debacle, albeit he fought for Athens. After 18 years of fighting, Athens fell to Sparta and its allies in 402 BCE, as did its traditional democracy.

Clearly, popular election of unqualified generals is a dubious procedure, as the educated elite understood. In Book 7 of Plato's *Republic*, Socrates asks, "If you were heading out on a journey by sea, who would you ideally want to decide who was in charge of the vessel? Just anyone or people educated in the rules and demands of seafaring?" As one can see, Plato was no fan of democracy, preferring enlightened and rigorously trained philosopher-kings as guardians of his ideal society. His was a meritocracy, albeit within a repressive totalitarian state, wherein the masses' welfare was regarded as within the exclusive purview of those best trained to oversee it. In fact, there would be little mirth and raucous behavior in Plato's well-ordered republic, nor would there be any demagoguery or dissent. It was a Nazi ideal state well before Nazism existed.

To me, democracy is a terribly flawed system, but so is totalitarianism. Oddly, both methods of governance run afoul of the same problem, as in charismatic egotists seeking to satiate personal desires rather than doing what is best for the state. Perhaps the most suitable answer is a representative democracy wherein local leaders are appointed by the masses. These representatives then select from among themselves the people best suited to lead. We see this parliamentary system in play worldwide, and it somewhat limits the potential of demagogues to gain power. After all, most politicians understand leadership and the motivations of their peers, albeit that a demagogue can still arise occasionally.

By most measures, I became an intellectual. However, I never felt informed and competent enough to select a president, although I consistently voted. I know the issues in depth, but the nuances of governance are a precise science. Few know its details and intricacies, except those with practical experience with the system. Such individuals can thus discern what is and is not possible within how government operates and who is best suited to bear the mantle of leadership. I am content to appoint representatives to govern local public affairs, concurrent with my capacity to fire them when and if they make poor choices. Those bad choices include the appointment of a lousy national leader.

As it currently stands, demagoguery is alive and well in America, and there are few or no elected leaders willing to impede its negative and self-serving aspects. In fact, we have appointed an inexperienced egotist to the nation's highest office, someone with a long history of corruption and improper behavior. His followers laud their "Orange Jesus" based on their inherent disdain for the existing political order and for governance in general. They readily dismiss their leader's many foibles, frequent missteps, and ribald lies, granting him dispensations they would never extend to the child of a lesser god. When asked why his followers respond with anger and insults. "They" represent the worst impulses in all of us and are a perfect example of how democracies often destroy themselves.

So, here we are: a deeply divided and fractious nation nearly ready to burst into Red and Blue countries. To me, the only fix possible is a democratic parliamentary system, a governmental structure far from perfect but perhaps better than what we have created. Our approach is neither democratic nor a republic, and it is fraying badly in many places. The founders knew the system they patched together would need tweaking over time, and they included mechanisms to permit changes. Perhaps it is time to try something we have not done before this nation slides into an abyss that some have willingly created. Is anyone up for a peaceful revolution of reason? It is doubtful, and some are openly calling for a civil war. Yet no fight is ever civil, and only fools plunge in where angels will not follow. Alas, America has no shortage of foolish people, including this writer. Amen.

74

Lords of the Flies

Many of us grew up very close to nature in the Upper Valley, with long walks through and beside cow pastures occasionally providing excellent analogies to the human condition. Of course, cattle defecate, like all animals, with the freshest, smelliest, and juiciest cow pats attracting the most and largest flies. You can check it out firsthand and find that this is the case, with some piles of poop attracting minion dung flies. They can sometimes assume plague-like densities and woe unto the person who strays too close to that nastiness.

American politics seems strikingly similar in some ways to walking through cattle fields. Take the ongoing Trump tweeting hysteria. Here is a guy who likes to constantly excrete the most enormous manure piles possible, with every extreme claim,

74.1 Cow-pat politics and reporting plague America.

outright lie, and dubious position designed to generate the largest imaginable stench when pooped out via X number of tweets. So, McCain isn't a hero, "anchor babies" is an acceptable term, Hispanic immigrants are all criminals, and so it goes . . . spew after oozy spew. And even after he was beaten in the 2020 election, the manure just didn't stop coming, with public whining joining the excrement to increase its stench.

Of course, the press is neither imaginative nor principled, behaving like flies in their knee-jerk stimulus–response behaviors. Thus, reporters and analysts buzz about smelly old Trump tweets and pronouncements, leaving lesser poopers to wither unattended. Indeed, FOX, CNN, and others have endless special reports whenever Trump breaks wind and releases a messy mass. The talking heads make the loudest imaginable buzz over every word. Hell, it's so much easier for the press to follow what gets good ratings than to do anything akin to public service, and so the drumbeat goes. Instead, the press stirs and distributes the manure to better spread its polluting stink hither and yon.

For example, Tucker Carlson and Sean Hannity knew that the crazies they were hosting to promote the Big Lie were absolutely wrong about their election fraud claims, as did their master, Rupert Murdoch. However, they happily let the deceitful tails wag the election-lie dog to appeal to their audience's prejudices and anger at losing an election. In fact, Carlson wanted her fired when FOX correspondent Jacqui Heinrich fact-checked one of Trump's election claims. How dare any FOX reporter tell the truth? A better question would be, how could anyone believe such whoppers as FOX spews?

These kinds of antics led to the debacle of January 6, 2021, a genuine attempt to overthrow our government with the brainwashed and foolish leading the charge. Are Murdoch, Carlson, and Hannity any less culpable than Trump for what happened on January 6? Not in my book. They are even worse, having knowingly lied to please their audience and to line their pockets. There can be no greater sins, but nothing will be done. After all, this is America, the land of the free, deluded, and malcontent. This is where the press lies on command and, all the while, knows its own dreary rectitude. Deeper moral and ethical issues need not concern them when ratings are everything.

Those eager beaver poop eaters love hyperbole and don't reflect much on what is being said while they attend to all the noise and hullabaloo, devouring every morsel. Some like and even admire the pungent fragrance of what is being served up, finding it a refreshing change from the bland odor they are accustomed to. "Yes, sir, it's a great idea to put up a big fence to keep them damn Mexicans out. Get 'er done! It don't make no never mind how we pay for it." And so the tea flows.

I'm amused by it all, cow-pat politics in America. Sure, people are pissed off, but many don't know why. They blame our collective ills on out-groups, politicians, foreigners, lawyers, Liberals, and everyone but the person they see in the mirror. Truth is, America is suffering from gross irresponsibility and stupidity, as in looking toward others for faults that are clearly our own. It's the teachers' fault my kid is not doing well in school. It's the cop's fault I got busted for driving under the influence or for stealing. It's the boss's fault my job sucks. We eat and poop this crap daily; such is our myopia and lack of self-reflection.

The fact that Trump's dung has attracted so many flies is ample proof that we are lost, for no thinking creatures could ever tolerate such a stench, let alone devour it. Ultimately, those who care about the country and this world must save it through their thoughts and deeds. We can only hope there are enough folks to take up the slack and do the things needed for the species to survive, beginning with the person reading these words. There will always be hoards of stench-loving folks who prefer to buzz around piles of festering feces rather than work for the common good. Cattle are brighter than that. Despite the lush growth simulated by the reeking fertilizer, they will not graze near manure pats. They know what messes to avoid, far more so than do most reporters . . . and folks like me. Amen.

75

Threads Fray

Even the finest and most intricately woven threads fray with time, especially when a tapestry is exposed to high stress and hard use over the ages. While pondering this basic truism, the fate of the United States drifts through my mind. Over 160 years ago, a great civil war killed 620,000 Americans and maimed 1.5 million more. The issues included states' rights, secession, slavery, economics, and largely incompatible sociocultural practices between different regions of the country. These issues might have been alleviated or ameliorated with a more comprehensively drafted constitution. Still, the history of slavery teaches us that even the definition and scope of freedom were impossible for the nation's founders to agree upon, let alone the collective whole.

Thus, many compromises were made, covering differences that would one day reveal themselves in tragic ways.

Concerning slavery, many of our nation's founders seemed to feel that all men were not truly created equal because they owned people. Nor were those they possessed endowed by their Creator with certain unalienable rights. So, the founders applied patches of mutual disregard for problematic issues instead of fully integrating threads that were difficult to weave together. Alas, the inherent flaws weakened the nation's underlying unity as the regional differences festered and, after some 80 years, the fabric finally gave way. The resultant tear morphed into a savage and terrible conflict that devoured more lives and treasure than the nation's founders imagined.

The country endured the Civil War and was patched back together via stitches of iron, gunpowder, and blood. However, long-standing differences festered beneath the imposed patches, weakening to this day the threads of unity binding this nation together. Indeed, it is dubious to consider America as an amalgamation of fully united states. In truth, it never has been, but whatever differences existed during the last 160 years were accorded a lesser place than the general notion that we are better off united than divided. There is currently bitter and open political discord throughout America, stoked by nationalistic chest-thumping and populist stridency. Rampant hatred penetrates our private and public discourse. It is often fanned by our nation's foes, vested forces within, and via the agency of twisted and intolerant ideologies that do not permit compromise. Rural Red America and urban Blue America are separated by education, belief, color, creed, geography, wealth, and much more. Some call themselves Conservatives, and others subscribe to a Liberal philosophy. Add an undemocratic electoral system that favors thinly populated states over citified regions, and the current turmoil was inevitable. The center has given way to the extremes, and our star-spangled banner has become threadbare and tattered.

In fact, I participate in pointless cyber wars regularly. I recall one wherein some anonymous keyboard hero said, "We got the guns, and it is you communist Libs who will get your asses handed to you when the shooting starts!" I asked my erstwhile opponent how he thought the founders described themselves, Liberal or Conservative. He should have said American, but he told me, "They sure weren't no damn Liberal snowflakes." I told him nearly all of the founders described themselves as avowed Liberals, as befits people seeking to overthrow an entrenched political order based on kingship. I also advised him that one of my kinfolks fought during the Revolutionary War, suffering two musket wounds to the face that left him disfigured for life. He told me to go if I didn't love America, and I told him to make me. I offered my address and contact info, saying, "My kin have been here since 1634, and I'll be damned if an ignorant piss-ant will tell me to leave!" And so it went, with me receiving three death threats before the 2020 election. Well, that was down from six during the 2016 national elections. You see, I'm part of the problem.

Leadership can rise to the occasion and focus on what is needed to unify this diverse country. Conversely, it can flame divisions by embracing demagoguery, corruption, and deceit. Indeed, anger, deception, and mockery act as crude scissors that can separate us by race, region, belief, and much more. Some are called socialist snowflakes by those who happily suckle down Social Security checks and other governmental benefits, not realizing their hypocrisy. Others are dubbed con-dumb cultists and Trumpanzees, as if such mockery befits a supposedly well-educated mind. And sprinkled throughout is mutual loathing as "us" gathers against "them," with posting boards dripping the venom of paid foreign trolls and homegrown haters. I am one of the latter and openly confess to my inveterate desire to be absolutely divorced from the God-awful them, those savage apes that deserve only the very worst that God has to offer. I would happily see two Americas, one free of the "goobers" and blessed by ideals that separate church from state, protect equal rights, and ensure our fundamental freedoms.

Therein resides the primary problem. Many Americans on all sides feel the same way about protecting their individual viewpoints and rights, with all concerned not wanting "them" to trample on "our" civil liberties and ways of life. This mutual distrust and disrespect are precisely why the Russians and their kindred can easily interfere in our politics. They realize that the

United States is far more vulnerable than many would-be patriots like to think. The threads that unite us are as weak as before the Civil War. If we are lucky, there will be no armed conflict this time. Instead, one can predict a semi-amicable dissolution as the Northeast, Pacific Coast, and others form the blue United States. In contrast, the South and rural states craft a red confederation. I don't believe the nation's enemies would gain anything from such a division because both entities would be relatively wealthy and well-armed.

Moreover, each entity would have greater internal unity than the nation currently enjoys. However, something would be lost because the United States is actually an idea. The premise is based upon instilling and protecting the themes of life, liberty, and the pursuit of happiness, all anchored within a structure that provides justice, tolerance, and equality. Is this something we should even contemplate giving up?

Regrettably, tolerance and equality within the United States were stillborn from the beginning, and justice is a matter of local perceptions and values. These ideals were all sacrificed on the altar of phony idealism, religiosity, selfishness, and salesmanship, the cynical means to political ends. We thus have a situation wherein rigid adherence to label-defined beliefs and personal branding is deemed far more important than accepting differences. There is no compromise, no shades of grey. There is no united "us" or "we," none of the shared ideals that can hold us together as one people. I see all this from an abstract intellectual perspective, but I simply cannot overcome my loathing of "them!" After all, "they" are utterly ignorant and uncultured barbarians, the end result of inbreeding and watching too much FOX noise and religious evangelicalism. Yes, I realize my rectitude, and it is indeed a tragedy when those who can see willingly elect not to look.

How perfidious we humans are, happily bashing each other through word and deed and then calling ourselves righteous. Disabled people are mocked while racial tensions bubble up and explode. Children are shot down in churches and schools while some simpletons yammer about making America great again by supplying more guns. And heaven knows that those Chinese, Mexicans, Russians, and many others are just waiting to devour our land and sell us cheap goods! Moreover, by all means, let us heap all opprobrium upon those useless "woke" people, the supporters of transgender rights, and all such nonsense. Meanwhile, our underlying problems go unresolved because "some" isn't enough. It is all or nothing.

Those who have helped fan these flames may harvest the whirlwind one day. The foreign trolls, haters, and innocent alike will all get burned if the center gives way, and perhaps that is how it should be. God's lessons can be harsh and painful, as the Civil War proved. Yet it is our own hands, hearts, and deeds that make matters this way. The answers and the problems reside within that image we see in a mirror. Will we dare to compromise, or will we burn? It's our choice, and I am not all that optimistic right now about the United States. Many Americans cannot see the forest because of all the damn trees, and I am but one. God willing, perhaps we can muddle through. Amen.

76

Guns, Guns, Everywhere a Gun

Americans have no right to be safe from gun violence within this vast land of unbridled opportunity. It has been ordained that owning guns is a personal right in the United States, which trumps any desire or need to be secure from their potential ill-use. We cannot be safe in our homes, streets, schools, churches, or temples. In fact, there are about 120.5 guns for every 100 people in the United States, making us the most armed society in the world. About 40 percent of all households have at least one gun on hand, and about 30 percent of all Americans claim to own at least one gun. However, only 3 percent of all Americans own roughly 33.3 percent (133 million) of the 400 million guns we have in circulation. Most gun collections number between 8 and 140 weapons, typically about a dozen. I have been in such households, one of which was the site of an accident that killed a 14-year-old boy.

Gun owners tell me to get a pistol or shotgun if I feel threatened or unsafe, and thus to make my personal safety predicated upon a willingness to harm another. In effect, I can buy security at the risk of making others less secure. Hell, I am far more likely to shoot myself or an innocent person than I am to shoot a criminal. In fact, it seems about 500 Americans get accidentally killed with guns yearly versus the 260 criminals "legally" killed by gun owners. For each justifiable homicide with a firearm, there are 34 gun homicides, 82 gun suicides, and 2 accidental gun deaths. Well, so much for the good guy with a gun argument. A whopping 24,292 folks committed suicide with guns in 2020, 53 percent of the 45,979 suicides that happened that year. In addition, 19,384 (78 percent) out of the 24,576 homicides in 2020 were associated with gun use. Meanwhile, there are roughly 700–1,000 police-caused firearm deaths. Overall, 45,000-plus die by guns yearly, while another 110,000-plus are wounded.

Being from New Hampshire, I became familiar with guns early on. We had a beat-up old .22 long rifle that could only be coaxed into working by great effort. Of course, deer hunting and other seasons were a big deal for most kids where I grew up. The same is true in many states, and at Penn State it was often useless to try to conduct any classes when the deer-hunting season started. Hunting has long been a way of life in the United States, and the herds have adjusted to the yearly culling. Some may not like Bambi getting shot down, but Bambi may starve if the deer population is too large and winter is too harsh. I am not a big fan of hunting, but I can understand the tradition and need.

Furthermore, most hunters are trained to some degree in firearm use, and thus they only suffer 1.5 incidents per 100,000 hunters each year (about 100 deaths and 900 injuries). Yet hunting is a damn-sight different than cowboys with a mad-on trying to be tough guys. In fact, we typically have about 10 mass shootings per year, and here we see people hunting people.

The essential point is that gun ownership doesn't seem to make folks safer. Besides, the current type of shoot-'em-up "freedom" is not how I want to live. Alas, personal choices can be limited in this land of liberty. In short, a minority tells the majority how it must live because their individual rights to possess firearms dominates all else. Some may consider this a consummately selfish and myopic perspective, but I think there is something more pernicious underlying the attitude. It is a mentality based on fear and the simplistic notion that deadly force is the font from which personal freedom springs. Ergo, the collective whole must sacrifice its security so that some may feel protected or empowered. Most of those seeking protection fear the government far more than bad guys and regard firearms as a means of preventing malicious governmental control.

I know many responsible gun owners who are not a threat to anyone. They are good and kind people by any standard. I also know nut-cases who own all sorts of weapons, and they are a clear and present danger to anyone nearby. Good Lord, my friend Tony is certifiable, and the miscreant packs a TEC-9. When he is brandishing that damn thing, I do not feel safe, nor should any living thing. Tony is bipolar, and folks like him should not own anything sharp, let alone firearms. However, unlike trucks, buses, cars, planes, or other potentially dangerous tools, one doesn't need any demanding tests, psychological histories, or additional sets of criteria to own a gun. If you're not yet a convicted felon, that's usually good enough. Thus, Mad Tony packs legal heat. He is half crazy when sober, which is less than half the time. The walls of his trailer are pockmarked with bullet holes. Yeah, he's out there, just waiting to cook off. However, it's all legal. I bet many of you know folks like Tony.

This is an odd country, a land wherein personal freedom impedes one of the most fundamental rights we should share: freedom from fear. There is a bar down the way, and the drunks stagger by late at night. I sometimes wonder whether Mad Tony or someone like him will be one of the rowdies. His seething rage could become the death knell for some poor soul, a cop, or a classroom full of kids. However, this is how freedom works in America, with the rights of the individual being held paramount over the common welfare. There are no easy answers here. Most countries address firearm issues far differently than the United States, but here, the collective "we" are being forced to suffer the dreadful malevolence of Mad Tony and his cohorts. Every day the blood spills, sometimes by the bucket full. And so it goes in this land of the free.

One day, America may be liberated from this threat. This assumes we grow enough as a people to recognize that the chaos occurring in our communities needs to be addressed. Gun ownership will be a right with requirements when reason rules. The prerequisites will include a psychological assessment, an actual background check, and required gun-safety training courses. In some countries, guns are safely secured in municipal and/or state-controlled arsenals, where target shooters, sportsmen, and others can store and retrieve their weapons. I am not sure such a system would work in the United States, but it could reduce some ongoing madness.

Yet in having strict requirements, all gun owners will have been tested in weapon safety protocols, and those with dubious psychological or criminal histories will be banned from gun use or ownership altogether. Illegal gun possession violations will be harsh, as in 5- to 10-year sentences. Gun use while committing crimes will merit 20 years to life in prison. These measures may curb the criminal urge to procure and/or use guns for wicked ends, but I doubt it. These proposals for reducing gun violence are admittedly problematic; but, as it stands, the nation is in chaos, and no one feels safe. Either we act rationally, or we suffer collectively from the ongoing madness. The essential point is that if we do nothing, nothing changes. Then you may meet the dark side of Mad Tony one day, and that will be no fun at all. Amen.

77

On Wearing Labels

To my way of thinking, people who label themselves or others as Liberal or Conservative have their heads planted firmly up their butts. The folks who call others Fascists or Communists are just as bad. They are judges without judgment. Instead, these spewers of ribald belief are like those preening and prideful debutant dupes who wear such heavy makeup that they look like circus clowns, mere caricatures of people. Truth is, most of us are conservative about some issues, liberal about others, and neutral concerning many subjects, with individual experiences directing us where they will. For example, I embrace equality, unions, gun control, progressive taxation, Social Security, the separation of church and state, reproductive choice, and other typically liberal notions. On the other hand, I also strongly support the rule of

77.1 Need our political leaning be polar extremes?

law, our armed forces, states' rights, the free practice of religion, the existence of a Creator, and many policing agencies, which are issues often considered conservative territory. Moreover, I am open to gay marriage, universal health care, and similar matters. However, I am not amenable to many ideas and/or behaviors, such as pedophilia, slavery, bestiality, torture, political correctness, fraud, laissez-faire capitalism, and much more.

I suspect everyone reading these words has both conservative and liberal preferences regarding different issues, so why paint ourselves with generalized labels that only mean something to people who can barely think at all? Ergo, if you're calling yourself a Liberal or Conservative, use appropriate adjectives: such as foolish, stupid, simple-minded, blind, inane, reactionary, myopic, and so on. One can thus be a foolish Conservative or myopic Liberal. Still, one can hardly ever be a "pure" Conservative or

Liberal unless one adds an adjectival equivalent to "idiotic." For example, one can be mostly "this" on specific issues, but ample room exists for being "that" on other subjects. As for me, I've finally decided I'm neither Conservative nor Liberal. I'm mildly misanthropic with some idealistic tendencies, which means hope still exists. As for you self-described Liberals and Conservatives, please consider the following before applying labels to your clown makeup.

Webster's dictionary defines liberal as "not opposed to new ideas or ways of behaving that are not traditional or widely accepted." With this comes the notion that Liberals believe "that government should be active in supporting social and political change." Liberals are thus "open to new behavior or opinions and willing to discard traditional values." Of course, there are degrees to which some folks will not accept some parts of a label while embracing others. For example, I don't mind people deciding they are transgender. Yet, I find it unacceptable for a biological man to compete against a natural woman in weight-lifting or many other sports. Hmmm, I wonder if one can be a Conservative-Liberal.

The term "Liberal" has become anathema to some, but our nation's founders certainly embraced liberal ideals, as befits a group that wanted to change an existing order. For example, George Washington advised:

As Mankind becomes more liberal, they will be more apt to allow that all those who conduct themselves as worthy members of the community are equally entitled to the protections of civil government. I hope ever to see America among the foremost nations of justice and liberality.

Of course, some of our Liberal-minded founders also owned slaves, so how they defined themselves is not exactly the same as how we would describe these people based on today's standards. Definitions change with time, so it is folly to think we could fully understand how someone from a different time believed.

Conservative is "holding to traditional attitudes and values and cautious about change or innovation, typically in relation to politics or religion." This perspective is based on preserving the existing order, whatever this order may be. Thus, a conservative is averse to change and holds tightly to extant and entrenched legal, social, political, and religious ideologies. Many conservatives sided with King George and the established British-based colonial governance in early US history. Indeed, they were very much against the Revolution, and several fought our nation's founders tooth and nail. Many current self-described American Conservatives believe the US Constitution should be interpreted as perceived by its creators, a challenging task given the passage of time and the accompanying shifts in the meaning of various terms.

Much more can be added to each description, but these are the essentials in terms of basic definitions. Oddly, many people who describe themselves as Conservative or Liberal do not know how the words are defined or their history. However, that should not be surprising, given the ineptitude and superciliousness that comes with willfully wearing labels. Look at those ridiculous hats and T-shirts folks wear at political events, even to the extent of being tattooed. To me, these folks are advertising their ignorance, which they have a perfect right to do. After all, we can't ban stupidity. So, are you a Conservative or a Liberal? Or could you be smart enough to avoid using either label? After all, playing the role of a clown does get tedious after a while. Besides, fashions change quickly, and whatever colors we wear today may be shifted to entirely different attire tomorrow. And then what becomes of all our makeup or tattooes? Oh, the human condition is far from easy. Amen.

78

Existential Threats

In 2016 a truck was used to horrible effect in slaughtering 84 people on Bastille Day in Nice, France, providing yet more proof that the weapons of terrorism come in many forms. A disgruntled man revved up a truck's engine and plowed through a vast crowd, killing and maiming as many as possible. Was it another Muslim attack? Well, not by an organized group. The crime was perpetrated by a wife-beating Tunisian petty criminal who had nothing going for him except three kids. Now they will have to pay for his sins and be forever marked, mocked, and maybe even killed. And so it goes when passion, stupidity, and malintent merge. We saw much the same thing here in the good old United States on January 6, 2021, the desecration of our capital building by an unthinking mob of raging seditionists.

As Islamic State in Iraq and Syria (ISIS) is crushed under a continuous barrage of air and land attacks, its ardent supporters reach out to disaffected Muslims with a straightforward aim. They wish to provoke a Muslim–Christian Armageddon, though most of the world's political leaders perceive the possibility and work hard to avoid its eventual realization. ISIS has harvested a whirlwind of enhanced strikes over their recent assaults. Still, the organization will happily trade several hundred lives for the deaths of dozens of French and other citizens. Such is the grim mathematics of war when you're on the losing side. Yet as it currently stands in 2023, ISIS is losing leader after leader, sometimes to drone strikes, but more often to Special Forces assassinations. As for the rank and file, they are now the hunted and not the hunters.

One wonders if their acts of terrorism are getting ISIS any closer to its ultimate goal of a complete and hostile breakdown in relationships between the Muslim and Christian worlds. I would have said no for now, but Western demagogues provide ample evidence that preying on religious hatred is not restricted to radical Muslims. For example, the leadership of "make America great again" (MAGA), which borrows freely from Hitler's playbook, has already instituted widespread scapegoating and public loathing via "anti-woke" opprobrium and other means that find their way into the popular press. Indeed, some zealots openly scorn Mexicans, Chinese, women, gays, the disabled, and, most especially, Muslims.

Millions of Americans eagerly cheer hate-filled words, with millions more applauding from the wings. Our home-grown haters thus do ISIS's work for them, stoking the fires of ethnic and religious hatred that lead to the immolation of all concerned. Furthermore, MAGA has amply demonstrated that there are enough seething and bellicose Americans to tip the US into a far more cooperative attitude concerning participating in another mindless war. Of course, it is not MAGA alone that seeks to sow chaos, for any number of vested energy, commercial, religious, and international interests like to stir the pot. Yeah, there is no shortage of haters in America, and I am most assuredly one of them. You see, I hate the haters, which makes me as vile as they are.

Even as their losses explode and territory shrinks, ISIS sees hope in the likes of eager-beaver political dupes who willingly participate in their plans. Of course, the group despises the status quo because ISIS now faces utter extermination, a fate they have foisted upon many others. Indeed, their identified head-cutters are now prime targets, and many have faced the harshest justice. They originally planned on melting away, if need be, only to reform in other regions. However, their ongoing losses in leadership, equipment, and fighters have been staggering, and they are now teetering on the brink of abject failure. Nonetheless, ideas are hard to kill permanently, and their last and best hope resides therein. They will simply endure until the time is right to rise anew.

A wise leader would suffer the losses ISIS and ISIS-inspired attacks cause and keep striking back until the group loses enough adherents, territory, cohesiveness, and influence to forfeit a viable future. This is a difficult task, but it is now being managed successfully. A fool would act disproportionately to ISIS' actions and thus cause so much slaughter of innocents and general outrage that it fosters ISIS's goals. Yet many of "our" cyber heroes blithely talk about exterminating entire groups of people, albeit they do so from the comfort of some pulpit or comfy news studio. In short, our home-grown zealots and ISIS walk hand-in-hand, for they thrive on hatred, violence, and discord. One would think we could find a better way, but I have little confidence in that prospect.

We humans usually understand and restrain our darker sides, but we also tend to revel in the release of our suppressed tendencies. If there were still public executions, there would be crowds of people to watch the gory spectacles, just as there would still be an audience for the gladiatorial games of old Rome. Indeed, mixed martial arts (MMA) amply proves the latter point, albeit the carnage wrought is governed by something akin to rules that prevent deaths. Pre-2020, there were seven deaths from sanctioned MMA fights. Nine more came from unregulated bouts, but the numbers are still relatively low considering the number of people who engage in martial arts. Still, we watch the MMA contests while they unfold, eager to see some big-mouth lout laid low or a prima donna get the skids put to her. The urge seems to be born in the blood.

So, what is a terrorist to do to get noticed in this modern world? Well, cutting off heads seemed to do the trick, and thus it became the rave wherever ISIS once ruled. However, many decapitators have been blown to bits, shot up, or otherwise terminated as the West and others extract their pound of flesh. If they are lucky, the head-cutters die quickly, but often that is not the case. An arm may be torn off, or perhaps a leg. Great agonies and blood loss follow, although it usually ends within 20 minutes. Still, that is not an attractive way to die, although what could decapitators expect? Moreover, sometimes their entire family pays the piper, for guilt is transferred to the next of kin in some ethnic groups.

One wonders if our politics has evolved even slightly since biblical times, but I believe so. We have chained slavery, made "rules" of war, and even punished war crimes. But nearly everyone reading these words knows the dark tendencies that many of us harbor deep within. The rape or murder of a loved one may well release a beast of vengeance in a formerly kind man or woman that would lay low not only the killer but perhaps his or her entire family. Supposedly, we have laws and beliefs that help us chain our savage tendencies, yet they often churn away, seeking recourse via bloodletting.

If I were from an advanced species, I would not share any high tech with a genus of bipedal hominids such as humans. After all, look at their history of savagery with primitive means. Is this a lot any advanced species would like to see running amok through the entire universe with starships and energy weapons?

Well, perhaps not right now. Yet I have this odd faith we will get there. Indeed, maybe one day we will live by the golden rule and thus will begin a new age for our kind. Amen.

79

Pigs and Politics

During this Tuesday's presidential primary, a 600-pound hog somehow found its way to a polling place in Pelham, NH (February 9, 2016). I found the incident most appropriate, for that porcine is at least as bright as those inbred, red-hat-wearing MAGA miscreants who voted for the Con. I bet that big, old sow did indeed get a ballot, a nice pink one to match her Grand Old Party proclivities. Yeah, and she probably managed to mark the ballot in the right place, though getting that vote into the counting machine required some help. The good news is that the police were seen escorting the hog away for questioning, something about an ID issue. Yeah, I bet that porcine wasn't registered, and it looks like she wasn't even carrying a wallet.

I am usually very proud of New Hampshire, but I have to agree with the *New York Daily News*. Yes, there are "Mindless Zombie" voters in New Hampshire, and lots of them. Some are my kith and kin! Hell, I see one every time I glance in the mirror, lame sot that he is. And to those many New Hampshire zombies that voted for Trump and company goes the distinction of enshrining the man who will divide and destroy. We've made many mistakes in our history but never placed Satan incarnate upon the throne. Oh, my goodness, what will we do? Hmmm, perhaps I'm being a bit hyperbolic, and I should see more humor in the situation.

Yet it is not all that amusing, except for the hog voting. For the life of me, I see no logic whatsoever in supporting a big-mouthed whiner in a three-piece suit who isn't exceptionally bright or talented. He is a beast of petty ego that the press finds solace in because they always appeal to the lowest common denominator. Trump feeds the press a steady diet of bullshit, and they buzz about for more. They made him, and with every extreme utterance he provided them with more crap. Ain't reciprocity grand?

And now we have former New York City mayor Mike Bloomberg spewing up political verbiage about running, and once again, the flies are buzzing. Will we become a nation of oligarchs wherein vested rich pricks run the show? Some will say we have always been "managed" by the elite. Zombie voters in New Hampshire don't seem to think it matters all that much . . . when we can think at all. Some of them are indeed my friends, and they will be pissed off to the max when they read this. I can live with their angst, but I cannot live with Trumpism and Trumpanzees.

To me, New Hampshire has cast this nation adrift, and into the coming tempest, we shall all go. And make no mistake about it: this travail will be no fun. Come the eventual revolution, New Hampshire will most definitely not be given the right of primacy in the electoral process. That right will shift from state to state, with New Hampshire consistently voting dead last. We deserve nothing more and a whole lot less. As for me, I voted for Sanders, who may be able to defeat the dreaded Trump. Yeah, that'll happen when pigs can fly, but it's possible. After all, pigs can already vote in the Granite State! Amen.

PS: This piece predicted a lot of what has unfolded sans the misery of January 6, 2021. It did not take a prophet to see where enshrining the likes of Trump would lead. However, one day, time itself shall still his nasty maw, and then the press will have to work for a living. That would be nice. Still, they'll find another patch of bullshit to land upon and devour, and then the nation must muddle through as best it can.

80

Blood Sport

I had a bizarre dream last night, utterly brutal in its theme and meaning and full of color, sound, and fury. Several wild animals were chained to tree trunks that lined the far side of an open field. There was a doe, ferret, large wildcat, goose, tubby woodchuck, raccoon, squirrel, and other forest creatures securely tethered by chains to their respective posts. A large and raucous crowd was gathered about 30 yards away on the opposite side of the field, and I was among the unwashed masses. The observers were really into the gory spectacle, and many stank of booze and body odor.

Occasionally, a particular animal would suddenly lurch out and attack one of the others. However, their placement was so contrived that it put one creature or the other at a significant advantage or disadvantage. For example, the doe was built for speed and agility, a God-given ability to avoid attackers. This was taken away by stout chains that held the deer in place, and thus even the ground-hugging woodchuck could nip the doe's lower legs if so inclined. The poor animal's legs got increasingly mauled as the utterly savage exhibition proceeded, a singularly gruesome process to watch. Good Lord, blood poured from long, gaping wounds, and the deer was getting eaten alive.

This greatly amused those watching from across the field. They hooted and howled with each inflicted wound. I found the odd blood sport cruel and barbaric, senseless savagery that went out with the Middle Ages. The wild cat took it especially hard, being repeatedly set upon by creatures it could usually easily avoid or kill. The cat had the fiercest bite and inflicted deep, bloody wounds on several compatriots. However, the chains ensured the cat could not flee far or jump very high, not that it tried to. In fact, the feline was savagely attacked by all the other animals at one time or another. The raccoon got a particularly savage bite into the cat's upper left arm that shattered the bone, leaving the wildcat limping on a mangled and disgustingly deformed appendage. But the worst damage to the cat was inflicted by the ferret. At one point, the fierce little beast tore a piece of the wildcat's upper jaw off, a gruesome injury. I turned away in disgust at the sight of its battered and dying body while the crowd roared.

Even during the dream, I knew the underlying theme, as in debate politics CNN style. The ratings' beasts were all tethered to their respective podiums, and ardent "journalists" asked each candidate schoolyard gibes designed to bring out conflict, the role of picadors in bullfighting, and many other blood sports. Thus, one candidate was goaded to go after another or defend against some petty insult or gibe. One picador exclaimed the equivalent of, "Donald says your face looks terrible, just butt-ass ugly. What do you think about that?"

And so it went, with some monitoring the audience response to every word. Of course, Donald, the wildcat (?), supposedly got pretty ripped up, much to the amusement of many. Yet I did not see it that way. The candidates got the attention they so eagerly craved, and the audience got scammed, as it always does. I found the staged event much ado about ratings more than anything else, the press's incessant need to make news rather than to report it. To be perfectly honest, I did not watch the debate live, for I do not feed feral pigs if avoidable. We already have too many of the damn things running about, so why provide them with food? My imagination addressed the "real" content issues during this dream, albeit via a disturbing and bloody metaphor.

Reflecting on the dream and debate, I think of Alice and the Cheshire Cat. One day, the only thing left of Donald, or some other politico, will be the fading image of glaring eyes, a mocking mouth, and some famously-quaffed vanity hairdo. The press is on the hunt, and such a tethered target as Trump can only endure. He will survive and prosper but be painted and tainted, forever a vile and egotistical demagogue to most thinking folks. He will never have excellent ratings, which hardly matters in securing political power. It isn't like America is actually a democracy.

As for others, the best we can hope for is that some of the wounded animals crawl out of the bloody carnage still alive, becoming some of the few who managed to survive the press's cull. As for me, I'll have none of it. What is being conducted in these media contests is neither a debate nor news. It is puerile entertainment, an appeal to all that is vulgar and violent, those lowest possible denominators that the press so loves. We usually get what we deserve during this life, albeit often not what we most need. Well, maybe I can get back to bed. There is much to do today, and I am exhausted. Soon, I must live through the nightmare of debate reviews, with helpful talking heads telling me how I feel, what I saw, and what it all means. Yeah, we hardly need to think about issues with such advice from our monitors. Amen.

81

Buying Favor

I've been reading about the most prolific and wealthy political donors who help to pollute our electoral system with vast wads of money. I need some of that largess big time. Oh, the sources of America's political perfidy change with time and fortune, but make no mistake about it . . . some would readily select and buy our leaders for us. A few power brokers own entire stables of politicos, all eager to do their paymaster's bidding. Indeed, our Supreme Court has ruled that the uber-rich can buy whoever they want, equating their political contributions with "free speech." After all, it isn't like America ever crafted an actual working democracy. At its core, the United States has always been an oligarchy wearing democratic drag.

Our top political cash-cows for the current 2020 election cycle "donations" includes the following (listed by name and contributions): Sheldon G. and Miriam O. Adelson ($218,168,500, Republican, Las Vegas, gambling), Michael R. Bloomberg ($152,509,750, Democrat, media), Thomas and Taylor Steyer ($72,119,974, Democrat, business), Richard and Elizabeth Uihlein ($68,314,982, Republican, Uline, business), Kenneth C. Griffin ($67,423,384, Republican, business), Timothy Mellon ($60,097,555, Republican, business), and Dustin and Cari Moskovitz ($50,568,012, Democrat, business). These are among the 25 people who have paid $14,558,850 or more, which is enough to buy a vested interest in any politician. Lord only knows who will be the top cash cows next year, but it is a safe bet some of these same names will show up.

Some of these rich folks are brilliant, such as James Simons, a mathematician and theorist who has written scholarly articles for academic journals. Others, such as Sheldon Adelson, are not scholars by any measure but shrewd and hard-working business aficionados who know how to turn big profits. The majority are elderly, white Republicans who contributed mightily to right-leaning political causes and for little gain in the last election. They are countered by primarily elderly, white Democrats, who lack much organizational prowess but are equally fervent in equating money with political power.

Yet what bothers me most about ALL these wealthy folks is that they would be better served in giving some of their hard-earned money to people who really need it, like me! I am awash in a sea of red ink, and that tide keeps rolling in. And there you rich folks go, wasting billions of dollars on two causes that do little more than create the kind of discord that ensures the nation doesn't get a damned thing done. I am a much better deal: you can readily discern this fact by the words you're reading! You all know I am openly self-serving, but at least I am not afraid to say so.

You rich people buy and sell political influence by the millions and make yourselves popes of the moment. Then the lameass politicos bend their knees, kiss your shiny rings, and rush to curry more favor from other rich pricks. They say sweet words that please you, and all the while, our country goes to hell in a handbasket. Gosh, I am a much better deal than that because I will tell you like it is, not merely what you want to hear! Are your egos too bloated to entertain what is true? Are you sure spreading your preferred ideology is more important than the ongoing corruption drowning our political system in a sea of lies and discord? Yeah, some of you folks ought to be ashamed of yourselves. And that little sage advice I just offered ought to be worth at least a few million, or perhaps enough to pay my damn credit card bill. I may be a lowly beggar, but at least I am honest!

So, instead of giving to some damn political action committee to do the devil's work concerning our nation's welfare, help folks in ways that count. Yes, some rich people are already into philanthropy, although many seem to hate it when giving comes through social programs. I just don't get that. On the one hand, some of you rich bastards give to beat the band to scholarship funds, building programs, and education. Yet you get all strange about having the government doing the same damn thing. Some of you claim big government is a sin, at least the parts of it that you don't own. Others say politicos make terrible business decisions, except for the politicos you bought off. Yet as rich as you guys may be, it is clear that the multitude can do even more than you folks. Someone will have to sit down and explain all of this to me because I do not get your outrage about social programs.

So, instead of swift-boating a Kerry, mangling a Mitt, or dumping Trump, why don't you guys give to the "Save the George Fund?" It is tax-deductible, and you could foster the creation of witty chapters like this here, at least during those times when I can stay upright and am dead-ass sober. Yeah, I am a disabled person, one of those useless eaters. Of course, needy kids deserve your help much more than lame sots like me, as do wounded veterans, battered women, and the like. The essential point is, you folks just coughed up billions in political donations, and what did you buy? Well, you got an increasingly divided nation, a congress that can't get a damn thing done, and the possible ruination of America's future. What a deal!

Some rich pricks should be wacked with a big stick, but let's not go there. Instead, let's consider what needs to be done to help the country. And please don't tell me it's giving even more money to damn politicians! That dog cannot hunt to save its own life. The system has become corrupted enough and reached the utter failure stage. As soon as some of these clowns get elected, they're already back at work raising money. You already know that because they come knocking on your doors! Their collective mantra is to hell with our national needs during these times of greed. You rich geeks have been a big part of that problem and not the solution, which is something you need to be told.

Put your mendacity aside and help set things right for a change. I think you know what causes are worth a damn, and they are not associated with parties, PACs, or politics. They are related to your neighbors, children, and folks in need. If you guys can't see that, you're just not looking hard enough. And, of course, there are always lame-ass folks like me, and keeping us off the streets is always good for the country. Please send me whatever donations you see fit, but do it soon. Now, get it done . . . or I'll write even more of these essays! Amen.

82

Illegal Aliens

William Holton, my paternal grandfather many times removed, came from Ipswich, Suffolk County, England, to New England in 1634 aboard the ship *Francis*. By 1638 he was given a land grant in Hartford, Connecticut, consisting of some 38 acres. Now mind you, I am reasonably sure the area's original inhabitants were not consulted about how their seized lands were distributed. However, our forefathers had firearms, heavy artillery, cavalry, ample numbers, and good military organization. Indeed, we had a much more developed lethal technology than the natives; thus, they didn't stand much chance. "The People" fought mightily against our incursions, especially when my ancestors began to migrate to northern New England. In fact, the natives killed two of my kin in separate engagements, but the blood flow definitely went against the People.

It strikes me that we had no legal claim to the land other than what was granted by others who had no legal claim. We took what we wanted because we had the power to take it. The issue was simple and brutal. Their territory became "ours" through the force of arms and ruthless policies of ethnic cleansing and extermination. Yeah, we even gave the natives knowingly infected garments and the like, thus using biological warfare on a population that had no resistance to it. The casualties were massive. This is the typical Western way of doing things, although other cultures are equally piratical. As a result, many of our ancestral histories are linked to pillagers and opportunists who slaughtered the indigenous people who called the North American continent home for at least 600 generations. Yes, nowadays, we feel a tad guilty about some of our dastardly deeds, such as biowarfare and butchering entire villages. However, our occasional guilt pangs don't do the displaced and dead much good.

Thus, it seems peculiar that many of my kith are so ardently against "illegal immigrants." For heaven's sake, nearly ALL Americans are the sons and daughters of illegal immigrants, even those from families that settled here over 400 years ago. It is as if we have no sense of our own history, no inherent culpability for some of the dreadful events that unfolded on this land that we eventually dubbed the United States of America. Then again, perhaps we fear getting the same treatment we served up to so many others by those brown heathens entering the country. No,

I've no idea what supports our blatant hypocrisy on this issue other than a bit of myopia and a healthy degree of ignorance.

Now don't get me wrong. I love my country deeply, despite our flaws, inconsistencies, and moral lapses. This brief chapter is a perfect example of why I love the United States, for where else would one be allowed so critically to examine our past? That gift of freedom is precious, rare, and can form the basis of countless great things. Yet against this, we must weigh our short-sightedness concerning familial histories and our overweening rapaciousness. We are also undoubtedly possessed by a species of vanity and arrogance typical to many conquerors. Hence, we often wallow in our ancestry and form organizations celebrating our glorious past. We laud our families' many outstanding ac-complishments, works, and deeds and hardly pay any heed at all to those we displaced and annihilated. Then we troop off to our churches and thank God for our bounty . . . as if God hears the invocations of those who steal and murder.

And now we want to protect our ill-gained booty from those damn Hispanics, even though among our blood-soaked prizes were Texas, California, and the entire southwest. Yeah, we kicked Mexico's ass in a few unjust wars to secure those vast tracts of land. The way I look at it, the Hispanics are merely coming back to settle on the turf *they* took from the natives. Of course, many Hispanics have a high percentage of Native American blood. Thus, their right to the land is probably more morally sound than our United States claims. So, I have no problems with the Hispanics returning to settle in what we call the United States. I

LOOKING FOR GOD

consider most of those who oppose them as ignorant, red-neck, sons-of-bitches who have no sense of history, justice, or morality. We have met our enemies, and they are us!

My paternal family has roots that stretch way back, but I am also a child of more recent Italian immigrants who settled in White River Junction, Vermont, in the 1910–1920 era. They worked hard, endured privations and prejudice, and built a legacy that includes me, tragic though that happenstance is. Thus, I see both the old and the new sides of the immigration debate, and I'll be damned if I laud the singularly stupid ideas of closing *our* borders and building great walls and fences. Yeah, ask the Chinese how well that approach worked out for them. Moreover, the real strength of America is in its diversity, and ongoing influxes into the gene pool are needed. Indeed, new blood can be very beneficial, as the success of this country amply demonstrates.

Yet rather than fight about all this, I say we let the Native Americans decide what kind of immigration policy the collective "we" should employ. Let the original owners of this land determine how it is best to be shared or if it is to be shared. They may have a far better sense of perspective than any of the illegal immigrants who currently call themselves Americans . . . including me. Yes, let the natives be the deciders and not the children of those who took what wasn't theirs.

I am not sure the mortal sins of the past can ever be expiated by any amount of recognition or penance. However, we can damn sure prevent a future that mirrors a dubious history, and hence the call to build walls is a fool's errand. It is not like the country has enough workers, let alone people willing to harvest the crops, do day labor, and undertake thousands of other jobs that we entitled folks simply do not wish to take on. The immigrant communities I have known are universally hard-working. That is more than I can say about many of the kids of the Daughters of the American Revolution or the progeny of other elitist groups. Given a choice, I opt to support those immigrants who risk life and limb to find happiness within a hostile land of bigots. They are welcome in my house any time, not that I have much to share. After all, my kin took the homes of others by force, so the least I can do is share my home in peace. That seems like a fair thing to do. Amen.

83

On Killing a Soul

As any thinking person could have easily predicted, Trump screamed fraud after he got defeated by Biden during the 2020 election. That deceitful claim has been dubbed "The Big Lie" by the press, pundits, and politicos alike. Even FOX has openly confessed its rectitude in supporting stolen election claims that its management and anchors knew were deceptions. However, many Republicans are still falling all over themselves to pay Trump homage as he seeks to maintain control over a party that now stands for less than nothing. Indeed, the GOP is happily purging themselves of anyone who dares speak, write, or even think a contrary word to the accepted lies of the day. They have also become a party that embraces violent seditionists, the most depraved of what America offers. Before jumping into this issue, let us examine the basic 2020 election facts as derived from numerous sources: Biden got 81,283,501 votes (51.3 percent) while Trump managed 74,223,975 (46.8 percent), thus losing the popular vote by 7,059,526. Both candidates won 25 states, although Biden won 306 electoral votes to Trump's 232 because he won several well-populated states. This was a difference of 74 electoral votes, not that the electoral system is just or democratic.

Now, this was not a particularly close election by historical standards. Trump got beaten like a drum by nearly all measures. Nonetheless, Trump and Cult 45 continued screaming fraud, bringing up numerous court cases and demanding several recounts. Indeed, Trump and his allies brought over 60 election fraud cases and suits before state and/or Federal courts, and they were *ALL* dropped or dismissed. This was even the case when Trump-appointed judges, including an essentially conservative Supreme Court, made rulings. In most cases, there was a dismal lack of proof for the complainant's contentions, which caused several lawyers to be scolded by judges. Some claims have even earned damaging counter-litigation, with news services apologizing to offended parties and facing massive fines (e.g., Dominion Voting Systems versus FOX, NEWS MAX, etc.).

Numerous lengthy and tedious recounts were also conducted nationwide, all confirming the reported results. Trump and his cronies didn't like that outcome, so they threatened and cajoled state officials to "find" extra votes. That was a legal no-go zone and an effort that could still end up in election interference charges. Time will tell. The Trumpians have given up holding their "own" private recounts, as happened in the Arizona farce wherein some hired number-crunching guns also found no fraud. Shortly after that, Trump gave up on the notion that vested parties could craft vested victories . . . something no fair-minded person would have ever believed or approved of. Yet we are well past the time of reason in United States politics.

Nonetheless, over 60 percent of all Republicans still (2023) believe the Big Lie, despite the veritable sea of contrary evidence and the spate of public hearings. This lot is willfully ignorant, and that choice cannot be fixed. Indeed, many Republican representatives were elected while their Orange Jesus lost, so do we throw out those "tainted" babies with the dirty electoral wash water? The Trumpanzees do not consider such things. Subtleties seem to elude them at every turn regarding their favorite TV reality star. Instead, they believe a demonstrable falsehood because Trump told them to believe it, much like some claim a given thing must be true because the Bible says it is. Only here we have Trump playing the part of God and his followers taking on the dreary roles of willful dupes.

In effect, the Trumpanzees have freely subordinated their wills and judgment to that of their egotistical master, having been reduced to a cult of zombie zealots who will do anything their leader says. This includes many would-be Christians who blithely opt to ignore Trump's many lies, constant cheating, and ongoing criminality. Yeah, this follow-the-leader mentality even extends to breaking into our nation's Congress building and attempting to overturn the election results by force. We all saw it, empty-minded "believers" screaming, beating officers, and threatening to kill folks in the name of their Orange Jesus. Some even paraded Confederate flags through the Capitol Building, insulting the thousands of Americans who died to quash the Stars-and-Bars.

The inescapable fact is that a weak and malicious man-child lost an election, and his petty ego demanded that he burn down the nation rather than accept his dismal failure. Sadly, the United States is still burning while fires of division char the nation's structure. I am from a somewhat Blue state located deep within a Blue region. I despise the predominantly Red state seditionists that tried to take our capitol by force, and I would have exposed them to the same containment measures as might have been employed on people of color. Yeah, there would have been thousands of casualties, all for the sake of one foolish and failed man's bloated self-image. The unwashed are still being busted en masse, and the sentences being handed out are getting markedly longer. Meanwhile, some yammering fools still try to justify their mendacity by foolishly claiming that they were sanctioned to kill, maim, and destroy by their Lord and Master.

In the background, Trump continues to stoke the fires. He is indeed the devil's plaything, something he revealed early on through deeds and words. I remember Trump openly calling for beating a heckler some time ago. Furthermore, he wanted the person trashed so savagely that a stretcher would be needed to haul him away. Trump's zombified and drooling supporters hooted and howled, revealing their souls as being as shallow, rabid, and ugly as their master's. They proved that point during the turmoil in Washington, openly violating everything our country stands for. A good part of the nation's population has gone mad, like the mindless lock-step populace that supports the likes of Putin and Kim.

I am conflicted about what to do. Part of me yearns to see Trump dead, as in God taking him by disease or violence. Furthermore, I would like to see him die slowly and painfully, which betrays a sickness within my soul. Alas, I may even celebrate his demise by dancing in the street, much like folks did after Trump was defeated during the 2020 election. Yes, these are very sick thoughts. However, these ravings are emblematic of how divided and angry our nation has become, for I am not alone in harboring violent feelings. Mutual hate and disrespect have become our overlords. Barring his death via nature's call, I hope that Trump is simply pushed off the political stage before doing even more harm. Alas, God's universe includes the very worst of possibilities. These brutal pruning tools can exterminate the innocent, guilty, and everyone else by the millions.

My thoughts are terribly dark. Should I even write about killing Trump? It is an honest feeling that comes from deep within, for Trump is an existential threat to much of what I find precious. Yet is slaying a destructive demagogue ever justifiable? I must ponder long and hard. Doing the right thing is not always easy, for morality is often the unhappy bride of pragmatism. Would it have been right to kill Hitler when he was in the crib?

One can contemplate such issues indefinitely, but in the meantime, baby Hitler grows up to be a monster and runs amok.

Moreover, Trump continues bringing absolute ruin to many within and outside our nation, with the gleeful zombies thinking that the ongoing destruction is a great idea. Indeed, the likes of Marjorie Taylor Greene are openly calling for a national divorce of Red and Blue states, the very dissolution of the United States. Of course, she is not alone in that view, although her vacuous brain cannot articulate the reasons why.

I am sure many other folks have found ample reasons to want Trump dead. In fact, I freely confess that I would give my life to end Trump's evil if given the opportunity. This is a sinful admission, although the chances of it ever happening in my case are zilch, given increasing disabilities and limitations. Hell, I have become a cripple. Besides, do I truly wish to die with the blood of anyone on my hands, be he or she a demon or saint? There are some inescapable truths to consider. Killing another makes one into a killer by definition, no matter the motive or justification. The bottom line is that a life was taken, and it is difficult for any person with a conscience to be a supporter of life while justifying murder. That is an inescapable truth.

God usually does things for a reason, and she also gives us free choices. Free choice can be a bitch when demagogues are directing the actions of a flock of brain-dead, willful, and angry malcontents. Yet is acting as judge, jury, and executioner morally sound? Let's play it all out. Let's assume you or I had the capacity, inclination, and opportunity to pull the trigger, for many of us harbor a bit of the Beast. So, bang-bang, and down the demon goes, his face and head torn to bloody shreds. Of course, I would never flee from responsibility for my perfidy or offer lame justifications. I am no Ed Snowden, a man who lacks any sense of honor. Heck, I know that killing that lame prick would be wrong and that if one does such a thing, he or she should face death or whatever else the courts dictate. One does not run from personal responsibility.

No, it is certainly not a fear of retribution that stills my savagery, but something more profound. I am not alone in my brutal inclinations. Many folks are contemplating Trump's demise; a few may be well along in their planning. Oh, what to do? Some of us need to pay a bit of penance for our savage inclinations, and God seems to have already lined up a massive dose of atonement for me through pain and disability. Yeah, that last heart event was a bitch, as are the current lumber disc collapses. They are agonizing. Yet I have no complaints whatsoever. Time is precious, and the misery felt at any moment does nothing to lessen my gratitude for still being here. So, is it right for me or anyone else to take time from Trump, despite the clear and present danger he represents to this country and the world? Perhaps not.

All the fool needs are clown-face makeup and oversized shoes to reveal what he truly is, and then a few of the zombie sheeple supporting him would finally recognize what is actually there. Maybe we malignant haters should hit Trump with clown pies instead of buckshot, puffy pastries that leave permanent multi-colored hues. There could be blues, purples, and greens, all etched on that horrid countenance. Then we would have bright, cheerful patterns that elicit smiles, not scowls. Now, some of you may think I'm pretty damn lame to be voicing these views so stridently. All I can say in my defense is that you're reading these lines for a purpose. If they influence you in any positive way, then that is not such a terrible outcome. My choice is to walk away from the notion of killing Satan incarnate. You may decide far differently, but please understand the price one must be willing to pay to put an action into effect. To kill is to die in more ways than merely physical. One must simply find another way. And so it goes . . . Amen.

PART IX

PEOPLE

84

A Home for Big Tom

I have shoveled the fifth load of dead plants, potting soil, and garbage into the 55-gallon rubbish bucket. I'm tired and dripping sweat. Sadly, my brother Tom won't need his room anymore, which must be cleaned. Memories yank at my tears while I work. Among the debris, I find an old letter Tom wrote to my parents when he was stationed in San Francisco, some military badges, and ball bearings from the machine shop he worked in for 23 years. I set these pearls aside and shovel more dirt and debris into the bucket. Most of the cacti are alive, but his other plants died of neglect. Tommy would have never let this happen a few years ago, but that was then. I toss their withered carcasses into the bucket until it is filled.

The filled bucket weighs over 100 pounds, and I grunt as I carry it down the stairs. My gray-haired mother looks up, ever the brood hen. "You better take it easy, George." My father sits in a reclining chair, silent and sullen. I am thankful sweat conceals my tears, and grunts hide my sobs. I tell myself Tom isn't dead. He's just in a group home. They'll take good care of him there. He'll be happy. Just watch where you're stepping, or you'll take a header, and that's all Mom and Dad need. At the bottom of the stairs, I put my load down, open the door, and drag the bucket onto the front porch of my parents' dilapidated duplex.

I carry the bucket past Peter's entrance to his half of the duplex. My younger brother has long been the rock that has kept our nuclear family anchored, with me being very much a prodigal child. The plastic handles dig into my fingers as I haul the container down the front porch steps, around Peter's side porch, and to the garbage tailor. I put the bucket down and suck in some humid air. Nancy, my sister, and Peter made it possible for Tom to remain at home for as long as he did. So, it's the least I can do to clean up the decay.

Poor Tommy has had no luck. First came the brain tumor when he was just 22, then two brain operations, massive radiation treatments, epilepsy, seizures, and diabetes. And now, 22 years after the X-ray treatments that saved his life, he is diagnosed with radiation-induced leukoencephalopathy. It has produced an advancing form of dementia that is untreatable. While I rest, I think about how he was and is.

Tom once weighed over 400 pounds, a hulking bear of a man. He could lift massive steel grinding wheels that weighed more than him onto ball-bearing-making machines without using jacks or lifts. Now, Tom takes slow, shuffling baby steps, forgets things, slurs words, is incontinent, falls, gets stuck in chairs and on toilet seats, and cannot muster the motor skills and strength to stand. And he is only 48 years old. It seems so wretchedly unfair. I wipe the sweat from my brow and heft the bucket over the tailor's side. Its contents tumble out as clouds of brown dust billow up. I shake the bucket empty and carry it back to Tom's room.

On the way up the stairs, I glance at Mom and Dad. Henry is 79, and his body is covered with scars: open heart surgery, prostate cancer, lymphatic cancer, aneurysms, abdominal surgery, and a fused hip. His alcoholism sometimes made life miserable, but I don't fault him. As mentioned earlier, he was the victim of an autocratic father who frequently beat him, a bigoted man who wore his anti-Latin prejudice on his sleeve. Yet my Italian mother bore my father's illness gracefully and gave him five kids. First came Tom, then Mary, Nancy, myself, and Peter. Mom was the eye of the storm, but at 74, her optimism is failing, and her anxiety increasing.

The stench of urine in Tom's room is nauseating, so I open another window to create a cross-breeze. I start putting his flower books in an old bookcase and stumble across a black-and-white photograph of his third-grade class. I see the circled picture of a little boy with light eyes, dark curly hair, and a forced smile,

84.1 This is a red guzmania and it is one of hundreds of pictures found in Tom's room, presumably taken when he was stationed in Hawii

another echo from the past. I sob as Tom's history drifts through my mind. Even his birth was complicated, the instruments denting his head. Yet he was a precocious child who once bit a young dog after the dog had bitten him.

Yet most of his life was miserable. Tom's teachers thought he was retarded in grade school. When asked, "What letter is this?" he would run up to the chalkboard and look. "It's an A!" he would answer while his classmates chuckled. He got scolded and then branded as odd by his peers. Tom's teachers eventually blundered into discovering his vision was abnormal, a double stigmatism. He finally got glasses, but the sensitive child had already seen enough humiliation to become withdrawn. He came to love far more than the company of his classmates the wildflowers and plants he discovered in the woods. The flowers' brightness penetrated his despair and gave him joy, but even this tiny solace became a target of ridicule. His peers called him "Flower Boy," "Posy," and all the other taunts associated with a love that isn't macho. Tom eventually lashed out when he was

16, simultaneously beating up two punks. Part of me wishes he had broken their legs.

Life at home provided him few pleasures, although Mom tried her best. Tom often had to fetch our father from local bars when Dad didn't come home after a day's work in the Tip Top Bakery. Dad would call him names, act belligerently, and often do things that still haunt his conscience. I remember the day Dad repeatedly slapped Tom's face, whack after whack. He just stood there and absorbed the blows. "Go on," he bellowed, "Hit me again!" In my mind's eye, I see Tom trooping up the stairs after the beating. I see his beet-red face, his tears flowing down. Anger fills me, and I attack the chore at hand. I scoop up dirt, some half-eaten food, and more dead plants.

I start cursing as the dust flies. Why are you so cruel, God? I pick up a round piece of metal to throw away, but it is part of a uniform, yet more memories. Tom joined the Army in 1965, during the beginning of the Vietnam War. He was eventually stationed in Hawaii as a supply sergeant because his eyes were too bad for combat. Hawaii provided Tom with lush tropical plants, balmy weather, and long black beaches to stroll on. He went from hell to paradise. He was going to re-enlist, but at 270 pounds, "Big Tom" simply could not stay within the acceptable weight limit, and they mustered him out. So, he returned home and got a machinist job with the Split Ball Bearing Company. But a frontal brain tumor that had taken up residence grew. Tom had vicious headaches, and he became increasingly antisocial and temperamental. Then came the day he snapped. He was 23, and I was 15. The memory haunts me.

Tom and Dad throw verbal barbs at one another over the dinner table. Dad is half in the bag. "Come on," Mom pleads, "Let's just eat." Tom explodes at a comment and heaves a plate. He picks up a heavy steel dustpan and crumples it in his big hands like tin foil. "Protect Mom," I think. I get up, ready for battle. Tom heads toward the living room, casting anything in his way aside. I pick up a full half-gallon bottle of Wesson food oil and hurl it in his direction. It bounces off the back of his head with a thud. He staggers forward. He glances back at me, a vacant look in his eyes. Then he retreats up the stairs and into his room.

An hour later, the stairs creak. Tom is coming, and I'm afraid. He turns to face us at the bottom of the stairs. His right eye is swollen, and he's dizzy and confused. Did I do that? Dad takes him to the Mary Hitchcock Memorial Hospital for treatment. One week they say he is crazy, and the following week they tell us he has a brain tumor. It's a walnut-sized beast that has wedged itself between his skull and his right frontal lobe. They tell us it's only a 50/50 operation, and he hovers between life and death. I crawl under my bed and cry. Why did I have to hit him? I dwell on our sibling rivalry. I see my toy tanks deployed on the floor while he sleeps in a chair, their plastic guns trained in his direction. My soldiers are also moving in for the kill. He wakes to the sound of my, "Rat-a-tat-tat, kerpow! kerpow!" A bemused smile covers his face.

Tom survives the operation, and we visit him in the hospital. The right side of his head bulges three or four inches from his skull, straining at the bandages. He is angry and irrational. The doctors say it will pass, but some of it doesn't. At home, he becomes childish and moody; he keeps to himself and broods. Dad no longer abuses him. He feels guilt mixed with sorrow. Mom becomes perpetually anxious, and she frets over Tom. He soon returns to work but continues having vicious headaches. Two years after the operation, he experiences a grand mal seizure that almost kills him, so he returns to the hospital. They discover that the tumor has returned, and another operation has to be done.

The doctors also use radiation this time because the tumor has become malignant. They employ as much radiation as the human body can endure. It's that or death. Tom lives to see his hair fall out and his teeth turn soft, but the radiation destroys the tumor. He goes back to work, and his personality actually improves. Tom shops and plays Bingo with Mom and Dad but seldom interacts with people outside the family. He watches cartoons, reads comic books, and keeps to himself. His room is his fortress of solitude and gradually goes to dirt and decay.

I pick up a biplane model skillfully fashioned out of Coca-Cola cans. It's a present from Barbara, one of Tom's few close friends. She is 12 years older than Tom and lives only a few hundred feet from our house. It was a platonic romance between two shut-ins, but their links endured. Barbara was tightly held in a cage that her domineering mother forged. My brother was confined in a cage of psychic bars and physical anguish. Yet they communed. They smiled, laughed, and looked forward to meeting. I find the biplane's propeller and repair the model. It, too, is a pearl that must be preserved.

I sit and ponder Tom's slow decline. He taught me how to hit a baseball when we were children. "You have to look and see where the ball is going. You can't close your eyes and just swing at the thing!" His advice worked, but he gradually became more uncoordinated in the years following his radiation treatments. He also became more temperamental and bitter. On hot days, he started wearing bed sheets around the house, like some great sheik. I muse at the thought, but there was a time it was mortifying. I look around. Just a few more shovels full to go.

I don't feel put upon. If anything, Peter and Nancy have done the heavy lifting. When Tom got diabetes and had a series

84.2 A CocaCola biplane made by Tom's dear friend Barbera that was rescued from his room

of minor seizures, Nancy and Peter cared for him. Nancy's nursing skills kept Tom's diabetes in check, and Peter ensured Tom got to his medical checkups. Tom continued to work, shop, and play Bingo, but he had little energy to do much else, even tend his garden. Barbara remained his best friend, but perhaps her mother saw a threat in their happy relationship, just a tiny chance that her bird would fly away. So, she moved to another town, taking her caged prisoner with her.

I bend down to move the full bucket and get a sharp pain in the right side of my head. I wince. It is one of several jolts I have had from moving heavy loads. They are harsh reminders of a cerebral vascular problem that ended my 11-year coaching career at the University of New Hampshire. There was no way of knowing it then, but I had two crushed discs in my neck that were only discovered some years later. I recall how despair became my master, how I went bankrupt, how I endured constant pain, and how I was not physically able. I remember contemplating suicide, a couple of pills, and the suffering is over. Then I think about when Big Tom visited me while I was laid up despite his declining health. 'What are my flea bites compared to his gunshot wounds?' I asked myself. I recovered, but Tom didn't. He fell at work, shattering his tibia, but he was back on the job eight months later.

An incident from my last visit home comes to mind as I look at where Tom's bed once was. Tom went to his room to get some Christmas wrapping paper and has been gone for a while. My mother glances at me while I sit in a chair. Her troubled look says more than words. "Do you want me to check on him?" I ask. She nods. I go up the stairs and into Tom's room. His legs are folded underneath his shrinking, but still huge, body. No, he can't get up. I strain to lift his 300-plus pounds off the filthy floor and set him on his broken bed. I can still feel his trembling hand clutching onto mine. I still see him lying on the bed, utterly helpless and insensible. I am shaken.

A few days later, I talked to Tom. He is eating a fistful of candy, his diabetes is acting up, and I feel he's trying to kill himself. He is seated in an over-stuffed chair that has a yellow floral pattern covering. I am sitting on a couch beside the chair. The bubble lights on the Christmas tree percolate, and the tinsel glitters.

"Tom, you've got to stop eating all this candy."

He hears me but says nothing.

"Hey, if I had been through half of what you've been through, I'd be depressed too. But when you eat like this, it screws you all up. And you know how much that bothers Mom."

He does not reply. I get frustrated.

"Goddammit, Tom. I know you've been dealt some lousy cards, but you've got to try to help yourself."

Tom remains silent. I look down. I know Tom may be unable to help himself, and I feel empty. I get up and walk away while Tom stares off into space. Did he hear a word I said? I go next door and talk to Peter, and he is also perplexed by Tom's condition. Peter tells me Tom is getting a medical workup if his condition doesn't improve soon, and I am relieved. That conversation was right before I left to continue my graduate studies at

UNH. And now the prodigal son has returned to help clean the decay. I am ashamed about how little I have done to help Tom. I rationalize as I look at the artifacts of his life. I tell myself no one knew he was this sick.

Tom's condition worsened before the summer began. He became incontinent, and his personality went dead flat. The psychiatrists couldn't understand why he lacked emotion. They also noted marked decreases in his intellect and short-term memory. So, he was put into the Mary Hitchcock Memorial Hospital for tests. His spinal protein levels were eight times normal, indicating widespread destruction within his central nervous system. They thought he might have hydrocephaly, but that diagnosis was rejected after an MRI. It wasn't a suitable protein for multiple sclerosis, nor were there any signs of another tumor, so more tests were done. Finally, Tom was diagnosed with delayed onset radiation-induced dementia. He wasn't depressed after all.

The doctors told my parents that many brain tumor patients treated with massive radiation dosages are afflicted with Tom's disease. Radiation kills fast-growing cancer cells but also scars the linings of nerve cells, which are poor at repairing or regenerating themselves. It can take years for the neurological damage from radiation to become noticeable, as in Tom's case, but the condition is irreversible. Tom may get worse or, at best, stabilize where he is. However, I remain skeptical of the diagnosis because my experiences with doctors have shown they can be fallible. However, perhaps I'm just rationalizing that my brother's fate need not be sealed, that there's still a chance he'll recover.

I gather the empty pots and put them in the attic. I lug the last bucket out of the room and dump it. The floor is now cleared enough to vacuum and mop. Peter comes home from his job at the Post Office and helps me finish up. Most of my tears have dried, but Tom's fate pains me. "I feel like he's dead," I say as I wring out the mop. Peter says he knows how I feel. But Tom isn't dead. He has been placed in the England Group Home, in Salisbury, New Hampshire, about 40 miles from his home in West Lebanon. It was the only alternative, but the family still felt guilt. We know Tom yearns to come home. "I wanna work on my garden," he says. "I'm goin' ta grow tomatoes." We all rationalize, especially Mom: "He likes it there, George. He really does. And they're so good to him."

During the next Christmas vacation, I visit Tom in the group home. His 273-pound frame is sunk into a well-padded recliner. His mouth is slightly agape, and his balding head is held askew while he watches television. Jerry sticks his cartoon sidekick Tom in the rear with a diminutive foil. The wounded cat's eyes leap out of his head. He screams and jumps several feet into the air, clutching his behind. My brother lets out a monotone laugh. "Ha, ha, ha." I fight back tears. Tom is watching a parody of his life, only he does not scream out in pain despite all the jabs he has received.

"How do you like it here, Tom?"

"Itsh not too bad."

"I understand Gloria and you are going to plant a garden."

"Yeah."

"You must be psyched."

"Yeah."

"What are you going to plant?"

"I'm not sure."

He focuses back on the television. Unkempt graying whiskers cover his bespectacled face and his flesh sags. Later, we looked through a photo album I helped put together with Laury Beth, Peter's youngest. Donna wisely chose an album for Tom's Christmas present, and he is enjoying it immensely. We are seated at the kitchen table while a few of the home's clients and staffers hover about. Tom smiles while turning the pages. Gloria, the friendly director of the privately owned seven-patient home, does a double take when she sees the photograph of a handsome, powerfully built young man with dark curly hair. He is wearing a floral Hawaiian shirt and smiling at the camera.

"Who's that handsome fella?" Gloria asks.

"Thash me," Tom replies.

"Come look at this," Gloria says to her daughter and son-in-law, two staffers who work in the group home. They look at the picture, then quickly glance at one another.

"You were a good-looking guy," the daughter offers Tom.

"Yeah," Tom replies.

"Were?" I think. I'm miffed, perhaps unreasonably, for it is hard to be reasonable when you're struggling to keep your eyes dry.

"My brother is a person."

"And a very good person," Gloria says while patting Tom's big forearm.

We have included photographs of Tom's days in the service. While stationed in Hawaii, he took hundreds of pictures of tropical plants. Photos of bright red orchids, immense tropical flowers, and lush jungle plants fill parts of the album. His eyes light up while he slowly turns each page, and he seems more alive than he has been in years. We look at Schofield Barracks, some army buddies, then a collage of pictures of cats and dogs. He points at an old photo of a German Shepherd.

"That's Gretchen!" he chirps.

"That's right. And who is this cat?"

"It's Satan. And, and, and thish is Kelly."

"Kelly was a neat cat."

"Yeah."

"She could fetch. Do you remember that?"

"Yeah."

He is beaming, and it's a rare show of emotion. Tom loves animals, and Gloria's black lab is his constant companion. The two walk through the woods around the group home, not going too far before encountering the steel fence surrounding the grounds. Whenever Tom has money, he shuffles down to the local market, a Mom and Pop store about 300 yards from the home. He'll buy sweets there and eats so much he gets sick. Then his diabetes will act up, his neurological symptoms will worsen, and he'll become vacant for a few days. So, no one gives him money anymore, just little gifts. Barbara still writes him. She still sends him hand-made Christmas presents. Barbara is still caged and may remain that way after her mother dies. I hope not because she is a kind, caring person who deserves a good and full life.

Peter and my sisters Nancy and Mary have allowed Tom to enjoy whatever time he has left. They visit him every week and often bring him home to see Mom and Dad. I have been removed from the situation, maybe by fate or choice. But I care about my brother. There is still a love we have, a love that was forged out of some shared misery, but a love nonetheless. Indeed, Tom helped to keep our family together, for it had every reason to fall apart. He was the cause we rallied around and Tom continues to be the star-crossed teacher of many great lessons.

I know there will come a day when Big Tom needs me, and I will be by his side. He may not recognize me nor understand what I say, but I'll bring him a gigantic floral arrangement. There will be red, orange, and yellow starbursts at the end of thin green contrails. There will be roses and tulips, orchids and irises, and all will be surrounded by the tiny white buds of baby's breath. I will tilt Tom's head up so that he can see the bright colors, and perhaps he will smile before his soul drifts away, finally freed from a cage that can no longer confine it. Amen.

Postscript

Tom was to see seven more years of life, but they were punctuated by seizures, strokes, and decreasing control of his body. He was moved from one care home to another as his needs increased, with a sizeable thalamic stroke being a devastating addition to his woes. I have written about Tom's demise, but it is too painful to publish, especially considering the possible reaction of my siblings. In the end, Tom could only move one arm a little bit, and he had lost the ability to swallow, speak, or care for himself. His body began to reject the formula used to feed him via a stomach tube, and the family decided to stop feeding and hydrating Big Tom. He made it clear that he was OK with that fate, so I retreated from my position that his life is maintained or ended humanely, with the latter being my preferred choice.

Five days followed of utter misery, for his was not the easy death the doctors had assured us it would be. I will not go into the details of those final days, but the entire family was there to support him throughout. Peter and I were at his bedside during the very end. I held his right hand while that final seizure tore at him, and I cried, "It's over, Tom. You are free." He gasps, not yet being able to release himself. Joanny takes out a stethoscope and seems sure he is dead or will be soon. But he gasps again, his head and face frozen in a grimace. I can see the life flowing from those eyes. I feel the awfulness, the terror, the full scope of this release called death. And just when I think it is finally over, he gasps again, and then yet again. He is wide-eyed but ashen: his life has fled. Tom's mouth is agape, not the relaxed repose one expects to see. The time is 3:31 p.m., September 3, 2001. Yet Tom died loved, and that love remains. Indeed, even after 20 years, the tears flow with every recall. Amen.

85

When The Walls Fall In

Two friends found Denise's lifeless body in her bedroom, naked, cold, and sprawled out on her bed. Her head, shoulders,
and torso rested against the headboard and the nearby wall
behind it while her lower body lay on the bed. She often slept
that way and was known to use a similar posture when writing
longhand. I will not describe the details of how she was found
or the condition of her apartment other than to note she had
probably been dead for no more than a few days. Besides, the sad
details of her discovery will not change the harsh reality of her
passing. Moreover, privacy extends beyond death, or does it? I
know the medical examiner is busily dissembling Denise's corpse
today, observing and taking samples while the causal agency of
her demise is determined. It is all so cold and clinical, but therein

dwelled the soul of a dear friend. And now she is gone, suddenly and without much warning.

Good Lord, this is the third death in three weeks in River House, and some of us in this retirement community are ill at ease. However, Denise's death did not surprise everyone who knew her. She was petite and trim, a former horse trainer thrown badly enough to suffer severe brain and back damage. She battled those injuries and subsequent epilepsy, still managing to secure a nursing degree despite her ills. Denise married an emergency doctor, but they parted after 12 years, sans any children and with few regrets she would expound upon. All the while, her demons festered within, and mental illness soon began consuming her. Observing her ordeal was beyond sad, but she tried to find and give some joy during her life.

I met Denise quite a few years ago, and we became close friends at one point. Denise was not beautiful, nor was she homely. Her thin brown hair was cropped short, spectacled eyes and extremely casual attire, a sort of jockess look that befitted her sometimes frenetic nature. She readily wore her moods, and one could tell from a glance if she was happy, depressed, or something else, albeit depression was an all-too-frequent visitor. Indeed, Denise had attempted suicide in the past, although she had heart and other health issues that occasionally had her knocking on heaven's door. However, if I recall correctly, she wasn't old, being just under 60.

She had two therapy cats, and they quickly became pals with all who knew them. The poor animals, frightened and perplexed by a situation they could not fathom, were desperate for attention when friends found Denise's body. Mom was wrapped in a sleep that knows no waking, which is a state she had straddled many times. Cutting, overdosing, mixing medications, she did one thing after another to quell the demons. She was a font of energy and action when the battle went well, often working for hours preparing delicious meals for neighbors and friends. Yet the demons kept returning, and some saw where it would lead. I retrieved the computer and other items I had lent her and skulked away to avoid the inevitable. Yes, I was more of a coward than a friend when all was said and done.

Oh, I had tried, but I could not say or do anything to help make Denise love herself. And I often could not blame Denise for being down, angry, or frustrated. I saw firsthand the ills she battled, having witnessed one of her grand mal seizures. There was violent shaking, unsteady breathing . . . Get everything heavy out of the way. God, I hope she is getting enough air. Move the coffee table, or her legs will hit it. Make sure her air passage is clear. On and on, the torment went . . . like something out of a horrible nightmare. Yet I am sure the ordeal was less than four minutes because my perception of time had extended. However, I maintained calm while Denise struggled to regain her senses.

"It's OK, my friend," I softly say. "I've seen seizures many times. Hang in there."

She went to sleep after recovering, and I waited for some time before leaving. She had experienced many such seizures, including another grand mal while shopping. The meds they gave her to contain the epilepsy were powerful, and she detested taking them. Add to this various psych meds, pot, and alcohol, and Denise was often fairly well buzzed. She made promises and often broke them, but who could blame her? Denise barely existed on Social Security disability insurance, self-medicated as needed, and struggled to find happiness and purpose. She often tried feeding everyone in sight, recently inviting some people for a Turkey Day dinner. That was her way, and Denise was an excellent cook. However, she never answered the door when people arrived for the expected Turkey Day feast, and the apprehensive guests left. They half-suspected she was passed out on the couch and huddled into a ball, such was her habit.

She once tried to run for an Activities Club office and was well known for being an exemplary chef and party organizer. I asked her not to run because I knew where rejection could lead, and my fears were well placed. She publicly lost the vote, and this was merely another blight heaped upon her. She became more withdrawn for a while but seemed to recover. Then she had a nasty spat with a dear friend over something Denise should not have said, although the two made amends. All the while, I became more distant. Yes, it was clear she was spiraling, and I did my gutless best to avoid the entire situation. Soon, I did not even visit, partly because Denise seldom answered the door and partly because I had seen where melancholy can lead.

Now she is gone, and I am not sure events had to transpire as they did. Yet I doubt there was anything I could have said or done, although my increasing avoidance was the last thing she needed. Indeed, she required quite the opposite. They say that to have ever been is to always be from the perspective of what created this reality we are bound to. We all produce great and small influences that ripple out into time and space in myriad ways, and Lord knows that Denise made more than a few positive waves. I saw her happy at times, an all too rare occurrence. A tear rolls down my cheek, and a prayer comes to mind.

Be at peace, my friend. Know that you were loved, although some of us did not know how to express that love in ways that could ease your torment. Know that you will be missed and that your life most assuredly mattered to many. Be at peace in the knowledge that the cats will be cared for and that they will be kept together. They never judged you, became angry, or bitter. They offered you the unconditional love that some of us could not share. Perhaps that is the final lesson you left us. Life accords us chances, but it is up to us to take advantage of them. I wish I had done so. You leave this table of life we share, and I pray God grants you the solace, grace, and comfort you seldom found during your life. Amen.

Postscript

The autopsy revealed that Denise had severe heart issues, but one does not push cause-of-death matters with family members. We helped her sisters clean the apartment, with bits and pieces of her life distributed to friends and relatives. It was a sad and dreary task that friends do for friends. The cats found solace with an older couple, a retired military man and his wife, who were seeking a pair of felines. And so life goes in the Hollow.

86

Preachers, Paths, and Purposes

I was going downtown from Penn State's Sparks building in 1996, a trip that goes right by the Willard Preacher (also known as Gary Cattell). The lifelong State College resident is famous or infamous, depending on one's point of view. Cattell usually sets up camp on the large, open stoop in front of the Willard Building at about noon, surrounded by paved grounds, bike racks, shrubbery, and milling students. He has been sermonizing there since 1982, gaining much notoriety. Cattell isn't big or small, a blinding intellect or a nascent fool. He is average in every way but one. The preacher talks ad nauseam, his bespectacled eyes, sandy gray hair, and increasingly weathered face displaying time's toll. Cattell certainly isn't a slave to fashion and often wears a hoodie, t-shirt, simple shorts or pants, ankle socks, and athletic shoes.

His wife is a school teacher, and Cattell helped raise their four kids into adulthood. Preaching is his job, albeit donations are slim pickings when raising a family. Still, Cattell feels compelled to proselytize, and his family has followed the life plan. He will rave incessantly about the decadence of partying, the evils of drugs, and/or the depravity of the homosexual lifestyle. Some students eagerly engage him, while others simply listen. I usually find his act tediously pedantic and plow on by without regard for the sideshow. Indeed, I try to ignore this preacher's tirades, although they are designed to get a rise out of people. For example, on this occasion, he was excoriating the Muslim faith. He asked, "How can anyone who believes and acts like THEM come unto God?" I blurted out, "Who the hell are you to judge?" He began quoting scripture, but I tossed him a dismissive open palm and moved on.

In the past, I've heard this frequently angry man say many terrible things about gays, liberals, and other folks. Yeah, he doesn't seem to love anyone who doesn't live according to his evangelical Christian version of Hoyle. Yet I do not begrudge the Willard Preacher his daily exercise in free speech. Besides, his invective-filled ravings are not unlike those we hear from any number of similar self-anointed political saviors. This is the calling of Cattell's heart, albeit a dubious industry considering his familial responsibilities and existential needs. Still, it is his choice.

Yet, I wonder what gives such people the moral authority to openly berate their brothers and sisters. It seems one would win more converts with kindness and concern rather than condemnation and anger. However, we nonbelievers get a steady diet of hellfire and brimstone, which will not grow productive crops of adherents. Besides, the central tenets of Christianity include love, selflessness, and humility, which are subjects we hear precious little of from the mouths of some preachers. Indeed, many of the self-anointed spit out razor blades at every turn, and one can't help but notice that a net of love can catch more lost souls than a bombastic web of venom, threats, and fear.

Now, I know that many evangelicals claim they are simply performing an act of love when they point out the errors of our heathen ways. They are trying to save our souls from eternal damnation by guiding us toward some sacred light. I can appreciate these sentiments, but I can't help thinking about what fuels the vision of this light they wish to share. Many have told me it's "the" WORD of God as expressed in the Bible that has shown them the light. Yet no matter their source, words are subject to different interpretations. Indeed, many divergences in Christians' paths are based on distinct and conflicting textual interpretations. Moreover, no one can be sure who has the market cornered on the right way to find the philological light that reveals divine inspiration versus speculative delusion.

Nonetheless, we're told by some folks that they have somehow seen this light and thus found the absolute and singular truth. They have hence discovered the eternal and unchanging, and they will share this great absolute IF we but believe as they believe and act as they act. Well, one of the only absolutes I've ever found is that anyone who claims to know the truth usually isn't worth listening to. There is always something beyond what we currently know, although one of the real joys of life is that it often gives us enough time to find at least some answers. And that's the greatest danger in thinking you've already seen "the" WORD. Such a belief can stop one from looking wherever he or she hasn't searched. This is the stuff of closed minds and hearts, the path that leads to the banal rejection of other beliefs, other ways of life, and other sources of knowledge. It is the stuff of intolerance and book burning.

I wish I were smart enough to advise people about finding God, truth, or whatever the glue is that binds reality together. But I'm not that wise. Moreover, I hope I'm never smart enough to tell a Buddhist, Muslim, Hindu, gay, or liberal person that they are damned for not believing as I do. The only meaningful advice I can offer is to constantly search for knowledge in all the directions life accords you. I'm one of those fools who believe we can find enlightenment in conversations with children, on mountaintops, or at the beach. We can also find wisdom in test tubes, mathematical equations, and the study of humanistic endeavors. I'm even crazy enough to think we can find truth in a mirror, and if we look real hard . . . perhaps a tiny bit of what it is that links us all together.

The main problem is figuring out what is and isn't true . . . or even if there is such a thing as truth. There are also many problems in determining the best way to conduct our lives, and this isn't something any single source can reveal. Yet there will always be those like the Willard Preacher, who often tell those around him what is wrong and righteous. Finding the answers to these questions is like putting together a vast puzzle. We can only get the big picture if we step back and see how the pieces we've found fit together. This is a quest that'll last an entire lifetime. There are bits and pieces of the puzzle in the Bible, the Koran, and the works of Plato, Newton, and Einstein. There are also answers in the Talmud and the many Eastern philosophies. Yet friends, family, and experiences will teach us more than any book or preacher could if our hearts and minds are open enough to listen. Eventually, we may even grow wise enough to tell our children not to damn those whose thoughts, words, and actions don't damn others, which is a lesson many would-be preachers have yet to learn. Amen.

87

Al-Baghdadi, a
Marked Man

This morning we're watching multiple volleys of cruise missiles
fired from United States naval vessels (9/13/14), demonstrating
the destruction modern warships can serve up. Dozens of bomb-
ers, drones, and other aircraft are adding to the firepower being
dumped on ISIS, which has become an existential threat to people and nations far and near. I despise the death and destruction
raining down, though a part of me lauds the systematic obliteration of those who have joined ISIS. They are head-hunters in the
most literal sense, psychopaths who show no mercy to anyone
designated an "enemy," be they man, woman, or child. Let ISIS

harvest what it sows, albeit the weapons used will kill and maim saints and sinners.

However, to defeat this group, one must understand what compels it. To do that, we must study Abu Bakr al-Baghdadi, the current leader of ISIS. The man is clearly destined to die by fire and violence, yet the vicious cause he leads will linger long after al-Baghdadi is gone. He is just 45 and has been involved in Islamic militancy movements since 2003, though not often as a fighter. No, this man is not an empty-headed thug. He has a Bachelor of Arts, Master of Arts, and Doctoral Degree in Islamic Studies and is a respected scholar. Moreover, he has written widely on Islamic law. Abu Bakr al-Baghdadi is a devout Sunni Muslim, and is affiliated with the Salafi movement. Salafism proposes that only the Qur'an and Hadith's strictest and most literal interpretations are acceptable. This is especially true concerning the observance of legal and religious requirements, which collectively form the basis of Sharia law.

In 2006 al-Baghdadi became a member of the Mujahideen Shura Council, and it is from his work with this group that he would eventually be bestowed with the title of "Caliph." The term *shura* is associated with mutual consultation and/or counsel, whereby collective decisions are made by recognized religious authorities regarding secular and spiritual affairs. Sharia law is codified and applied here, a process that can vary depending on how one interprets the Qur'an and Hadith. Yes, there is no separation of church and state in Sharia law. Alas, al-Baghdadi's ultra-conservative renditions of the law are reactionary and puritanical, devoid of any of the mercy so widely called for by the Prophet. Ergo, beheading, stoning, and holy war are all sanctioned in various situations via passages found in one holy book or another, as was the case with Europe's Crusades.

Regarding military credentials, al-Baghdadi's are not impressive, having been captured by the United States in 2004 as a civilian internee. According to their reports, some bright intelligence operatives found him a minimal threat, much more of a scholar than a warrior. He was thus released, probably in 2005, although records vary. Regrettably, the pen can be far mightier than the sword, as al-Baghdadi proved. By 2010 he was anointed as the leader of the Islamic State of Iraq (ISI), and he soon began a much more active military role. Infamous for inciting suicide and car bombings, al-Baghdadi became the bane of Iraq's Shia-led government. By 2012 he had well-established links with fundamentalist groups fighting against Assad in Syria, and in 2013 al-Baghdadi became head of the Islamic State in Iraq and Syria (ISIS). He was married to three wives at once, divorced, remarried, and fathered children.

In 2014, al-Baghdadi was named the Caliph of the new Islamic State, which had hitherto been known as ISIS. Caliph is a quasi-political and religious title for one who rules a Caliphate under strict adherence to Islamic law. This is the outcome of Shura writ large, complete with the formulation of Sharia-sanctioned maiming (flogging) and death (stoning or beheading) for what are commonly regarded as minor offenses. This can include a woman not wearing the traditional hijab (head scarf), adultery, and damaging the environment. As may be expected, al-Baghdadi's ascension has caused great consternation in the Arab world because the title of Caliph can ONLY be bestowed by a collective agreement among all Muslim nations and not merely by the proclamation of any single country or group.

These Islamic legalisms do not bother the Rolex-watch-wearing al-Baghdadi, who appears to buy into his press hype. In fact, al-Baghdadi claimed he would march on Rome, making Italy and Spain part of his new Islamic state, a place all Muslims should flock to. This bravado indicates extremely delusional thinking, but al-Baghdadi also has aspirations much closer to his current haunts, with Jordan, Saudi Arabia, and Lebanon all coming under explicit threat. Indeed, his formation of a Caliphate titillates many conservative Muslims living in those nations al-Baghdadi claims, thus forming a fifth column.

The problem is, many young people, regardless of their faith, are drawn toward creating a new and pure state, an Islamic utopia wherein the wretched corruption and excesses of the existing order can be eschewed for an idealistic way of life. After all, what could be nobler and more pursuit-worthy than forging a society based on religious precepts, especially for someone long marginalized or discriminated against by his or her community? Here is where life's outcasts get to rewrite their present and future, becoming religious heroes versus disgruntled youths or lamentable losers. Thus, a mild-mannered and spiritual mechanic can easily be transformed into a decapitator, an instrument of state-sanctioned terror.

Indeed, the dark side of many lost souls comes pouring out when granted a holy pat on the head, a weapon, a coerced mate, and adequate training. They kill and maim without thought or compassion, letting their demons within have free reign as they unleash the contents of their dark souls on the innocent and guilty alike. They commit unspeakable crimes in the name of a faith they ill-understand and gather riches so that al-Baghdadi and his cronies can continue to forge their perfect state. They are a blight, a plague in the biblical sense. Yet they are also very willing to die for their beliefs. Indeed, one of al-Baghdadi's sons (Hudhayfah al-Badri) was sacrificed in 2018 while attempting an Inghimasi-style suicide attack. This assault is where an explosives-lined vest destroys the bomb wearer, enemy soldiers, vehicles, and/or civilian targets.

Killing al-Baghdadi will not stop ISIS, for another talking-head will take up the leadership role. He is but a symbol, albeit a brilliant man who is better excised than allowed to fester. The holy warriors' quest is for an ideal, and the only thing that will stop them is death. That can mean killing our own, for thousands of ISIS fighters are born of our kind. Indeed, there are 2,000-plus Western holy warriors, including 100 Americans, 500 French, and 400 Britons. Another 15,000 come from Somalia, Korea, Turkmenistan, Tajikistan, Uzbekistan, Egypt, Libya, Tunisia,

Lebanon, and other places. To a person, they have richly earned a common fate.

The holy warriors will run for the hills or melt into local populations as the bombs fall and tanks rumble, and they will soon be unable to gather in large groups. They will switch from offense to defense and strive to hide their equipment and resources. However, small groups are far more vulnerable to attacks than large ones, and weapons that must be hidden away cannot be quickly and easily deployed as needed. Soon, those thousands of people the holy warriors tormented will become their tormentors. This is already happening in "liberated" areas of Iraq and Syria, and the decimation will continue until some kind of Faustian balance is achieved.

And so it will go while the holy warriors are systematically hunted down. They will be given no mercy because they showed none. They will be given no refuge because they made so many people into refugees. In the end, they will reap what they have sown, and nary will a tear be shed to mark their passing. Ah, but the ideas that compelled them will never die, so it will fall upon others to repeatedly do what is now being done. Indeed, the killing may never stop. That is another story and one that has no easy answers. As for al-Baghdadi, he lives on borrowed time, more of a symptom than a cause. The cause is religious hatred, and that has few cures. Amen.

Postscript

On October 27, 2019, al-Baghdadi (aged 48) reportedly killed himself and two of his children during a raid by United States Special Forces. Two of his wives also appear to have died. According to CENTCOM, al-Baghdadi detonated a suicide vest during the Barisha raid in Syria's northwestern Idlib Province. One suspects that far more than a suicide vest was involved, given the level of destruction at the operation site. He was given Islamic funeral rites, and his body was buried at sea. Baghdadi's replacement is Abu Ibrahim al-Hashimi al-Qurashi, so the madness continues. Despite losing tens of thousands and nearly all its territory, some 10,000 ISIS full- or part-time fighters remain, albeit as of 2023 they are still being pursued. There are hundreds of thousands of sympathizers, so ISIS could be reconstituted to full strength rather quickly.

88

A Profile in Strength: Walter Plumber

It would be anyone's worst nightmare. Walter Plumber vividly recalls waking up in an operating room at Mass General during a procedure to stabilize his shattered neck vertebrae. He remembers the doctors screwing eye bolts into the top of his skull. He also remembers asking the nurse for water. However, Plumber doesn't remember drifting off into unconsciousness again as the neurosurgical team attached the equipment needed to place his shattered neck in traction. His would be an ordeal that would last a lifetime.

Plumber's operation was only one in a series of traumatic events on August 20, 1954, a month before his fourteenth birthday. Since that day, Plumber's life has been one grueling struggle after another. Throughout his incredible ordeal, Plumber has been determined to become an active member of the greater community around him. It's a quest he spent his entire adult life trying to obtain, and the pursuit has made excellent progress.

The 49-year-old Plumber vividly recalls the day of his accident, although it happened over 35 years ago. He was diving into Lee, NH's Lamprey River, from a flat rock that hung over a steep, grass-covered bank. Like many places in New Hampshire, this swimming hole was well known to the local kids, and Plumber had visited it many times. Having been raised on a farm, he enjoyed swimming and an active lifestyle. Plumber was showing two 9-year-old boys how to dive when his footing slipped on the wet rock used as a diving perch. Plumber's feet flew out from underneath him, and he twisted while falling backside first. The side of his head missed the rock but hit the bottom of the river's steep bank. He continued sliding down the bank and soon plunged underneath the suffocating water, unable to slow his descent.

"I had taken a deep breath before I hit the water and waited until I surfaced to breathe," Plumber related. "I learned to do that in a Red Cross class, and it kept me from drowning." But after Plumber surfaced, he was confronted by a grave problem. He said, "I knew right away I was hurt because I couldn't move, but the two kids I was with thought I was only kidding."

Even after all these years, the silver-haired Plumber still protects the identities of his two compatriots. He insists, "My accident wasn't their fault, and I don't want them to feel bad about it by reading their names in the paper." Plumber repeatedly asked the boys for help but finally had to resort to some quick thinking. "I promised them on my Scout's honor that I needed help, and then they knew I wasn't joking," he said. This was a day when Scout's honor meant something in rural communities.

The boys rushed to aid their stricken friend and went into the turbid waters to rescue him. "They both pulled me to the shore, but I couldn't feel anything," Plumber related. And there he lay in the water, pondering the situation. "I thought I had pinched a nerve, but my mind was still working quickly."

One of the boys ran to a nearby house, and the Lee ambulance was called to the scene. "In those days, they used a hearse to save and bury people," Plumber said. "But they couldn't get it down the steep river bank." A flurry of activity followed as local people and rescue workers sought to save the stricken child, which required considerable time and effort.

As some workmen cut down brush and cleared a path to the stricken boy, Dr. Irving Brown showed up from his office in Newmarket, New Hampshire, to administer emergency medical care. Plumber explained how lucky he was that Brown was contacted so quickly.

"Dr. Brown just happened to be on duty at the time," Plumber said. "He knew exactly what to do because he had been in a MASH [mobile army surgical hospital] unit during the Second World War that dealt with many spinal cord injuries." Indeed, Brown had dealt with numerous severe neurological injuries as a battalion surgeon on the notorious Anzio beachhead.

He quickly improvised a stabilizer for Plumber's neck with two nylon stockings filled with sand and prepared him for transport. Plumber's parents, Stanley and Marian, arrived on the scene as Dr. Brown and the hearse drivers cautiously lifted their severely injured son out of the muddy waters of the Lamprey River.

"I was joking with my parents and trying to be calm," Plumber recalled. But morbid thoughts drifted through his fully conscious mind. "I remembered how chickens were killed on my father's chicken farm," he said. "First, their necks were stretched and then suddenly twisted."

Plumber was carefully loaded into the hearse by its drivers and Dr. Brown. He heard Brown advise the driver to avoid shaking the boy too much en route to the nearby Exeter Hospital. Plumber recalled, "It was a smooth ride, and I wasn't in much pain."

However, Plumber realized how serious his plight was in the X-ray room. "The full extent of the situation hit home when they cut off my bathing suit," he said. "I couldn't feel them doing it, and it made me think I had a spinal cord injury."

Another fortuitous event then intervened on Plumber's behalf that did a great deal to save his life. The renowned Dr. Henry Saltonstall of the Massachusetts General Hospital happened to be working in the Exeter Hospital on the day of Plumber's accident. Saltonstall was affiliated with Massachusetts General Hospital's newly formed spinal cord trauma unit at the time of Plumber's accident. He was familiar with the staff that treated spinal cord injuries and was soon working to get his patient the very best of care.

"I could hear Dr. Brown and Dr. Saltonstall talking about the X-rays," Plumber said. "I didn't understand the details but knew the situation was serious. Then they stabilized my neck with cloth pads and told me I was being taken to Boston." Plumber recalls the doctors ordering the ambulance driver to go slow, stressing safety over speed. But his ordeal was far from over. Just before the ambulance reached Boston, Plumber started to go into shock and vomited. Unable to move, he was choking on half-digested corn. "The attendant had to use a hand suction device to clear my wind-pipe and mouth," Plumber said. "But he did a good job because I'm still here to talk about it."

Once the ambulance reached the Massachusetts General Hospital Plumber was rushed into a surgical theater. A team of doctors hung over the stricken boy and prepared him for emergency surgery. "They gave me a shot that knocked me out," Plumber said. "I recall waking up in the operating room after that. They were drilling holes in the top of my head, but I was terribly thirsty. I asked for water and then drifted off."

But Plumber was to become semi-conscious again before the doctors finished his operation. He said, "When I came to again, they were saying the eye hooks were in and were asking for wires. I got mad as hell that they hadn't given me any water and called the doctors every name in the book!" related Plumber. A nurse finally gave the injured boy some ice to chew on while the doctors attached wires from a special traction frame to the eye hooks embedded in his skull. Plumber drifted off into semi-consciousness again and didn't entirely leave that state for several days.

"My mother had come down from Newmarket to be with me in the hospital," he said. "She would put on the Red Sox games and talk to me by the hour."

However, Plumber was only partially coherent, unable to move, and tormented by the traction device that stabilized his neck. He said, "I'd hallucinate about baseball games or swimming." Plumber stayed in this hazy, dream-filled state for almost two weeks. Then one day in the early fall, his mother was in Plumber's hospital room, listening to a Red Sox game on a portable radio. "I finally snapped out of it when I heard the announcer saying Ted Williams had just hit a home run," Plumber said. "I told my mother that he must have really got a hold of that one."

Plumber's wits returned quickly after that event, but his physical condition rapidly declined. "I used to haul around 100-pound bags of feed on my father's farm," he said. "I was over 6 feet tall and weighed 182 pounds, but my weight fell to under 100 pounds a few months after the accident." A psychologist was assigned to Plumber to monitor his mental health. She would play a paper spin-the-arrow baseball game with her young patient, but Plumber would have none of it. "It frustrated me," he said. "So, I expressed my displeasure at being treated like a child in no uncertain terms."

In late November, Plumber heard several people gathering outside his room and knew something was up. He could hear his mother's voice, his psychologist, and some doctors. "I knew what they were going to tell me before they came in the room," Plumber said. "Dr. White told me I'd be paralyzed for life, but

I had already figured that out." Plumber told Dr. White, "If it had to happen, too bad it happened to someone without money. At least a millionaire could pay the bills." Dr. White told his youthful patient he had three choices in life. He could "become a bastard" and make life miserable for everyone. The boy could commit suicide in some fashion. Or Plumber could make the best out of life that he could.

Plumber selected the last alternative, but not all spinal cord injury patients respond similarly. "One partially paralyzed guy beside me managed to slash his wrist with a razor blade," Plumber said. "He bled to death before anyone could help him." Plumber went on to see two other spinal cord patients commit suicide, but he wanted to live. "I wanted to be seen as a human being and to become part of the community," he said. "I accepted that I was disabled and accepted it totally."

Plumber ascribes his realistic view of life to a book he read as a child. "Every kid ought to read *Bambi*," he said. "There's life and death and an acceptance of the natural order of things in that book. It helped me accept the truth of what I was facing." However, Plumber's ordeal had only begun. He spent the following year in the Massachusetts General Hospital. Plumber was on his backside so long he developed huge bed sores on his buttocks that became infected. He said, "Then they put me out on my stomach for six months straight, and I had to learn to eat while lying down."

The neurological team at Massachusetts General formed an intensive rehabilitation program for the 12 patients they were treating for spinal cord injuries during Plumber's prolonged stay. He said, "They let us patients pick the nurses, doctors, and even the janitor." Plumber gradually reacquired the partial use of his arms, but could not write or pick up pieces of paper. His atrophied hand muscles still bear mute witness to their loss of function. However, Plumber had also lost all feeling and movement in his torso and lower body and constantly needed intensive personal care.

After his neck had healed enough, young Plumber was allowed to visit his parents on weekends. His mother, Marian, would care for his feeding and personal grooming needs, while Plumber's father, Stanley, carried him up and down stairs and to and from his wheelchair. "Next to being kept alive, my family was the most important thing," Plumber said. "My dad was always realistic about my condition, but my mother didn't accept it for about five years. She always thought I was going to get better."

Plumber was sent to the Crotchet Mountain Rehabilitation Center in Greenfield, New Hampshire because local schools and other facilities were inaccessible to someone with severe handicaps. "There were about 24 children of different ages when I first arrived at Crotchet Mountain," Plumber said. "We were all taught together in a single room by one school teacher, so I missed a lot. The teacher and I taught each other Algebra II, but there's no doubt I was denied a lot of education."

After three and one-half years of care at Crotchet Mountain, Plumber returned home and lived with his parents. "I'm blessed that my father was so big and strong," he related. "He weighed

255 pounds and could pick me up like a feather." Yet Stanley Plumber wishes he could have done even more to help his disabled son. "I didn't have much money," the elder Plumber related. "But my wife and I did all we could to help Walter." Indeed, Walter Plumber explained how critical his parents' care was. In the 1950s, quadriplegics were either homebound or institutionalized if a physically able person wasn't around who could lift them when necessary. He said, "My mother became a nurse, and my father carried me whenever necessary."

With time, Plumber desired to be part of society again. "I wanted to get out into the world," he said. "But there were very few places I could go without much help." Luckily, other strong individuals besides his father were willing to help the disabled youth find some social outlets in his wheelchair-bound existence. Plumber poignantly remembers a basketball playoff game he attended in Goffstown, NH. His father's foreman, Lincoln Gowen, had a son named Kenny, a close friend of Plumber's. After a brief deliberation, Gowen decided to take Plumber to see his son compete in the playoff game. "He and two other people carried me up three flights of stairs so I could see Kenny play in the game," Plumber said as a few tears appeared in his hazel-colored eyes. "He and my family treated me like a human being, and it became my goal to be accepted as one by the whole community."

Yet tragedy once again sought to smother the struggling quadriplegic. In 1961 Plumber's mother died of breast cancer, and the entire burden of his care fell into his father's already busy hands. "My mother was a very religious woman and accepted that she was going to die," said Plumber. "My father and I were both realists, so we also accepted the fact of her death and continued on as best we could."

For 10 years, Stanley Plumber cared for his quadriplegic son's every need as best he could. "He would help me get around," Plumber said. "My care must have been a terrible burden, but I never once heard him complain or be bitter. A traveling nurse would come by from time to time, but my father took care of most of my needs." Stanley Plumber still offers no complaints about the long hours caring for his son while simultaneously running the family's chicken farm. "I just adjusted my hours and worked a little harder," he said. "I only wish I could have done more for him."

But Plumber still yearned to get into the real world despite his handicaps. He wanted to study and learn, as well as watch sporting events. "My friends would pick up psychology textbooks from the UNH library, and I'd read them," he said. "I had to make it up (missed education) on my own." Plumber learned to turn the pages of books despite his immobile hands but says, "Papers and pens are still my worst enemy." Plumber's father is still impressed with how much his son has managed to learn despite his disabilities.

"He's only got the use of his biceps and a few shoulder muscles," the elder Plumber related. "But he works hard to learn what he can. He's done well with very little physically." Most importantly, Walter Plumber learned how to listen and to be able to recall in intricate detail what was said. He related, "I wanted to live as everyone else did and was determined to learn how. Memory was my single greatest tool in doing that."

In 1971 "Sue" became Plumber's personal care attendant. Plumber won't divulge her last name to protect his care provider's privacy. "Sue has made life much more livable for me," Plumber said about his friend of 18 years. "To her, my care is more than just a job; you do not know how thankful that makes me feel. She has given me the help I needed to leave the nest." Indeed, thanks to Sue's help Plumber has left the nest in a big way. In the middle 70s, Plumber became involved in improving accessibility to public facilities for disabled people. He became an advocate, and he was not to be ignored. Plumber dictated letters, joined in group lawsuits, and worked in other ways to improve disabled people's lives and opportunities.

By 1978 Plumber made a decision about what he was going to do with his life. "Given my disabilities, it would have taken close to 10 years to get a college degree, so I decided on something more immediate," he said. "I became committed to being able to move and to help other disabled people become part of society," Plumber proclaimed. "I decided to teach myself counseling techniques so that I could help other people who were disabled to enjoy life."

Plumber put his studies to good use and chaired the Seacoast Peer Group for local disabled residents from 1981 to 1988. He became deeply involved with the Granite State Independent Living Foundation (GSILF) and fought for accessibility rights for disabled people. Lesly Washburn, the GSILF peer support group coordinator, was effusive in her praise for Plumber's efforts. Washburn said, "He will dictate letters and make sure they are sent to congressmen about issues that concern him and other disabled people." Washburn is also impressed by both Plumber's outlook and perseverance. "He is very determined and is up to date on current political affairs," said Washburn. "But more importantly, he's looked up to by disabled and able-bodied people alike."

Donna Marie, UNH's ACCESS (assessing career challenges in education through special services) coordinator, is also familiar with Plumber's efforts. She said, "Walter has a great resourceful background and is very approachable." Marie is also effusive in her praise of Plumber's personal character. "He's very social, conscientious, and understanding," she said. "Walter is community-oriented and always available to help the ACESS program and other disabled people."

Plumber's condition continues to plague him at times. Last year, he experienced a severe urological infection that limited his availability. His condition slowly deteriorated and ultimately required reconstructive surgery. Plumber has healed well but relinquished his position with the Seacoast Peer Group due to his lengthy hospital stays. Since Plumber left the peer group, its name has been changed to Fun on Wheels. Plumber has returned to the group to help out as an advisor, but his concerns are not solely directed toward the less able in society.

"I remember swimming in clean water as a boy and playing in a pollution-free world," Plumber said. "Now I see what's happening to the land, and it bothers me. It bothers me that things like AIDs and drugs have become so much a part of the society around me." Plumber plans on getting involved in these areas via letters or whatever else he can do to change the current situation. "Just because I'm in this chair, it doesn't mean I've lost any love for the world," he said. "I struggled to be part of this society, and I think both able and disabled people ought to work towards making life better."

Yes, Plumber certainly is trying to make life better. He skillfully pilots his electric wheelchair to meetings and events with a specially modified joystick that he has learned to use with considerable aplomb. His chair has a lap tray for Plumber to hold his towel-covered water bottle, watch, and wallet. Plumber's red baseball cap and broad, friendly features have become familiar to many Durham, NH residents, but he's also known in other seacoast communities. Plumber's recognized because he refuses to stay home and wallow in despair. "I do what I can do, and don't dwell on what I can't," Plumber insists.

After three days of interviews, Plumber made a crucial observation. He said, "When people first see me, they notice the chair. After a while, the chair disappears, and only then do they see the person sitting in that chair," an exceptional person in many ways. His dedication was to become part of a dynamic life and not just another victim of tragic happenstance. He has succeeded marvelously and provides a wonderful example for us all. Amen.

89

The Honesty of Death

A childhood acquaintance died (3/23/16), and I remain unsure how to feel about his passing. Honestly, I did not like "Jeremy," not one tiny bit. Nor do I lament his death. That admission paints me as an unforgiving prick, and perhaps that is appropriate. After all, what is to be gained by disliking the dead? We played football together, and I spent many hours competing in war games with him and a mutual friend. Malcolm, Jeremy, and I could often be found reaching over a table during the wee hours, moving tiny markers over hexagon grids. I grew to be best of friends with Malcolm, whose life was eventually ended when the back end of a tractor-trailer rolled over onto his motorcycle on a busy Texas highway. However, there was to be no deep and lasting friendship with Jeremy. Indeed, the right-wing memes I originally planned to use in this chapter were all collected and shared by Jeremy, but my editor reminded me I had no rights to them.

The reasons I grew to dislike Jeremy, if one wishes to call them reasons, were many and sometimes petty. In seventh or eighth grade, our physical education (PE) teacher put a wrestling segment into his teaching plan. I loved it and was good at the activity. There was minimal formal coaching per se, and soon kids were being carted off with various injuries. I well recall my match with Jeremy. He rushed across the matt and head-butted me in the face. That did not work out well for him. I absorbed the impact and used the pain to trigger some adrenalin. I reached low, picked him up to chest level in a high crotch throw, and quickly executed a nearly perfect full-body slam. I put some real oomph into the landing, with Jeremy's backside being well-planted into the mat. He did not get up. Jeremy was taken to the doctor and missed a week of school.

I didn't feel bad about the incident and figured I had finally found a sport I could excel at. Sadly, too many kids were getting beaten up, so we ended our wrestling section of PE. Back to racket sports and other activities that I absolutely sucked at. Yet this incident had nothing to do with my dislike of Jeremy. Sure, he had head-butted me, but my angst began during those marathon war games. He would often order his mother around rudely and condescendingly, showing off in a manner that indicated he had been brought up as a little prince. "Get me a drink," he would bark, "and make sure it's cold this time." He found the incidents amusing, but they pissed me off. I am positive Jeremy deeply loved his mom, yet here was a vile display of arrogance I found utterly unforgivable.

He made snide comments towards me and disparaged others, occasionally being a bully. Over time, my antipathy toward him slowly increased, despite our being teammates in football and sharing many friends. All kids can be rude and selfish, and I was no exception. However, his pronouncements had a certain haughtiness and egotism, as if Jeremy thought he was indeed fit to judge. He did not openly invite conflicts with me, nor did I with him. Yet he sometimes made jibes, something Jeremy was keen to do with many people. We hung with different crowds, and our lives went their separate ways. He became a cop in Lebanon, NH, and I was a student at UNH.

Jeremy visited Malcolm at UNH on one occasion, and the three of us shared some drinks over a table. Jeremy had picked up the smoking habit and tried to play tough guy. I recall him blowing smoke into my face, a singularly disrespectful gesture. I grabbed the ashtray and contemplated burying it in the side of his face and skull. I was ready to harm him, but fate, discretion, and/or happenstance intervened. The moment passed, but the desire to maul Jeremy remained. His actions and words were such that I knew we could not be in the same universe, let alone the same room. It was best to avoid him because it would end in a sea of blood and endless legal hassles. Darkness was within me, and it took several years to cage the beast. It still lurks within but is now much better controlled.

As noted above, Jeremy became a cop in Lebanon, NH, for a while, a role he was ill-suited to undertake by nature. In fact, he eventually got canned, with Malcolm once telling me that an underage girl was involved. I had no reason to doubt Malcolm; such an event would not surprise me. However, the incident was hushed up, or so it seems, and I cannot attest to its veracity. A bit later, Jeremy and Malcolm started a limo service that carted people to and from the Upper Valley and Boston. The venture eventually failed, and I soon lost contact with Malcolm and Jeremy. In time, I regained contact with Malcolm but not with Jeremy. Contacting him was never high on my list of things to do. Several years ago, I found Jeremy on Facebook, and his life had taken some regrettable health and career turns.

Jeremy had donned an essentially conservative ideology, albeit he dubbed himself a Libertarian. Indeed, his tendency to mock others found many kindred spirits in the Trumpian clan that infested United States politics during the 2015–2024 era. Jeremy graduated from New Mexico State University in 1976 and married in 1978. That ended with a divorce, and Jeremy moved to Phoenix, Arizona, in 1990. He seems to have fallen in love with the place, being exposed to wide-open skies rather than the verdant hills and mountains of the Upper Valley. He grew to like George Bush and survivalism, that old-fashioned notion that people are meant to live as isolated and self-sufficient monads instead of being citified codependents.

It seems Jeremy had a diverse string of jobs dotting his past, not that I understand why. He once had a personality that invited being dismissed, although I don't know what the case was during his later career. Indeed, Jeremy could have been very good at his job. His health declined by age 55, and he became morbidly obese. So, Jeremy was far from living a good life, not that I take any pleasure from that. Indeed, I have not entirely decided why I disliked him, other than we were as oil and water. He became disabled, slovenly, and leaned heavily on friends. This was not at all the rugged life of independence that he envisioned. Then it all ended on Wednesday, March 23, 2016. He supposedly died of natural causes, though I was told differently by some mutual friends. In any case, he was in lamentable health and financially strapped, and thus a sea of woes awaited him.

So, I read the full-length obituary and was dismayed by its fawning nature, albeit a common theme in obituaries. After all, how often do we read, "She was a miserable bitch who beat her kids and threw heavy objects at people?" Jeremy was definitely not the saintly person being portrayed and probably not nearly the sinner I had remembered. I have since written a brutally critical and honest obit for myself, lest folks get the wrong ideas. One of Jeremy's last postings on Facebook kind of says it all, albeit he lifted the passage from a YouTube video:

> I have but one request to make at my departure from this world; it is the charity of silence. Let no man write my epitaph; for as no man who knows my motives, dare now vindicate them, let no prejudice or ignorance asperse them. Let them rest in obscurity and peace! Let

my memory be left in oblivion, and my tomb remain un-
inscribed, until other times and other men can do justice
to my character. (MisterE 1024)

No, I did not grant Jeremy the charity of silence, although I
will not write an epitaph for him or inscribe his tomb. Indeed,
I will not even post his picture or his real name. That would be
unjust according to his lofty standards. Instead, I will ask one
and all if holding on to resentment and anger is worth the in-
vestment of time and energy that it takes. Some of us cling to
the hatred of a parent, relative, or acquaintance, and often for
some valid reasons. Yet we hold that anger close long after the
object of our opprobrium has passed. Likewise, some of us grow
to despise a job or occupation, even when it is long confined to
being in the rearview mirror of our life's direction. Some of us
even magnify a past wrong into something that blights our future, never quite grasping that we have made a conscious choice
to do so. I see the folly in making such choices, yet we all do it.
As for Jeremy, I am pleased he grew to love New Mexico, as is
evidenced by the many pictures he posted of its vast open expanses. He searched for beauty and serenity and found some in
his new abode.

Humans are strange creatures, but when we meet sentient
compatriots, we will see that some behaviors are cross-species
and consummately universal. I imagine dislike and hatred are
among them, although let us hope that love and forgiveness are
also prized. So, I wish you fair sailing, Jeremy, wherever you may

be. I was not one of your biggest fans, but I opted to memorialize you via this chapter. Would that I could have forgiven . . . Would that I could have cared . . . Would that I could have been your friend . . . The things we could have shared. Amen.

90

Shady Brady, a Dealer's Lament

Shady Brady's apartment is above a flower shop in New Hampshire's Seacoast region. He wears a short dark beard and mustache, has brown eyes, and a Roman nose that displays a partial Italian heritage. In fact, Shady doesn't know his precise genealogy, having been cast adrift when he was a baby. Yet he wants little about his past and appearance to appear in this chapter and for a good reason. Shady is an excellent friend and bad enemy, especially when buying and selling drugs. Yet he was game for this story you're reading, and he knew I could and would write the tale.

90.1 Shady Brady sure looked like this guy, but one never knows

So, he lights up the big joint he just rolled and asks me to take a hit. I'm initially apprehensive about taking notes while getting stoned, but it's the only way to do the story. Plus, I welcome good marijuana. I take a long, slow drag of the sweet, spicy-smelling herb and melt into the comfortable armchair. Oh yeah, this is good stuff. However, I don't want to get too stoned because there is work to be done. I need a dealer's viewpoint on the recent Zero Tolerance Law. It bothers me greatly that some New Hampshire-based dealers are starting to arm themselves, and I want to understand why. Yeah, this is the "live free or die" state, but that does not mean the motto should be taken so literally.

"It's damn good reefer," Shady tells me, but that fact has already become abundantly clear. Being stoned certainly isn't an unpleasant feeling, nor is it the first time I've ever indulged in this illegal activity. Though it isn't a healthy pursuit, I doubt it will even be the twenty-thousandth time I've smoked pot. However, it will be the first time I've tried putting down a self-confessed dealer's perspective into the written word. I scribble away while he talks.

"This is only $50.00 a quarter, but I can get quantity if you like," he says. "I think it's a home-grown type of Hawaiian. Sure smells like it." I tell him the story is the primary goal, and I don't have extra money to spend on marijuana; maybe next week. He laughs and says, "So, you're serious about the story. I know you're cool, brother, but don't be blabbin' my name around! I got you like you got me." I nod, knowing we're now mutually guilty of at least a misdemeanor. Yeah, but Shady knows me as a friend, and we've been on many adventures over the years. I am surprised he is being a tad paranoid, but he has good reasons to avoid being overly trusting.

"This is a crazy ass idea, but let's get it done," Shady tells me. He winces, his back having been badly injured at work. Then he goes on. "At first, I sold a few bags to cover the cost of my head stash, but it's grown beyond that now." Shady sells between two ounces and a pound of high-quality marijuana every week. In a year, he makes from $8,000 to $10,000 in profit, or so he claims. That is tiny potatoes compared with some dealers, but Shady doesn't like the risks of moving prodigious quantities of marijuana. "It's damn dangerous to move 10 or 20 pounds nowadays," he says.

He breaks out his special head stash and puts some top-shelf marijuana on the desk. I think this is one hell of a way to go through life, but Shady is a mess. A heavy roll of roof tiles had been loaded on his shoulder from a truck, and the sudden load badly damaged some discs in his lower back. Indeed, a major operation was needed to repair the damage. His back never appropriately healed after the surgery, and he claims the herb helps a bit. Oddly, Shady hates pain narcotics, though he does them on occasion. While he cleans and manicures the pungent herb, we discuss the growing legal dangers of dealing marijuana.

"The anti-drug laws ain't going to stop people from smoking weed," Shady insists. "Hey, stoners are going to get stoned. The laws just make life more violent." He adds, "I never used to own a gun, but I just bought a Ruger." Shady tells me that the new high stakes have forced his hand. With the Zero Tolerance Law in effect, he insists "We have to fight. What the fuck choice do we have?"

Indignantly, he proclaims, "If those stupid bastards in Congress wanted to make me act like a goddamned toots [cocaine] dealer, they've done it." He knows that if he's caught, the authorities will automatically impound his car and possessions, slap up to $50,000 in fines, and put him away for many years. But Shady defiantly states, "I'd rather die fighting than face that hassle, and I will." I tell him I hope not, and he advises me that the suppliers are also arming themselves to the teeth, something many of them were loath to do.

90.2 Shady Brady with his 2nd wife, Cathy Lee

We start on the second joint, but I'm too much of a "light-weight" to keep up with Shady while trying to take notes. He's not worried about the cops. "No one's going to put me in the pen for selling herb, smoking herb, or speaking my piece about it," he says. "It's no more wrong to get baked than to get drunk." The double-standard society uses concerning drug laws utterly infuriates him. "I don't drink, and I don't do toots. I don't do downers or uppers, like all those droopy-titted housewives you see. All I do is herb, and I ain't gonna be punished for it."

I play the devil's advocate and tell Shady he'll go to jail if they catch him. His answer is simple, "Dead men don't go to jail." Shady insists he would prefer being shot versus submitting to incarceration. "I'm sick of it," he says solemnly. He shakes his shaggy head and adds, "If the pigs try to take away my home, family, and possessions, there will be a war. It ain't me that's imposing my will on them! It's them that are trying to impose their will on me."

Yet to shoot an officer––is anything worth doing that, I ask. "Lots of people got shot in 'Nam because the government said it was OK," Shady informs me. He explains, "I had to fight to survive from day one. It's that or take a beat down. No one gave a shit about me until I was adopted, and that was the first time I knew love." Shady then discusses his experiences, many fights, and brushes with the law. He grew up in a school of tough knocks for sure, and that is something he desperately wants his kids to avoid. So, we dive into the subject.

What about your wife and children? I ask. Do you want your kids to get high all the time? He tells me his family is "My entire reason for being alive." He says, "My wife occasionally smokes, but we never smoke in front of the kids. When they come of age, they'll make their own decisions. But I expect one or the other will try drugs for themselves." Shady claims it's the same truth many American families will have to deal with, although he would prefer his kids get into sports.

I tell him kids could be buying the marijuana he sells to local people. Maybe his children will, too, someday. Shady replies, "I don't think any young kid should be doing drugs, but they're going to get them if I sell dope or not. I just dread my kids getting a hold of some toots." Cocaine seems to scare Shady, and we start to talk about it.

"Toots is terrible shit," Shady tells me. "I know you've seen how crazy it makes people." Shady feels the new anti-drug law has lumped marijuana users into the same category as cocaine users. "Herb's weaker than alcohol, but toots is a bitch," he says. Shady knows of several people who have died from cocaine use in one way or another, as do I. He tells me, "One guy overdosed, one drowned, three died in car accidents, and one tried to rip off the wrong kind of people."

"It's stupid to treat marijuana users like cocaine freaks," Shady claims. "When you get baked, you sit back, turn on the tunes, and shoot the shit, like we're doing now. But when doing toots, you always think of ways to get more. Plus, you're wired enough to do some crazy shit to get it!" Shady supports the legalization of marijuana but not cocaine. "Legalizing pot would put me out of business, but I wouldn't need the damn gun," he says, glancing toward a desk drawer. "Legalizing cocaine would result in a need for everyone to carry guns."

I ask him what the solution is, and he offers a smile. "There ain't any solution," he tells me. The way Shady sees it, politicians lack the courage to legalize marijuana and waste their time and resources battling "the wrong dragons." He frowns and says, "I don't want to hurt anyone. You know that. I thought those days had ended. But if the DEA [Drug Enforcement Administration] comes for me, I'll drop a few of those bastards." I believe him but push the issue.

What about your family, I ask? What will they do if the DEA gets their breadwinner? Shady's eyes light up, and he angrily tells me, "My life doesn't mean a damn if my kids got to grow up in a country that ain't free!" He talks about the right to choose and how that right is being denied to marijuana users. Shady feels people have as much of a right to smoke marijuana as to drink alcohol or smoke cigarettes. To him, this is a matter of living free or dying.

But marijuana is terrible for your health, I tell him. Shady nods and says, "I know this shit clogs up my lungs, but alcohol rots the liver, and butts give you lung cancer." We start laughing for some unknown reason, and I forget what I want to ask him, a common occurrence for marijuana users. He turns on some new tunes and relights the rest of the second joint. Finally, I remember my question.

What about the anti-drug campaigns? Are they a good thing? To my surprise, Shady nods and tells me all drugs can be harmful if overused. He adds, "I just wish they'd show a drunk's rotten liver or Spuds McKenzy falling down a flight of stairs in a drunken stupor." We roar with laughter, and I ponder about what a sight that would be . . . little spuds bumpily-bumping all the way down a steep flight of stairs, head over heels.

Shady switches the topic to Nancy Reagan's Just Say No campaign. His laughter turns abruptly to anger. He yells, "That #%&? just wanted to rescue her rich-bitch character after everyone got pissed about her $450,000 dinner sets and $10,000 evening gowns." Shady rages for almost 15 minutes on the evils of the Reagans and closes by saying, "Hey, I'm still here selling dope, and they're down the river."

We've talked for about two hours when someone raps on the door. "Who the hell is it?" shouts Shady. "It's the fucking pigs," comes the boisterous reply behind the door. Shady laughs and says, "Someday, it may be the pigs, but that's Bob." I'm somewhat relieved by the revelation but perplexed about what to do. Shady tells me to stay put as he approaches the door and lets in his friend.

"Don't mind him: he's only a narc," he tells Bob while glancing in my direction. "A damn big un," Bob replies while briefly checking me out. I can see business is about to be transacted, and having already gotten the story, I opt to leave. Shady asks me if I'd like a joint for the road, but I'm stoned enough already. I thank him for his hospitality and assure Shady I'll protect his identity. He says, "I know you will. We both got some honor."

I trudge down the stairs, relishing the glow and still musing about Spuds taking a tumble. I regret not taking the joint, but next week will provide enough funds for a bag. And it is excellent weed. Shady is more than my dealer. He is my friend. Shady doesn't make much money selling pot but cannot do much work until his back heals. That may not happen for a long time, given the damage that was done, so there Shady is, puffing on a joint, listening to tunes, and regretting owning the Ruger he just bought. He doesn't want to hurt anyone; let us hope he never does. And so it goes . . . Amen.

Postscript

This article was written during the spring of 1989, and Shady's path diverged from my own shortly after this time. I went to Penn State to get my PhD, leaving my New Hampshire Seacoast friends in my wake. Shady's first wife eventually divorced him because he couldn't keep his dick in his pants, and thus he can only visit his kids now. That is a tragedy because he was a good father. I tried to find Shady after I returned from PSU in 2001, but that search didn't go too well. Alas, I found out in March 2023 that Shady,

> David . . ., 51, of Hampton Falls, passed away peaceful-
> ly on Thursday, March 8, 2018, at his home, attended
> by his loving wife . . . David always had a smile on his
> face. David also loved riding his Harley really fast. David
> was a straight shooter. To know him was to love him . . .
> He was also a talented musician and loved jamming with
> his friends on his guitar or bass. David had many great
> friends and will be sadly missed.

I discovered two of his kids had become accomplished athletes, as he had wished. Esophageal cancer claimed Shady's life, but dying loved is the most we can ask for. Fair sailing and following seas, my friend. Amen.

91

Flying Low with Coony

"Raccoon" Reynolds looks like the Zig-Zag man imprinted on my rolling papers, albeit that his mustache is not upturned. He usually knows his drugs, but this is some nasty shit he brought over. It doesn't look like the crystal meth I've traditionally bought, yet that's what Coony says this stuff is. Christ, it's in crystalline form, all right, but the crystals are dirty brown, not off-white or opaque like the pure stuff I prefer. It nearly burned out my nostrils when I tried snorting a line, like putting bleach up my nose. Most crystal meth burns slightly but doesn't make folks wince and tear up. Yeah, this crap has a lot of duff in it, as many imports do. I don't know what this crap is, although Coony tried doing me a favor when he snagged it.

91.1 The Zig-Zag man from rolling paper fame, and a fair rendition of Coony

I'll chop up another line and let Coony try it out. It chops up nicely, but even this line I'm making looks brownish. I wish Mike would bug out of here. Christ, I can't stand that bloated shit-head. Here he is, hovering around my kitchen table like a hungry puppy, hoping to grab handouts. No, I don't like that guy at all. I'd prefer to put a plastic bag over his head, tape it closed, and toss him off a bridge. Now don't think like that, or you may just do it. Well, this line ought to do Coony right. I'll just hand him this mirror and tooter and let him do it.

"Try it for yourself," I tell him.

He snorts the line, his eyes tear up, and he clutches his nose.

"Wheeeewww!" Coony exclaims. "It is a bit harsh, Dino, but that's 'cause it's that Mexican shit. Ah, mind lettin' me try another line?"

Another line? God, you do hate yourself.

"It's your nose," I reply. Yes, I'll chop up some more of these noxious brown crystals for you, but I'm not happy with this crap. Better tell Coony now.

"I don't like payin' a hundred bucks for shit I can't even use. I mean, I thank you for picking it up and everything. But this stuff is bogus."

I hand Coony the mirror. He does another line. His eyes tear up, and he cringes.

"Fuckin' a; that is strong," he says hoarsely. "But I can fuckin' feel it workin' already. I'll keep the stuff if you don't want it. Won't be able to pay you for a few days, though. We ain't had much business on the boats lately. I was gettin' sick of gill-nettin' anyways."

"Sure, Coony, but keep the money," I reply. Coony did me many favors over the years, including giving me money when I was out of work due to a bad knee injury. One hand washes the other, as the Italians say.

I wish I had spent my money on some cocaine or pot. Look at Coony brushing away tears, and he still wants this shit. Coony is a spectacle: shoulder-length brown hair tied together in a ponytail, full beard and mustache, tattered leather jacket and cap, eight-inch Bowie knife, and steel-colored eyes set into those permanently dark eye-sockets of his. I've known him for four or five years, close to when I moved out of the UNH dorms and into downtown Durham, NH. He isn't big, just 160 pounds, but he can be dangerous. Yeah, we make a good tag team.

He swilled that beer down in just a few gulps. Shit, he's been a case-a-day man ever since I met him in The Wildcat—a nice little bar and pizza joint in the middle of downtown Durham, NH. Was that in 1972? Yeah, my sophomore year at UNH. Hmmm, it's very unusual for Coony to indulge in amphetamines like this. That's way out of character. He likes downers like Valium and Demerol, although he ain't too fond of pot.

"Mind if I try a line?" Mike asks.

I nod and cut a little chunk of the stuff into tiny bits. I don't like Mikey, but he doesn't object to my crazy friends and partying. But as a neighbor, I would rather he weren't here. In fact, he likes to get involved in my antics, whether invited or not. Perhaps that's why I'm making this line so huge. This ought to burn his frigging face off! Yeah, here's the mirror sucker.

"Go nuts."

Shit, he's trying to toot up the whole damn line in one nostril! I knew he would! Ho, ho, ho, look at that fool's face! He dropped my tooter. Now he's grabbing his nose and yelping like a wounded dog. Coony's laughing his ass off too! Hell, now Mikey is doing a little jig around my kitchen table. Ho, ho, ho, ho! This is excellent entertainment.

"Die, you mother-fucker. Die!"

Hell, it's worth a hundred dollars to see old Mikey get his free buzz. Ho, ho, ho.

"Fuck, you guys!" Mike yells, while Coony and I laugh.

"Nice buzz?" I ask. "Want another line?"

"No way!" Mike says. "Hey, I know how we can do this stuff."

91.2 Coony at peace

"Yeah?" Coony asks.

"Sure, I'll be right back."

What the fuck is he up to now? Oh no, what's that he's got in his hand. Shit, it's a fucking syringe, old-school style! Oh crap, Coony's eyes are lit up like damn Christmas tree ornaments. Here we go again. Shit, I better put the skids to this plan. Coony's crazy enough to boot this shit. I've seen it before.

"I don't know if this is such a good idea," I say. "Shit, you guys don't know if this crap's pure. I mean, the stuff is fucking brown. I don't . . ."

"All we got to do is heat it real good before we shoot it up," Mike interjects.

"That's right," Coony says. "Have ya got anything for me to tie off with, Dino?" He gets up to scrounge around for some shooting equipment.

"Ah, no."

"I'll be right back," Mike says before scurrying into his room again. I hate that fucking guy! No skin off my back if he offs himself, but Coony is a friend. Well, have to try talking some reason into him, but that ain't easy.

"This is a terrible idea, Coony. The crap is toxic."

The bastard is pretending not to hear me. That's how it always is when I'm playing "citizen." There he goes, grabbing my candle from the window sill. He is lighting the damn thing. And here comes Mike with a garter belt and an oversized spoon. Coony is already taking his jacket off. He just can't wait to die. Go ahead, roll up that sleeve, you asshole. And there's Mike, chopping up a bunch of that shit on my mirror. I don't want any part of this.

"Chop that shit up real good," Coony says to Mike while he wraps the garter belt around his arm. Coony repeatedly squeezes his fist open and closed to get his blood vessels to distend. "I don't want no chunks getting stuck anywhere," he says. "Can't be dyin' in Dino's kitchen."

"Sure you can," Mike says with a chuckle.

I shake my head. I've often partied with Coony: he knows I don't mainline. But I understand why he does this shit. It's those frigging parents of his. They abandoned him when he was about 12, and his grandmother couldn't handle him. She tried, though, and Coony has some good values––on those occasions when he's semi-sober. Plus, she loves him, and that matters a whole lot. I wonder what she would think if she could see him now?

"Don't worry," Mike says while chopping the crystals into a powder. "I've done this before. You doin' any, Dino?"

"That shit?"

"You only live once," Mike says with a laugh.

"You only die once, too," I retort.

"Oh, you're the big tough guy," Mike replies.

"Want to find out?" Come on, shit-head. Just push me a bit more, and I'll rip your fuckin' head off. Just a little bit more.

"Lighten up," Mike sneers.

"Jesus, I got me a huge fuckin' blood vessel poppin' out," Coony interjects. Yeah, you got a big blood vessel to shoot at, Coony. Christ, I remember that time we tore a five-dollar bill in half. The guy who survived would get the other half from his dead buddy and have a few shots on him. I'm going to win that bet for sure at this rate. Of course, one never knows.

"Just hold your water," Mike says. "I gotta cut this up some more."

Yeah, chop that shit up real good, you bastard. There he goes putting it in the spoon with the razor blade. Now he's turning on my tap. Fuck, I wish he'd ask me if shooting up in my kitchen is OK. He's turning on the faucet just enough to release a tiny trickle of water. Old Mikey must have done this many times be-fore. Will surprises never cease? I didn't know he was a damn mainliner. Now he's adding water to the crystals and swirling the spoon.

"Yes, sah!" Mike exclaims. "It's already dissolving. I think we got us some good stuff here."

"Yeah," I say, "bet you'd like Draino just as well."

Mike and Coony are laughing, but this ain't funny to me.

"You ain't gonna join us, Dino?" Coony asks.

"No fuckin' way!"

"Heh, heh," Mike says. "Now look who's the wimp."

You cream puff. I'll look right through those blue eyes of yours, pal. Go ahead, sucker. Blinking already? And now that smirk is gone from your face. Oh, you're just fine with words, Mikey, but you don't want to really play, do you? That's right. You better look away, old Mikey, because one day I may cut off your dirty blond mop with a dull butter knife.

"I'll heat it up a bit more," Mike says, holding the spoon over the stubby candle's flame. He gently swirls the mixture around.

"You don't want to get meth too hot," Coony warns. "Too much heat breaks that shit down."

"I know what I'm fucking doing . . . I think," Mike says.

They're both laughing. Fools! I'll just fold my arms across my chest and look unhappy. Maybe Coony will get the message. That's an interesting old hypodermic Mike's got. It has a glass barrel with calibration marks and a rubber-tipped glass plunger. There's an O ring on the top of the plunger. It must be there so the thing can make injections and blood withdrawals. The needle looks like stainless steel but is only about an inch and a quarter long.

"Where'd you get that thing," I ask Mike as he hands the spoon to Coony.

"Oh, a friend gave it to me a few years ago. I don't know where he got it. Probably from a dead junkie."

We all laugh.

"Is it clean?" I ask.

"Cleaner than the stuff we're using," Mike chuckles while drawing the spoon's contents into the syringe. "We gotta move it, Coony. We don't want this stuff coming out of solution. Want me to shoot you up?"

"Nah, I can do it," Coony replies. He takes the loaded syringe from Mike and taps the bubbles out of its barrel.

Christ, Coony's sticking that hypodermic's business end into his arm. This is nasty bullshit. He's gotten into that vein now with the needle. What the fuck is he doing? I see. He's not injecting the shit all at once. Yeah, you've seen this before. Oh, gross. He's sucking some of his blood into the hypodermic barrel to let it mix with the crystal meth. Just get it over with! Now he's injecting about half the stuff into his arm. And now he's sucking more blood into the syringe. This is grossing me out big time.

"How is it?" Mike asks nervously.

"WAH FUCKIN' WHO!" Coony exclaims as he finally empties the hypodermic's contents into his arm. "It's givin' me a real good head rush.

91.3 Coony enjoying food and libation with friends

"Real good?" Mike asks.

Get that needle out of your arm, Coony. Yeah, that's it. Now he's putting the damn thing on the table. I wonder if he'll drop dead? Now he's loosening the garter belt. Shit! He's closing his eyes, and he ain't moving. Don't die on me, Coony. Ah, there's a smile etching its way across his face.

"It's good shit, Mike," he says. "Mother of fuckin' Christ, I can feel my heart poundin' away already. You're gonna like this stuff."

Good, Coony is taking in a few deep breaths. He'll be OK. Look at Mikey. He's studying Coony to see if he is going to have a bad reaction or not. Typical. If Coony goes down, you will too, Mikey. Your fate will be his—I swear it. After all, it was your fuckin' idea to shoot this shit up, and you let Coony be the guinea pig. I'll smash your skull and claim that I found you shooting up Coony. Why are you looking at me like that, Coony?

"No shit, Dino, you gotta try this shit," he says. "I'm speedin' my fuckin' brains out."

"Nah, I don't think so."

"Well, by Jesus, I think I'll try me some of that stuff," Mike says.

"Not in here," I say.

"What's your problem?" Mike asks.

"You are," I fire back, glaring through his eyes and deep into the back of his skull.

"Fuckin' A, this is really good shit, Mike," Coony interjects while glancing around the room. "I think I'll do me another."

"Why don't you come over to my place? Dino's getting all uptight. He needs some Fem-Iron, I guess."

I look at the hypodermic needle on my table and smile at Mike.

"I bet I could shove that thing up your ass sideways," I say.

"Oh, I'm petrified," Mike sneers. "Come on, Coony. Let's go to my place."

"I think that's a good fuckin' idea," Coony says while leaping to his feet. "Christ, what a fuckin' head rush. You're gonna like this shit."

"Stop by later, Coony," I say.

"If my head's still fuckin' on, I will."

That's right, Mikey, pick up that hypodermic and candle and get the hell out of here. And Coony is snagging the garter strap, spoon, and ersatz crystal meth. Shit, he's shaking a bit. I wonder what he'll be up to tonight? Go on, go to your destiny. You never listen to me anyway. Oh well, $100 down the tubes and two possible Dead on Arrivals, though Mikey would be no great loss. Still, not a good night. Course, there's been worse. That gun-in-the-mouth shit Juan pulled was nuts, but that wasn't in my place. I can't believe he actually pulled the damn trigger. Yeah, the cocaine blues takes no prisoners.

I can hear Coony and Mike laughing from across the hall. Fucking Mike is waiting for Coony to do another injection just to make sure. Ah, now Mikey is finally doing one himself. Shit, that crap didn't kill him. Yeah, Mikey is doing another shot, but he still lives. Christ, they're getting wound up tighter than a drum. At least Coony has the downing effect of mass dosages of alcohol to help compensate for the meth's effects. But Mikey is speeding along, spewing out words at an astonishing rate. What's this? Mikey is bitching about the way I treat him. Well, why don't you fucking cry about it? Ho, ho, ho. Good old Coony tells Mike he doesn't want to hear about it.

"You got a problem with Dino? You go talk to him about it," Coony says. "He'll set you straight."

Shit, Coony's doing a third shot! Oh, Christ, at least he's still talking. Now Mike wants to go out. They're debating about where to go. Yeah, go to Nicks, Coony. You got friends who'll watch out for you there. Christ, they're taking the meth and "shooting works" with them. Yeah, that's the kerchunk sounds of Coony's steel-tipped boots zipping down the stairs. I'll just sit back here and roll me up a big old joint. It's only 8:00 p.m. I wonder if I'll ever see Coony again? Most likely. He's a tough little bastard.

Oh, yeah! This pot tastes good. I remember tearing some knee ligaments in a lifting accident and couldn't do my coaching job in UNH's weight room. Coony would come over to my apartment to drink beers and visit. He'd even offer money to help tide me over until my knee healed. Ah, but I was too damn proud, and I told Coony that my school loans would cover my head. Shit, he knew I was lying. Then one morning, I hear a rustling sound outside my door, and I get myself up to see who wants in.

I hear the kerchunks of steel-tipped motorcycle boots going down the stairs while I limp along, and then I notice that an envelope has been forced under the door. I discover ten ten-dollar bills in the envelope, but nothing else, not even a note. I limp down the stairs and look out the front door of the apartment house. There's Coony, trooping off toward town. I yell out his name, but he doesn't turn around. Christ, that money allowed me to get a bunch of groceries. Yeah, he's got a good heart—a real good heart. I remember that he stopped by a week later. I offer him a beer, and we talk.

"Coony, that was nice of you."

"What was?"

"I mean, the money."

"What the fuck are you talkin' about?" he said unconvincingly.

"I got you some beers with part of it. Want one?"

"Does a cow have tits?"

"I'll pay ya back."

"Just give me a fuckin' beer, Dino. You don't owe me Jack Shit."

"You're good people, Coony."

"Ain't so bad yourself."

No, he isn't such a bad guy. However, he sure as hell doesn't have good judgment, especially when he's shit-faced, which is most of the time. Hell, I remember when he went after me, and I'm twice his weight. He must have been feeling particularly rambunctious.

"Shey, Dino," he says with a slur. "Are you really that fuckin' strong?"

"I am, Coony."

"Well, I'm a good shcraper. I-I bet I can out-wrestle you."

"You don't want to do that, Coony."

"Jusht 'cause you're big, it don't mean you can fight."

He gets up and stares down at me.

"Don't worry . . . I won't hurt you too bad," he says.

984

I sigh and shake my head.

"I'm not going to fight you," I say.

"Hah, jusht as I figured . . . you're big but can't fight."

I look down.

"Come on," Coony said while taking a stance.

I shock the shit out of him. I leap up and swiftly reach my right arm under his crotch and my left over his right shoulder. I lift him to my chest swiftly, and he flails about, trying to break the hold. I get Coony in a high body-slam position and hold him there momentarily. He is thrashing and kicking away for dear life, but the fun is only beginning. I slam him onto the flat surface of my kitchen table, crushing the beer cans on it and sending eating utensils flying. I don't stop there, though.

I keep my grip on Coony, pick him back up, and repeat the treatment. More debris falls off the table, and a chair goes flying that Coony has managed to latch on to. Then I pick Coony up again and do a jumping, full-weight body slam onto the kitchen table. The table collapses, and I find myself on top of Coony. He's barely moving. I start laughing like a madman and look down at Coony. He is almost buried underneath my bulk.

"Jesus fuckin' Christ," he blurts out. "I always wanted to know how a friggin' pancake felt."

I get up and give Coony a hand getting to his feet. He is wobbly and shaken but not hurt too badly. My kitchen looks like a disaster area, and judging from the angry yells from the apartment below, I'm sure the show must have been loud.

"It's a good thing I'm shit-faced. . . . 'cause this musht hurt," Coony says while balancing himself on unsteady legs.

"You all right?" I ask.

"Did I leave any beers in the fridge?"

"A couple."

"Then I'll be all right," he says while staggering to my couch.

I continue to muse and, finally, fall asleep on the couch. Hours pass, and I hear someone gently knocking on my door. I groggily ask my visitor to come in and am relieved to see it is Coony. He looks awful. His face is ashen, and his breathing is rapid and labored. He's shaking, trembling, like some kid who just woke up from a bad dream. Oh, shit—this ain't good.

"C-c-can I, c-c-can I crash here?" he asks. He rocks back and forth on unsteady legs.

"You OK?"

"I-I don't know. I'm all fucked up, Dino. I-I don't know what's fuckin' up."

I gesture toward my coach. He's walking stiffly and balancing himself by leaning on furniture. His equilibrium is gone. Oh no, I bet he's overdosed. Shit, he almost fell off the damn couch. He's sweating his ass off! Christ, this will be the third OD I've seen in this place. Come on, look at me, you little bastard. Yeah, his pupils look like pinpricks, all right. It also looks like he'll chuck, and his eyelids are quivering.

"You guys do any more of that shit?" I ask.

He nods.

"You goin' to make it, buddy?"

He shrugs his shoulders.

"For Christ's sake, Coony, you're sweating like a pig."

"J-j-just need some downers. G-g-got any b-b-beers left?"

"Only one," I say. I reach into the fridge and pull out the last tallboy.

Shit, he can't even coordinate his movements enough to pull the flip-top can open. He's looking at me with a vacant expression. Yeah, you want me to open the damn can. Sure, I will. There you go. Are you happy now? Why don't I just hand you a loaded pistol instead? God, Coony, I wish I knew the right words to say to you. Don't die on me, you little bastard.

"Is it OD time, Coony?"

"N-n-not if I can just down out a bit," he says before taking a big swig of beer.

"Why do you do this?"

Go ahead, close your eyes, and shake your head. You always shut me out when I try to discuss your urge to die. And you're trembling and shaking. Whew, that breath of yours could melt a diamond. Smells like alcohol mixed with a slow death. Look at you, staring off into space. I don't know what you see, but I imagine it's a dreadful future. There will be more nights like this, I bet. But one day, you're not going to come back. No, not tonight, though. I won't let that happen.

"Talk to me, you mother fucker! Are you going to make it?" I yell, my voice shaking the room.

He says nothing, and his eyes slowly close again.

"Coony, I should never have given you that shit back. I should have just dumped it. Why does it have to be like this?"

He's just sitting there, lost in some world I can't penetrate. I'll just watch him for a few minutes. I wonder if I should call an ambulance. Jesus, he'd get busted, and so would I. Well, maybe not. Christ, he's holding that can in a death grip. Why does it have to be like this? I just don't get it.

You're not a man without talents, Coony. You can cook far better than the average ham-and-egger, and your chili is the best I've ever tasted. I'm sure you could make a living as a cook or a chef. You can also draw. I recall your drawing of a pouncing bald eagle with outstretched talons and wings. That thing was so detailed and lifelike that commercial art is not outside your abilities. Yet even when you're coherent, you don't listen to me when I say these things. And now you're out of it.

I know you like the freedom of being a lobster-man and a logger. All your bosses ever ask is that you show up for work. They don't care if you're an alcoholic or druggie. As long as you do your job, everyone is happy. And you're a damn good worker. You put in 12-hour days loading logs onto skidders or disappear for weeks at a time doing deep-sea trawls off George's Bank. So long as you have beers, you can do just about any manual chore . . . but you could do so much more.

The only hard work I ever do is in a weight room, and I doubt I'd have the endurance to do what you do. I'm unsure what I will do for a career, and I'm not optimistic that UNH is helping me much. My home life was no bed of roses, but I love myself more than you do, pal. My dad is an alcoholic, and it's clear I have inherited his disease. I also have a lousy self-image due to my size. Perhaps that's why we get along so well. Shared misery can make strong friendships. But . . . Hey, your breathing is becoming awfully unsteady. Oh, shit.

"Coony, are you OK?!" I yell.

He's totally out of it. Let go of that beer, you bastard. I got to get a pulse. Yeah, it's rapid but steady. I got to get him moving.

"You little bastard! You better not die on me!"

Shit, I better shake him harder.

"Fuckin' talk to me, Coony!"

Yeah, that's good. Coony's eyes barely open, and he's taking a little breath now.

"Are you going to make it?"

He's mouthing some words, but no sounds are coming out. I'll shake him again. Shit, he could be in trouble. There we go. He's looking at me. Christ, you're a mess.

"Come on, Coony, are you going to live?"

"It don't matter," he whispers. "It just don't fuckin' matter."

I wonder what you are seeing and feeling, my friend.

"Nothin' matters, Dino," he softly says. "You know that."

Postscript

Coony survived the night, and so too did Mike. Eventually, Coony got into a legal jamb and escaped to Oregon. He tried to stay under the radar because of pending charges in New Hampshire and reportedly lived a quiet life as a property caretaker for some years, just he and his dog. However, his intravenous drug-use days came back to haunt him, and he developed Hepatitis C. Word has it that Coony discovered Jesus about this time, although I have no idea if that is true. In any case, Coony got leukemia, but he refused treatments. Some locals visited him, bringing him cards and good wishes. We had long lost touch by the 1980s, and I was unaware he died in 2003. Nor did I get the other half of our five-dollar bill to tell me that was the case, although I retain my half. I moved on to become a weightlifting coach in the late 1970s, and then I became an academic in the 1990s at Penn State. In fact, coaching saved me from oblivion and/or incarceration. I'd wish Coony had found solace in drinking beers instead of booting up mystery crap. He had a lot of life lessons and talent locked up within, and I still miss the miscreant. Deep down, he was "good people," far better than most fools who would judge him. This is a snapshot of what it's like to live on the edge, and it isn't a place that most people should even visit. Fair winds and following seas, Coony. Amen.

PART X

THE HUMAN CONDITION

92

Bang, Bang, Shoot Them Up!

The nation's founders were far from perfect, as is typical of everyone, given the human condition. Indeed, our Constitution is proof of the founders' fallibility and strengths, although they clearly recognized that theirs was a work in progress. Thus, unlike the final word we read in the Bible, the Constitution was designed to be a "living" document in that the rights and laws it presents can be changed and amended. However, the cost of changing those laws is often measured in blood and misery, as with slavery. Simply put, the founders didn't address the rotting elephant in the room because of political expediency. Thus, a great Civil War eventually devoured 618,222 to 750,000 lives and maimed perhaps twice that number. There were many other omissions, poorly stipulated rights, and outright mistakes in the Constitution, not the least of which is the Second Amendment.

Currently, firearms are the number one cause of death in children under 18, having passed motor vehicle deaths in 2020. As CNN reported:

> Firearms accounted for nearly 19 percent of childhood deaths (ages 1–18) in 2021, according to the Centers for Disease Control and Prevention Wonder database. Nearly 3,600 children died in gun-related incidents that year. That's about five children lost for every 100,000 in the United States. In no other comparable country are firearms within the top four causes of mortality among children, according to a KFF [Kaiser Family Foundation] analysis.

Mahatma Gandhi once said, "The true measure of any society can be found in how it treats its most vulnerable members." By that standard, the United States has become an abject failure because it cannot protect its kids.

Clearly, there was once a need for an armed militia in the United States, given the numerous threats early American settlers faced and the lack of a significant standing army. That was then, some 245 years ago. Moreover, the idea that guns can protect freedoms from our own government is absurd, as the military has repeatedly proven. Yes, George Washington quickly demonstrated this case during the Whiskey Rebellion, as have many other presidents when there was a perceived need to clear protestors or impose laws. The military has tanks, missiles, warships, and all manner of weapons that can easily defeat rifles and pistols, automatics or not. Currently, most threats come from within our nation, as in the mob of degenerates who violated our nation's Capitol on January 6, 2021. Over 900 of these miscreants face justice, albeit some politicos want us to forget the debacle altogether. Many of these willfully myopic and forgetful representatives and senators are the same people who wish to ignore the numerous deaths and injuries that gun violence brings us daily.

By all measures, the United States is the number one nation in gun ownership, with 120 firearms owned for every 100 people, over twice the rate of any other country. The United States has 327 million citizens holding 393 million guns, albeit only 44 percent of people own firearms. In fact, there is an average of eight guns per gun owner in the United States. We also dominate the statistics in terms of yearly gun violence, leading the world in firearm-related homicides (19,000), suicides (24,000), and legal killings by police and federal authorities (350). In 2020, nearly 40,000 Americans died via guns, while 43,000 died from breast cancer. In terms of mass killings and injuries from firearms, the number of victims per incident has increased from 7 in 2009 to 13 in 2019. So, while people may crow about their rights to own guns, none of us are free from gun violence . . . whether or not we are armed. What a deal.

The grim firearm statistics mean nothing to most gun owners. They clutch onto guns like an infant suckles a mother's breast. Many of the pro and con gun arguments are tedious, and I'll not rehash them here. It is not a simple matter of giving up freedom for security, for MANY nations with stringent gun laws have more personal rights than we in the United States. Other countries with relatively homogenous societies have more liberal gun laws than we do, albeit with much better background controls than the United States. The United States is racially, ethnically, politically, and economically diverse, and its populace is often reactionary. Thus, the more guns there are, the greater the odds of their being used for mendacious purposes. The numbers bear out this obvious fact. Ergo, the current outcome is that guns have made us less secure in many ways.

Odds are odds, and in a mixed population such as the United States, one wherein inherent conflicts are built into our ethnic and racial backgrounds, well . . . bang, bang, shoot 'em up, one, two, three. Add in the fact that nearly all crazies in the United States can quickly get guns, and the problem gets magnified. For example, a person like me is far too volatile to own guns, and Lord knows how many people I might have shot down if I possessed one. Indeed, I once publicly welcomed seeing Trump shot in the face . . . preferably with a shotgun. Yet I'm hardly alone in being half-crazed, although I also recognize the danger of my nature by not owning a firearm. Some of you reading these words are like me, so don't pretend to be holier than thou! We all have demons within, and guns can give them a lethal presence.

Today, what would have ended up as a fistfight 40–50 years ago can quickly become multiple murders. The number of deadly firearms available to ALL Americans is a fundamental problem in the United States, and I have yet to hear anything approaching a solution. We are not the USA of the founding fathers, an elite all-white-boys club that included some amazingly short-sighted sots. We are the USA of today, one wherein desire, violence, and greed rule the day. We are like children playing with razor blades. Is it any wonder our streets, churches, and even schools sometimes run red? Oh, but what the hell do I know? After all, I'm half-crazed.

I shudder at the thought of any of my nephews and nieces being shot down while attending church, school, or simply walking home from a friend's house. Yet these tragedies happen nearly every day now. Meanwhile, the gun sucklers insist on doing nothing. After all, they are too worried about the government infringing on their personal rights to care about children's rights to be free from gun violence. Why not have means tests for gun ownership, much like the checks done before issuing badges to the police or licenses to bus drivers? Let there be a strict background check, psych profile, and other attestations of basic competency and psychological well-being. Furthermore, why not make firearms safety classes a requirement for gun ownership? As it stands, even a demented psycho like me can own a gun, and that is a problem that needs to be corrected ASAP. Amen.

93

The Battle of the Bulges

I like my bathroom scale because it goes up to 325 pounds. It also gives a reading that is 15 to 18 pounds lighter than it should be for those rare fatties who push its upper limits, like me, so I'm especially fond of that sucker. The scale even has a magnified readout dial that protrudes far enough out from the front so that even folks with profoundly bulging bellies can read the thing. I stepped on it a few days ago, something I hadn't done since the winter feasting and party times ended. The numbers on the dial whizzed by at an astonishing rate, and I was reminded of the special effects used to represent the star ship *Enterprise* going into warp drive. "She just can't take anymore, Captain!" I heard a hysterical Scotty scream.

There was a blur and a loud "ka-chunk" sound as the scale's innards banged up against their design limits. The dial bounced crazily around before settling at 302 pounds. Hmmm, it is possible, but it seemed best to use the usually accurate balance-beam scale in the University of New Hampshire's field house just to make sure. After all, my poor old weight meter could have an over-stressed spring or two, especially after all the years it has been in my service. So, I waddled on up to Lundholm Fieldhouse, which I had done for 11 years when I worked as UNH's weight-lifting coach, and I asked the weight room's current proprietor if I could use the scale.

"Sure you can," Fred said. "You been lifting?"

"Nah, I'm just a bit heavy."

"You look it."

"Thanks, Fred."

I began by setting the scale's counterweight on the 300-pound mark and then gently stepped onto the scale itself. The balance beam's indication arrow instantly pegged itself to the high side of the readout limiter with a loud 'ka-thunk' sound.

"Wow," Fred said with a wry smile.

"Wow, indeed," I replied.

I budged the pound marker over as a small gathering of athletes watched . . . 305, no, 310? No again! That frigging beam must be magnetized or something. How about 315? What? No again! One kid chuckled. I was not amused.

"Hey, buddy, I might be able to lose weight, but there ain't a damned thing you can do about that face."

I moved the pound marker toward the 320 mark. At last, the indicator showed a tiny sign of not being magnetized after all. It actually budged a bit. Finally, at 323 pounds, the marker achieved balance. I looked around. The athletes were gawking at me.

"What's the matter with you guys? Haven't you ever seen a 5-foot-8-inch guy who weighs a svelte 323 pounds before?"

"Svelte?" a 288-pound offensive lineman asked.

A few days later, I had a skin-caliper test done in UNH's Exercise Physiology lab to determine my body fat percentage. After all, my 323 pounds could be a mass of highly relaxed muscle; if so, my weight need not be a matter of concern. However, even the guy taking the skin-fold measurements was surprised. "Your body fat is 36 percent," he piped, "Thirty-six percent!" He paused and added, "That's three times more than most guys and twice as much as most women. You going on a diet?" So much for my relaxed muscle theory, plus the guy mentioned that God-awful D word. My percentage of body fat is coming precariously close to my age, which is 39 . . . as it always has been. I have 116.5 pounds of fat dangling from my body, enough to make another person. However, an even scarier realization has recently donned on me; I'm only 68 inches tall and almost 58 inches around! I am achieving unity in my measurements and could evolve into a sphere one day. Ah, but I will not be a celestial body, at least in terms of looks.

Alas, it's this endless quest of mine that keeps me fat. You see, I believe the perfect pizza awaits me somewhere in our world. I can see it now even as I write this line. It is a vast steaming rectangle of gastronomic delight. I can smell the pungent aroma of parmesan and Romano cheese mixed with the oh-so-delicate scent of Canadian bacon and pepperoni. The pizza's sauce-covered surface is still bubbling; the bacon and pepperoni sizzle. And the crust, oh, it is undoubtedly the mother of all crusts. It is a full three-quarter of an inch in thickness and has been baked to a golden brown. What are Brooke Shields or Marilyn Monroe when compared with such a sight?

Until I find this paragon of all pizzas, this Golden Fleece of my imagination, I must forever search. I must devour all pizzas on the theory that one of them may be the right one, the singular pizza that can at long last satiate my inveterate appetite in a single meal. Then a horrible thought suddenly grabs me. What if someone has already eaten my perfect pizza? What if some vile interloper has purloined that which drives me on? And what if he's a skinny guy, a guy whose minuscule physique would make a mockery of my quest? I shiver at the thought. However, we cannot live a life full of such fear and doubt. So, I go on, eating pizza after pizza in my endless search. And I know that one day, maybe my last day on earth, I will find my gastronomic 10.

Yes, my quest has had its cost. Little kids gawk at me in wonderment. They point, wide-eyed and open-mouthed, as if I were an earth-bound float in the Macy's Thanksgiving Day parade. "Wow, Mommy, did you see that guy? He was reeeally fat!" And the fat jokes; I'm sick to death of those things. No, they don't have to kill a whole herd of cows just to make my belt, and there isn't quite enough material in my pants to cover an entire living room set. And no, I usually don't get confused with a dry-docked tug boat when I wear red pants and a gray shirt. Jokes and stares are the lot of all true fatties, but I guess I am a spectacle. Just consider my measurements:

CHEST: 52.5 inches
GUT: 54.0 inches
HIPS: 57.5 inches
UPPER LEG: 30.0 inches
NECK: 19.25 inches
LOWER LEG: 18.5 inches
HEIGHT: 68.75 inches
UPPER ARM: 17.0 inches
WEIGHT: 323 pounds

Now, I'm not just your average drinks-too-much-beer-and-does-too-little fatty. I used to be a weightlifter, something I have done since I was 16. Moreover, I could easily bench press a barbell loaded to my body weight for 15 or so repetitions, not that I have too far to push a barbell at my size. Before I wrecked the discs in my lower back, I could full squat 560 pounds for repetitions, military press 385 pounds for a double, and push-jerk 440 pounds overhead. Yep, I was a pretty strong fatty, but ants can easily outsprint me: a flight of stairs makes me pant more than a nude picture of Christie Brinkley, and it takes a cosmic calendar along the lines of Stonehenge to clock my time in the

100-yard waddle. Yeah, fatties don't do things very quickly . . . except for eating.

My obesity is inherited. My Italian mom, Rosina Leonedria Albanese, was over 235 pounds in her prime. Heck, at one time, there wasn't a male relative on her side of the family who was under 280 pounds. My Aunt Cilia tipped the scales at over 350 pounds, and her daughter Cookie, very appropriately named, touched the golden 400 mark. My 400-pound-plus big brother looked like an even bigger version of myself before an illness dragged his weight down to a mere 235 pounds. However, my English dad is only about 165 pounds, which indicates his ethnic heritage and the fact that he wasn't quite quick enough to get in his fair share at the dinner table.

Ah, and make no mistake about it, every meal was a momentous occasion in my family's life. You see, my mother was a fabulous cook. Now I know that all mothers are viewed as great cooks by their kids, but even other kids thought my mom was a chef-and-a-half. On a pasta day, she'd get up early and strain freshly picked tomatoes by hand into a large kettle before adding garden-grown oregano and a touch of mint to the simmering mixture. A few cans of tomato paste would thicken the sauce, and a tiny bit of sugar cut the acidity. Then work would start on the meat. Oh, just the thought of those meatballs has me salivating. They were made of lean hamburger, parmesan and Romano cheese, bread, eggs, and spices that my mother carefully blended and then rolled into inch-and-a-half globes. They were fried dark brown before being added to the sauce. A lean cut of braised pork and several large chunks of pepperoni were added to the brew to enhance its flavor.

The aroma was captivating as the sauce simmered and thickened over the next 8 to 10 hours. Kids we seldom hung out with would come over to visit. People we hardly knew would hover around on the sidewalk beside our house in a trance-like state, vainly hoping to get an invitation to supper. Happily, all intruders were kept at bay by Gretchen, our get-them-by-the-throat German shepherd, a dog who would protect her right to any leftovers with deadly force. Then came dinner time! Everyone had their own seat, but it was a melee after that. No time for two-bit dinner talk here. There was serious eating to be done. I'd wolf down a dozen meatballs and four vast servings of pasta at a feed. My stomach ached from eating, but with time it expanded enough to hold enormous quantities of food. In 1973, I ate 56 pieces of pizza in 64 minutes during a Pizza Hut all-you-can-eat special in Dover, New Hampshire. What a deal for 99 cents!

My collegiate Pizza Hut pig-outs bring back memories of my mother's family reunions at Bear Brook State Park. They were like big gatherings of Richard Simmons' diet plan failures, bulging old Italians stuffing sauce-covered meats, buttered garlic bread, and vats of wine into their vast stomachs. The only exercise was playing bocce ball and running away from Uncle Ralph, a strange man who had the nasty habit of tugging on the front of your pants and shaking off the hot ashes at the end of his cigar into your drawers. As the day wore on, talk would shift to the food that had been prepared. Woe be unto the fiancé or other would-be family members that made a thin sauce, used the wrong kind of cheese, or didn't cook the meatballs for the proper length of time. Such affronts were not publicly mentioned, but the perpetrators received that God-awful look, that evil eye, that go-somewhere-else glance from the assembled critics. Such is the price of membership in a family that worships food.

Yeah, I'm fat for many reasons, but being that way has its costs. For instance, not many women are attracted to men who have bulges in all the wrong places, and I have plenty. Even so, we fatties still have the urge to merge, and not all of us like to consign ourselves to dating people with similar waist sizes. After all, it takes more than insatiable appetites to hold two people together. Besides, there are physical problems that two romantically inclined fatties have to consider when it comes to procreation. The fact that two balloons can touch at one point proves that sex between fatties is possible, but it is more of a chore than an act of pleasure.

A desire to broaden the availability of female companionship is one of the things that motivated me to endure almost a year of dieting when I was 29. It was a terrible experience. Every day I would eat a can of Campbell's Chunky soup, a can of tuna fish, one orange, one apple, and a huge salad. It totaled about 1,100 calories. My weight dropped from 322 pounds to 175 pounds at one point, but it finally stabilized at about 205 pounds. My appearance improved enough to become involved in some tempestuous relationships, but all the while, there was a gnawing urge to resume my pizza quest. Yeah, being thinner has its physical rewards, but the work it takes to get and stay that way is something that most folks can never understand. In fact, 95 percent of all morbidly obese people regain all the weight they lose while dieting.

You see, dieting is barely controlled starvation, and the miserable experience affects every aspect of your life. I even have a recurring dream that kicks in whenever I diet for a few months. I'll be eating a pizza, and although it tastes great, it is not perfect. Suddenly, I'll feel this presence watching me, so I'll look around to see who has discovered me pigging out. However, no one is there. So, I'll start eating again . . . and then the presence returns. This pattern continues until I wake up, eating being associated with guilt.

Moreover, my waking hours aren't much better when I'm dieting. A desire for a wider variety of female company has often motivated diets. Still, when you're in the midst of starvation, a slowly simmering turnip is far more attractive than a gyrating Madonna. This may be why the relationships I've established while dieting have been so unsuccessful. It's hard to say, "I love you," to someone when all you really want is a hot pizza and a full stomach.

After the misery of dieting is over, one gets the dubious reward of trying to maintain a lower body weight. Unfortunately, my body isn't happy being lighter and seeks every opportunity to expand. After my diet, I gain weight if I eat over 2,600 calories, which isn't all that much food, not even one large pizza. No person can live forever without overeating on occasion, and I'm no exception. However, whenever I pigged out during or after a diet, I'd feel unremitting guilt, much as I did in my dreams. So, I'd have to atone for my sins. I'd take some Ex-Lax or a diuretic or spend hours steaming in a sauna. Happily, I'm over that sickness now, but I never found a mate who loves short, fat guys. Yet hope springs eternal. After all, a woman is likelier to love a fat man who can smile than a half-starved dude with a year's supply of Ex-lax and the will to use it.

Bouts of binging and purging aren't the only hazards of being obese. My blood pressure has been as high as 164/106, and in 1985 I had a cerebral vascular event while moving some light weights around at work. There was a convulsion, slurred speech, numbness on the left side of my body and the right side of my face, a general lack of coordination, and one terrified fat man. Some doctors said I had bisected a vertebral artery in my neck; some said I was crazy, and others didn't know which end was up. All I know for sure is that the event sparked a migraine headache syndrome that becomes especially bad when I try to lift heavy weights. This condition cost my career as UNH's weightlifting instructor, ultimately leading me into academia.

The doctors have told me *ad nauseam* that I've got to lose weight, but I keep telling them I've already lost thousands of pounds. And it's true. I've lost 50 or more pounds on over 10 occasions and once lost 142 pounds in about a year! I've been as heavy as 359 pounds and as light as 175 pounds within the last 20 years. Yep, it's been a singularly unpleasant yo-yo existence of starvation and gluttony. Yeah, I know that bouncing your weight up and down like a super-ball is dangerous, and I know my heart may explode one day, and I know I'll never be the cover guy on *Playgirl Magazine*, and I know I can't fit in a Ford Fiesta, and I know I won't be a jockey in the Kentucky Derby. I know all about the bad things that result from being fat. However, I've tried dieting, and it hasn't worked. I have returned to the folds, like 95-plus percent of all fatties.

I realize that my attitude about pizza is probably the main reason I'm still a porker, but being fat isn't all bad, especially now. On a hot summer day, the sun beats down unmercifully on all the parts of my skinny friends, but not me. My entire lower body, including all the essential bits, is forever shaded from the sun's dangerous ultraviolet rays by a fleshy front porch. And with ozone depletion becoming a severe problem, it may one day come to pass that sunlight sterilizes folks. Thus, while most guys are having their gonads fried to a shrivel by ultraviolet radiation, mine will still be in the shade, forever undamaged by our environmental perfidy . . . "And so it was written that only the fat shall inherit the earth."

There are several other significant advantages to being fat that doesn't require ozone depletion. We fatties can handle cold weather far better than most normal-sized folks. We also stay put better in hurricanes and tornadoes; we have excellent traction on slippery roads; we get much better buys on the various all-you-can-eat specials; we float a lot better; we make exceptional grape stompers in the wine industry; we're great anchor people in tugs-of-war, and, of course, we have perfect aerodynamic forms.

So, being fat isn't all a big minus. However, those damn norms, those lucky geeks who have never had to fight the Battle of the Bulges, continue to treat us fatties like dirt. They sneer at us, call us names, and often recoil at our appearances. Man, it does hurt. It's like an Afro-American being called the "N" word, only we fatties don't have powerful lobbyists who can get anti-fatty discrimination legislation passed by Congress. Oh, a few groups of disgruntled heavyweights have banded together to demand better treatment. They strut their huge stuff in fashion displays, insist they have souls under their ample mounds of flesh on talk shows, and occasionally whine before a group of sympathetic Congress people.

However, all the carping we fatties do produces little good because behind the seemingly compassionate gaze of those we complain to are tiny minds thinking, "My God, I've never seen someone that fat up this close. I wonder how he can fit on a toilet seat?" I can't write about the perceptual filters that norms use because I've never been one, but perhaps they should try to employ their imaginations a bit more than they have to date. Consider a morbidly obese lady wearing a long, flowing white dress while walking across a street. Some people will see Moby Dick, others will see Mount Everest, and a few will see a moving van. However, those intelligent and imaginative individuals will see a wonderfully majestic floating cloud or the billowing sails of a fleet clipper ship as she plies the waters of the North Atlantic.

Yeah, I guess it all comes down to a matter of perception. Some folks believe Oprah Winfrey is a fatty, but that's mainly because the woman is surrounded by emaciated Hollywood types. You know, the beautiful people, those whose souls are as deep as a mud puddle and just as cloudy, the same ones who worship the twin gods of Silicone and Face Lift. However, if Oprah were to come to one of my family reunions, she would be the runt of the litter. Yet I must confess she has felt the sting of ostracism that many of us true fatties know. Tabloids ridicule her, comedians poke fun, and she bears it all with a smile.

We fatties have learned to smile and laugh even when we're crying inside, and maybe that's why we keep getting grief. Perhaps we should band together and hang out in Fat Packs. There could be a minimum weight requirement of 300 pounds, and who will give a bunch of angry porkers any grief? We could rule the pizzerias, the streets, the cities, and eventually the world! Then would come our swift retribution, for we would force-feed the beautiful people until they were like unto us. If you norms want to prevent this just fate, I would advise you to lighten up a bit and let us fatties be! After all, giving fatties gruff doesn't make the norms that dish it out any wiser or us fatties any thinner.

I can feel another pizza attack coming on, and it's a big one. All this writing about food has got me ready to go into a feeding frenzy that would put a Great White shark to shame. Maybe today will be the day that I finally find my perfect pizza. And if any beautiful person gives me a dirty look or says something mean while I'm picking up my two large extra-sauce, extra pepperoni, extra Canadian bacon pizzas, he or she had better look out. Hungry people can do strange things, and I am forever hungry. However, if a norm treats me right, and moves cautiously when coming close to my pizzas, then I just may let him or her sit down at the table for a bit and have a couple of pieces . . . if that person is quick enough. Amen.

94

Twilight Echoes

I enjoy talking with Ellen, a fellow resident/inmate of Quail Hollow's River House building. The elderly residential facility was built in West Lebanon, New Hampshire, and is located amid nature incarnate, with all manner of wildlife paying us regular visits. At 83, Ellen is much younger in thought and form than her chronological age indicates. A roughly 2-foot tall, wooden gray wolf statue guards her door. He is sitting on his haunches and howling, with a silk scarf adorning his head. "Though she be but little, she is fierce," says a framed sign that adorns her door. Here is a woman who has lived fully, having been everything from an art curator to a motorcycle mama, with the role of a doting parent being the task she loved best. She can be overbearing occasionally, acting as an overprotective mother figure,

94.1 Here is Ellen in her 40s during a NASCAR race

which she very much is. That is her way, whether one accepts it or not. Ellen's face is a bit weathered by time's winds, with character lines etched here and there. Ah, but those pretty blue eyes are still bright and lively, with happy expressions sweeping over her face, graced by a warm, pleasant smile.

We laugh, tell each other stories, and occasionally indulge in old bad habits . . . the sins of youth brought forward. At 70, I am a relative kid in our senior housing facility, with the vagaries of fate having brought us into this rural community. The River Building houses roughly 140 mostly older folks within single- and double-bedroom apartments. The long hallways of the interior are relatively generic and institutional, though the well-manicured grounds and surrounding forest are beautiful. Our neighbors include wild turkeys, fleet deer, bushy-tailed foxes, and even a she-bear with cubs. It is a fine place to spin out our remaining years, with frequent gatherings and activities allowing great camaraderie and amusement before the final curtain falls. Indeed, we often lose people we care about deeply here, which is only natural given our age and health issues.

Ellen and I can be at complete ease with one another, even though we often forget what we're talking about, sometimes in mid-sentence! And may God help us if we have to come up with a name because that game can go on *ad nauseam*. "Oh, what was his name? You know who I mean: the guy who lives down the hall." It must greatly amuse mutual friends who overhear parts of our somewhat confused and disjointed conversations. We laugh about the growing memory issues, musing about how God sometimes reminds us there are medical concerns afoot. Regrettably, the problems are all too real, but they wax and wane in our cases.

Ellen has a brain tumor, a slowly growing meningioma pressing on her frontal lobes. That kind of tumor is seldom malignant, but its pressure causes poor balance, falls, and memory and cognitive problems. It can also make one not care much about clothing and other incidentals, which can be liberating. According to magnetic resonance imaging (MRI) studies, parts of my brain have atrophied, and some doctors believe I have frontotemporal dementia (FTD) or a similar malady. I doubt they are correct, other than to note that I seldom remember conversations or names anymore. Writing stories like this is still possible, but recalling whom I spoke to about what topics a day or two ago often eludes me. The more pressing problem is emotional volatility, which comes to the forefront when I'm challenged or castigated. Alas, that is Ellen's way, so we drift in and out of overt amity at times, albeit an enduring and underlying friendship seems to eventually conquer all.

There are medical procedures that may be able to help Ellen, but at her age she is not an ideal candidate for brain surgery. The brain atrophy I supposedly have has no cure and very few treatments. The annoying memory issues can be endured, although the behavioral elements are scary, as in explosive flashes of intense emotion that are hard to control sans drugs. However, there is usually none of that when I am with Ellen unless she decides to play the part of Mom. That brooding instinct aside, I typically feel at complete peace with her, as I believe she does with me. Our maladies influence similar brain areas, and we understand our current limitations and deficits, at least for now. Indeed, we help one another navigate life, being very supportive whenever possible.

It is an odd Mutt-and-Jeff platonic friendship. Ellen is a tiny urbane Jew, elegant in her upbringing and education. Her mother was a poet and her father an artist, with Ellen having known great wealth and much love. She speaks of her two sons and three grandchildren as her most precious possessions. The rest is all gone, the fine homes, private plane, and ample money. Her last husband developed Alzheimer's disease, and he obliterated the family's legacy, leaving Ellen to drift on the uncertain tides of relative poverty. She ponders the possibility of visiting him one

94.2 Ellen is looking fine at a young 50

last time, yet there are great resentments and many fears about his declining condition baring the way.

I was born poor and remain so. My persona is paired with the body of a hulking guy who eats too damn much. Oh, I've managed to get a good education, including a PhD. I've run a business, been a weightlifting coach, experienced marriage, and written several books, although I've not done the things I was capable of or had a fully productive life. At present, I'm more or less crippled but modestly content. I don't fret about forgetting, falling, and pain. That has become the norm, much like it is for others who live here.

The residents at Quail Hollow often help one another, fully understanding that some neighbors and friends are close to the end of their rodeos. The ambulance often comes by to cart

94.3 At 63 Ellen still enjoyed the good life, as she does to this day

away someone who has fallen or gotten ill. After the meat wagon leaves, we hover around like scared deer, with many wondering who is heading out this time. It is thus not a big deal if we cannot recall a friend's name or get a bit disoriented about what we are doing and why we are doing it. This happens frequently and causes us more amusement than misery. Hell, I've even forgotten the central idea of this chapter!

Hmmm, I think it has something to do with the human spirit. I believe the essential notion is that many of us opt to smile and laugh while life unfolds, finding pleasure in one another's company while we still can. Sure, life and happenstance have swept many of us far from our intended course, but here we are, still enjoying our Friday night parties or simply shooting the breeze. We do not fear the inevitable because dread and regret are a complete waste of time and energy, which are finite resources for many elderly folks. Yes, we certainly empathize with one another. We are sorrowful when a friend breaks a hip or leaves for a nursing home. We walk by the newly empty apartments while work crews prepare them for new residents, lamenting the departure of those we cared about.

Some acquaintances suddenly and unexpectedly enter that final sleep that knows no waking, and we miss them dearly. The entire house is disturbed for a few days as if a great rock tumbled into our serenity pond. However, most of us do not lament for too long. There is little time for that. Indeed, most of us would much rather commune, despite injuries, worn-out joints, and the bitter loss of family and friends. You see, we are still very much alive. The glass remains half full, though some neutral observers may find it mostly empty, and by a lot! Ah, it is all a matter of perspective, and we can surely opt to enjoy the precious moments that remain.

Lack of money limits some of our options. Yet Ellen and I can still share beautiful memories, despite our increasingly fractured and moody natures. We laugh about old loves and misbegotten adventures and sometimes regret lost friends, pets, and innumerable poor choices. We muse about what life has wrought and even find humor in our frailties. "Are you sure about that?" is not a question we frequently ask, nor need we do so. Hell, we are hardly ever sure about anything. It is not a perfect friendship because our maladies can become ascendant, and one of us, usually

94.4 We see Ellen as of March, 2023. At 84, her eyes still glitter

me, withdraws to recuperate. Indeed, some ailments demand solitude, as anyone with chronic illnesses comes to understand.

However, we have many shared moments, and that precious time is worth more than all the treasure and fulfillment we could have accrued in several lifetimes. Those moments allow us to ride on imagination's wings, share old memories, and find joy in one another's company. There will come a time when we are but dim and fading memories buried deep within the minds of those we once loved. However, those echoes that defined our lives will reverberate anew in a child's laugh, lovers' kiss, or the simple acknowledgment that life is best when lived fully. As for now, we are very much alive and enjoying every second that God grants us. Amen.

95

Living in the Moment

We often gather, setting up tables and chairs in a large second-floor common area that can accommodate up to 40 people. This is not an easy task for seniors because the average age in Quail Hollow's River House is about 75, and most of us geriatrics are well past our best bulling and hauling days. Yet we somehow manage, with ample excellent and experienced cooks to prepare a multi-course feast that pleases the palates of all concerned. Soft music plays in the background, the wine and booze flow at a healthy rate, and the conversations range far and wide. And for a while, many cares and concerns about health, finances, and other issues drift away, being relegated to lesser priorities as we collectively opt to live in the moment. And make no mistake, some serious concerns are hovering in the background.

95.1 Preparing for a dinner with librations. Here are Derek and Candice

For example, my friend Richard has to go in for yet another tongue biopsy this week because a possibly cancerous lesion was found. The lesion is painful, as will be the biopsy. This has happened before, and a good part of Richard's tongue was removed, with him having to endure a long recovery. However, Richard is a brave and determined fellow who has survived the tests of time and circumstances. He is a former marine and is still no slouch as he passes well by his eightieth year. Richard does not walk so much as he marches, one foot quickly following the other while he strides down the long hallways that serve our apartment complex. His travails began six or seven years ago with prostate cancer, which metastasized and spread to his bladder. They suspect the lesions may proliferate someday, but he is winning the fight

95.2 The room slowly fills asRiver House occupants settle in for a meal

for now. In addition, fluid began gathering around Richard's heart, with painful bouts of draining needed to ensure better breathing. Nonetheless, he tends his garden, paints Americana pictures, plays golf, and brings back vegetables that he shares with one and all. He and his wife live large and enjoy life, often joining us at our potlucks.

My former neighbor Mary is a strong-willed and independent woman living with Stage 4 lung cancer, the small-cell type that cannot be operated on. She has been fighting the disease for five years and is undergoing long-term chemotherapy with a new experimental drug. The medication has its downside (e.g., eye and other lesions) but seems to be holding the beast in check. She frequently goes out shopping with her daughter and often displays a cheerful attitude that can be infectious. Indeed, she recently established a relationship with Ray, which may lead to something special. Several other residents at the house and I indulged in an animated cocktail hour a few weeks ago that left me absolutely pie-eyed and staggered. In contrast, Mary, Ray, and most others practiced a more moderate approach to partying. "I told you not to drink so much," she recalled with a smile.

And then there is me, one of many residents battling conditions that generally do not have good outcomes. In my case, there is advanced heart disease and the beginning of dementia caused by atrophy of my frontal and temporal lobes. They don't know what to call it, but I'm coping with the condition the best I can. One has a conversation and promptly forgets most or all of it by the following day, as I'm constantly reminded. Names and events evaporate while moods vacillate wildly. Yeah, our "use-by" dates are approaching, but you won't find a lot of despair here. Some feel bad for themselves, although most of us do not dwell upon the things we cannot change.

Most of us have decided to embrace the moment and strive to find what is good about life while retaining the fleeting gift of time. We are older and have developed the capacity to empathize via the agency of many shared life experiences. Indeed, Ellen often laughs about her failing memories, with her frontal lobe meningioma occasionally derailing her train of thought, sometimes in mid-sentence. She gets flustered, and then her bright blue eyes light up. "Where was I going with that?" she asks with a laugh. "Well, it isn't like I'll remember what you were saying," I reply.

95.3 Jane, Pat, and Candice join the crew as the party proceeds

A smile crosses our faces, a mutual realization that we are doing our best to enjoy our lives despite travails and doubts.

There are a few self-appointed judges in our group, petty opinionates who feel an incessant and boorish need to make pronouncements about a person, place, or thing. They are as excitable schoolchildren and sometimes every bit as cruel. I detest their actions and often tell them so, even amid a party or other social affair. We have too little time to waste even a second on that nonsense. Indeed, most of our lives are complicated enough, and we need not find distraction in trivial bitching, whining, and carrying on like entitled queens and kings passing judgments. No, this is a time to spend our moments more wisely, and most of us opt to do so.

And that is the essence of this chapter. All lives are like sentences punctuated by periods. No one gets out of this ongoing story alive, but we write this tale as our will and happenstances allow. Moreover, our children and work can ripple into the future in countless ways. Lastly, we may even have souls that exist after we slip our failing bodies, although relatively few of us bank on that possibility. Most of us live in the present and strive to enjoy our precious moments with those who help give our lives meaning. For some, family and friends are what matters most. For others, it is a hobby or a good book. For folks like me, it is jotting down these lines that you are reading.

Believe me, there is little fear of the inevitable here. Dreading death and disability is a complete waste of our time, and time is the only currency we have to spend, be we rich, poor, or indifferent. In fact, some of those in the above pictures have passed on, and we grieve their loss. Yet we go on. Indeed, many go out for a daily commune at a long table that graces our lobby. This is our "table of life." We greet one another, share food, tell stories, discuss politics, and commiserate when that is needed. Sadly, we must eventually leave the table when our curtain call comes. We grieve for the departed, lamenting the meat wagon's arrival to cart away someone we know. However, others soon join our group, and life goes on.

As for me, I have opted to leave the table of life for the time being, although not life itself. Some complained about my behavior, which has become stridently direct. Indeed, if I perceive someone as a horse's ass, I will say so. It is not something I can control, and I will not take drugs to curtail what all medical evidence indicates will only progress. Instead, I will focus on writing chapters like this, using whatever skills I still have to contribute to the common welfare. My withdrawal from the table does not mean I care less for my fellow residents who are patiently cued in God's waiting room. After all, I have become a drag to some folks, and we cannot have that, not if we care about one another.

And to be sure, we sincerely care for one another. We truly do. If someone is confused or needs advice, we do our best to help. If someone needs to see a doctor or nurse, we aid that person. If someone needs to withdraw due to illness or other issues, that is perfectly acceptable. However, mostly, we simply care. The true beauty of the human condition is that people can form communities that improve our collective lives. This is where the "I" becomes the "we," and out of that admixture comes a grace that makes our remaining time all the more precious. And for that, we thank our Creator. Amen.

96

Ave Maria

Italy has 60,262,770 people, which is undoubtedly wrong by the time you read this line. Alas, at least 25,673,442 of these people contracted COVID during the recent outbreaks, although estimates indicate even more were infected, with the total being 35–40 million. 188,933 of these people died from or with COVID, albeit the Italians were too overwhelmed by the disease to count home and nursing facility deaths, which were many. The Italian government and the World Health Organization understand that the listed number of COVID deaths is a marked underestimate, with an additional 165,285 Italian victims being uncounted based on overall excess death figures during the worst pandemic. The number of Italian COVID deaths is thus closer to 325,000 to 355,000, although those with lasting damage and long COVID are in the millions. In World War II, Italy lost 301,400 soldiers and 155,600 civilians, and thus COVID is perhaps the second worst disaster the country has suffered in the last 100 years. And I care very much for the Italians because they are the blood of my blood.

As mentioned earlier, my mother took on the baptismal name of Rosina Leonedria Abanese. Her parents were children of Italy (Naples and Sicily) who came to America in 1912 to build a new life. It was not an easy task. Indeed, my maternal grandmother was taken by the Spanish flu in 1918, and now yet another plague reaches out to consume lives. Yet out of her parents' passion arose a beautiful, blue-eyed child who would occasionally sing, often in Italian. I well recall her heartfelt chords of Ave Maria. The tones touched me profoundly when I was a child, and at that point, I realized what it was to be Italian. Yes, my name is George Holton Elder, but I have the heart and soul of an Italian. Indeed, I am proud of that blood and spirit, for it built vast empires, crafted great works of art and created some of the finest music ever known.

And that heart of mine bleeds for what COVID has done to my kindred spirits in Italy. Italy has endured countless trials and tribulations for thousands of years, and yet another threat now looms large. I see the many patients attached to every manner of machine and monitor, struggling for breath against the clutches of a consuming sickness that devours lives by the thousands. The exhausted doctors and nurses strive to keep the faint embers of mortality glowing. Yet life after life slowly gives way while lungs fill with fluid, and we pray that a loving embrace awaits these souls after the torments of a cruel passing.

Many of us will enter that battle soon enough, but I tell you this: we will enter into that fight unafraid and filled with the passions that created us. We will not give in to doubts and anxiety over uncertainties that we haven't the power to control. Instead, we will stand tall and voice the contents of our hearts, as millions of Italians did during this crisis's worst days. They sang from the balconies and windows, filling the air with the rich sounds of classical and modern music. They sang loud and proud, showing us that the desire to live cannot be overcome by the fear of death. And these brave souls give us all an example to follow during any crisis, with Hemingway's "grace under pressure" defining their courage and resolution.

Instead of being afraid, we will do what I am right now. I'm listening to music; and this time, Ave Maria. My soul soars with each passage, and I feel the presence of my mother and ancestors. That heartfelt communion is happening all over Italy at this very moment. Living souls sing out from balconies and porches as ancient spirits touch their rekindled selves, those parts of their being that are forever linked to the hills, rivers, shores, mountains, and plains of *Bella Italia*. The voices vary in tone and strength but are united in purpose and heart. They are singing for life, and God indeed hears such prayers. So, sing loud! Sing Proud! Sing together and walk into the future as Italians should, unafraid and touched by love's kindness and God's grace. Long live Italy! Amen.

97

Ouch!

Semester break was over, and I recall busily loading pairs of 45-pound plates onto the back seat and floor of the car, all in preparation for my return to UNH. Where I went, so too did my weightlifting sets. Well, I let the plates drop a bit, just an inch or so. But that was more than enough. The tip of my right middle finger got caught between the two plates while they jumped off the seat, and I have to say, that rebound crunch was the worst pain I have ever experienced. Yeah, I've broken bones, crushed multiple spinal discs, passed numerous kidney stones, had a massive heart attack, torn up both knees, and experienced other nasty things. Yet that small injury to the tip of my finger was by far the most excruciating. Later X-rays revealed I had crushed the end of my finger into four or five distinct pieces, losing half my fingernail. I cursed. I screamed. I even did a war dance while clutching the mauled digit and whimpering like a child. Thus began a painful healing process that was to last for about four months, and I now find myself musing about it all.

A few weeks ago, I had another heart attack (in April 2021). For me, there is usually little agonizing pain associated with the events but tremendous disability. One cannot get enough air, and my heart rate plunged into the upper 20s in the emergency room. My heart fluttered, beating irregularly and assuming extreme bradycardia that lasted over four hours. The crash cart was beside me in the room, and the monitors were constantly going off. One often knows when death hovers during a heart attack, with one hint being that catching sufficient breath is not easy. Yet the intermittent slipping feeling and accompanying loss of consciousness bring the message home.

I would describe the pain level as uncomfortable but not exquisite. Now, crushing disks in your neck and lower back can produce exquisite pain that can drop you to the ground and make you wish for unconsciousness. Yeah, I've done that three or four times. Similarly, torn knee ligaments and cartilage can be a real bear, along with broken bones, cuts, bruises, and all the other happenstances that everyday life can bring. Granted, all this pales compared to what war and violence can cause, such as savage burns, shattered limbs, and far worse.

Yet of all the injuries I have suffered during a lifetime of moving hefty loads, that little smashed fingertip is the one that makes me cringe. It was certainly no threat to life or much else, yet it crowds out memories of broken bones, mangled joints, and even life-threatening events. I suspect this odd phenomenon is not unique to me and that some of you also have a moment of pain trapped in your memory's net. I know soldiers who were "blown up" by improvised explosive devices in Iraq. Although missing body parts, some claim that relatively minor injuries are what they recall the most. One guy vividly recalled getting most of his foot blown off, but what bothered him most was when he got part of his hand crushed in a car door. "I didn't break anything, but that f'n hurt for weeks! With the foot, I felt something, but soon enough, I was out to lunch. My foot sure as heck hurt when I woke up!"

The thing is, fear of pain and existential threats do not always walk hand-in-hand. People often dread things that cannot kill or seriously harm them, which are sometimes out of all proportion to the danger they face. My heart is a mess, and I know the next time may be my last. Oddly, I do not fear that distinct possibility. Yet to this day, I dread getting a finger mauled. I know it is a silly and irrational fear that is terribly unlikely to happen. However, the experience changed a perceptual filter enough to make a very remote possibility into a palpable dread. We humans are odd creatures.

How much worse must it be for someone who suffers a grievous injury and tremendous pain, such as what cancer is now doing to some of my dear friends. They take toxic drugs, get burned by radiation, undergo the needed surgeries, and then go on. One recently said, "It isn't like I have a choice. Besides, life is worth fighting for." I admire their courage and note that most endure painful treatments to secure more time. Yes, life is worth fighting for, despite our actual or exaggerated fears.

Yeah, I still feel occasional chest and mid-back zingers from angina, and we have become old friends. Yet is the pain I feel worse than surgery to repair a shattered hip, remove a diseased lung, or excise an aggressive oral tumor? I think not. Pain is a part of life; we feel it for good existential reasons. Yet we can take our fears, amplify them with memories of pain, and make the resultant amalgam much more prominent than it needs to be. Indeed, we can magnify a fear of harm or death into something that blots out our potential to enjoy the day. My fires are burning very low, but I will drag my sorry ass down to the boat dock in a few days. There I will commune with God and thank her for helping me to survive this last travail. Life is a beautiful thing, despite the vagaries of happenstance and fate. Be at peace, my friends, and don't let fear ruin your day. Amen.

98

Flying Kites

Seeing friends angry, depressed, or anxious bothers me greatly, far more so than it once did. Our capacity to empathize often improves as we age, one of the few things that can improve over time. Of course, this assumes that we allow our sensitive side to be seen by others and felt within. Empathy tends to improve because experience teaches us powerful lessons about loss, joy, pain, happiness, and all the rest while our days unfold. The laugh of newborns, the wonder of children, joyful graduations, fearsome surgeries, and all the other happenstances of life move our souls. We share the moments with others, their related memories sparking anew while they contemplate our ongoing experiences. Yes, this is sharing writ large.

This is also the "normal" course of life, although exceptions exist. Some people are born or become creatures of the self. They seldom consider anything other than their reflections and personal concerns and could care less about others. Sure, these people occasionally commune, but they are often painfully negative. Many tend to complain incessantly and become tedious to the core. They simply cannot see outside themselves and their immediate problems. Happily, such impoverished souls are a minority, for age typically gives us the impetus and consideration to commiserate and empathize.

Ellen was depressed today, her usually gleaming blue eyes looking downcast. At 78, time and life have weathered and tested her. She has survived a dangerous back surgery, divorces, breast cancer, the loss of financial security, and a host of other ills. Now, she faces neck surgery due to pinched nerves and impinged blood vessels. If she turns just so, down she goes in a heap. These falls happened a few times recently, and nothing good can come from that tendency in the future. Thus, the surgery is not as elective as some may think, although Ellen doesn't want to hear that. Moreover, a brain tumor still lurks that can also impact her balance. The meningioma makes Ellen forget every manner of thing, although it has been reasonably stable and slow growing.

Alas, Ellen's usual optimism has evaporated lately, but who wouldn't be depressed given her situation? Getting old isn't for the weak of heart or spirit. Time tests us, usually far more so than do tiffs, battles, and the various accidents of our youth. We elderly folks often feel trapped within a razorblade storm, suffering wounds whenever we dare lift our heads. Indeed, we sometimes lose sight of the positives life offers due to fear of getting cut. Our "now" becomes tainted by despair, and then we dare not hope. We withdraw deep into the self and simply want the game to end. No more cuts, No more pain. No more running from the pouring rain.

Yet if we try, the reasons for existence reveal themselves. They did so today while I was with Ellen. The winds came on strong at about 6:30 p.m. and fluttered the leaves on the birch trees outside Ellen's living room. The sun shining through them created an utterly fascinating rippling effect as the leaves' different hued front and back surfaces alternated. Then two goldfinches abruptly darted from one tree to its neighbor, reminding Ellen and me of everything there is to be thankful for: gold on wings, dancing greenery, blue skies, puffy white clouds, and gyrating branches––a veritable symphony of colors and movement.

Oh, that wind shook the trees mightily, forcing our attention to shift from the moment's sadness. I told Ellen that the ongoing activity was God tapping us on the shoulder. "Look at me. Look at me," God advised. We were reminded to gaze outside ourselves and our woes, to see instead what beauty we can while we can. Then the wind's impetus and God's good graces caused our thoughts to turn toward flying kites, something we often did as children. Ellen has a granddaughter, and I asked her if she had ever flown a kite with her. Well, she hasn't.

Perhaps grandparents should take the opportunity to fly kites and the like with their grandkids more often, assuming the kids will do most of the work involved. After all, some of us cannot run, and getting kites aloft isn't always easy. It will also be a chore helping Ellen to remember what she is doing, but we quickly formulated a plan for an adventure with her granddaughter in some easily accessible place where kites can be flown. I am not at all sure it will ever happen. However, we went from inward-turning despair to a quest for sharing an adventure with a loved one. We must make it happen, but the wind's call was strong.

God speaks to us in many ways. It may be the sound of thunder, scorching heat, or the melodic chirping of songbirds. However, when God asks us to ponder possibilities, we should try our best. Moreover, sharing adventures can help get us out

98.1 It is in every elderly person's interest to play with their children, such as flying kites

of our self-imposed constraints. We can turn outward instead of inward, a viable and vibrant choice for many. You young ones reading this line may want to take your aging progenitors out and about. And you older folks ought not to anchor yourselves so firmly to couches and beds if possible. Go out and play! Live, share, and find some joy in shared moments. Amen.

99

Reminders

So, we're gathered around our new multipurpose pedestal tables and seated atop equally new wheeled chairs. The tables have a deep gray ersatz marble finish on top, while the padded wooden chairs are graced with dark mahogany stain. All is nice and comfy. The recently installed gray rug has an abstract royal blue *fleur-de-lis* pattern, and quaint couches, sofas, and end tables complete the second-floor lounge's revamped setting. It's a much-welcomed change from our former ratty standard wherein large holes punctured our stained carpet, and we well-weathered residents of the Hollow appreciate the improvements. Many of us meet in the lounge daily, finding mutual pleasure in communing, telling stories, and sharing meals. I am sitting beside a moderately portly woman in her mid-70s who needs oxygen, be-ing usually tethered to tanks or other breathing aids. However, Sandy is now free of that encumbrance.

"Wow, no O2 today," I say.

"I've been off it for over two weeks," Sandy says. "You know that."

"I do?" I reply.

"Yes. We talked about it when I went off the tanks, and you've seen me several times since then. Of course, you know."

The observations hit hard, but Sandy must be correct. However, I have no memory of seeing her without the O2 tanks, let alone recall us talking about it. Good Lord, I'm struggling to find the memories and images of those happenings, but there is absolutely nothing there . . . not even the dimmest of recollections. This forgetting problem seems to be occurring more frequently, with conversations and interactions drifting into complete emptiness. Specialists call this episodic memory, though my increasing loss of name recollection abilities indicates some semantic memory elements are also in play.

Nonetheless, I can still commune via these words. Moreover, sometimes I write and think well. That is why I am unconvinced that my lapses are part of developing dementia, although the doc-tors claim this is definitely the case. Still, the cognitive function tests and magnetic resonance imaging results could have been misinterpreted, as is common in many neurological disorders. Yet I must confess to not recalling some of what I have written.

The passages "sound" like me, but I don't remember when and why I wrote them. It is disconcerting, almost like part of me is doing its own thing.

No, I cannot deny something is very wrong. There are painfully obvious memory gaps that are increasing in number and severity. Issues with emotional control, impulse restraint, and poor judgment are also becoming vexing. Man, I went right after a woman who started joking about my memory issues when I didn't recall Sandy's O2 status. A person's loss of contextual memory isn't something to mock, and I will not be an object of ridicule. It was utterly infuriating! I became increasingly pissed off, loud, and angry. However, having seen the torment unfold, my companions quickly deflected the budding angst. I regained my composure, although my outburst reminded me that a problem was afoot.

Still, I doubt this behavior is caused by frontotemporal dementia (FTD), which they once claimed was the case. This is the condition Robin Williams had, which is a grim diagnosis. He opted not to live with it, but checking out posthaste is not my way, albeit I can understand why some do. Moreover, my MRI report states, "disproportionate frontoparietal and left medial occipital atrophy, with sparing of the temporal lobes." So, they switched gears and called it a major cognitive disorder instead of FTD. Hell, how can anyone take a diagnosis that is so nebulous seriously? Of course, names do not matter when a particular malady is much like a close relative. It is part of an unwanted family, any member of which can ruin your whole day.

Yeah, I am disconcerted by the lapses, but one strives to avoid allowing the negative to become overwhelming. Instead, one reacts. I am thus making appropriate preparations while doing so is still under my control. A guardian ad litem will be appointed, and I laid the groundwork for that need. My friend Al is ideal for the job. The shrinks will know when I should activate that protocol, but I'd have to be a damn site more demented than is currently the case if I didn't prepare for the possibility. The fact I can still do so means the glass remains half full. The memory gaps indicate the empty parts: lost and unconsolidated recollections. Yet there are some glaring problems. For instance, I cannot balance a bankbook to save my life and have repeatedly started buying the same books. It is a bitch of a situation to ponder and impossible entirely to ignore. Indeed, my doctor called yesterday, something about a missed appointment or test or some such thing.

However, one must always avoid freaking out, and they have given me trazodone to help achieve that end. Oh, but I will not take it. I am simply drifting into the present, which isn't the worst thing that could happen. The ability to commune will remain intact for some time. Indeed, the loss of contemplative depth may be a blessing. It allows me to express myself more concisely, clearly, and vividly, albeit not in my typical arcane style. How long this will remain the case is unclear. As for my books and articles, I think about making them freely accessible to anyone who wants them. The time to fret about the things of necessity (e.g., money) is waning. The time to give freely from one's soul is eternal and immediate. That is what living fully is all about, and I will do so for as long as possible. I feel blessed, as I have for many years. Depression doesn't have my number, and fear remains a choice.

I look around me whenever I feel overwhelmed. Poor Anita's brain tumor is growing out from a hole radiation burned through her skull. Yet she smiles and carries on with the help of her sister, Irene. Bev can hardly walk, and her heart function is down in the 30 percent range. She still does her art and helps organize all manner of events. Hiram has fought bladder cancer for many years and has now opted for hospice care at home. I am surrounded by examples of people striving to live fully while dealing with problems that would crush lesser souls. No whining needs to apply because I have seen how to live well while facing that final period punctuating every line. All is well, with the nagging reminders being like small ripples in a pond. They disturb the surface for a bit but slowly drift away--if we let them. Amen.

100

Mowing the Lawn

Early May 2021 brought turmoil to Israel and the occupied territories, a dreary constant in the human condition. Israeli planes flattened entire buildings in Gaza while Hamas launched thousands of missiles into Israel proper. Oh, the typical ratio of deaths will be one or two Israeli Jews for every 100-plus Palestinians, which the Israeli Defense Forces (IDF) once called "mowing the lawn" or "cutting the grass" before the terms became politically incorrect. Sometimes, the Palestinians die by the thousands, but they resist. This time, the causal agency was Jewish settlers forcing Palestinians out of their homes, sometimes by very harsh means. This is also a recurring theme, and one wonders if it will ever change.

I find it odd that two nationalities are fighting over a land neither owns. All things on this planet are aspects of the Divine: to God alone, they ultimately belong. God freely gives life, land, bounty, time, and everything else. Yet we perceive many of these things as being ours and not theirs, with sharing being a seemingly alien concept. So, the tanks rumble, and rockets fly, while children aplenty hide and die. Yes, God's lessons can be brutal, although some never quite get the point. The point here is that the Jews and Palestinians must learn to share the land in life, or they will surely share it in death.

The two-state solution is the only viable resolution for the ongoing misery. Everyone knows it, yet past and ongoing traumas prevent all concerned from embracing reasonable answers. The Jews were tormented for centuries, subject to every manner of brutality. Indeed, the Romans tore the Jews from their homeland and scattered them to the winds some 2,000 years ago. Then Hitler became the last in a long line of anti-Semites to slaughter the Jews en masse. The souls of 6 million dead screamed for a homeland, and so Israel was forged from torment and hardened by tragedies and savagery that defy our imaginations. After all, who can imagine the unimaginable?

Alas, the homeland the Jews created was already occupied by the Palestinians, and they were not keen on being displaced. Many families had lived on the land for 1,000 years or more: this was the only home they knew. That situation has not changed for 80 years, despite the many wars and conflicts that have raged since the 1940s. And thus, the IDF periodically mows the lawn, striking down those Palestinians who dare threaten Israel's existence, innocent and guilty alike. Once enough blades have been cut down, there is a temporary peace, at least until the lawn looks a bit overgrown.

The real problem is that this one-sided game may take on an entirely new character one day. If COVID has taught us anything, an essential lesson is a virus cannot be contained. Israel is well-equipped to deal with biological warfare but not novel viruses. These can be easily manufactured, as some suspect was the case with COVID. So, all of a sudden, people begin dying in a few small towns in Israel, Jews and Palestinians alike. No one knows who started the biological fire, nor can it be squelched easily or quickly because it is both fast-moving and highly lethal. Multitudes die as the disease runs its course, with the virus eventually breaking out worldwide.

Tell me, who will Israel strike back at? What will the IDF do while its soldiers and people die by the millions? Will they mow the lawn yet again? Will they slaughter people already dying of a plague that no one can control? The makers of the virus will not care. They may even be among its first victims, with their sole impetus being to strike down the venal landscapers who dared to mow down their families. And so, a festering sore becomes an existential illness that consumes everything in its wake.

This is not a vague possibility. This increasingly realistic scenario can only be prevented by embracing reason. Regrettably, people of belief often eschew logic, preferring final solutions and mowing the lawn. To them, the possibility of annihilation is not nearly as important as building a new kibbutz for their kith and kin. They do not perceive the long game. Instead, they are bound by traumatic memories and ongoing violence. They quote a sacred passage and then take more of what God freely gives us all to share.

Indeed, God gave of its being to create all that we were, are, or could ever be. That was the ultimate act of sharing that has carried us through to the present day. If we do not learn to share freely, we will inherit only the worst fates. That choice is ours to make, and I suggest that the time to act is now. Will the collective "we" do so? I doubt it, but I know that fatally flawed species always go extinct. God gives us chances, but we must take advantage of them. To share is to live; it is well past time for the Israelis and Palestinians to embrace that idea. Amen.

101

The Sensitive Beast: A Bouncer's Lament

I don't know exactly why I care about people, but the most evident proof I do is to be found in this chapter you're reading. Of course, we all change over time if we allow ourselves to. Yet my early course was about as wayward as it gets. I wanted to be tough and fierce, so I donned a convincing tough-guy act. Indeed, my lamentable actions showed what a miserable and cruel species we humans can be, yet that violent person is certainly not who I am today. Nonetheless, I find myself hoping and working against cold and harsh reality that the species will somehow survive and evolve, all this coming from a bloated man who once played the role of a miscreant bouncer.

101.1 Known as 'Dino,' here is the author around the time of his bouncer days

Ah, the life of a bouncer. Now, that job can give someone a unique perspective on the human condition. The requirements for being a bouncer are simple. You should look the part and also be willing to "handle" people, the latter being far more critical than the former. I was both. I weighed 322 pounds but stood only 5-foot-8 inches tall. I had a 53-inch-plus chest, 53-inch gut, and 32-inch thighs: a truncated giant. I was also extremely strong, not that strength is any substitute for knowledge and experience regarding tiffs and the like. However, I was powerful enough to maul most people, and I knew better than to tangle with more formidable foes. I could push 440 pounds overhead and once absconded with a washer and dryer from my dorm. Yeah, they were held for ransom in my room after ripping me off once too often. I disguised them under a doily, finding the entire exercise wildly amusing.

I was also mean at times, which was no act. Being the son of a drunk does that to you. My first memory was of my old man smashing the rocking chair my mother comforted me on. She used to sing while he ranted and raved, but that went out with the chair—like so much kindling. Some of my brothers and sisters experienced far worse. I became angry and resentful. On my fourteenth birthday, I helped my inebriated dad up the stairs to his bedroom, with him cursing my birthday every step of the way. It made a deep impression, though most of my angst was added to the growing pile of psychic fuel that defined my early character. I grew to hate my father. Eventually, I grew to hate myself.

This helped instill the confrontational spirit needed to be a good bouncer. One has to be physically willing to enforce decorum; although I wasn't overtly aggressive until about 17. Before that age, I was unsure of myself, but then the anger and resentment grew enough to overcome doubt and fear. The beast within finally reared its head. Retribution was mine, and it was bittersweet. I know what tasting my enemies' blood is like because I have bitten them deeply. I have heard anguished screams while bending necks backward, ever teasing their breaking point. I reveled in such mischief. It is an excellent thing I lacked martial arts training because that would have made me a killer.

In college, I carried my past with me. Everyone in my dormitory was soon aware of my dubious ways, and I enjoyed playing the role of a badass. Of course, a Mixed Martial Arts fighter could have kicked my ass. Still, I was hard to hurt, having ample muscle mass buried beneath layers of protective fat. Moreover, I could smash my fists into cinder blocks, bricks, and other hard objects with resounding thuds, sans any formal instruction and replete with bloody and cracked knuckles. I did the exercise regularly to toughen my fingers and hand bones, with the odd activity intimidating those who witnessed it. Yeah, it was an act, something done to avoid conflict. Yet the result was a killer right hand.

"Just don't get him drunk," they used to say. My budding viciousness had tangible rewards. After some of its brothers razzed me, I once entered a rowdy fraternity house with a baseball bat. They fed me free drinks all night long. Mine was the arrogance of power, as in threatening people with desks, picking up full-grown men by their necks, and seeing fear in folk's eyes. The mayhem somehow soothed my insecurities and fears. In truth, I was becoming a nascent psychopath, just one or two incidents away from incarceration. One would think being a bouncer would have encouraged crossing the line and becoming a brute, but it did not quite work out that way.

Like all college students, I was perpetually short of money. I went to a local bar in town, Nicks, and asked the Greek owner if he needed a bouncer. Nick already knew me. He had heard about my antics from his employees, and my appearance completed the interview. Nick even offered me a discount price on pizzas! I've often thought that heaven itself couldn't compare with a good pizza, so Nick had my complete loyalty. He was a friendly old guy with a very thick accent. "You'll do veddy, veddy good"--not that a bouncer has much to do.

My main task was to check IDs at the door to the subterranean disco section of Nicks. Occasionally, I had to ask a person to leave who was getting too rowdy, but no one gave me too hard a time. That's why Nick hired me in the first place. A bouncer's job is to *discourage* trouble and not start it. I was good at preventing problems as long as I stayed sober. Drinking freed the beast within, and Nick definitely didn't want that. No one did, including me.

After a while, I got used to the regulars, and they got used to me. That's when I started studying the human condition. Perhaps I was trying to find answers to my inner problems, but young people mixed with alcohol provide more mystery than edification. Oh, we had a great cast of characters. There were foreign students armed with big wallets, townies, athletes, servicemen, horny guys, horny girls, and your typical hodgepodge of frequent student drinkers. Some of these people did things

101.2 Nick's had a crowded dance floor, repleat with a steady disco beat that the author came to deplore

that taught me a great deal about myself. Others drove me to distraction.

I recall this "wing nut," an air force man, who came in Nicks at around 7:00 p.m. every Friday night. "Paul" would always come in alone, get shit-faced, and dance with his chair for hours on the disco floor. He was pretty good at dancing with a chair, doing spins, quick chop-steps, and sometimes even slow dancing. Alas, as Paul got drunker, he occasionally crashed into other gyrating customers. Paul would apologize and then go right back to doing his thing. I always found this behavior very amusing, but Nick was not impressed. "He do dat 'gain, you trow his ass out, eh?" Yes, Nick.

Sure enough, Paul repeated his bizarre dance the following week, and I was forced to act. I was reluctant to do so because the guy was basically harmless. He was 160–170 pounds soaking wet and was no buffed and dangerous dude. However, I was duty-bound to act.

"I'm sorry, but you can't do that here," I said.

"Do what?" he replied with a slurred voice.

"Dance with a chair."

"Christ, I was just getting to know her."

I started laughing but remembered how serious Nick had been, "You trow his ass out." I put on my nasty face and abruptly grabbed the chair.

"Look, you can't dance with this chair."

"Hey, you can't cut in on me like that. I saw her first!"

Pretending you're mad at someone while laughing is hard, but I tried.

"You're gonna get yourself hurt if you don't let go of this goddamn chair," I growled.

"Oh, I didn't know she was yours. I didn't mean anything by it. No offense," Paul chirped.

Paul released his grip on the chair and promptly grabbed another one from a nearby table. He introduced himself to the chair, bowed, and started dancing with it. All of this greatly amused the disco's patrons. However, I was beginning to feel like a fool. There I was, holding a chair in the middle of a damn disco floor while some wing nut was dancing circles around me with another chair. Paul didn't know, but humiliation can free the beast. I put down the chair I was holding and abruptly grabbed Paul by the throat. His dance ended.

I walked him backward across the disco floor and toward the wall. Paul's feet barely touched the ground, and the conversation was one way. I was guttural.

"You miserable little bastard. You don't make fun of me! Ever! I ought to fuck you up so bad you won't dance for a year."

Then I noticed I was choking him out. Paul's face was red, and he was gasping, so I relaxed my grip. Killing customers is taboo in bouncing circles—it's awful for business. Paul spoke to me, his voice made harsh by my ill-treatment.

"Look at my face!" he hoarsely yelled. "Look at my face!"

He had a pot-marked face, severely marred by acne.

"What girl would want to look at this?"

I felt small and wicked.

"For Christ's sake, I only want to have a good time. I'd rather have people laugh than puke when they see me."

The bouncer could think of no reply.

"You know what it's like to be ugly. Look at yourself. God, you're fat as a pig. So, why don't you just lighten up?"

"Buddy, you ain't ever gonna get a girl by dancing with a chair. Besides, you might hurt somebody," I said.

"Any more than I'm hurting myself?"

Tears welled up in Paul's eyes, and he suddenly bolted toward the stairway that led to the exit. I went after him, but fat men don't move fast. I opened the exit door in time to see his backside disappearing down the street, lost in the gloomy darkness. I never saw Paul at Nick's again. I never got to say I was sorry or that dancing with chairs is no sin. Ah, the misery of loneliness and a lousy self-image. How much they are a part of me and of many others who hang out at bars. It was a good lesson but a harsh one.

I lived across the street from Nicks, above an old grocery store managed by Johnny Grimes. Maybe that's why I got so friendly with the townies that frequented Nicks. They looked at me as just another local, a rather conspicuous one. Most of the townies liked me because my tough guy act was convincing, a trait that many of them found admirable. They also appreciated that I would readily share my weed and even drop them joints from the fire escape while they were gathered in the back of my apartment building. Some of my townie friends were worse badasses than myself, and a few were downright criminals. However, most were just drunks and druggies, blithely living within a world of illusions, pretenses, and contrived images.

Juan was a frequently drunk but good-hearted fellow, lean, dark-haired, and of average height. Yeah, he looked Hispanic but was a Yankee to the core. I would often talk with him in front of Nicks, and Juan raved incessantly, lost in some chaotic world I only fully understood when I was pie-eyed. But Juan was also a crazy mother when he was buzzed, and that was all too often. Yeah, that was his act. He once nipped a coed on the breast because a fellow townie, Matty, bet him $50 that he wouldn't dare. At first, the girl laughed, but after some reflection, she very understandably became upset about the incident. In fact, she filed a sexual assault charge on Juan, and he soon found himself hiding out from the cops.

A few weeks later, Juan turned himself in and was charged accordingly. The townies had a nasty habit of getting into each other's business. Pretty soon, Matty was chided for having goaded the drunken Juan into committing such a stupid act. After all, Juan was rather helpless at times, especially when he was shit-faced. A few locals demanded that Matty pay up on the bet, and he fumed mightily about being held responsible for Juan's stupidity. A month or two later, Matty and Juan were drinking in the bar next to Nick's, and they soon argued.

The fray started after Matty repeatedly broke Juan's cigarettes and called him yellow. Unfortunately, the bouncer in the bar didn't react in time, and Juan abruptly lashed out at Matty.

Regrettably, Juan held a glass tumbler in his hand at the time, and it shattered in Matty's face. There was lots of blood. It took some 70-odd stitches to repair Matty's nose and upper lip. Several townies jumped Juan immediately after the incident and began pummeling him. Juan got away, ran across the street, and scurried up to my apartment. His hands and clothing were covered with Matty's blood when I saw him. He was frightened out of his mind, nervously glancing toward the door.

The townies knew better than to bring their fights into my abode, so Juan was safe for now. He made a call, escaped town, and soon found himself hiding from the law again in a local barn. The cops wanted to bust him for criminal assault this time. Juan was bummed, having nowhere to go and few friends left. One day, he snuck over to my house and asked me what to do. Yet what the hell does a bouncer know? I told him to try to find a reason, a positive purpose for his life that he could pursue. However, I asked him to accomplish something I had not done, and we both knew it. Yeah, Juan was a guy that needed professional counseling, and I was not the right guy to see. Juan put a gun in his mouth four days later and killed himself. I liked the guy a lot. Why the hell didn't I do more to help him?

Matty drank at Nick's often after Juan's suicide and was frequently melancholy. He grew a skimpy mustache and goatee to cover his facial scars, but the wounds ran deeply into his soul. I remember talking with him about Juan's death on the street outside the bar.

"Yeah, I didn't expect it either," I said.

"It bummed me out."

"Still bummed?"

"We were good friends, you know."

"I know."

"But we were."

"I know. Jaun felt the same way about you."

"Do ya think it was my fault, Dino?"

"Nah, I think it had something to do with pretending."

"Pretendin'?"

"Yeah, we all pretend our acts are real. We become an image of what we want to be, not what we truly are. Then we do something stupid and just can't live with it afterward. Look at what the guys did to Juan after he hit you. Shit, and they were bawling at his wake . . . the fuckin' hypocrites. I sure as hell didn't help him much when I gave him my two-cent advice. We all fucked up, including Juan."

"Yeah, we did. Juan could sure play the guitar, though," Matty sadly replied.

"That he could."

"He was a great guitarist."

"I know. One of the very best I've ever heard."

"We were friends."

Matty looked down and walked away without saying goodbye. He was right. Juan had talents and demons, an outstanding musician plagued by chronic alcoholism. There were a lot of townies like that, all striving to find a way of life that fits. Over the coming months, Matty drank more frequently, and his behavior became increasingly reckless. He was spiraling toward oblivion, and there were plenty of warning signs. I had to ask him to leave Grimes' store once because Matty was asking for a fight with a kid who could have wiped the floor with him. A few months later, he got into a jam with some dude from my hometown outside Nicks. The fight got way out of hand, and Matty got his lights punched out, his head hitting a curb stone. I saw the ambulance lights from my room and went downstairs to check the scene.

Matty was bloodied and staggered, but he was being drunkenly obnoxious to the ambulance drivers, police, and friends. He refused treatment, so his buddies asked if they could take Matty to my apartment until he sobered up. Sure. Why not? Juan had come in for a landing when the going got tough, so why not Matty? His friends laid him down on my couch and cleaned the blood off his face. I noted that he was bleeding from the ear, a terrible sign. Man, Matty was a mess. However, he behaved like a jerk, as drunks are prone to.

"Fuck you guys!" he screamed time and again. "Just leave me the fuck alone. Ohhh, my head is frigging, killing me. Leave me alone!" This went on for over an hour. I finally ordered Matty to stop insulting people in my apartment. He listened and calmed down.

I was tired, so I told everyone, "Hey, look, if the guy wants to die, let him. I just want to get some sleep." Matty's friends then left, and he slept on my couch. I could hear him moan occasionally as the hours passed, so I checked on him once or twice. He mumbled that he was doing OK. Then came the morning, and I went to make a 6:30 a.m. check on my unwelcome guest. To my surprise, he had already left. Matty came by at about 8:30 to apologize for his behavior, and I decided to sit him down for a talk.

"You're lucky you didn't get killed last night," I said.

"I know, my fuckin' head is killing me," he said, his eyes wincing from the pain.

"You still feelin' bad about Juan?"

"Yeah, always will."

"I don't know what to say, but I'll tell you what I told him."

"What was that?"

"Try to find a purpose for your life. Fuck, I know I don't have one, but I think finding a purpose is like having a rudder. It kind of gives you direction."

We talked a lot that morning. We spoke about Juan, drinking, doing too many drugs, and these silly games we play that can become all too real. But soon, it came time for Matty to leave for work. Later that night, the cops told me Matty was undergoing brain surgery for a subdural hematoma in a local hospital. Things didn't work out well for him. There was a lot of damage, followed by an infection. Today, Matty doesn't even recognize me, let alone remember our conversations. He has the mind of a child, emotionally, intellectually, and perceptually. It pains me to see him. His words are constantly slurred and mumbled, and he still seeks solace in the bottle.

"Eh, Buddy—can you buy me a drink?"

The townies know better than to feed Matty's addiction because alcohol and anti-seizure meds do not mix well. I have no idea how his life has gone and may look Matty up. Then again, he could have already gone the way of so many of my friends.

Direction and purpose are things that most bouncers can't think about too much, or they won't be bouncers for very long. A regular named Charlie once told me that most people are given direction and purpose through their upbringing and that those who develop doubts are the ones who end up getting lost. He said, "Of course, the people who are smart enough to doubt are also the ones who are bright enough to accomplish the most. That is if they can think of exactly what they want to accomplish." Good old Charlie. He was a white-bearded, big-bellied college professor who was just as lost as we were on occasion, albeit he certainly had direction in his academic work. I liked that guy a lot, as I did his daughter. Charlie was smart as a whip, even while four sheets to the wind.

Charlie was the real deal, but many 10-cent intellectuals also hung around at Nicks. I enjoyed talking with them. We discussed everything from Aristotle's definition of God, thought on thought, and contemporary politics. I wasn't just a big dumb bouncer. I fancied myself as a semi-erudite bouncer who could empathize with the fellow he was throwing out on his ear. However, empathy can only take you so far in bouncing or life. There comes a time when you simply have to be cruel, yet another grim aspect of the human condition.

My final time to be cruel at Nick's was forced upon me. I was working the disco door again, and the place was hopping. I was supposed to keep the numbers down due to fire code regulations, but I was usually very bribable. Hey, if someone handed me a couple of dollars or a fiver, there was room for him or her. However, I did make sure that no one was underage. On this particular night, four very drunk girls, who must have been about 16 or 17, came trooping down the stairs with their boyfriends in tow to get into the disco. Ah, but the bouncer was in their way.

Usually, I give a person the benefit of the doubt, yet not a drunken teenage girl with someone else's ID. And she was the one who was vouching for her friends!

"What do you mean this isn't me?" she indignantly asked.

"Your hair's blond, kid, not red."

"I dyed it!"

"Along with your eyes?"

"Fuck that. They let me in next door!"

"This ain't next door."

"You let me by, you fat bastard."

"You better take a hike."

"Fuck off, I'm goin' in."

"I don't think so."

I was getting pissed off. One of the girls' boyfriends saw this and advised his erstwhile friend to give up her quest. He was the only wise person in the group. I followed the kids while they retreated up the stairs and watched them disappear into the bar next to Nick's. I chatted with our upstairs' bouncer outside, and he said, "They tried it with me too. Obnoxious little bitch, isn't she?" We laughed, but no bouncer likes being hassled by under-age drunks. The job's bad enough as it is.

After taking in some fresh air, I returned to the disco, lamenting the rock-hard beat we had to endure every working night. It was busy as hell, and a line soon formed outside the upstairs' door to the disco. Nick had been on me about keep-ing the numbers down, so I was ruthless about letting people in. Then I heard a commotion at the top of the stairs, and the un-derage group walked in, led by the girl who gave me a hard time. Apparently, they had shoved other patrons aside, but I was in no mood for nonsense. I sighed and then donned my angry face.

They were all very drunk by now. I glared at the oncoming teenyboppers, but they kept coming down the stairs. The girls' boyfriends held back, waiting to see if their fearless leader could melt the bouncer. I think most guys know better than to bug bouncers, but all too many girls think there's an open season on them. They use their gender as a shield, though that crap did not work with me. I became the door and stared at the lead girl while she approached.

"You can't come in here," I said coldly.

"Get the hell out of my way."

"I think you better leave," I growled.

"Fuck that."

I held my arms up and said, "Look, I don't want any trouble with . . ."

Then she kneed me in the groin. The beast was instantly released. I hit the entitled brat in the upper chest with an open hand, and she flew backward into her girlfriends, sending them reeling. A girl suddenly fell forward over one of her friends. I caught the kid in midair and threw her up a few stairs. Then I found myself wailing on the girls while they tried retreating up the stairwell. I kicked them. I punched them. I slapped one girl across the face so hard it bounced her off the stair railing. Their boyfriends ran away.

In short order, I was standing outside the entrance to the disco, watching the battered girls drunkenly pull off a strategic retreat. I was fuming. The upstairs bouncer laughed at the bizarre spectacle, but I was not amused. A guy in the waiting line said something about it not being proper to beat on girls, but another guy clapped. Hey, a bouncer has to do what a bouncer has to do. Suddenly, one of the waiting patrons grabbed one of the girl's jackets, ran across the street, and tossed it atop a laundromat. The kids chased the guy, and soon others joined the mayhem. Chaos ensued, and I retreated back to my station.

I talked to Nick about the incident after the place closed. "You do a good job on them. A veddy, veddy good job. I give you five-dollar tip." I told Nick I could have hurt the girls, and he said they had assaulted me, not vice versa. Maybe he was right, but I asked myself, what gives me the moral authority to hurt people? Why must the bouncer be the final arbiter of bar-room etiquette? Why must my acting role conflict with my changing beliefs? I quit that night and never bounced again.

I continued to hang around bars for a while, forever studying how people behaved and interacted. My back was always to the wall, having learned how best to place myself respective of potential threats. I retain the habit and probably always will. Ultimately, I realized that bars aren't the best places to study the human condition. They are places people go to have their conditions altered, either through alcohol or infinitely variable social interactions. Perhaps bars exist to allow people a reprieve from the human condition's ugliness, but I learned this salvation is illusionary at best. People tend to create ugliness, carrying it with them wherever they go. There is no escape from the human condition and no reprieve.

Be that as it may, purpose can indeed give one's life meaning, and when I became a weightlifting coach at UNH, my life changed for the better. Ah, but that's another story, and a great one. Regrettably, karma finally caught up with me. By age 35, I was physically disabled by weightlifting accidents and a cerebral vascular problem. Gone are my days of sublime physical arrogance. They were slowly replaced by a life of growing infirmity, weakness and pain. I hurt when I get up in the mornings and when I go to bed at night. Justice is a bitch, and I have much to atone for. I still study the human condition while I plod through life, and it continues to mystify me. One day, I may discover that the human condition isn't ugly at all, and the only problem lies in the perceptual lens I've been using. Perhaps it needs a bit of cleaning, for issues harbored within influence what we tend to see around us. Amen.

About the Author

Dr. George H. Elder is an irascible and increasingly disabled recluse living in rural New Hampshire near where he was born and raised. He has a Ph.D. from Penn State in Speech Communication and a Master's in nonfiction writing from UNH. Mostly, he is a dreamer with a long and colorful history of lucid, astral, and other unique dream experiences, many of which involved an active search for the source of creation. Indeed, Elder's spiritual quest and psychic adventures have few equals, with prophecies that range from the mundane to existential. His irreverent and temperamental attitude was anathema to many in the academy. Still, he was a gifted scholar who authored numerous articles in the popular press and scientific textbooks that examine the neuropsychological basis of human communication and dream science. He also addressed subjects such as religion, ancient philosophy, love, nature, nurture, time, politics, drug use, street life, and many other issues that he shares in this text. Elder has been a college teacher, custodian, upper-level scholar, drug addict, weight lifting coach, bouncer, and much more, and through it all, he has displayed an honesty that pulls no punches and openly confesses to Elder's occasional rectitude and failings. This is a man one can learn from. Indeed, Elder believes the person reading these words has the power to change the future for the betterment of humanity.